IDENTIFICATION OF LEARNING DISABILITIES: RESEARCH TO PRACTICE

The LEA Series on Special Education and Disability
John Wills Lloyd, Series Editor

IDENTIFICATION OF LEARNING DISABILITIES: RESEARCH TO PRACTICE

Renée Bradley
Louis Danielson
*Office of Special Education Programs,
U.S. Department of Education*

Daniel P. Hallahan
University of Virginia

EDITORS

LAWRENCE ERLBAUM ASSOCIATES, PUBLISHERS
2002   Mahwah, New Jersey   London

Lawrence Erlbaum Associates, Inc., Publishers
10 Industrial Avenue
Mahwah, NJ 07430

Cover design by Kathryn Houghtaling Lacey

Library of Congress Cataloging-in-Publication Data

Identification of learning disabilities: research to practice/Renée Bradley, Louis Danielson, Daniel P. Hallahan, editors.
    p. cm. -- (The LEA series on special education and disability)
    Includes bibliographical references and index.
    ISBN 0–8058–4447–3 (alk. paper) -- ISBM 0–8058–4448–1 (pbk.: alk. paper)
        1. Learning disabilities. 2. Learning disabled children--Education. I. Bradley, Renée.
        II.Danielson, Louis C. III. Hallahan, Daniel P., 1944–IV. Series.

LC4704.I34 2002
371.92'6--dc21

2002066822

TABLE OF CONTENTS

FOREWORD

Much has happened in the special education field in the past 26 years. In 1975 the U.S. Congress passed Public Law 94–142, the Education for All Handicapped Children Act. This legislation was noteworthy for a number of reasons. First, it mandated appropriate public education for all children, even those with disabilities, challenging the prevailing notion that children should "fit the school" and that children with disabilities who did not "fit" could be excluded. In addition, PL–94–142 designated specific learning disabilities as a legitimate category of special education, thus ensuring services. Third, the legislation came about primarily because of litigation and advocacy, specifically legal challenges by parents such as the 1972 landmark case, *The Pennsylvania Association for Retarded Children v. the Commonwealth of Pennsylvania*. In that case parents argued successfully that the U.S. Constitution guarantees every child the right to a free and appropriate public education, and the Court agreed. Finally, PL 94–142 specified protections targeting due-process procedures and discriminatory assessment practices, mandated the development of individualized educational plans for all students receiving special education services, and directed placement in the least restrictive educational settings. These rights and protections are the basis of current practices under the Individuals with Disabilities Education Act (IDEA).

The reauthorization of IDEA will be considered by the U.S. Congress in 2003. Like any legislation, reauthorization is conducted within social, economic, and political contexts. PL 94–142 was strongly influenced by the civil rights movement, and the reauthorization of IDEA will likewise be considered within the current social-political context. Arguments have waged over definition, etiology, and identification practices, and even over the reality of learning disabilities (LD), a category that serves the largest number of students and that has been controversial since Sam Kirk proposed it in 1963. Concerns have persisted regarding the numbers of students identified as learning disabled, the diversity of problems considered LD, identification procedures and practices, and the appropriateness and effectiveness of interventions and remedial programs. Too often, however, the controversies have been based on beliefs and ideologies rather than on evidence. Fortunately, the present volume, *Identification of Learning Disabilities: Research to Practice,* provides a comprehensive and substantive basis for informed decisions.

This book boasts several unique aspects, not the least of which is how quickly and efficiently it was accomplished. It began with a small working meeting in Washington, DC, in May 1999. Organized by the Office of Special Education Programs (OSEP), the meeting brought together people with different perspectives on LD: parents, researchers, practitioners, and administrators. Products of that meeting were the commissioning of a set of papers addressing basic issues in LD and the nomination of researchers qualified to write them. These papers provided the substance for a large summit conference held in Washington in August 2001. At that meeting, representatives from many constituencies, including professional and parent organizations, were given the opportunity to respond to the papers and to consider policy implications. In a followup to the summit, a small research forum reached consensus on a number of important aspects of LD. And given the history of LD, it is remarkable that consensus could be reached on a number of basic points, and that the whole process took such a short time.

The chapters in this book cover topics that are basic to understanding LD. Long and substantive, they provide comprehensive reviews of the research evidence underlying different aspects of LD. The respondents bring different perspectives to the chapters, as some are themselves researchers, and others are parents, practitioners, or administrators. A final chapter summarizes major findings and presents consensus statements. The complete volume provides the basis for understanding LD and the policies needed to provide effective services. The volume as a whole deserves careful reading as background to the reauthorization of IDEA.

It is not appropriate in a foreword to review the content in detail, but in my view several points of consensus are especially important. The first and perhaps most important concerns the validity of the concept of specific learning disabilities. Despite its controversial and often contentious history, there is clear agreement that learning disabilities are real, that they are different from other disabling conditions, that the disorders are intrinsic to the individual, that they may be evidenced in different areas of functioning although most commonly in reading, mathematics, and writing, and that they reflect underlying cognitive processing disorders. The content in these chapters helps put to rest questions about the reality of LD.

A second major issue involved the models and practices used in identifying individuals as learning disabled. There was considerable if not unanimous consensus that current methods, specifically discrepancy models, need rethinking. Unexpected discrepancies between ability and achievement may be defensible on a conceptual level, but problems with measurement and with implementation make operational models suspect. Consistent with an emphasis on instruction, there was considerable support for identification based on responsiveness-to-intervention approaches. Such approaches are especially relevant to LD in schools where identification has implications for eligibility and instruction. There are other reasons for identifying individuals as LD, however—such as research and advocacy—and criteria and methods may vary according to purpose. Thus, a range of criteria and identification methods may be needed.

Finally, as evidenced in this volume, we know a good deal about problems in reading, particularly problems in reading acquisition. Many of the authors in this book have carried out research funded by the Office of Special Education Programs and the National Institute of Child Health and Human Development, and their efforts have increased our understanding of reading and of reading problems. It is important to emphasize, however, that reading problems are not the only content areas in which LD is expressed. Thus, there is real need for in-depth study of problems in mathematics, writing, and other skill areas.

This volume arrives at an important time in the education of students with LD. The content is comprehensive, substantive, current, and sometimes provocative. Overall the book provides a solid basis for considering the reauthorization of IDEA and future policy and implementation decisions regarding students with LD. It also brings cohesiveness to a field that has been not very cohesive. Prior to the efforts represented in this book I would have been tempted to say that consensus in LD was an oxymoron. LD has been controversial, characterized more by disagreement than by agreement. As a field we have argued over conceptualization and definition, over methods and measures for identifying individuals as LD, over the appropriateness and efficacy of treatments or interventions, even over whether there really is such a condition as LD. Many of these issues have now been resolved. The consensus reached in *Identification of Learning Disabilities: Research to Practice* is impressive. OSEP and the authors and respondents whose work appears in the book deserve our thanks. The next step is to include the translation of these insights into policies that lead to effective instructional programs in schools.

Barbara K. Keogh, Ph.D.
University of California–Los Angeles

ACKNOWLEDGMENTS

This book represents the efforts and patience of many people who worked for two years to improve the identification of children with learning disabilities (LD). First, acknowledgment is due to the members of the workgroup that laid out the two-year process and identified the issues and authors for the papers in this volume. Their names are listed in the introduction. Second, the authors and respondents need to be acknowledged. These authors produced high-quality papers and responses, presented them at the LD summit, and endured the process of preparing these manuscripts for inclusion in this book. All of their work was accomplished under very tight deadlines. The third group to acknowledge is the staff at American Institutes for Research (AIR) who provided logistical, technical, and editorial support throughout this two-year initiative. A few staff deserve particular recognition: Christina Diamond and Heidi Corwin for their assistance with the LD summit, Eric Spears for production of this volume, and Maury McInerney for his attentiveness to the overall initiative. Special thanks to Stephanie Jackson who provided support throughout the initiative by serving as the coordinator for the AIR staff and was a lifesaver for the Office of Special Education Programs (OSEP). She enabled this initiative to successfully fulfill its primary goal of synthesizing the current research and making it readily available for future discussions and decision making. Thanks also to Marilyn Crocker whose expertise in group facilitation was invaluable during several important meetings during the initiative.

A small group of researchers, listed in the final chapter, dedicated an enormous amount of time to summarizing the research and developing some key consensus statements regarding the identification of children with learning disabilities. Their work will have a tremendous impact on future discussions in this area.

Many thanks to all of the national organizations concerned with learning disabilities and their representatives for supporting this initiative and for their participation in the second roundtable discussion. Special thanks to the National Council on Learning Disabilities which assisted with the organization and follow-up work of the roundtable.

Finally, thanks to the folks at the Office of Special Education and Rehabilitative Services (OSERS). Although this initiative spanned across two administrations, the leaders in both the prior administration—Assistant Secretary Judith Heumann of OSERS and Director Ken Warlick of OSEP—and in the current one—Assistant Secretary Robert Pasternak and Stephanie Lee—recognized the value of and need for this work and supported the initiative. Special thanks also to Jeremy Buzzell of OSEP who helped with the initiative from the summit to the roundtables and with this publication.

DISCLAIMER

The Learning Disabilities Initiative was organized and facilitated by staff in the U.S. Office of Special Education and Rehabilitative Services (OSERS), Research to Practice Division of the Office of Special Education Programs. The goal of the initiative was to synthesize the most current research and to make that information available to serve as a foundation for future discussions and decision making.

The papers and responses in this book review the current research and represent the opinions of the authors. The final chapter, based on that work, represents the opinions of those researchers participating in the consensus meeting.

This publication is not an official publication of OSERS. U.S. Department of Education opinions represented are those of the authors, respondents, or researchers and do not necessarily represent opinions of OSERS or the U.S. Department of Education and no endorsement should be inferred.

INTRODUCTION

HISTORICAL CONTEXT

In 1975, Congress enacted the Education for All Handicapped Children Act (Public Law 94-142), now known as the Individuals with Disabilities Education Act (IDEA), to support states and localities in protecting the rights of, meeting the individual needs of, and improving the results for infants, toddlers, children, and youth with disabilities and their families. This landmark civil rights law and state grant program established procedures for ensuring that all individuals with disabilities have the right to an individualized, free appropriate public education in the least restrictive environment.

In the 27 years since the passage of Public Law 94-142, significant progress has been made toward meeting major national goals for developing and implementing effective programs and services for early intervention, special education, and related services. Before IDEA, many children with disabilities were denied access to education and opportunities to learn. For example, in 1970, U.S. schools educated only one in five children with disabilities, and many states had laws excluding certain students, such as children who were deaf, blind, emotionally disturbed, or mentally retarded.

Today, over 6 million children and youth with disabilities receive special education and related services. IDEA is responsible for many improvements in the lives of children with disabilities and their families. The majority of children with disabilities are now being educated in their neighborhood schools in regular classrooms with their nondisabled peers. High school graduation rates and employment rates among youth with disabilities have increased dramatically: graduation rates increased by 14 percent from 1984 to 1997, and today's post-school employment rates for youth served under IDEA are twice those of older adults with similar disabilities who did not have the benefit of IDEA. Post-secondary enrollments among individuals with disabilities receiving IDEA services also have sharply increased: the percentage of college freshmen reporting disabilities has more than tripled since 1978. The past 27 years have witnessed significant changes as the nation has moved from paying little or no attention to the special needs of individuals with disabilities, to merely accommodating these individuals' basic needs, and eventually to providing programs and services focused on improved results for all children with disabilities and their families.

Public Law 94-142 guaranteed that a free appropriate public education would be made available to each child with a disability in every state and locality across the country. The law articulated a compelling national mission to improve access to education for children with disabilities. Changes resulting from the law included new efforts to improve how children with disabilities were identified and educated, to evaluate the success of these efforts, and to provide due-process protections for children and families.

Public Law 94-142 was a response to Congressional concern for two groups of children: the more than 1 million children with disabilities who were excluded entirely from the education system and the children with disabilities who had only limited access to the education system and were therefore denied an appropriate education. This latter group comprised more than half of all children with disabilities who were living in the United States at that time. These issues of improved access became guiding principles for further advances in educating children with disabilities over the last quarter of the 20th century. The last reauthorization of IDEA in 1997 moved the shift from focusing on access to services to focusing on results and accountability.

Currently, IDEA recognizes 13 disability categories, one of which is specific learning disability. In general, if a child is suspected of having a disability, the child is referred for a full and individual initial evaluation. The evaluation procedure includes the administration of a variety of assessment tools designed to gather relevant functional and developmental information about the child that may assist in determining the existence of a disability and the needs of the child. Following the evaluation, a group of qualified professionals and the parent of the child must determine whether the child has a disability. If a determination is made that the child has one or more of the disabilities and because of the disability needs special education and related services, an Individualized Education Program must be developed for the child. In addition, states must make available a continuum of alternative placements to meet the needs of children with disabilities for special education and related services. IDEA also requires that, to the maximum extent appropriate, children with disabilities be educated with children who are nondisabled. For specific information regarding these procedures, refer to the final Regulations of the Department of Education 34 CFR §§300.530–§300.553.

Although Part B of IDEA is permanently authorized, both Part C and Part D need to be reauthorized periodically. As reauthorization of IDEA approaches in 2002, attention likely will be drawn to how federal legislation can support improved results for children with disabilities. Improving the identification of children with learning disabilities has been a major concern in the field for many years and will likely be a major issue in this upcoming reauthorization. Prior to the last reauthorization in 1997, during the comment period, the Office of Special Education Programs (OSEP) received a letter from the National Joint Committee on Learning Disabilities (NJCLD). The NJCLD letter highlighted a series of concerns regarding the effectiveness of current identification procedures for children with learning disabilities. After a series of discussions, and largely because of the expected significant changes in the 1997 reauthorization, the then-current assistant secretary of the Office of Special Education and Rehabilitative Services, Judith Heumann, promised to address NJCLD's concerns following the 1997 reauthorization.

This commitment was recognized in the final regulations for IDEA 1997. Attachment 1 to the March 1999 final regulations noted that "While there is merit to many of the proposed changes to definitions and terms, modifications to the substance of existing definitions should be subject to further review and discussion before changes are proposed. For example, as indicated in the preamble to the NPRM [notice of proposed rulemaking] (10/22/97), the Department plans to carefully review research findings, expert opinion, and practical knowledge over the next several years to determine whether changes should be proposed to the procedures for evaluating children suspected of having a specific learning disability..." (3/12/99). The following year, the assistant secretary directed OSEP to design and carry out a plan to fulfill this promise.

THE LEARNING DISABILITIES INITIATIVE

Background

Early in 2000, OSEP staff began initial plans for developing a process for a discussion on learning disabilities. The OSEP staff realized that the category of "learning disabilities" was heterogeneous and multifaceted and a process was needed that reflected this diversity. A primary goal of the work was to synthesize and organize the most current and reliable research available on key issues in the identification of learning disabilities so that future decision making could be based not on anecdotes and opinion but on a rigorous research base. A secondary goal was to make sure that the process fully involved a broad variety of perspectives from other research agencies, national organizations, and stakeholders. OSEP also made a commitment to address both the scientific aspects and the broader political nature of the issue.

Sidebar A. Office of Special Education Programs, Research to Practice, Learning Disabilities Initiative Group Members.

Elaine Bonner Tompkins Council of Chief State School Officers	**Dan Hallahan** University of Virginia
Anita Booth Special Education Teacher	**Barbara Keogh** University of California—Los Angeles
Sandra Britt Parent	**Ann Kornblet** Parent
Martha Brooks Delaware Department of Education	**Diane Martin** Dasher Green Elementary School
Lynne Cook University of California—Northridge	**Cecil Mercer** University of Florida
Don Deshler University of Kansas	**Rune Simeonsson** Frank Porter Graham Child Development Center
Doug Fuchs Vanderbilt University	**Margaret Trader** Maryland State Department of Education
Jack M. Fletcher University of Texas—Houston Health Science Center	**Joe Torgesen** Florida State University
Frank M. Gresham University of California—Riverside	**Sharon Vaughn** University of Texas at Austin

Committee Work

In May 2000 OSEP brought together a diverse group of stakeholders, including parents, practitioners at the state and local levels, representatives from policy organizations, and researchers. To ensure even greater diversity of perspectives, OSEP included both researchers funded by OSEP and researchers from other agencies that have conducted research related to this area.

Eighteen researchers (see Sidebar A) came together for an intensive planning meeting. OSEP staff presented the following draft plan to the workgroup: (1) commission a set of papers on critical issues in the identification of learning disabilities and organize formal responses to each of the papers, (2) hold an issues conference to present and facilitate discussion, and (3) disseminate the proceedings and results of the process. The planning group fully supported the draft plan but felt strongly about adding a step following the conference and prior to publication of the proceedings. To facilitate conversation on the impact of the information in the papers and from the summit, the group revised the plan to include a roundtable discussion with key organizations and stakeholders as the third step in the process.

Sidebar B. White paper issues.

Historical Perspective
Early Identification
Classification Approach
Decision Making
Discrepancy
Alternative Responses to Intervention
Processing Deficits
Clinical Judgment
Is LD Real?

The next task of the workgroup was to select issues in the identification of learning disabilities that the commissioned white papers would address, as well as prospective authors. After much discussion, the group selected nine issues for the white papers (see Sidebar B). In selecting potential authors, the group looked for researchers who were recognized in the field and could comprehensively address a particular issue. Additional discussions evidenced a desire for a variety of expert opinions on each issue. To address this, the workgroup decided that each issue paper would have at least three research respondents representing diverse perspectives and one practitioner respondent. Potential respondents were identified. This book is a compilation of those nine papers and 36 responses.

The Issues Conference

On August 27 and 28, 2001, OSEP sponsored a by-invitation-only learning disabilities summit called Building a Foundation for the Future. The workgroup wanted this summit to accomplish two main goals: (1) to share the highlights from the papers and responses and (2) to provide an opportunity for a limited number of key stakeholders to begin a discussion on the identification of children with learning disabilities based on the most current research. Participation at the summit was limited to ensure opportunity for discussion; invitations were sent out by OSEP primarily through national organizations. The audience was composed of 250 parents, teachers, school administrators, researchers, higher education faculty members, members of professional organizations, and policy makers.

Each session was formatted to include a presentation of the paper by the primary author and at least three respondent reactions to the paper followed by a facilitated question, answer, and discussion period. Each of the nine sessions was also taped for web broadcast two days after the event to convey the information to a broader audience.

Stakeholder Roundtables

The final phase of the Learning Disabilities Initiative is to hold a series of roundtable discussions with targeted stakeholder groups including researchers, members of national learning disabilities organizations, and general education groups. Most of these roundtables are still in progress. The goal of these roundtables is to provide an opportunity to analyze the issue papers and summit presentations and discuss implications for research, policy, and practice. The workgroup also anticipated that these small roundtable discussions might begin to move the field to a common voice regarding how the identification of children with learning disabilities may be improved.

The first roundtable discussion was held in November 2001 with a select group of researchers including white paper authors, the paper respondents, and members of the learning disabilities workgroup. OSEP wanted to ensure that the information gathered, shared, and used for future decision making was based on the most up-to-date research. The commissioned papers reviewed available research on the specific area identified. Although there is consensus among the papers, conflicting research and conflicting interpretation of that research are also presented. The critical component of this process is the availability of research for decision making. For this research to be useful and have an impact on practice it must be summarized and presented in a user-friendly format.

OSEP also realized the need for this book to have a summary chapter of the research presented. The work of this research roundtable is reflected in the final chapter of this publication. That chapter provides eight consensus statements based on the available research regarding the identification of children with learning disabilities. The Learning Disabilities Initiative has been criticized for overemphasizing early reading and neglecting the other domains of learning disabilities. However, the emphasis on early reading throughout this work was not an intended focus but simply reflects the current state of research in the identification of learning disabilities. The lack of research in the other domain areas reveals a substantial need for future targeted research in learning disabilities.

The second roundtable discussion, held in October 2001, brought together members of NJCLD, including representatives from all of the national learning disabilities organizations and a few related organizations. They met to choose a format that would allow each of the organizations to respond to the issues addressed in the publication and summit presentations. These organizations pinpointed four areas of concentration: identification, eligibility, interventions, and professional development. Each organization responded to these four areas and then reconvened to work on establishing a more common voice on a few critical components. At press time for this book, those groups were still working on a final product. Additional roundtables, primarily with regular education stakeholders, are scheduled. One of the challenges throughout this process has been to keep the papers, presentations, and roundtables focused primarily on the issue of the identification of students with learning disabilities. This challenge was especially apparent in working with the NJCLD organizations, as they traditionally want to address all of the multiple issues affecting children with learning disabilities.

ORGANIZATION OF THE BOOK

This book presents the most current research on nine issues concerning the identification of children with learning disabilities. The book also fulfills one of the major goals of the two-year Learning Disabilities Initiative sponsored by OSEP: making broadly available the best information to build a foundation for future decision making.

Each of the first nine chapters is organized as follows: the major issue paper which reflects the most current research on that topic, followed by four respondent papers reflecting a variety of viewpoints on the topic presented. The first nine chapters address the following issues: the historical perspective; early identification and intervention; the classification approach; approaches to decision making; the discrepancy approach; alternative responses to intervention; processing deficits; the role of clinical judgment; and an analysis of learning disabilities versus low achievement. The inclusion of the respondents in this publication adds diversity and expands on the issues discussed in the primary papers. The final chapter summarizes the results of the researcher roundtable, presenting eight consensus statements derived from the nine papers and a discussion about future implications of this work on research, policy, and practice.

Albert Einstein once said, "The significant problems we face cannot be solved at the same level of thinking we were at when we created them." In this age of accountability and research-based decision making, the research presented in this volume and the discussion of the implications of the current knowledge level on research, practice, and policy should serve as a foundation to improve our level of thinking and greatly affect the quality of future decisions regarding the identification of children with learning disabilities.

CHAPTER I: LEARNING DISABILITIES: HISTORICAL PERSPECTIVES

Daniel P. Hallahan, University of Virginia, &
Cecil D. Mercer, University of Florida

Although the federal government's involvement in learning disabilities through task forces, legislation, and funding has only been evident since the 1960s and 1970s, we can trace learning disabilities' roots back to at least the early 1800s. Thus, learning disabilities may be one of the newest categories officially recognized by the U.S. Department of Education, but the origins of its conceptual foundation are as longstanding, or nearly as longstanding, as many of the other disability categories.

We have divided the history of learning disabilities into five periods: European Foundation Period (c. 1800 to 1920); U.S. Foundation Period (c. 1920 to 1960); Emergent Period (c. 1960 to 1975); Solidification Period (c. 1975 to 1985); Turbulent Period (c. 1985 to 2000). Others before us (Lerner, 2000; Mercer, 1997; Wiederholt, 1974) have also divided the history into roughly similar periods.[1]

EUROPEAN FOUNDATION PERIOD (c. 1800 TO 1920)

During the European Foundation Period, there were two main lines of work relevant to the field of learning disabilities. First, several groundbreaking discoveries in the field of neurology occurred during this time. Second, toward the end of this period, significant seminal articles and books on reading disabilities were published.

Research on Brain-Behavior Relationships

We can trace the origins of the field of learning disabilities back to research in Europe on acquired brain pathology in adults. Men whose names still grace the pages of neurology textbooks conducted this research. One of the primary objectives of this research was the attempt to match up areas of the brain to particular behaviors. A German physician, Franz Joseph Gall, is credited as the first major figure to explore the relationship between brain injury and mental impairment. Gall based much of his theorizing on observations he made of brain-injured soldiers. In a letter published in 1802, he conjectured that three separate parts of the brain are each responsible for what he termed: (a) vital sources (movement and sensation), (b) moral qualities (inclinations of the soul), and (c) intellectual qualities (Head, 1926; Wiederholt, 1974). Of particular relevance to learning disabilities, Gall is known for noting the effect of brain damage on what today would be termed *Broca's aphasia*.

Gall's contributions in linking brain injury and aphasia, however, were largely overshadowed by his association with the phrenology school of thought, the belief that skull shape determines mental and personality attributes. In later years, many considered him a quack. One exception was John Baptiste Bouillaud, Dean of the Medical School of the College of France (Wiederholt, 1974).

In the 1820s, Bouillaud furthered Gall's work through autopsies of several patients with brain injury. Bouillaud did not ascribe to Gall's position on phrenology, but he did agree with much of what he had to say regarding the localization of brain functioning. Although Gall had hypothesized that the control of movement and sensory perception are located in the brain stem, Bouillard concluded that they are located in the cortex. In addition, he asserted that the frontal anterior lobes of the brain control speech.

In the 1860s, Pierre Paul Broca did much to debunk the phrenologists through postmortem observations of adults with brain injury. In particular, Broca is generally known for being the one who did the most to promote the idea that speech functions primarily reside in the left side of the brain.[2] He based his case on autopsies of several patients who had had impaired speech while alive. Broca concluded that a small section of the left side of the brain was responsible for speech. This area, which is located in the inferior left frontal lobe, has come to be called *Broca's area*; persons who have a particular constellation of speech problems involving slow, laborious, dysfluent speech are referred to as having Broca's aphasia. Some have questioned specific aspects of Broca's observations (e.g., Grodzinsky, in press), and neuroscientists now believe that damage to the right side of the brain can play a role, although limited, in causing speech problems. However, Broca's claims have largely withstood the test of time.

Carl Wernicke, a Polish-born physician whose family moved to Germany at an early age, was another major figure who explored brain localization during this period. In 1874, he published a book describing 10 case studies of brain-injured patients with language problems. However, the language disorders they possessed were different from those of Broca's patients as was the particular area of the brain affected (Wernicke, 1874). In contrast to Broca's subjects, Wernicke's patients had fluent and unlabored speech, but the sentences spoken were often meaningless. In addition, his cases had difficulties in recognizing and comprehending words. He called this disorder sensory aphasia, which has become known as *Wernicke's aphasia*. The particular area of the brain, now referred to as *Wernicke's area*, consists of a section of the left temporal lobe.

Research on Reading Disabilities

In 1872, Sir William Broadbent reported on the case of an intelligent adult patient who:

> after head symptoms, completely lost the power of reading either printed or written characters, while he could write readily and correctly from dictation or spontaneously. His conversation was good and his vocabulary extensive, but at times he was at a loss for a name, and he was quite unable, when asked, to name the simplest and most familiar object presented to his notice. The loss of power to read was of course a part of this more general loss of power to name. (Broadbent, 1872, p. 26)

Five years later, Adolph Kussmaul (1877) reported on the case of an adult patient with no apparent disabilities other than a severe reading deficit. He asserted that "a complete text-blindness may exist, although the power of sight, the intellect, and the powers of speech are intact." In emphasizing the specificity of the reading problems, in isolation from other types of potential problems, Kussmaul gave birth to the idea of *specific* reading disability. Kussmaul labeled the condition *word-blindness*:

> In medical literature we find cases recorded as aphasia which should not properly be designated by this name, since the patients were still able to express their thoughts by speech and writing. They had not lost the power either of speaking or of writing; they were no longer able, however, although the hearing was perfect, to understand the words which they heard, or, although the sight was perfect, to read the written words which they saw. This morbid inability we will style, in order to have the shortest possible names at our disposition, *word-deafness* and *word-blindness*... (Kussmaul, 1877, p. 770)

A reciprocal academic relationship between two physicians—John Hinshelwood from France and W. Pringle Morgan from England—was the catalyst for extending this work on acquired word-blindness in adults to congenital word-blindness in children. Hinshelwood's first foray into research on word-blindness was with an adult whom he saw in 1894 and followed until his death in 1903. After his death an autopsy was performed, and Hinshelwood concluded that the section of the brain affected was the left angular gyrus, which is immediately posterior to Wernicke's area.

Hinshelwood's paper describing this patient, published in 1895 in *Lancet,* prompted Morgan to report on what is believed to be the first published case of a child with congenital word-blindness.[3] Morgan's case was a 14-year-old boy who had a history of severe reading problems:

> He seems to have no power of preserving and storing up the visual impression produced by words—hence the words, though seen, have no significance for him. His visual memory for words is defective or absent; which is equivalent to saying that he is what Kussmaul has termed "word blind"…

> Cases of word blindness are always interesting, and this case is, I think, particularly so. It is unique, so far as I know, in that it follows upon no injury or illness, but is evidently congenital, and due most probably to defective development of that region of the brain, disease of which in adults produces practically the same symptoms—that is, the left angular gyrus.

> I may add that the boy is bright and of average intelligence in conversation. His eyes are normal, there is no hemianopsia, and his eyesight is good. The schoolmaster who has taught him for some years says that he would be the smartest lad in the school if the instruction were entirely oral. (Morgan, 1896, p. 1378)

Hinshelwood, in turn, used Morgan's case as an impetus to turn his attention to congenital, in addition to acquired, word-blindness. From the late 1890s into the early 20th century, Hinshelwood gathered data on several cases of acquired and congenital word-blindness and published his observations in his classic volume, *Congenital Word-Blindness* (Hinshelwood, 1917). He was one of the first to note at least two important aspects of reading disability in children. First, he noted the preponderance of males with the condition. Out of the 12 cases he presented in the book, 10 of them were males. Furthermore, he cited an article published in *Lancet* in 1904 by Stephenson, in which the author had commented that of the 16 cases reported up until then in the literature, 13 of them were males.

Second, Hinshelwood highlighted the potentially inherited aspect of reading disability. He reported on six cases within two generations of the same family:

If we analyze the symptoms manifested by these six cases, we are struck with their similarity. The symptoms of all six children were practically identical in kind, but only differed in degree. Their defect was strictly confined to their inability to recognize by sight, words and letters, with one exception, that of Case XI, where the inability was extended to numbers also. (Hinshelwood, 1917, p. 72)

Furthermore, he cited a growing body of literature published in several journals (e.g., *Lancet, The Ophthalmoscope, Ophthalmic Review*) of cases of congenital word-blindness occurring within close relatives. Similar to the literature on gender, the cases were relatively few in number; however, evidence was accumulating to suggest that congenital word-blindness was primarily manifested in males and was often inherited.

Hinshelwood also addressed the issue of diagnosis and prevalence of word-blindness, foretelling current-day debates over these issues:

In my first contribution on this subject I said: "I have little doubt that these cases of congenital word-blindness are by no means so rare as the absence of recorded cases would lead us to infer. Their rarity is, I think, accounted for by the fact that when they do occur they are not recognized." ... In educational circles there was even a tendency to exaggerate the frequency...and I find...the statements "that these cases...are of very common occurrence," and that "one in every thousand of the children in our elementary schools at least shows this defect." ...

The truth is that this great divergence of opinion...is simply due to the fact that some later writers have extended the term congenital word-blindness to include slight degrees of defect in the visual word center, while the earlier writers had reserved it only for those grave cases which could be regarded as pathological. (Hinshelwood, 1917, pp. 76–82)

Hinshelwood postulated that the primary disability these children had was in visual memory for words and letters. Thus, his educational recommendations, although not very specific, dealt with training children to increase their visual memory for words. Furthermore, he was a strong advocate for intensive, individualized one-on-one instruction: "It is not possible to teach such children in ordinary elementary schools.... The first condition of successful instruction in such cases...is that the child must have personal instruction and be taught alone" (Hinshelwood, 1917, p. 99).[4]

U.S. FOUNDATION PERIOD (C.1920 TO 1960)

By about the 1920s, clinicians and researchers in the United States began to take an interest in the work of the Europeans who had been studying brain-behavior relationships and children and adults with learning difficulties. The U.S. researchers focused their efforts on language and reading disabilities and perceptual, perceptual-motor, and attention disabilities.

Language and Reading Disabilities

In the United States, there were several key figures from medicine, psychology, and education during this period who used the research of Hinshelwood and other Europeans as a springboard for their own work. Primary among these were Samuel Orton, Grace Fernald, Marion Monroe, and Samuel Kirk.

Samuel Orton. Samuel Orton was arguably the key figure in setting the stage for the study of reading disabilities in the United States. The primary professional society devoted to reading disabilities, the International Dyslexia Association, was originally named the Orton Dyslexia Society.

In January of 1925, Orton, then a neuropathologist at the State Psychopathic Hospital in Iowa City, set up a 2-week, mobile clinic in Greene County, Iowa. As a part of this "experiment," local teachers were invited to refer students "who were considered defective or who were retarded or failing in their school work" (Orton, 1925, p. 582). Fourteen of the 88 students were referred primarily because they had great difficulty in learning to read. Orton highlighted the fact that many of these students scored in the near-average, average, or above-average range on the Stanford-Binet IQ test—one had an IQ of 122, four had IQs between 100 and 110, five had IQs between 90 and 100, one had an IQ of 85, and four had IQs between 70 and 80.

Hinshelwood had also noted that many of his cases of congenital word-blindness were intelligent, but with the advent of IQ tests Orton was able to lend a certain degree of objectivity to this notion. Furthermore, presaging later references to the Matthew effect, Orton speculated that the IQ score might not always reflect true intellectual ability in students with reading disabilities. In describing what he termed a typical case, a student with an IQ of 71, he stated: "I was strongly impressed with the feeling that this estimate did not do justice to the boy's mental equipment, and that the low rating was to be explained by the fact that the test is inadequate to gage the equipment in a case of such a special disability" (Orton, 1925, p. 584).

After his seminal article in 1925, Orton continued to study children with reading disabilities over the next several years, with his work being summarized in his classic book, *Reading, Writing, and Speech Problems in Children* (Orton, 1937). Although he relied heavily on Hinshelwood's prior work, Orton's views differed from Hinshelwood's in at least three important respects. First, Orton had a much more liberal view of the prevalence of reading disabilities. Whereas Hinshelwood had bristled at the notion that one per thousand of students in elementary schools might have "word-blindness," Orton offered that "somewhat over 10 per cent of the total school population" (Orton, 1939, p. 59) had reading disabilities. He noted that Hinshelwood had argued for restricting the diagnosis of word-blindness to those cases in which there would be no question about whether there was pathology present. Orton argued, however, that Hinshelwood:

> did not...offer any usable criterion as to how such a separation of the pathological cases could be made, and our experience in studying and retraining several hundred such cases over a period of years has convinced us that [they] cannot be so divided but rather that they form a graded series including all degrees of severity of handicap. (Orton, 1937, pp. 71–72)

Second, although they both thought reading disabilities were often inherited, Hinshelwood pointed to agenesis of the angular gyrus in the dominant hemisphere as the site of the problem. Although Orton considered the angular gyrus of the dominant hemisphere as "essential to maintaining a normal reading skill" (Orton, 1937, p. 39), he viewed reading as a complex activity that involved several areas of the brain. Rejecting the idea of defects in brain development, Orton focused instead on the inheritance of mixed cerebral dominance, or motor intergrading, as being behind many cases of reading disabilities.

Orton linked mixed dominance to the major symptoms he frequently observed in the clinic: (a) reversals of letters such as *p* and *q* and *b* and *d*; (b) confusion of palindromes such as *was* and *saw*; (c) reading from right to left, manifested by reversals of paired letters, syllables within words, or whole words within sentences; and (d) a propensity to "mirror read and/or write." He theorized that the nondominant hemisphere of the brain stored mirror engrams of the engrams recorded in the dominant hemisphere. For example, in reading the word *was*, the dominant hemisphere would store *was* in the dominant hemisphere while at the same time storing *saw* in the nondominant hemisphere. In those who have complete hemispheric dominance, the dominant hemisphere controls language and, therefore, the mirrored engrams are suppressed. In the case of mixed dominance, however, the mirrored engrams often emerge causing the child to reverse letters or words.

Third, Orton's emphasis on cerebral dominance and reversals led him to propose a different term than word-blindness to describe the children whom he was seeing in his clinic:

> The term "congenital word-blindness" because of its association with the acquired condition and the implications therefrom, does not seem to be properly descriptive of this disability, and I would therefore like to offer the term "strephosymbolia" from the Greek words, [*strepho*], twist, and [*symbolon*], symbol…. The prefix "strepho" has been chosen to indicate the turning or reversals…. "Symbolon" is used in its original meaning of "word," "sign" or "token,"…. Strephosymbolia thus seems nicely suited to our cases in which our analysis points to confusion, because of reversals, in the memory images of symbols resulting in a failure of association between the visually presented stimulus and its concept. (Orton, 1925, p. 610)

Ironically, neither term—word-blindness, strephosymbolia—fared well historically, the former primarily because of its focus on the visual aspect of reading, the latter primarily because of its emphasis on mixed cerebral dominance and reversals. Although few subscribe to Orton's views on cerebral dominance and reversals today, he has had an enduring influence in the realm of remediation techniques in at least two respects. First, he was one of the first to advocate focusing on phonics instruction with students with reading disabilities. He criticized the then-current "look and say" or "sight reading" method of reading instruction for the general population and proposed that:

> logical training for these children [those with strephosymbolia] would be that of extremely thorough repetitive drill on the fundamentals of phonic association with letter forms, both visually presented and reproduced in writing, until the correct associations were built up and the permanent elision of the reversed images and reversals in direction were assured. (Orton, 1925, p. 614)

Orton later emphasized that teaching letter sounds was not enough, that there was a need for sound blending:

> We have repeatedly seen children referred to us as reading disability cases with the statement that the phonetic method had been tried but had failed. In these cases examination has revealed the fact that while the teaching of the phonetic equivalents may have been fairly complete, the next step, that of teaching the blending of the letter sounds in the exact sequence in which they occur in the word, had not been attempted or had been poorly

carried out. It is this process of synthesizing the word as a spoken unit from its component sounds that often makes much more difficulty for the strephosymbolic child than do the static reversals and letter confusions. (Orton, 1937, p. 162)

Second, Orton was one of the first to introduce the idea of multisensory training. In particular, he stressed the use of the kinesthetic function by having students trace letters while sounding them out (Orton, 1937). And Orton's ideas served as a stimulus for the work of Anna Gillingham and Bessie Stillman, whose book, *Remedial Work for Reading, Spelling, and Penmanship* (1936) emphasized building the following linkages: visual-auditory, auditory-visual, auditory-kinesthetic, and kinesthetic-visual. Gillingham and Stillman believed "it is essential to establish each linkage with patient care, even into the thousandth repetition" (Gillingham & Stillman, 1936, p. 36).

Today, practitioners still use many of the ideas of Orton and Gillingham and Stillman. These practices have come to be referred to as the Orton-Gillingham Approach. Basically, the Orton-Gillingham Approach is a phonics-based, multisensory method using the visual, auditory, and kinesthetic modalities for reading-decoding and spelling instruction.

Grace Fernald. Fernald was another figure associated with a multisensory approach to reading disabilities. As part of her rationale, she provided a brief history of the use of the kinesthetic modality to teach reading, including references to Plato in the third century B.C. Horace in 65 B.C., Quintilian in 68 A.D., Charlemagne in the 8th century, and Locke in the 17th century (Fernald, 1943).

Fernald differed from Orton and Gillingham, however, in her opposition to a phonics-based emphasis on sounding out letters and words. Instead, she emphasized reading and writing words as wholes.

Fernald actually predated Orton with respect to advocating for a multisensory approach to reading disabilities. In 1921, she coauthored an article describing remedial treatment of six cases of students with reading disabilities at the University of California–Los Angeles (UCLA) Clinic School (Fernald & Keller, 1921). Fernald and Keller developed what came to be known as the VAKT (visual-auditory-kinesthetic-tactual) method, which is composed of five stages. First, the teacher asks the child to pick some words that he or she would like to learn. The teacher then writes the word on the board, and the child says the word to him- or herself and traces the letters with the first two fingers of the dominant hand. Once learned, the teacher erases the word and the student writes the word, saying the syllables. The second stage is the same as the first except sentences are used rather than individual words.

In the third stage, the child selects a book he wants to read. The student and teacher work through the book, one paragraph at a time. Words the student has not already learned are exposed through an adjustable slit in a piece of cardboard. If the student is unable to read the word, the teacher reads it aloud, and then the student says the word and writes it without looking at the copy. If the student still has problems writing the word, the teacher writes it and the student learns it as in the first stage. In the fourth stage, the slit is widened to include phrases, and the exposures are so brief that the student is not able to read word by word. After achieving recognition of the phrases, the child reads the entire paragraph to himself and reports on what he read. In the final stage, the teacher has the child read alone.

Over the years, the UCLA Clinic School expanded and by the early 1940s there were about 20 children admitted each academic year, with an additional 60 to 80 cases seen in the summer. Students received intensive instruction in basic school subjects, with a focus on reading instruction. In 1943, Fernald authored *Remedial Techniques in Basic School Subjects*, in which she summarized work in the clinic as well as in "experimental" classrooms established in the public schools, some of which contained a high concentration of children for whom English was a second language (Fernald, 1943).

Fernald kept extensive records on the progress of the students. Although lacking control groups, she reported notable gains for reading, spelling, penmanship, foreign language, and arithmetic. In addition, she reported follow-up data for many of the students, which were equally impressive. Whether Fernald's results warrant the following assertion she made in the preface to her book is arguable, but it is interesting to contrast her confident optimism with some of the present-day lamentations about the ineffectiveness of special education:

> Since no abilities are required for the mastery of reading, writing, and arithmetic which are not already possessed by the ordinary, normal individual, it seems obvious that there is no such thing as a person of normal intelligence who cannot learn these basic skills. The follow-up records of our cases over a period of years show that the application of established psychological principles makes success in the fundamentals possible for any normal individual. (Fernald, 1943, p. *v*.)

Marion Monroe. Having served as Orton's research associate for his mobile clinic, Marion Monroe tried out his methods along with the methods of Fernald and Keller. While in Iowa, she developed diagnostic tests and used the results to guide instruction. Using a combination of kinesthetic tracing techniques and sound blending, she reported success with 29 children with reading disabilities (Monroe, 1928).

From Iowa, Monroe took a position at the Institute for Juvenile Research, a residential facility for delinquent boys with mental retardation. At the Institute, Monroe developed a *synthetic phonetic approach*, which began with having the child identify initial consonants and then vowels for pictures mounted on cards. After success with this, the teacher introduced sound blending and had the child read stories. In addition, the teacher used tracing whenever it was deemed necessary.

In her book, *Children Who Cannot Read* (1932), Monroe reported on several "experiments" in which she tested out her methods. In the first study, she compared three groups: Group A (89 students) was referred to the clinic and received instruction under close supervision there or in their home school, Group B (50 students) received instruction in their home school from teachers who came regularly to the Institute for teaching suggestions, Group C (50 students) received ordinary instruction in their home school. The major differences between Groups A and B with respect to treatment was that the teachers for the latter group delivered instruction more sporadically (before or after school or during free periods) and under less supervision: "The remedial work done in Group B, therefore, was not so intensive as that of Group A, and was subjected to a greater variety of disrupting influences" (Monroe, 1932, p. 138). Group A's mean IQ was 101, Group B's was 89, and Group C's was 92. Over the course of the year, Group A gained 1.39 years in reading achievement, Group B gained 0.79 years, and Group C only gained 0.14 years.

Monroe also reported on four field-based projects in cities near Chicago where she was invited to train teachers to work with students with reading disabilities. In the first two, teachers were trained to provide one-on-one instruction. In City A, 15 teachers worked with 15 children over 2 months, providing an average of 13.8 hours of one-on-one instruction. The group made an average gain of 0.67 years in reading achievement. In City B, after 5 weeks of instruction and an average of 10.1 hours of one-on-one instruction, 30 children averaged 0.81 years growth in reading achievement.

In the last two field-based projects, students were taught in small special classes, which met with a trained teacher two or three times a week for 30- to 40-minute periods. In the first one, 41 students from grades 2 through 8 in City B made an average gain of 0.7 years in 2 months. In the second one, 10 students from a special school for truant children met daily in two groups of five for 3 months, which resulted in an average gain of 1.0 year in reading achievement.

Monroe's summary of the studies is prescient with respect to what many learning disabilities researchers today report, especially concerning the need for intensive instruction by well-trained teachers:

Two hundred and thirty-five children were given remedial training by one hundred and thirty-one teachers. Progress in reading was made in a large percentage of cases studied, not only when children were trained under carefully controlled laboratory conditions, but also under conditions possible in public schools. Progress in reading was made under individual instruction and also in small groups of children....

The remedial-reading methods were found to be direct and readily understood. Public school teachers learned to apply the methods in the course of conferences and demonstration lessons.

The rate of progress in reading under remedial instruction was found to be a function of the child's intelligence, his age, the number of hours spent in training, the number of months during which treatment was continued, the severity of the disability, the personality and behavioral difficulties encountered in applying the remedial training, and the closeness of supervision of the remedial techniques. Children and teachers varied greatly with regard to these factors....

The children with whom the remedial work failed were those whose reading difficulties were complicated by behavior disorders which the teachers were unable to control, or those to whom the remedial work was given irregularly and without persistent, systematic, or sympathetic treatment. (Monroe, 1932, pp. 157–158)

Although Monroe's studies lacked the kind of methodological rigor demanded by today's standards, e.g., random assignment and limited use of control groups, the impressive gains she reports are difficult to disregard completely. She was far ahead of her time with respect to the care she took to document the efficacy of her methods. Furthermore, in addition to furthering the work of Orton and Fernald through systematic investigation, she pioneered two practices that are fundamental to the field of learning disabilities today.

First, Monroe introduced the notion of discrepancy between actual achievement and expected achievement as a way of identifying students with reading disabilities. She calculated a "reading index" by comparing the student's reading grade (the average of four tests: Gray's Oral Reading Paragraphs, reading comprehension as measured either by the Haggerty Test for cases less than third grade achievement or by the Monroe Test, word analysis from the Iota Word Test from the Monroe Test, and word discrimination from the Word Discrimination Test from the Monroe Test) to an average of the student's chronological, mental, and arithmetic grade. For example, a boy who chronologically is at a grade of 3.6, who on the basis of the Stanford-Binet has a mental grade of 4.0, and who has an arithmetic grade of 3.5 would have an average of 3.7. If his grade scores on the four reading tests average

2.0, then his reading achievement would only be 2.0/3.7, or 54%, of his expected achievement. Monroe advocated using 80% as a cut-off for having a reading disability, and using this cut-off she estimated that about 12% of the population had reading disabilities.

Second, Monroe went beyond using standardized tests just to identify children with reading disabilities. She advocated analyzing the specific types of reading errors children made on the tests in order to guide instruction, thus introducing the notion of what would later be called *diagnostic-prescriptive teaching.* She developed individual profiles of errors made on three reading tests (Gray's Oral Reading Examination, the Iota Word Test, and the Word Discrimination Test from her own test). The errors included faulty vowels, faulty consonants, reversals, addition of sounds, omission of sounds, substitution of words, repetition of words, addition of words, omission of words, refusals, and words aided. Based on the types of errors the child presented, Monroe had specific remedial training suggestions.

Samuel Kirk. In 1929, Samuel Kirk began graduate school in psychology at the University of Chicago. As part of his training, he spent time as a resident instructor at the Institute for Juvenile Research, where Marion Monroe worked. Kirk's duties were varied, but there was one fortuitous experience that was life-changing for Kirk and the eventual field of learning disabilities:

> At this school I taught in the afternoon and served as a recreational worker after school. In the evenings I helped the nurses put the boys to bed and see that they stayed there. In reading the clinical folders of one of these children from the famous Institute for Juvenile Research, I noticed that the boy was labeled as "word blind," a term I had never heard before in my psychology courses. He was ten years old, a nonreader, and had a recorded IQ of 82. This clinical folder referred to Marion Monroe's monograph [Monroe, 1928] on reading disabilities, Hinshelwood's book [1917] on congenital word blindness, and Fernald's kinesthetic method. After reading these references, which I found the next day in the university library, I arranged to tutor the boy at nine o'clock in the evening, after the boys were supposed to be asleep. This boy, who was eager to learn, sneaked quietly out of bed at the appointed time each night and met me in a small space between the two dormitory rooms..., actually, in the doorway of the boy's toilet. By making this arrangement we both knew we were violating a regulation, since the head nurse had directed me not to allow the boys out of bed after nine. In the same vein as the Boston Tea Party, and knowing the consequences of civil disobedience, I decided to take a chance

and violate the directions since the cause was good. I often state that my first experience in tutoring a case of reading disability was not in a school, was not in a clinic, but in a boy's lavatory. (Kirk, 1976, pp. 242–243)

After 7 months, the boy was reading at the third grade level and he was released from the Institute to attend regular school. Monroe, hearing of Kirk's success, invited him to confer with her about his tutoring. She then tutored Kirk in diagnosing and remediating severe cases of reading disabilities.

For his master's thesis, Kirk (1933) compared the Fernald kinesthetic method with the look-and-say method, finding them equal with regard to number of trials required for learning but retention being better for the manual tracing method. Kirk was then employed as a psychologist at another residential facility for children with mental retardation, Wayne County Training School in Northville, Michigan, an institution that was to become a testing ground for many instructional techniques used for children with learning disabilities.

While at Wayne County, Kirk pursued his doctorate at the University of Michigan. Influenced by a number of theoretical notions coming out about the brain and learning, including Orton's theory about cerebral dominance, Kirk studied brain-behavior relationships, with his dissertation focused on surgically creating lesions in rats and testing them for handedness and strephosymbolia (Kirk, 1935, 1936). Kirk later noted that this foray into neurophysiology had little direct bearing on his future work in learning disabilities other than to result in an aversion to terms such as "brain dysfunction," "strephosymbolia," and "dyslexia": "I feel that it is more parsimonious to give a designation in behavioral terms by stating, for example, that the child has not learned to read" (Kirk, 1976).

Kirk teamed up with Thorleif Hegge, who had recently emigrated from Norway and was brought to Wayne County as the director of research. Hegge and Kirk, along with Kirk's wife, Winifred Day Kirk, coauthored *Remedial Reading Drills* (Hegge, Kirk, & Kirk, 1936). Influenced by Orton, Fernald, and Monroe, as well as the principles of learning from the school of functional psychology at the University of Chicago, the approach taken in the remedial drills was a

carefully programmed phonic system which emphasizes sound blending and kinesthetic experiences. The program is based upon the following principles: minimal change; overlearning; prompting and confirmation; one response for each symbol; and social reinforcement. Kirk (1940) followed up this earlier interest in reading with a book on teaching slow-learning children to read. (Wiederholt, 1974, p. 32)

Kirk moved on to the Milwaukee State Teachers College and then to the University of Illinois in the late 1940s to head up the special education program. In 1949, he established the first experimental preschool for children with mental retardation. In so doing, "to be able to analyze the communication problems of younger children at the outset or before the remediation, it became necessary for us to develop tests to isolate some of these abilities and disabilities" (Kirk, 1970, p. 108).

Kirk worked for the next decade on refining an assessment approach for pinpointing specific disabilities in children. Influenced by Monroe's use of profiles (Kirk, 1976), he aimed to come up with an instrument that would provide profiles of intra-individual differences on key psycholinguistic abilities. The result was the first edition of the *Illinois Test of Psycholinguistic Abilities* (*ITPA*) (Kirk, McCarthy, & Kirk, 1961). We return to the *ITPA* in our discussion of the next time period (c.1960 to 1975).

Perceptual, Perceptual-Motor, and Attention Disabilities

As with the research on language and reading disabilities, the early research on perceptual, perceptual-motor, and attention disabilities was focused on adults with brain injuries, and much of it was conducted by Europeans, many of whom had immigrated to the United States. Key figures during this period were Kurt Goldstein, Heinz Werner, Alfred Strauss, Laura Lehtinen, William Cruickshank, and Newell Kephart.

Kurt Goldstein. As a physician and director of a hospital for soldiers who had incurred head wounds during World War I, Kurt Goldstein studied many cases of brain injury over several years. Studying his patients, whom he referred to as "traumatic dements," within a clinical framework, he reported that they tended to display a consistent constellation of behaviors: hyperactivity, forced responsiveness to stimuli, figure-background confusion, concrete thinking, perseveration, meticulosity, and catastrophic reaction (Goldstein, 1936, 1939).

Forced responsiveness to stimuli was characterized by the soldiers' indiscriminant reactions to stimuli, a seeming inability to distinguish essential from inessential. It was as though they were driven to respond to things in their environment, thus displaying a high degree of distractibility.

One can consider figure-background confusion as a particular manifestation of forced responsiveness to stimuli. Being from the German Gestalt School of psychology, Goldstein was interested in his patients' perception of form and figure-ground relationships. He interpreted much of the soldiers' distractibility as a deficiency in discriminating figure from background. In the case of reading, for example, they would have problems focusing on a word or phrase in the context of hundreds of words on a page of print.

Goldstein hypothesized that abstract thinking, because of its primary place in the hierarchy of intellectual behaviors, was one of the first aspects of cognition to be affected by brain injury. He noted that whenever one of the patients

> must transcend concrete (immediate) experience in order to act—whenever he must refer to things in an imaginary way—he then fails.... Each problem which forces him beyond the sphere of immediate reality to that of the "possible," to the sphere of representation, insures his failure. (Goldstein, 1939, p. 29)

Goldstein's patients had a tendency to repeat the same behaviors over and over again. This perseveration could be verbal or motor. Goldstein conjectured that it was a way that the damaged organism could rescue itself from disorganization.

Another symptom used to ward off disorganization was meticulosity. Many of the soldiers became very rigid in their daily living habits, structuring their time schedules and objects in their environment. Goldstein theorized that this penchant for routine was used by the patients to protect themselves from overstimulation and disorganized perceptions. If the patients were unsuccessful in dealing with overstimulation and disorganization, they could experience a "catastrophic reaction," a total emotional breakdown similar to a severe temper tantrum. Goldstein attributed such outbursts to the patients' inability to make sense of the chaotic perceptual world in which they lived.

Goldstein highlighted the resiliency of the brain-damaged organism in automatically being able to compensate for disturbed functions. His conceptualization of the brain was in the Gestalt tradition of looking at the total array of behaviors rather than individual symptoms, which was in contrast to those seeking to localize specific functions with particular areas of the brain.

Heinz Werner, Alfred Strauss, Newell Kephart, and Laura Lehtinen. Goldstein's findings served as the basis for the research of Heinz Werner, a developmental psychologist, and Alfred Strauss, a neuropsychiatrist. With the rise to power of Hitler, Werner and Strauss both fled Germany, with Werner going first to the Netherlands and Strauss to Spain. Eventually, both ended up in the United States at the Wayne County Training School. There they teamed up to focus on whether brain damage in children with mental retardation resulted in the same symptoms as what Goldstein had found in adults who were not retarded.

Using a dichotomy introduced earlier by Larsen (1931), Strauss and Werner divided residents at Wayne County for their studies into those with exogenous versus endogenous mental retardation. Children with exogenous mental retardation were considered to have a brain disease or injury of some kind whereas those with endogenous mental retardation were presumed retarded because of heredity or a poor learning environment.

Through a series of laboratory-based studies, Werner and Strauss found the exogenous group to exhibit more forced responsiveness than the endogenous group to visual and auditory stimuli (Strauss & Werner, 1942; Werner & Strauss, 1939, 1940, 1941). For example, in one study (Werner & Strauss, 1941) they presented children with a series of slides, exposing each slide for only a fraction of a second. Each slide contained a drawing of a familiar figure such as sailboat or a cup, embedded in a background such as wavy or undulating lines. After each slide, the child was asked to identify what he or she had just seen. The exogenous group was more likely to refer to the background and was less able to identify the figure correctly. In addition to their laboratory studies, using a behavior rating scale they found children classified as exogenous to be more disinhibited, impulsive, erratic, and socially unaccepted (Strauss & Kephart,[5] 1939).

Werner and Strauss's studies did not go without criticism. The focus of the criticism was on the procedures used to identify participants as exogenous versus endogenous mentally retarded. They diagnosed the child as having exogenous mental retardation if none of the immediate family members was retarded and if there was a history of prenatal, natal, or postnatal disease or damage to the brain. Additionally, a child could be diagnosed as exogenous mentally retarded purely on behavioral characteristics that previous research (e.g., Goldstein's studies) had found associated with brain injury. For example, if the child was hyperactive and distractible in the classroom, then he or she was considered to have exogenous mental retardation. This reliance on behavioral symptoms for the diagnosis of exogenous mental retardation caused some to point out the possible circularity of forming their groups on the basis of symptoms that were very similar to the ones on which they were then attempting to differentiate the children (Sarason, 1949).

Criticisms of Werner and Strauss's work were undoubtedly valid with respect to their attributing brain disease or injury as the cause of forced responsiveness to stimuli, hyperactivity, distractibility, and so forth. However, this does not deny the fact that Werner and Strauss had found consistent behavioral differences between the exogenous and endogenous groups, regardless of whether the differences were caused by brain injury or not:

> It is important to point out here that up until this time mental retarda-
> tion was perceived as a relatively homogenous state.... Consequently no
> differential or individual educational or psychological programming was
> initiated on their behalf. Dispelling the long-standing notion that there
> were no individual differences among the retarded, the work of Werner
> and Strauss, therefore, had revolutionary impact. (Hallahan & Kauffman,
> 1976, p. 6)

This impact was manifested in the form of differential educational programming
for the exogenous group. Prompting the Wayne County researchers to look at individualizing instruction for the exogenous group was a survey they did of the first
500 admissions to Wayne County (Strauss & Kephart, 1939). They found that 4 or
5 years after admission to Wayne County, the IQs of the exogenous group declined
2.5 points whereas the IQs of the endogenous group increased 4.0 points. Furthermore, they investigated those children whose IQ scores could be traced back prior
to institutionalization and found that the exogenous group showed a steady decline before and after institutionalization; but the endogenous group showed a
decline in IQ until admittance, whereupon the trend was reversed and their IQs
rose (Kephart & Strauss, 1940).

The Wayne County research team hypothesized that the endogenous group, in contrast to the exogenous group, was receiving an appropriate education. Noting the
highly stimulating nature of the educational program at the school, they concluded
that it was not a good fit for children who were highly distractible, impulsive, and
hyperactive. Their first primary recommendation was to provide an environment
in which inessential stimuli were attenuated and essential stimuli were accentuated
(Werner & Strauss, 1940). This was followed by more elaboration on the teaching
methods (Strauss, 1943), culminating with two classic volumes: *Psychopathology
and Education of the Brain-Injured Child* (Strauss & Lehtinen, 1947) and *Psychopathology and Education of the Brain-Injured Child: Progress in Theory and Clinic* (Vol.
2; Strauss & Kephart, 1955). The first volume, in particular, described a number of
educational recommendations for children with exogenous mental retardation. The
focus of the recommendations was on providing a distraction-free environment
for the students:

> The class group is small—twelve children is the maximum number....
> The classroom for these children is large enough to permit each child to
> be seated at a considerable distance from any other. There is only a mini-
> mum of pictures, murals, bulletin boards, and the usual stimulating vi-
> sual materials of the average classroom. (Strauss & Lehtinen, 1947, p. 131)

To avoid auditory distractions, they recommended the class be on the second floor where the windows were in front of a little used court, and to avoid visual distractions, they suggested covering the lower part of the windows with paint. In addition, they discouraged the teachers from wearing "distracting influence of ornamentation such as bracelets, earrings, dangling necklaces, and flowers in the hair" (Strauss & Lehtinen, 1947, p. 131).

In addition to focusing on manipulating the environment, Strauss and Lehtinen placed a heavy emphasis on remediating students' perceptual disturbances:[6]

> We cannot state too strongly that all these factors [e.g., emotional disturbance, immaturity, boredom, absence from school] can and do contribute toward reading difficulties in brain-injured children but beyond these factors one should seek for evidence of general or perceptual disturbances which, if present, should be clinically regarded as the primary causal agents and therefore the ones to be attacked. (Strauss & Lehtinen, 1947, p. 174)

William Cruickshank. While pursuing a doctorate at the University of Michigan, Cruickshank worked on research at Wayne County. There, he was heavily influenced by the ideas of Werner and Strauss:

> There were others, but two…became particularly significant in my life: Dr. Heinz Werner and Dr. Alfred A. Strauss. These two men, along with their wives, became important persons to me and my wife, professionally and socially, and so remained until the two died. Strauss, the idea man, Werner the laboratory scientist so well epitomized in Sinclair Lewis' *Arrowsmith*. Both were patient; both were thoughtful to suggest and to raise questions which had to be answered. Both were energetic and constantly pointed other directions in which my professional life might go— theirs! The inoculation took well, and their thinking has been mine for more than thirty years. (Cruickshank, 1976, p. 102)

Cruickshank was key in building a bridge from the Wayne County research group's work with children with mental retardation to children of normal intelligence, many of whom today would be identified as learning disabled. The construction of this bridge began with research on children with cerebral palsy.

After receiving his doctorate, Cruickshank took a position at Syracuse University in 1946. Along with his first doctoral student, Jane Dolphin, Cruickshank embarked on a series of studies. They found that students with cerebral palsy and near-normal, normal, or above-normal intelligence performed similarly to Werner and Strauss's children with exogenous mental retardation (Dolphin, 1950; Dolphin &

Cruickshank, 1951a, b, c, d). These studies were followed by even more extensive studies of perceptual and figure-background abilities in children with cerebral palsy of near-normal, normal, or above-normal intelligence (Cruickshank, Bice, & Wallen, 1957; Cruickshank, Bice, Wallen, & Lynch, 1965). Again, the children with cerebral palsy displayed more forced responsiveness to the background than did a control group who did not have cerebral palsy.

Finding the same behavioral characteristics in children with cerebral palsy as had been found in children with exogenous mental retardation led Cruickshank and Dolphin (1951) to recommend the same educational program for students with cerebral palsy as had been developed for those with exogenous mental retardation a la Strauss and Lehtinen (1947). In particular, their recommendations focused on the provision of a distraction-free environment.

In the late 1950s, Cruickshank took the notion of educational programming for distractible and hyperactive children one step further, a step that placed his work right in the middle of the developing field of learning disabilities. He initiated a demonstration-pilot study, the Montgomery County (Maryland) Project, for 1 year. The results, along with extensive descriptions of the students and teaching methods used, were published in *A Teaching Method for Brain-Injured and Hyperactive Children* (Cruickshank, Bentzen, Ratzeburg, & Tannhauser, 1961). The project included four classes (two experimental and two control) of 10 children each. The 40 children (37 males) were matched on chronological age, IQ, instructional or achievement levels, previous experience in special education, perseveration, hyperactivity, and evidence of neurological damage. At the beginning of the year, the students ranged in age from about 6½ to 9½ years and had IQs from 51 to 107. Thus, several of the students had IQs in the normal range, and several more were thought to have depressed IQ scores because of behavioral characteristics such as distractibility. Cruickshank et al. wrestled with criteria to use for inclusion in the study and ended up focusing on hyperactivity:

> The authors of this study and members of the Diagnostic Team struggled for many hours to obtain a meeting of the minds regarding definitions. They were hindered by the stereotypes of the several professions and by the literature which employed such terms as *brain injury, brain damage,* and *brain disorder....*

> The children about whom this monograph is concerned are those who are defined as hyperactive, with or without the diagnosis of brain damage. Specific brain injury is difficult to delineate in every instance....

Hyperactivity is herein defined to include…short attention span, visual and auditory distractibility, and disturbances of perception leading to dissociative tendencies. (Cruickshank et al., 1961, pp. 9–10)

Even though they focused on hyperactivity, the extensive case histories Cruickshank et al. presented indicate that many of the children, today, would be considered learning disabled and/or learning disabled with comorbid attention deficit hyperactivity disorder (ADHD).

Similar to the educational program recommended by Strauss and Lehtinen (1947), the Montgomery County Project focused on providing an environment that would help students cope with their distractibility and hyperactivity. Thus, the program emphasized (a) reducing irrelevant stimuli, (b) enhancing relevant stimuli, and (c) providing highly structured assignments. For example, students frequently used cubicles to shield them from irrelevant stimulation; windows were opaque; the classrooms were painted in a uniform color; closets and cabinets were enclosed; and materials such as calendars, handwriting charts, paintings, murals, and so forth were only put on display when needed. On the other hand, there was an attempt to make teaching materials used during instruction as colorful and stimulating as possible:

> …what is meant by a structured program? For example, upon coming into the classroom the child will hang his hat and coat on a given hook— not on any hook of his choice, but on the same hook every day. He will place his lunch box, if he brings one, on a specific shelf each day. He will then go to his cubicle, take his seat, and from that point on follow the teacher's instructions concerning learning tasks, use of toilet, luncheon activities, and all other experiences.… The day's program will be so completely simplified…that the possibility of failure experiences will be almost completely minimized. (Cruickshank et al., 1961, p. 18)

It is fair to say that the primary focus of the Montgomery County project, at least as described in the 1961 publication, was on controlling the learning environment in comparison to academic instruction. The academic instruction recommendations tended to be dominated by readiness training in the form of perceptual and perceptual-motor exercises, handwriting, and arithmetic, with relatively little attention devoted to reading. Also, there was relatively little reference to phonics instruction.

Results after 1 year indicated that the program was effective in increasing perceptual-motor abilities as measured by the Bender-Gestalt test and in reducing the degree of distractibility as measured by a visual figure-background test. However, no effects were found for academic achievement or IQ. A 1-year followup found the perceptual-motor and attention advantages for the experimental group students had been eliminated.[7]

EMERGENT PERIOD (C.1960 TO 1975)

From about 1960 to 1975, learning disabilities began its emergence as a formal category. It was during this period that (a) the term *learning disabilities* was introduced; (b) the federal government included learning disabilities on its agenda; (c) parents and professionals founded organizations for learning disabilities; and (d) educational programming for students with learning disabilities blossomed, with a particular focus on psychological processing and perceptual training.

Introduction of the Term *Learning Disabilities*

Kirk's definition. Most authorities credit Samuel Kirk as the originator of the term learning disabilities. In the first edition of his *Educating Exceptional Children*, which became arguably the most widely used college introductory text for special education of its era, Kirk (1962) defined learning disabilities as follows:

> A learning disability refers to a retardation, disorder, or delayed development in one or more of the processes of speech, language, reading, writing, arithmetic, or other school subject resulting from a psychological handicap caused by a possible cerebral dysfunction and/or emotional or behavioral disturbances. It is not the result of mental retardation, sensory deprivation, or cultural and instructional factors. (Kirk, 1962, p. 263)

Addressing a group of parents of "perceptually handicapped" children a year later, Kirk (1963) again used the term learning disabilities. Several of the parents at the conference had approached Kirk before he spoke, saying that they needed help in selecting a name for their proposed national organization (Kirk, 1976). Ironically, Kirk first talked of his distaste for labels but then proceeded to introduce a term that has become, by far, the most frequently used label in special education:

> I have felt for some time that labels we give children are satisfying to us, but of little help to the child himself. We seem to be satisfied if we can give a technical name to a condition. This gives us the satisfaction of closure. We think we know the answers if we can give the child a name or a label— brain injured, schizophrenic, autistic, mentally retarded, aphasia, etc. As indicated before, the term "brain injury" has little meaning to us from a management or training point of view. It does not tell me if the child is smart or dull, hyperactive or underactive.... The terms cerebral palsy, brain

injured, mentally retarded, aphasic, etc. are not actually classification terms. In a sense they are not diagnostic, if by diagnosis we mean an assessment of the child in such a way that leads us to some form of treatment, management, or remediation. In addition, it is not a basic cause since the designation of the child as brain injured does not really tell us why the child is brain injured or how he got that way.

Recently, I have used the term "learning disabilities" to describe a group of children who have disorders in development in language, speech, reading, and associated communication skills needed for social interaction. In this group, I do not include children who have sensory handicaps such as blindness or deafness, because we have methods of managing and training the deaf and the blind. I also exclude from this group children who have generalized mental retardation (Kirk, 1963).

Motivated by Kirk's speech, the parents immediately formed the Association for Children with Learning Disabilities (ACLD), now known as the Learning Disabilities Association of America (LDA), which is generally acknowledged as the largest and most influential learning disabilities parent organization in the United States.

Bateman's definition. In 1965 a student of Kirk's, Barbara Bateman, offered the following definition:

> Children who have learning disorders are those who manifest an educationally significant discrepancy between their estimated potential and actual level of performance related to basic disorders in the learning process, which may or may not be accompanied by demonstrable central nervous system dysfunction, and which are not secondary to generalized mental retardation, educational or cultural deprivation, severe emotional disturbance, or sensory loss. (Bateman, 1965, p. 220)

Bateman's definition was historically significant because it reintroduced Monroe's earlier notion of using a discrepancy between achievement and potential as a way of formally identifying students with learning disabilities. Whereas the notion of a discrepancy went relatively unnoticed or unused during Monroe's time, discrepancy was to become intimately linked to identifying learning disabilities shortly after Bateman's emphasis on it.

Federal Involvement

Task Force I and II definitions. By the early 1960s, the federal government began to take interest in developing a definition of learning disabilities. Several federal agencies[8] and the Easter Seal Research Foundation cosponsored three task forces, the first two of which focused on definition. The title of the project, "Minimal Brain Dysfunction: National Project on Learning Disabilities in Children," reflected the division in the field at the time over the relevance and validity of attributing neurological causes to learning disabilities. This division was also evident in the definition that emanated from Task Force I, composed primarily of medical professionals, versus the definition developed by Task Force II, composed primarily of educators. Task Force I elected to define minimal brain dysfunction whereas Task Force II defined learning disabilities. The decision of Task Force II to provide an alternative definition to Task Force I is all the more significant in that Task Force I's charge was to come up with a definition whereas Task Force II was not charged with arriving at a definition. Instead, it was to focus on educational recommendations. However, it was the consensus of Task Force II that "because special educators in the field of learning disabilities must base educational management and teaching strategies on functional diagnostic information, a redefinition of this group of children for educational purposes was required" (Haring & Bateman, 1969, p. 2).

Task Force I defined minimal brain dysfunction as a disorder affecting

> children of near average, average, or above average general intelligence with certain learning or behavior disabilities ranging from mild to severe, which are associated with deviations of function of the central nervous system. These deviations may manifest themselves by various combinations of impairment in perception, conceptualization, language, memory, and control of attention, impulse, or motor function....
>
> These aberrations may arise from genetic variations, biochemical irregularities, perinatal brain insults or other illnesses or injuries sustained during the years which are critical for the development and maturation of the central nervous system, or from unknown causes. (Clements, 1966, pp. 9–10)

Task Force II could not agree on a single definition of learning disabilities. Instead, it put forward two definitions; the first stressed the notion of intra-individual differences included in Kirk's definition, the second stressed discrepancy between intelligence and achievement contained in Bateman's definition. The first definition held that

Children with learning disabilities are those (1) who have educationally significant discrepancies among their sensory-motor, perceptual, cognitive, academic, or related developmental levels which interfere with the performance of educational tasks; (2) who may or may not show demonstrable deviation in central nervous system functioning; and (3) whose disabilities are not secondary to general mental retardation, sensory deprivation, or serious emotional disturbance. (Haring & Bateman, 1969, pp. 2–3)

The second definition stated that

Children with learning disabilities are those (1) who manifest an educationally significant discrepancy between estimated academic potential and actual level of academic functioning as related to dyfunctioning [sic] in the learning process; (2) may or may not show demonstrable deviation in central nervous system functioning; and (3) whose disabilities are not secondary to general mental retardation, cultural, sensory and/or educational deprivation or environmentally produced serious emotional disturbance. (Haring & Bateman, 1969, p. 3)

National Advisory Committee on Handicapped Children (NACHC) definition. Toward the end of the 1960s, the U.S. Office of Education (USOE) formed a committee to issue a report on learning disabilities and to write a definition of learning disabilities that might be used as a basis for legislation for funding programs. The committee, chaired by Samuel Kirk, offered a definition similar to Kirk's 1962 definition:

Children with special (specific) learning disabilities exhibit a disorder in one or more of the basic psychological processes involved in understanding or in using spoken and written language. These may be manifested in disorders of listening, thinking, talking, reading, writing, spelling or arithmetic. They include conditions which have been referred to as perceptual handicaps, brain injury, minimal brain dysfunction, dyslexia, developmental aphasia, etc. They do not include learning problems that are due primarily to visual, hearing or motor handicaps, to mental retardation, emotional disturbance, or to environmental disadvantage. (USOE, 1968, p. 34)

Legislation for learning disabilities. The original version of the Education of the Handicapped Act (EHA), passed in 1966, did not include learning disabilities as one of the categories of handicapping conditions eligible for special education assistance. Even though parents of children with learning disabilities advocated including their children in the law, they were outmaneuvered by parents of children with other, more traditional disabilities, who

> convinced key Congressional staff persons that the definition of LD was so broad that it could include any economically disadvantaged child whose circumstances resulted in educational problems. They argued that such children, already assisted by the Congress through Title I of the Elementary and Secondary Education Act, would use up all the resources needed by children who were, in fact, disabled. (Martin, 1987)

By 1969, advocates supporting legislation proposed by the Bureau for the Education of the Handicapped (BEH) were able to exert enough pressure to have legislation passed for learning disabilities—the Children with Specific Learning Disabilities Act of 1969. This act, which adopted the NACHC definition of learning disabilities, supported service programs for students with learning disabilities for the first time in the form of model projects. As part of the leverage to convince Congress of the need for funding for learning disabilities, advocates used the NACHC report, which stated that few of the estimated 1% to 3% of the school-age population with learning disabilities were receiving services.

In 1970, Public Law 91-230 consolidated into one act a number of previously separate federal grant programs related to the education of children with disabilities. Under this law Congress still did not recognize learning disabilities as a formal category eligible for support to local schools through Part B (Grants to States) of EHA. However, Part G of the law, the earlier law for Children with Specific Learning Disabilities, continued to provide authority to the USOE to award discretionary grants for learning disabilities to support teacher education, research, and model service delivery programs (Martin, 1987).

Two significant programs established by BEH under Part G were the Child Service Demonstration Projects (CSDPs) and the Leadership Training Institute in Learning Disabilities (LTI). From 1971 to 1973, 43 states set up CSDPs. The LTI, housed at the University of Arizona, prepared documents on broad topics related to service, research, and training in learning disabilities (Bryant, 1972; Bryant, Kass, & Wiederholt, 1972), and staff of the LTI provided consultant services to the CSPDs (Wiederholt, 1974). This program followed BEH's strategy for early childhood models and technical assistance (E. W. Martin, personal communication, January 16, 2001).

Parent and Professional Organizations Founded

During the late 1950s, parents of children who would have qualified as learning disabled had there been such a category were starting to make inroads into having their children served. Parents were beginning to bend the ear of sympathetic and progressive educational administrators. Parent advocacy groups at the local and state level were starting to spring up around the country.

In April of 1963, several of these groups gathered together in Chicago for a conference entitled, "The Conference on Exploration into Problems of the Perceptually Handicapped Child." As noted earlier, Kirk addressed this group and introduced the term, learning disabilities. The following year, the Association for Children with Learning Disabilities was formally established.

In 1968, the first major professional organization dealing with learning disabilities, the Division for Children with Learning Disabilities (DCLD) of the Council for Exceptional Children (CEC) was founded. Its first president was Raymond Barsch.

Educational Programming: Dominance of Psychological Processing and Visual Perceptual Training

The Emergent Period witnessed a proliferation of training programs specifically designed for children with learning disabilities. The vast majority of these educational approaches assumed that children with learning disabilities suffered from psychological processing and/or visual-perceptual processing deficits. We divide the educational programs into those focused on language disabilities and those focused on visual and visual-motor disabilities.

Language disabilities. During this period, Kirk's conceptualization of language disabilities, using the *ITPA*, had a major impact on the field. The development of the *ITPA* grew out of an earlier project of Kirk's focused on preschool children with mental retardation (Kirk, 1976). In 1949, Kirk began a study of the effects of early intervention on the development of children with mental retardation, setting up experimental and contrast classes in both an institutional and a community setting. The children were studied for 3 to 5 years, and the results were generally successful[9] (Kirk, 1958). In directing the early intervention study, Kirk and his colleagues worked on coming up with diagnostic tests that would be useful for instruction. Because no measures were in existence, they began to develop tests to determine the individual perceptual, linguistic, and memory disabilities of the children.

Frustrated with these early attempts to build a diagnostic test of discrete abilities, Kirk enrolled in a course taught by Charles Osgood at the University of Illinois. Kirk and his colleagues eventually used Osgood's (1957) communication model as a basis for the first experimental edition of the *ITPA* (Kirk et al., 1961), with a revised edition published in 1968 (Kirk, McCarthy, & Kirk, 1968). The *ITPA* consisted of 12 subtests divided along three dimensions: (a) channels of communication, (b) psycholinguistic processes, and (c) levels of organization. Channels referred to the modalities (auditory-vocal or visual-motor) through which sensory information is received and then expressed. Psycholinguistic processes included reception, expression, and organization. Organization was the internal manipulation of information of concepts and linguistic skills. Levels of organization included the representational, dealing with symbolic behavior, and the automatic, dealing with habit chains. The 12 subtests were: visual reception, auditory reception, visual association, auditory association, verbal expression, motor expression, visual sequential memory, auditory sequential memory, visual closure, auditory closure, grammatic closure, and sound blending.

Depending on the particular profile that a child showed, a teacher was to concentrate remediation on various areas. Several authors came up with training activities for use with the *ITPA* (Bush & Giles, 1969; Karnes, 1968; Kirk & Kirk, 1971; Minskoff, Wiseman, & Minskoff, 1974).

Although use of the *ITPA* was widespread throughout the 1960s, by the 1970s it began to wane in popularity. Numerous critics of the *ITPA* surfaced (e.g., Engelmann, 1967; Hallahan & Cruickshank, 1973; Hammill & Larsen, 1974; Mann, 1971; Ysseldyke & Salvia, 1974). The criticism focused on the psychometric properties of the instrument as well as the efficacy of the training procedures.

Even though the *ITPA* fell out of favor,[10] it was historically important for at least two reasons. First, it reinforced the notion that children with learning disabilities have intra-individual differences. Second, it underlined the concept of using assessment to guide instruction, sometimes called diagnostic-prescriptive teaching. Both of these ideas had been championed by Monroe (1932) earlier, but they did not gain widespread popularity until the extensive use of the *ITPA*.

While the *ITPA* was the dominant approach to language problems of children with learning disabilities in the 1960s, there were other language theorists who also garnered considerable support. Perhaps the most notable was Helmer Myklebust. Myklebust's original work was in the area of the deaf. However, he found that many children referred to his clinic had normal hearing acuity, but they exhibited poor auditory comprehension.

A driving force behind Myklebust's orientation was his belief that many children with learning disabilities, which he referred to as "psychoneurological learning disabilities," had problems in interneurosensory learning, the ability to combine information from two sensory modalities. For this reason, he eschewed Fernald's VAKT approach (Hallahan & Cruickshank, 1973).

Myklebust teamed with Doris Johnson to develop remedial techniques, primarily for receptive and expressive language problems (Johnson & Myklebust, 1967). Some of their suggestions for remediating receptive language problems were that: (a) training comprehension skills should come before training expressive skills, (b) whole words and sentences should be trained rather than nonsense words or isolated sounds, and (c) words sounding different should be taught before words that have sounds that are difficult to discriminate.

Johnson and Myklebust focused on two types of expressive language problems relevant to children with learning disabilities: reauditorization deficits, or problems in word retrieval, and syntax deficits. For reauditorization deficits they suggested such things as rapid naming drills using real words. For problems with syntax, rather than teaching grammatical rules, they provided "a series of sentences auditorially, sufficiently structured with experience so the child will retain and internalize various sentence plans" (Johnson & Myklebust, 1967, p. 137).

Visual and visual-motor disabilities. There was a proliferation of training programs developed in the 1960s for visual perceptual and/or visual-motor disabilities. The most notable figures promoting these programs were Newell Kephart, Marianne Frostig, Gerald Getman, Raymond Barsch, Glen Doman, and Carl Delacato.

Newall Kephart probably did the most to create an upsurge in interest in visual and visual-motor problems in children with learning disabilities. His major publication was *The Slow Learner in the Classroom* (Kephart, 1960, 1971), which contained his theoretical ideas as well as numerous perceptual-motor training exercises.

Influenced by his earlier tenure at the Wayne County Training School, Kephart came up with even more extensive theoretical conceptualizations and practical suggestions than had his mentors, Strauss, Werner, and Lehtinen. Kephart based his work heavily on the then-popular theories of visual perceptual development of Heinz Werner (1948, 1957), Harry Harlow (1951), and John and Eleanor Gibson (1955). For example, he relied on Werner's theory that perceptual development in children progresses from being undifferentiated to being broken down into parts to the integration and reformulation of the parts into a whole.

The most important aspect of Kephart's theory was what he referred to as the "perceptual-motor match," which he based largely on Brown and Campbell's (1948) servomechanistic model of perceptual development:

> When the output pattern has been generated, it is sent down the efferent nerves...and response results. On the way,...a portion of the output pattern is...fed back into the system at the output end. The presence of feedback in the perceptual process makes the system a servomechanism. (p. 60)

The perceptual-motor match relied on two assumptions: (a) motor development precedes visual development, and (b) kinesthetic sensation resulting from motor movement provides feedback, which can be used for monitoring visual-motor activities. Based on these assumptions, especially the former, Kephart advocated that motor training precede visual perceptual training.

Another important aspect of Kephart's approach was his belief that laterality, the ability to discriminate the left from the right side of the body, is necessary in order for children to discriminate left from right out in space. He viewed children who had difficulties with reversals (e.g., problems discriminating *b* from *d*) as needing training in laterality.

Marianne Frostig, who founded the Marianne Frostig Center of Educational Therapy in Los Angeles, California, and was its executive director from 1947 to 1970, developed *The Marianne Frostig Developmental Test of Visual Perception* (Frostig, Lefever, & Whittlesey, 1964) as well as a commercial training program (Frostig & Horne, 1964). The paper-and-pencil test assessed (a) eye-motor coordination, (b) figure-ground visual perception, (c) form constancy, (d) position in space, and (e) spatial relations. The Frostig-Horne program had specific exercises for each of these areas.

Gerald Getman, an optometrist who had collaborated with the noted developmental psychologist Arnold Gesell at Yale University in the 1940s (e.g., Gesell, Ilg, Bullis, Getman, & Ilg, 1949), began offering summer training programs for practitioners in the 1950s on remediation of visual-motor disabilities in children.[11] He and his colleagues published a manual of training activities for children with visual-perceptual and visual-motor problems (Getman, Kane, Halgren, & McKee, 1964). The activities focused on general coordination, balance, eye-hand coordination, eye movements, form perception, and visual memory.

Raymond Barsch[12] developed what he called the "Movigenic Curriculum" (Barsch, 1967). One of Barsch's major theoretical assumptions was that efficient movement in the environment was necessary for survival. Thus, many of the 12 areas of his curriculum focused on movement: muscular strength, dynamic balance, body awareness, spatial awareness, tactual dynamics, kinesthesia, auditory dynamics, visual dynamics, bilaterality, rhythm, flexibility, and motor planning.

Glen Doman, a physical therapist, founded the Institutes for the Achievement of Human Potential in Philadelphia, Pennsylvania, in 1955. He along with Carl Delacato, an educational psychologist, developed a controversial approach to treating children with brain injury.[13] Their program of "neurological organization" was based on three assumptions: (a) the development of the individual, ontogeny, recapitulates the development of the species, phylogeny; (b) children with brain injury need to be trained to have cerebral dominance; and (c) training procedures need to change the brain itself, not just symptoms (Delacato, 1959, 1963, 1966).

The Doman-Delacato program enjoyed considerable popularity for a time, but it eventually met with overwhelming criticism from the field (Robbins & Glass, 1969). In 1968, a number of professional organizations[14] issued a statement criticizing the Institutes on four major points: (a) the promotional methods placed parents in an awkward position if they decided against using the treatment; (b) the training regimens were very demanding, which might cause parents to neglect other family needs and restrict the child from engaging in age-appropriate normal activities; (c) the claims for success were not backed up by credible research; and (d) the theoretical foundation of the methods were questionable.

Although no official statements came out against the perceptual and perceptual-motor training programs of Kephart, Frostig, Getman, and Barsch, they were the topic of several research studies. Most of these studies found that, although these programs were sometimes effective in improving perceptual and/or perceptual-motor development, they were ineffective in improving academic performance (Cohen, 1969, 1970; Hammill & Larsen, 1974). Probably because of the ubiquitous research-to-practice gap in education, the use of perceptual and perceptual-motor training hung on for a period of time, but by the mid-1980s its use had waned considerably.

SOLIDIFICATION PERIOD (c. 1975 TO 1985)

The period from about 1975 to 1985 was a period of relative stability as the field moved toward consensus on the definition of learning disabilities as well as methods of identifying students with learning disabilities. It was a period of considerable applied research, much of it funded by the USOE, that resulted in empirically validated educational procedures for students with learning disabilities. There was some upheaval with respect to professional organizations, but this unrest was relatively brief.

Solidification of the Definition

In 1975, Congress passed Public Law 94-142, the Education for All Handicapped Children Act. With this law, learning disabilities finally achieved official status as a category eligible for funding for direct services.

U.S. Office of Education 1977 definition. By the early 1970s, the NACHC definition of 1968 had become the most popular one among state departments of education (Mercer, Forgnone, & Wolking, 1976). This no doubt figured into the USOE's virtual adoption of the NACHC definition for use in the implementation of P.L. 94-142:

> The term "specific learning disability" means a disorder in one or more of the psychological processes involved in understanding or in using language, spoken or written, which may manifest itself in an imperfect ability to listen, speak, read, write, spell, or to do mathematical calculations. The term includes such conditions as perceptual handicaps, brain injury, minimal brain dysfunction, dyslexia and developmental aphasia. The term does not include children who have learning disabilities which are primarily the result of visual, hearing, or motor handicaps, or mental retardation, or emotional disturbance, or of environmental, cultural, or economic disadvantage. (USOE, 1977, p. 65083)

The 1977 USOE definition, with minor wording changes, has survived until today as the definition used by the federal government. However, that does not mean that other definitions have not been promulgated by parent and professional groups. Examples of two developed during this period were those of the National Joint Committee on Learning Disabilities (NJCLD) and the ACLD.

NJCLD definition. In 1978, the major learning disabilities professional organizations as well as the ACLD formed the NJCLD in order to attempt to provide a united front in addressing issues pertaining to learning disabilities. In 1981, the NJCLD developed the following definition:

> Learning disabilities is a generic term that refers to a heterogeneous group of disorders manifested by significant difficulties in the acquisition and use of listening, speaking, reading, writing, reasoning or mathematical abilities. These disorders are intrinsic to the individual and presumed to be due to central nervous system dysfunction. Even though a learning disability may occur concomitantly with other handicapping conditions (e.g., sensory impairment, mental retardation, social and emotional disturbance) or environmental influences (e.g., cultural differences,

insufficient-inappropriate instruction, psychogenic factors), it is not the direct result of those conditions or influences. (Hammill, Leigh, McNutt, & Larsen, 1981, p. 336)

In formulating this definition, the NJCLD was purposeful in its exclusion of any mention of psychological processes, which were integral to the USOE definition. By not mentioning psychological processes, the NJCLD distanced itself from perceptual and perceptual-motor training programs, which had lost favor in the research community.

Federal Regulations for Identification of Learning Disabilities

When P.L. 94-142 was implemented in 1977, in addition to the inclusion of a definition of learning disabilities, the federal government issued regulations pertaining to the identification of students with learning disabilities. Because the federal definition was not explicit about how states and local school systems were to identify students as learning disabled, the regulations were intended to provide an operational definition for use in identification. The USOE first proposed a formula that defined a severe discrepancy as "when achievement in one or more of the areas falls at or below 50% of the child's expected achievement level, when age and previous educational experiences are taken into account" (USOE, 1976, p. 52405).

Public response to the notion of a formula was overwhelmingly negative. Thus, no formula was included in the definition or regulations. However, the USOE stayed with the idea of an ability-achievement discrepancy in the regulations:

(a) A team may determine that a child has a specific learning disability if:

    (1) The child does not achieve commensurate with his or her age and ability levels in one or more of the areas listed in paragraph (a) (2) of this section, when provided with learning experiences appropriate for the child's age and ability levels; and

    (2) The team finds that the child has a severe discrepancy between achievement and intellectual ability in one or more of the following areas:

        (i) Oral expression;

        (ii) Listening comprehension;

        (iii) Written expression;

        (iv) Basic reading skill;

        (v) Reading comprehension;

        (vi) Mathematics calculation; or

        (vii) Mathematics reasoning

(USOE, 1977, p. 65083)

Empirically Validated Educational Procedures

The heavy criticism of psycholinguistic process and perceptual process training programs toward the end of the previous period had left the field of learning disabilities with a relative void of research-based educational practices. Beginning in the 1970s several learning disabilities researchers began to turn their attention to developing educational methods for students with learning disabilities. A major impetus for this effort was the USOE's funding of five research institutes from 1977 to 1982. These institutes were housed at Columbia University, the University of Illinois at Chicago, the University of Kansas, the University of Minnesota, and the University of Virginia. In addition to the work of the institutes, another major body of influential intervention work was that which focused on Direct Instruction.

Columbia University. The Columbia institute, directed by Dale Bryant, focused on information processing difficulties of students with learning disabilities (Connor, 1983). The institute conducted research in five areas: memory and study skills (led by Margaret Jo Shepherd), arithmetic (Jeanette Fleischner), basic reading and spelling (Bryant), interaction of characteristics of the text and the reader (Joanna Williams), and reading comprehension (Walter MacGinitie).

University of Illinois at Chicago. The main foci of the Illinois institute, directed by Tanis Bryan, were on the social competence and attributions about success and failure of children with learning disabilities (Bryan, Pearl, Donahue, Bryan, & Pflaum, 1983). Social competence was an area that had largely been ignored by researchers up to this point. By focusing on social competence, the Illinois team validated the ACLD's concern for social skills evident in their definition of learning disabilities. Bryan and her colleagues established that students with learning disabilities have deficits in the pragmatic use of language, which interferes with their ability to make and keep friends. For example, they found that such students have problems in adapting their communication style to fit the listener, are less persuasive in conversations, and are less apt to request clarification when faced with ambiguous information.

With respect to attributions, the Illinois researchers found that students with learning disabilities tend to attribute their failures to lack of ability, but attribute their successes to luck or the task being relatively easy. Furthermore, mothers of children with learning disabilities believe that their children's successes are due more to luck than ability and that their failures are due more to lack of ability than to bad luck.

The University of Kansas. Researchers at the Kansas institute, directed by Donald Deshler, focused on educational interventions for adolescents with learning disabilities (Schumaker, Deshler, Alley, & Warner, 1983). The focus on adolescents filled a void in the research literature on learning disabilities. By focusing on older children, the Kansas team reinforced the ACLD's concern for the lifelong nature of learning disabilities evident in their definition. The Kansas researchers first conducted epidemiological studies to determine the characteristics of adolescents with learning disabilities. Among other things, they found that many of these students have deficiencies in study skills, learning strategies, and social skills.

Based on what they had found to be the characteristics of adolescents with learning disabilities, the Kansas team developed a variety of educational strategies for working on academic problems, called the Learning Strategies Curriculum. They also field-tested a number of social skills strategies.

University of Minnesota. Directed by James Ysseldyke, the Minnesota institute primarily focused on two areas: (a) the decision-making process related to identification of students with learning disabilities, and (b) curriculum-based assessment (CBA) procedures (Ysseldyke, Thurlow, et al., 1983). With respect to identification, they raised concerns about whether students identified as learning disabled could be reliably differentiated from low achievers:

> After five years of trying, we cannot describe, except with considerable lack of precision, students called LD. We think that LD can best be defined as "whatever society wants it to be, needs it to be, or will let it be" at any point in time. Who have other researchers studied? The 1% of the school-age population that some experts think are LD or the 85% of the school-age population other experts think are LD? We think researchers have compiled an interesting set of findings on a group of students who are experiencing academic difficulties, who bother their regular classroom teachers and who have been classified by societally sanctioned labelers in order to remove them, to the extent possible, from the regular education mainstream. (Ysseldyke, Thurlow, et al., 1983, p. 89)

Led by Stanley Deno, the Minnesota researchers working on CBA were interested in developing a method of assessing students' progress in the curricula to which they were exposed. They saw this as providing more educationally useful information than the typical, nationally-normed, standardized tests of achievement. Deno and his colleagues found that students with learning disabilities and their teachers benefit from CBA.

University of Virginia. The Virginia institute, directed by Daniel Hallahan, focused on children with learning disabilities who also had attention problems (Hallahan et al., 1983). The Virginia researchers documented metacognitive problems in the students and developed cognitive behavior modification techniques for the remediation of those problems. In particular, they had students use self-monitoring techniques while engaged in academic work. Their findings indicated that self-monitoring of attention generally results in increased academic productivity.

The Virginia institute also focused on providing strategies for direct use on academic tasks. Led by John Lloyd, this research on academic strategy training resulted in a number of specific techniques for instruction in reading and math.

In assessing the impact of the institutes as a group, Keogh (1983) noted that four of the institutes approached learning disabilities as a strategic, information processing problem and developed educational interventions accordingly: "I am impressed by the effectiveness of the experimental interventions developed and tested. In this sense these data are among the most optimistic to be found in the literature" (Keogh, 1983, p. 123).

McKinney (1983), likewise, noted that

> the central concept that emerges from this research is that many LD students have not acquired efficient strategies for processing task information and therefore cannot use their abilities and experience to profit from conventional instruction. Most of this research, however, also demonstrates that they are capable of acquiring the strategies that account for competent performance and that they can improve their academic skills and adaptive functioning when they are taught task-appropriate strategies. This conceptualization of learning disabilities contrasts with the traditional view that emerged during the 1960's that LD students suffered from relatively enduring deficits in the development of specific abilities, such as perception and language, which impaired their capacity to perform academic tasks. (McKinney, 1983, p. 131)

McKinney, however, was critical of some of the Minnesota institute's conclusions regarding identification of learning disabilities:

> First, the conclusions of this institute and the implications they draw suggest that LD students are not handicapped in any significant way apart from underachievement. In my opinion this conclusion is not supported by the evidence presented in the Minnesota report or by that obtained by the other four institutes....

Second, the conclusions of this group imply not only that special education services for LD students are ineffective but that they are unnecessary
and potentially do more harm than good. The evidence for this implication appears to be based on research of placement team decision making
as opposed to research on instructional processes and intervention.

Third, …the idea that we provide intervention at the point of referral has
intuitive appeal, …and may be worthy of additional consideration…; but
the issues of what constitutes intervention, exactly who receives the intervention, who provides the intervention, and whether parents are involved
in planning the intervention were not discussed in the report. (McKinney,
1983, pp. 137–138)

Whether Keogh's and McKinney's praise of some of the institutes' work and
McKinney's criticisms of some of the Minnesota institute's work are justifiable is
debatable. There is no doubt that all of the institutes' work has remained influential up until the present day in terms of theory and practice. With particular reference to the Minnesota work, there are those, today, who agree with McKinney's
criticisms and those who do not. We address some of these influences and disagreements in our discussion of the Turbulent Period.

Direct Instruction. In the 1970s, Sigfried Engelmann, Wesley Becker, and their colleagues developed a number of intervention programs for language, reading, and
math (Englemann, Becker, Hanner, & Johnson, 1978, 1988; Englemann & Osborn,
1977). Often referred to as Direct Instruction, these programs emphasized the systematic teaching of language subskills and the integration of these subskills into
broader language competence. Several studies, including large-scale evaluations
such as Project Follow-Through (Abt Associates, 1976, 1977) found Direct Instruction highly effective.

Learning Disabilities Professional Organization Turmoil

Toward the end of the 1970s and beginning of the 1980s, several members of DCLD
began voicing dissatisfaction with their parent organization, CEC. Among other
things, they complained that DCLD was not receiving its fair share of services from
CEC. In addition, they were upset with CEC's policy of not allowing individuals to
be members of DCLD without being a member of CEC. More relevant to our
discussion of the history of the learning disabilities field, however, were philosophical
differences brewing between the leaders in DCLD. Many of the younger, rising leaders in learning disabilities were disenchanted with the older guard's tacit, and sometimes explicit, acceptance of assessment and intervention approaches embracing
perceptual and psychological processing, such as the *ITPA*.

In 1982, the Council for Learning Disabilities (CLD) was founded as an organization separate from CEC. Several key figures in the old DCLD immediately organized and petitioned CEC to start a new division. In 1983, the Division for Learning Disabilities (DLD) of CEC was established, with its first president being Sister Marie Grant.

Over the years the philosophies of the two organizations have become more and more similar. Today, there are virtually no philosophical differences between the two organizations, and many professionals, especially academics, belong to both organizations. In fact, some have pointed out that having two organizations—CLD, with about 3,000 members, and DLD, with about 10,000 members—makes it difficult to provide a united front with respect to advocacy for learning disabilities.

TURBULENT PERIOD (c.1985 TO 2000)

During the most recent period of learning disabilities history, several things have occurred that have solidified the field of learning disabilities even further, but several issues have also threatened to tear the field apart. Driving much of the concern for the latter issues is the extraordinary growth in the prevalence of learning disabilities. From 1976–1977 to 1998–1999, the number of students identified as learning disabled has doubled. There are now more than 2.8 million students identified as learning disabled, which represents just over half of all students with disabilities (USOE, 2000). Although some (Hallahan, 1992) have argued that there may be good reasons for some of this growth, most authorities acknowledge that there is a very good chance that many children are being misdiagnosed as learning disabled.

Areas in which there has been further solidification are definition, the research strands of the learning disabilities research institutes, research on phonological processing, and research on biological causes of learning disabilities. Issues contributing to the turbulence in the field include concern about identification procedures, debate over placement options, and denunciation of the validity of learning disabilities as a real phenomenon by constructivists.

Learning Disabilities Definitions

Early during this period, several new and revised definitions surfaced: the ACLD (now the LDA) definition of 1986, the Interagency Committee on Learning Disabilities (ICLD) definition of 1987, and the NJCLD revised definition of 1988. In the meantime, the definition in federal law covering learning disabilities remained virtually unchanged.

ACLD/LDA definition (1986). The LDA definition is distinctive for its emphasis on the lifelong nature of learning disabilities, its lack of an exclusion clause, and its reference to adaptive behavior:

> Specific Learning Disabilities is a chronic condition of presumed neuro-logical origin which selectively interferes with the development, integra-tion, and/or demonstration of verbal and/or nonverbal abilities. Specific Learning Disabilities exists as a distinct handicapping condition and var-ies in its manifestations and in degree of severity. Throughout life, the condition can affect self-esteem, education, vocation, socialization, and/or daily living activities. (ACLD, 1986, p. 15)

ICLD definition (1987). The ICLD, consisting of representatives from several fed-eral agencies, was charged by Congress to report on several issues. Although Con-gress did not direct them to do so, they did formulate a definition. Their definition was essentially the same one as the 1981 NJCLD definition, except for two changes. It mentioned deficits in social skills as a type of learning disability, and it added attention deficit disorder as a potential comorbid condition with learning disabili-ties:

> Learning disabilities is a generic term that refers to a heterogeneous group of disorders manifested by significant difficulties in the acquisition and use of listening, speaking, reading, writing, reasoning, or mathematical abilities, or of social skills. These disorders are intrinsic to the individual and presumed to be due to central nervous system dysfunction. Even though a learning disability may occur concomitantly with other handi-capping conditions (e.g., sensory impairment, mental retardation, social and emotional disturbance), with socioenvironmental influences (e.g., cultural differences, insufficient or inappropriate instruction, psychogenic factors), and especially with attention deficit disorder, all of which may cause learning problems, a learning disability is not the direct result of those conditions or influences. (ICLD, 1987, p. 222)

NJCLD revised definition (1988). The NJCLD revised definition was in response to the LDA definition's emphasis on the lifelong nature of learning disabilities and the ICLD's listing of social skills deficits as a type of learning disability. The NJCLD revised definition agreed with the former but disagreed with the latter:

> Learning disabilities is a general term that refers to a heterogeneous group of disorders manifested by significant difficulties in the acquisition and use of listening, speaking, reading, writing, reasoning, or mathematical abilities. These disorders are intrinsic to the individual, presumed to be

due to central nervous system dysfunction, and may occur across the life span. Problems of self-regulatory behaviors, social perception, and social interaction may exist with learning disabilities but do not by themselves constitute a learning disability. Although learning disabilities may occur concomitantly with other handicapping conditions (for example, sensory impairment, mental retardation, serious emotional disturbance) or with extrinsic influences (such as cultural differences, insufficient or inappropriate instruction), they are not the result of those conditions or influences. (NJCLD, 1988, p. 1)

Individuals with Disabilities Education Act (IDEA) Reauthorized definition (1997). The definition in federal law has remained virtually unchanged since the one included in P.L. 94-142:

A. IN GENERAL.—The term "specific learning disability" means a disorder in one or more of the basic psychological processes involved in understanding or in using language, spoken or written, which disorder may manifest itself in imperfect ability to listen, think, speak, read, write, spell, or do mathematical calculations.

B. DISORDERS INCLUDED.—Such term includes such conditions as perceptual disabilities, brain injury, minimal brain dysfunction, dyslexia, and developmental aphasia.

C. DISORDERS NOT INCLUDED.—Such term does not include a learning problem that is primarily the result of visual, hearing, or motor disabilities, of mental retardation, of emotional disturbance, or of environmental, cultural, or economic disadvantage. (IDEA Amendments of 1997, Sec. 602(26), p. 13)

Continuation of Research Strands of the Learning Disabilities Research Institutes

As we noted earlier, Keogh (1983) noted that four of the learning disabilities research institutes funded by the USOE in the late 1970s and early 1980s (Columbia University, University of Illinois at Chicago, University of Kansas, University of Minnesota, and University of Virginia) approached learning disabilities as a strategic, information processing problem and developed their interventions within this framework. She pointed out that the institutes' data on outcomes were very promising. McKinney (1983) reported that the institutes' intervention research demonstrated that students with learning disabilities are capable of learning task-appropriate strategies that enable them to succeed in academic learning and adaptive functioning. Although it is conjecture, it is easy to postulate that the institutes' rigorous research standards and encouraging findings provided a springboard for future research.

Columbia University. The Columbia institute's research in reading most likely helped facilitate the proliferation of reading intervention research that has occurred in the field of learning disabilities. For example, Lyon (1998) reported that the National Institutes of Health (NIH) has received more than $25 million to study how students with and without disabilities learn to read. Today, findings from the NIH studies are having a significant impact on the reading instruction provided youngsters with learning disabilities. Judith Birch of Columbia University recently teamed with numerous NIH researchers to develop a very informative video series that presents research-based practices in teaching reading to students with learning disabilities.

University of Illinois at Chicago. The Chicago institute's research introduced social competence as an area worthy of investigation. The importance of this affective side of learning disabilities was very timely in that it quickly captured the attention of many educators. For example, during the 1980s, social skill deficits were featured in three nationally disseminated definitions of learning disabilities (i.e., ACLD/LDA in 1986; ICLD in 1987; NJCLD in 1988).

Gresham (1988) reported that 75% of all published articles in social skills were published between 1983 and 1988. Given the concern for safety in America's schools, such affective topics as social competence, self-concept, dependency, loneliness, suicide, drug usage, and impulsivity are certain to attract more attention. These topics are discussed in the recent learning disabilities literature and research (Mercer, 1997). Unfortunately, the goal of developing highly effective interventions for social skills still remains elusive (Forness & Kavale, 1996; Vaughn, McIntosh, & Spencer-Rowe, 1991; Vaughn & Sinugab, 1998).

University of Kansas. The work of the Kansas institute has not only continued but also expanded. Since 1978, the University of Kansas Center for Research on Learning (the parent organization for the Institute for Research in Learning Disabilities) has continued to focus on the mission of designing and validating interventions for adolescents and young adults with learning disabilities. In this organization, more than $20 million of contracted research has been conducted on adolescents and young adults with learning disabilities (Deshler, Ellis, & Lenz, 1996).

University of Minnesota. It is fair to say that the research on assessment at the Minnesota institute has made diagnosticians more aware of the specific weaknesses of standardized tests and the decision-making processes based on assessment data.

The assessments in special education continue to be an area of substantial controversy (e.g., over-representation of minorities in special education) and more research in needed.

The Minnesota research initiative that focused on CBA has also influenced many assessment practices nationwide in special education. CBA refers to any approach that uses direct observation and recording of a student's performance in the school curriculum as a basis for obtaining information to make instructional decisions (Deno, 1987). Specific procedures include assessing students' academic skills with repeated rate samples using stimulus materials taken from the students' curriculum. The primary uses of curriculum-based measurement (CBM) are to establish district or classroom performance standards, identify students who need special instruction, and monitor individual student progress toward long-range goals. Over the years, researchers have garnered considerable evidence supporting the positive association between data-based monitoring and student achievement gains. In a meta-analysis of formative evaluations, Fuchs and Fuchs (1986) found that data-based programs that monitored student progress and evaluated instruction systematically produced 0.7 standard deviation higher achievement than nonmonitored instruction. This represents a gain of 26 percentage points. Moreover, CBM measures have good reliability and validity (Fuchs, 1986; Tindal & Marston, 1990).

University of Virginia. The work at the Virginia institute appears to have provided a springboard for much further research on attention deficits, metacognition, and instruction. Since 1980, attention deficits have been featured in the subsequent editions of the *Diagnostic and Statistical Manual of Mental Disorders* (DSM–IV). Moreover, there is a high degree of comorbidity between learning disabilities and ADHD (Lyon, 1995b).

Metacognitive deficits have also continued to receive much attention. For example, from a knowledge base of 11,000 statistical findings across 28 categories, Wang, Haertel, and Walberg (1993/1994) found that the metacognitive and cognitive processes of students ranked second and third on their influence of student learning. Cognitive behavior modification techniques highlighted by the Virginia institute are an integral part of many widely used instructional materials. For example, teacher modeling using think-alouds is an integral part of the University of Kansas learning strategies (Deshler et al., 1996) and Doug and Lynn Fuchs have used self-monitoring in some of their intervention packages.

Research on Phonological Processing

Given that the majority of individuals with learning disabilities experience reading difficulties, the research on phonological awareness has the potential to improve the assessment and intervention practices used to treat learning disabilities. Adams (1990) reported that the discovery of the nature and importance of phonemic awareness is considered to be the single greatest breakthrough in reading in the 20th century.

Definition and nature of phonemic awareness. The National Reading Panel (2000) noted that phonemes are the smallest units of spoken language and that phonemic awareness is the ability to focus on and manipulate phonemes. Reid Lyon, Chief of the Child Development and Behavior Branch of the National Institute of Child Health and Human Development (NICHD) of the NIH, periodically reports on the research findings of NIH studies concerning reading development for children with and without reading difficulties. In a 1998 report to the U.S. Senate Committee on Labor and Human Resources, Lyon (1998) discussed the following specific findings related to phonemic awareness, early intervention, and poor readers:

> In contrast to good readers who understand that segmented units of speech can be linked to letters and letter patterns, poor readers have substantial difficulty developing this "alphabetic principle." The culprit appears to be a deficit in phoneme awareness—the understanding that words are made up of sound segments called phonemes. Difficulties in developing phoneme awareness can have genetic and neurobiological origins or can be attributable to a lack of exposure to language patterns and usage during the preschool years. The end result is the same however. Children who lack phoneme awareness have difficulties linking speech sounds to letters—their decoding skills are labored and weak, resulting in extremely slow reading. This labored access to print renders comprehension impossible. (p. 8)

Applications of phonemic awareness research. Phonemic awareness skills allow for early assessment. For example, phonemic assessments in kindergarten and first grade serve as powerful predictors of children who will have reading difficulties. Lyon (1998) has noted that these assessments are efficient (i.e., they take approximately 20 minutes) and predict with 80% to 90% accuracy who will become good or poor readers.

It is also recognized that the development of phonemic awareness is a necessary but not sufficient condition for learning to read fluently. Phonemic awareness training must be combined with other types of reading instruction to improve reading skills of poor readers to average levels.

Lyon (1998) has highlighted the need for multiple interventions:

> We have learned that for 90% to 95% of poor readers, prevention and early intervention programs that combine instruction in phoneme awareness, phonics, fluency development, and reading comprehension strategies, provided by well trained teachers, can increase reading skills to average reading levels. However, we have also learned that if we delay intervention until nine-years-of-age, (the time that most children with reading difficulties receive services), approximately 75% of the children will continue to have difficulties learning to read throughout high school. (p. 9)

Definition of dyslexia. Phonemic awareness research has already had an influence on the definition of dyslexia. In 1994, the Research Committee of the Orton Dyslexia Society (now known as the International Dyslexia Association), along with representatives from the National Center on Learning Disabilities and the NICHD, set forth the following working definition of dyslexia:

> Dyslexia is one of several distinct learning disabilities. It is a specific language-based disorder of constitutional origin characterized by difficulties in single word decoding, usually reflecting insufficient phonological processing abilities. These difficulties in single word decoding are often unexpected in relation to age and other cognitive and academic abilities; they are not the result of generalized developmental disability or sensory impairment. Dyslexia is manifested by variable difficulty with different forms of language, often including, in addition to problems reading, a conspicuous problem with acquiring proficiency in writing and spelling. (Lyon, 1995a, p. 9)

It will be interesting to see if phonemic awareness research will be a factor in shaping future definitions of learning disabilities or federal regulations pertaining to identification of learning disabilities.

Biological Causes of Learning Disabilities

Since the 1960s, most definitions of learning disabilities have made reference to a neurological basis for learning disabilities. However, it was not until the 1980s and especially the 1990s that evidence began to accumulate to support a biological basis for learning disabilities. Researchers have used two different sources of evidence to support the conclusion that learning disabilities may be the result of neurological dysfunction: postmortem studies and neuroimaging studies. Furthermore, evidence has begun to mount that hereditary factors are implicated in many cases of learning disabilities.

Postmortem studies. Albert Galaburda and Norman Geschwind and their colleagues (Galaburda & Kemper, 1979; Galaburda, Menard, & Rosen, 1994; Galaburda, Sherman, Rosen, Aboitz, & Geschwind, 1985; Geschwind & Levitsky, 1968; Humphreys, Kaufmann, & Galaburda, 1990) made postmortem comparisons between the brains of people with and without dyslexia. When they first started this research, it was difficult to assess its reliability because the number of cases was so small. By the 1990s, however, they had accumulated data on more than a dozen cases, and their results were demonstrating a consistent pattern. In most brains of the nondyslexic group, the left planum temporale (a section of the left temporal lobe, including a large segment of Wernicke's area) is larger than the planum temporale in the right temporal lobe. The left and right planum temporales in the brains of those with dyslexia, in contrast, are the same size or the planum temporale in the right hemisphere is larger than the one in the left hemisphere.

Neuroimaging studies. Using magnetic resonance imaging (MRIs) and computerized axial tomography (CAT) scans, researchers have found the same symmetry or reversed symmetry for the planum temporales of adults with dyslexia (Hynd & Semrud-Clikeman, 1989; Kusch et al., 1993; Larsen, Hoien, Lundberg, & Odegaard, 1990). Studies of brain metabolism, using positron emission tomography (PET) scans and fMRIs, have also begun to reveal differences between individuals with and without dyslexia (Flowers, 1993; Flowers, Wood, & Naylor, 1991; Gross-Glenn et al., 1991; Hagman et al., 1992; Shaywitz et al., 1998). Again, the left hemisphere appears to be the locus of the abnormal functioning, with some of the evidence pointing to Wernicke's area.

Hereditary factors. The 1990s also witnessed an increase in evidence pointing to the hereditary nature of learning disabilities. Researchers have found that about 40% of first-degree relatives of children with reading disabilities have reading disabilities themselves (Pennington, 1990). An approximately equal degree of familiality has also been found for speech and language disorders (Beichtman, Hood, & Inglis, 1992; Lewis, 1992) and spelling disorders (Schulte-Korne, Deimel, Muller, Gutenbrunner, & Remschmidt, 1996). Furthermore, studies of heritability, comparing monozygotic versus dizygotic twins, have found a high degree of concordance for reading disabilities (DeFries, Gillis, & Wadsworth, 1993), speech and language disorders (Lewis & Thompson, 1992), and oral reading ability (Reynolds et al., 1996).

Concern over Identification Procedures

At least two issues related to identification have occupied the learning disabilities literature at the end of the twentieth century. The first pertains to the use of the discrepancy between achievement and intellectual potential; the second is the issue of over-representation of minorities in the learning disabilities category.

Discrepancy between achievement and intellectual potential. By the 1990s, the majority of states had adopted a discrepancy between achievement and intellectual potential as part of their identification procedures (Frankenberger & Franzaglio, 1991). However, during this same time period many learning disabilities researchers began to question seriously the use of discrepancy. These critics have cited at least four reasons for their objections. First, they argue that studies that were instrumental in justifying a discrepancy approach in the first place were flawed. Researchers conducted epidemiological studies on the Isle of Wight in which they used regression scores between reading and performance IQ scores to differentiate students who had specific reading retardation (discrepant readers) from those who had general reading backwardness (nondiscrepant readers) (Rutter & Yule, 1975). Finding a "hump" in the lower end of the distribution of residual reading scores for those with specific reading retardation, some researchers used these data as evidence of the validity of using discrepancy to define students with learning disabilities. Several researchers, however, have leveled criticisms at the Isle of Wight studies, e.g., inability to replicate the results and ceiling effects on the reading test, which could have led to an inflated number of discrepant readers and resulted in the "hump." (See Vellutino, Scanlon, & Lyon, 2000, for a more in-depth discussion of these criticisms.)

Second, some have cited the Matthew effect (better readers learn more about their world and, therefore, are likely to score higher on IQ tests) as a problem. They have pointed out that the IQ scores of students with reading disabilities may be under-estimated (Siegel, 1989).

Third, using a discrepancy approach makes it very difficult to identify children as learning disabled in the early elementary grades. This is particularly problematic because research has generally shown that intervention is more effective the earlier it is implemented (Fletcher et al., 1998)

Fourth, researchers have been unable to discriminate between students with a discrepancy from those with low reading achievement but no discrepancy on measures considered important for reading, e.g., phonological awareness, orthographic coding, short-term memory, word retrieval (Fletcher et al., 1994; Foorman, Francis, Fletcher, & Lynn, 1996; Stanovich & Siegel, 1994). Although low achievers do not differ from those with a discrepancy on these variables, this does not mean that low achievers do not differ from students identified as learning disabled, using broader identification criteria (Fuchs, Mathes, Fuchs, & Lipsey, 1999).

Researchers have just begun to explore alternatives to the discrepancy approach to identification. One alternative would rely on the assessment of phonological processes (Torgesen & Wagner, 1998). Another, referred to as the treatment validity approach, would involve assessment of students' levels of academic performance and learning rates on curriculum-based measures (Fuchs & Fuchs, 1998).

Disproportionate representation of minority students. Since at least the time of Lloyd Dunn's classic article, "Special Education for the Mildly Retarded: Is Much of It Justifiable?" (Dunn, 1968), there has been concern over identification of children from minority backgrounds in special education. Although most of the concern has been focused on the categories of mental retardation and emotional disturbance, there is also some evidence of disproportionate representation in learning disabilities. For 1998–1999, 4.49% of all students (aged 6 to 21 years) were identified as learning disabled. Following are the percentages for different ethnic groups: White (4.27%), African American (5.57%), Hispanic (4.97%), Asian/Pacific Islander (1.70%), American Indian/Alaska Native (6.29%, U.S. Department of Education, 2000). These figures indicate substantial over-representation of African Americans and, especially, American Indian/Alaska Natives in the learning disabilities category and a very large under-representation of Asian/Pacific-Islanders.

Researchers have not yet been able to disentangle the reasons why disproportionate representation in learning disabilities and other areas of special education exists. Factors that researchers have cited as potential causes are racially biased tests, racially biased professionals, and inadequate community resources, such as health care and educational opportunities (Hallahan & Kauffman, 2000). Most authorities do agree that disproportionate representation is a complex problem, and the federal government has begun to highlight it as a major problem:

> The complexity of this issue requires an integrated and multifaceted effort to promote greater educational access and excellence for racial/ethnic minority students that involves policy makers, educators, researchers, parents, advocates, students, and community representatives. The disproportionate representation of racial/ethnic minority students in special education programs and classes points to the need to:
> ■ make available strong academic programs that foster success for all students in regular and special education;

- implement effective and appropriate special education policies and procedures for referral, assessment, eligibility, classification, placement, and re-evaluation;
- increase the level of home/school/community involvement in the educational process; and
- use diverse community resources to enhance and implement educational programs. (U.S. Department of Education, 1997, p. I-47)

Debate Over the Continuum of Placements

In the mid-1980s, the Assistant Secretary of Education, Madeleine C. Will, proposed the regular education initiative (REI). The mother of a child with Down syndrome, Will (1986) called for general educators to take more ownership for the education of students who were one or more of the following: economically disadvantaged, bilingual, or disabled. The REI launched a movement toward inclusion of students with disabilities, including those with learning disabilities, that continues to this day. At the same time, it triggered a debate about placement options that also continues to this day.

Views on placement options have ranged from full inclusion[15] to a preservation of the continuum of placements. The following two excerpts illustrate the two different views. The first attacks the concept of the least restrictive environment (LRE):

Three generations of children subject to LRE are enough. Just as some institution managers and their organizations—both overt and covert—seek refuge in the continuum and LRE, regional, intermediate unit, and special school administrators and their organizations will continue to defend the traditional and professionally pliable notion of LRE. The continuum is real and represents the status quo. However, the morass created by it can be avoided in the design and implementation of reformed systems focusing all placement questions on the local school and routinely insisting on the home school as an absolute and universal requirement. In terms of placement, the home-school focus renders LRE irrelevant and the continuum moot. (Laski, 1991, p. 413)

The second responds to full inclusion advocates' frequent use of battle metaphors to defend their position:

For many…[defenders of a continuum of placements] regular education remains a foreign and hostile territory, neglecting many children with disabilities. PL 94-142, with its declaration of a free and appropriate education and its cascade of services and the LRE principle, represented in 1975 the capturing of the beachhead for children with disabilities. It is time to

gather our energies and courage; validate comprehensive integration strategies; pressure mainstream administrators and teachers to make greater
accommodations; move inland! But as we mount this new offensive, we,
like any general worthy of his rank, must make certain that the beachhead
remains secure. It's the beachhead, after all, that provides supplies and, in
a worst-case scenario, guarantees a safe retreat. The cascade of services is
a source of strength and safety net for the children we serve. Let's not lose
it. (Fuchs & Fuchs, 1991, pp. 253–254)

In keeping with the REI philosophy, this time period also spawned a concern for
students with learning disabilities' access to the general education curriculum, their
inclusion in high stakes testing, the use of pre-referral strategies, and the use of
cooperative teaching practices. However, not all learning disabilities professionals
have been completely sold on the value of these concerns and practices. In
particular, some have voiced objections that too much focus on inclusive practices
has resulted in students with learning disabilities not receiving enough intensive,
specialized instruction:

The reason why children with learning disabilities are not getting enough
of the intensive, structured instruction is that many schools, for all intents
and purposes, are offering inclusion in the regular class as the only type of
model for our kids. They give lip service to the full continuum of placements, in order to remain legal, but in reality they push an inclusion model
over other options: "You have a learning disability, this is what we have for
you—full time in a regular class." This one-size-fits all thinking is reminiscent of what we had prior to PL 94-142: "You have a learning disability;
this is what we have for you—a self-contained class." ...

Recently, the Council for Exceptional Children released a report entitled,
"Conditions for Special Education Teaching." This survey of special education teachers, general education teachers, and special and general education administrators tells an alarming tale. It's no wonder that special
education teachers are leaving the profession in droves. Almost a third of
special education teachers spend 20 to 30 percent of their time on paperwork related to identifying students and developing IEPs. And 12% spend
more than half their time doing this. This doesn't even count other types
of paperwork, like taking attendance, writing notes to parents, and so forth.
Fifty-eight percent report spending 10 to 20% of their time in meetings
related to IEPs, and 25% report spending 20 to 30% of their time in such
meetings. And this doesn't count the time required to collaborate with
general educators. From the way these data are reported it's not possible
to arrive at a precise measure of how much time is spent in either

meetings or paperwork, but a not unreasonable estimate would be that about half the special education teachers report spending about half their time in IEP-related meetings or paperwork.

So where's the time for instruction? There isn't any. Thirty-one percent of special education teachers report they spend less than 1 hour per week in individual instruction. Twenty-two percent spend ... 1 to 2 hours per week in individual instruction. And ... 15% spend *zero* time in individual instruction. (Hallahan, 2000)

Postmodernism and Learning Disabilities

Kauffman (1999) has expressed concern and displeasure about the current status of special education. Specifically he has stated, "I am not very happy with most of what I see in our field today. I think we are in a period of considerable upset and danger, and our future could look rather bleak depending on how we respond to current pressures" (p. 244).

Kauffman's words of unrest are, in part, due to the spread of postmodernism and its position that special education is fundamentally flawed and needs reconceptualization. The position of postmodernists is in stark contrast to the point of view of Kauffman and others who believe that special education is basically a sound system that needs incremental improvements guided by scientific inquiry. Various terms, such as incremental improvement versus substantial reconceptualization (Andrews et al., 2000), modern versus postmodernism/cultural relativism (Sasso, 2001), modern versus postmodernism/constructivism (Kauffman, 1999), and modern versus postmodernism (Kavale & Forness, 2000), have been used to describe these two camps; however, in this discussion, modern and postmodernism are used. The major tenets and implications of the two positions are apparent when their respective views on the nature of knowledge, disability, special education, and expected outcomes for students with disabilities are examined.

Nature of knowledge. The modern position holds that the current state of knowledge is promising and provides a solid basis on which to build. The modern position supports the use of the scientific method of inquiry to increase knowledge and features experimental research designs and quantitative analysis. Postmodernism rejects the modern view of science in favor of alternative ways of knowing. Postmodernism primarily supports a socially constructed view of knowledge in which logical inquiry is a social enterprise. This social negotiation approach to knowing is used to focus on topics such as racism, systems, researchers as change agents, and the redefining of ethical and moral behavior.

Critics of postmodernism (Kauffman, 1999; Kavale & Forness, 2000; Sasso, 2001) maintain that the most questionable tenet of postmodernism is the rejection of science because it is thought of as untrustworthy or evil. The concern emerges because the rejection of science insulates socially constructed knowledge from compelling criticism and allows points of view to be endorsed that promote agendas that could be scientifically challenged.

The implications of postmodernism concerning the nature of knowledge have much potential to influence the field of learning disabilities in a negative manner. For example, there has been a rapid growth of scientific knowledge about the nature and treatment of learning disabilities during the past decade. If this knowledge were not recognized as valuable, it probably would not be used to improve the identification and treatment of individuals with learning disabilities in our public schools.

Nature of disability. The modern position views disability as a phenomenon that is within the individual and is consistent with the medical model view of wellness and illness. The disability is owned by the individual and needs to be treated, accommodated, and/or endured. Postmodernism views disability primarily as a social construction that is based on incorrect immoral assumptions about difference. Although the notion of a disability is not totally rejected, most postmodernists believe that disability exists more in the perceptions of the beholder than in the bodies of the beheld (Andrews et al., 2000). The aim is to change the flawed constructions of disability. Kauffman (1999) maintains this position undermines the concepts of disability. Sasso (2001) provides an interesting perspective on the postmodern view of disability:

> Having apparently decided that teaching competency skills to children with disabilities is too difficult, they have decided that instead of changing children with disabilities, they will change everyone else. Thus, their reasoning goes, schools, the community, courts of law, the government, indeed all of society must be made to change to accommodate and accept individuals with disabilities. As with most initial claims of postmodernists, the basic goal of attitude change appears reasonable. When translated to practice, the illogic of these critics becomes apparent. (pp. 188–189)

The postmodernism view of disability has significant implications for individuals with learning disabilities. The social construction of disability risks minimizing or trivializing an individual's disability. One of the most caring acts that educators can do is to apply current and forthcoming research-based assessments and interventions to identify and teach individuals with learning disabilities to read, write, problem solve, socialize, communicate, and be independent. The social construction process must not overlook the biological construction process.

Nature of special education and outcomes. The modern view of special education is to use instruction in order to enhance the functioning, knowledge, skills, and socializations of individuals with disabilities. Modernists hope that these cumulative interventions eventually enable individuals with learning disabilities to have successful and rewarding postschool experiences. Although the postmodern view of special education mentions the importance of enhancing performance, the primary focus is on changing social constructions that limit individuals with disabilities. Postmodernists value the outcome of creating a caring adaptable society that treats differences and needs without labels, stigmas, or exclusion (Andrews et al., 2000).

It would seem that modern and postmodern conceptions regarding the nature of special education and related outcomes should naturally blend together. Unfortunately, the strong and radical feelings between these two positions foster extreme viewpoints and minimum common ground. Sasso (2001) points out that the overall purpose of postmodernism is to dismantle special education, to undermine the epistemic authority of the science of disability and valorize "ways of knowing" incompatible with it.

The intensity of this special education divide is captured in Sowell's (1995) words:

> Those who accept this vision [postmodernism] are deemed to be not merely factually correct but morally on a higher plane. Put differently, those who disagree with the prevailing vision are seen as being not merely in error, but in sin. For those who have this vision of the world, the anointed [postmodernists] and the benighted [modernists] do not argue on the same moral plane or play by the same cold rules of logic and evidence. The benighted are to be made "aware," to have their "consciousness raised," and the wistful hope is held out that they will "grow." Should the benighted prove recalcitrant, however, then their "mean-spiritedness" must be fought and the "real reasons" behind their arguments and actions exposed. (pp. 2–3)

If individuals with learning disabilities are to receive the very best education possible and be accepted by a caring and loving community, educators must join to stop yet another "education war" that truly deters special education from being the helping profession it was created to be.

REFERENCES

Abt Associates. (1976). *Education as experimentation: A planned variation model,* Vol. 3A. Cambridge, MA: Author.

Abt Associates. (1977). *Education as experimentation: A planned variation model,* Vol. 4. Cambridge, MA: Author.

Adams, M. J. (1990). *Beginning to read: Thinking and learning about print.* Cambridge, MA: MIT Press.

Andrews, J. E., Carnine, D. W., Coutinho, M. J., Edgar, E. B., Forness, S. R., Fuchs, L. S., et al. (2000). Bridging the special education divide. *Remedial and Special Education, 21,* 258–260, 267.

Anderson, P. L., & Meier-Hedde, R. (2001). Early case reports of dyslexia in the United States and Europe. *Journal of Learning Disabilities, 34,* 9–21.

Anonymous. (1966). *Minimal brain dysfunction in children: Terminology and identification.* Washington, DC: U.S. Department of Health, Education, and Welfare.

Association for Children with Learning Disabilities. (1986). ACLD definition: Specific learning disabilities. *ACLD Newsbriefs,* 15–16.

Barsch, R. H. (1967). *Achieving perceptual-motor efficiency: A space-oriented approach to learning.* Seattle, WA: Special Child Publications.

Bateman, B. (1965). An educational view of a diagnostic approach to learning disorders. In J. Hellmuth (Ed.), *Learning disorders: Vol. 1* (pp. 219–239). Seattle, WA: Special Child Publications.

Beichtman, J. H., Hood, J., & Inglis, A. (1992). Familial transmission of speech and language impairment: A preliminary investigation. *Canadian Journal of Psychiatry, 37*(3), 151–156.

Broadbent, W. H. (1872). On the cerebral mechanism of speech and thought. *Proceedings of the Royal Medical and Chirurgical Society of London* (pp. 25-29). London: Anonymous.

Brown, G. S., & Campbell, D. P. (1948). *Principles of servomechanisms.* New York: John Wiley.

Bryan, T., Pearl, R., Donahue, M., Bryan, J., & Pflaum, S. (1983). The Chicago Institute for the Study of Learning Disabilities. *Exceptional Education Quarterly, 4*(1), 1–22.

Bryant, N. D. *Recommendations for programmatic research.* (1972). Washington, DC: U.S. Office of Education.

Bryant, N. D., Kass, C. E., & Wiederholt, J. L. (1972). *Final Report: Leadership Training Institute in Learning Disabilities.* Washington, DC: U.S. Office of Education.

Bush, W. J., & Giles, M. T. (1969). *Aids to psycholinguistic teaching.* Columbus, OH: Merrill.

Clements, S. D. (1966). Minimal brain dysfunction in children: Terminology and identification: Phase one of a three-phase project. *NINDS Monographs, 9,* Public Health Service Bulletin No. 1415. Washington: DC: U.S. Department of Health, Education, and Welfare.

Cohen, S. A. (1969). Studies in visual perception and reading in disadvantaged children. *Journal of Learning Disabilities, 2,* 498–507.

Cohen, S. A. (1970). Cause versus treatment in reading achievement. *Journal of Learning Disabilities, 3,* 163–166.

Connor, F. P. (1983). Improving school instruction for learning disabled children: The Teachers College Institute. *Exceptional Education Quarterly, 4*(1), 23–44.

Cruickshank, W. M. (1976). William M. Cruickshank. In J. M. Kauffman & D. P. Hallahan (Eds.), *Teaching children with learning disabilities: Personal perspectives* (pp. 94–127). Columbus, OH: Charles E. Merrill.

Cruickshank, W. M., Bentzen, F. A., Ratzeburg, F. H., & Tannhauser, M. T. (1961). *A teaching method of brain-injured and hyperactive children.* Syracuse, NY: Syracuse University Press.

Cruickshank, W. M., Bice, H. V., & Wallen, N. E. (1957). *Perception and cerebral palsy.* Syracuse, NY: Syracuse University Press.

Cruickshank, W. M., Bice, H. V., Wallen, N. E., & Lynch, K. S. (1965). *Perception and cerebral palsy* (2nd ed.). Syracuse, NY: Syracuse University Press.

Cruickshank, W. M., & Dolphin, J. E. (1951). The educational implications of psychological studies of cerebral-palsied children. *Exceptional Children, 18,* 1–8, 32.

DeFries, J. C., Gillis, J. J., & Wadsworth, S. J. (1993). Genes and genders: A twin study of reading disability. In A. M. Galaburda (Ed.), *Dyslexia and development: Neurological aspects of extra-ordinary brains* (pp. 187–204). Cambridge, MA: Harvard University Press.

Delacato, C. H. (1959). *The treatment and prevention of reading problems: The neurological approach.* Springfield, IL: Charles C. Thomas.

Delacato, C. H. (1963). *The diagnosis and treatment of speech and reading problems.* Springfield, IL: Charles C. Thomas.

Delacato, C. H. (1966). *Neurological organization and reading.* Springfield, IL: Charles C. Thomas.

Deno, S. L. (1987). Curriculum-based measurement. *Teaching Exceptional Children, 20*(1), 41–42.

Deshler, D. D., Ellis, E. S., & Lenz, B. K. (1996). *Teaching adolescents with learning disabilities: Strategies and methods* (2nd ed.). Denver: Love.

Dolphin, J. E. (1950). A study of certain aspects of the psychopathology of cerebral palsy children. Unpublished doctoral dissertation, Syracuse University.

Dolphin, J. E., & Cruickshank, W. M. (1951a). Pathology of concept formation in children with cerebral palsy. *American Journal of Mental Deficiency, 56,* 386–392.

Dolphin, J. E., & Cruickshank, W. M. (1951b). Tactual motor perception of children with cerebral palsy. *Journal of Personality, 20,* 466–471.

Dolphin, J. E., & Cruickshank, W. M. (1951c). The figure-background relationship in children with cerebral palsy. *Journal of Clinical Psychology, 7,* 228–231.

Dolphin, J. E., & Cruickshank, W. M. (1951d). Visuo-motor perception of children with cerebral palsy. *Quarterly Journal of Child Behavior, 3,* 198–209.

Dunn, L. M. (1968). Special education for the mildly retarded—Is much of it justifiable? *Exceptional Children, 35,* 5–22.

Engelmann, S. (1967). Relationship between psychological theories and the act of teaching. *Journal of School Psychology, 5,* 92–100.

Engelmann, S., Becker, W. C., Hanner, S., & Johnson, G. (1978). *Corrective reading program: Series guide.* Chicago: Science Research Associates.

Engelmann, S., Becker, W. C., Hanner, S., & Johnson, G. (1988). *Corrective reading program: Series guide* (Rev. ed.). Chicago: Science Research Associates.

Engelmann, S., & Osborn, J. (1977). *DISTAR language.* Chicago: Science Research Associates.

Fernald, G. M. (1943). *Remedial techniques in basic school subjects.* New York: McGraw-Hill Book Company.

Fernald, G. M., & Keller, H. (1921). The effect of kinaesthetic factors in the development of word recognition in the case of non-readers. *Journal of Educational Research, 4,* 355–377.

Fletcher, J. M., Francis, D. J., Shaywitz, S. E., Lyon, G. R., Foorman, B. R., Stuebing, K. K., & Shaywitz, B. A. (1998). Intelligent testing and the discrepancy model for children with learning disabilities. *Learning Disabilities Research & Practice, 13,* 186–203.

Fletcher, J. M., Shaywitz, S. E., Shankweiler, D. P., Katz, L., Liberman, I. Y., Stuebing, K. K., et al. (1994). Cognitive profiles of reading disability: Comparisons of discrepancy and low achievement definitions. *Journal of Educational Psychology, 86,* 6–23.

Flowers, D. L. (1993). Brain basis for dyslexia: A summary of work in progress. *Journal of Learning Disabilities, 26,* 575–582.

Flowers, D. L., Wood, F. B., & Naylor, C. E. (1991). Regional cerebral blood flow correlates of language processes in reading disability. *Archives of Neurology, 48*, 637–643.

Foorman, B. R., Francis, D. J., Fletcher, J. M., & Lynn, A. (1996). Relation of phonological and orthographic processing to early reading: Comparing two approaches to regression-based, reading-level-match designs. *Journal of Educational Psychology, 88*, 639–652.

Forness, S. R., & Kavale, K. A. (1996). Treating social skill deficits in children with learning disabilities: A meta-analysis of the research. *Learning Disability Quarterly, 19*, 2–13.

Frankenberger, W., & Franzaglio, K. (1991). A review of states' criteria for identifying children with learning disabilities. *Journal of Learning Disabilities, 24*, 495–500.

Frostig, M., & Horne, D. (1964). *The Frostig program for the development of visual perception: Teacher's guide*. Chicago: Follett.

Frostig, M., Lefever, D. W., & Whittlesey, J. R. B. (1964). *The Marianne Frostig Developmental Test of Visual Perception*. Palo Alto, CA: Consulting Psychology Press.

Fuchs, D., & Fuchs, L. S. (1991). Framing the REI debate: Abolitionists versus conservationists. In J. W. Lloyd, N. N. Singh, & A. C. Repp (Eds.), *The regular education initiative: Alternative perspectives on concepts, issues, and models* (pp. 241–255). Sycamore, IL: Sycamore Publishing.

Fuchs, D., Mathes, P. G., Fuchs, L. S., & Lipsey, M. W. (1999). *Is LD just a fancy term for underachievement? A meta-analysis of reading differences between underachievers with and without the label.* Unpublished manuscript.

Fuchs, L. S. (1986). Monitoring progress among mildly handicapped pupils: Review of current practice and research. *Remedial and Special Education, 7*(5), 5–12.

Fuchs, L. S., & Fuchs, D. (1986). Effects of systematic formative evaluation: A meta-analysis. *Exceptional Children, 53*, 199–208.

Fuchs, L. S., & Fuchs, D. (1998). Treatment validity: A unifying concept for reconceptualizing the identification of learning disabilities. *Learning Disabilities Research & Practice, 13*, 204–219.

Galaburda, A. M., & Kemper, T. L. (1979). Cytoarchitectonic abnormalities in developmental dyslexia: A case study. *Annals of Neurology, 6*, 94–100.

Galaburda, A. M., Menard, M. T., & Rosen, G. D. (1994). Evidence for aberrant auditory anatomy in developmental dyslexia. *Proceedings of the National Academy of Science USA, 91*, 8010–8013.

Galaburda, A. M., Sherman, G. F., Rosen, G. D., Aboitz, F., & Geschwind, N. (1985). Developmental dyslexia: Four consecutive patients with cortical anomalies. *Annals of Neurology, 18,* 222–233.

Geschwind, N., & Levitsky, W. (1968). Human brain: Left-right asymmetries in temporal speech. *Science, 161,* 186–187.

Gesell, A. F., Ilg, G., Bullis, G., Getman, G. N., & Ilg, F. (1949*). Vision: Its development in infant and child.* New York: Hoeber.

Getman, G. N., Kane, E. R., Halgren, M. R., & McKee, G. W. (1964). *The physiology of readiness: An action program for the development of perception for children.* Minneapolis: Programs to Accelerate School Success.

Getman, G. N., & Kephart, N. C. (1956). *The perceptual development of retarded children.* Unpublished manuscript, Purdue University.

Gibson, J. J., & Gibson, E. J. (1955). Perceptual learning: Differentiation or enrichment? *Psychological Review, 62,* 33–40.

Gillingham, A., & Stillman, B. W. (1936). *Remedial work for reading, spelling, and penmanship.* New York: Sachett & Wilhelms.

Goldstein, K. (1936). The modification of behavior consequent to cerebral lesions. *Psychiatric Quarterly, 10,* 586–610.

Goldstein, K. (1939). *The organism.* New York: American Book.

Gorton, C. E. (1972). The effects of various classroom environments on performance of a mental task by mentally retarded children and normal children. *Education and Training of the Mentally Retarded, 7,* 32–38.

Gresham, F. M. (1988). Social competence and motivational characteristics of learning disabled students. In M. Wang, M. Reynolds, & H. Walberg (Eds.), *The handbook of special education: Research and practice* (pp. 283–302). Oxford, England: Pergamon Press.

Grodzinsky, Y. (in press). The neurology of syntax. *Behavioral and Brain Sciences.*

Gross-Glenn, K., Duara, R., Barker, W. W., Loewenstein, D., Chang, J., Yoshii, F., et al. (1991). Positron emission tomographic studies during serial word-reading by normal and dyslexic adults. *Journal of Clinical and Experimental Neuropsychology, 13,* 531–544.

Hagman, J. O., Wood, F., Buchsbaum, M. S., Tallal, P., Flowers, L., & Katz, W. (1992). Cerebral brain metabolism in adult dyslexic subjects assessed with positron emission tomography during performance of an auditory task. *Archives of Neurology, 49,* 734–739.

Hallahan, D. P. (1992). Some thoughts on why the prevalence of learning disabilities has increased. *Journal of Learning Disabilities, 25,* 523–528.

Hallahan, D. P. (2000). *William M. Cruickshank: If He Were Alive Today.* Washington, DC: International Dyslexia Association Annual Conference.

Hallahan, D. P., & Cruickshank, W. M. (1973). *Psychoeducational foundations of learning disabilities.* Englewood Cliffs, NJ: Prentice-Hall.

Hallahan, D. P., Hall, R. J., Ianna, S. O., Kneedler, R. D., Lloyd, J. W., Loper, A. B., et al. (1983). Summary of research findings at the University of Virginia Learning Disabilities Research Institute. *Exceptional Education Quarterly,* 4(1), 95–114.

Hallahan, D. P., & Kauffman, J. M. (1976). *Introduction to learning disabilities: A psycho-behavioral approach.* Engelwood Cliffs, NJ: Prentice-Hall.

Hallahan, D. P., & Kauffman, J. M. (2000). *Exceptional learners: Introduction to special education* (8th ed.). Boston: Allyn & Bacon.

Hammill, D. D., & Larsen, S. C. (1974). The effectiveness of psycholinguistic training. *Exceptional Children, 41,* 514.

Hammill, D. D., Leigh, J. E., McNutt, G., & Larsen, S. C. (1981). A new definition of learning disabilities. *Learning Disability Quarterly, 4,* 336–342.

Hammill, D. D., Mather, N., & Roberts, R. (2001). *Illinois Test of Psycholinguistic Abilities (ITPA-3)* (3rd ed.). Austin, TX: Pro-Ed.

Haring, N. G., & Bateman, B. (1969). Introduction. In N. G. Haring (Ed.), *Minimal brain dysfunction in children: Educational, medical, and health related services.* (pp. 1–4). Washington, DC: U.S. Department of Health, Education, and Welfare.

Harlow, H. F. (1951). Learning theories. In W. Dennis (Ed.), *Current trends in psychological theory.* Pittsburgh: University of Pittsburgh Press.

Head, H. (1926). *Aphasia and kindred disorders of speech.* London: Cambridge University Press.

Hegge, T. G., Kirk, S. A., & Kirk, W. D. (1936). *Remedial reading drills.* Ann Arbor, MI: George Wahr.

Hinshelwood, J. (1895). Word-blindness and visual memory. *Lancet, 2,* 1564–1570.

Hinshelwood, J. (1917). *Congenital word-blindness.* London: H. K. Lewis & Co. LTD.

Humphreys, P., Kaufmann, W. E., & Galaburda, A. M. (1990). Developmental dyslexia in women: Neuropathological findings in three patients. *Annals of Neurology, 28,* 727–738.

Hynd, G. W., & Semrud-Clikeman, M. (1989). Dyslexia and brain morphology. *Psychological Bulletin, 106,* 447–482.

Individuals with Disabilities Education Act Amendments (IDEA) of 1997. (1997). Public Law 105-17.

Interagency Committee on Learning Disabilities. (1987). *Learning disabilities: A report to Congress.* Bethesda, MD: National Institutes of Health.

Jenkins, J. R., Gorrafa, S., & Griffiths, S. (1972). Another look at isolation effects. *American Journal of Mental Deficiency, 76,* 591–593.

Johnson, D. J., & Myklebust, H. R. (1967). *Learning disabilities: Educational principles and practices.* New York: Grune & Stratton.

Karnes, M. B. (1968). *Activities for developing psycholinguistic skills with preschool culturally disadvantaged children.* Washington, DC: Council for Exceptional Children.

Kauffman, J. M. (1999). Commentary: Today's special education and its message for tomorrow. *The Journal of Special Education, 32,* 244–254.

Kavale, K. A., & Forness, S. R. (2000). History, rhetoric, and reality: Analysis of the inclusion debate. *Remedial and Special Education, 21,* 279–296.

Keogh, B. K. (1983). A lesson from Gestalt Psychology. *Exceptional Education Quarterly, 4*(1), 115–127.

Kephart, N. C. (1960). *Slow learner in the classroom.* Columbus, OH: Charles E. Merrill.

Kephart, N. C. (1971). *Slow learner in the classroom* (2nd ed.). Columbus, OH: Charles E. Merrill.

Kephart, N. C., & Strauss, A. A. (1940). A clinical factor influencing variations in IQ. *American Journal of Orthopsychiatry, 10,* 342–350.

Kerr, J. (1897). School hygiene, in its mental, moral, and physical aspects. *Journal of the Royal Statistical Society, 60,* 613–680.

Kirk, S. A. (1933). The influence of manual tracing on the learning of simple words in the case of subnormal boys. *Journal of Educational Psychology, 24,* 525–535.

Kirk, S. A. (1935). Hemispheric cerebral dominance and hemispheric equipotentiality. In Anonymous, *Comparative Psychology Monographs.* Baltimore: Johns Hopkins Press.

Kirk, S. A. (1936). Extrastriate functions in the discrimination of complex visual patterns. *Journal of Comparative Psychology, 21,* 145–159.

Kirk, S. A. (1940). *Teaching reading to slow learning children.* New York: Houghton Mifflin.

Kirk. S. A. (1958). *Early education of the mentally retarded: An experimental study.* Urbana, IL: University of Illinois Press.

Kirk, S. A. (1962). *Educating exceptional children.* Boston: Houghton Mifflin.

Kirk, S. A. (1963). Behavioral diagnosis and remediation of learning disabilities. In Anonymous, *Proceedings of the conference on exploration into problems of the perceptually handicapped child.* Chicago: Perceptually Handicapped Children.

Kirk, S. A. (1970). *Lecture in Final Report of Institute for Leadership Personnel in Learning Disabilities.* University of Arizona: Anonymous.

Kirk, S. A. (1976). Samuel A. Kirk. In J. M. Kauffman & D. P. Hallahan (Eds.), *Teaching children with learning disabilities: Personal perspectives* (pp. 239–269). Columbus, OH: Charles E. Merrill.

Kirk, S. A., & Kirk, W. D. (1971). *Psycholinguistic learning disabilities: Diagnosis and remediation.* Urbana, IL: University of Illinois Press.

Kirk, S. A., McCarthy, J. J., & Kirk, W. D. (1961). *Illinois Test of Psycholinguistic Abilities* (Experimental ed.). Urbana, IL: University of Illinois Press.

Kirk, S. A., McCarthy, J. J., & Kirk, W. D. (1968). *Illinois Test of Psycholinguistic Abilities* (Rev. ed.). Urbana, IL: University of Illinois Press.

Kushch, A., Gross-Glenn, K., Jallad, B., Lubs, H., Rabin, M., Feldman, E., et al. (1993). Temporal lobe surface area measurements on MRI in normal and dyslexic readers. *Neuropsychologia, 31,* 811–821.

Kussmaul, A. (1877). Word deafness and word blindness. In H. von Ziemssen & J. A. T. McCreery (Eds.), *Cyclopedia of the practice of medicine.* (pp. 770–778). New York: William Wood.

Larsen, E. J. (1931). A neurologic-etiologic study on 1000 mental defectives. *Acta Psychiatrica et Neurologica, 6,* 37–54.

Larsen, J. P., Hoien, T., Lundberg, I., & Odegaard, H. (1990). MRI evaluation of the symmetry of the planum temporale in adolescents with dyslexia. *Brain and Language, 39,* 289–301.

Laski, F. J. (1991). Achieving integration during the second revolution. In L. H. Meyer, C. A. Peck, & L. Brown (Eds.), *Critical issues in the lives of people with severe disabilities* (pp. 409–421). Baltimore, MD: Paul H. Brookes.

Lerner, J. W. (2000). *Learning disabilities: Theories, diagnosis, and teaching strategies* (8th ed.). Boston: Houghton Mifflin.

Lewis, B. A. (1992). Pedigree analysis of children with phonology disorders. *Journal of Learning Disabilities, 25,* 586–597.

Lewis, B. A., & Thompson, L. A. (1992). A study of developmental speech and language disorders in twins. *Journal of Speech and Hearing Research, 35,* 1086–1094.

Lyon, G. R. (1995a). Toward a definition of dyslexia. *Annals of Dyslexia, 45,* 3–27.

Lyon, G. R. (1995b). Research initiatives in learning disabilities: Contributions from scientists supported by the National Institute of Child Health and Human Development. *Journal of Child Neurology, 10*(Suppl. 1), 120–126.

Lyon, G. R. (1998). *Overview of reading and literacy initiatives (Report to Committee on Labor and Human Resources, U.S. Senate).* Bethesda, MD: National Institute of Child Health and Human Development, National Institutes of Health.

Mann, L. (1971). Psychometric phrenology and the new faculty psychology. *The Journal of Special Education, 5,* 3–14.

Martin, E. W. (1987). Developmental variation and dysfunction: Observations on labeling, public policy, and individualization of instruction. In M. D. Levine & P. Satz (Eds.), *Middle childhood: Development and dysfunction* (pp. 435–445). Baltimore: University Park Press.

McKinney, J. D. (1983). Contributions of the institutes for research on learning disabilities. *Exceptional Education Quarterly, 4*(1), 129–144.

Mercer, C. D. (1997). *Students with learning disabilities* (5th ed.). Upper Saddle River, NJ: Merrill.

Mercer, C. D., Forgnone, C., & Wolking, W. D. (1976). Definitions of learning disabilities used in the United States. *Journal of Learning Disabilities, 9,* 376–386.

Minskoff, E. H., Wiseman, D. E., & Minskoff, J. G. (1974). *The MWM Program for Developing Language Abilities.* Ridgefield, NJ: Educational Performance Associates.

Monroe, M. (1928). Methods for diagnosis and treatment of cases of reading disability. *Genetic Psychology Monographs, 4,* 341–456.

Monroe, M. (1932). *Children who cannot read.* Chicago: The University of Chicago Press.

Morgan, W. P. (1896). A case of congenital word blindness. *The British Medical Journal, 2,* 1378.

National Joint Committee on Learning Disabilities. Anonymous. (1988). *Letter to NJCLD Member Organizations.*

National Reading Panel. (April, 2000). *Report of the National Reading Panel: Teaching children to read (NIH Publication No. 00-4654).* Bethesda, MD: National Institute of Child Health and Human Development, National Institutes of Health.

Orton, S. T. (1925). "Word-blindness" in school children. *Archives of Neurology and Psychiatry, 14,* 581–615.

Orton, S. T. (1937). *Reading, writing, and speech problems in children.* New York: W. W. Norton & Company, Inc.

Orton, S. T. (1939). A neurological explanation of the reading disability. *The Educational Record, 20*(Supp. No. 12), 58–68.

Osgood, C. E. (1957). A behavioristic analysis of perception and language as cognitive phenomena. In J. S. Bruner (Ed.), *Contemporary approaches to cognition* (pp. 75–117). Cambridge, MA: Harvard University Press.

Pennington, B. F. (1990). Annotation: The genetics of dyslexia. *Journal of Child Psychology and Child Psychiatry, 31* (2), 193–201.

Pinel, J. P. J. (1997). *Biopsychology* (3rd ed.). Boston: Allyn & Bacon.

Reynolds, C. A., Hewitt, J. K., Erickson, M. T., Silberg, J. L., Rutter, M., Simonoff, E., et al. (1996). The genetics of children's oral reading performance. *Journal of Child Psychology & Psychiatry & Allied Disciplines, 37*, 425–434.

Robbins, M., & Glass, G. V. (1969). The Doman-Delacato rationale: A critical analysis. In J. Hellmuth (Ed.), *Educational therapy: Vol. II.* Seattle: Special Child Publications.

Rost, K. J., & Charles, D. C. (1967). Academic achievement of brain injured and hyperactive children in isolation. *Exceptional Children, 34*, 125–126.

Rutter, M., & Yule, W. (1975). The concept of specific reading retardation. *Journal of Child Psychology and Psychiatry, 16*, 181–197.

Sarason, S. B. (1949). *Psychological problems in mental deficiency.* New York: Harper.

Sasso, G. M. (2001). The retreat from inquiry and knowledge in special education. *The Journal of Special Education, 34*, 178–193.

Schulte-Korne, G., Deimel, W., Muller, K., Gutenbrunner, C., & Remschmidt, H. (1996). Familial aggregation of spelling disability. *Journal of Child Psychology and Psychiatry, 37*, 817–822.

Schumaker, J. B., Deshler, D. D., Alley, G. R., & Warner, M. M. (1983). Toward the development of an intervention model for learning disabled adolescents: The University of Kansas Institute. *Exceptional Education Quarterly, 4*(1), 45–74.

Shaywitz, S. E., Shaywitz, B. A., Pugh, K. R., Fulbright, R. K., Constable, R. T., Mencl, W. E., et al. (1998). Functional disruption in the organization of the brain for reading in dyslexia. *Neurobiology, 95*, 2636–2641.

Shores, R. E., & Haubrich, P. A. (1969). Effect of cubicles in educating emotionally disturbed children. *Exceptional Children, 36*, 21–26.

Siegel, L. S. (1989). IQ is irrelevant to the definition of learning disabilities. *Journal of Learning Disabilities, 22*, 469–486.

Skeels, H. M. (1966). Adult status of children with contrasting early life experiences. *Monographs of the Society for Research in Child Development, 31*(Serial No. 105).

Skeels, H. M., & Dye, H. B. (1939). A study of the effects of differential stimulation on mentally retarded children. *Proceedings: American Association on Mental Deficiency, 44,* 114–136.

Slater, B. R. (1968). Effects of noise on pupil performance. *Journal of Educational Psychology, 59,* 239–243.

Sommervill, J. W., Warnberg, L. S., & Bost, D. E. (1973). Effects of cubicles versus increased stimulation on task performance by first-grade males perceived as distractible and nondistractible. *The Journal of Special Education, 7,* 169–185.

Sowell, T. (1995). *The vision of the anointed: Self-congratulation as a basis for social policy.* New York: Basic Books.

Stanovich, K. E., & Siegel, L. S. (1994). Phenotypic performance profile of children with reading disabilities: A regression-based test of the phonological-core variable-difference model. *Journal of Educational Psychology, 86,* 24–53.

Strauss, A. A. (1943). Diagnosis and education of the cripple-brained, deficient child. *Journal of Exceptional Children, 9,* 163–168, 183.

Strauss, A. A., & Kephart, N. C. (1939). *Rate of mental growth in a constant environment among higher grade moron and borderline children.* Anonymous.

Strauss, A. A., & Kephart, N. C. (1955). *Psychopathology and education of the brain-injured child, Vol. II: Progress in theory and clinic.* New York: Grune and Stratton.

Strauss, A. A., & Lehtinen, L. E. (1947). *Psychopathology and education of the brain-injured child.* New York: Grune and Stratton.

Strauss, A. A., & Werner, H. (1942). Disorders of conceptual thinking in the brain-injured child. *Journal of Nervous and Mental Disease, 96,* 153–172.

Tindal, G. A., & Marston, D. B. (1990). *Classroom-based assessment: Evaluating instructional outcomes.* Upper Saddle River, NJ: Merrill/Prentice Hall.

Torgesen, J. K., & Wagner, R. K. (1998). Alternative diagnostic approaches for specific developmental reading disabilities. *Learning Disabilities Research & Practice, 13,* 220–232.

U.S. Department of Education. (1997). *Nineteenth annual report to Congress on the implementation of the Individuals with Disabilities Education Act.* Washington, DC: Author.

U.S. Department of Education. (2000). *Twenty-second annual report to Congress on the implementation of the Individuals with Disabilities Education Act.* Washington, DC: Author.

U.S. Office of Education. (1968). *First annual report of National Advisory Committee on Handicapped Children.* Washington, DC: U.S. Department of Health, Education, and Welfare.

U.S. Office of Education. (1976). Proposed rulemaking. *Federal Register, 41*(230), 52404–52407.

U.S. Office of Education. (1977). Assistance to states for education of handicapped children: Procedures for evaluating specific learning disabilities. *Federal Register, 42*(250), 65082–65085.

Vaughn, S., McIntosh, R., & Spencer-Rowe, J. (1991). Peer rejection is a stubborn thing: Increasing peer acceptance of rejected students with learning disabilities. *Learning Disabilities Research & Practice, 6,* 83–88.

Vaughn, S., & Sinugab, J. (1998). Social competence of students with learning disabilities: Interventions and issues. In B. Y. L. Wong (Ed.), *Learning about learning disabilities* (pp. 453–487). San Diego, CA: Academic Press.

Vellutino, F. R., Scanlon, D. M., & Lyon, G. R. (2000). Differentiating between difficult-to-remediate and readily remediated poor readers: More evidence against the IQ-achievement discrepancy definition of reading disability. *Journal of Learning Disabilities, 33,* 223–238.

Wang, M. C., Haertel, G. D., & Walberg, H. J. (1993/1994). What helps students learn? *Educational Leadership, 51*(4), 74–79.

Werner, H. (1948). *Comparative psychology of mental development.* New York: International Universities Press.

Werner, H. (1957). The concept of development from a comparative and organismic point of view. In D. B. Harris (Ed.), *The concept of development* (pp. 125–148). Minneapolis: University of Minnesota Press.

Werner, H., & Strauss, A. A. (1939). Types of visuo-motor activity in their relation to low and high performance ages. *Proceedings of the American Association on Mental Deficiency, 44,* 163–168.

Werner, H., & Strauss, A. A. (1940). Causal factors in low performance. *American Journal of Mental Deficiency, 45,* 213–218.

Werner, H., & Strauss, A. A. (1941). Pathology of figure-background relation in the child. *Journal of Abnormal and Social Psychology, 36,* 236–248.

Wernicke, C. (1874). *Der aphasische symptomenkomplex.* Breslau, Poland: Cohn & Weigert.

Wiederholt, J. L. (1974). Historical perspectives on the education of the learning disabled. In L. Mann & D. Sabatino (Eds.), *The second review of special education* (pp. 103–152). Philadelphia: JSE Press.

Will, M. C. (1986). Educating children with learning problems: A shared responsibility. *Exceptional Children, 52*, 411–415.

Ysseldyke, J. E., Algozzine, B., Shinn, M. R., & McGue, M. (1982). Similarities and differences between low achievers and students classified as learning disabled. *The Journal of Special Education, 16*, 73–85.

Ysseldyke, J. E., & Salvia, J. A. (1974). Diagnostic prescriptive teaching: Two models. *Exceptional Children, 41*, 181–186.

Ysseldyke, J. E., Thurlow, M., Graden, J., Wesson, C., Algozzine, B., & Deno, S. L. (1983). Generalizations from five years of research on assessment and decision making: The University of Minnesota Institute. *Exceptional Education Quarterly, 4*(1), 75–93.

ENDNOTES

[1] In this chronicle of the field of learning disabilities, we have drawn upon original sources as well as other prior histories of the field: Hallahan & Cruickshank, 1973; Lerner, 2000; Mercer, 1997; Wiederholt, 1974. The writing of any history, especially when it is restricted to a certain page-length, reflects the particular point of view, or bias, of the author(s). Therefore, we encourage the reader to consult these other histories to supplement the information in the present paper.

[2] Actually, in 1836, a little-known country doctor named Dax presented a paper to a medical society in France, in which he noted that over the course of his career he had seen about 40 cases of brain-injured patients with speech problems, and none of them had damage solely in the right hemisphere. "His report aroused little interest, and Dax died the following year unaware that he had anticipated one of today's most important areas of neuropsychological research" (Pinel, 1997, p. 412).

[3] Anderson and Meier-Hedde (2001), in an excellent summary of several early case studies of dyslexia, have questioned Morgan's legitimacy as the first to report on word-blindness in children. They note that James Kerr, Medical Superintendent to the Bradford School Board, delivered a presentation 6 months prior to Morgan's publication in which he reported on a child with word-blindness. However, when Kerr's essay was published in 1897, the reference to the boy with word-blindness was terse. He listed several cases of various kinds, including a " boy with word blindness, who can spell the separate letters, is a trouble..." (Kerr, 1897, p. 668). In any case, it is fair to say that Morgan was probably the first to *publish* on word-blindness in children.

[4] As we discuss later, the need for intensive instruction has re-emerged at the end of the 20th century as a theme among some learning disabilities researchers.

[5] Newell Kephart later became a major historical figure in the learning disabilities field in his own right, with his advocacy for perceptual-motor training for children with learning disabilities. We discuss his work in a later section.

[6] Although recommending a general focus on perceptual training, Strauss and Lehtinen did not provide many specific perceptual training recommendations. For example, their discussion of perceptual training was nowhere near as detailed as those of Newell Kephart, Marianne Frostig, and Gerald Getman, whom we discuss later. Furthermore, although Strauss and Lehtinen did make some mention of the value of phonics instruction, they primarily discussed it in the context of auditory perceptual problems and offered few suggestions for phonics instruction.

[7] In the 1960s and 1970s there were several other studies that assessed Strauss and Lehtinen's and Cruickshank's recommendations, focusing specifically on the use of reduced environmental stimulation, primarily through the use of cubicles (Gorton, 1972; Jenkins, Gorrafa, & Griffiths, 1972; Rost & Charles, 1967; Shores & Haubrich, 1969; Slater, 1968; Sommervill, Warnberg, & Bost, 1973). In general, these studies showed improvements in attending skills but no improvements in academic achievement.

[8] Bureau of Education for the Handicapped, U.S. Office of Education, Department of Health, Education, and Welfare; Neurological and Sensory Disease Control Program, Department of Health, Education, and Welfare; National Institute of Neurological Diseases and Stroke

[9] Kirk (1976) stated that this study brought about renewed interest in Howard Skeels' (Skeels & Dye, 1939) original study, in which institutionalized young children with mental retardation were provided stimulation by institutionalized teenage girls with mental retardation. Encouraged to do a followup, Skeels (1966) found evidence that the effects of the program lasted into adulthood. Kirk also stated that the Skeels study and his served to help convince Congress years later to fund Head Start and preschool programs for children with disabilities.

[10] Recently, the *ITPA* has been revised (Hammill, Mather, & Roberts, 2001). Ironically, the senior author of the *ITPA-3*, Donald Hammill, was one of the strongest critics of the original *ITPA*. The *ITPA-3* focuses more exclusively on language and does not include subtests devoted to visual perception.

[11] At the invitation of Kephart, these programs were moved in 1956 from Minnesota, where Getman lived, to the Adult Education Department of Purdue University, with Kephart serving as the faculty sponsor (Hallahan & Cruickshank, 1973). Collaboration with Kephart also resulted in an unpublished monograph at the end of the summer in 1956, *The Perceptual Development of Retarded Children* (Getman & Kephart, 1956). Kephart and Getman also organized a camp for children with brain injury and their parents during the summers of 1957 and 1958. This close relationship between Getman and Kephart is evident in the similarity between their 1956 monograph and Kephart's *Slow Learner in the Classroom* (1960).

[12] Barsch, like Kephart, also collaborated with Getman. Together, they established a summer camp for children and parents at Stevens Point, Wisconsin, in 1960. Barsch also collaborated with Alfred Strauss when the latter was the director of the Cove Schools in Racine, Wisconsin (Hallahan & Cruickshank, 1973).

[13] We discuss the Doman-Delacato program here with perceptual and perceptual-motor approaches because many of their remedial activities did focus on motor and perceptual-motor training. However, it also differed in many ways, especially with respect to focusing on the family as a whole and purportedly training the brain rather than behavioral symptoms.

[14] American Academy for Cerebral Palsy, American Academy of Physical Medicine and Rehabilitation, American Congress of Rehabilitation Medicine, Canadian Association for Retarded Children, Canadian Rehabilitation Council for the Disabled, National Association for Retarded Children

[15] Definitions of full inclusion vary, but two features included in most conceptualizations of full inclusion are that students with disabilities should be educated totally in the regular classroom and in their home school.

RESPONSE TO "LEARNING DISABILITIES: HISTORICAL PERSPECTIVES"

Sandra Britt, Minter City, MS

The serious study of the Hallahan and Mercer discussion of the historical perspective of learning disabilities (LD) is critically important to any consideration of reforming current legislation, policies, and procedures affecting persons with LD. Changes in the identification and treatment of persons with LD should only occur after thoughtful consideration of lessons learned from the past and recent research findings, always keeping as the ultimate goal the best interest of persons with LD. Change must not be determined to accommodate political agendas.

This white paper calls attention to the fact that LD, even though one of the newer disability categories in the federal law, is not a passing, recent "fad." Its origin dates back into the 1800s with European roots. It is interesting to note that early research into LD was centered in the medical community, specifically in the field of neurology. Recent years have seen a lessening of involvement of the medical field, with LD often considered to be an educational problem with limited regard for biological connections.

In 1975 Public Law 94-142 was passed and became what is often called "the special education law." P.L. 94-142 officially included LD as a disability category and made children identified with LD eligible for services in the educational system. This "special education" law may have further distanced LD from the medical field.

In 1977 the Association for Children and Adults with Learning Disabilities (ACLD), now the Learning Disabilities Association of America (LDA), formed the ACLD Scientific Studies Committee, under the leadership of John Wacker, a parent of two children with LD. This committee felt that research on the brain dysfunction that causes LD should have priority with the federal government. On the theory that "if it's a brain dysfunction, then it must be a physiological condition," the Scientific Studies Committee began contacting key staff members of the health-oriented institutes in Washington (Cannon, 1997).

It soon became apparent that there was little research targeted toward understanding, much less diagnosing and treating, the physiological aspect of the hidden handicap that has come to be known by the "umbrella term," *learning disabilities*. It was considered by the health agencies—and for that matter, by just about everyone in Washington—to be an educational problem. One federal institute knew practically nothing about what another was doing or had done to study the subject. There were incidence figures ranging from 1% to 25%. Obviously, a major coordinated and multidisciplinary effort was needed to assess the status of knowledge of LD and determine what was needed (Cannon, 1997).

Public Law 99-158, the Health Research Extension Act of 1985, was passed. This legislation mandated that the Director of the National Institutes of Health establish an Interagency Committee on Learning Disabilities (ICLD) to review and assess federal research priorities, activities, and findings regarding LD (including central nervous system dysfunction in children). This mandate further required that the ICLD report to the Congress on its activities and include in the report: the number of persons affected by LD and the demographic data that describe such persons; a description of the current research findings on the cause, diagnosis, treatment, and prevention of LD; and recommendations for legisation and administrative actions to increase the effectiveness of research on LD and to improve the dissemination of the diagnosis, treatment, and prevention of LD (Cannon, 1997).

The ICLD published their *Report to Congress on Learning Disabilities*, as was required by P.L. 99-158. As a result of this legislation and the work of the ICLD, the National Institute of Child Health and Human Development (NICHD) was charged with developing a systematic, long-term perspective, longitudinal, and multidisciplinary research program to define the different types of LD, to identify the various causes of these disabilities, and to map the developmental course of each of these disabilities, to determine how best to treat each type of LD and to ultimately understand how to prevent these disabilities. NICHD continues to oversee research centers on LD across the country (Lyon, Alexander, & Yaffe, 1997). The findings to date of all LD research under this program must be available for study and consideration as important changes in LD policies are discussed and planned. Since problems with definition and identification existed at the time of the convening of the ICLD, it is believed prudent and necessary to review all information and findings from current research efforts.

Major issues facing the LD field, according to Hallahan and Mercer, include concern about identification procedures, debate over placement options, the denunciation of the validity of LD as a real phenomenon, and the extraordinary growth in the prevalence of LD. The diagnosis of LD requires clinical judgment derived from multiple data. No specific test, test battery, nor formula can substitute for clinical judgment. To help ensure valid diagnostic decisions, appropriately trained professionals require extensive clinical training. The validity of the LD diagnosis increases when the responsibility for making the judgment is placed with clinicians who hold advanced professional degrees in generally accepted fields. The diagnosis must provide a full description of how the individual learns and what types of learning are affected by the condition, together with intervention methods that can offset these areas of deficit. No one would dispute the need for new diagnostic procedures; however, until new ones are developed that truly identify the handicapping condition, this is the model we must continue to use.

It is hoped that information coming out of the various research institutes under NICHD leadership will answer many of the questions on these issues, particularly the validity of LD as a legitimate disorder that truly interferes with the ability of its victims to function adequately in many areas of life. Because LD is a lifelong handicapping condition, once it has been validly diagnosed, the *existence* of this handicap need not be questioned again. While the manifestations of the condition may change over time, the inherent condition persists. Reassessment is needed to monitor progress and develop appropriate plans, but it is unnecessary to verify whether an individual has specific learning disabilities (LDA, 1990).

In regard to the increase in the numbers of persons identified as having LD, it is hoped that this discussion will include the possible effects of education reform, including mandated higher standards and high stakes assessments. It is reasonable to assume that school systems may very well identify students who are performing below their expectation as having LD in order to disaggregate their academic scores from the whole, thus showing the school system in a better light.

The discussion of phonemic awareness research is of considerable interest, in particular these comments from the white paper:

> Phonemic awareness training must be combined with other types of reading instruction to improve reading skills of poor readers to average levels. Lyon (1998) has highlighted the need for multiple interventions: 'We have learned that for 90% to 95% of poor readers, prevention and early intervention programs that combine instruction in phonemic awareness, phonics, fluency development, and reading comprehension strategies, provided by well trained teachers, can increase reading skills to average reading levels.' ...It will be interesting to see if phonemic awareness research will be a factor in shaping future definitions of learning disabilities or federal regulations pertaining to identification of learning disabilities (this volume).

The use of the discrepancy between achievement and intellectual potential in the identification of persons with LD has long been discussed, but a reasonable alternative has not yet appeared. This seems further supported by the white paper, which states, "Researchers have just begun to explore alternatives to the discrepancy approach to identification" (this volume). Without support from research, perhaps it is premature to rush into adopting a new identification procedure. While the pitfalls of the use of the discrepancy are recognized, there is some concern that a drastic change from this practice, just for the sake of change, may be a case of "throwing the baby out with the bath water." Open, honest dialogue on this subject is desperately needed and desired, with change only coming when there are indications of significantly better ways to identify persons with LD.

The overidentification of children from minority backgrounds in special education is a concern, especially the statement, "there is also some evidence of disproportionate representation in learning disabilities." Hallahan and Mercer state, "Researchers have not yet been able to disentangle the reasons why disproportionate representations (of minority students) in learning disabilities and other areas of special education exists" (this volume). The lack of research-based information will limit any scholarly approach to this significant problem. This important issue, like others mentioned, would appear to be not only a special education issue, but perhaps even more one of interest and concern to general education. It is hoped that general education and representatives from minority groups will be brought into these discussions so that they will be major players in the discussion and decision making from the beginning.

LDA (1990) developed a strong position paper supporting the continuation of continuum of placement options rather than full inclusion of all students with LD in the general education classroom (inclusion). This position continues to be enthusiastically supported by LDA. This is an important issue and again must be discussed along with general education. Full inclusion of students in the general education classroom without the ability and opportunity for both general education and special education to collaborate and cooperate seems doomed for failure and the students are the losers. Another component of this discussion is teacher education. Perhaps failures of the inclusion movement have often been the results of the assignment of teachers who are not trained to teach students with disabilities, especially general education teachers. Again, data gathered over the last few years when school systems have been "experimenting" with full inclusion would be useful to this discussion.

Again, when we discuss appropriate treatment and interventions for persons with LD, we must rely heavily on the research discussed earlier. The dissemination of research findings is the proof of the value of such research. There is a tremendous need for research-based programs for students with LD in classrooms across the country.

I heartily agree with Hallahan and Mercer in their final paragraph—a rally cry to us all: "If individuals with learning disabilities are to receive the very best education possible and be accepted by a caring and loving community, educators must join to stop yet another 'education war' that truly deters special education from being the helping profession it was created to be" (this volume).

REFERENCES

Cannon, L. (1997). Preface. *Learning Disabilities: A Multidisciplinary Journal, 8*(1), iii–iv.

Learning Disabilities Association of America. (1990). Eligibility position paper and supporting documents. *LDA Newsbriefs*, May, 2a–8a.

Lyon, G. R., Alexander, D., & Yaffe, S. (1997). Progress and promise in research in learning disabilities. *Learning Disabilities: A Multidisciplinary Journal, 8*(1), 1–6.

RESPONSE TO "LEARNING DISABILITIES: HISTORICAL PERSPECTIVES"

Beth Harry, University of Miami

I found this paper very informative and very comprehensive with regard to the history and development of the field of learning disabilities (LD). The outline of the arguments around definitional issues points to some of the central controversies surrounding LD.

My main concern with the paper is the need to develop the issues related to minorities and to show how they relate to the rest of the discussion. As it stands, the placement of this issue under the section on identification results in the impression that it is a somewhat discrete concern, resulting mainly from difficulties in identification. From my perspective, the impact on minorities is integrally related to issues of definition and measurement. Postmodern perspectives, which the author also treats somewhat separately, are, to my view, deeply intertwined with the minority issues and with the issues of definition and measurement. My comments will be focused first on minorities and then on how this aspect relates to postmodern perspectives.

Discussion of how LD interacts with minority status is very complex and moves in different directions at once. On the one hand, both the definition of LD and the manner of assessing it work against minorities being categorized with LD (Collins & Camblin, 1983). The placement data reported by the Office for Civil Rights (OCR) showed that, throughout the 1980s and early 1990s, the only over-representation of minorities in LD was of Hispanics in certain states where representation of that ethnic group was high (Finn, 1982; U.S. Department of Education [USDOE], 1994. That pattern declined in the mid- to late nineties (USDOE, 1999). The white paper refers to the 2000 Report to Congress, which indicated that some minorities are now becoming over-represented in the LD category. This is relatively new and points to the fact that LD placement has escalated for all ethnic groups (including Whites) except for Asian Pacific Islanders. I will comment first on the traditional trend—that minorities were under- rather than over-represented in this particular category.

The traditional low rate of LD among minorities was related to a central feature of the definition: the notion of 'unexpectedness.' It was this notion that led to the exclusionary clauses of the LD definition. For learning difficulties to be seen as unexpected, two sets of conditions needed to be ruled out—general cognitive or sensory impairments and environmental disadvantages that could account for slow rate of learning. To establish that normal general intelligence in fact is present, the field has used certain tests that purport to measure intelligence and has then compared scores on these tests to scores on tests of academic achievement. If members of a group are more likely to score below the normal range on an IQ test, it is more difficult for them to meet the requirement of an IQ/achievement discrepancy. It is well known that African Americans have tended to score lower than Whites on these tests. These tests, regardless of the many statistical analyses that have shown minimal to no discrimination against minorities, are patently discriminatory to the common sense perceptions of anyone who examines a sample of the items. It is not that the items directly discriminate against race, per se, but that they discriminate against any group of children whose daily and educational experiences have provided them with less opportunity to master the material. For example, questions that seek an individual's recall of factual material commonly included in school curricula (as in the information section of the Wechsler Intelligence Scale for Children [WISC]) require that an individual was present and attentive when this information was being taught. It also requires that the material was properly taught. Questions that seek an individual's opinions about what constitutes moral behavior (as in the "comprehension" section of the WISC) require that the individual was brought up in a home and community that honored the required moral tenets or that the child's schooling included training in these beliefs. Questions that seek an individual's knowledge of similarities between items require that the individual has had first hand exposure to those items (such as knowing that a piano has strings and has both black and white keys). Such questions also require facility in particular discourse patterns, such as defining items by their properties rather than by their functions (as in saying that the similarity between two musical instruments is that they have strings as opposed to saying "You play 'em" [Harry, Klingner, Sturges, & Moore, in press]).

It is not enough to say that children in poor, minority communities in the United States should have inculcated the information on IQ tests simply through being members of the society. Anyone who has spent time in such communities knows that many children go no further than several blocks from their own homes and come into contact with adults from other communities only in school, which oftentimes presents them with negative experiences that they would rather avoid than learn from. As one teacher in an inner-city school exclaimed: "They think the world ends at their neighborhood!" (Harry et al., in press).

Thus, the discrepancy criterion has worked against, at least, African American children. With a lower IQ score, this group of children is less likely to meet the criterion of showing a discrepancy between general intelligence and academic achievement. The second exclusionary clause—that delay in academic progress should not be related to environmental disadvantage—has also served to exclude many children from poor and minority backgrounds. When this clause is followed, school personnel typically do not seek LD as a cause of learning difficulties with such children. I believe that the general lack of over-representation in LD was largely the result of these two exclusionary clauses. For several decades, LD was a disability category reserved for middle class children, mostly White, whose poor academic achievement stood out as unexpected in the context of their family and community settings and of their own verbal and general skills.

Poor achievement of minorities and particularly minorities of low socioeconomic status, however, has persisted over the years. There has been a clear trend toward use of the LD category for what traditional LD researchers would see as "garden variety" low achievers. There are many reasons for the move toward broader use of LD, many of which suggest good intentions on the part of referring school personnel. First, low achievement and IQ levels that do not meet the criteria for mental retardation usually leave children in the regular program without specialized services. Second, levels that fall slightly below the criteria for mental retardation are often seen as too ambiguous by practitioners concerned about biased testing. Third, LD is seen as a more favorable category than mental retardation, and fourth, the instruction received in an LD classroom is more likely to be in synch with that of the regular classroom. On a less positive note, it is also true that many regular educators have come to view referral to special education as an escape from having to address children's learning challenges.

In accomplishing the increased use of LD, practitioners have addressed the exclusionary clauses in different ways. The environmental disadvantage clause, I believe, is generally disregarded. The discrepancy clause, however, is addressed by more devious means—typically by the manipulation of the measures being used. It is common in the field to hear psychologists speak of using "softer" tests to "get the IQ up," so that there can be room for the establishment of the required discrepancy.

Overall, the point needs to be made clearly that issues of definition and measurement are an integral part of the relationship between LD and minority status. This brings us to the question of postmodern views of LD. The casting of scholars into specific camps of modern or postmodern oversimplifies the debate. For example, I do not see that there is any necessary incompatibility between acknowledging the role of social decision making in determining disability and acknowledging that individuals have different capabilities and limitations. The question is not whether differing abilities exist, but whether, and at what point, a society wishes to determine that such difference should be designated as a disability and what the outcomes of that designation should be. This is most evident with the high incidence disabilities, whose existence is particularly difficult to measure. We need only look at the American Association on Mental Retardation's (AAMR's) decision to change the IQ cut-off point for mental retardation to see that what constitutes this disability within our society has been different between one period of time and another. The same is true of the changing definitions of LD. It is clear, as Groce's research showed several decades ago (Groce, 1985), that deafness would not be a disability in a community where the condition and accommodations for it are commonplace.

Nor is there any incompatibility between understanding the role of social decision making and providing instruction tailored to the needs of individual children. Right now, ironically, the presence of special education programs in no way guarantees such tailoring. Indeed, one of the most detrimental effects of the reification of the concept of LD is that regular education teachers have come to believe that they have no skills for teaching children who do not learn at the same pace as their peers. The increasing use of LD placement as a panacea for learning difficulties has led to increasingly poor quality of such placements. In Florida, where a program known as "Varying Exceptionalities" houses children designated with any of three high incidence disabilities (emotional handicap, LD, and mild mental retardation), it is common to see 18–24 children in these classrooms with one special education teacher and, in the inner-city schools, no paraprofessional assistance.

I would suggest that the white paper move toward some reconciliation of the apparent divide between postmodernists and modernists. This divide, I believe, is more rhetorical than real. There is no moral advantage in being critical of the status quo. The fact is that the traditional definitions of LD tended to reserve the category for children from privileged backgrounds. The trend toward ignoring or manipulating the exclusionary clauses has tended to push the pendulum in the opposite direction, resulting in dramatic increase in the use of the LD category and in diluted and ineffective services. While there is, no doubt, a group of children whose learning difficulties are really due to some built-in deficits that produce genuinely unexpected difficulties, this is not the case with the vast majority of children designated LD. As a researcher who has been observing instruction and classroom management in inner-city schools for the past 3 years, I believe that the main treatment needed is the improvement of regular education and an end to the reliance on having to call children disabled in order to provide them with individually tailored instruction.

References

Collins, R., & Camblin, L. D. (1983). The politics and science of learning disability classification: Implications for Black children. *Contemporary Education, 54*(2), 113–118.

Finn, J. D. (1982). Patterns in special education placement as revealed by the OCR surveys. In K. A. Heller, W. H. Holtzman, & S. Messick (Eds.), *Placing children in special education: A strategy for equity* (pp. 382–381). Washington, DC: National Academy Press.

Groce, N. (1985). *Everyone here spoke sign language.* Cambridge, MA: Harvard University Press.

Harry, B., Klingner, J., Sturges, K., & Moore, R. (in press). Of rocks and soft places: Using qualitative methods to investigate the processes that result in disproportionality. In D. Losen & G. Orfield (Eds.), *Issues in the disproportionate placement of minorities in special education programs.* Cambridge, MA: Harvard Education Publishing Group.

United States Department of Education, Office for Civil Rights (1994). *1992 Elementary and secondary school civil rights surveys: National summaries.* Washington, DC: DBS Corporation.

United States Department of Education, Office for Civil Rights (1999). *1997 Elementary and secondary school civil rights surveys: National summaries.* Washington, DC: DBS Corporation.

RESPONSE TO "LEARNING DISABILITIES: HISTORICAL PERSPECTIVES"

Edwin W. Martin, Former Assistant Secretary for Special Education and Rehabilitative Services, U.S. Department of Education

In an age where one is frequently disappointed by receiving less than expected, Hallahan and Mercer provide more—a comprehensive history of learning disabilities beginning around 1800 and continuing to 2000. In addition, the authors provide information on related subjects: brain injuries, cerebral palsy, attention deficit disorders, and more. They divide their account into five time periods, 1800–1920; 1920–1960; 1960–1975; 1975–1985, and 1985–2000, acknowledging that the system is similar to that used by Lerner (2000), Mercer (1997), Weiderholt (1974), and Hallahan and Cruickshank (1973).

The earliest period, which they entitle the "European Foundation Period," presents a "straight ahead" review of the literature with little editorializing. The "U.S. Foundation Period" (c.1920–1960) provides a more detailed account of Samuel Orton's work and assumptions as well as those of Grace Fernald, Marion Moore, and Samuel Kirk and provides information on the basic teaching strategies and some of the research associated with their theories. The authors, while primarily reporting and describing, do help the reader understand some of the linkages between these pioneers. "Perceptual, Perceptual-Motor, and Attention Disabilities" receive careful attention, demonstrating the linkages of later educational methods to earlier work by psychologists such as Goldstein (1936, 1939) and Werner and his colleague, the neuropsychiatrist Strauss (1939). While ultimately pointing out the movement of the educational field away from these theories and those of a number of educational practitioners whose work is described carefully, Hallahan and Mercer recognize the very significant impact that perceptual-motor theories and instructional methodologies had for many years. This includes its impact on later descriptive definitions of learning disabilities, which while more language oriented, continued to identify underlying psychological processes as critical to understanding the learning and classroom behavior of learning disabled students (see Kirk and U.S. Office of Education definition [1968], Haring and Bateman [1969]).

As one trained in speech pathology and psychology, I find interesting the parallels between these theoretical and teaching developments and those current at approximately the same time in the speech field, i.e., attributing speech disorders to underlying disabilities in perceiving and discriminating sounds. Therapies based on training those skills were replaced by more language-oriented approaches when research failed to find correlation between this skill training and improved speech performance. To some degree, we in special education have come full circle as we focus on phonemic awareness and synthesis in research-supported approaches to understanding reading disorders, although few practitioners or researchers are working on skill training in these areas independent of language context.

THE FEDERAL ROLE

Hallahan and Mercer identify the 1960–1975 period as the "Emergent Period" and focus considerable attention on the term *learning disabilities* and on its several definitions over time. They also introduce the topic of "Federal Involvement" in discussing the development of these definitions and the evolution of federal legislation.

Their discussion of the "Minimal Brain Dysfunction: National Project on Learning Disabilities in Children" and its task forces correctly identifies the divisions in assumptions between the two task forces, one primarily medical practitioners and one primarily of educators. In discussing the sponsors within the Department of Health, Education and Welfare (HEW), there is an minor misidentification of the Bureau of Education for the Handicapped (BEH) as a sponsoring agency, however; the actions of Task Force I occurred before the establishment of the BEH in 1967 and involved earlier entities in the U.S. Office of Education.

Education legislation affecting children with disabilities is reported, as is some of the resistance to including children with learning disabilities in the federal definition of "handicapped children" that was necessary for federal funding. I believe some additional attention could have been given to the impact of the federal government on the development of special education programming for children with learning disabilities, both positive and negative. (Has there ever been a respondent, who like this author had a special interest and involvement in a given topic, who did not think that topic deserved more attention?)

Beginning in the middle 1960s, before the federal definition included learning disabilities, the Office of Education's special education units began to provide funding to colleges and universities to train specialists in teaching such children. They did this by funding some programs under the label of "other health impaired" that was included in the federal definition. Still other programs were in a vague category of "interrelated programs," and managed to secure some of the funds that might have gone to programs for training teachers of children with mental retardation, speech disorders, or behavioral disorders. It might be noted that the advocates within and outside the government for these other disability areas fought these activities vigorously. Nevertheless, some funding did help university programs grow and federal funding inevitably led to increased status and more general acceptance. When the 1969 legislation included children with learning disabilities as eligible for funds in the areas of personnel training and research, the professional field made another large step forward in its development within special education and colleges of education. (One might note that similar developments in early childhood education and education of severely handicapped children resulted from federal recognition and funding.)

The powerful impact of a few people involved in the federal legislative and administrative process can be demonstrated by the historical development of the learning disabilities area. In 1966, when the first Education of the Handicapped Act (Title VI of the Elementary and Secondary Education Act, P.L. 89-750) was being considered by the Congress, one person, Patria Winalski, played a key role in keeping the term learning disabilities out of the federal definition of children requiring special education by virtue of having a handicap. Winalski, then a HEW staff person responsible for an advisory committee on deafness, was close friends with John Forsythe, counsel to the Senate Labor and Public Welfare committee that had jurisdiction over education legislation. As the mother of a child who was deaf, she feared that this new area of interest, learning disabilities, would be so broadly defined that it would open the door for "handicapped funds" to be used for minority and other economically disadvantaged children. Although there were advocates for including learning disabilities, both parents and professionals (the writer was staff director of the House of Representatives' ad hoc Subcommittee on the Handicapped at the time), Winalski's ally Forsythe was in the more powerful position.

In 1969, as Deputy Director of the BEH, it was possible for the writer to advocate legislation for education of children with learning disabilities. A program passed that provided funds for teacher training, research, and model demonstration programs. The good news stopped there—once again Winalski and Forsythe prevented the definition being included in the basic grants to the states program of the Education of the Handicapped Act. It was not until 1975 that BEH advocacy resulted in that inclusion in P.L. 94-142, the Education of All Handicapped Children Act (Martin, 1993).

One example of the significance in public policy of a well placed advocate or opponent is drawn from the 1980s, when Edward Sontag was director of the Office of Special Education Programs, the successor to the BEH. A decision was made at that time to end support for the research institutes studying learning disabilities. Hallahan and Mercer do an excellent job of describing the role of those institutes and present their opinion that the institutes played a significant role in advancing understanding of education of children with learning disabilities and that they had a continuing influence through the patterns of research they initiated (which, fortunately, were able to continue in most instances under other funding). At the time it seemed incredible to this writer that there would be no systematic research effort going on in the Office of Special Education Programs in the area of learning disabilities, given that about half the children in special education classes were identified as having learning disabilities.

A final illustration may be seen in the National Institute for Child Health and Human Development, led by Reid Lyon (1998), which has played a tremendously significant role in filling this void by funding a research centers program studying various aspects of learning disabilities ranging from genetics to education. Over the years the Office of Special Education Programs has also expanded its research support, through individual project and program grants, without reestablishing the centers. Above the National Archives in Washington, there is an inscription: "Past is Prologue." Educators need to be aware of the power of public policy on their mission and involved in directing its purposes for the good of children with disabilities.

INCLUSION FOR BETTER OR WORSE?

In a section entitled "Debate over the Continuum of Placements," the authors point out differing opinions within the special education community on the desirability of full inclusion and preserving the continuum of placements. It is the one place where I wish the authors had provided more emphasis, although it is appropriate to note that in their data-based review, there would not be much research to guide their discussion. They do present some arguments pro and con, including a statement from Hallahan in a 2000 paper, "William M. Cruikshank: If He Were Alive Today," presented at the International Dyslexia Association annual conference. In discussion with teachers and other professionals this writer has had as an officer and president of the Division for Learning Disabilities (DLD), I have been struck by the overwhelmingly negative reports by teachers of children with learning disabilities. They find the education system is frustrating their attempts to help children as they feel they can. Teachers report being overburdened by paperwork, but also being hampered by assumptions within their systems that children with learning disabilities have "mild" disorders that can be treated in the regular classroom with relatively minor modifications. They report be required to serve too many children, thereby reducing the amount of time they have for individualized instruction, and being expected to serve children with a variety of mild conditions, thereby being faced with a population whose heterogeneous learning needs can not be satisfactorily met in a "one fits all" system.

Recently, the Council for Exceptional Children (CEC) Has documented similar sentiments across the gamut of special education teachers in a report called, "Conditions for Special Education Teaching." Hallahan and Mercer cite some of its conclusions in their discussion. For several years, the presidents of the DLD (Don Deshler, Dan Hallahan, Jean Schumaker, and this writer, along with the next two presidents, Charles Hughes and Naomi Zigmond) have worked together to apply the resources of the division to help teachers, primarily by focusing attention on research-based methods of teaching children with learning disabilities—procedures that demonstrate some positive results with children who frequently show little or no progress in ordinary education programs. In 2000 the DLD had a special conference in Charleston, South Carolina, to provide this kind of information to teachers and more than 300 oversubscribed the meeting. A similar conference was planned for San Antonio in the fall of 2001. To a number of leaders in special education and in the area of learning disabilities, there is a connection between inclusion efforts, with their worthy philosophy, and the failure of these new programs to provide the sufficient, specialized instruction that is needed for success. Their expression of concerns very much swims against the tide of massive movement toward inclusion and a prevailing view that it is the only appropriate way to offer special education, although there is little if any research data demonstrating inclusion is more effective than, for example, small group instruction.

At the CEC conference in Vancouver, British Columbia, in April 2000, this writer organized a panel of a number of the field's most distinguished research leaders and asked them to present informally their thoughts about inclusion and about education of children with disabilities. All of the speakers had been recipients of the CEC Research Award or a similar award given by a CEC division or had had articles selected as "The Outstanding Research Article" for a given journal. It may be instructive to mention their names: James Kaufmann, (Division of Behavior Disorders), Don McMillan (Division of Research), and DLD members Hallahan, Naomi Zigmond, Barbara Keogh, and Doug Fuchs. It should give every professional food for thought that none of these research specialists felt that inclusion provided a sufficient basis for a comprehensive special education program designed to meet the individual learning needs of children.

In their final section, Hallahan and Mercer make a logical transition from their discussions of placement and the nature of learning disabilities to define and discuss what they see as the current clash between "modernism" and "postmodernism." They cite Kauffman's (1999) views and concerns about postmodernism and cite contributors to Andrews et al. (2000) as expressing views that societal perceptions are the root of disability. The authors make a brave and reasonably successful effort to make sense of what linguists might call "high level abstractions." They also suggest that the clash of values and assumptions of morality and immorality that is part of our current scene need to be moderated and replaced with a search for common ground on behalf of the children all propose to serve.

This paper, while not the first historical account, is impressively comprehensive. It relies heavily on scholarly description but adds the authors' interpretations when they are necessary to establish significance. What is impressive is that Hallahan and Mercer do this so well and with no violence to the facts.

REFERENCES

Andrews, J. E., Carnine, D. W., Coutinho, M. J., Edgar, E. B., Forness, S. R., Fuchs, L. S., et al. (2000). Bridging the special education divide. *Remedial and Special Education, 21,*258–260, 267.

Goldstein, K. (1936). The modification of behavior consequent to cerebral lesions. *Psychiatric Quarterly, 10,* 586–610.

Goldstein, K. (1939). *The organism.* New York: American Book.

Hallahan, D. P. (2000). *William M. Cruickshank: If He Were Alive Today.* Washington, DC: International Dyslexia Association Annual Conference.

Hallahan, D. P., & Cruickshank, W. M. (1973). *Psychoeductional foundations of learning disabilities.* Englewood Cliffs, NJ: Prentice-Hall.

Haring, N. G., & Bateman, B. (1969). Introduction. In N. G. Haring (Ed.), *Minimal brain dysfunction in children: Educational, medical and health related services* (pp.1–4). Washington, DC: U.S. Department of Health, Education and Welfare.

Lerner, J. W. (2000). *Learning disabilities: Theories, diagnosis and teaching strategies* (8th edition). Boston: Houghton Mifflin.

Lyon, G. R. (1998). *Overview of reading and literacy initiatives (Report to Committee on Labor and Human Resources, U.S. Senate)*. Bethesda, MD: National Institute of Child Health and Human Development, National Institutes of Health.

Martin, E. W. (1993). Learning disabilities and public policy: Myths and outcomes. In G. R. Lyon, D. B. Gray, J. F. Kavanagh, & N. A. Krasnegor (Eds.) *Better understanding learning disabilities: New views from research and their implications for education and public policies* (pp.325–342). Baltimore: Paul H. Brookes.

Mercer, C. D. (1997). *Students with learning disabilities* (5th ed.). Upper Saddle River, NJ: Merrill.

U.S. Office of Education. (1968). *First annual report of National Advisory Committee on Handicapped Children*. Washington, DC: U.S. Department of Health, Education and Welfare.

Werner, H., & Strauss, A. A. (1939). Types of visuo-motor activity in their relation to low and high performance ages. *Proceedings of the American Association on Mental Deficiency, 44,* 163–168.

Wiederholt, J. L. (1974). Historical perspectives on the education of the learning disabled. In L. Mann & D. Sabatino (Eds.), *The second review of special education* (pp. 103–152). Philadelphia: JSE Press.

RESPONSE TO "LEARNING DISABILITIES: HISTORICAL PERSPECTIVES"

Jim Ysseldyke, University of Minnesota

Those who provide a historical perspective on a topic have a choice of chronicling events or analyzing those events. In their paper "Learning Disabilities: Historical Perspectives," Hallahan and Mercer have done a nice job of chronicling the history of learning disabilities. Their listing of events, changing definitions, and areas of focus is parallel to that provided by others (e.g., Doris, 1993; Lerner, 2000; Satz & Fletcher, 1980; Shaywitz & Shaywitz, 1994). With the exception of their comments about over-representation, the continuum of placements, and constructivism, what I thought was missing in the paper was analysis, specifically an analysis of how some things changed over time while other things remained the same; an analysis of which events in history were entirely predictable in the context of the time, contrasted with those that were unexpected; an assessment of the relationship of events in time, along with an evaluation of continuity and change; or a set of guiding hypotheses or questions. In my response/reaction, I have chosen to provide an analysis of the history chronicled by Hallahan and Mercer.

As I read the history of learning disabilities (LD), I see a response to a problem: the failure of significant numbers of students to achieve in school, primarily in reading. There have been repeated efforts to differentiate a specific subgroup of those who fail, subtypes of the subgroup, and specific kinds of instruction that work with the specific subgroup or its subtypes. The history of LD chronicled by Hallahan and Mercer reflects: (1) the search for a specific condition (or category), (2) the search for a cause of the condition, and (3) the search for a cure or remedy for the condition.

THE SEARCH FOR A CONDITION (OR CATEGORY)

At least since the early days of American education, significant numbers of students have failed to profit to the extent thought reasonable from curricular offerings. Specifically, unacceptable numbers of students have experienced difficulty

learning to read. In the late 1800s psychologists, administrators, and teachers began labeling them as mentally retarded, emotionally disturbed, hearing impaired,
brain-injured, word-blind, and as evidencing minimal cerebral dysfunction. In the
1960s a subgroup was given the name learning disabled. Names and labels were
assigned assuming that the students so labeled were alike, and that doing so would
further our communication in instruction and research. Counting early definitions of conditions like congenital word-blindness, traumatic dements, and mixed
cerebral dominance, Hallahan and Mercer cite at least 19 definitions of LD.
Admittedly, some of the definitions are statements of causes (as in children with
strephosymbolia or children with attention-hyperactivity disorders) and others are
more reflective of "conditions" with names of their own (e.g., congenital word-
blindness, dyslexia).

In my opinion, all the inventing and defining has not gone well largely because
fundamental principles have been ignored in efforts to delineate a condition called
LD. In their classic 1975 chapter on criteria for classification systems, Cromwell,
Blashfield, and Strauss specify two conditions necessary for a classification to make
sense: universality (all members of the class must have at least one thing in common) and specificity (there must be at least one thing that differentiates members
of the class from nonmembers of the class). The history of LD has been characterized by an unproductive search for universals and specifics. For example, while it is
generally agreed that all members of the class have a discrepancy between ability
and achievement (some call it unexplained difficulty in acquiring academic skills),
the magnitude of the discrepancy has been open for debate, and no widely accepted level is evident in what has been written about the history of LD. Equally
frustrating is the simple fact that there is no agreement on the characteristics specific to the condition that are not evidenced by poor readers, low achievers, or
students who evidence other disability conditions).

I am reminded of the statement of Tom Lovitt at the roundtable conference on LD
held in Minnesota at the beginning of the Minnesota LD institute. Lovitt stated:

> I believe that if we continue trying to define learning disabilities by using
> ill-defined concepts, we will forever be frustrated, for it is an illusive [elu-
> sive] concept. We are being bamboozled. It is as though someone started
> a great hoax by inventing the term and then tempting others to define it.
> And lo and behold, scores of task forces and others have taken the bait.
> (1978, p. 3)

The failure to define a universal and specific condition is most recently reflected in
the efforts of assessment personnel to identify "real students with learning disabilities." Most definitions are discrepancy definitions. Hallahan and Mercer indicate

that solidification was reached in the early 1990s around a deficit/discrepancy model, yet I think the 1990s are actually characterized by a movement away from a discrepancy model and a general consensus that a discrepancy approach lacks validity (Algozzine & Ysseldyke, 1987; Fletcher et al., 1998). Alternatives are being proposed. Fuchs and Fuchs (1998) advocate a treatment validity approach in which the value of an eligibility assessment process is judged by its capacity to simultaneously inform, foster, and document the necessity for and effectiveness of special treatment (p. 204–205). While this approach does not help us with definitional issues, it does help with eligibility decisions and is consistent with the 1975 Cromwell, Blashfield, and Strauss contention that information about individual characteristics is useful only if it leads to assignment of treatments with known outcomes. What is gaining broad consensus is the Fuchs & Fuchs (1998) argument for curriculum-based identification and a dual discrepancy model (level and rate of performance/progress) and their argument for a distinction between ineffective instruction and unacceptable individual learning, made by comparing to peers and looking at growth rate. This is consistent with the early 1980s arguments of the Minnesota Institute for Research on Learning Disabilities (IRLD).

I will not belabor definitional issues. It looks like nearly all of the papers being presented at this summit address definition, discrepancy, or whether LD is real. I do want to digress though to address one matter Hallahan and Mercer chose to report. They cite McKinney's opinions about the work of the Minnesota IRLD. "The conclusions of this institute and the implications they draw suggest [to him] that LD students are not handicapped in any significant way apart from underachievement." Further, "the conclusions of this group imply [to him] not only that special education services for LD students are ineffective, but that they are unnecessary and potentially do more harm than good." Once again we have quotations of what McKinney thought we said or his opinion of what we said. I am reminded of the statement of Edna St. Vincent Millay: "It is not true that life is one...thing after another—it's the same ... thing over and over again." Based on work reported in more than 140 technical reports, we reported a failure to find reliable differences in performance on psychometric measures between students labeled LD and low achievers who did not have a discrepancy. We argued that there are students with LD, and that they do evidence disabilities (specifically in learning to read). We argued that schools are assigning the LD label to too many students, and that the decision-making process is at best inconsistent. We have not argued that there is no such thing as LD; in fact using currently accepted scientific methods, it is impossible to prove the nonexistence of anything. We argued though that the concept of LD was over-sophisticated. We argued that curriculum-based measurement (CBM) approaches are a reasonable alternative to norm-referenced–test-based approaches to making entitlement and instructional decisions. We argued that there was plenty of evidence that specific interventions worked for LD students, *but not exclusively for them.* Since learning is learning, there is no reason for us to expect that there be unique interventions for LD students—and of course there are not. We have not argued that special education harms students with LD. There just is not evidence in the aggregate to support either side of that contention. Our failure to find psychometric differences has been challenged (Kavale, Fuchs, & Scruggs, 1994) using meta-analytic procedures we considered to be incorrect (Algozzine, Ysseldyke, & McGue, 1995).

THE SEARCH FOR CAUSE

Hallahan and Mercer chronicle a long series of efforts to identify the causes of LD, concentrating on reading disabilities. They identify a myriad of presumed process and ability causes of the condition. For all practical purposes, the terms ability and process have been treated as identical in special education. There are ultimately as many abilities or processes as there are things that one does or acts that one engages in. To some, the processes are hypothetical constructs; to others they are substantive realities. Throughout history different names have been assigned to explanatory processes or abilities. Plato and Aristotle called them powers. Others called them virtues, potentiae, faculties, capacities, dispositions, traits, or constructs. All were "used to explain the hows in reading, arithmetic, perception, hog calling, and psychological depression" (Mann, 1979, p. 4). When all is said and done, there are no process disorders or dysfunctions specific to the condition of LD, though the federal definition of the condition requires evidence of such.

The other content I found missing in the white paper was reference to the contention that LD is the product of teaching failures. There is a camp of folks in our profession who have made that argument. Becker (1973) was a strong proponent of such a view. He stated

> As long as the educational climate was such that teaching failures could be blamed on the children, there was no pressure on the teacher to learn more effective means of dealing with children... With the recent advent of the label learning disability (for children with normal IQ who fail to learn) there is no teaching failure which cannot be blamed on the child. (p. 78)

THE SEARCH FOR CURES (OR REMEDIES)

I thought Hallahan and Mercer were more thorough in their chronicling of definitional debate and the search for causes of the condition than they were in their chronicling of treatment efforts. I found missing the chronicling of evidence-based interventions for students who are failing to learn to read, write, compute, and get along with others. If one looks at the history of services to students with LD, then the history is characterized more by the search for a condition and its cause than by investigation of intervention effectiveness. Yet if one looks at advances in educating students who experience learning difficulties, then the advances have been major. If one looks at the effectiveness of special education, it is difficult to find positive outcomes in the aggregate. If one looks at the effectiveness of educational services for students with disabilities, then there is plenty of evidence of major advances. I concur with the observation that the work of the LD institutes and subsequent research based on those efforts has made major advances in identification of approaches that are effective. The LD institutes made major contributions to our understanding of interventions that work with students identified as LD—as well as non-disabled students. Not chronicled is the early work of regional resource centers that focused primarily on LD students, demonstration centers that focused on LD, and the many projects focused on identification of approaches and procedures that worked for LD students in regular classes (e.g., Baker & Zigmond, 1990). The other major contribution of the LD institutes was in the training of more than 50 professionals who went on to make major contributions to research on treatment approaches and who are among the leading researchers of the day.

Clearly, there are treatment approaches that work with LD students. Yet those treatments are not uniquely effective with LD students. Gresham, MacMillan, and Bocian (1996) compare LD students, low achieving students, and students with mild mental retardation and identify some differences among them, but conclude that the differences probably are not educationally relevant in terms of different placement options or interventions. Hallahan and Mercer reviewed interventions with LD students. They did not review research on Direct Instruction (Carnine, Silbert, & Kame'enui, 1997) or other forms of direct teaching of academic skills. They did not review the findings of the recent National Reading Council that concluded that instruction in phonemic awareness and phonics is the preferred methodology for young students who fail to learn to read. Had they reviewed interventions that work across categories, it would be logical to expect reference to these powerful lines of work that clearly have impacted the field. Our recent examination of methodologies for interpreting trends in the performance of students with disabilities reveals evidence of effectiveness, yet not specifically and exclusively for students labeled LD.

ON OVER-REPRESENTATION

Hallahan and Mercer provide a set of figures on the percentages of different kinds of students classified LD and indicate that "these figures indicate substantial over-representation of African-American, and especially, American Indian/Alaska natives in the learning disabilities category and a very large under-representation of

Asian/Pacific Islanders" (this volume). I do not know where Hallahan and Mercer got their figures. In Table 1 I show figures as reported by the Office of Civil Rights (OCR) and the Office of Special Education Programs (OSEP), on data collected independently and using different survey methods. The percentages are even larger than Hallahan and Mercer suggest, though the conclusion is the same.

Table 1. Percentage of Students in Disability Categories Reported by OCR and OSEP (1998)

	LD	MR	ED	Total
American Indian				
OCR	7.45	1.28	1.03	9.76
OSEP	7.29	1.19	1.00	9.48
Asian–Pacific Islander				
OCR	2.23	0.64	0.26	3.13
OSEP	2.25	0.57	0.27	3.09
Black				
OCR	6.49	2.64	1.45	10.58
OSEP	6.58	2.63	1.56	10.77
Hispanic				
OCR	6.44	0.92	0.55	7.91
OSEP	6.46	0.78	0.66	7.90
White				
OCR	6.02	1.18	0.91	8.11
OSEP	6.08	1.12	0.98	8.18
National				
OCR	6.02	1.37	0.93	8.32
OSEP	6.08	1.30	1.01	8.39

Note.—LD = learning disabilities; MR = mental retardation; ED = emotional disturbance.

Concluding Remarks

In the early days of schooling in America, significant numbers of students failed to profit from schooling. In the 1950s about 25–30% of children failed to learn to read by the end of third grade. In the early days of schooling we identified categories of students who failed (Horn, 1924), and in the 1960s one of those categories was named "learning disabled."

In 2001, 25–30% of students fail to learn to read by the end of third grade, and in some urban areas and for some groups of students with disabilities, the dropout rate exceeds 50% of the student body that should graduate. In the 1970s about 7.4% of students were considered disabled (an unknown percent of those who failed were considered disabled), with 25.7% of disabled students considered LD. By 2000 about 12% of students were considered disabled (again, an unknown percent of those who fail to achieve), and more than half of those considered disabled were considered LD. Over time a discrepancy approach has been used to identify those who are LD, though the magnitude of discrepancy necessary has varied from state to state. One who analyzes history might be tempted to ask what happened.

In my spare time I am a professor. In my real life I fish. In my spare time I have argued that LD is politically determined. In my real life I fish walleye, the Minnesota state fish. The Minnesota Department of Natural Resources (DNR) controls the walleye harvest on Minnesota's largest lake, Mille Lacs. They do so as part of a political settlement with the Mille Lacs Ojibwa. They do so by putting what are called slot limits on fish that can be harvested by non-Ojibwas. Earlier this year the slot limit was 16–20 inches. Those who fish could keep fish within this slot limit and one trophy fish over 28 inches. The fishing has been too good. In the eyes of the DNR, too many walleye have been harvested. So, effective as I began to write this response was a new slot limit. The DNR changed the slot to 16–18 inches and eliminated the taking of trophy fish. All other fish have to be returned to the mainstream. Why? To control the harvest. The definitions of a "keeper walleye" and a "trophy walleye" were made on the basis of political rather than biological or scientific factors. As I prepared the very final draft of this paper, the DNR responded to the cries of resort owners that they were suffering economically because people quit renting their boats to fish for walleye. Just this morning they passed a new regulation permitting keeping of one fish longer than 30 inches. The definitions of "keeper walleye" and "trophy walleye" changed in response to political considerations. In education, definitional debate is more political than scientific, and it is designed primarily to control the numbers of students who are entitled to service.

Significant numbers of students are failing to acquire academic skills, specifically in reading. Those who evidence a politically specified deficit between presumed ability and norm-referenced, test-identified achievement are entitled to receive services. Those who evidence disabilities but no discrepancy are not entitled to service. Why?

In 1979 Lester Mann reviewed the history of efforts to train processes and concluded that review with this statement:

> Those urgent needs should be for us the training or remediation of our pupils in those skills required for productive living in and outside of school—and, when possible, the impartation of knowledge and wisdom to them that will make their lives more than a pursuit of mere reinforcements. In so doing, as we engage our pupils in instruction, we will also engage those processes of theirs that are appropriate to that instruction. For if our pupils come along, surely their processes will not be left behind. (p. 542)

In chronicling the history of LD, we have an opportunity to celebrate advances in educating students with reading, writing, math, communication, and social skills deficits. This runs the possibility of leading readers to the conclusion that we need to focus our energies on implementing evidence-based treatments with those students. Chronicling our frustrations in defining the condition and identifying its causes leads to frustration. It also runs the risk of leading readers to the conclusion that we need to do a better job of typing, subtyping, and identifying causes.

As a nation we have demonstrated a collective political inability to stop using ineffective reading curricula (whole language damages beginning readers) and ineffective teachers (constructivist and discovery learning advocates who don't teach and who don't use methods of demonstrated efficacy). I believe there is a connection between curriculum casualties and teacher-disabled students and the rise in the numbers of students who need special interventions. I believe we will serve the same students if we take the lowest quartile on the basis of achievement as if we continue to insist that students demonstrate a learning disability. There are evidence-based treatments for those children.

I agree strongly with Hallahan and Mercer's concluding contention that "one of the most caring acts that educators can do is to apply current and forthcoming research-based assessments and interventions to identify and teach individuals with learning disabilities to read, write, problem solve, socialize, communicate, and be independent" (this volume). In fact, I think we should do this even for those not considered LD.

REFERENCES

Algozzine, B., & Ysseldyke, J. E. (1987). Questioning discrepancies: Retaking the first step twenty years later. *Learning Disability Quarterly, 10,* 301–313.

Algozzine, B., Ysseldyke, J., & McGue, M. (1995). Differentiating low achieving students: Thoughts on setting the record straight. *Learning Disabilities Research and Practice, 10,* 140–146.

Baker, J. M., & Zigmond, N. (1990). Are regular education classes equipped to accomodate students with learning disabilities? *Exception Children, 56*(6), 515–527.

Becker, W. (1973). Applications of behavior principles in typical classrooms. In National Society for the Study of Education (Ed.), *Behavior modification in education: The seventy-second yearbook of the National Society for the Study of Education.* Chicago, IL: NSSE.

Carnine, D., Silbert, J., & Kame'enui, E. J. (1997). *Direct instruction reading* (3rd ed.). Columbus, OH: Merrill.

Cromwell, R. L., Blashfield, R., & Strauss, J. S. (1975). Criteria for classification systems. In N. Hobbs (Ed.), *Issues in the classification of children: Vol. 1* (pp. 4–25). San Francisco: Jossey Bass.

Doris, J. (1993). Defining learning disabilities: A history of the search for consensus. In G. R. Lyon, D. B. Gray, J. F. Kavanaugh, & N. A. Krasnegor (Eds.), *Better understanding learning disabilities* (pp. 97–116). Baltimore: Brookes.

Fletcher, J. M., Francis, D. J., Shaywitz, S. E., Lyon, G. R., Foorman, B. R., Stuebing, K. K., et al. (1998). Intelligent testing and the discrepancy model for children with learning disabilities. *Learning Disabilities Research and Practice, 13,* 186–203.

Fuchs, L. S., & Fuch, D. (1998). Treatment validity: A unifying concept for reconceptualizing the identification of learning disabilities. *Learning Disabilities Research & Practice, 13,* 204–219.

Gresham, F. M., MacMillan, D. L., & Bocian, K. M. (1996). Learning disabilities, low achievement, and mild retardation: More alike than different? *Journal of Learning Disabilities, 29*(6), 570–581.

Horn, J. L. (1924). *The education of exceptional children: A consideration of public school problems and policies in the field of differentiated education.* New York: Century.

Kavale, K., Fuchs, D., & Scruggs, T. (1994). Setting the record straight on learning disabilities and low achievement: Implications for policymaking. *Learning Disabilities Research and Practice, 9,* 70–79.

Lerner, J. (2000). *Learning disabilities* (8th ed.). Boston: Houghton-Mifflin.

Lovitt, T. (1978). *Reactions to planned research.* Paper presented at the Roundtable Conference on Learning Disabilities. Minneapolis, MN: Institute for Research on Learning Disabilities.

Mann, L. (1979). *On the trail of process.* New York: Grune & Stratton.

Satz, P., & Fletcher, J. (1980). Minimal brain dysfuntions: An appraisal of research concepts and methods. In H. E. Rie & E. D. Rie (Eds.), *Handbook of minimal brain dysfunctions: A critical view* (pp. 669–714). New York: Wiley.

Shaywitz, B. A., & Shaywitz, S. E. (1994). Learning disabilities and attention disorders. In K. F. Swaiman (Ed.), *Pediatric neurology* (2nd Ed., pp. 1119–1151). St. Louis: Mosby.

CHAPTER II: EARLY IDENTIFICATION AND INTERVENTION FOR YOUNG CHILDREN WITH READING/LEARNING DISABILITIES

Joseph R. Jenkins, University of Washington &
Rollanda E. O'Connor, University of Pittsburgh

We can all agree that reading is one of the principal tools for understanding our humanity, for making sense of our world, for advancing the democratic ideal, and for generating personal and national prosperity. We can agree that ability to read allows us to achieve three important goals: building knowledge (e.g., learning about the physical world); acquiring information for accomplishing tasks (e.g., installing a VCR); and deriving pleasure and feeding our interests (e.g., how our favorite athletic team has fared). Lacking reading ability, our lives would be very different. They would not be as rich.

Students with reading/learning disabilities (R/LDs) face enormous challenges learning to read. Many never reach a level of reading proficiency that allows them to build knowledge, acquire information, feed their interests, or enrich their lives. In some cases, their attempts to read result in such a degree of discouragement and frustration that reading subtracts rather than adds to their lives. For students with R/LDs, their early struggles in learning to read are a harbinger of dismal educational outcomes. Overall, students with learning disabilities leave elementary school with severely deficient reading and writing skills (deBettencourt, Zigmond, & Thornton, 1989; Deshler, Schumaker, Alley, Warner, & Clark, 1982) and leave secondary school with little or no improvement in these areas (Zigmond, 1990), with many dropping out before graduation (deBettencourt & Zigmond, 1990). This is why early identification and prevention of reading difficulties is important.

This paper summarizes (a) our current understanding of the difficulties encountered by children with R/LDs as they start down the road to reading and (b) research on early identification and intervention. The focus is children in kindergarten through second grade, although research on older children is included when it informs the understanding of problems in early reading acquisition. The paper is divided into four sections: background on skilled reading and reading disability (RD); early identification of children with R/LDs; intervention research on this population; and final thoughts on intervention approaches. We also offer short lists of sensible actions for practitioners working in this field.

BACKGROUND: SKILLED READING AND READING DISABILITY

Comprehension is the immediate goal of reading. Successful reading comprehension sits atop three essential pillars: the ability to read words; the ability to comprehend language; and the ability to access background and topical knowledge relevant to specific texts. Lacking any one of these foundations, reading comprehension suffers. Having an R/LD means having trouble with one or more of the foundation skills. Reading, language skills, knowledge, and word reading ability are all mutually dependent and reciprocally related (Stanovich, 1986). Weakness anywhere in the system can spell trouble for growth in the other foundation skills, and for reading development.

Reading Comprehension and Word Reading

Students with an R/LD may have weaknesses in any of the three foundation areas. However, during the beginning stages of learning to read, the most salient characteristic of these students is difficulty in acquiring efficient word-level reading skill. Thus, this paper focuses on assessment and treatment of word-level reading problems.

Two aspects of word reading are important for comprehension: accuracy and speed. Accurate word reading is critical to reading comprehension because the meanings that readers construct from text come via the words. No words, no meaning. If individuals cannot read words accurately, their comprehension suffers. Speed of word recognition is also strongly related to reading comprehension; individuals skilled in reading comprehension can read single words faster than individuals with poor reading comprehension (Perfetti & Hogaboam, 1975). Perfetti (1985) explained this relationship in terms of verbal efficiency and the sharing of limited cognitive resources.

According to Perfetti's verbal efficiency theory, both word recognition and comprehension processes consume attentional resources, which are known to be finite. The more attentional resources consumed by lower level processes (i.e., word identification), the fewer resources available for comprehension. Individuals who develop highly efficient word identification processes release cognitive resources for constructing and integrating meaning during reading. By contrast, individuals with inefficient word-reading skill (indicated by slow word recognition) must divide their attention between word identification and comprehension, and comprehension suffers. A major difference between skilled and unskilled readers, according to verbal efficiency theory, is efficiency at word-level processing. Whereas skilled readers read words in a split second (literally) without using conscious attention, the word reading of poor readers is inaccurate, slow, or both. Poor readers' inefficient word-level processing drains the very attentional resources needed to maximize comprehension.

By the end of grade 4, when the majority of children with R/LDs have been identified, these students already demonstrate pronounced deficits in word reading relative to their more skilled peers. The magnitude of this difference is illustrated in a study by Jenkins, Fuchs, Espin, van den Broek, and Deno (2000). These researchers asked fourth-grade students to orally read a passage of third-grade difficulty. Figure 1 shows the accuracy and fluency (i.e., mean number of words read in 1 minute) by students with R/LDs and more skilled peers (i.e., classmates who had average or above scores in reading comprehension). In 1 minute of reading, skilled comprehenders read three times more words than did students with R/LD. Accuracy levels were 98% and 86%, respectively, for the skilled and R/LD groups. These kinds of results underscore how disadvantaged elementary school students with R/LD are in word reading. It is not difficult to imagine how these students' inefficient word reading might overload working memory, making it difficult for them to connect and integrate text ideas into a coherent meaning representation.

Jenkins et al. (2000) illustrated the potential ramifications of slow word reading on comprehension. Using a procedure developed by Brown and Smiley (1977), they estimated that one new idea unit was introduced approximately every six running words in their experimental passage. Because skilled readers on average read the passage at a rate of 155 words per minute, they encountered approximately 26 idea units per minute (i.e., 155/6). By contrast, the R/LD group encountered approximately 9 idea units per minute (52/6). The temporal contiguity of ideas encountered by the two reader groups was sizable (26 vs. 9 per minute), a difference that may have consequences for comprehension. Interestingly, the 155-words-per-minute rate of the skilled readers is close to the speed with which TV news anchors read the news, which may be an optimal rate for processing verbal information. Considered in light of verbal efficiency theory, the less efficient word reading of students with R/LD overloads working memory and undermines reading comprehension.

Figure 1. Accuracy and fluency of fourth graders.

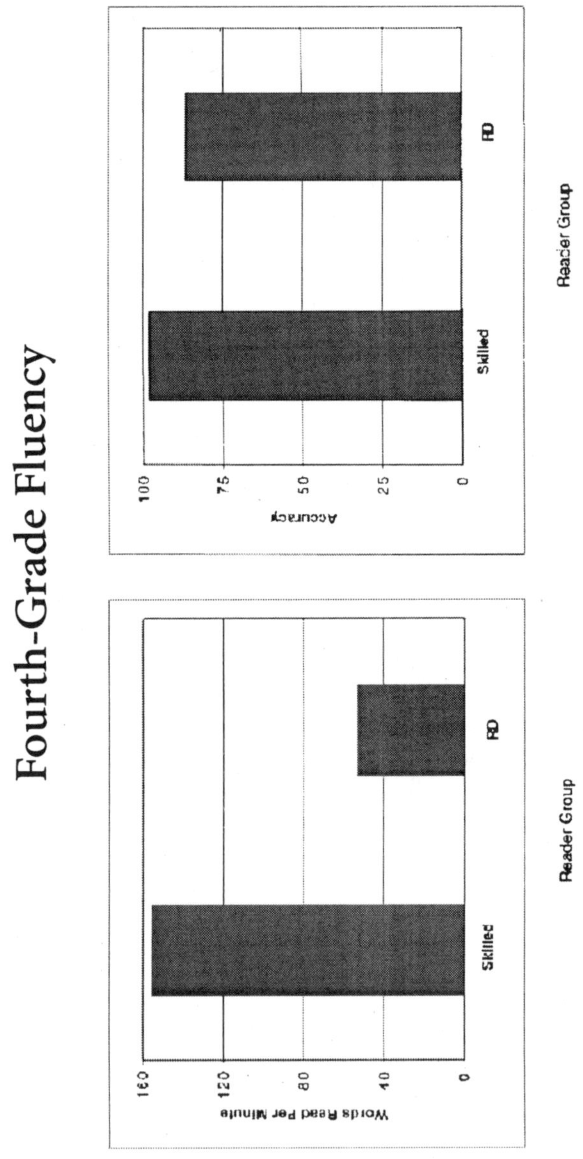

Fourth-Grade Fluency

Note: RD = reading disability

Ways to Read Words

Because word-reading accuracy and speed are important, it is worthwhile to consider some of the ways we read words. We could "read" unfamiliar words by guessing their identity from sentence contexts, but guessing hardly qualifies as reading. Moreover, guessing words from context is a notoriously unreliable process (Adams, 1990). There are better ways to read words. For example, we can read unfamiliar words by analogy, noting their similarity to a familiar word (Goswami & Bryant, 1990). Using an analogy strategy, we might read the pseudoword *flad* by recognizing its similarity to known words like *had, mad,* and *sad.* Alternatively, we might read the pseudoword *feab* using a graphophonemic conversion strategy (i.e,, decoding) to assemble a pronunciation for the word. Decoding is sometimes referred to as phonological or alphabetic reading skill (Torgesen, Wagner, & Rashotte, 1997), because it involves mapping phonemes onto appropriate letters and letter combinations.

For skilled readers, pseudowords like *feab* present no challenges. We can read these words very fast, in a fraction of a second. Nor are we challenged by a pseudoword like *regnessem,* although we read it more slowly than *feab,* probably because it is longer, has three syllables instead of one, and bears little resemblance to any known word. Though skilled readers can read words by analogy and decoding, most words are read by sight. For example, *messenger* is read much faster than *regnessem* even though both words have the same number of letters and syllables. In fact, *regnessem* is *messenger* spelled backwards. The difference in the time required to read *regnessem* versus *messenger* demonstrates the advantage of having stored a *word-specific* memory. Automatic (i.e., instant) word reading requires having words readily available in memory. The fact that skilled readers can instantly read most words tells us they have *vast* stores of word-specific memories (think Home Depot warehouses filled with words). Reading words by sight is sometimes referred to as orthographic reading, in contrast to phonological or alphabetic reading in which words are read by recoding or translating individual graphemes to their phonemes (Torgesen et al., 2001).

Words become sight words when their *complete* spellings and pronunciations are stored in memory. In the sentence, "After he delivered the package, the messenjer rode off on his bicycle," we can read the word *messenjer* very fast, but not as fast as *messenger.* Even when *messenjer* is embedded in a sentence, we notice something amiss in its spelling that draws our attention to this word, momentarily interrupting meaning construction. The spelling, off by only one letter, disrupts the flow of reading, because it does not match the spelling of *messenger* in memory.

Ehri (1998) has argued that sight words, such as *messenger*, are stored and remembered by their specific grapheme-phoneme connections, not just as letter strings and a pronunciation. Memory would be quickly overloaded if words were stored by spellings alone, without phonetic values. For example, if words like *messenger* and *sword* retained their pronunciations but were spelled *egrsemsn* and *wdrso* (same letters, absent their phonemic values), our sight word vocabularies, which now number in the thousands, would be severely shrunken. Fortunately instead, we are able to store and retrieve words from memory using both letters and their phonemic values. According to Ehri, skilled readers store sight words in memory on several levels. These levels include the smallest units (phoneme-grapheme linkages) as well as larger sound-spelling units (rimes, syllables, and whole words). To accomplish this feat, readers must have sufficient generic graphophonemic knowledge to allow them to represent the specific spelling-phonological connections for specific words.

Fluent reading is essentially a function of volume of sight word knowledge. The fact that skilled readers can instantly read most any word they see tells us they have vast stores of word-specific memories. The primary difference between fluent and nonfluent readers is the difference in the number of words they can read by sight.

The Basis for Orthographic (Word) Reading Skill

What's needed to establish sight words? Two requirements stand out: repetitions and decoding skill. A study by Reitsma (1983) demonstrates the importance of both repetitions and decoding skill on the development of sight words by beginning readers. By the middle of first grade, after acquiring some decoding skill, children in a laboratory study significantly decreased reading times for words they had encountered as few as four times. With additional word repetitions, reading times decreased further. These children had begun to develop word-specific memories after encountering the words only a few times.

That high frequency words like *the, is,* and *and* become sight words is not surprising, given the number of times these words are encountered in text. However, most words that we can read by sight appear only occasionally. Individuals must read extensively in order to encounter specific words often enough to allow their instant recognition (reading by sight). Anderson, Wilson, and Fielding (1988) estimated that the number of words read during independent reading by fifth-grade students ranges from 0 to more than 4 million words annually. Individuals differ greatly in their amount of independent reading; those who avoid reading encounter and learn fewer words.

A second group of children in Reitsma's (1983) study did *not* show savings in reading times following several encounters with the same words. These were children near the beginning of first grade. Reitsma attributed their lack of word learning to insufficient graphophonemic knowledge. They were unable to take advantage of repeated encounters with target words to form word-specific memories. It is no accident that early alphabetic reading (decoding) and orthographic reading (word identification) skills are highly related (0.70 and 0.90, respectively, in Compton, 2000; Shankweiler et al., 1999).

Studies like Reitsma's demonstrate the importance of decoding ability for word learning. Some of the most convincing evidence for the important role of decoding ability for developing sight word knowledge comes from studies of exception word reading. Exception words are those that are not strictly decodable using graphophonemic knowledge (e.g., island, yacht, sword, aisle, guide). Coltheart (1978) proposed a dual-route theory to describe how exception and regular words are processed, with regular words read through application of graphophonemic knowledge, and exception words read as visual wholes. However, research on word reading has raised doubts about dual-route theory. Decoding ability seems to be at the heart of (i.e., necessary for) learning to read both regular *and* exception words. Figure 2 (from Tunmer & Chapman, 1998) shows this relationship graphically. Individuals may be skilled in both exception word reading and decoding, or skilled in neither. Some students can decode well, but perform poorly on exception word reading. Presumably, they lack adequate exposure to exception words. The necessary relationship that ties decoding to exception word reading is revealed by the observation that only skilled decoders are skilled exception word readers (Gough & Walsh, 1991). Thus, decoding skill appears to be important for learning all kinds of words.

Why is decoding skill important for developing a large sight vocabulary? Or, what does the process of working out pronunciations for unfamiliar words have to do with filling mental warehouses with sight words? One hypothesis is that decoding functions as a self-teaching tool which allows children to work out the pronunciation of an unfamiliar word on several occasions, and eventually secure the once unfamiliar word in orthographic memory (Share, 1995). In effect, the capacity to decode an unfamiliar word is like having a tutor available to pronounce unfamiliar words. After children have encountered and successfully decoded an unfamiliar word on several occasions, they begin to form a word-specific memory, which results in faster word recognition, much like the first-grade children in Reitsma's study.

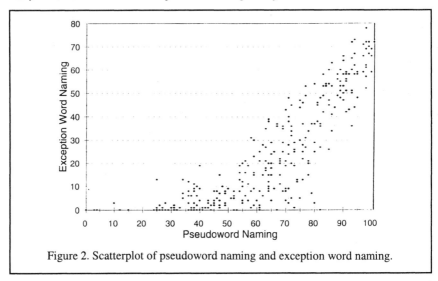

Figure 2. Scatterplot of pseudoword naming and exception word naming.

A second possible explanation for the strong relationship between decoding and sight word reading derives from the act of decoding itself. In assembling a pronunciation for a novel word, the reader must attend to every letter in the word, thereby bonding each letter or letter combination with the phonemes that compose the word. Forming specific connections between a word's phonemes and graphemes enables a word to be read by sight (Adams, 1990).

A third possibility is that decoding skill is a proxy for graphophonemic knowledge. If, as Ehri (1992) has proposed, skilled readers fix sight words in memory using the words' complete spellings (i.e., storing every grapheme-phoneme connection in a word), readers must have sufficient graphophonemic knowledge to allow them to represent these word-specific connections. Even in learning exception words, individuals need a minimum level of graphophonemic knowledge to exploit existing regularities (e.g., even in exception words like *sword* and *yacht*, some phonemes map to graphemes in a regular fashion). More than likely, a level of decoding skill beyond simple graphophonemic knowledge is necessary for readers to establish high-quality, word-specific orthographic memories that include multiple levels of orthographic-phonological links (involving phonemes, onsets, rimes, and syllables; Ehri, 1998; Perfetti, 1992).

A fourth possibility is that individuals who easily acquire decoding skill are the same individuals who easily remember word-specific spellings and their pronunciations. Those individuals who easily induce graphophonemic knowledge may also detect and remember the specific graphophonemic elements of newly encountered words.

The Basis for Decoding Skill

Given the necessity of decoding skill for skilled word reading, we can ask, What is necessary for decoding? Two foundation skills stand out: knowledge of spelling-sound relations (i.e., graphophonemic knowledge) and phonemic awareness. Both appear to be necessary . The essential role of graphophonemic knowledge in decoding is obvious, but that of phonemic awareness is less so. Byrne and Fielding-Barnsley (1991) found that phonemic awareness accounted for significant variance on a word-choice task, after controlling for letter-sound knowledge. Their research is consistent with the large body of research indicating that children who lack phonological awareness are likely to become poor readers (Bradley & Bryant, 1983; Fletcher et al. 1994; Juel, 1988; Share, Jorm, MacLean, & Matthews, 1984; Wagner & Torgesen, 1987; Wagner et al., 1997)

Figure 3 shows a typical relationship between phonemic segmentation skill and decoding ability at the end of grade 1 (Vadasy, 2001). Inspection of this figure reveals that phonemic segmentation skill and decoding have the same kind of necessary relationship as that observed between decoding and exception word reading. Some children performed well in both phonemic segmentation and decoding nonwords; others performed poorly on both tasks. However, only students with phonemic segmentation skill were successful in decoding, even though strong phonemic segmentation did not necessarily guarantee strong decoding.

Thus, both phonemic awareness and graphophonemic knowledge appear necessary, but not sufficient, for successful decoding. For many children, instruction in *how* to utilize this knowledge may also be important (Iversen and Tunmer, 1993). Fielding-Barnsley (1997) found that children who had both phonemic awareness and graphophonemic knowledge benefited from instruction that asked students to say and write the sounds within printed words as they learned to read them.

Skilled Reading and Reading Disabilities

To summarize, research on skilled reading has disclosed the following foundational skills that go into making a skilled reader: phonological awareness, graphophonemic knowledge, decoding or alphabetic reading skill, orthographic or sight reading skill, and fluency, along with language comprehension. It has also revealed the nature of the relationships among these components. Sight word reading appears necessary for maximizing reading fluency and comprehension; decoding skill appears necessary for developing a large storehouse of sight words; and knowledge of spelling-sound rules plus phonemic awareness appears necessary for alphabetic reading skill. The foundational skills are like localities along a road, where reaching distant towns depends on passing through towns on the way (Spear-Swerling & Sternberg, 1994).

What do we know about students with RD in relationship to these components of skilled reading? Research has shown that students with RD are challenged in these very areas. Their reading is not as fluent as that of skilled reader, as shown in Figure 1. Their orthographic reading skill (sight word knowledge) is substantially below that of their age-level peers (Felton & Wood, 1992). Their decoding skills are especially weak (Felton & Wood, 1992; Rack, Snowling, & Olson, 1992; Shankweiler et al., 1999). Finally, they are slow to develop phonological awareness, and their graphophonemic knowledge is less secure (Juel, 1988; Wagner, Torgesen, Laughon, Simmons, & Rashotte, 1993).

The most widely accepted view of reading disabilities traces the reading problems of young children with specific R/LDs to weaknesses in processing phonological information. This weakness includes difficulties in developing phonological awareness (Shankweiler & Liberman, 1989) as well as difficulties in accessing phonological name codes (as evidenced in slower naming speeds for known stimuli like numbers and letters; Wolf & Bowers, 1999), poorer memory for phonological stimuli (e.g., recalling a series of orally presented numbers; Torgesen, Wagner, & Rashotte, 1994), or speech perception (e.g., repeating multisyllabic nonwords; Brady, 1991). In general, students with reading disabilities have been found to perform poorly in all these areas, although not every individual with R/LD will experience difficulty in every area. These phonological processing problems surface in the earliest stages of learning to read, where children experience particular difficulty in developing alphabetic reading skills (i.e., decoding). As we noted earlier, alphabetic reading skill probably plays a prominent role in the development of orthographic (sight word) reading skill, which in turn affects the development of fluency and comprehension.

Some of the most convincing evidence that students with R/LDs have specific deficits in alphabetic reading skill comes from studies using reading-level match designs. In such studies, older (e.g., grade 4) students with R/LDs are matched with younger (e.g., grade 2) typically developing readers on orthographic reading skill (e.g., the Word Identification Word Identification subtest of the Woodcock Reading Mastery Test, or WRMT; Woodcock, 1987). Both groups are then tested for alphabetic reading skill, typically measured by performance on a nonword reading measure (e.g., WRMT, Word Attack). The logic of this design is that if students with R/LDs are merely *delayed* in orthographic and alphabetic reading skills, they should perform on both tasks like younger typically developing readers. However,

Figure 3. Relationship between phonemic segmentation skill and decoding.

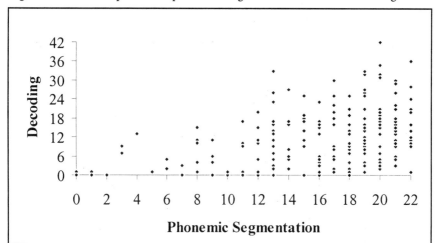

if they have a specific *deficit* in alphabetic reading, their performance on the nonword measure will be significantly below that of the younger typically developing readers with whom they have been matched on orthographic reading skill.

In reviewing this literature, Rack et al. (1992) concluded that students with R/LDs demonstrate nonword reading deficits relative to their younger, reading-level control group, especially in studies that control for regression effects. Since Rack et al.'s review, similarly designed research with German-speaking children with dyslexia consistently found a specific nonword reading deficit (Landerl, Wimmer, & Frith, 1997; Wimmer, 1993, 1996). These findings are important because German is considered to be an "orthographically shallow" language in which grapheme-phoneme pronunciation rules are highly consistent, unlike English which is considered an "orthographically deep" language. Whereas the nonword deficit for English-speaking students with R/LD is reflected in reading accuracy and rate, German dyslexics are relatively *accurate* readers of nonwords; however, their reading *speed* for nonwords is greatly impaired relative to that of younger, reading-level match controls (Landerl et al., 1997).

Thus, German readers with R/LD more readily acquire decoding accuracy (although this achievement is also a struggle for them). Their relative advantage over English readers in decoding accuracy is probably the result of systematic phonics instruction along with the German language's transparent graphophonemic relationships. German readers' alphabetic reading difficulty shows up as a deficit in decoding speed. Relative to German readers, English readers with R/LDs have more difficulty in acquiring decoding accuracy, probably because the graphophonemic regularities in their reading corpus is more opaque. The important point is that across languages with alphabetic orthographies, the reading problems of students with R/LD manifest most prominently as nonword reading deficits in speed and sometimes accuracy. These reading problems appear to arise from phonological dysfunction. Reading-related phonological processing problems can be observed in the development of phonological awareness, difficulty in learning graphophonemic relations, and difficulty in using phonemic awareness and graphophonemic knowledge to decode unfamiliar words, all of which negatively affect acquisition of a sight word reading vocabulary (orthographic reading skill), fluency, and comprehension.

EARLY IDENTIFICATION OF STUDENTS AT RISK FOR READING/LEARNING DISABILITIES

Identifying early those children most likely to encounter reading problems may constitute the first step in reducing the incidence or severity of RD. Because schools tend not to identify these children until the middle elementary grades, these children's reading difficulties grow stronger roots, and possibly become more intractable. For the most effective intervention, schools must find ways to identify these children much earlier than they usually do.

Research on early identification originates from studies of potential causes of reading difficulties, in which a range of children's preliteracy skills are measured in kindergarten or first grade, and then the strength of the correlations between these skills and reading ability is calculated either concurrently, or 1 or 2 years later. As one might expect, virtually all studies in which letter knowledge was measured in preschool, kindergarten, or early first grade documented its significant contribution to reading. Other contributing factors have been explored, such as vocabulary (Bowey & Patel, 1988; Mantzicopoulos & Morrison, 1994; Scarborough, 1990, 1995), short-term memory for language-related information (Baddeley, 1986; Leather & Henry, 1994; Mann & Ditunno, 1990; Rapala & Brady, 1990), and efficient retrieval of verbal labels (Badian, 1993; Bowers & Swanson, 1991; Doi & Manis, 1996; Seidenberg & McClelland, 1989; Wagner et al., 1987; Wolf, 1991), however, findings on the unique additional variance in reading that each factor contributes have been inconsistent. Some of these differences appear to depend on whether or which control variables were used (e.g., indices of IQ, socioeconomic level, age, or phonological awareness), and whether these skills and reading achievement were measured concurrently or predictively.

Since the mid-1980s, most studies that focus on predictive correlations have also included measures of phonological awareness (e.g., Berninger, 1986; MacLean, Bryant, & Bradley, 1988; Majsterek & Ellenwood, 1995; Mann & Ditunno, 1990; Share et al., 1984; Stanovich, Cunningham, & Cramer, 1984; Uhry, 1993; Wagner,

Torgesen, Laughon, Simmons, & Rashotte, 1993). These measures include matching tasks, in which children match spoken words with similar beginning or ending sounds or rhymes; representational tasks, in which children tap the syllables or phonemes they hear within words spoken by an examiner; production tasks, in which children blend speech sounds together to generate words, or articulate the first, last, or all phonemes within spoken words; or deletion tasks, in which children listen to a word (e.g., baseball, street) and say the word without a particular syllable (e.g., /base/) or phoneme (e.g., /s/). A convergence of findings across these studies builds a strong case that the combination of phonological awareness and letter knowledge accounts for a large portion of the attributable variance in reading—generally 40–60% of the variance concurrently and 1–2 years later. In addition to reports of the relative stability of phonological processing over the elementary years (Elbro, Borstrom, & Petersen, 1998; Wagner et al., 1993), MacDonald and Cornwall (1995) found that phonological awareness measured in kindergarten was still more predictive of word identification and spelling 11 years later than was socioeconomic status or vocabulary.

Because sensitivity to the phonemic elements of spoken words is necessary for reading acquisition (see Figure 3), researchers have examined various ways to assess children's phonemic sensitivity as a means of early identification of RD. Yopp (1988) compared the strength of correlations and factor loadings of a range of measures of phonological awareness and a reading analogue task with kindergartners, and found that rhyme production was too easy, deletion too difficult, and segmenting the most highly correlated with reading analogue scores. Because her participants were kindergartners, she was unable to measure "real" reading. Segmenting tends to develop among typical readers during kindergarten and early first grade (Kaminski & Good, 1996; Vandervelden & Siegel, 1997), and so measures used with preschoolers, such as rhyme (MacLean et al., 1988) or alliteration (Bradley & Bryant, 1983), are often predictors of later predictors (i.e., segmenting). Murray, Smith, and Murray (2000) tested the validity of a measure of phoneme identity ("Do you hear /s/ in *moon* or *soon?*") to predict prereading children's ability to read with phonetic cues (choosing between the printed words *mad* and *sad* when *sad* was spoken). Their measure correlated more strongly with trials to criterion on phonetic cue reading than the Comprehensive Test of Phonological Processing (Wagner, Torgesen, & Rashotte, 1999) or the Yopp-Singer segmenting test (Yopp, 1988); however, again, the dependent variable was not "real" reading achievement, and the measures were used concurrently, rather than predicting reading later in time.

Despite a strong correlational knowledge base connecting children's phonological language skills to later reading acquisition, predicting exactly which children will develop RD has proved problematic. The relative accuracy of prediction varies with the specific measures used as predictors and as outcomes, the timing of their administration, and the degree and direction of classification error the researchers consider acceptable, such that differences among selection processes have resulted in confusion over how reliably and early children with RD can be identified (Felton, 1992; Hurford et al., 1993; Torgesen, Burgess, Wagner, & Rashotte, 1996). Moreover, as Tymms (1999) suggested, "assessment has its work cut out simply getting a good general measure," given the tendency of many kindergartners to become easily distracted or bored.

Degree of Prediction Error

Two types of errors reduce the prediction of RD. Errors of underprediction occur when the predictive measures miss children who subsequently develop RD. Coleman and Dover (1993) developed the RISK screening battery, which required teachers to estimate the ability of each of their kindergarten students along several different dimensions, including school competence, task orientation, social competence, behavior, and motor ability. The overall accuracy of the scale was high (94% of children correctly identified); however, 21% of the children who later needed special education services were overlooked by this screening tool. Over half of the missed children were girls, suggesting the possibility of teacher bias related to gender. Mantzicopoulos and Morrison (1994) investigated the accuracy of the SEARCH procedure developed by Silver and Hagin (1981) for identifying children at the end of kindergarten who were likely to develop RD. SEARCH, which uses 10 measures of reading readiness (visual and auditory discrimination, immediate visual recall, visual-motor copying, rote sequencing, articulation, sound-symbol associations, directionality, finger schema, and pencil grip) underidentified relatively advantaged youngsters (missing 50%), while overidentifying children from low socioeconomic backgrounds.

Measures of vocabulary or concepts about print, although moderately related to later reading achievement, can lead to underprediction of RD because some children who will develop RD, especially those who are older than their peers at the time of testing or those who come from homes rich in literacy experiences, perform better on these measures than non-RD children who are younger or who come from more impoverished literacy circumstances. Measures that underpredict RD are of concern for those interested in early intervention because they directly undermine the intent of early intervention efforts (i.e., identifying those students who require early, intense, and targeted instruction).

The second type of error, overprediction, occurs when predictive measures mistakenly identify non-RD children as at risk for becoming RD. Indeed, most efforts to identify reading problems before children receive reading instruction overpredict RD (Badian, 1994; Catts, 1991; Felton, 1992; O'Connor & Jenkins, 1999; Torgesen et al., 1996; Uhry, 1993). Sixty-nine percent of the children predicted to be at risk in Felton's (1992) study, for example, were good readers by third grade; only 58% of Badian's (1994) at-risk preschoolers had confirmed reading problems 2 years later.

Over time, attempts at early identification of RD have been linked to the theoretical models of the causes of learning disability as understood at that time. Uhry (1993) used measures of sound categorization, segmenting, fingerpoint reading, and writing in kindergarten to predict poor readers in first grade. She established cutoff scores for the measures, which increased the potential usefulness of the battery; however, establishing a low cutoff score missed 28% of the future poor readers, and raising the cutoff scores to correctly identify most at-risk students resulted in a prediction that 42% of her private school sample would develop reading difficulties. Torgesen et al. (1996) used measures of phonological awareness, rapid naming, and letter knowledge in kindergarten and first grade to predict beginning second-grade reading. Although measures administered in first grade were more predictive than in kindergarten, they still missed 35% of the poor readers 1 year later.

Nicolson and Fawcett (1996) developed the Dyslexia Early Screening Test (DEST), a set of screening measures and cutoff scores widely used in the United Kingdom at school entry. Rather than identify a small set of predictive measures with cutoff scores, their test yields a profile of current ability across rapid naming, phonological and letter tasks, copying, and balance, which is summed to a risk index. With cross-validation, however, they needed to adjust the cutoff scores for this index to avoid problems of underprediction, particularly for children who began kindergarten at an age greater than 6.5 years.

Some of the language measures that have the highest correlation with subsequent reading achievement (e.g., phonological segmentation) are difficult for many typically developing children when tested early in kindergarten, leading to substantial overprediction errors. Other language measures, such as receptive or expressive vocabulary, have strong relations with reading comprehension by second or third grade, but may weaken classification accuracy for first-grade reading because they exert a protective factor in a discriminant function, making children with RD with strong vocabularies more difficult to detect—even though, on average, children with RD earn lower verbal scores (O'Connor & Jenkins, 1999). When early intervention services are in short supply, overprediction may squander limited educational resources. Part of the challenge facing researchers is to identify early-developing reading-related skills, and design age-based measures that are at an appropriate level of difficulty. As Badian (1998) noted, "as the nature of reading changes, so change the predictors" (p. 478).

Solving the Problem of Floor Effects

Researchers have tried to solve the problem of overprediction by fine-tuning measures to make them more sensitive to small differences among children, or to growth in the same children over time. For example, even though kindergartners' ability to segment spoken words is tied ($r = 0.62$) to their reading achievement in grade 1 (Share et al., 1984), segmentation ability nevertheless overpredicts RD because many normally developing readers are unskilled segmenters in kindergarten, leading to floor effects for the measure. To better distinguish children with RD from late-developing segmenters without RD, researchers have attempted easier levels of segmenting, such as syllable tapping (Badian, 1998), alliteration matching (Bradley & Bryant, 1983), or first sound production (Good, Simmons, & Kame'enui, 2001). Although these tasks correlate with reading, they lose substantial predictive power when administered late in kindergarten (O'Connor & Jenkins, 1999). Others have used discrimination indexes or item-response theory to order the items within a segmenting task (Wagner et al., 1999) from easier to more difficult. This approach allows children with low skill levels to engage in some of the testing items; however, the number of low-level items is limited.

Another approach to controlling the difficulty of segmenting is to adjust the tasks to offer more opportunity to learn, or to assess growth in a skill, rather than merely static achievement. Spector (1992) used a dynamic segmentation measure that provided children with varying levels of prompts to help them perform the task. Dynamic segmentation proved more predictive of later reading achievement than did static segmentation. Kaminski and Good (1996) provided variable scoring on the items of their segmenting test, so that children received credit for partially segmenting a word (e.g., identifying the /f/ or the /sh/ in fish), with more points for completely correct attempts. Scoring adjustments that reflect partial knowledge of a complex task (e.g., isolating the first phoneme within a word) and progress toward a goal (i.e., to completely segment a three- or four-phoneme word) may also provide teachers with insight into children's instructional needs.

Recent Efforts to Predict RD in Kindergarten

O'Connor and Jenkins (1999) tested over 400 children in kindergarten and followed their reading development through first grade, layering the investigation by testing various cohorts from diverse geographic, community, and economic conditions. They began with measures that have been identified in studies that sought component skills with high concurrent (Badian, 1993; Perfetti, Beck, Bell, & Hughes, 1987; Tunmer, Herriman, & Nesdale, 1988) or predictive (Felton, 1992; Hurford et al., 1993; Juel, 1988; Share et al., 1984) correlations with reading, including timed letter recognition, first sound identification, syllable and phoneme blending and segmenting, deletion, short-term memory for sounds, and rhyme production. Next, they set criteria by calibrating indicators of RD on one cohort of children; testing the parameters on a new cohort; and exploring the relative accuracy of predictors gathered over time. Across the three cohorts, rapid letter naming and segment phonemes were included among the subset of strong predictors of RD at all three screening points (beginning and end of kindergarten and beginning of first grade). The stability of these two tasks across three test periods in this study may be tied to their capacity to detect fine-grain individual differences. Their letter naming task represented not only children's accuracy of letter knowledge, but also their speed in accessing that knowledge. Likewise, their segmenting measure tapped various levels of insight into the phonemic structure of words, because items were not scored simply as right or wrong; rather, credit was awarded for gradations of phonemic awareness (isolating the initial sound in a word, separating onset from rime, complete phonemic segmentation), much like that of Kaminski and Good (1996). In addition, borrowing from Spector's work (1992), they provided corrective feedback to children during administration of the measure, which offered learning opportunities within the task itself. They suggested that the combination of graduated scoring and corrective feedback increased the predictive validity of the segmentation task by reducing floor effects that otherwise would have been pronounced, particularly for the November kindergarten test period, had scores been based solely on complete phonemic segmentation.

This sensitivity to children's partial and developing knowledge of segmentation probably contributed to reduced overselection rates (4–17% across cohorts) relative to earlier prediction studies. It also reduced ceiling effects associated with tasks like identifying the first sound in words, a task that was difficult in November for all three cohorts, but mastered by April for many students, including a few children who later developed RD. Depending on the timing of the screenings and the cohort, overprediction ranged from 4 to 17% and underprediction from 0 to 9%, but like Nicholson and Fawcett (1996), O'Connor and Jenkins warned that the patterns that predict poor reading among children of typical kindergarten age may not apply as well to older kindergarten children (> 6.1 years in September) who are repeating the grade. Some children who repeated kindergarten had learned enough about letter names and segmenting first sounds to score above established cutoff criteria, even though their performance still fell below the average of first-time kindergartners.

It appears, then, that for prereaders in kindergarten, tests that incorporate some form of learning, such as providing feedback on test items (O'Connor & Jenkins, 1999), variable scoring to indicate partial knowledge (Kaminski & Good, 1996; O'Connor & Jenkins, 1999), or trials to criterion (Murray et al., 2000; Spector, 1992) may be more sensitive indicators of future reading achievement.

Using Screening Measures to Establish Intervention Criteria

Prediction studies attempt to select (a) *all* children (i.e., no underprediction) whose reading scores at the end of first or second grade reveal a pattern of RD and (b) few children (i.e., small overprediction) whose later reading scores do not reveal an RD pattern. None of the studies we have reviewed have met these stringent expectations. Discriminant analysis provides information about the extent to which tasks in kindergarten distinguish children who eventually develop an RD profile. To take the next step in developing a screening instrument requires establishing criterion, or cutoff, scores for each of the primary predictors. Few research studies provide specific criteria for interpreting scores on predictive measures, and specific measures are rarely cross-validated with other samples.

Selecting *specific* tasks that are most useful in distinguishing children who will exhibit RD is dependent on the timing of the screening effort. Second, cutoff scores on various screening measures that accurately distinguished RD in one cohort tend to have reduced predictive validity for other same-age cohorts. In studies that included cross-validations (Badian, 1998; Fawcett, Singleton, & Peer, 1998; O'Connor & Jenkins, 1999), the researchers liberalized the preceding criterion scores with each successive cohort in order to capture every child who subsequently developed an RD profile. As expected, raising criterion scores increased overprediction rates, sometimes substantially.

As we noted before, which error is most egregious depends on the consequences. Some researchers recommend screening later than kindergarten to reduce the overidentification (Torgesen, Burgess, Wagner, & Rashotte, 1996). Accuracy rates of the predictive tasks for correctly classifying RD and non-RD groups tend to be higher with later screening. Moreover, the accuracy of prediction in kindergarten is somewhat dependent on the instruction children receive in first grade. This phenomenon was documenting in a year-long study conducted by Perfetti, Beck, Bell, and Hughes (1987) in which ability to blend and segment at the beginning of first grade was predictive of reading at the end of the year for children who received instruction organized around whole language, however, early phonemic awareness lost predictive power in classes that included frequent instruction in phonics as part of the reading approach, perhaps because the instruction in sound-symbol relations and word analysis quickly established the alphabetic principle for most children who had not already acquired it.

Badian (1998) suggests that many children predicted to fail by her kindergarten measures in fact succeeded because of the instructional approach in first grade. This approach was based on Bradley and Bryant's (1985) instructional procedures for children at risk for reading problems, which included integrating letter sounds with phonological blending, segmenting, and spelling. She believed that her rate of overprediction would have decreased if children had received a less structured reading program.

Tradeoffs between increased accuracy of identification and provision of early intervention affect the choice of a screening window. Another alternative is to incorporate some of the features of early intervention (e.g., stronger emphasis on letter knowledge, phonological blending and segmenting, and activities to promote the alphabetic principle) in general kindergarten routines, so that children are less likely to score poorly on kindergarten screenings because of lack of exposure, and are more likely to succeed in first grade.

Reasonably accurate prediction of RD is essential for evaluating the outcomes of early intervention. It is obvious why the predictive net must capture all or most of the children with RD—they are whom treatment is meant to help. Unless we set liberal cutoff scores (resulting in sizable overidentification), no set of predictors appears to be 100% accurate in identifying all children who eventually develop RD. Moreover, if RD samples in early intervention studies include many non-RD children, researchers and practitioners may be misled by the *cure rate* for children who did not really have RD. Prediction batteries that can be administered more than once over time may decrease overprediction by allowing the evaluators to determine growth in response to good instruction, as well as absolute levels of skills.

Some researchers (e.g., Fawcett et al., 1998; O'Connor, 2000; Simmons, Kuykendall, King, Cornachione, & Kame'enui, 2000) advocate layered approaches to screening and intervention, such that prediction of reading problems and increasingly intense interventions are interfaced over time. The interplay between small-group instruction on early literacy skills and ongoing measurement may ease the problem of overidentification, while offering low-cost early intervention to the children captured in the predictive net. Some sensible actions to identify the children most likely to need intensive support in reading are shown below.

Early Identification of Reading/Learning Disabilities: Sensible Actions

1. Assess the prerequisite skills of letter naming and phonemic awareness early in kindergarten (e.g., November).
2. Use measures that can be administered in 5 minutes or less to avoid fatigue (e.g., letters named in 1 minute; segments identified in 10 spoken words).
3. For children who have not acquired knowledge of letter names, assess often (e.g., monthly) to determine whether children are acquiring this knowledge in the current program.

4. For children who cannot segment or blend, assess easier levels of segmenting (e.g., first sound) and blending (e.g., stretched sounds), and then increase the difficulty level of the measurement tasks as children acquire the easier levels.

5. Use assessment information to provide targeted help to children who need it.

6. Watch children as they attempt to write or spell words for clues into their understanding of the alphabetic principle.

7. Record progress in letter and phonemic knowledge in ways that encourage closer monitoring of children who appear most at risk.

EARLY INTERVENTION FOR STUDENTS AT RISK FOR READING/LEARNING DISABILITIES

Because alphabetic reading skills provide the basis for developing orthographic reading skills, and because students with R/LDs encounter difficulty acquiring alphabetic reading skills, early intervention researchers have concentrated their efforts on teaching these skills and their prerequisites, specifically phonological awareness and graphophonemic knowledge. That is, researchers have attacked the very phonological weaknesses that are thought to cause word-level reading problems. In the sections that follow, we review research on teaching phonological awareness, decoding, and fluent reading.

Teaching Phonological Awareness

Individual differences in prereaders' phonological awareness are one of the best predictors of later success in learning to read (Elbro, 1996; MacLean et al., 1988; Share et al., 1984). The strong relationship between phonological awareness and reading achievement remains even after children have received several years of reading instruction (Wagner et al., 1997), suggesting a reciprocal relationship between the two skills (Ehri, 1979; Perfetti et al., 1987). However, it is the early predictive value of phonological awareness along with its theoretical status as a prerequisite for gaining insight into the alphabetic principle that has attracted the interest of prevention-oriented researchers.

Working inside and outside classrooms, teachers and researchers have used a variety of activities to teach phoneme awareness. Some instructional programs have emphasized sound categorization or phoneme identity (e.g., classifying pictures of objects on the basis of common beginning, middle, or ending sounds; Bradley and Bryant, 1985; Byrne & Fielding-Barnsley, 1993). Some researchers have used concrete visual aids such as Say-It-And-Move-It tasks (e.g., moving a plastic tile to represent each sound in a spoken word; Ball & Blachman, 1991) or a task modeled after Elkonin (1973)—given pictures of objects or spoken words (e.g., fan), children are asked to move a disk to or mark one in a series of boxes as they say each phoneme in the word (Blachman, Ball, Black, & Tangel, 1994; Vadasy, Jenkins, & Pool, 2000). Others have used a variety of metaphonological tasks (e.g., rhyming games, clapping for words in a sentence, syllables in a word, or phonemes in words; synthesizing the speech of a puppet who spoke only in segmented speech; identifying the initial sound in names and words; Lundberg, Frost, & Petersen, 1988; O'Connor, Jenkins, Slocum, & Leicester, 1993; O'Connor, Notari-Syverson, & Vadasy, 1996; Torgesen, Morgan, & Davis, 1992). A comprehensive listing of resources for assessing and instructing phonological awareness can be found in Torgesen and Mathes (2000).

Major questions pertaining to teaching phonological awareness include the following: Can phonological awareness be taught to children before they begin reading instruction? Does teaching phonological awareness either before formal reading instruction or alongside formal reading instruction affect either beginning decoding or word reading? Does combining phonological awareness and alphabetic instruction result in stronger effects on phonological awareness and reading than teaching phonological awareness alone? Does early phonological awareness instruction affect later reading development of students who are at risk for reading problems? Do the effects of early phonological awareness training persist beyond the earliest stages of reading development?

To address these questions, Bus and van Ijzendoorn (1999) conducted a meta-analysis of 32 published articles that tested the effects of phonological awareness training. Bus and van Ijzendoorn reported training effect sizes of $d = 0.73$ and 0.70 on measures of phonological awareness and reading, respectively. However, effect sizes on reading real words were smaller than on simpler forms of reading (e.g., determining which of two printed words matches a spoken word) ($d = 0.34$ vs. 0.85, respectively). Students whom Bus and van Ijzendoorn categorized as experiencing problems in the early stages of learning to read showed significantly smaller effects on measures of phonological awareness than students classified as "normal" ($d = 0.54$ vs. 1.16, respectively), but the two groups showed similar effects on reading measures ($d = 0.60$ vs. 0.40, respectively). Further, effects of phonological awareness training on reading, measured 18 months after the end of treatment, were not significant ($d = 0.16$).

Meta-analyses like Bus and van Ijzendoorn's are useful in estimating treatment effects across many studies (e.g., students given phonological awareness training show a better grasp of the segmental features of language than do untrained students). Meta-analyses can also provide information about particular variables (e.g., treatments combining phonemic awareness and letter-sound instruction yield larger reading effects than phonemic awareness by itself). However, because meta-analyses combine effects from many disparate studies that vary in context (e.g., preschool, kindergarten, or primary school), vary in type of training (e.g., purely phonetic, combined with letters, or within reading instruction), and depend on the researchers' classification of studies (e.g., should "normal populations" include urban students from low-income families who often are at risk for reading failure?), they do not answer other questions of importance to prevention-oriented researchers. For example, does phonemic awareness training with at-risk kindergarten students lead to better reading outcomes at the end of first grade, and is the answer to this question qualified by the type of reading program (code vs. whole language emphasis) that students receive? Individual studies focusing on particular research questions must be consulted to fill out the picture painted by meta-analyses. Below, we examine some of the major questions pertaining to phonemic awareness instruction, along with a selection of the highest quality studies addressing these questions.

Do children benefit from phonemic awareness instruction in preschool and kindergarten? Targeted phonemic awareness instruction with prereading children (preschool and kindergarten) leads to significant gains in phonological awareness and in word-level reading skills (e.g., Ball & Blachman, 1991; Bradley and Bryant, 1985; Byrne & Fielding-Barnsley, 1993). In these studies research staff provided phonemic awareness instruction outside the classroom to typically developing youngsters, with some groups taught to represent sounds with letters of the alphabet. Groups who received a combination of phonemic and alphabetic tasks showed significantly stronger performance on reading measures. In fact, few studies of prereaders report effects from pure phonemic awareness training (without teaching letter sounds) on reading tasks administered immediately after training (Cunningham, 1990) or following a year of formal reading instruction (Lundberg et al., 1988).

Phonemic awareness instruction has also proven beneficial when delivered by kindergarten teachers rather than research staff. In one study, kindergarten teachers and their assistants gave 11 weeks of phonemic awareness training (10–13 hours of instruction in 15–20-minute lessons) to low-income, inner-city youngsters (Blachman et al., 1994). The experimental group used Say-It-And-Move-It and Elkonin-like segmentation tasks, and received direct instruction in letter names and sounds. Children who had mastered several letter names and sounds also used letter tiles to form words in the Say-It-And-Move-It task. Compared to a control group that did not receive phonological awareness lessons, the experimental group performed significantly higher at the end of the year on measures of phoneme segmentation, spelling, and an experimenter-designed measure of reading phonetically regular words and nonwords. The groups did not differ on the Word Identification subtest of the WRMT. O'Connor et al. (1996), who unlike Blachman et al. (1994) included students with disabilities in their treatment, reported similar results in a kindergarten study of teacher-implemented phonological awareness instruction.

Does explicit phonemic awareness instruction add to the effects of phonics instruction for beginning readers? Whereas many typically developing students easily acquire phonemic insight, graphophonemic knowledge, and the application of these skills to decode words, students with R/LDs encounter difficulties with these skills right from the start. This fact has led some prevention researchers to conclude that merely incorporating phonemic awareness training in kindergarten is insufficient to overcome the challenges faced by students at risk for R/LD. Rather, kindergarten programs should also include systematic instruction of early reading skills.

Fuchs and colleagues conducted three kindergarten studies examining the contributions of explicit phonemic awareness instruction, decoding instruction, and their combination. In their first study, Fuchs et al. (2001) compared three groups: an untreated control; one that received phonemic awareness instruction; and one that received both phonemic awareness and decoding instruction. Classroom teachers and peer-tutoring dyads conducted all instruction. Phonemic awareness instruction was based on *Ladders to Literacy* (O'Connor, Notari-Syverson, & Vadasy, 1998). Decoding instruction was delivered through PALS, a peer-mediated format developed by the researchers. On phoneme awareness tests at the end of kindergarten, the treatment groups did not differ, but outperformed the control. On word identification, decoding, and spelling tests, however, the decoding plus phonological awareness group surpassed the other two groups, which did not differ from each other. By October of grade 1, the pattern of effects on phonological and reading tasks was similar to the earlier results, but the groups no longer differed significantly.

In their second study, Fuchs et al. (2001) compared three kindergarten groups: decoding (PALS), decoding plus phonemic awareness, and an untreated control. In non-Title 1 schools, the two treatment groups performed comparably at the end of the year on reading and spelling outcomes, and both groups surpassed the control group. Finally, in a third study, Fuchs and Fuchs (2001) compared four kindergarten groups: decoding with and without phonological awareness training; phonological awareness alone; and a control group. Again, the researchers found no evidence that phonological awareness training added to the effects of their decoding program. Together, these three kindergarten studies raise questions about the added value of phonemic awareness instruction in learning to read words, when students also receive systematic decoding instruction.

In a related study using another version of PALS, Mathes, Torgesen, & Allor (2001) examined how the quantity of phonological awareness instruction affected first graders' reading growth. The PALS treatment emphasized phonics and story reading, but also included practice in segmenting spoken words into sounds. Low achieving students who received PALS along with computer-assisted phonological awareness training performed no better than students who received PALS alone. More phonological awareness practice did not add value.

If struggling readers' critical deficit is a lack of phonemic awareness, why were they not helped by training in this skill? One possibility is that explicit instruction of phonics implicitly teaches phoneme awareness. That is, instruction that clearly specifies grapheme-phoneme relationships, gives practice in converting graphemes to phonemes, and assists students in assembling word pronunciations from strings of graphemes may be sufficient to establish the level of phoneme awareness necessary for learning to read. In any case, these three kindergarten studies found strong word-reading effects from explicit phonics instruction, whether or not it was supplemented with explicit phonemic awareness training.

The absence of a phonemic awareness training effect in the context of an explicit phonics intervention is a reminder that care is needed in interpreting the necessary relationship between phonemic awareness and alphabetic reading skill. Although alphabetic reading skill may depend on phonemic awareness, the two skills may develop concurrently, rather than sequentially, under certain instructional conditions.

Not to be overlooked in the kindergarten studies by Fuchs and colleagues is the large number of low achieving students (i.e., those most at-risk for R/LD) who registered no gains in reading, even with explicit decoding and phonemic awareness instruction. This brings us to the next question.

For students at risk for R/LDs, does phonological awareness instruction in kindergarten result in better phonological awareness and reading performance? Few researchers report the percentage of children who, despite training, fail to acquire segmental language and decoding skills (i.e., nonresponders), and those researchers who do report this statistic find that as many as 30% of low achieving kindergarten students do not show increased phonological awareness (Torgesen et al., 1992) and 50% show no increases in reading performance (Fuchs et al., 2001). Of course, these students might show a stronger response with longer and/or more intense instruction. By and large, studies reporting long-term reading effects of early training in phonemic awareness have been conducted with typically developing youngsters, not students at risk for R/LD (Bradley and Bryant, 1985; Byrne & Fielding-Barnsley, 1993, 1995; Lundberg et al., 1988).

Does the type of reading instruction students receive affect their need for explicit teaching of phonological awareness? Teaching students phonological awareness in kindergarten may be less important if they subsequently receive explicit and systematic instruction in phonics. By contrast, if first graders are left to figure out the code on their own (e.g., in a classroom with insufficient phonics instruction), kindergarten instruction in phonological awareness and graphophonemic relations may be critical. Because many studies combine phonological awareness and phonics instruction, it is difficult to separate the contributions of each. However, the value added by phonological awareness instruction may be diminished when phonics is explicitly taught (Fuchs & Fuchs, 2001; Fuchs et al., 2001). Consistent with this possibility are findings from first-grade studies that show initial level of phonemic awareness, often a strong predictor of reading success, loses its predictive power in classrooms with strong code-based instruction (Compton, 2000; Perfetti et al., 1987).

How much phonological awareness is needed? It will also be important to determine how much phonological awareness is enough for getting a start on word reading. By plotting performance on onset-rime segmentation against word-reading ability, Stahl and Murray (1994) concluded that segmenting into onset-rime is necessary for reading. On the basis of their analysis of phonemic segmenting and reading, O'Connor et al. (1996) concluded that children may need to be able to isolate two or more phonemes correctly within spoken words to facilitate reading. In a study that measured children from kindergarten through third grade, Good et al. (2001) established minimum scores for kindergarten segmenting of 25–35 segments per minute (i.e., children could provide most sounds in three-phoneme words) as indicators of children who would pass the Oregon state reading assessment at the end of third grade. Beyond three-phoneme segmentation, faster segmenting (e.g., 10 words in less than 1 minute) or deeper segmenting (e.g., four- and five-phoneme words) does not appear to improve reading outcomes at the end of first grade (Good et al., 2001; O'Connor & Jenkins, 1999). Merely isolating the first sound in words appears to be insufficient for reading words through a decoding process, and if segmenting advances no further than first-sound identification, this level may encourage the "use the first sound and guess" strategy for word identification that persists well into the elementary years for many children with RD.

Even though important questions remain unanswered about teaching phonological awareness (e.g., the contribution of phonemic awareness training to reading acquisition under different reading instructional approaches), we recommend a conservative approach (e.g., providing such training to kindergarten children). A short list of sensible actions follows:

Fostering Phonemic Awareness: Sensible Actions

1. Teach phonemic awareness early—in preschool, kindergarten, and first grade.
2. With novices, begin instruction using larger (easier) linguistic units (e.g., words, syllables) and progress to smaller units (i.e., phonemes), but be sure that children can segment words into phonemes by the end of kindergarten.
3. Teach phonemic awareness in conjunction with letter sounds.
4. Encourage spelling/writing early in literacy instruction because it prompts children to notice the segmental features of language.
5. Emphasize the sounds in spoken words when teaching phonics.
6. Assess students' phonemic awareness regularly until children attain proficiency, and permit no one to lag behind in developing this insight.
7. Provide students with whatever additional help they need to become sensitive to the segmental features of spoken language.

Teaching Alphabetic Reading Skill (Decoding)

Because students with R/LD have poorly developed alphabetic reading skill, and because this skill serves as a platform for acquiring orthographic reading proficiency, instructional researchers have sought effective ways to help students master decoding. Research has focused on three important questions—the relative effectiveness of more- and less-explicit instruction in establishing decoding and word-reading skill, the relative value of an instructional focus on phonemes or rime units, and the effects of layered interventions for at-risk readers.

Do beginning readers develop better decoding skills from more- versus less-explicit phonics instruction? When researchers have compared more and less explicit approaches to teaching phonics on *decoding* outcomes, they consistently report an advantage for more explicit approaches (National Reading Panel, 2000). We illustrate these findings by examining three particularly strong studies. Besides the level of explicitness of phonics instruction, these studies differ on several other dimensions: length (1 to 3 years); instructional arrangements (individual tutoring or classroom-level instruction); and type of comparison group (a well-specified alternative treatment or an undefined control group).

Torgesen et al. (1999) compared three approaches to beginning reading instruction for students whose performance on phonological processing measures were predicted to be in the bottom 10% of readers. Research staff tutored the students from mid-kindergarten through grade 2. The Phonological Awareness at an oral-motor level plus Synthetic Phonics (PASP) group received *Auditory Discrimination in Depth,* or ADD (Lindamood & Lindamood, 1984). ADD emphasizes how phonemes are produced and teaches grapheme-phoneme conversions explicitly (in isolation), along with how to use this knowledge to decode words. An Embedded Phonics (EP) group received less explicit phonics, with grapheme-phoneme instruction delivered in the context of learning to read and write sight words. A Regular Classroom Support (RCS) group received tutoring in the activities and skills taught in the regular classroom. The final group was a No-Treatment Control (NTC).

The primary focus of the study was on the PASP and EP groups. As students in these two groups acquired graphophonemic knowledge and word-reading skill, they spent an increasing proportion of lesson time on text reading. However, whereas PASP students spent 80% of lesson time on word-level activities and 20% on text-level activities, EP students spent 43% and 57% on word- and text-level activities, respectively. At the end of grade 2, the ADD group significantly outperformed the other groups in decoding and word identification; the EP, RCS, and NTC groups did not differ.

Other early intervention researchers have reported similarly strong effects in decoding for at-risk first-grade students who receive explicit phonics tutoring. However, in these latter studies the effectiveness of tutorial instruction was contrasted with regular classroom instruction alone (e.g., Vadasy, Jenkins, & Pool, 2000) or as demonstration of changes in reading ability of tutored students (Vellutino et al., 1996).

Early intervention has not been limited to supplemental tutoring. Blachman, Tangel, Ball, Black, and McGraw (1999) found strong effects from small-group instruction from classroom teachers, beginning in kindergarten and continuing through grade 1 for some students, and through grade 2 for those still struggling at the end of first grade. Kindergarten instruction focused on phonemic awareness and letter sounds, consistent with Blachman et al. (1994). In first grade, children were assigned to classes on the basis of their phonemic awareness and word-reading ability so that teachers could teach relatively homogeneous small groups. Following a review of kindergarten lessons, first-grade instruction consisted of daily 30-minute lessons, following a five-step reading program: (1) review and introduction of graphophonemic relations; (2) sound-blending letters to form words and using a letter board to spell words; (3) fluency building using flash cards; (4) reading phonetically controlled text; and (5) writing to dictation. Time spent reading stories and rereading increased as students acquired proficiency on word-level skills. Second-grade teachers continued using the five-step program with students reading below grade level. Control students received an equivalent amount of basal reading instruction. Treatment children significantly surpassed control children on phonemic awareness, decoding, word identification, and spelling tests at the end of grades 1 and 2.

In contrast to Torgesen et al. (1999) and Blachman et al. (1999) who examined multiyear treatments, Foorman, Francis, Fletcher, Schatschneider, & Mehta (1998) studied progress of Title I first- and second-grade students in a single-year comparison of three classroom approaches. Direct Code (DC) teachers gave explicit instruction in phonemic awareness and explicit phonics (42 phonic rules) using Open Court's *Collection for Young Scholars* (1995). Students practiced in decodable texts, and also read from Big Books to develop oral language and comprehension skills. In a second approach, Embedded Code (EC), teachers emphasized phonemic awareness and a common list of spelling patterns (word families) as well as a variety of comprehension strategies. Students learned an analogy strategy for reading new words with familiar spelling patterns, and read from predictable books. In the third treatment, Implicit Code (IC), teachers followed a whole-language philosophy. They emphasized comprehension and integrated reading, writing, and spelling activities, but did not provide explicit phonics instruction. Growth curve analyses over four first-grade measurement points revealed significantly stronger progress by the DC group on phonological awareness and word reading. The DC group also significantly surpassed the other groups on an end-of-year word-reading measure (a combination of nonword and real-word tests), and scored higher on passage comprehension than the EC group did. EC and IC groups did not differ on any outcomes. DC seemed especially stronger in assisting the lowest achieving students to acquire some word-reading skill.

In these three studies, groups that made the largest gains in decoding received decontextualized instruction in phonemic awareness and grapheme-phoneme relationships, and were shown how to use graphophonemic information to read words. This is not entirely surprising, as Brophy (2000) noted: "... bear in mind that most assessments of the relative effectiveness of explicit versus implicit methods of teaching anything, regardless of subject matter, have favored the explicit methods" (p. 176). More at issue is the transfer effects of instructional explicitness of decoding skill on subsequent skills farther downstream in the reading process (e.g., word identification, fluency, and comprehension).

Do explicit phonics treatments result in stronger word identification skill for beginning readers? Most explicit phonics treatments that obtain significant effects on decoding also find effects on word identification. However, effect sizes on word identification measures are often smaller than those observed for decoding. For example, using nonword tests for decoding and real-word tests for word identification, we figured respective effect sizes for decoding versus word identification to be

0.86 versus 0.33 for Blachman et al. (1999) at grade 1; 0.60 and 0.25 for Fuchs et al. (2001) at kindergarten; 0.88 versus 0.48 for Torgesen et al. (1999) PASP and EP at grade 2; 1.16 and 0.87 for Vadasy et al. (2000) at grade 1.

Findings on the value of explicit decoding instruction for word identification divide according to the stage of reading development of the students studied. For beginning readers, more explicit phonics approaches yield stronger word-reading skill (Foorman et al., 1998; Torgesen et al., 1999). By contrast, more- and less-explicit decoding approaches yield similar word-reading outcomes in research on older, remedial R/LD readers (Torgesen et al., 2001; Wise, Ring, & Olson, 2000). Should we conclude that explicit decoding instruction "works" for beginning readers but not for remedial readers? Such a conclusion would be premature. Nevertheless, age-qualified results serve as a reminder to exercise caution in forming general conclusions about the benefits of explicit phonics instruction.

Several studies comparing more and less explicit phonics approaches are exceptionally well designed and methodologically sound, but they are few, and comparing approaches to reading instruction is a tricky business. While it is possible to characterize different reading programs on a single dimension (for example, degree of phonics explicitness), each program is composed of many properties that can influence learning (e.g., quality of examples, attention to reviews, scaffolding of student learning). Moreover, few of the more prevalent approaches that special education teachers use have been examined. Comparative research using explicit programs like Reading Mastery, Corrective Reading, or Read Well are needed.

Should decoding instruction emphasize phonemes or phonograms (word families)? In principle, there are advantages to each approach. Focusing on phonemic units (/a/, /sh/, /ea/) forces learners to attend to every letter, something readers must eventually do. By contrast, instruction that focuses on phonograms (-at, -ate, -art) regularizes vowel pronunciations for words within a family. Teaching phonograms also helps learners chunk letter groups in ways that can speed word recognition.

In their study of beginning at-risk readers, Foorman et al. (1998) found faster word learning in classrooms teaching phoneme-level decoding than classrooms emphasizing either phonograms or whole language. Notably, first graders receiving phonograms instruction performed no better than those receiving whole-language instruction. More evidence favoring a phoneme emphasis comes from a training experiment by Berninger et al. (2000) who compared several kinds of instructional modeling for word reading (letter-phoneme; onset and rime-pronunciation; letter spelling–whole-word pronunciation), singly and in combination. Treatment groups also received decontextualized instruction on graphophonemic relations and phonemic awareness, using Berninger's (1998) "Talking Letters" and practiced assisted text reading. On a test of the taught words, all experimental groups outperformed a contact control group (who received phonological and orthographic awareness instruction along with assisted text reading), but did not differ from each other. However, on a test of transfer words, the letter-phoneme pronunciation group, the spelling–whole-word pronunciation group, and the group that received a combination of both these kinds of instructional modeling differed significantly from the control group. Groups given instructional modeling of onset and rime-pronunciations fared no better than students who received no word-level instruction. Thus, both Foorman et al.'s (1998) classroom research and Berninger's et al. (2000) clinical research found an advantage for phoneme over onset-rime instructional emphases.

However, the instructional advantage of phonemes over onset-rimes may depend on the child's reading level. Working with older (7- to 12-year-old) students with severe reading disabilities, Lovett has reported inconsistent results for these approaches across several studies. However, in her longest running study, Lovett et al. (2000) compared various combinations of graphophonemic and phonograms emphases, as well as pure versions of each, with the constraint that all groups received 70 hours of intervention. Children were given graphophonemic instruction followed by phonograms instruction, phonograms instruction followed by graphophonemic instruction, graphophonemic instruction alone, or phonograms instruction alone. Overall, Lovett et al. found no advantage for graphophonemic versus phonograms instruction. Combining the two approaches, however, produced performance superior to that of either approach by itself. In addition, on a few measures of word reading, graphophonemic instruction followed by phonograms instruction appeared stronger than the reverse order. Thus, in deciding between graphophonemic and phonogram instructional approaches, the jury awaits more definitive evidence.

Should beginning reading instruction be confined to decodable texts? Some reading authorities believe that beginning reading instruction, particularly for children at risk for reading problems, should employ text that is consistent with the phonics that children have been taught (Carnine, Silbert, & Kame'enui, 1997). With the exception of a few high-frequency irregular words necessary for creating stories (e.g., *said, the*), only words made up of previously taught letter-sound correspondences should appear in sentence or story reading. Other authorities contend that consistency between phonics and text is an open question (Allington & Woodside-Jiron, 1998). Only two studies have addressed this issue. Juel and Roper-Schneider (1985) found a decoding advantage for typically developing first graders taught with phonetically transparent text, relative to students who received the same phonics instruction but read from less phonetically consistent text. The groups did not differ on an end-of-year reading achievement test.

More recently, Peyton, Jenkins, Vadasy, and Sanders (2001) studied three groups of at-risk first graders. Two groups received supplemental one-to-one reading instruction from nonteacher tutors, using the same phonics program, *Sound Partners* (Vadasy et al., 2001). During the story reading component of the lessons, students in the more-decodable group read texts that were highly consistent with the phonics program (i.e., a high proportion of the words appearing in the texts were composed of taught letter-sounds alone). Those words that could not be decoded from previously taught graphophonemic correspondences were taught in isolation before they appeared in stories. In contrast, students in the less-decodable group read stories composed primarily of high-frequency words, with an emphasis on predictable text. A control group received regular instruction from classroom and Title 1 teachers, but were not given the supplementary one-to-one lessons. At the end-of-year reading, the tutored groups surpassed the control group on a broad array of decoding, word reading, accuracy in context, and comprehension measures. However, the more- and less-decodable groups did not differ significantly on any measure. In interpreting these findings, it must be remembered that the more- and less-decodable text treatments were supplemental to classroom reading instruction, in which students read from a variety of texts that bore little relationship to the supplemental phonics lessons. Under these circumstances, text differences may not carry the weight that some authorities claim.

How can schools organize assessment and instruction to prevent and/or ameliorate R/LDs? Most early intervention research on R/LD has compared the relative effectiveness of specific instructional approaches (e.g., Foorman et al., 1998, Torgesen, et al., 1999). Results of these studies remind us again how much students vary in their responsiveness to instruction. Even with explicit and intense decoding instruction, researchers find between 15 and 30% of at-risk students still perform significantly below average in decoding and word identification (e.g., Torgesen et al., 1999; Vellutino et al., 1996). If these students are to become competent word readers, they will require longer, more intense, or different treatments than they received. In line with this thinking are two recent studies that attempt to adjust treatment length and intensity according to student response.

Blachman et al. (1999) provided longer treatments to students who required more help by reconstituting and linking kindergarten and first-grade instruction for at-risk students, and then extending treatment into second grade for students who had not completed the intervention program. Because Blachman et al. did not report standard scores for the lowest performing students, we cannot determine the number of students who finished grade 2 still reading at an unsatisfactory level. Nevertheless, the lowest achieving treated students strongly outperformed their counterparts in the control group (ES = 1.4 and 1.24 in decoding and word identification, respectively). On a nonword decoding test, treated students in the bottom quartile tripled the performance level of control students. Blachman et al. obtained these results by organizing homogeneous, small-group instruction (including the assignment of students to classroom), designing lessons that emphasized phonemic awareness and alphabetic reading skills, and adjusting treatment duration according to students' progress. Students did not receive supplemental services from remedial and special education teachers. Despite these impressive results, it is unlikely that even high-quality general education, no matter how well organized, will be sufficient to meet the needs of students with R/LDs.

O'Connor, Fulmer, Harty, and Bell (2001) provide a model for primary schools attempting to accommodate students at risk for R/LDs who do not thrive even within high-quality general education classrooms. Focusing on grades 1 and 2, these researchers linked professional development for general and special education teachers, redesigned classroom literacy instruction, periodically assessed student performance, and provided supplemental instruction for struggling students. Literacy instruction addressed phonological and print awareness, oral language, word analysis, comprehension, writing activities, and fluency. In Layer 1 of O'Connor et al.'s intervention, classroom teachers received professional development to help them deliver literacy instruction that was geared to the needs of struggling students. Layer 2 of the intervention used periodic reading assessments to identify children requiring additional help. Research personnel provided small, homogeneous group instruction (2–3 students) to struggling students for 25–30 minutes, three times per week. Depending on students' needs, small-group instruction emphasized either alphabetic reading skills (e.g., letter sounds, sounding-out, word analysis) or fluency (e.g., reading and rereading decodable texts).

At the end of second grade, reading scores of average and low achieving students (including students with disabilities) who received the layered intervention were compared to those of control students. Treated students performed significantly higher on word identification, nonword reading, fluency, and comprehension. The fluency scores of the lowest performing students (Figure 4) indicate a strong advantage for those in the intervention group over those in the control group. Whereas 23 control students read fewer than 50 words per minute, 16 intervention students fell below this criterion. When criterion performance was set lower, at 25 words per minute, 11 control versus only 2 intervention students failed to achieve this criterion. Together, the studies of Blachman et al. (1999) and O'Connor et al. (2001) suggest that schools can reduce the number of students who fail to respond to interventions by lengthening the intervention period and by providing supplemental instruction for students experiencing the most difficulties.

Not surprisingly, many important questions remain unanswered or partially answered regarding the teaching of decoding. Here are some things we don't know. Is it important to confine beginning reading practice to decodable text? What level of decoding skill is necessary for fast, accurate word identification and comprehension? How should we teach those children who do not reach adequate levels of decoding and word-reading skill despite receiving our strongest treatments? Research like O'Connor et al.'s (2001) is sorely needed to identify specialized intervention approaches for students who do not respond to enhanced classroom instruction.

Even though important questions remain about teaching phonics (e.g., the relative emphasis on decontextualized phonics instruction and text reading practice), we recommend a conservative approach (i.e., providing sufficient explicit phonics instruction for students to read nonwords easily). A short list of sensible actions follows:

Promoting Alphabetic Reading: Sensible Actions

1. Teach grapheme-phoneme conversions explicitly right from the start.
2. Teach graphophonemic relations directly and systematically, not with worksheets.
3. Assess graphophonemic knowledge frequently until children attain proficiency.
4. To bolster word-level reading skill, encourage spelling/writing, right from the start.
5. Teach sounding-out, right from the start.
6. Provide beginning readers with ample opportunity to practice reading words that are consistent with their phonics instruction.
7. As students' decoding of short words reaches proficiency, teach strategies for reading multisyllabic words.
8. Find ways to provide more instruction in decoding for those who need it.

Promoting Orthographic Reading Skill (Fluency)

Fluent reading is an important aspect of reading ability for two reasons. First, slow, effortful reading ruins motivation to read and reduces the chances that individuals will choose reading over other activities. Second, reading fluency and comprehension are intertwined; slow reading detracts from comprehension. Children should achieve a level of word reading that is relatively effortless.

Relative to age peers, students with RD have far fewer words stored in memory, in part because their limited decoding skills result in fewer successful independent learning trials, and in part because they spend less time reading and cover less ground when they do read. And most discouraging to these students (and their teachers) is the extraordinarily high number of encounters with specific words needed to secure the words in orthographic memory. Lacking breadth of word knowledge, students with RD exhibit slow, halting, error-laced reading—that is, reading that lacks fluency. Although we understand a considerable amount about factors that contribute to fluency, a number of important questions remain about ways to facilitate its development in students with RD.

What level of decoding is necessary before broad reading will boost fluency? Because it is the principal mechanism by which individuals gain repeated exposure to words in print, wide reading is essential for developing fluency. However, in the early stages of reading acquisition, bypassing decoding instruction in favor of wide reading is a recipe for failure. Nevertheless, we lack information about the level of decoding proficiency necessary if wide reading is to have its intended effect on fluency. Chall (1996) proposed that reading fluency develops after students have mastered basic decoding skills. Research is needed on the effects of text reading practice for students at different stages of decoding proficiency.

How does text difficulty affect the development of fluency? That is, what level of reading accuracy in texts is required for students to develop fluency from practice in those texts? A variant on the previous question, this one focuses more on the reader-text interaction than on absolute levels of decoding proficiency. Instructional reading level (i.e., the minimum level of reading accuracy in a text for the student to benefit most from direct instruction) is said to range from 90 to 95%, depending on the reading authority.

Instructional level is itself something of an ambiguous term because it does not specify the nature of instruction. For example, must the first reading of texts used in repeated readings achieve a 95% level to maximize word learning and fluency growth? Is a 95% accuracy level required for "assisted reading" interventions (e.g., reading with the assistance of audiotapes or a more able reader)?

How should fluency instruction be organized? Teachers can organize fluency practice in a variety of ways. Studies examining repeated reading and continuous (nonrepeated) reading suggest that both produce gains (Dowhower, 1987; Samuels, 1979; Shany & Biemiller, 1995). Repeated reading provides students with multiple repetitions of the same words within a short time. Continuous reading exposes students to a wider volume of words (i.e., more different words). Very few studies comparing repeated and continuous reading have been performed with struggling readers, and only one of these was conducted with children in the age range covered by this paper. Vadasy (2001) obtained equivalent growth from repeated and

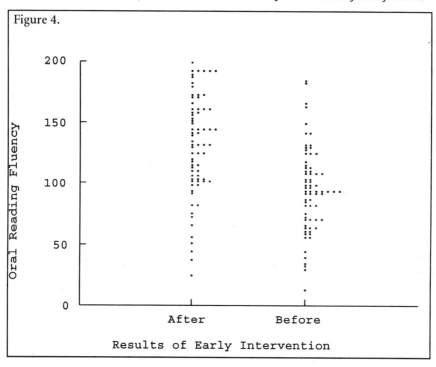

Figure 4.

Results of Early Intervention

continuous reading treatments with second-grade poor readers, consistent with findings obtained with slightly older (third grade) readers (Rasinski, 1990; Vaughn et al., 2000).

Criteria used in repeated readings treatments are also at issue, without a clear advantage for either performance criteria (number of words read per minute) or number of readings. Research is needed on target fluency levels used in repeated readings and the number of rereadings that optimize fluency development. Finally, attempts to improve fluency through reading word lists instead of texts also show beneficial effects, and it is not clear if text or word list practice produces better outcomes (Tan & Nicholson, 1997; van den Bosch, van Bon, & Schreuder, 1995).

How can we encourage students with R/LD to increase their volume of reading? Information is needed about how to make reading practice easier and more enjoyable for students who struggle with reading. Some possible areas to examine include the effectiveness and appeal of assisted reading with audiotape or computer software, and providing students with reading material that matches their interests—topical books and magazines, biographies, and books with the appeal of Harry Potter.

Does word study add to the effects of text reading practice? Assuming that increased text reading (with the aid of adults, tapes or software, or rereading opportunities) can raise the volume of words encountered in text, it should result in expanded reading vocabulary and faster word recognition. We still must determine whether extensive text practice by itself is sufficient to improve fluency, especially for students who do not learn words easily. For these students, some portion of reading instruction may still need to be reserved for word study. How should such word study by conducted to maximize its effects by focusing on words misread in text; words that have been categorized in ways to make spelling and pronunciation patterns more explicit; or subword units (Mercer, Campbell, Miller, Mercer, & Lane, 2000)?

Even though important questions remain unanswered about how best to promote reading fluency (e.g., an emphasis on repeated readings practice or on wide reading), teachers can make fluency an instructional focus. A short list of sensible actions follows:

Building Fluency: Sensible Actions

1. Find ways to make text reading easier for students with RD, using various forms of assisted reading (audiotapes, computer programs, choral reading, and partner reading).
2. Experiment with texts of various levels of difficulty.
3. Motivate students to read more by taking into account their interests, the variety of reading materials available to them, and the personal, linguistic, and cultural relevance of texts. Consult with the school librarian or someone knowledgeable about children and literature.
4. Develop areas of interest and teach students to feed those interests through reading.
5. Experiment with supplements to text reading such as word and subword study, word lists, and the proportion of time devoted to text- and word-level practice.
6. Measure students' text fluency regularly to inform instructional decision making.

FINAL THOUGHTS

Our understanding of RD derives primarily from an amalgamation of stage and verbal efficiency theories that link phonological processes to alphabetic reading skill to orthographic reading skill to language and reading comprehension. Empirical backing for the theoretical framework consists mainly of correlational research, supplemented with experiments that invite causal interpretations. This theoretical framework guides much of the research on early identification and early intervention for students with R/LD. Although we have learned much about early identification and treatment of young children with R/LD, we still have far to go. We know that some level of phonemic awareness is necessary for acquiring decoding skill, and that decoding skill is necessary for acquiring the enormous sight vocabulary needed for fluent reading. We also know that the majority of students with reading disabilities are weak in phonemic awareness, have difficulty decoding, and lack fluency.

However, it is fair to ask, have the assessment and instructional practices derived from this framework led to better outcomes for students with R/LDs? In our view, the answer is a qualified yes. "Yes," because early assessment of phonological awareness has increased our accuracy in identifying children who subsequently exhibit reading problems; because early training of phonological awareness facilitates decoding; and because explicit decoding instruction produces better orthographic reading skill. Nevertheless, we must qualify our "yes" answer because of lingering questions about the long-term benefits of early phonological training, explicit decoding instruction, and fluency training. For example, early intervention researchers report strong effects for phonological awareness training on decoding when measured immediately after phonological training, but statistically negligible effects 18 months later. Immediate effects resulting from a specific treatment approach are educationally important only if teachers can exploit them to produce long-term advances in reading skill.

Another cause for concern is the sizable number of children who exhibit small or indiscernible response to early intervention. Besides students who respond weakly to our interventions, we may also find children who respond well by learning the foundation skills that are the targets of early intervention, yet still fail to grow in reading ability at rates that keep them within the range of normal reading development over time. We may find other children who with ongoing, intense intervention by research or school staff can keep pace with peers in first or second grade, but falter as reading demands become more complex in the middle elementary years. Other students may struggle with reading throughout their schooling and into adulthood—regardless of early identification, early intervention, and relentless support. For some individuals, reading disability may be a chronic condition.

Finally, even with the explosion of early intervention research in R/LD, the practical knowledge derived about intervention is far more modest than many had hoped for. The good news is that researchers have been able to document a variety of specific intervention approaches that yield significantly better outcomes. Examples of interventions that surpass generic classroom instruction include Blachman's five-step instructional program for struggling first graders (Blachman et al., 1999);

O'Connor's experimental multilevel intervention program (O'Connor et al., 2001); *Peer-Assisted Learning Strategies* (Fuchs et al., 2001); Open Court's *Collection for Young Scholars* (Foorman et al., 1998); Phonological Awareness plus Synthetic Phonics (Torgesen et al., 1997), *Read, Write, and Type* (Torgesen, Wagner, Rashotte, & Herron, undated); *Spell Read P.A.T.* (Rashotte, MacPhee, & Torgesen, in press); and *Sound Partners* (Vadasy et al., 2000). These approaches which incorporate instruction in phonological awareness, explicit phonics, text reading, and spelling/writing lead to two generalizations. Classroom instruction and specialized interventions (e.g., tutoring) that include these elements (in particular, explicit phonics) reduce the number of children who demonstrate an R/LD profile at the end of treatment (kindergarten, first grade, or second grade). Longer and more intense treatments tend to give stronger effects, though some children still struggle with reading.

Without minimizing the importance of these generalizations, we cannot overlook the fact that similar generalizations existed before the current rash of early intervention studies. Decades ago, major studies of beginning reading instruction (Chall,1967; Bond & Dykstra, 1967; Becker & Gersten, 1982) concluded that beginning reading instruction characterized by explicit phonics, ample amounts of text reading, and spelling/writing produces better reading outcomes for novice and at-risk learners. Moreover, few practitioners would be startled by the conclusion that longer and more intense interventions lead to better outcomes for at-risk learners.

Alternative Approaches to Understanding and Treating Reading/Learning Disability

Are there alternative conceptualizations of reading acquisition that have potential for guiding interventions for students with R/LD? Granted, any alternative must make room for direct code instruction. The overwhelming volume of research attesting to its benefit has erased doubts about the role of explicit phonics instruction. Teachers are on board; Baumann, Hoffman, Duffy-Hester, and Ro (2000) report that more than 99% of primary-grade teachers believe explicit phonics instruction is essential. This is an important milestone.

Although word reading constitutes the primary roadblock for children with R/LD, special educators would commit a serious error were they to focus exclusively on word-level reading, shortchanging other aspects of reading competence. Word reading is not the end goal of literacy instruction; teaching phonics, even if combined with fluency-oriented instruction, will not suffice (i.e., there are limits to the amount of reading improvement possible from word-level training alone). Children must also gain proficiency in reading purposefully and selectively; reading between the lines; integrating text information with background knowledge; linking ideas within and across texts; establishing standards for coherence; monitoring and evaluating comprehension; repairing comprehension failures; finding, explaining, and learning information from text; and appropriating authors' ideas and discourse conventions for talking and writing about text. Fortunately, students need not accomplish all these skills in the primary grades, any more than they need to fully master decoding or fluent reading, but they should get a start on becoming mentally active, strategic readers and on learning how reading is used to cultivate knowledge, accomplish tasks, and enrich the mind.

Remaining alert to the larger goals of reading instruction compels us to think beyond teaching alphabetic and orthographic reading skills, necessary and critical though they be, to consider the nonphonics, nonfluency, text-level component of literacy instruction. How much emphasis should the text-level component receive in the early grades? What theoretical model should guide text-level instruction? Are there approaches to teaching text-level skills and dispositions that produce better outcomes for students with R/LD? Far less attention has been paid to this aspect of literacy learning and teaching, especially as it relates to students with R/LD.

Some of the most promising research from an alternative conception derives from a social constructivist perspective, exemplified in Englert and colleagues' Early Literacy Project (ELP; Englert, Raphael, & Mariage, 1994; Englert et al., 1995). Relative to instructional approaches derived from phonological processing and verbal efficiency perspectives, the ELP gives minimal consideration to explicit teaching of phonological awareness, phonics instruction, and fluency building. Although the ELP supplements literacy lessons and activities with phonics teaching, most code instruction is embedded within writing activities. The instructional emphases of phonologically driven, information-processing approaches, and social-constructivist teaching models show remarkably little overlap, each focusing on different but equally important aspects of literacy. Each approach has potential for complementing the other.

Success rates, even for state-of-the-art early intervention programs are not so high that researchers and practitioners can afford to dismiss alternative theoretical perspectives. The sizable number of unanswered and partially answered questions that we catalogued earlier testifies to our limited understanding of early intervention. Successful treatment and prevention of R/LD is the goal. Achieving that goal will take all our best ideas. Remaining open to different theoretical perspectives is both sensible and necessary, especially in the face of children who do not respond satisfactorily to conventional intervention approaches. Creative, responsive, relentless instruction will be needed for these children, and it must arrive before children with R/LD give up on the reading enterprise.

REFERENCES

Adams, M. J. (1990). *Beginning to read: Thinking and learning about print.* Cambridge, MA: MIT Press.

Allington, R. L., & Woodside-Jiron, H. (1998). Decodeable text in beginning reading: Are mandates and policy based on research? *ERS Spectrum, 16,* 2, 3–11.

Anderson, R. C., Wilson, P. T., & Fielding, L. G. (1988). Growth in reading and how children spend their time outside of school. *Reading Research Quarterly, 27,* 334–345.

Baddeley, A. (1986). *Working memory.* New York: Oxford University Press.

Badian, N. A. (1993). Phonemic awareness, naming, visual symbol processing, and reading. *Reading and Writing: An Interdisciplinary Journal, 5,* 87–100.

Badian, N. A. (1994). Preschool prediction: Orthographic and phonological skills, and reading. *Annals of Dyslexia, 44,* 3–25.

Badian, N. A. (1998). A validation of the role of preschool phonological and orthographic skills in the prediction of reading. *Journal of Learning Disabilities, 31,* 472–481.

Ball, E. W., & Blachman, B. A. (1991). Does phoneme segmentation training in kindergarten make a difference in early word recognition and developmental spelling? *Reading Research Quarterly, 26,* 49–66.

Baumann, J. F., Hoffman, J. V., Duffy-Hester, A. M., & Ro, A. M. (2000). The first R yesterday and today: U.S. elementary reading instruction practices reported by teachers and administrators. *Reading Research Quarterly, 35,* 338–377.

Becker, W. C., & Gersten, R. (1982). A follow-up of Follow-Through: The later effects of the direct instruction model on children in fifth and sixth grades. *American Educational Research Journal, 19,* 75–92.

Berninger, V. (1986). Normal variation in reading acquisition. *Perceptual and Motor Skills, 62,* 691–716.

Berninger, V. (1998). *Process assessment of the learner: Guides for intervention and Talking Letters Teacher Guide.* San Antonio, TX: Psychological Corporation.

Berninger, V., Abbott, R., Brooksher, R., Lemos, Z., Ogier, S., Zook, D., & Mostafapour, E. (2000). A connectionist approach to making the predictability of English orthography explicit to at-risk beginning readers: Evidence for alternative, effective strategies. *Developmental Neuropsychology, 17,* 241–271.

Blachman, B. A., Ball, E. W, Black, R. S., & Tangel, D. M. (1994). Kindergarten teachers develop phoneme awareness in low-income, inner-city classrooms. Does it make a difference? *Reading and Writing, 6,* 1–18.

Blachman, B. A., Tangel, D. M., Ball, E. W., Black, R., & McGraw, C. K. (1999). Developing phonological awareness and word recognition skills: A two-year intervention with low-income, inner-city children. *Reading and Writing: An Interdisciplinary Journal, 11,* 239–273.

Bond, G., & Dykstra, R. (1967). The cooperative research program in first-grade reading instruction. *Reading Research Quarterly, 2,* 5–142.

Bowers, P. G., & Swanson, L. B. (1991). Naming speed deficits in reading ability: Multiple measures of a singular process. *Journal of Experimental Child Psychology, 51,* 195–219.

Bowey, J. A., & Patel, R. K. (1988). Metalinguistic ability and early reading achievement. *Applied Psycholinguistics, 9,* 367–383.

Bradley, L., & Bryant, P. E. (1983). Categorizing sounds and learning to read: A causal connection. *Nature, 301,* 419–421.

Bradley, L., & Bryant, P. E. (1985). *Rhyme and reason in reading and spelling.* International Academy for Research in Learning Disabilities Monograph Series No. 1. Ann Arbor: University of Michigan Press.

Brophy, J. (2000). Beyond Balance: Goal awareness, developmental progressions, tailoring to the context, and supports for teachers in ideal reading and literacy programs. In B. M. Taylor, M. G. Graves, & P. van den Broek (Eds.), *Reading for Meaning* (pp. 170–192). New York: Teachers College Press.

Brown, A. L., & Smiley, S. S. (1977). Rating the importance of structural units of prose passages: A problem of meta-cognitive development. *Child Development, 48,* 1–8.

Bus, A. G., & Van Ijzendoorn, M. H. (1999). Phonological awareness and early reading: A meta-analysis of experimental training studies. *Journal of Educational Psychology, 91,* 403–414.

Byrne, B., & Fielding-Barnsley, R. (1991). Evaluation of a program to teach phonemic awareness to young children. *Journal of Educational Psychology, 83,* 451–455.

Byrne, B., & Fielding-Barnsley, R. (1993). Evaluation of a program to teach phonemic awareness to young children: A 1-year follow-up. *Journal of Educational Psychology, 85,* 104–111.

Byrne, B., & Fielding-Barnsley, R. (1995). Evaluation of a program to teach phonemic awareness to young children: A 2- and 3-year follow-up and a new preschool trial. *Journal of Educational Psychology, 87,* 488–503.

Carnine, D., Silbert, J., & Kame'enui, E. (1997). *Direct instruction reading* (3rd ed.). New York: Merrill.

Catts, H. (1991). Early identification of dyslexia: Evidence from a follow-up study of speech-language impaired children. *Annals of Dyslexia, 41*, 163–177.

Chall, J. S. (1967). *Learning to read: The great debate.* New York: McGraw-Hill.

Chall, J. S. (1996). *Stages of reading development.* (2nd ed.). Fort Worth, TX: Harcourt-Brace.

Coleman, J. M., & Dover, G. M. (1993). The RISK Screening Test: Using kindergarten teachers' ratings to predict future placement in resource classrooms. *Exceptional Children, 59*, 468–477.

Coltheart, M. (1978). Lexical access in simple reading tasks. In G. Underwood (Ed.), *Strategies of information processing.* London: Academic Press.

Compton, D. L. (2000). Modeling the response of normally achieving and at-risk first-grade children to word reading instruction. *Annals of Dyslexia, 50*, 53–84.

Cunningham, A. E. (1990). Explicit versus implicit instruction in phonemic awareness. *Journal of Experimental Child Psychology, 50*, 429–444.

deBettencourt, L., & Zigmond, N. (1990). The learning disabled secondary school dropout: What teachers should know. What teachers can do. *Teacher Education and Special Education, 13*, 17–20.

deBettencourt, L., Zigmond, N., & Thornton, H. (1989). Follow-up of postsecondary-age rural learning disabled graduates and dropouts. *Exceptional Children, 56*, 40–49.

Deshler, D., Schumaker, J., Alley, G., Warner, M., & Clark, F. (1982). Learning disabilities in adolescent and young adult populations: Research implications. *Focus on Exceptional Children, 15*, 1–12.

Doi, L. M., & Manis, F. R. (1996, April). *The impact of speeded naming ability on reading performance.* Poster presented at the annual meeting of the Society for the Scientific Study of Reading, New York.

Dowhower, S. L. (1987). Effects of repeated reading on second-grade transitional readers' fluency and comprehension. *Reading Research Quarterly, 22*, 389–406.

Ehri, L. C. (1979). Linguistic insight: Threshold of reading acquisition. In T. Waller & G. MacKinnon (Eds.), *Reading research: Advances in research and theory* (Vol. 1, pp. 63–114). New York: Academic Press.

Ehri, L. C. (1992). Reconceptualizing the development of sight word reading and its relationship to recoding. In P. B. Gough, L. C. Ehri, & R. Treiman (Eds.), *Reading acquisition* (pp. 107–143). Hillsdale, NJ: Erlbaum.

Ehri, L. C. (1998). Grapheme-phoneme knowledge is essential for learning to read words in English. In J. L. Metsala & L. C. Ehri (Eds.), *Word recognition in beginning literacy* (pp.3–40). Mahwah, NJ: Lawrence Erlbaum Associates.

Elbro, C. (1996). Early linguistic abilities and reading development: A review and a hypothesis. *Reading and Writing: An Interdisciplinary Journal, 8*, 453–485.

Elbro, C., Borstrom, I., & Petersen, D. K. (1998). Predicting dyslexia from kindergarten: The importance of distinctness of phonological representations of lexical items. *Reading Research Quarterly, 33*, 36–60.

Eloknin, D. B. (1973). USSR. In J. Downing (Ed.), *Comparative reading: Cross-national studies of behavior and processes in reading and writing* (pp. 551–579). New York: MacMillan.

Englert, C. S., Garmon, A., Mariage, T., Rozendal, M., Tarrant, K., & Urba, J. (1995). The Early Literacy Project: Connecting across the literacy curriculum. *Learning Disability Quarterly, 18*, 253–275.

Englert, C. S., Raphael, T. E., & Mariage, T. V. (1994). Developing a school-based discourse for literacy learning: A principled search for understanding. *Learning Disability Quarterly, 17*, 2–32.

Fawcett, A. J., Singleton, C. H., & Peer, L. (1998). Advances in early years screening for dyslexia in the United Kingdom. *Annals of Dyslexia, 48*, 57–88.

Felton, R. H. (1992). Early identification of children at risk for reading disabilities. *Topics in Early Childhood Special Education, 12*, 212–229.

Felton, R. H., & Wood, F. B. (1992). A reading level match study of nonword reading skills in poor readers with varying IQ. *Journal of Learning Disabilities, 25*, 318–326.

Fielding-Barnsley, R. (1997). Explicit instruction in decoding benefits children high in phonemic awareness and alphabetic knowledge. *Scientific Studies of Reading, 1*, 85–98.

Fletcher, J. M., Shaywitz, S. E., Shankweiler, D. P., Katz, L., Liberman, I. Y., Stuebing, K.K., Francis, D. J., Fowler, A. E., & Shaywitz, B. A. (1994). Cognitive profiles of reading disability: Comparisons of discrepancy and low achievement definitions. *Journal of Educational Psychology, 86*, 6–23.

Foorman, B. R., Francis, D. J., Fletcher, J. M., Schatschneider, C., & Mehta, P. (1998). The role of instruction in learning to read: Preventing reading failure in at-risk children. *Journal of Educational Psychology, 90*, 37–55.

Fuchs, D., & Fuchs, L. S. (2001, June). *The respective contributions of phonological awareness and decoding to reading development in Title 1 and Non-Title 1 schools.* Paper presented at the annual meeting of the Society for the Scientific Study of Reading, Boulder, CO.

Fuchs, D., Fuchs, L. S., Thompson, A., Al Otaiba, S., Yen, L., Yang, N., Braun, M., & O'Connor, R. E. (2001a). Is reading important in reading-readiness programs? A randomized field trial. *Journal of Educational Psychology, 93*, 251–267.

Fuchs, D., Fuchs, L. S., Thompson, A., Yen, L., Al Otaiba, S., Nyman, K., Yang, N., & Svenson, E. (2001b). *A randomized field trial to explore the effectiveness of beginning reading program that excludes phonological awareness training.* Paper presented at the annual meeting of the American Educational Research Association, Seattle.

Good, R., Simmons, D., & Kame'enui, E. (2001). The importance and decision-making utility and a continuum of fluency-based indicators of foundational reading skills for third-grade high stakes outcomes. *Scientific Studies in Reading, 5*, 257–288.

Goswami, U., & Bryant, P. (1990). *Phonological skills and learning to read.* London: Erlbaum.

Gough, P. B., & Walsh, M. (1991). Chinese, Phoenicians, and the orthographic cipher of English. In S. Brady & D. Shankweiler (Eds.), *Phonological processes in literacy* (pp. 199–209). Hillsdale, NJ: Lawrence Erlbaum Associates.

Hurford, D. P., Johnston, M., Nepote, P., Hampton, S., Moore, S., Neal, J., et al. (1993). Early identification and remediation of phonological-processing deficits in first-grade children at risk for reading disabilities. *Journal of Learning Disabilities, 27*, 647–659.

Iversen, S., & Tunmer, W. E. (1993). Phonological processing skills and the Reading Recovery program. *Journal of Educational Psychology, 85*, 112–126.

Jenkins, J. R., Fuchs, L. S., Espin, C., van den Broek, P., & Deno, S. (2000, February). *Task and performance dimensions of word reading.* Paper presented at the Pacific Coast Research Conference, La Jolla, California.

Juel, C. (1988). Learning to read and write: A longitudinal study of 54 children from first through fourth grades. *Journal of Educational Psychology, 80*, 437–447.

Juel, C., & Roper-Schneider, D. (1985). The influence of basal readers on first grade reading. *Reading Research Quarterly, 20*, 134–152.

Kaminski, R. A., & Good, R. H., III. (1996). Toward a technology for assessing basic early literacy skills. *School Psychology Review, 25*, 215–227.

Landerl, K., Wimmer, H., & Frith, U. (1997). The impact of orthographic consistency on dyslexia: A German-English comparison. *Cognition, 63*, 315–334.

Leather, C. V., & Henry, L. A. (1994). Working memory span and phonological awareness tasks as predictors of early reading ability. *Journal of Experimental Child Psychology, 58*, 88–111.

Lindamood, C. H., & Lindamood, P. C. (1984). *Auditory Discrimination in Depth.* Austin, TX: Pro-Ed.

Lovett, M. W., Lacerenza, L., Borden, S. L., Frijters, J. C., Steinbech, K. A., & De Palma, M. (2000). Components of effective remediation for developmental reading disabilities: Combining phonological and strategy-based instruction to improve outcome. *Journal of Educational Psychology, 92,* 263–283.

Lundberg, I., Frost, J., & Petersen, O. (1988). Effects of an extensive program for stimulating phonological awareness in preschool children. *Reading Research Quarterly, 23,* 263–284.

MacDonald, G. W., & Cornwall, A. (1995). The relationship between phonological awareness and reading and spelling achievement eleven years later. *Journal of Learning Disabilities, 28,* 523–527.

MacLean, M., Bryant, P., & Bradley, L. (1988). Rhymes, nursery rhymes and reading in early childhood. In K. Stanovich (Ed.), *Children's reading and the development of phonological awareness* (pp. 11–37). Detroit: Wayne State University Press.

Majsterek, D. J., & Ellenwood, A. E. (1995). Phonological awareness and beginning reading: Evaluation of a school-based screening procedure. *Journal of Learning Disabilities, 28,* 449–456.

Mann, V. A., & Ditunno, P. (1990). Phonological deficiencies: Effective predictors of future reading problems. In G. Pavlides (Ed.), *Perspectives on dyslexia* (Vol. 2, pp. 105–131). New York: Wiley.

Mantzicopoulos, P. Y., & Morrison, D. (1994). Early prediction of reading achievement: Exploring the relationship of cognitive and noncognitive measures to inaccurate classifications of at-risk status. *Remedial and Special Education, 15,* 244–251.

Mathes, P. G., Torgesen, J. K., & Allor, J. H. (2001). The effects of peer-assisted literacy strategies for first-grade readers with and without additional computer-assisted instruction in phonological awareness. *American Educational Research Journal, 38,* 371–410.

Mercer, C., Campbell, K., Miller, D., Mercer, K., & Lane, H. (2000). Effects of a reading fluency intervention for middle-schoolers with specific learning disabilities. *Learning Disabilities Research and Practice, 15,* 179–189.

Murray, B. A., Smith, K. A., & Murray, G. G. (2000). The test of phoneme identities: Predicting alphabetic insight in prealphabetic readers. *Journal of Literacy Research, 32,* 421–447.

National Reading Panel. (2000). *Summary report.* Washington, DC: National Institute of Child Health & Human Development.

Nicolson, R. I., & Fawcett, A. J. (1996). *The dyslexia early screening test.* London: The Psychological Corporation.

O'Connor, R. E. (2000). Increasing the intensity of intervention in kindergarten and first grade. *Learning Disabilities Research and Practice, 15,* 43–54.

O'Connor, R. E., Fulmer, D., Harty, K., & Bell, K. (2001, April). *Total awareness: Reducing the severity of reading disability.* Presented at the American Educational Research Conference, Seattle, WA.

O'Connor, R. E., & Jenkins, J. R. (1999). The prediction of reading disabilities in kindergarten and first grade. *Scientific Studies of Reading, 3,* 159–197.

O'Connor, R., Jenkins, J. R., Slocum, T., & Leicester, N. (1993). Teaching phonological awareness to young children with disabilities. *Exceptional Children, 59*(6), 532–546.

O'Connor, R. E., Notari-Syverson, N., & Vadasy, P. (1996). Ladders to literacy: The effects of teacher-led phonological activities for kindergarten children with and without disabilities. *Exceptional Children, 63,* 117–130.

O'Connor, R. E., Notari-Syverson, N., & Vadasy, P. (1998). *Ladders to literacy: A kindergarten activity book.* Baltimore: Paul H. Brookes.

Open Court Reading. (1995). *Collections for young scholars.* Chicago and Peru, IL: SRA/McGraw-Hill.

Perfetti, C. A. (1985). *Reading ability.* New York: Oxford University Press.

Perfetti, C. A. (1992). The representation problem in reading acquisition. In P. Gough, L. Ehri, & R. Trieman (Eds.), *Reading Acquisition* (pp. 145–174). Mahwah, NJ: Erlbaum.

Perfetti, C., Beck, I., Bell, L., & Hughes, C. (1987). Phonemic knowledge and learning to read are reciprocal: A longitudinal study of first grade children. *Merrill-Palmer Quarterly, 33,* 283–319.

Perfetti, C.A., & Hogaboam, T. (1975). Relationship between single word decoding and reading comprehension skills. *Journal of Educational Psychology, 67,* 461–469.

Peyton, J., Jenkins, J.R., Vadasy, P. F., & Sanders. L. (2001). *Effects of more- and less-decodable text on reading development of at-risk first grade students.* Manuscript in preparation. Seattle, WA: Washington Research Institute.

Rack, J. P., Snowling, M. J., & Olson, R. K. (1992). The nonword reading deficit in developmental dyslexia: A review. *Reading Research Quarterly, 27,* 29–53.

Rapala, M. M., & Brady, S. (1990). Reading ability and short-term memory: The role of phonological processing. *Reading and Writing: An Interdisciplinary Journal, 2,* 1–25.

Rashotte, C. A., MacPhee, K., & Torgesen, J. (in press). The effectiveness of a group reading instruction program with poor readers in multiple grades. *Learning Disability Quarterly.*

Rasinski, T. V. (1990). Effects of repeated reading and listening-while-reading on reading fluency. *Journal of Educational Research, 83,* 147–150.

Reitsma, P. (1983). Printed word learning in beginning readers. *Journal of Experimental Child Psychology, 36,* 321–339.

Samuels, S. J. (1979). The method of repeated readings. *The Reading Teacher, 32,* 403–408.

Scarborough, H. S. (1990). Very early language deficits in dyslexic children. *Child Development, 61,* 1728–1743.

Scarborough, H. S. (1995, March). *The fate of phonemic awareness beyond the elementary school years.* Paper presented at the biannual meeting of the Society for Research in Child Development, Indianapolis, IN.

Seidenberg, M. S., & McClelland, J. L. (1989). A distributed, developmental model of word recognition and naming. *Psychological Review, 96,* 523–568.

Shankweiler, D., & Liberman, I.Y. (1989). Phonology and reading disability: Solving the reading puzzle (pp.1–33). *IARLD Monograph Series.* Ann Arbor, MI: University of Michigan Press.

Shankweiler, D., Lundquist, E., Katz, L., Stuebing, K. K., Fletcher, J. M., Brady, S., Fowler, A., Dreyer, L. G., Marchione, K. E., Shaywitz, S. E., & Shaywitz, B. A. (1999). Comprehension and decoding: Patterns of association in children with reading disabilities. *Scientific Studies of Reading, 3,* 69–94.

Shany, M. T., & Biemiller, A. (1995). Assisted reading practice: Effects on performance for poor readers in grades 3 and 4. *Reading Research Quarterly, 30,* 382–395.

Share, D. L. (1995). Phonological recoding and self-teaching: Sine qua non of reading acquisition. *Cognition, 55,* 151–218.

Share, D., Jorm, A., MacLean, R., & Matthews, R. (1984). Sources of individual differences in reading acquisition. *Journal of Educational Psychology, 76,* 1309–1324.

Silver, A. A., & Hagin, R. A. (1981). *SEARCH manual.* New York: Wiley.

Simmons, D. C., Kuykendall, K., King, K., Cornachione, C., & Kame'enui, E. (2000). Implementation of a schoolwide reading improvement model: "No one ever told us it would be this hard!" *Learning Disabilities Research and Practice, 15,* 92–100.

Spear-Swerling, L., & Sternberg, R. (1994). The road not taken: An integrative theoretical model of reading disability. *Journal of Learning Disabilities, 27,* 91–103, 122.

Spector, J. E. (1992). Predicting progress in beginning reading: Dynamic assessment of phonemic awareness. *Journal of Educational Psychology, 84,* 353–363.

Stahl, S. A., & Murray, B. A. (1994). Defining phonological awareness and its relationship to early reading. *Journal of Educational Psychology, 86,* 221–234.

Stanovich, K. (1986). Matthew effects in reading: Some consequences of individual differences in the acquisition of literacy. *Reading Research Quarterly, 21,* 360–406.

Stanovich, K., Cunningham, A., & Cramer, B. (1984). Assessing phonological awareness in kindergarten children: Issues of task comparability. *Journal of Experimental Child Psychology, 38,* 175–190.

Tan, A., & Nicholson, T. (1997). Flashcards revisited: Training poor readers to read words faster improves their comprehension of text. *Journal of Educational Psychology, 59,* 276–288.

Torgesen, J. K., Alexander, A. W., Wagner, R. K., Rashotte, C. A., Voeller, K., Conway, T., & Rose, E. (2001). Intensive remedial instruction for children with severe reading disabilities: Immediate and long-term outcomes from two instructional approaches. *Journal of Learning Disabilities, 34,* 33–58, 78.

Torgesen, J. K., Burgess, S., Wagner, R. K., & Rashotte, C. (1996, April). *Predicting phonologically based reading disabilities: What is gained by waiting a year?* Poster presented at the annual meeting of the Society for the Scientific Study of Reading, New York.

Torgesen, J. K., & Mathes, P. G. (2000). *A Basic Guide to Understanding, Assessing, and Teaching Phonological Awareness.* Austin, TX: Pro-Ed.

Torgesen, J., Morgan, S., & Davis, C. (1992). Effects of two types of phonological awareness training on word learning in Kindergarten children. *Journal of Educational Psychology, 84,* 364–370.

Torgesen, J. K., Wagner, R. K., & Rashotte, C. A. (1994). Longitudinal studies of phonological processing and reading. *Journal of Learning Disabilities, 27,* 276–286.

Torgesen, J. K., Wagner, R. K., & Rashotte, C. A. (1997). Prevention and remediation of severe reading disabilities: Keeping the end in mind. *Scientific Studies in Reading, 1,* 217–234.

Torgesen, J., Wagner, R., Rashotte, C., & Herron, J. (undated). Summary of outcomes from first-grade study with *Read, Write, and Type* and *Auditory Discrimination in Depth* instruction and software. Tallahassee, FL: Florida State University.

Torgesen, J. K., Wagner, R. K., Rashotte, C. A., Rose, E., Lindamood, P., Conway, T., & Garvan, C. (1999). Preventing reading failure in young children with phonological processing disabilities: Group and individual responses to instruction. *Journal of Educational Psychology, 91*, 579–593.

Tunmer, W. E., & Chapman, J. W. (1998). Language prediction skill, phonological recoding ability, and beginning reading. In C. Hulme & R. M. Joshi (Eds), *Reading and Spelling: Development and Disorders* (pp. 33–67). Mawah, NJ: Erlbaum.

Tunmer, W., Herriman, M., & Nesdale, A. (1988). Metalinguistic abilities and beginning reading. *Reading Research Quarterly, 23*, 134–158.

Tymms, P. (1999). Baseline assessment, value-added and the prediction of reading. *Journal of Research in Reading, 22*, 27–36.

Uhry, J. (1993). Predicting low reading from phonological awareness and classroom print. *Educational Assessment, 1*, 349–368.

Vadasy, P. F. (2001). *Approaches to comprehension instruction*. Unpublished manuscript. Seattle, WA: Washington Research Institute.

Vadasy, P. F., Jenkins, J. R., Firebaugh, M., Pool, K., O'Connor, R., Wayne, S., & Peyton, J. (2001). *Sound Partners: A Reading Tutoring Program for First-Grade At-Risk Readers.* Seattle, WA: Washington Research Institute.

Vadasy, P. F., Jenkins, J. R., & Pool, K. (2000). Effects of a first-grade tutoring program in phonological and early reading skills. *Journal of Learning Disabilities, 33*, 579–590.

van den Bosch, K., van Bon, W., & Schreuder, R. (1995). Poor readers' decoding skills: Effects of training with limited exposure duration. *Reading Research Quarterly, 30*, 110–125.

Vandervelden, M. C., & Siegel, L. (1997). Teaching phonological processing skills in early literacy: A developmental approach. *Learning Disabilities Quarterly, 20*, 63–81.

Vaughn, S., Chard, D. J., Pedrotty-Bryant, D., Coleman, M., Tyler, B., Linan-Thompson, S., & Kousekanani, K. (2000). Fluency and comprehension interventions for third-grade students. *Remedial and Special Education, 21*, 325–335.

Vellutino, F. R., Scanlon, D. M., Sipay, E., Small, S., Pratt, A., Chen, R., & Denckla, M. (1996). Cognitive profiles of difficult-to-remediate and readily remediated poor readers: Early intervention as a vehicle for distinguishing between cognitive and experiental deficits as basic causes of specific reading disability. *Journal of Educational Psychology, 88*, 601–638.

Wagner, R. K., Balthazor, M., Hurley, S., Morgan, S., Rashotte, C., Shaner, R., Simmons, K., & Stage, S. (1987). The nature of prereaders' phonological processing abilities. *Cognitive Development, 2*, 355–373.

Wagner, R. K., & Torgesen, J. T. (1987). The nature of phonological processing and its causal role in the acquisition of reading skills. *Psychological Bulletin, 101*, 192–212.

Wagner, R. K., Torgesen, J. K., Laughon, P., Simmons, K., & Rashotte, C. A. (1993). Development of young readers' phonological processing abilities. *Journal of Educational Psychology, 85*, 83–103.

Wagner, R. K., Torgesen, J. K., & Rashotte, C. A. (1999). *The Comprehensive Test of Phonological Processing.* Austin, TX: Pro-Ed.

Wagner, R. K., Torgesen, J. K., Rashotte, C. A., Hecht, S. A., Barker, T. A., Burgess, S. R., Donahue, J., & Garon, T. (1997). Changing causal relations between phonological processing abilities and word-level reading as children develop from beginning to skilled readers: A 5-year longitudinal study. *Developmental Psychology, 33*, 468–479.

Wimmer, H. (1993). Characteristics of developmental dyslexia in a regular writing system. *Applied Psycholinguistics, 14*, 1–33.

Wimmer, H. (1996). The nonword reading deficit in developmental dyslexia: Evidence from German children. *Journal of Experimental Child Psychology, 61*, 80–90.

Wise, B. W., Ring, J., & Olson, R. K. (2000). Individual differences in gains from computer-assisted remedial reading. *Journal of Experimental Child Psychology, 77*, 197–235.

Wolf, M. (1991). Naming speed and reading: The contribution of the cognitive neurosciences. *Reading Research Quarterly, 26*, 123–141.

Wolf, M., & Bowers, P. (1999). The double-deficit hypothesis for the developmental dyslexias. *Journal of Educational Psychology, 91*, 415–438.

Woodcock, R. W. (1987). *Woodcock Reading Mastery Tests—Revised.* Circle Pines, MN: American Guidance Service.

Yopp, H. K. (1988). The validity and reliability of phonemic awareness tests. *Reading Research Quarterly, 23,* 159–177.

Zigmond, N. (1990). Rethinking secondary school programs for students with learning disabilities. *Focus on Exceptional Children, 23,* 1–24.

CLASSROOM PREVENTION THROUGH DIFFERENTIATED INSTRUCTION: RESPONSE TO JENKINS AND O'CONNOR

Barbara R. Foorman, The University of Texas-Houston Health Science Center &
Christopher Schatschneider, University of Houston

Jenkins and O'Connor (this volume) provide us with an excellent review of the literature on early identification and intervention for young children at risk for reading difficulties. First, critical elements of skilled reading are delineated: phonological awareness, graphophonemic knowledge, decoding or alphabetic reading skill, automatic word recognition, fluency, and language comprehension. Second, research on early screening is reviewed and "sensible actions" for identifying children at risk for reading/learning disabilities are listed. Finally, the early intervention literature is reviewed and "sensible actions" for achieving each critical element of skilled reading are proposed. In the concluding section, Jenkins and O'Connor urge us to expand the instructional emphases of phonologically driven, information-processing approaches to accommodate alternative theoretical perspectives such as that of constructivist teaching in our efforts toward the common goal of prevention and treatment of reading/learning disabilities.

My response is organized around three major points. First, an early emphasis on writing should be common ground for *both* information-processing and constructivist approaches because skillful reading entails mastery of one's writing system (Rayner, Foorman, Perfetti, Pesetsky, & Seidenberg, in press). Second, prediction of risk status for reading difficulties involves a somewhat different set of variables and assessment schedule than identification of reading disabilities. Third, this distinction between risk and disability has implications for intervention.

Skillful Reading Entails Mastering One's Writing System

Cultures invent writing systems to map speech onto print. The mapping may be at the level of morphemes as in Chinese characters, at the level of syllables as in Japanese kana, or at the level of phonemes as in the English alphabet. As literate members of societies teach their children to read, they help them master the writing system through reinvention of the sound-symbol connections. The invented spellings of young writers reveal the intentions and conventions of the mapping. Take, for example, Moats' (1995) example of a first grader's spelling of *think* across the year: TGK, TANGK, THINGK, THIGK. The ability to phonemically segment sounds in speech and represent them conventionally develops over time. This is apparent from (a) the transition from /t/ to the digraph /th/, (b) the misrepresentation of the nasal /n/ with the letter *g* from the spelling of the phoneme /ng/, and (c) the changing spelling of the co-articulated vowel plus sonorant, *in*.

By organizing phonics instruction around speech sounds and their orthographic representations, we can instructionally facilitate the student's reinvention of the alphabetic writing system. But many basals approach beginning reading instruction from a perspective of grapheme-to-phoneme rather than phoneme-to-grapheme. This can lead to confusion. For example, in one basal the following keywords are used to teach *o*: *of, once, on, orange, off, open, out*. Moats (2000) warns that "If children are shown that words starting with the letter *o* begin with as many as six different sounds, including the /w/ in *once*, they may surmise that letters are irrelevant to sound and must be learned by some magical memory process" (p. 150). But, even in basals thoughtfully oriented around speech sounds, there are decisions. Should rules be taught for all the spelling patterns for each of the approximately 40 phonemes of American English? For the "long a" alone there are eight patterns (as in *make, rain, say, they, baby, eight, vein, great*). Or, do all phonemes need attention? For example, should the vowel sounds in *book* and *moon* be taught separately or taught in the same lesson and then contrasted? What about "short o" as in *fox* and *frog*? A reasonable approach is to keep *fox* as the keyword but to create a "set for diversity" (Gibson & Levin, 1975) within the lesson by contrasting spelling patterns with the two phonemes, noting that in the northeastern part of the United States *fox* and *frog* (and *card* and *caught*) all share the same vowel sound (see Foorman, Breier, & Fletcher, in press, for further discussion).

In sum, Jenkins' and O'Connor's call for an emphasis on writing need not be a plea for appreciation of a constructivist paradigm. There is no reason to appeal to extremes in order to establish the need for specific instructional practices. Writing is at the heart of mastering the alphabetic system. Writing starts with the encoding of speech to print. From its initial phonological emphasis, writing develops to entail verification of orthographic patterns that merge phonological, morphological, and conventional information. A complete representation of a word's spelling in memory will enhance the speed and accuracy with which it is recognized (Ehri, 1998; Perfetti, 1992). Thus, the writing of words supports the reading of words and, over time, builds toward the writing of text, which can support the comprehension of text. An early emphasis on writing is common ground whatever one's philosophical perspective.

PREDICTING RISK VERSUS DISABILITY

Jenkins and O'Connor discuss the tradeoffs between underidentification and overidentification of reading disabilities. They point out that no set of predictors is 100% accurate and recommend setting liberal cutoff scores so that no child who develops reading disability is missed. Although this approach results in sizable overidentification, we agree with this strategy so long as the identification results in a risk status that triggers differentiated instruction within regular education rather than a special education label. Jenkins and O'Connor recommend two ways that overidentification can be minimized. One way is to administer prediction batteries serially so as to measure growth in response to instruction. The other way is to interweave screening and intervention so that response to intervention can readily be discerned and the predictive net adjusted accordingly. Both approaches make sense and are embodied in the *Texas Primary Reading Inventory* (TPRI; Texas Education Agency, 2000), an early reading assessment used in 92% of the approximately 1,100 districts in Texas. The development and implementation of the TPRI will be described briefly to illustrate how use of the instrument in Texas relates to national concerns about identification and intervention.

The TPRI (Foorman, Fletcher, & Francis, in press) was developed in the 1997–1998 school year as a result of legislation requiring that all children in kindergarten through grade 2 be individually administered a diagnostic instrument by their teacher for the purpose of informing instruction. The legislation expressly excluded early reading assessment from the accountability system or the teacher appraisal and incentive system in Texas. The goal was to identify children at risk for reading difficulties and to encourage early intervention.

The TPRI consists of a screen and an inventory. The inventory is aligned with the state curriculum standards and consists of the following components:

- Book and Print Awareness—knowledge of the function of print and of the characteristics of books and other print materials
- Phonemic Awareness—the ability to detect and identify individual sounds within spoken words
- Graphophonemic Knowledge—the recognition of the letters of the alphabet and the understanding of sound-spelling relations
- Reading Accuracy and Fluency—the ability to read grade-appropriate text accurately and fluently
- Reading Comprehension—the understanding of what has been read

The purpose of the screening component is to identify children who do *not* need the inventory so that the teacher can focus her time on the children who do. As discussed earlier, cut points for the screening items were purposely set low so that overidentification rather than underidentification would occur. As a consequence, overidentification rates in kindergarten and grade 1 range from about 35% in kindergarten and beginning of grade 1 to about 25% at the end of grade 1 and to less than 15% at the beginning of grade 2. These rates could be reduced but then rates for underidentification, purposely kept below 10% on the TPRI, would increase. Such an approach of minimizing underidentification is sensible when the consequence of overidentification is that the teacher administers the inventory to the child.

The screen consists of those measures most predictive of reading success in a longitudinal sample of 945 children in a metropolitan school district in Texas assessed four times a year for assessment of literacy-related growth and at the end of grades 1 and 2 for reading and spelling achievement (TPRI Technical Manual, 1998). The items on the screen were those items selected on the basis of Item Response Theory (IRT) from a larger battery of items that discriminate success and failure on reading outcomes at the end of grades 1 and 2. The larger battery included measures of phonological awareness, phonological (working) memory, rapid naming of letters and objects, expressive and receptive syntax, vocabulary, knowledge of letter names and sounds, and perceptual skills. For predictions involving grades 1 and 2, the Woodcock-Johnson Broad Reading cluster, which consists of letter-word identification and cloze-based reading comprehension, was used. The criteria for risk were arbitrarily set at grade equivalents of 1.4 or lower at the end of grade 1 and 2.4 or lower at the end of grade 2 on the Woodcock-Johnson (Woodcock & Johnson, 1989). In grade 1 this grade equivalent represents the 22nd percentile for Basic Reading and the 18th percentile for Broad Reading. In grade 2 it represents the 35th percentile. The cut point was deliberately set higher in grade 2 because of the greater stability of the prediction equations and the limited time available to reach the Texas goal of reading on grade level or above by the end of grade 3.

The TPRI screening items are the following: phonological awareness and its theoretically related construct of letter-sound knowledge in kindergarten and the beginning of grade 1; and word reading at the beginning and end of grade 1 and beginning of grade 2. These predictors are similar to those identified in the longitudinal studies by O'Connor and Jenkins (1999) and by Wood, Hill, & Meyer (2001) and could easily be identified in other completed longitudinal studies (e.g., Torgesen, in press; Vellutino, Scanlon, & Lyon, 2000). These longitudinal studies all reveal that the predictiveness of phonological awareness skills depends on how and when such skills are assessed—relations that are obscured when correlations are averaged across studies, as in Scarborough (1998). In the analysis of phonological awareness tasks used in the TPRI—tasks drawn from a prepublication version of the *Comprehensive Test of Phonological Processing* (Wagner, Torgesen, & Rashotte, 1999)—Schatschneider, Francis, Foorman, Fletcher, & Mehta (1999) found that phonological awareness was a unitary construct that varied on a continuum of complexity. The simplest assessments involve initial sound comparison and rhyming, while the most complex assessments involve segmenting and blending of multiple phonemes. Moreover, assessments at the beginning of kindergarten may be less reliable than assessments in the middle or end of kindergarten, reflecting the child's need to acclimate to the learning environment (Fletcher et al., in press).

Two other measures proved predictive but were not included in the TPRI (Schatschneider, Fletcher, Foorman, & Francis, 2001). One of these—letter naming—was predictive at the beginning of kindergarten but not by the middle and end when the TPRI is first administered, because of ceiling effects. The other variable—rapid naming of letters—is comparable in its predictiveness to phonological awareness and knowledge of letter sounds from the end of kindergarten to grade 1 or grade 2 outcomes. Rapid naming of letters was not included on the TPRI screen because of difficulty in obtaining adequate reliability of administration, especially when teachers are the administrators and the children are in kindergarten or the beginning of grade 1. Finally, what about vocabulary as a predictor of risk? It is one of the marker variables that Torgesen (in press) recommends in the assessment of reading disability, along with phonological awareness, rapid naming of letters, and phonological memory. Vocabulary did not add substantially in the prediction equations of Schatschneider et al. (2001), but this study was a normative sample where children were not selected for reading disabilities. When large samples of children with reading disabilities are studied, individual differences (subtypes) emerge as a result of variability in vocabulary, phonological memory, and rapid naming (e.g., Fletcher, Foorman, Shaywitz, & Shaywitz, 1999; Morris et al., 1998). Phonological awareness difficulties are present in each subtype and are characterized by word recognition difficulties.

In sum, there is substantial agreement among researchers of longitudinal studies about predictors of risk status for reading difficulties. There is also agreement about marker variables that should trigger evaluation for a reading disability. The TPRI is an example of one state's scaling up of longitudinal research to create a screen to identify risk status and an inventory to chart progress on mastering curriculum standards.

IMPLICATIONS FOR INTERVENTION

We have converging evidence about how to make valid and reliable predictions of risk status in kindergarten and grade 1. The next step is to examine the effectiveness data on early reading interventions. There are many critical components of effective reading interventions, including (a) the intensity, duration, and supportiveness of intervention; (b) the timing of intervention; and (c) student-teacher ratio, requisite knowledge level of intervention teachers, and the content of intervention. Elsewhere (Foorman, Breier, & Fletcher, in press; Foorman & Torgesen, in press), we and many others have argued that

- Early intervention—in kindergarten and grades 1 and 2—is more effective than later intervention because of the intensity and duration of treatment required if later intervention is to be effective and the difficulty of remediating fluency rates (see Torgesen et al., 2001; Torgesen, Rashotte, & Alexander, in press).
- Small-group intervention is just as effective as one-on-one intervention and well-trained paraprofessionals can be as effective as certified teachers (Elbaum, Vaughn, Hughes, & Moody, 2000).
- The content of effective reading interventions, like that of effective classroom reading instruction, is explicit instruction in the alphabetic principle integrated with reading for meaning and opportunities to read and write that are based on what is being taught (National Reading Panel, 2000; Snow, Burns, & Griffin, 1998).

The most cost-effective early intervention is prevention—prevention in the form of differentiated classroom instruction. Now that identification of risk can be in the hands of teachers, as in the Texas example of the TPRI, we need to assist teachers in translating results of early reading assessment to instruction. The TPRI has an Intervention Activities Guide that offers instructional activities for the content of the inventory. Because of statewide requests for more structured activities, the 2001–2002 edition of the TPRI includes a Differentiated Instruction Guide that provides lessons that explicitly address mastery of state curriculum standards. Focus groups around the TPRI indicate that teachers want help in (a) how to group and regroup children for instructional purposes, (b) what the content of group instruction should be, and, most important, (c) what to do with the rest of the class while they work with groups. With respect to the latter request—what to do with the rest of the class—the classroom-based techniques of peer-assisted learning strategies have great potential (e.g., Fuchs, Fuchs, Mathes, & Simmons, 1997; Greenwood, Delquadri, & Hall, 1989).

With respect to the content of classroom instruction, the research of our team and of others is informative (Foorman, Francis, Fletcher, Schatschneider, & Mehta, 1998; Foorman et al., 2001; Juel & Minden-Cupp, 2000). We studied the interaction of child characteristics (e.g., low phonemic awareness) with curriculum (e.g., degree of explicitness of instruction in the alphabetic principle) in 285 Title I-served children in 66 first- and second-grade classrooms in eight schools. Direct instruction in phonemic awareness and phonics had the effect of normalizing the distribution of reading scores such that even students who brought to the classroom low phonemic awareness and word-level skills were able to become successful readers. The overall failure rate of children who received direct instruction (based on the percentage of children remaining below the 30th percentile) represents less than 6% of the population from which these children were selected (Torgesen, 2000). This is a substantial reduction in the approximately 15–20 percent of students with reading disabilities in the United States (Fletcher & Lyon, 1998). However, approximately one third of these Title I-served students remained below the 30th percentile. The number that remain delayed in pullout interventions that emphasize phonological decoding (Torgesen, 2000) or context-based decoding such as Reading Recovery (Center, Wheldall, Freeman, Outhred, & McNaught, 1995; Hiebert, 1994; Shanahan & Barr, 1995) is only slightly lower.

Remember that the overidentification rate from prediction studies is also approximately one third. This suggests the following strategy: Put resources into kindergarten and grade 1 to maximize learning to read for all children through whole-class instruction coupled with differentiated small-group instruction. Delay pullout intervention until the middle of first grade, at the point when overidentification rates begin to fall and response to classroom instruction can reliably be determined. Use response-to-treatment criteria to gauge the mix of phonological skills and text-based instruction for individual children. Pullout intervention can be small-group (i.e., 1:3 ratio) but groups will need to be reconstituted as individuals master skills at different rates. Consequently, it may make sense to shorten the duration and increase the intensity of intervention in the beginning of grade 2 so that groups can be reconstituted as needed after each grading period. This approach is similar to the layered approach of O'Connor, Fulmer, Harty, and Ball (2001), but it differs from other models more widely in use such as Success for All (Slavin, Madden, Dolan, & Wasik, 1996) and Reading Recovery (Clay, 1993) in its ratio, intensity, and directness.

In conclusion, helping teachers use the results of early assessment to group children based on instructional needs is a priority for professional development of kindergarten and first-grade teachers. This approach provides a preventative double dose of classroom instruction. A triple dose of pullout intervention becomes relevant for some children in the second half of grade 1 and early grade 2 when the determination of risk status becomes more reliable and response to classroom instruction is apparent. Jenkins and O'Connor provide us with a layered model for intervention in the form of supplemental instruction that is effective in schools and should be scaled up to meet the national need for early identification and intervention for reading difficulties.

REFERENCES

Center, Y., Wheldall, K., Freeman, L., Outhred, L., & McNaught, M. (1995). An experimental evaluation of Reading Recovery: A critique. *Educational Psychology, 12,* 263–273.

Clay, M. (1993). *Reading recovery: A guidebook for teachers in training.* Portsmouth, NH: Heinemann.

Ehri, L. C. (1998). Grapheme-phoneme knowledge is essential for learning to read words in English. In J. L. Metsala & L. C. Ehri (Eds.), *Word recognition in beginning reading* (pp. 3–40). Mahwah, NJ: Erlbaum.

Elbaum, B., Vaughn, S., Hughes, M. T., & Moody, S. W. (2000). How effective are one-to-one tutoring programs in reading for elementary students at risk for reading failure? A meta-analysis of the intervention research. *Journal of Educational Psychology, 92,* 605–619.

Fletcher, J. M., & Lyon, G. R. (1998). Reading: A research-based approach. In W. M. Evers (Ed.), *What's gone wrong in America's classrooms* (pp. 49–90). Stanford, CA: Hoover Institution Press.

Fletcher, J. M., Foorman, B. R., Boudousquie, A., Barnes, M., Schatschneider, C., & Francis, D. J. (in press). Assessment of reading and learning disabilities: A research-based, treatment-oriented approach. *Journal of School Psychology.*

Fletcher, J. M., Foorman, B. R., Shaywitz, S. E., & Shaywitz, B. A. (1999). Conceptual and methodological issues in dyslexia research: A lesson for developmental disorders. In H. Tager-Flusberg (Ed.), *Neurodevelopmental disorders* (pp. 271–306). Cambridge, MA: MIT Press.

Foorman, B. R., Breier, J. I., & Fletcher, J. M. (in press). Interventions aimed at improving reading success: An evidence-based approach. *Developmental Neuropsychology.*

Foorman, B. R., Fletcher, J. M., & Francis, D. J. (in press). Early reading assessment. In W. Evert (Ed.), *Testing America's schoolchildren*. Stanford, CA: The Hoover Institution.

Foorman, B. R., Francis, D. J., Chen, D. T., Carlson, C., Moats, L., & Fletcher, J. (2001, April). *The necessity of the alphabetic principle to phonemic awareness instruction*. Paper presented at the Society for Research in Child Development, Minneapolis, MN.

Foorman, B. R., Francis, D. J., Fletcher, J. M., Schatschneider, C., & Mehta, P. (1998). The role of instruction in learning to read: Preventing reading failure in at-risk children. *Journal of Educational Psychology, 90,* 37–55.

Foorman, B. R., & Torgesen, J. K. (in press). Critical elements of classroom and small-group instruction promote reading success in all children. *Learning Disabilities Research and Practice.*

Fuchs, D., Fuchs, L. S., Mathes, P. G., & Simmons, D. C. (1997). Peer-assisted learning strategies: Making classrooms more responsive to academic diversity. *American Educational Research Journal, 34,* 174–206.

Gibson, E. J., & Levin, H. (1975). *The psychology of reading.* Cambridge, MA: The MIT Press.

Greenwood, C. R., Delquadri, J. C., & Hall, R. V. (1989). Longitudinal effects of classwide peer tutoring. *Journal of Educational Psychology, 81,* 371–383.

Hiebert, E. H. (1994). Reading Recovery in the United States: What difference does it make to an age cohort? *Educational Researcher, 23*(9), 15–25.

Juel, C., & Minden-Cupp, C. (2000). Learning to read words: Linguistic units and instructional strategies. *Reading Research Quarterly, 35,* 458–492.

Moats, L. C. (1995). *Spelling: Development, disability, and instruction.* Baltimore, MD: York Press.

Moats, L. C. (2000). *Speech to Print.* Baltimore, MD: Brookes Publishing.

Morris, R. D., Stuebing, K. K., Fletcher, J. M., Shaywitz, S. E., Lyon, G. R., Shankweiler, D. P., Katz, L., Francis, D. J., & Shaywitz, B. A. (1998). Subtypes of reading disability: Variability around a phonological core. *Journal of Educational Psychology, 90,* 347–373.

National Reading Panel. (2000). *Teaching children to read: An evidence-based assessment of the scientific research literature on reading and its implications for reading instruction.* National Institute of Child Health and Human Development, Washington, DC.

O'Connor, R. E., Fulmer, D., Harty, K., & Ball, K. (April, 2001). *Total awareness: Reducing the severity of reading disability.* Paper presented at the annual meeting of the American Educational Research Association, Seattle, WA.

O'Connor, R. E., & Jenkins, J. R. (1999). The prediction of reading disabilities in kindergarten and first grade. *Scientific Studies of Reading, 3*, 159–197.

Perfetti, C. A. (1992). The representation problem in reading acquisition. In P. G. Gough, L. C. Ehri, & R. Treiman (Eds.), *Reading acquisition* (pp. 107–143). Hillsdale, NJ: LEA.

Rayner, K., Foorman, B., Perfetti, C. A., Pesetsky, D., & Seidenberg, M. S. (in press). Psychological science can inform the teaching of reading. *Psychological Science in the Public Interest.*

Scarborough, H. S. (1998). Early identification of children at risk for reading disabilities: Phonological awareness and some other promising predictors. In B. K. Shapiro, A. J. Capute, & B. Shapiro (Eds.), *Specific reading disability: A view of the spectrum* (pp. 77–121). Hillsdale, NJ: Erlbaum.

Schatschneider, C., Fletcher, J. M., Foorman, B. R., & Francis, D. J. (2001). Kindergarten predictors of reading outcomes: A dominance. Manuscript submitted for publication.

Schatschneider, C., Francis, D. J., Foorman, B. F., Fletcher, J. M., & Mehta, P. (1999). The dimensionality of phonological awareness: An application of item response theory. *Journal of Educational Psychology, 91*, 1–11.

Shanahan, T., & Barr, R. (1995). Reading Recovery: An independent evaluation of the effects of an early instructional intervention for at-risk learners. *Reading Research Quarterly, 30*, 958–996.

Slavin, R. E., Madden, N. A., Dolan, L., & Wasik, B. A. (1996). *Every child, Every school, Success for All.* Thousand Oaks, CA: Corwin Press, Inc.

Snow, C. E., Burns, M. S., & Griffin, P. (Eds.) (1998). *Preventing reading difficulties in young children.* Washington, DC: National Academy Press.

Texas Education Agency. (2000). *Texas Primary Reading Inventory.* Austin, TX: Texas Education Agency.

TPRI Technical Manual (1998). Austin, TX: Texas Education Agency.

Torgesen, J. K. (in press). The prevention of reading difficulties. *Journal of School Psychology.*

Torgesen, J. K. (2000). Individual differences in response to early interventions in reading: The lingering problem of treatment resisters. *Learning Disabilities Research and Practice, 15*, 55–64.

Torgesen, J. K., Alexander, A. W., Wagner, R. K., Rashotte, C. A., Voeller, K., Conway, T., & Rose, E. (2001). Intensive remedial instruction for children with severe reading disabilities: Immediate and long-term outcomes from two instructional approaches. *Journal of Learning Disabilities, 34*, 33–58.

Torgesen, J. K., Rashotte, C. A., & Alexander, A. (in press). Principles of fluency instruction in reading: Relationships with established empirical outcomes. In M. Wolf (Ed.), *Time, fluency, and developmental dyslexia*. Parkton, MD: York Press.

Vellutino, F. R., Scanlon, D. M., & Lyon, G. R. (2000). Differentiating between difficult-to-remediate and readily remediated poor readers: More evidence against the IQ-achievement discrepancy definition for reading disability. *Journal of Learning Disabilities, 33*, 223–238.

Wagner, R. K., Torgesen, J. K., & Rashotte, C. A. (1999). *Comprehensive test of phonological processing*. Austin, TX: Pro-ed.

Wood, F., Hill, D., & Meyer, M. (2001). *Predictive assessment of reading*. Winston-Salem, NC: Author.

Woodcock, R. W., & Johnson, M. B. (1989). *Woodcock-Johnson Psychoeducational Battery-Revised*. Allen, TX: DLM Teaching Resources.

FROM AN "EXPLODED VIEW" OF BEGINNING READING TOWARD A SCHOOLWIDE BEGINNING READING MODEL: GETTING TO SCALE IN COMPLEX HOST ENVIRONMENTS

Edward J. Kame'enui & Deborah C. Simmons, University of Oregon

The field should be gratified and duly enlightened by the paper written by Joseph R. Jenkins and Rollanda E. O'Connor entitled "Early Identification and Intervention for Young Children With Reading/Learning Disabilities." These authors provide nothing short of an exploded view of the complex elements that punctuate the complicated process of reading in an alphabetic writing system, especially for young children with reading/learning disabilities (R/LDs). For both the mechanically minded and the mechanically disinclined, an exploded view of most things is good, because it permits a look at the working parts that make up the whole apparatus and invokes an appreciation of the complexity of the whole. In fact, we need more exploded views of things that work for us in important ways, like the zipper that "cleverly exploits the principle of the inclined plane to join or separate two rows of interlocking teeth" (Macaulay, 1988, p. 21) or the gearbox that keeps an engine running at "its most efficient rate while allowing the car to travel at a large range of speed" (Macaulay, 1988, p. 44). Exploded views remind us that an operation or process, however ordinary and natural in appearance, often betrays a complexity in both form (e.g., zipper with rows of interlocking metal teeth) and principle (e.g., the inclined plane).

Not surprisingly, some authors and illustrators, like David Macaulay (1988), have perfected the exploded view of things through detailed cutaway diagrams. Individual parts of a device or apparatus are separated and placed strategically to indicate their relative position. Jenkins and O'Connor's careful review of research studies, attention to methodological details, and insightful integrative analysis have given us an exploded view of reading that rivals the detail of Macaulay's visual and conceptual guide to the workings of mechanical clocks and watches, the microchip, and the cams and cranks of an automobile (Macaulay, 1988).

Like a machine with levers, gears, wheels, and cranks interconnected in complex linkages, reading in an alphabetic writing system involves parts (e.g., the eyes) that must move (e.g., the eye moves 4–5 times per second) with exactly the right amount of force (e.g., the eye jumps 7–9 characters each time it moves; Rayner & Pollatsek, 1989) to excite neurons to form perceptually relevant linguistic representations at exactly the right moment (Duane, 1999). But this complex orchestration of physical, visual, auditory, and neural elements does not occur of its own accord for the majority of learners. It needs a driving force—the push of an extrinsic agent such as a parent or teacher, or the intrinsic pull of words etched in marble that echo the reader's inner voice long after the physical representation of the words have disappeared.

Jenkins and O'Connor observed, "We can all agree that reading is one of the principal tools for understanding our humanity, for making sense of our world, for advancing the democratic ideal, and for generating personal and national prosperity" (Jenkins & O'Connor, this volume). Jenkins and O'Connor also make clear that the agreement on democratic ideals that reading allows is one thing, but agreement on how best to address the difficulties young children with R/LDs encounter is more difficult. There is clear agreement, perhaps even consensus, that earlier rather than later is critical to the development and implementation of reading interventions. But how early? Under what conditions? By whom? With what tools, strategies, and programs? How often and for how long? At what criterion levels of performance? For what skills and strategies? In what contexts and with what levels of intensity should reading interventions be initiated and sustained to obtain reading achievement?

Jenkins and O'Connor offer important, trustworthy answers and "sensible actions" for practitioners. However, they also raise important unanswered questions that require sustained, large-scale, longitudinal programs of research before the field is able to yield trustworthy and sensible actions to address them. For example, Jenkins and O'Connor assert, "Despite these impressive results, it is unlikely that even high-quality general education, no matter how well organized, will be sufficient to meet the needs of students with R/LDs" (Jenkins & O'Connor, this volume). Jenkins and O'Connor's pessimism is well founded; there is little trustworthy evidence that supports general education "getting to scale" with effective, scientifically based reading practices and programs that meet the needs of students with R/LDs. But this reality only begs bigger, more important questions: Why is this the case? Why is it so difficult to build capacity in complex host environments known as schools, especially for young children who face reading and learning difficulties (Kame'enui, Simmons, & Coyne, 2000; Simmons et al., 2000)?

Getting Schools as Complex Host Environments to Scale

Elmore (1996) has argued that "[g]etting to scale with good educational practice" is not easy because of a "deep, systemic incapacity of U.S. schools, and the practitioners who work in them, to develop, incorporate, and extend new ideas about teaching and learning..." (p. 1). Getting research-based innovations to scale requires changing the very *core of educational practice,* which includes determining (a) how knowledge is defined, (b) how programs design and communicate knowledge (e.g., universal designed instruction or specially designed instruction), (c) how teachers relate to students regarding knowledge, (d) how teachers relate to other teachers in their daily work, (e) how students are grouped for instruction, (f) how time and content are allocated, and (g) how students' work is assessed.

According to Elmore (1996), the difficulty of getting educational innovations to scale is *not* because schools are resistant to change. In fact, schools are "constantly changing—adopting new curricula, tests, and grouping practices, changing schedules, creating new mechanisms for participation in decision-making, adding or subtracting teaching or administrative roles, and myriad other modifications" (Elmore, 1996, p. 4). Almost two decades ago, Fullan (1982) asserted that schools routinely undertake reforms for which they have neither the institutional nor the individual competence to carry out. Rather than getting research-based innovations to scale, Elmore (1996) observed, schools end up *trivializing* significant reforms by creating superficial structures (e.g., new administrative structures are introduced, additional personnel are hired) around the very "core of educational practice" they are attempting to change. Nor is the difficulty of getting to scale the failure of educational research to supply schools with new ideas about what to do and how to change. The supply of ideas has been more than ample and has created a more insidious problem in which good and bad ideas are implemented without adequate evidence that improved learning is likely to result, especially for young children with R/LDs.

To change the core of educational practice requires "understanding the conditions under which people working in schools seek new knowledge and actively use it to change the fundamental processes of schooling" (Elmore, 1996, p. 4). This requires considering schools "complex host environments" in which policies, pedagogies, practices, procedures, and passionate personalities interact in complex ways. These complex host environments also require diligent attention to the particulars, such as (a) connecting the "big ideas"(e.g., phonological awareness, alphabetic principle, orthographic reading) from the research base on beginning reading as Jenkins and O'Connor so carefully delineated, to the fine grain of practice; (b) pushing hard in a few strategic places in the system of relations surrounding the problem, then carefully observing the results; (c) creating strong professional and social normative structures for good teaching; (d) embracing and promoting the perspective that successful teaching is not an individual, idiosyncratic trait, but a set of learned professional competencies acquired over the course of a professional career; (e) finding the connective tissue to bind teachers together in a relationship of mutual obligation that supports them in sorting out issues of practice; and (f) harnessing the institutional incentives in ways that lead to the improvement of practice, particularly in beginning reading.

Kame'enui and Simmons (2000) and colleagues (Simmons et al., 2000; Kame'enui, Simmons, and Coyne, 2000) have developed a schoolwide beginning reading model that has unique promise to address concerns that Jenkins and O'Connor raise about getting schools to scale with effective practice and programs for young children with R/LDs. In Figure 1, we portray the tension between two complex systems (i.e., the symbolic system—the alphabetic writing system, and the organizational system—schools as host environments) that must be addressed if the goal of "All children reading at grade level by grade 3" is to be attained. In addition, an unexploded view of the schoolwide beginning reading model is given in Figure 2. This graphic reveals the five stages and two levels of the beginning reading model. The two levels capture the essential tension that Jenkins and O' Connor identify; that is, the tension between addressing the needs of "all" children (identified as the "School Level" in the model), as well as the needs of "each" child (identified as the "Student Level" in the model) concurrently in reforming schoolwide practice.

The model has eight tenets: (1) Address reading success and reading failure from a schoolwide systemic perspective and recognize that schools are complex host environments; (2) embrace a prevention framework by intervening early and strategically during the critical window of instructional opportunity; (3) recognize and respond to the multiple contexts of reading achievement and include articulated goals, research-based programs, student progress monitoring, prioritized instructional time, quality instructional delivery, differentiated instruction, and effective organization and grouping; (4) develop and promote a comprehensive system of instruction based on a research-based core curriculum and enhancement programs; (5) anchor instruction and practice to the converging knowledge base of effective reading practice; (6) build capacity by using school-based teams to customize interventions to the host environment; (7) rely on and foster the ability of the school principal to serve as the instructional leader; and (8) use ongoing performance indicators (the Dynamic Indicators of Basic Early Literacy Skills; DIBELS) of student performance to identify students at risk, plan instructional groups, and modify instruction according to levels and rates of learning.

Figure 1. Two complex systems in Schoolwide Beginning Reading Improvement Model.

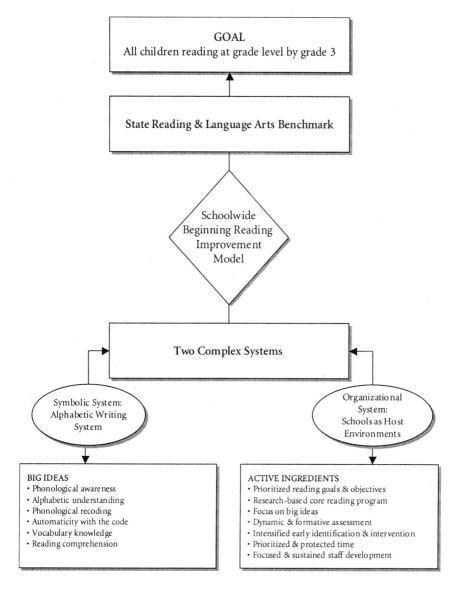

Figure 2. Stages and levels of a Schoolwide Beginning Reading Improvement Model

	Stage I: Conduct School Audit and Assess Student Performance	Stage II: Analyze School and Student Performance	Stage III: Design Instructional Interventions	Stage IV: Set Goals and Monitor Progress Formatively	Stage V: Evaluate Intervention Efficacy and Adjust Instruction
School Level	**Conduct School Audit** ■ Use Planning and Evaluation Tool (Kame'enui & Simmons, 2000).	**Identify Reading Priorities and Develop Action Plan** ■ Review Audit ■ Identify strengths and areas of development based on Audit summary scores ■ Identify and develop three priorities ■ Establish Action Plan	**Design Core Instructional Interventions** ■ Specify the following: — Goals — Core Curriculum Program — Time for Reading — Instruction Grouping and Scheduling — Instructional Implementation — Progress-Monitoring System	**Establish and Implement Progress-Monitoring System** ■ Identify valid and reliable dynamic reading indicators ■ Establish absolute and relative goals ■ Commit resources ■ Determine schedule ■ Interpret and communicate results	**Evaluate School-Level Performance** ■ Evaluate effectiveness three times per year ■ Examine components of interventions in Stage III ■ Make instructional adjustments ■ Determine whether and for whom to maintain or adjust intervention
Student Level	**Assess Student Performance** ■ Use Dynamic Indicators of Basic Early Literacy Skill (DIBELS; Kaminski & Good, 1998).	**Analyze Individual Performance and Plan Instructional Groups** ■ Identify students who require: — Benchmark Intervention — Strategic Intervention — Intensive Intervention	**Customize Intensive and Strategic Interventions** ■ Specify the following: — Goals — Core or Specialized Curriculum Materials — Time for Reading — Instructional Grouping and Scheduling — Instruction — Progress-Monitoring System	**Customize Progress-Monitoring System for Intensive and Strategic Interventions** ■ Intensive: Monitor progress every 2 weeks ■ Strategic: Monitor progress every month ■ Benchmark: Monitor progress three times per year	**Intensify Intervention** ■ Determine students who are and are not "learning enough" ■ Chart instructional profiles for students making little or no progress ■ Adjust components of interventions in Stage III

Participants in the schoolwide beginning reading model receive a four-day intensive knowledge and application session in which they study and apply research-based findings on three big ideas in beginning reading: (a) phonemic awareness, (b) alphabetic understanding, and (c) automaticity with the code. In later sessions, participants are introduced to the topics of vocabulary development and text comprehension (Adams, 1990; National Reading Panel, 2000). The principles and practices are designed to provide a professional grounding and foundation. During the four-day session, participants conduct a schoolwide audit and learn to assess student performance formatively. Schools then summarize their overall level of reading implementation quantitatively, prioritize areas of improvement, and develop a "Reading Action Plan" to direct schoolwide beginning reading improvement.

In addition, participants learn to administer and interpret DIBELS (Kaminski & Good, 1998), which is used to identify children whose performance differs significantly from their same-age peers and who may need early intervention. DIBELS measures align with the "big ideas" in early reading and include (a) Letter-Naming Fluency, (b) Onset-Recognition Fluency, (c) Phonemic-Segmentation Fluency, and (d) Nonsense-Word Fluency. Once students are able to read words in connected text (typically mid-first grade), 1-minute, curriculum-based measures of oral reading fluency (R-CBM) are used as indicators of general reading competence. These measures provide "vital signs of growth in basic skills comparable to the vital signs of health used by physicians" (Deno, 1992, p. 6). The validity and reliability of DIBELS and R-CBM are well established (Good, Simmons, & Kame'enui, 2001; Kame'enui, Simmons, Good, & Harn, 2001; Kaminski & Good, 1998).

A critical technological feature of the professional development intervention consists of a web-based system for managing student performance data. This system is linked to the DIBELS data system (http://dibels.uoregon.edu/), a web-based data base for entering DIBELS scores, tracking student performance, and generating reports for individual teachers. Reports include (a) histograms of the distribution of student performance on each measure, (b) percentile rankings for a school district, (c) box plots depicting performance across points in time, (d) scatterplot graphs of cross-month and cross-year comparisons, and (e) specification of instructional status and recommendations for each student. This system is designed for benchmark assessment of all students and accepts data for the DIBELS assessments of kindergarten and grade 1, as well as the R-CBM measures of oral reading fluency for grades 1–3.

In addition, participants attend a follow-up professional-development session immediately after the first student performance data are collected at the beginning of the school year. During this session, teachers learn to analyze individual student performance and plan instructional groups. Student performance on DIBELS and R-CBM is compared to the benchmark goals to identify children who may be at risk of reading disability or delay. Performance expectations are derived from research-based criterion levels of performance (Good et al., 2000; Hasbrouck & Tindal, 1992), and students are identified as potentially at risk relative to how other students in their school and district perform and in comparison to research-based criteria.

A second focus of this professional development session is the design of differentiated instruction. Of foremost importance to the model is the fit of the instructional reading intervention with the students' needs and school's resources; therefore, schools invest serious and sustained energy at this stage. In this analysis, the decisions focus on (a) specifying and implementing core instructional interventions and (b) customizing strategic and intensive interventions for students not benefiting adequately from the core curriculum or who are at high risk of reading difficulty.

A third professional development session focuses on setting goals and monitoring progress formatively. Professionals learn to evaluate intervention efficacy and adjust instruction. The effects of instruction are evaluated directly and interventions intensified as indicated by the student performance data from DIBELS. In this session, teachers address the following questions: Are the instructional interventions working for the full range of learners? Are students learning enough? What instructional adjustments must be made to enhance beginning reading performance? What other resources are needed to improve?

The schoolwide beginning reading model involves two specific technology applications: (a) a web-based centralized data management system and (b) web-based technology support (see http://dibels.uoregon.edu/). Individual schools enter student performance data three times per year, generating school, grade, class, and individual reports. From the reports, instructional recommendations are provided and linked to web-based instructional vignettes, instructional strategies, and recommended programs.

Conclusion

As Jenkins and O'Connor astutely recognize, the convergence of research in beginning reading makes clear that we can change the reading trajectories of young children with R/LDs. Intervention must be early, precise, and differentiated enough at the rights points in time and delivered with the right level of focus, effort, and intensity. However, establishing and sustaining this kind of intervention in schools will require further research and, in good time, an "exploded view" of an empirically robust schoolwide beginning reading model. The parts have been identified, and we can visualize their complex linkages. Getting all parts in place and working with precision in schools as complex host environments is our next major challenge as a field.

REFERENCES

Adams, M. J. (1990). *Beginning to read: Thinking and learning about print.* Cambridge, MA: The MIT Press.

Deno, S. L. (1992). The nature and development of curriculum-based measurement. *Preventing School Failure, 36*(2), 5–10.

Duane, D. D. (Ed.) (1999). *Reading and attention disorders: Neurobiological correlates.* Baltimore: York Press.

Elmore, R. F. (1996). Getting to scale with good educational practice. *Harvard Educational Review, 66,* 1–26.

Fullan, M. (1982). *The meaning of educational change.* New York: Teachers College Press, Columbia University.

Good, R., Kaminski, R., Shinn, M., Bratten, J., Shinn, M., & Laimon, D. (2000). *Technical report #7: Technical adequacy and decision making utility of DIBELS.* Eugene, OR: University of Oregon, Early Childhood Research Institute.

Good, R., III, Simmons, D. C., & Kame'enui, E. J. (2001). The importance and decision-making utility of a continuum of fluency-based indicators of foundational reading skills for third-grade high-stakes outcomes. *Scientific Studies of Reading, 5,* 257–288.

Hasbrouck, J. E., & Tindal, G. (1992). Curriculum-based oral reading fluency norms for students in grades 2 through 5. *Teaching Exceptional Children, 24,* 41–44.

Kame'enui, E. J., & Simmons, D. C. (1999). *Toward successful inclusion of students with disabilities: The architecture of instruction.* Reston, VA: Council for Exceptional Children.

Kame'enui, E. J., & Simmons, D. C. (2000). *Planning and evaluation tool for effective schoolwide reading programs.* Eugene, OR: Institute for the Development of Educational Achievement.

Kame'enui, E. J., Simmons, D. C., & Coyne, M. D. (2000). Schools as host environments: Toward a schoolwide reading improvement model. *Annals of Dyslexia, 50,* 33–51.

Kame'enui, E. J., Simmons, D. C., Good, R. H., & Harn, B. A. (2001). The use of fluency-based measures in early identification and evaluation of intervention efficacy in schools. In M. Wolf (Ed.), *Time, fluency, and dyslexia* (pp. 307–331). New York: York Press.

Kaminski, R. A., & Good, R. H., III. (1996). Toward a technology for assessing basic early literacy skills. *School Psychology Review, 25*(2), 215–227.

Kaminski, R. A., & Good, R. H., III. (1998). Assessing early literacy skills in a problem-solving model: Dynamic indicators of basic early literacy skills. In M. R. Shinn (Ed.), *Advanced applications of curriculum-based measurement.* New York: Guilford.

Macaulay, D. (1988). *The way things work.* Boston: Houghton Mifflin Co.

National Reading Panel. (2000). *Report of the national reading panel: Teaching children to read: An evidence-based assessment of the scientific research literature on reading and its implications for reading instruction.* Washington, DC: National Institute of Child Health and Human Development.

Rayner, K., & Pollatsek, A. (1989). *The psychology of reading.* New Jersey: Prentice Hall.

Simmons, D. C., Kame'enui, E. J., Good, R. H., III, Harn, B. A., Cole, C., & Braun, D. (2000). Building, implementing, and sustaining a beginning reading model: School by school and lessons learned. *Oregon School Study Council, 43*(3), 1–30.

EARLY IDENTIFICATION AND INTERVENTION FOR YOUNG CHILDREN WITH READING/LEARNING DISABILITIES

Phyllis Raynor, Montgomery County Public Schools, Maryland

Jenkins and O'Connor presented a current understanding of the difficulties encountered by children with learning disabilities as they begin the process of learning to read. A review of the literature on early identification and intervention procedures included historical as well as current publications. The importance of reading fluency as related to the demands of current word cultures was clearly described. Certainly, a level of reading proficiency to ensure acquisition of basic reading skills for primary students at risk for reading/learning disabilities (R/LDs) can be enhanced through early identification and intervention programs.

For students at risk for R/LDs, learning to read can be a very frustrating experience, which in turn has far-reaching negative implications within the school, family, and community. Literacy, the ability to read and write, promotes knowledge acquisition, provides access to information for task accomplishment, and expands pursuits of pleasure, which feed our interests. Students who are unable to attain acceptable standards of literacy are essentially deprived of attaining their full academic potential.

Jenkins and O'Connor maintain that reading comprehension, which is based on a foundation of ability to read words, ability to comprehend language, and ability to access prior knowledge, is the primary goal for successful reading. Students with R/LDs lack efficient word recognition strategies, which affects reading fluency. The amount of energy expended on word identification detracts from comprehension. Inefficient word reading overloads working memory, which makes it difficult to connect ideas into meaningful understanding of text. Practically speaking, to attain adequate comprehension, word recognition skills need to be initially and explicitly taught to children who are at risk for reading disabilities.

SKILLED READING VERSUS R/LDS

During the early stages of learning to read, word-level reading skills are the most difficult skills to acquire for a student with R/LDs. In their discussion of word-level reading skills, Jenkins and O'Connor present three approaches to reading text. First, unfamiliar sight words in context are read by guessing, which is generally an unreliable process. Second, analogies, noting similarity with other words, can give some context to an unfamiliar word. Third, decoding—use of phonological or alphabetic reading skill—involves knowledgeable application of letter sounds (phonemes) to alphabetic symbols (graphemes). Skilled readers, although they use analogy and decoding, read most words by sight (orthographic reading). I agree with the arguments of Jenkins and O'Connor that sight words are stored by skilled readers using grapheme-phoneme connections. Memory would operate on overload if words were stored by spellings alone. Research supports the ability to store and retrieve words from memory through the use of alphabetic symbols and their respective letter sounds. Reading fluency is a function of basic sight vocabulary, which instead of being entirely committed to memory is enhanced by a level of grapheme-phoneme connections and repetitions. Observation of students during independent oral reading confirms their reliance on decoding as the backup when words are not recognized by sight. Extensive experiences in reading are required in order to encounter specific words, which become basic sight vocabulary. As most words read by sight, with the exception of identified high-frequency words (*the, and, is*), appear only occasionally, a sufficient level of graphophonemic knowledge is required. Jenkins and O'Connor discuss studies that demonstrate the importance of decoding ability in sight word recognition. The answer to what is necessary for decoding is (a) knowledge of symbol/sound relationships (graphophonemic knowledge) and (b) phonemic awareness. The reviewed research indicates that children who lack phonological awareness are likely to have reading disabilities. On the basis of practical classroom experience working with students at risk for reading disabilities, I agree with this discussion of designated phonological processing problems and the need to provide direct instruction in the early stages of learning to read.

EARLY IDENTIFICATION

Designated programs for early identification of students at risk for R/LDs have been known to initially reduce incidence or severity. Jenkins and O'Connor report that school district personnel tend not to identify students with reading disabilities until the middle elementary grades, even as late as fourth grade. However, efforts are under way in school systems and through private phonologically based reading programs to target students at risk as early as kindergarten. In Montgomery County,

Maryland, the board of education in Montgomery County Public Schools approved a comprehensive reading initiative to target improvement in the reading performance of elementary school students (Vance, 1998). Class size in grades 1 and 2 was reduced to a student-teacher ratio of 15:1 during a 90-minute block of reading. Training was provided for teachers to emphasize early literacy practices as part of their instructional program. Concepts of print, including phonemic awareness and letter/sound patterns, were emphasized as critical factors in language acquisition. The reading initiative was expanded to include grade 3 for the 2000–2001 school year. An emphasis on instruction in phonemic awareness was added to the kindergarten curriculum.

As a result of school systems' serious concerns that the amount of special education help available was insufficient to meet the needs of students at risk for learning to read, popular one-to-one tutoring programs such as Reading Recovery and comprehensive schoolwide reading/school reform programs such as Success for All have been introduced in public elementary schools. Private companies, such as Spell Read P.A.T. (Phonological Auditory Training), who offer private tutoring for children at considerable expense to their families, have been approached by elementary schools. A case in point in Newfoundland, Canada, is a study reported by Rashotte, MacPhee, and Torgesen (2001). Educators, parents, and students are reporting increased reading ability as a result of these intervention programs. For many school systems, the problem is not whether or when to implement programs for children at risk for reading disabilities, but what program will be effective yet economically feasible. The success of early intervention programs depends on program design and how best to deliver program components, which include teaching phonological awareness (awareness that spoken words are made up of individual sounds), emphasizing the alphabetic principle (written spellings systematically represent the phonemes in spoken words), and integrating these components with activities which develop reading comprehension and fluency skills.

Jenkins and O'Connor discuss problems in prediction of reading disabilities, which result in errors of underprediction and overprediction. Measures that underpredict are of concern, since early intervention efforts are intended to identify all students who require and who will benefit from early and direct instruction. Overprediction mistakenly identifies students at risk for reading disabilities, who in all probability could benefit from the early intervention strategies, but who would not necessarily be included in the targeted school population and would not necessarily require costly intervention services. Special education resource teachers face similar problems, which result in increased caseloads of students in need of special education intervention services. In both cases, the ideal solution would be to design age-appropriate measures to identify early developing reading-related skills.

In the meantime, students who present at risk for R/LDs should be included in early intervention instruction. Jenkins and O'Connor offer some sensible actions to identify the children most likely to need intensive support.

EARLY INTERVENTION

Because alphabetic reading skills are necessary to develop word recognition skills, Jenkins and O'Connor reviewed early intervention research on teaching phonemic awareness, decoding, and building fluency. Research reports that individual differences in prereaders' phonological awareness are one of the best predictors of later success in learning to read. However, further research is needed on students at risk for R/LDs. Questions need to be answered, such as how early to begin direct instruction in phonemic awareness, what are the effects of explicit instruction in phonological awareness, and how much phonological awareness is enough to start word reading. Sensible actions for fostering phonemic awareness are presented by Jenkins and O'Connor as well.

Research on the relative effectiveness of more and less explicit instruction to teach decoding skills and on whether decoding results in better word-level reading skills was also discussed. In the three studies reviewed by Jenkins and O'Connor, groups that made the largest gains in decoding received explicit instruction in phonemic awareness. To answer the question whether explicit phonics instruction results in stronger word identification skills, further research is needed. Initial reports indicate that more explicit phonics approaches yield stronger word-reading skills in beginning readers.

More definitive evidence is needed to determine which approach should be emphasized in early intervention programs: focusing on phonemic units (individual sounds such as /e/, /ea/, /sh/) or on phonograms (word families such as -at, -ate, -ar which regularize vowel pronunciations). In a study reviewed by Jenkins and O'Connor, a combination of the two approaches produced results superior to those produced by either approach alone. In my experience, a combination of approaches has resulted in a more successful delivery of instruction to students at risk for R/LDs.

In a review of several studies, Jenkins and O'Connor report that in spite of explicit and intense decoding instruction within the general education classroom, students vary in their responsiveness to instruction. A percentage of students who received extended lengths of treatment and explicit instruction continued to perform significantly below average in decoding and word recognition skills. However, another study suggested that schools can reduce the number of students who fail to respond to general high-quality classroom intervention by lengthening the intervention period and by providing supplemental instruction in small homogeneous groups several times each week. This generally means referral to special education resource services, which is the practice in my district's special education program. Jenkins and O'Connor provide a list of sensible actions for promoting reading through instruction in decoding skills.

As the primary goal of reading is comprehension, fluent reading becomes an important aspect of reading ability. A student who expends too much effort on word recognition ruins motivation to read, limits the amount of resources for understanding text, and reduces the chances of reading being a chosen activity. Research studies reviewed by Jenkins and O'Connor propose that reading fluency develops after students have mastered basic decoding skills. The level of reading accuracy in a text required for a student to benefit from independent reading ranges from 90 to 95%. One of my concerns is the scarcity of interesting, readable text for students with R/LDs. Controversy continues as to how teachers can best organize fluency practice. Information is needed to make text reading easier for struggling readers. Various forms of assistive technology (books on tape, computer programs, shared reading) have been suggested. Jenkins and O'Connor provide a list of sensible actions for building fluency.

Conclusion

Jenkins and O'Connor define problems in phonological awareness, decoding, and fluency, which affect acquisition of reading skills for children with R/LDs. Comprehension is the immediate goal of reading, which suffers as a result of problems in any of the three areas previously mentioned. Word reading is not sufficient to achieve satisfactory levels of literacy. Children must also be able to read purposefully and discriminately. Early identification and intervention programs for young children apparently are making a positive impact on reducing the severity of a reading disability. However, early intervention can only be as effective as the end results, which are not entirely clear. Long-term benefits of early training in phonological awareness and decoding have yet to be determined. In practice, concerns similar to those expressed by Jenkins and O'Connor are raised by special educators. Regardless of early identification, early intervention, and continued support, a small number of students struggle with reading throughout their schooling, even into adulthood. From a practitioner's point of view, the impact of insufficient reading skills on self-esteem, family, and community is extensive. In schools, it is heartbreaking to observe the struggles of children with R/LDs. I would concede that for some individuals, reading disability may be a chronic condition.

I appreciate the problems encountered in early identification attempts and in developing early intervention programs. Questions regarding designation of funds, teacher training, and appropriate instructional approaches must be resolved. As part of their final thoughts, Jenkins and O'Connor caution us to not be blindsided by relying exclusively on alphabetic and orthographic reading skills. Other nonphonics text-level approaches need to be explored as complementary and alternative approaches to teaching students with R/LDs. Students, with their unique learning styles, often benefit from a more eclectic approach to instruction.

On the basis of my experience, I concur that programs embedded in general education classroom instruction do not provide sufficient instruction for children who appear to have chronic reading problems. Special education resource services, which provide sufficient monies to purchase materials and which provide quality teacher training, are an important component of early identification and intervention programs for students with R/LDs.

REFERENCES

Rashotte, C., MacPhee, K., & Torgesen, J. (2001). The effectiveness of a group reading instruction program with poor readers in multiple grades. *Learning Disability Quarterly, 24,* 119–134.

Vance, P. (1998). 1998 update on the reading initiative. Memorandum to members of the Board of Education, Montgomery County Public Schools, Rockville, Maryland.

RESPONSE TO "EARLY IDENTIFICATION AND INTERVENTION FOR YOUNG CHILDREN WITH READING/LEARNING DISABILITIES"

Timothy A. Slocum, Utah State University

The scientific knowledge base for early identification and intervention with children who are at risk for reading problems has burgeoned in the past 15 years. A general outline of the understanding brought about by this explosion of knowledge is fairly easily summarized. Research in early identification and intervention has clarified the central importance of the roles of phonological awareness, knowledge of letter-sound correspondence, and phonological decoding. These three skill areas are critically important both as indicators of incipient problems in reading development and as instructional targets. Though the general thrust of research results in these areas is easily summarized, the detailed understanding of specific measures and instructional programs that is critical for early identification and intervention is complex and rapidly changing. Jenkins and O'Connor have done a service to the field by writing a clear summary of current knowledge in this important area. They provide useful summaries of current understanding of the development of reading skill, the state of the art in early identification of youngsters at risk for reading difficulties, and recent advances in early reading interventions. In addition, Jenkins and O'Connor touch on the importance of reading fluency and the role of the total volume of reading that students experience. These areas have received relatively little research attention and programmatic development in the past decade and should be targets for increased focus in coming years. The authors also briefly discuss several important methodological points that may have implications for future research. In this review, I will respond to and expand on Jenkins and O'Connor's comments in these areas.

ACCURACY OF CLASSIFICATION

One of the most fundamental methodological issue is how we summarize quantitative research results. Summaries that address our research questions clearly and directly are, of course, most useful. Research on education and psychology has been impeded by our overreliance on, and misinterpretation of, p-values. P-values, of course, do not directly describe the magnitude of a relationship, but only the likelihood of obtaining a given result under the null hypothesis. Use of p-values tends to support dichotomous conclusions about the absence or presence of a relationship. However, research that is oriented to identification and intervention is generally more concerned with the strength of relationships, not merely their existence. Strength or magnitude of a relationship is better described by effect size statistics. The field's understanding of early identification has made progress through a comparison of the magnitude of correlation coefficients (r and r^2 are effect size measures) of various potential predictors of reading problems. However, as Jenkins and O'Connor note, correlation is not the best statistic to describe the ability of a test to identify specific individuals who are likely to experience reading difficulties. They comment, "Despite a strong correlational knowledge base connecting children's phonological language skills to later reading acquisition, predicting exactly which children will develop RD [reading disability] has proved problematic." Correlation does not directly describe the accuracy of dichotomous classification (predicting which students will have a reading disability and which students will not). Jenkins and O'Connor are pointing out a mismatch between the question (accuracy of identification of individuals) and the summary statistics commonly used (r and r^2). Questions about the accuracy of classification are addressed by examining rates of accurate classification and rates of errors. Two kinds of errors are possible. One type of error is incorrectly predicting that a child will develop a reading disability. Jenkins and O'Connor refer to this as underidentification; it is also known as a false positive and is said to reflect a lack of specificity. The other type of error is one of failing to identify a child who does develop a reading disability. This kind of error is known as underidentification or false negative and is said to indicate a lack of sensitivity. These errors are not simply a function of the correlation between the predictor and the criterion measures. These errors also depend on

1. The acceptable level of performance on the criterion. A judgment must be made about what level of performance on the criterion measure will be considered to constitute a reading disability. The level at which this standard is set influences the amount and kind of errors that are made.

2. Relative importance of the two kinds of errors. For any specific predictor and criterion, we face a tradeoff between the two types of errors. We can minimize overidentification errors (false positives) by setting a high threshold on the predictor, but the low rate of overidentification would come at the cost of a higher rate of underidentification (false negative). Conversely, setting a low threshold for identification will reduce underidentification at the cost of higher levels of overidentification. The cut score cannot be set without (implicitly or explicitly) making a values-based decision about the relative importance of these two kinds of errors. Some of the implications of this tradeoff will be discussed below.

3. The specific shape and other characteristics of the scatterplot of the predictor and criterion. A given correlation coefficient can describe scatterplots with very different shapes and characteristics. A scatterplot may show a close relationship between predictor and criterion at low levels on the measures, but a weaker relationship at higher levels; it may show a necessary-but-not-sufficient relationship like that of Jenkins and O'Connor's Figure 3; it may reveal a curvilinear relationship; or it may show any of a nearly infinite variety of other relationships. Each of these shapes has different implications for accurate classification. For example, in Figure 3, it would be impossible to use the phonemic segmentation test to identify most of the students who will score below 12 on the decoding test. Even if you set a threshold as high as 18 (and accept a high rate of overidentification), you will still miss a substantial number of students who will score below 12 on the decoding test.

Thus, although correlation coefficient is a critical contributor to categorical prediction, by itself correlation can be misleading. Jenkins and O'Connor make the important point that to compare tests for early identification, we must know not only the predictive correlation with the criterion measure, but also (a) the standard for adequate performance on the criterion measure, (b) one or more cutoff scores recommended for classification, and (c) rate of underidentification and overidentification errors. Without this information, we cannot form strong judgments about the validity of early identification decisions based on test results. Put another way, a test does not have an inherent rate of over- or underidentification; errors of identification are a function of the test along with the decision rules for making identifications.

One of the important ideas from the discussion of classification decisions is that, other things being equal, there is a tradeoff between underidentification errors (false negatives) and overidentification errors (false positives). We must balance these two kinds of errors based on the consequences of each. Clearly, underidentification errors are tremendously costly. Each underidentification error represents a child who needs special services but does not receive them. If the consequences of overidentification are not terribly severe, then we can reduce underidentifications by accepting a higher level of overidentifications. The cost of overidentifications depends on the flexibility and responsiveness of the intervention program. If the intervention program includes a strong placement test and frequent progress monitoring, then students who do not need the program can be quickly identified and reassigned. This kind of program makes overidentification much less dire than it is in less responsive programs. In addition, layered programs that initially place students into a relatively simple intervention and go to a more intensive intervention only for students who do not respond to the first layer reduce the seriousness of overidentification. Thus, the structure of the program can have important implications for setting identification criteria.

Jenkins and O'Connor point out that accuracy of classification is systematically biased (too high) in the sample from which the classification criteria were derived. When we use a sample to set a threshold for classification, that threshold is optimized for that particular sample. Other samples will be somewhat different and the classification will tend to be less accurate on these other samples. Thus, early identification measures should be validated on a sample that is distinct from that which was used to set the criteria. This basic procedure is all too often ignored, and test users may be systematically misled as a result.

DANGERS IN DRAWING CONCLUSIONS

There is always tension between the desire to find the maximum possible generality in our findings and the desire to make strong and specific conclusions and recommendations. Jenkins and O'Connor explore an important area in which generally accepted conclusions from research may have been drawn too broadly. Numerous studies have found that phonological training along with letter-sound correspondence instruction has a positive effect on subsequent reading skills. However, several studies have found that this relationship may not hold if students receive high-quality phonics instruction. Thus, we may have to specify the nature of the reading instruction in order to draw conclusions about the effects of phonological training.

This example may provide a useful reminder about the importance of specific and powerful conclusions. As Jenkins and O'Connor point out, the conclusion that phonological skills are excellent predictors of subsequent reading success is considerably overstated. Through their close examination of attempts to optimize identification, Jenkins and O'Connor remind us that the quality of prediction depends on the specific phonological task, the specific age and developmental level of the student, the specific items, the specific scoring system, and whether the test assesses learning.

On the basis of the overall positive results for using phonological tasks for identification and intervention, we may be led to conclude that phonological tasks are sufficient for identification and as teaching targets. However, Jenkins and O'Connor report that phonological training alone may not be sufficient as a prereading intervention. In addition, Figure 3 suggests that although phonological skills are necessary for successful reading, a substantial number of students who have strong phonological skills (as measured by this particular test) still struggle with decoding. This may imply that both assessment and intervention should include but not be limited to phonological skills and perhaps that differential diagnosis and targeted intervention would be useful.

MORE UNANSWERED QUESTIONS

Jenkins and O'Connor point out the centrality of fluency in reading development. They also note that many fundamental questions about instructional practices have received scant research attention. These questions include (a) when, in the process of reading skill development, to begin explicit fluency practice, (b) determining the appropriate difficulty level (and other specific characteristics) of practice texts, (c) identifying optimal practice procedures, and (d) setting target rates. I would add that there are important basic issues about the role of fluency in typical and atypical reading development and its role as a support to reading development that are not well understood. The most foundational of these issues is the degree to which increases in fluency causes increases in comprehension. Although there are a strong theoretical rationale from a variety of perspectives for suspecting it, a large correlational literature that is consistent with it, and a few experimental studies that seem to confirm it, this causal relationship and the details of how and when it applies is not strongly established by the experimental literature. Thus, research on basic understanding of the role of reading fluency and development of educational interventions on fluency should proceed in tandem.

Jenkins and O'Connor also recognize the importance of the total volume of words that students read. Like the issue of fluency, the role of total volume of reading has not been the focus of sufficient research. Of course, there is a well-established correlation between volume of reading and reading comprehension, but the specific causal relations that underlie this correlation are not well understood. One of the important barriers to experimentation in this area is that interventions that powerfully increase the volume of reading have not been demonstrated. This is an area with a huge literature of recommended practices but an almost nonexistent empirical base. A recent systematic review of this literature (Forbush, 2001) located only five studies that met the criteria of (a) including an intervention designed to increase the volume of student reading and (b) providing some kind of outcome data related to the amount of reading that students completed. Of these five studies, three included neither baseline data nor a control group. Four of the five studies used students' self-report as their exclusive measure of reading volume. The National Reading Panel (2000) replicated the finding that the research base in this area is very weak. Clearly, both basic research and development of empirically validated interventions on the volume of reading are needed.

CONCLUSION

Jenkins and O'Connor have summarized a large body of important work in early identification and intervention. Their review confirms the central role of phonological skills, letter-sound knowledge, and phonological decoding in early reading development. It also emphasizes the important nuances that are necessary if the empirical research base is to support effective identification and intervention. The authors have linked these early reading factors with later reading development and have clarified the need for research and development on reading fluency and volume of student reading.

REFERENCES

Forbush, D. E. (2001). *Reading buddies: A student partnership to increase reluctant readers' reading participation.* Doctoral dissertation, Utah State University. Manuscript in preparation.

National Reading Panel. (2000). *Teaching children to read: An evidence-based assessment of the scientific research literature on reading and its implications for reading instruction.* Washington, DC: Author.

CHAPTER III: CLASSIFICATION OF LEARNING DISABILITIES: AN EVIDENCE-BASED EVALUATION

Jack M. Fletcher, University of Texas; G. Reid Lyon, National Institutes of Health;
Marcia Barnes, University of Toronto; Karla K. Stuebing, University of Texas;
David J. Francis, University of Houston; Richard K. Olson, University of Colorado;
Sally E. Shaywitz, Bennett A. Shaywitz, Yale University

INTRODUCTION

The purpose of this paper is to review research on the classification of learning disabilities (LD). We begin by briefly reviewing the nature of classification research. Then we discuss the evolution of definitions of LD, making explicit the classification hypotheses from which these definitions derive. An extensive review of the evidence for these hypotheses will be provided for the three components of classification implicit in the federal definition of LD: discrepancy, heterogeneity, and exclusion. We will show that classification hypotheses involving discrepancy and exclusion as embedded in federal (and state) policy have at best weak validity, often representing inaccurate and outdated assumptions about LD. There is evidence for heterogeneity of LD, but some reorganization of the types of LD identified in the federal definition may be necessary. Throughout the paper we identify alternative approaches to classification and identification, including weaknesses in any psychometric approach to the identification of LD. We suggest that classifications based on *inclusionary* definitions that specify attributes of different forms of LD are more desirable than current *exclusionary* definitions. Inclusionary definitions permit a focus on identification procedures that are intervention oriented as well as a focus on prevention, both of which are desirable and could contribute to improved results in remediating LD.

WHAT IS CLASSIFICATION?

Classification is the process of forming groups from a large set of entities based on their similarities and dissimilarities. It is not the same as identification, which is the process of assigning entities to an established classification. Valid classifications can be differentiated according to variables not used to form the groups. They are also reliable and have adequate coverage, i.e., permit identification of the majority of entities of interest. In classification research, groups are formed and evaluated for reliability, validity, and coverage. All classifications are hypotheses about the independent variables. Classification researchers evaluate the reliability, validity, and coverage of a hypothetical grouping of interest (Fletcher, Francis, Rourke, Shaywitz, & Shaywitz, 1993; Morris & Fletcher, 1988; Skinner, 1981).

Classification is fundamental to science and practice. It is virtually impossible to identify components of science or practice, regardless of the discipline and epistemological orientation, that do not involve classification. Although ubiquitous, classifications are often implicit and not explicitly identified. As part of science, however, all classifications are hypotheses that need to be empirically evaluated. Whenever a set of dependent variables is compared in relation to a set of independent variables (e.g., memory performance in children with and without LD), there is an explicit test of the hypotheses motivating the dependent variables (e.g., memory is weaker in LD), but also an implicit test of the independent variables (i.e., criteria for identifying children with and without LD) that derive from a hypothetical classification (Morris & Fletcher, 1988).

Even classifications that seem more straightforward, such as those used for defining children with and without traumatic brain injury, represent hypotheses at the level of the independent variables. To continue the memory performance example, if groups with and without traumatic brain injury differ in memory performance, evidence accumulates for the hypotheses that (a) memory is impaired in children with traumatic brain injury and (b) the criteria for defining traumatic brain injury are valid. The latter evidence would support the hypothetical classification of children along dimensions of brain injury (loss of consciousness, duration of coma, neuroimaging findings). Such evidence could be used to expand the classification towards hypothetical definitions of levels of severity (mild, moderate, severe); this classification and the criteria that lead to identification of children into severity groups could also be systematically evaluated along multiple dimensions: cognitive functions, prognosis, and response to intervention. The capacity of the classification to account for all children with traumatic brain injury (coverage) and to validly discriminate traumatic brain injury from other forms of brain injury (e.g., strokes, tumors) could also be evaluated. The keys are to recognize that there is a classification, to make it explicit, and to evaluate its reliability, validity, and coverage. When variation occurs in cognitive function, prognosis, or response to intervention among individuals with different levels of severity of traumatic brain injury, we can establish that the hypotheses leading to selection of these dependent variables were valid, but also that (a) the classification of injury severity has validity, and (b) the criteria used to operationalize the definitions of injury severity have validity (Fletcher et al., 1993).

In the area of LD, classification occurs at multiple levels: in identifying children as LD or typically achieving; as LD versus mentally deficient; within LD, as reading versus math impaired. Across classes of putative childhood conditions that produce underachievement, LD is identified as a particular type of "unexpected" low achievement and is distinguished from types where low achievement is expected due to emotional disturbance, social or cultural disadvantage, or inadequate instruction (Kavale & Forness, 2000). From a classification perspective, these levels of classification and the notion of LD as a form of low achievement that is unexpected represent hypotheses that should be evaluated.

That there are multiple underlying classifications of LD that are essentially hypotheses has not been consistently recognized. When the criteria for identifying LD began to evolve into policy in the 1960s, there was little research on which to base the underlying classifications and resultant definitions. This situation has gradually changed over the past 30 years, but the research that has emerged has had little impact on policy at the federal, state, and local levels. Indeed, the persistence of common assumptions about LD, its classification, and the perpetuation of resultant identification procedures are surprising given what has been learned about these disorders (Lyon et al., 2001). As we turn to research on the classification of LD, the question of how classifications should change as knowledge advances will emerge as a challenge to the field.

DEFINITIONS OF LEARNING DISABILITIES: IMPLICIT CLASSIFICATIONS MADE EXPLICIT

The evolution of definitions of LD can be traced to the turn of the last century and is closely linked to concepts of organically based behavioral disorders (Doris, 1993; Rutter, 1982; Satz & Fletcher, 1980). The concept of LD arose from observations of children who were hyperactive and impulsive, but for whom the cause of the disorder was not obvious. As these problems often occurred in children for whom there were a history or some other suspicion of a brain injury, it was often presumed that the cause of these unexpected behavior disorders was constitutional in origin. Thus, these children were described with terms such as organic driveness syndrome, minimal brain injury, and then in the 1960s, minimal brain dysfunction. The latter label, stemming from a meeting convened by the federal government in 1962

(Clements, 1966), recognized that many children with these behavioral difficulties also had difficulty mastering academic skills with associated processing difficulties despite adequate intelligence and opportunities to learn.

In a subsequent meeting in 1966 convened by the U.S. Office of Education (USOE; 1968), the concept of LD, as proposed by Kirk (1962), was formally defined and considered as inclusive of minimal brain dysfunction and related disorders. The notion of minimal brain dysfunction as a disorder not attributable to mental deficiency, sensory disorders, emotional disturbance, or cultural or economic disturbance was retained. Etiological terms were dropped and replaced by educational descriptors, although the notions of unexpectedness and the implicit attribution to constitutional factors were retained. Parental and professional advocacy efforts led to the provision of special education services through the 1969 Learning Disabilities Act. The legislative language in the 1969 Act later appeared in the Education for All Handicapped Children Act of 1975 (Public Law 94-142) and is now currently reflected in the 1997 reauthorization of the Individuals with Disabilities Education Act (IDEA). All these legislative proceedings used the 1968 definition of LD:

> The term "specific learning disability" means a disorder in one or more of the basic psychological processes involved in understanding or in using language, spoken or written, which may manifest itself in an imperfect ability to listen, speak, read, write, spell, or to do mathematical calculations. The term includes such conditions as perceptual handicaps, brain injury, minimal brain dysfunction, dyslexia, and developmental aphasia. The term does not include children who have learning disabilities which are primarily the result of visual, hearing, or motor handicaps, or mental retardation, or emotional disturbance, or of environmental, cultural, or economic disadvantage. (USOE, 1968, p. 34)

After P.L. 94-142 was passed and federal funds became available, states were expected to identify children with LD. It quickly became apparent that states needed assistance with criteria for identification of LD, leading to publication of the Procedures for Evaluating Specific Learning Disabilities in the *Federal Register* (USOE, 1977). These procedures recommended that LD be defined as:

> a severe discrepancy between achievement and intellectual ability in one or more of the areas: (1) oral expression; (2) listening comprehension; (3) written expression; (4) basic reading skill; (5) reading comprehension; (6) mathematics calculation; or (7) mathematic reasoning. The child may not be identified as having a specific learning disability if the discrepancy between ability and achievement is primarily the result of: (1) a visual,

hearing, or motor handicap; (2) mental retardation; (3) emotional disturbance, or (4) environmental, cultural, or economic disadvantage. (USOE, 1977, p. G1082)

Although states vary considerably in the IQ and achievement criteria used to designate a child as LD, discrepancy is used in either the definition and/or criteria by virtually all states, with the use of an IQ test to establish "aptitude" equally common (Frankenberger & Fronzaglio, 1991; Mercer, Jordan, Alsop, & Mercer, 1996). Discrepancy is the only inclusionary criterion; all other criteria are exclusionary and indicate simply what LD is not. Although there was little research at the time validating classifications of LD based on IQ discrepancy, researchers, practitioners, and the public commonly assume that IQ discrepancy is a marker for a specific type of LD that is unexpected and categorically distinct from other forms of underachievement (Kavale & Forness, 2000; Mercer et al., 1996; Stanovich, 1993). These beliefs reflect the common observation of unexpected underachievement in children who seem bright and capable.

The reification of IQ discrepancy in public policy is clearly apparent in the definition of LD in the 1992 and 1997 reauthorizations of IDEA, which continued the 1968 definition and added the following criteria from the 1977 recommendations to states:

(a) A team may determine that a child has a specific learning disability if:

(1) The child does not achieve commensurate with his or her age and ability levels in one or more of the areas listed in paragraph (a) (2) of this section, when provided with learning experiences appropriate for the child's age and ability levels; and

(2) The team finds that a child has a severe discrepancy between achievement and intellectual ability in one or more of the following areas: (i) Oral expression; (ii) Listening comprehension; (iii) Written expression; (iv) Basic reading skill; (v) Reading comprehension; (vi) Mathematics calculation; or (vii) Mathematics reasoning. (U.S. Department of Education, 1999, p. 12457)

IQ discrepancy is clearly a prominent classification hypothesis. Other components of the federal definition also reflect classification hypotheses. Here we note the *heterogeneity* hypothesis, where LD is represented as seven different types of unexpected low achievement that may overlap. In addition, there is the *exclusion* hypothesis, which suggests that low achievement in LD is different from low achievement due to (a) mental deficiency and sensory disorders; (b) emotional disturbance; (c) social, economic, and cultural disadvantage; or (d) inadequate instruction. In the next sections, we review each of these classification hypotheses.

DISCREPANCY HYPOTHESIS

The IQ-achievement discrepancy criterion is the most controversial and best-studied component of the federal definition of LD. From a classification perspective, it is a hypothesis that children with poor achievement below a level predicted by an IQ score (IQ discrepant) are different from children with poor achievement consistent with their IQ score (low achievement). IQ-discrepant children with LD have been proposed to differ from low achievers who are not IQ discrepant on several dimensions, including neurological integrity, cognitive characteristics, response to intervention, prognosis, gender, and the heritability of LD (Fletcher et al., 1998; Rutter, 1989; Siegel, 1992; Stanovich, 1991). There is an extensive body of research that can be used to evaluate this hypothesis. Although virtually all of the published studies involve reading disabilities (RD), we address LD in other domains later in this paper.

Isle of Wight Studies

The IQ-discrepancy classification hypothesis is not without support. The earliest empirical evidence validating IQ discrepancy came from the Isle of Wight studies in the early 1970s (Rutter & Yule, 1975). In this epidemiological study of RD, Rutter and Yule (1975) administered the Performance IQ Scale of the Wechsler Intelligence Scale for Children (WISC) and measures of reading. They defined two groups using a regression-adjusted definition: *specific reading retardation*, representing children with reading scores two standard errors below IQ, and *general reading backwardness*, representing children with reading scores that were deficient, but within two standard errors of IQ. In examining the distribution of residualized scores, they found an over-representation of children with general reading backwardness in the lower tail of the distribution of reading scores, representing a "hump." They also found evidence suggesting that the two groups of poor readers could be differentiated, thus accepting the existence of a group of children with specific RD:

> Reading retardation is shown to differ significantly from reading backwardness in terms of sex ratio, neurological disorder, pattern of neurodevelopmental deficits and educational prognosis. It is concluded that the concept of specific reading retardation is valid. (p. 195)

Is There A Bimodal Distribution?

The Isle of Wight studies were widely accepted because they seemed to support the IQ-discrepancy hypothesis. Since that time, more critical evaluation of this support has become necessary. Although methodological factors involving inadequate ceilings on the reading measures have been cited (van der Wissell & Zegers, 1985), the critical issue centers around the interest of Rutter and Yule (1975) in the question of whether specific forms of RD could be distinguished from reading failure attributable to all other causes. Given this hypothesis, no exclusionary criteria were applied and approximately 36% of the children in the group defined as backwards readers had known or suspected evidence of a neurological disorder; many also had IQ scores in the ranges associated with mental deficiency. At the time, Rutter and Yule (1975) wrote that "it could be argued that the association with general reading backwardness was to be expected on the grounds of the below average intelligence of that group of children" (p. 189). It is well known that the distribution of IQ scores in a population is bimodal when individuals are included who have sustained injury to the central nervous system (Robinson, Zigler, & Gallagher, 2000). Not surprisingly, epidemiological studies in Australia (Jorm, Share, Matthews, & Matthews, 1986), New Zealand (Silva, McGee, & Williams, 1985), Great Britain (Rodgers, 1983; Stevenson, 1988), and the United States (Shaywitz, Escobar, Shaywitz, Fletcher, & Makuch, 1992) that either excluded or had fewer children with brain injury have largely failed to replicate the Rutter and Yule (1975) finding of a bimodal distribution. This finding can be attributed to the prevalence of neurologically impaired children on the Isle of Wight, many with mental deficiency (Fletcher et al., 1998).

Can IQ-Discrepant and Low Achieving Poor Readers Be Differentiated?

Rutter (1989) observed that the critical test of the classification hypothesis does not depend on the presence of a bimodal distribution. Rather, the question is whether differences can be found that meaningfully differentiate IQ-discrepant and low achieving groups, which is a classification hypothesis. More recent studies of the validity of this hypothetical two-group classification, reviewed by Aaron (1997), Fletcher et al. (1993), Fletcher et al. (1998), Siegel (1992), and Stanovich (1991), have provided mixed evidence for the validity of the two-group classification. Many comparisons yielded null results, whereas others demonstrated small but statistically significant differences between the two groups.

When the studies are examined, they can be broken into domains involving prognosis, response to intervention, neurobiological factors, behavioral characteristics, achievement, and cognitive correlates. The bulk of the studies involve the behavioral, achievement, and cognitive domains, which are addressed in three meta-analyses summarized below. There is also research examining prognosis, response to intervention, and neurobiological factors. All six domains can be examined as evaluations of the validity of a two-group classification of poor readers based on presence or absence of IQ discrepancy.

Prognosis

Rutter and Yule (1975) reported that children who were backwards readers (i.e., low achieving) actually showed more rapid development of academic skills than children who were reading retarded (i.e., IQ discrepant). As the reading and spelling skills of the backwards readers were lower at baseline, and children were not randomly assigned to the two groups, the greater advances may reflect regression to the mean. Francis, Shaywitz, et al. (1996) examined this question using data from the Grade 9 follow-up of children in the epidemiological, population-based Connecticut Longitudinal Project. In this project, reading skills were assessed yearly beginning in Grade 1. The population is now being followed as adults.

Francis, Shaywitz, et al. (1996) composed three groups of children based on Grade 3 WISC–R full scale IQ and reading tests: not reading impaired (NRI), IQ discrepant using a 1.5 standard error regression-based criterion, and low achieving (not discrepant, but reading below the 25th percentile). Comparisons of the reading development of the three groups on the composite score from the Woodcock-Johnson Psycho-Educational Test Battery (Woodcock & Johnson, 1979) showed no differences between the two groups with RD in the rate of growth over time or the level of reading ability at any age despite the fact that about half the children in the IQ-discrepant group received special education services. As expected, both groups of poor readers differed significantly from the NRI group in growth rate and reading ability at all ages.

In Figure 1, these comparisons are carried through Grade 12. Again, there are clearly no differences in growth rates or level of reading ability at any age despite an 18-point difference in IQ between the two groups of poor readers. There was also no evidence that the poor readers narrowed the gap. More than 70% of those who read poorly in Grade 3 read poorly in Grade 12, showing that without intervention, LD in reading is a chronic, lifelong condition. These findings parallel those of Share, McGee, and Silva (1989), who reported results from another large longitudinal study in New Zealand. They found that IQ was not relating to reading achievement within age bands (7, 9, 11, 13 years) nor did IQ predict change over time. Share et al. (1989) concluded, "It might be timely to formulate a concept of reading disability that is independent of IQ. Unless it can be shown to have some predictive value for the nature of treatment or treatment outcomes, considerations of IQ should be discarded in discussions of reading difficulties" (p. 99).

Response to intervention

In turning to treatment, several studies examined outcomes in relationship to different indices of IQ or IQ discrepancy. Aaron (1997) reviewed earlier studies that sometimes included comparisons of groups defined as LD and low achieving, observing that both groups made little progress in their reading development, even

Figure 1. Growth in reading skills by children from 6–18 years of age (Grades 1–12) in the Connecticut Longitudinal Study based on the reading cluster of the Woodcock-Johnson Psycho-Educational Test Battery. The children were identified at 8 years of age (Grade 3) as not reading impaired (NRI), reading disabled according to a 1.5 standard error discrepancy between IQ and reading achievement (RDD), or low reading achievement with no discrepancy (25th percentile; low achieving). The figure shows that growth in the two groups with reading disability is similar (the growth curves are indistinguishable); that neither catches up to the NRI group; and that the differences between the NRI group and the two groups with reading disability are apparent well before Grade 3.

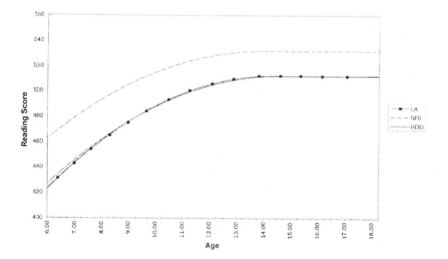

with remedial placements. More recent studies explicitly examine this hypothesis in remedial or prevention efforts. In a remedial study of children with poor reading skills in Grades 2–5, Wise, Ring, and Olson (1999) assessed the relationship of full scale IQ in response to different approaches to intervention. They found that full scale IQ predicted about 5% of the variance in word reading outcomes on one measure of word reading, but that this effect was not apparent on other measures of word reading or assessments of phonological processing ability at the end of intervention. Similarly, Hatcher and Hulme (1999) found no relationships of IQ and reading outcomes involving word recognition.

Studies that have attempted to prevent RD in kindergarten and Grade 1 have also found no relationships of reading outcomes with full scale IQ or verbal IQ (Foorman, Francis, Beeler, Winikates, & Fletcher, 1997; Foorman, Francis, Fletcher, Schatschneider, & Mehta, 1998; Torgesen et al., 1999; Vellutino, Scanlon, & Lyon, 2000). Foorman et al. (Foorman, Francis, Beeler, et al. 1997; Foorman, Francis, Fletcher, et al. 1998) and Torgesen et al. (1999) examined relationships of reading intervention outcomes and general verbal ability, while Vellutino et al. (2000) looked both at levels of IQ and IQ discrepancy based on full scale IQ. In Vellutino et al. (2000), IQ-discrepancy scores were computed and compared among a variety of subgroups formed on the basis of reading gains, response intervention, and other indices. They concluded that "…the IQ-achievement discrepancy does not reliably distinguish between disabled and non-disabled readers … Neither does it distinguish between children who were found to be difficult to remediate and those who are readily remediated, prior to initiation of remediation, and it does not predict response to remediation" (p. 235). These findings are especially important in showing that IQ discrepancy is not specifically associated with those who respond to intervention.

In all the above studies, measures of phonological awareness skills were robust predictors of response to intervention. Some of these studies found that levels of IQ predicted growth in reading comprehension ability (Hatcher & Hulme, 1999; Torgesen et al., 1999; Wise et al., 1999), but consider what IQ tests actually assess. The subtests that make up a verbal IQ scale are commonly found to represent a general verbal comprehension skill closely related to vocabulary (Fletcher et al., 1996; Sattler, 1993; Share et al., 1989, 1991). As such, it is not surprising that IQ would predict reading comprehension as vocabulary is an essential part of IQ and a strong predictor of reading comprehension skills (Adams, 1990). Indeed, if IQ tests included measures of phonological awareness, it is likely that such measures would predict response to intervention. Inclusion of such subtests would also virtually eliminate the possibility that children with RD could ever be IQ discrepant given the close linking of phonological awareness skills and RD. Altogether, the results do not provide much support for differences in response to intervention between children defined as IQ-discrepant and low achieving poor readers.

Neurobiological factors

A series of studies from a group of researchers at the University of Colorado has been completed on the heritability of RD that addresses the validity of the IQ-discrepancy hypothesis. Pennington, Gilger, Olson, and DeFries (1992) classified a large population of monozygotic and dizygotic twins in which at least one member was classified with RD and a set of control twins in which neither was RD into one of four groups: RD based on IQ discrepancy, RD based on low achievement, RD based on both IQ discrepancy and low achievement, and those not classified as RD.

Comparisons were made in three domains involving (a) genetic etiology, (b) gender ratios and clinical correlates, and (c) neuropsychological profiles. The researchers reported no evidence for differential genetic etiology based on type of definition. They also did not find evidence for significant differences in gender ratios, clinical correlates, and neuropsychological profiles.

More recent studies from this group have specifically tested the hypothesis that the genetic etiology of RD may vary by virtue of either IQ discrepancy or level of IQ. In a series of studies summarized by Wadsworth, Olson, Pennington, and DeFries (2000), genetic factors were more related to RD in children who have higher IQ scores than those with lower IQ scores. In Wadsworth et al. (2000), the overall heritability of reading disability was 0.58. Separating children defined as RD with full scale IQ scores above or below 100 resulted in heritability estimates of 0.43 for the lower IQ group and 0.72 for the higher IQ group, a statistically significant difference. These results indicate that environmental influences are particularly salient as a cause of reading difficulties in children with lower IQ scores.

These differences in heritability, while statistically and practically significant, are relatively small. Several earlier studies of the cohort with smaller samples yielded differences that did not reach statistical significance. Wadsworth et al. (2000) required almost 400 pairs of twins in order to detect the difference. It is not accurate to suggest that, because of these differences, classifications based on IQ discrepancy have value for components of LD other than the etiology of RD. As the researchers noted, the relatively high IQ of children with RD could be related to a more intractable genetically-based reading failure despite strong environmental support for IQ and for learning to read, whereas those children with RD who have relatively lower IQ scores may have more pervasive deficiencies in cognitive development and reading that reflect broader environmental disadvantages. For example, children in the lower IQ group in Wadsworth et al. (2000) had homes where there were fewer books and where mothers had fewer years of education. The researchers argued against excluding lower IQ children from intervention or remediation because they did not meet an IQ-discrepant definition, suggesting that the greater impact of environment influences on RD in this group suggests the need for emphasizing environmental intervention. Unfortunately, the traditional use of IQ and achievement criteria for LD in determining access to services has exactly the opposite effect.

There are also studies of children with RD that use functional imaging methods, such as functional magnetic resonance imaging (fMRI), which are reviewed in detail in the section on constitutional factors. While no study has a sample that is sufficiently large to actually compare IQ-discrepant and low achieving poor readers, it is noteworthy that no studies include only those children with IQ discrepancy. There is no evidence from these studies that children who meet IQ-discrepancy and low achieving definitions of RD have different neuroimaging profiles.

Meta-analyses of behavior, achievement, and cognitive ability domains

There are three meta-analyses that address the validity of IQ-discrepancy classifications for children with RD in the behavior, achievement, and cognitive ability domains and that constitute the bulk of studies of the IQ-discrepancy classification (Fuchs, Fuchs, Mathes, & Lipsey, 2000a; Hoskyn & Swanson, 2000; Stuebing et al., in press). The three studies were completely independent, but addressed slightly different questions. Fuchs et al. focused on the question of whether "the reading performance of underachieving children with and without the learning disabilities label is the same or different" (Fuchs, Fuchs, Mathes, Lipsey, & Eaton, 2000b, p. 2). To address this question, they identified and coded 76 studies that evaluated reading skills in children who were poor readers with and without the LD label. Fuchs et al. (2000a, b) reported a large effect size (0.76) showing poorer reading by groups with the label of LD in reading (presumably IQ-discrepant) relative to groups presumed to be poor readers without the LD label.

Hoskyn and Swanson (2000) coded 19 studies that met stringent IQ and achievement criteria. They focused specifically on studies where cognitive skills were compared in groups formed of those with higher IQ and poor reading achievement (IQ-discrepant) versus those with both lower IQ and poor reading achievement. They found negligible to small differences on several measures of reading and phonological processing (range = −0.02 –0.29), but larger differences on measures of vocabulary (0.55) and syntax (0.87). The groups were more similar than different, leading them to conclude that "… our synthesis concurs with several individual studies indicating that the discrepancy … is not an important predictor of cognitive differences between low achieving children and children with RD" (p. 117).

Stuebing et al. (in press) explicitly addressed the validity of the IQ-discrepancy classification hypothesis for RD in behavior, achievement, and cognitive domains. They reported on 46 studies that compared groups composed of poor readers who met explicit criteria for IQ discrepancy and low achievement. In the latter study, simply possessing the label of LD was not adequate, but some specification of the criteria used to designate children as IQ discrepant or low achieving was required. Fuchs et al. required the *label* of LD, with a presumption of IQ discrepancy, and some type of often unevaluated comparison group that presumably represented non-LD low achievers (e.g., placement in compensatory education). In contrast, Stuebing et al. required discrepancy criteria for the LD group and an indication that the low achieving group did not include individuals who might be IQ discrepant or typically achieving readers. These criteria were more liberal than Hoskyn and Swanson, but captured most of the 19 studies included in their meta-analysis.

Stuebing et al. (in press) found negligible aggregated effects for behavior (–0.05) and achievement (–0.12). A small effect size was found for cognitive ability (0.30). The effect sizes for the behavioral domain were homogeneous, but heterogeneity was apparent for the achievement and cognitive ability domains. When the heterogeneity was evaluated by examining the specific tasks within the achievement domain, those that involved word recognition, oral reading, and spelling showed small effect sizes indicating poorer performance by the IQ-discrepant groups. Tasks involving reading comprehension, math, and writing yielded negligible effect sizes. The small effect sizes for the former measures may reflect their similarity to the types of tasks used to measure poor reading in many studies. Similarly, constructs under cognitive ability closely related to reading yielded negligible effect sizes: phonological awareness (–0.13), rapid naming (–0.12), memory (0.10), and vocabulary (0.10). Not surprisingly, measures of IQ not used to define the groups yielded large effect size differences, while measures of cognitive skills like those measured by IQ tests (spatial cognition, concept formation) yielded small to medium effect sizes, the direction of both showing better performance by the IQ-discrepant group. Even with the inclusion of these measures of cognitive ability, the difference was only about three tenths of a standard deviation. Other analyses demonstrated (a) substantial overlap between the groups, and (b) that the size of the effects in different studies could be predicted by knowing the scores on the IQ and reading tasks used to define the groups (i.e., sampling variation across studies) and the correlation of these variables with the tasks used to compare the two groups. Stuebing et al. concluded that classifications of LD based on IQ discrepancy had at best weak validity.

The results of these three studies are quite consistent despite the differences in the research questions and the criteria for selecting studies. The most important difference was that unlike Stuebing et al. (in press), the other two meta-analyses did not differentiate IQ and achievement variables used to form the groups from those that served as dependent variables. It would be expected that variables used to define the groups would generate large effect sizes as IQ-discrepancy definitions select the poorest readers at each level of IQ (see Psychometric Issues below). To illustrate, Fuchs et al. (2000a, b) evaluated two constructs outside the reading domain that were not incorporated in the aggregated effect size estimate. The constructs yielded effect sizes consistent with Hoskyn and Swanson (2000) and Stuebing et al. (in press): 0.10 for phonological awareness and 0.26 for rapid naming. When measures of reading used to form groups were examined in Stuebing et al., a moderate effect size in reading showing poorer performance in children with IQ discrepancy was apparent. Altogether, these meta-analyses do not provide strong support for the validity of classifications based on IQ discrepancy.

Other Forms of LD and the IQ-Discrepancy Hypothesis

Discrepancy hypotheses have not received strong support in studies of RD, but LD is more than just RD. In this section, we review research on math disabilities, speech and language disorders, and psychometric issues relevant to any formulation of LD.

Specific math disability

As part of the Yale Center for Learning and Attention Disorders, Shaywitz (1996) evaluated the two-group classification hypothesis for computational disorders in math. The nature of these types of math disabilities (MD) is discussed below in the section on the heterogeneity hypothesis. Here we simply compare children who meet a 1.5 standard error IQ-discrepancy definition of MD with those who achieve below the 25th percentile, but whose math score on the Woodcock-Johnson Calculations subtest (Woodcock & Johnson, 1979) is within 1.5 standard errors of what would be predicted based on their full scale WISC–R score (Wechsler, 1974). These children do not meet criteria for RD using either IQ-discrepancy or low achieving criteria. They differ in full scale IQ (IQ-discrepancy $M = 107$, $SD = 12$; low achieving $M = 96$, $SD = 9$) and in math calculations (IQ-discrepant $M = 78$, $SD = 10$; low achieving $M = 85$, $SD = 4$). The nature and direction of the differences are exactly what would be expected given the properties of IQ-discrepancy definitions, where at each level of IQ the lowest performing children are identified into the IQ-discrepant group. Note also the reduction in the standard deviation relative to the population SD of 15, which is a product of subdividing a continuous distribution (Cohen, 1983).

Figure 2 shows a comparison of these two groups of children on a set of cognitive variables involving attention, language, problem solving, concept formation, and visual-motor skills. As Figure 2 shows, the IQ-discrepant group has higher performance levels on all variables. Note that neither group shows the severe impairment in phonological awareness associated with RD (see Figure 3 below). The group that is low achieving in math is noticeably poorer in vocabulary despite average reading skills. The critical issue, as for RD, is not that the groups differ; such differences in level of performance are expected because IQ tests are used to define the groups, and IQ is moderately to highly correlated with each of the measures (e.g., vocabulary) used to evaluate the children. Rather, the question is whether the pattern of differences separates the groups, implying that the correlates of math achievement differentiate the group. Testing the profiles for differences in shape did not yield a

Figure 2. Profile comparisons of cognitive skills from children with math but not word-reading disabilities, defined using IQ discrepancy (1.5 standard errors) and low achievement (< 25th percentile) criteria. As expected, the two groups differ in level of performance, but the shapes of the two profiles are similar.

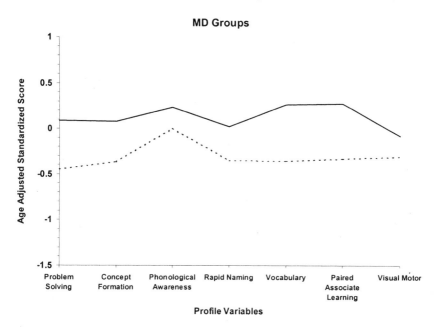

statistically significant difference and the effect size was negligible (0.06). As we have shown in the reading area (Fletcher et al., 1998), eliminating variability due to the difference in vocabulary eliminates the differences in level of performance apparent in Figure 2. The differences in Figure 2 are a product of the definitions and the correlates of poor math achievement do not appear to differ once the differences induced by the definition are taken into account.

Comorbid reading and math disability
Figure 3 compares IQ-discrepant and low achieving children with RD and MD on the same variables as Figure 2. In the upper panel, children with RD and no MD are depicted for contrast purposes, while the lower panel shows children with both RD and MD. In both panels, the striking impairment in phonological awareness is apparent. Note also the dip in vocabulary skills that characterizes both the low achieving groups. In the low achieving group that has only RD, the performance level in vocabulary is comparable with that of the low achieving MD group in Figure 2. Vocabulary is lowest in the low achieving RD-MD group. Again, these patterns reflect in part the relationship of IQ and vocabulary as opposed to specific

Figure 3. Profile comparison of cognitive skills from children with reading but not math disabilities (upper panel) and both reading and math disabilities (lower panel), defined using IQ-discrepancy (1.5 standard errors) and low achievement (< 25th percentile) criteria. The two groups differ in level of performance, but the shapes of the two profiles are similar.

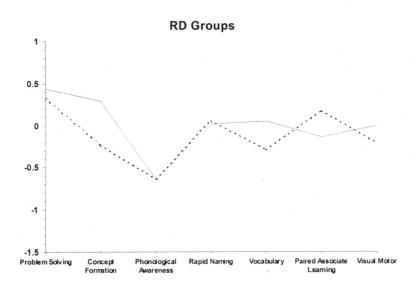

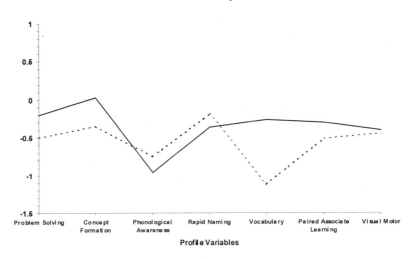

associations with either RD or MD. The comorbid RD-MD group is more impaired in language skills, but also shows impairment on some of the same measures as the group that is only MD.

Speech and language disorders

Disorders of oral expression and listening comprehension are included under the LD category, though speech and language disorders are also a separate category in special education under IDEA. Epidemiological studies directed by Bruce Tomblin have explored the validity of IQ-discrepancy definitions in children who have disorders of expressive and receptive language. These comparisons have not supported the validity of IQ-discrepancy hypotheses for children with oral language disorders.

To illustrate, Tomblin and Zhang (1999) used measures of nonverbal IQ and oral language ability to create three groups of children from their large epidemiological study: not impaired, specific language impairment (IQ > 87 and composite language skills < 1.25 standard deviations below age), and general delay (IQ d" 87 and composite language skills < 1.25 standard deviations below age). Comparisons of the three groups on a variety of expressive and receptive language measures showed that the two language-impaired groups differed on multiple dimensions from the non-impaired group. Differences between the two language-impaired groups were less robust: "children with general delay closely parallel the specifically language-impaired group except that the children with general delay were more impaired and noticeably poorer on the test involving comprehension of sentences (grammatical understanding)" (p. 367). The investigators go on to question whether even this latter difference in grammatical understanding is specific to either group, noting, "current diagnostic methods and standards for specific language impairment do not result in a group of children whose profiles of language achievement are unique." A consensus group convened by the National Institute of Deafness and Communication Disorders reached a similar conclusion (Tager-Flusberg & Cooper, 1999).

Psychometric Issues

Although we could continue a research program to evaluate the IQ-discrepancy hypothesis across multiple permutations, psychometric factors make it unlikely that any form of discrepancy can be effectively used. These factors raise questions about the viability of any approach to LD identification based solely on the use of test scores and cut-off points. Whereas to this point we have addressed the *validity* of LD classification, psychometric factors raise questions about the *reliability* of LD classifications.

Figure 4. Bivariate distribution of simulated IQ and achievement measures with a mean of 100, standard deviation of 1.5, and correlation of 0.6. Cutoffs depicting a 1.5 standard error discrepancy and low achievement (< 25th percentile) are drawn. Four segments are apparent: not reading impaired, only low achievement, only IQ discrepant, and both low achievement and IQ discrepancy.

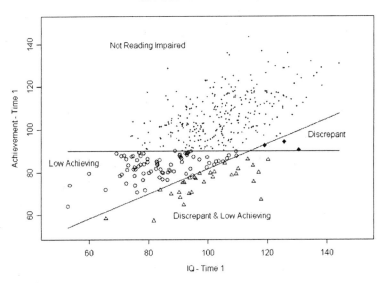

In Figures 4–6, we examine what happens when groups are formed using IQ-discrepancy definitions in simulated data constructed to follow the bivariate normal distribution with no true group structure. It is apparent that the instability in these "simulated groups" parallels the instability seen in true groups (Shaywitz et al., 1992), raising doubts about the validity of the "true groups" formed by IQ-discrepancy rules. Consider Figure 4, which plots the bivariate distribution of simulated ability and achievement measures with a mean of 100, standard deviation of 15, and correlation of 0.6, consistent with population estimates (Sattler, 1993). Figure 4 also shows the groups that emerge when a 1.5 standard error regression definition like that employed in Connecticut (see Figure 1) is used, along with an arbitrary cutoff for low achieving at the 25th percentile. In Figure 4, it is clear that the groups are clearly demarcated, with no overlap in group membership. Note that many data points are below the low achieving cutoff, but are not IQ discrepant. Another subgroup is below both the IQ-discrepancy and low achieving cutoffs. A few children are above the low achieving cutoff but below the IQ-discrepancy cutoff.

Figure 5. Bivariate distribution of simulated IQ and achievement measures with a mean of 100, standard deviation of 1.5, and correlation of 0.6. Cutoffs depicting a 1 standard deviation discrepancy and low achievement (< 25th percentile) are drawn. The subject designations are from Figure 4 and show how simulated cases shift across the four segments by virtue of the change in the definition of discrepancy.

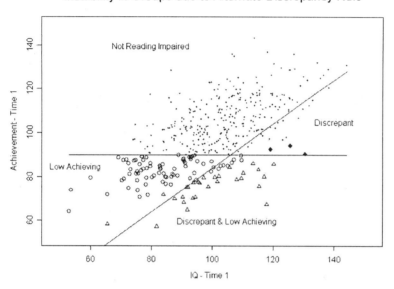

Figure 5 shows what happens when a different definition of discrepancy (one standard deviation) is used, analogous to how discrepancy is defined in many states, i.e., discrepancy without adjustment for the correlation of IQ and achievement. The symbols for the group represent their original locations in Figure 4. Note that the IQ-discrepancy cutoff is much steeper; the regression line in Figure 4 is actually slightly curved so that it is steeper at lower levels of IQ and flatter at higher levels of IQ. As a consequence, the unadjusted discrepancy definition identifies fewer children with lower IQs as discrepant (14% become low achieving) and identifies more children with higher IQs as "disabled" (6% of a large NRI group). The arbitrariness of the two discrepancy cutoffs is illustrated by asking what could possibly be the important differences in the 14% of children who change from IQ discrepant to low achieving at lower levels of IQ and other children who stay in these segments? Similarly, are the 6% of those who become "disabled" in Figure 5 truly impaired in reading? Fletcher et al. (1998) found no evidence supporting this hypothesis.

Figure 6. Simulated stability of group designations over time based on high stability (0.9) and reliability (0.8) for IQ and achievement measures. The subject designations are from Figure 4 and demonstrate the high instability associated with psychometric decision rules for identifying LD.

Instability in Groups in Simulated Data at Time 2

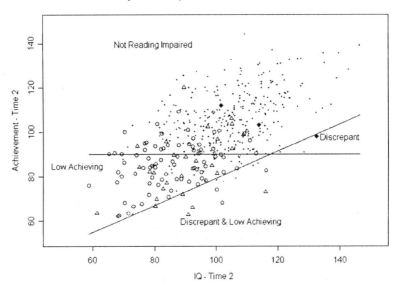

Figure 6 uses simulated data to show what happens to group membership over time. This figure was generated assuming high stability (0.9) in the traits measured and high reliability (0.8) for the measures of both traits. These assumptions mean that the traits vary little from person to person over time (i.e., individual differences are stable), and the traits are well-measured by the specific instruments. Thus, although there may be growth in the traits, growth does not differ much from one person to the other. These conditions should lead to a high degree of stability in classifications. Heterogeneity in growth would lead to instability in both individual differences over time and the classifications.

Figure 6 shows that classifications are not stable over time, despite the generally favorable conditions for stability. The instability is apparent in all four segments of Figure 6. In the group that is both IQ discrepant and low achieving, 38% move to the low achieving segment and another 38% move to the NRI segment. For the segment that is low achieving at Time 1, 14% move to the both IQ-discrepant and low achieving segment and 36% move to the NRI segment. In the Time 1 NRI segment, 3% move to the both IQ-discrepant and low achieving segment, 7% to the low achievement segment, and 1% to the IQ-discrepant-only segment. Finally, 67% of the only-discrepant segment moved to the NRI segment.

The lack of stability is also apparent when IQ and achievement scores are modeled from the Connecticut Longitudinal Study (Shaywitz et al., 1992). If IQ discrepancy and low achievement formed distinct and valid groupings, then one would expect stability in classifications over time, or at least instability that does not parallel the instability found in arbitrary classifications in simulated data. That IQ-discrepancy and low achieving classifications show instability that parallels the instability of arbitrary classifications in simulated data suggests that the IQ-discrepancy and low achieving distinctions are similarly arbitrary classifications, formed within a bivariate normal space and whose properties are largely driven by psychometric characteristics of this space rather than any inherent characteristics of the groups being formed.

Conclusions: Discrepancy Hypothesis

Concerns about the validity of the IQ-discrepancy classification hypothesis have led some to essentially reject the concept of LD (Ysseldyke, Algozzine, Shinn, & McGue, 1982), leading to fierce disagreements on whether LD and low achieving groups differ—all in defense of the concept of LD, not the validity of a hypothetical classification (Algozzine, Ysseldyke, & McGue, 1995; Kavale, 1995; Kavale, Fuchs, & Scruggs, 1994). The question is not so much whether children defined as IQ discrepant and low achieving are different, but how much they differ and whether the differences are meaningful for research and practice. The evidence reviewed above for prognosis, response to intervention, neurobiological factors, behavior, achievement, and cognitive abilities suggests that the IQ-discrepancy classification hypothesis lacks strong evidence for external validity. The psychometric evidence shows that the classification has problems with reliability. The criteria derived from the two-group classification produce groups of underachievers that are significantly overlapping; the differences that emerge are not strongly related to academic performance or to treatment and prognosis. Differences in behavior and cognitive abilities independent of the criteria used to form the groups are negligible. There is evidence for differences in the heritability of RD, but the differences are small, difficult to attribute solely to genetic factors, and with little evidence supporting the need to single out the IQ-discrepant group. There is no evidence from neuroimaging studies of a need to differentiate the groups; such studies routinely combine IQ-discrepant and low achieving children. Thus, consistent with the call of many researchers, the viability of the IQ-discrepancy classification hypothesis must be questioned.

HETEROGENEITY HYPOTHESIS

In federal and non-federal definitions, LD is rarely conceptualized as a single disability, but instead is represented as a general category composed of disabilities in any one or a combination of several academic domains. In the 1968 federal definition, seven domains are specified: (1) listening; (2) speaking; (3) basic reading (decoding and word recognition); (4) reading comprehension; (5) arithmetic calculation; (6) mathematics reasoning; and (7) written expression. While the inclusion of these seven areas of disability in the federal classification ensures that the category of LD accounts for a wide range of learning difficulties, the practice implies that what may be highly variegated learning problems should be lumped together. Even today, many studies simply define groups of children as "learning disabled" despite considerable evidence that the correlates of LD in reading, math, and other achievement domains vary at multiple levels of analysis. In this section, we will ask how well these seven domains cover the range of LD and raise questions concerning what domains should be included in the federal definition.

Listening and Speaking

Disorders of listening and speaking are essentially oral language disorders. Such disabilities are incorporated in IDEA under the speech and language category, so the need for including them as types of LD category is not clear. As oral language disorders, they represent examples of difficulties with expressive and receptive language. What is the point of duplication, especially since disorders of listening and speaking are not formal areas of academic achievement? Difficulties in listening comprehension typically parallel problems with reading comprehension (Shankweiler et al., 1999; Stothard & Hulme, 1996). Children cannot understand written language any better than they can understand oral language. Any phonological, syntactic, or semantic problems that hinder oral language comprehension will also affect the ability to read written text or even to comprehend when someone reads them the text. While some children with LD have oral language disorders, the duplication is far from perfect (Tomblin & Zwang, 1999). The basis for including disorders of listening and speaking in the federal classification of LD is not clear and leads to conceptual confusion in classifying and defining oral language disorders in IDEA.

Reading Disabilities

The federal definition specifies two areas of reading difficulties, basic reading (word recognition) and reading comprehension. That difficulties with word recognition represent a specific form of LD in reading is well established (Shaywitz, 1996). Children can also be identified with comprehension difficulties that do not involve the word recognition module. Much more is known about the nature and causes of disabilities in word recognition, as less reading research has been devoted to studying how children understand what they read.

What are not addressed in the federal definition are difficulties that involve the automatization of word recognition skills and speed of reading connected text. These problems also occur in children with accurate word recognition skills. Unfortunately, less is known about fluency deficits in reading despite recent development of hypotheses suggesting that deficiencies in reading fluency represent a separate subgroup of RD (Wolf & Bowers, 1999; Wolf, Bowers, & Biddle, 2001). In the next section, we review evidence for subgroups with RD specific to word recognition, comprehension, and fluency.

Word recognition (dyslexia)

Word-level RD is synonymous with dyslexia, a form of LD that has been described during the 20th century as word blindness, visual agnosia for words, and specific reading disability (Doris, 1993). The evolution of the concept of dyslexia, and its link with word-level RD, provide an excellent example of how definitions of LD can move from exclusionary to inclusionary. As an example of an exclusionary definition, consider the 1968 World Federation of Neurology definition that was in part the basis for the epidemiological studies of Rutter and Yule (1975):

> A disorder manifested by difficulties in learning to read despite conventional instruction, adequate intelligence, and socio-economic opportunity. It is dependent upon fundamental cognitive disabilities, which are frequently of constitutional origin. (Critchley, 1970, p. 11)

In contrast, consider the following definition of dyslexia formulated by a research committee of the International Dyslexia Society (Lyon, 1995; Shaywitz, 1996), which we have modified to be consistent with advances in research:

> Dyslexia is one of several distinct learning disabilities. It is a specific language-based disorder characterized by difficulties in the development of accurate and fluent single word decoding skills, usually associated with insufficient phonological processing and rapid naming abilities. These difficulties in single word decoding are often unexpected in relation to age and other cognitive and academic abilities; they are not the result of generalized developmental disability or sensory impairment. Dyslexia is manifest by variable difficulty with different forms of language, often including, in addition to problems reading, a conspicuous problem with acquiring proficiency in writing and spelling. Reading comprehension problems are common, reflecting word decoding and fluency problems.

This definition identifies dyslexia as a word-level RD proximally caused by phonological processing problems. It is inclusionary because it clearly specifies that a child is dyslexic who has (a) problems decoding single words in isolation, and (b) difficulties with phonological processing. These constructs are easily measured. The difficulty, of course, is specifying the level of impairment that would be of sufficient severity to constitute a disability. The definition is directly linked to intervention and it is now well established that treatments emphasizing the development of word recognition skills improve reading achievement in these children (National Reading Panel, 2000; Swanson, 1999). It reflects the developmental origins of dyslexia, so that prior to the expected onset of word recognition skills, interventions addressing the development of phonological processing skills should prevent word recognition difficulties. There is considerable research support for this expectation (National Reading Panel, 2000; Snow, Burns, & Griffin, 1998). The definition clearly permits the identification of children who are at risk for dyslexia and also permits identification of children who do not respond to preventative interventions and who may need different forms of remediation. No mention is made of discrepancy and IQ tests are not required for identification. It stipulates that dyslexia is differentiated from mental deficiency and sensory disorders, but criteria for these differentiations would be included in the identification of these disorders in an overall classification of low achievement. No distinctions or stipulations concerning cause or etiology are made, including constitutional factors, and exclusions are not identified.

The definition reflects a view of dyslexia that is different from those found in the media, where dyslexia is viewed as a rare, exotic disorder characterized by unusual perceptual characteristics (e.g., seeing words and letters backwards). Dyslexia as defined here is the most common form of LD and has its origins in the language system (Shaywitz, 1996; Vellutino, 1979). Lerner (1989) reported that 80% of all children served in special education programs have problems with reading, while Kavale and Reese (1992) found that 90% of children in Iowa with the LD label had reading difficulties. Most children who have reading problems have difficulty with word-level skills. It may not be the only problem that these children experience, but it is the problem that makes them poor readers. Most children served in special education programs as LD likely have word-level reading problems as part of their disability (Lyon, 1995).

Dyslexia as defined above is a disorder that is not associated with specific qualitative characteristics, but occurs on a continuum of normal development. Thus, dyslexia is the lower portion of this continuum (Shaywitz et al., 1992). A critical issue is where on the continuum sufficient severity of reading difficulty occurs that would lead to a designation of RD. This issue has not been adequately researched, but should be tied in some way to response to interventions of different kinds of intensity, not an arbitrary designation (e.g., 20th percentile) that the examples in Figures 4–6 show to be unreliable.

People with dyslexia often have other academic problems and also seem to have problems that are in the social and behavioral realm. This is not a problem with the definition, but with the classification of LD. The key is to have a classification that signals when a child has a form of LD, and which recognizes that they may have other academic and behavioral difficulties. Many children with this form of RD have problems with spelling, writing, reading comprehension, and math (Lyon, 1996). The spelling, writing, and reading comprehension problems can be explained on the basis of the disruption of phonological processing and word recognition skills. Spelling is closely tied to phonological processes; a person with poor word recognition skills cannot identify or spell words accurately because of poor understanding of the relationship of print and speech: the alphabetic principle. They will have reading comprehension problems because they can not process the text. When math is also impaired, the child typically has other problems involving oral language and working memory (Swanson & Siegel, in press). As we discuss below, reading comprehension and math problems in the absence of word recognition difficulties can also occur, which must be accounted for in our classification—not our definition of dyslexia.

Disorders like attention deficit hyperactivity disorder (ADHD) represent a different classification issue. While ADHD commonly co-occurs with dyslexia (Shaywitz, Fletcher, & Shaywitz, 1997), what is important is that the child with both dyslexia and ADHD looks dyslexic when their reading and language skills are examined and looks ADHD when their behavior is examined (Shaywitz et al., 1995). However, dyslexia is a problem with *cognitive* development; ADHD is a *behavioral* disorder with cognitive consequences (Barkley, 1997). Thus, the child has more than one disability, although children with both dyslexia and ADHD have more severe reading (and other cognitive) problems than children who have only dyslexia or ADHD. The treatment implication is that both disorders need to be addressed and that interventions addressing only one disorder may be less effective (Fletcher, Foorman, Shaywitz, & Shaywitz, 1999). ADHD is not a part of our classification of LD, as the primary defining characteristics do not reflect academic achievement.

Altogether, word-level RD is the best researched type of LD and the difference between the 1968 exclusionary definition and the modified 1994 inclusionary definition represent what we believe is a model for other forms of LD. As we see in the next sections, much progress needs to be made in other forms of LD, though we could formulate reasonable inclusionary definitions of most of these forms.

Reading comprehension disability

There is good evidence for disabilities in reading comprehension in cases where reading decoding is age-appropriate but reading comprehension lags. Estimates of the incidence range from 5% to 10% depending on the exclusionary criteria used to define the groups (e.g., Cornoldi, DeBeni, & Pazzaglia, 1996 vs. Stothard & Hulme, 1996). These estimates have not been studied in relation to age, but it is likely that specific reading comprehension problems are more apparent in older children and emerge after the initial stage of learning to read. Some may have a history of word recognition difficulties that have been remediated.

Studies on specific reading comprehension disability commonly have compared children with good word recognition accompanied by good reading comprehension skills with those who have good development of word recognition skills but poor development of reading comprehension (Nation & Snowling, 1998; Oakhill, Yuill, & Parkin, 1986; Stothard & Hulme, 1996). This is in contrast to studies that have investigated reading comprehension problems in groups that contain a large number of poor word decoders (e.g., Perfetti, 1985; Shankweiler et al., 1999), in which the sources of reading comprehension problems are difficult to address separately from the influences of difficulties in word decoding. Proficient reading comprehension presumes fluent decoding, so studies of reading comprehension must separately identify those weak in comprehension, but fluent in decoding.

IQ and the definition of reading comprehension disability. Research in the area of reading comprehension disabilities does not follow the classification guidelines that are embedded in the federal definition of LD. Most studies of children's comprehension difficulties have not attempted to relate general intellectual ability to reading comprehension. Not surprisingly, there are few studies that use IQ-achievement discrepancies to define groups of poor comprehenders. The discrepancy formula that is most often used in studies of reading comprehension disability is that between good basic reading achievement and poorer scores on standardized tests of reading comprehension, without reference to IQ. Such approaches have not been fruitful, though most of the research is on children who also have word-level RD (Fletcher et al., 1998). One study that used an IQ-achievement discrepancy model to classify poor comprehenders found that children with average intelligence and average word reading skills but poor reading comprehension had difficulties in listening comprehension, in working memory, and in metacognitive aspects of comprehension (Cornoldi et al., 1996). A survey of individual cases showed that children with reading comprehension disability were heterogeneous with respect to the specific pattern of cognitive deficits that they displayed in these skills.

In some studies of reading comprehension disability, IQ has actually been used as an outcome measure rather than as an exclusionary criterion for group membership. For example, children with specific reading comprehension disability have been found to have similar phonological skills and nonverbal intelligence as children with no comprehension disability, but lower verbal IQs (e.g., Stothard & Hulme, 1996). Such findings have been interpreted by some as providing evidence that general verbal cognitive deficits underlie the reading comprehension disability of good decoders/poor comprehenders. In a recent study of normally developing readers, however, verbal intelligence was found to account for only modest variation in reading comprehension performance (Oakhill, Cain & Bryant, in press; also see Badian, 1999). After accounting for verbal intellectual skills, significant variance in comprehension was predicted by text integration skills, metacognitive monitoring, and working memory with stability in these relationships over a 1-year period. Interestingly, these are the same skills that Cornoldi et al. (1996) found best characterized their group of poor comprehenders with IQs that were discrepant from reading comprehension achievement.

What does it mean to say that children with comprehension problems have lower verbal IQ? A simple assumption of a unidirectional relationship between intelligence and comprehension, such that higher verbal intelligence somehow paves the way for the development of good reading comprehension, is probably incorrect for two reasons. First, there is some evidence that the relationship between reading comprehension and intelligence may be bidirectional (Francis, Fletcher et al., 1996). Consider, for example, that reading experience may facilitate growth of verbal and even nonverbal intellectual skills (Stanovich, 1993). Second, tests of verbal intelligence measure vocabulary and verbal reasoning, and these are some of the same skills that are measured by tests of reading comprehension. A moderately strong relationship between verbal intelligence and reading comprehension, then, is not unexpected and is relatively uninformative. Furthermore, given that there are important aspects of comprehension that IQ tests do not capture, verbal IQ cannot be used as a proxy for reading comprehension disability.

Core deficits in reading comprehension disability. Most of the research on specific reading comprehension disability has focused on determining the core deficits that underlie the disability. These studies have generally taken three forms. One is to compare children who are good decoders but poor comprehenders to good decoders–good comprehenders, matched for age. More recent studies use reading level match designs in which the cognitive processes of good decoders–poor comprehenders are compared to those of younger children matched for reading comprehension level to the older disabled children. Finally, studies of remediation have asked whether training in skills hypothesized to contribute to the reading comprehension deficit actually improves reading comprehension. The findings from the three methods are largely consistent and are summarized below.

Some studies have shown that children who are good decoders–poor comprehenders may have more basic deficits in vocabulary and understanding of syntax that would impair reading comprehension (Stothard & Hulme, 1992, 1996). Other studies have shown that even when vocabulary and syntax are not deficient, deficits in reading comprehension still arise (Cain, Oakhill, & Bryant, 2000; Nation & Snowling, 1998). The results from these studies are consistent with findings discussed previously (IQ-achievement discrepancy group in Cornoldi et al., 1996, and normally-developing readers in Oakhill, Cain, & Bryant, in press). These deficits involve inferencing and text integration, metacognitive skills related to comprehension, and working memory. In contrast, phonological skills, short-term memory, and verbatim recall of text are typically not deficient (reviewed in Oakhill, 1993; Cain & Oakhill, 1999; Cataldo & Cornoldi, 1998; Nation, Adams, Bowyer-Crane, & Snowling, 1999; Oakhill, 1993; but see Stothard & Hulme, 1992).

More recent studies in this area have begun to question how poor comprehension early in a child's reading history may influence not only later reading comprehension, but also continued development of word decoding skills. Although decoding and comprehension disabilities have been shown to be dissociable, children who are good decoders but poor comprehenders may begin to fall behind in their decoding skills in the later school grades (Oakhill, Cain, & Bryant, in press). To the extent that these individuals are not very good at using reading as a means to an end, they may come to read less, and so truncate their exposure to less common words (Cunningham & Stanovich, 1999). Alternatively, their poor ability to use semantic cues (a component of comprehension) to decode less frequent words may constrain higher levels of lexical development (Nation & Snowling, 1998).

Findings similar to those discussed for children with reading comprehension disability have also been found in studies of children with brain injury. For example, Barnes and Dennis (1992, 1996) have evaluated the discourse and reading comprehension skills of children with spina bifida and hydrocephalus. These children are often characterized by intact word recognition skills, but deficient reading comprehension (and math) abilities. Using a variety of tasks, Barnes and Dennis have demonstrated that children with this form of brain injury have difficulty making inferences and problems assimilating nonliteral information from text, and that these difficulties in the reading domain parallel problems that the children have in oral discourse comprehension and production. Table 1 summarizes the characteristics of reading ability in children with spina bifida and hydrocephalus, children with word recognition difficulties and poor comprehension, and non-brain injured children who have intact word recognition skills but poor reading comprehension.

Table 1. Academic subgroups of LD

1. Reading Disability—Word Level
2. Reading Disability—Comprehension
3. Reading Disability—Fluency (?)
4. Math Disability
5. Reading Disability and Math Disability
6. Written Expression—Spelling, text, handwriting (?)

The comprehension-related deficits outlined in Table 1 have been replicated across studies that have used different criteria for group membership, including brain injury. Questions remain regarding whether metacognitive, inferential, and working memory processes are primary causes or consequences of the comprehension deficit and whether difficulties in these skills reflect deficits in more basic reading comprehension processes (Nation & Snowling, 1998; Nation et al., 1999; Perfetti, Marron, & Folz, 1996). Given that reading comprehension may be a more multidetermined process than reading decoding, it is not unexpected that advances in knowledge in this area have lagged behind word-level RD.

Given that it is a multifaceted process, the assessment of reading comprehension is a major problem. In contrast to tests of word recognition accuracy in which there is a relatively transparent relationship between the content of the tests and performance requirements for word reading, there is more controversy about what reading comprehension tests measure. Standardized reading comprehension tests differ from everyday reading contexts along several potentially important dimensions such as passage length, immediate versus delayed recall, and learning and performance requirements (Sternberg, 1991). Reading comprehension tests, like other tests of complex cognitive functions, may be limited both by a lack of ecological validity and by the absence of a model of the reading comprehension process that would guide test construction. Thus, it is not surprising that there is less consensus on how to define reading comprehension disability and how to best advance understanding of the reading comprehension process in terms of both its normal and disordered development.

Reading fluency

More controversial is the question of whether there is a specific subgroup of reading impairment that is characterized specifically by difficulties in reading fluency. Wolf and Bowers (1999, Wolf et al., 2001) have argued for a "rate deficit" group that does not have problems in the phonological domain, but often has difficulties with comprehension because of a more general difficulty rapidly processing information. The subtyping study of Morris et al. (1998) did find evidence for a rate deficit subtype that was not phonologically impaired, but which showed difficulty on any task that required speeded processing, including rapid automatized naming and tasks as mundane as canceling target letters as fast as possible from an array of letters. This subtype also had difficulties with reading fluency and comprehension, but not word recognition.

Studies of ADHD show that reading fluency problems are common in these children with ADHD and that these difficulties are related to their performance on measures of rapid automatized naming (Tannock, Martinussen, & Frijters, 2000). Some argue that these difficulties reflect common underlying brain-based problems with timing or rapid processing that occur across all forms of reading disability, but more research needs to be completed (Waber, Wolff, Forbes, & Weiler, in press).

Studies of children with brain injury also provide evidence that the accuracy and speed of word recognition can and should be differentiated. Barnes, Dennis, and Wilkinson (1999) matched children with traumatic brain injury on their word decoding accuracy. Comparisons of reading rate and naming speed showed that fluency was worse in children with traumatic brain injury, paralleling observations with non-brain injured children with rate deficits (Waber et al., in press; Wolf et al., 2001). Fluency was related to reading comprehension scores in both populations (Barnes et al., 1999; Morris et al., 1998).

This discussion of rate deficits represents an excellent example of how classifications and definitions must evolve in supporting the provision of services for children with academic deficits. Although there may be insufficient evidence to establish a form of RD that involves only fluency deficits, the possibility is under active investigation. If evidence continues to accumulate for a fluency disorder, the classification must be changed and definitions of reading disability expanded to incorporate these types of problems.

It is also apparent that a single definition will not work for these three putative forms of reading disability. It is already possible to specify the attributes of each disability. These attributes can be measured at the level of the academic skill as well as its associated correlates. As we will discuss below, it may be possible to measure these attributes and form inclusionary definitions that lead to specific procedures for identification and have important implications for intervention.

Math Disabilities

The federal definition of LD specifies disorders of math calculations and reasoning. Disabilities in math have been studied for as long but not as extensively as RD. Nonetheless, there is a burgeoning research base, particularly on children who have computational difficulties. There is clear evidence for a specific subgroup of children with LD in math calculations; whether there is also a subgroup that has impairment in math concepts is unclear and hardly studied. It is even possible that there are other subgroups of MD that have yet to be determined. Consider that the skills that fall under the heading of mathematics are broad and varied and it is unclear whether learning in one domain of mathematics is related to learning in another domain (Geary, 1994). Unlike reading, in which development produces changes in quantity and quality of decoding and comprehension, the development of mathematical competencies involves learning new categories of skills such as geometry and calculus (LeFevre, 2000). These new skills depend to some extent on previously learned math knowledge, but these areas of math also represent significant departures from prior learning.

As in the reading area, studies of adults with brain lesions show that fairly specific math skills can be either preserved or lost depending on the damage to the brain (Dehaene, 1999). Whether the development of math skills across different domains can be similarly fractionated is an open question. In normal development, for example, the acquisition of basic arithmetic skills may facilitate the acquisition of more advanced math skills across a number of math domains (Geary, Fan, & Bow-Thomas, 1992). Because of insufficient knowledge about development of some areas of math, the cognitive skills that lead to competence in those areas, and the potential importance of computation in facilitating these other areas of mathematical development, this section will deal primarily with evidence for LD in basic arithmetic calculation.

Computational abilities and disabilities

There is a rich literature on the acquisition of skills such as counting, basic understanding of quantity, and use of strategies that are important to the development of early computation ability (e.g., Ashcraft, 1992; Bisanz, Morrison, & Dunn 1995; Gelman & Gallistel, 1978; Nunes & Bryant, 1996; Rourke, 1993; Siegler & Shrager, 1984). This work was not motivated by a need to understand disordered development of computational skills, but to understand cognitive development through mathematical cognition and to understand the development of the math system itself. In the past decade, some math researchers have used the theories and methods of mathematical cognition and developmental psychology to study the emergence and development of MD. Until recently, this work largely proceeded without respect to the specificity of the disability, that is, whether RD and MD were comorbid or specific (e.g., Geary, Bow-Thomas, & Yao, 1992; Geary, Brown, & Samaranayake, 1991; Jordan, Levine, & Huttenlocher, 1995).

In contrast, studies of children with LD, including those involving math computations, have indeed been concerned with describing differences between groups of children with either specific RD or MD and both RD and MD (e.g., Ackerman & Dykman, 1995; Fletcher, 1985; Morrison & Siegel, 1991; Rourke, 1993; Swanson & Siegel, in press; White, Moffitt, & Silva, 1992). Children with specific MD appear much less frequently than children who have both RD and MD, and precise estimates are not available (Rourke, 1993). The existence of such children is clearly established in many studies where children are defined as having word recognition difficulties, both word recognition and math computation difficulties, and only math computation difficulties. The latter children do not have problems with language of the sort experienced by children with word-level RD. They typically have difficulty with different forms of nonverbal processing and concept formation (Rourke, 1993). To summarize, these studies have found cognitive deficits in marker skills such as verbal and visual working memory and visual-spatial skill that differentially characterize the different subgroups of children with LD (see Figures 2 and 3). Although these studies reveal the importance of considering the specificity and comorbidity of learning disabilities, they do not permit an analysis of the mechanisms by which the cognitive marker skills influence math learning. Furthermore, such subtyping studies were interested in the issue of LD in math versus reading rather than in understanding the basic math processes that contribute to scores on math achievement tests (Ginsburg, Klein, & Starkey, 1998).

A recent development in the research on MD has been the attempt to combine research strategies from the fields of cognitive development, mathematical cognition, and LD (e.g., Geary, Hoard, & Hamson, 1999; Jordan & Hanich, 2000). These studies: (1) follow children longitudinally from the beginning of their school careers to understand how MD plays out over time in terms of issues such as stability and comorbidity; (2) measure the development of early, informal arithmetic skills such as counting and problem-solving strategies for computing numbers that may be related to the later development of school-based or formal mathematical competence (Ginsburg et al., 1998); (3) relate cognitive marker skills or cognitive competencies that are purported to support the development of math to the acquisition of specific components of the math system such as knowledge of counting principles (Geary et al., 1999); and (4) analyze components of the developing math system and their supporting cognitive competencies with respect to whether the MD is specific or comorbid with RD. In some ways this new research strategy parallels earlier longitudinal studies of reading acquisition in typically achieving children and those with reading problems. As these studies proved critical to our understanding of RD at multiple levels, the current studies may similarly begin to reveal the explanatory status of hypothesized core number-related skills and supporting cognitive competencies with respect to the classification and prediction of MD.

What are the core number-related skills and supporting cognitive skills that have been hypothesized to account for difficulties with mathematics calculations? Disability in math computation may arise from problems in learning, representing, and retrieving math facts from semantic memory and/or from difficulties in the acquisition and use of developmentally-mature problem-solving strategies or procedures to perform mental or written calculations (Geary, 1993). Whether difficulties in the spatial representation and manipulation of number information constitute a third source of MD in children with and without frank brain injury (e.g., Geary, 1993) is unclear and not well studied (Barnes et al., in press).

Comorbid reading and math disability

It has been suggested that the core deficit of children with both RD and MD might be difficulty in retrieving math facts from long-term or semantic memory (Geary, 1993). In its more general form (i.e., not just involving math fact retrieval, but also retrieval of lexical information), this memory-based deficit may also be related to some of the features of reading disability (Geary et al., 1999). Longitudinal research and treatment studies suggest that this type of computation deficit may not improve much with age or remediation (Geary et al., 1991; Goldman, Pellegrino, & Mertz, 1988). In terms of supporting cognitive skills, these types of math disabilities are hypothesized to relate to working memory and also to long-term memory access (Geary, 1993; Geary et al., 1999; McLean & Hitch, 1999; Swanson & Siegel, in press).

In studies of older children there is some support for the hypothesis that co-occurring RD and MD may share a common underlying deficit in retrieval from long-term or semantic memory: Children who are slow readers make more errors in retrieving math facts from memory than children who are neither RD nor MD and more than children who have MD, but not RD (Rasanen & Ahonen, 1995). Younger children with both RD and MD difficulties have poor counting knowledge. They treat counting as a rote activity, rather than having a solid understanding of the principles of counting, and these children also have difficulty on working memory tasks and on tests tapping retrieval of verbal semantic information from long-term memory (Geary et al., 1999). Other studies suggest that children who are impaired in both reading and math computations typically show more severe and pervasive disturbances of oral language than children who are only impaired in word recognition. Their difficulties reflect problems learning, retaining, and retrieving math facts, which are essential to precise calculation; these problems lead to pervasive difficulties with math. Thus, Jordan and Hanich (2000) found that children with both reading and mathematics difficulties showed problems in multiple domains of mathematical thinking. Working memory is generally more severely impaired in children with both RD and MD than in either alone (Swanson & Siegel, in press).

Specific math disability

The error-prone use of developmentally immature procedures and strategies in simple arithmetic, and perhaps in written arithmetic, may underlie the form of MD that is not related to RD (Geary, 1993). Data on the validity of this source of MD is less strong at the present time than data on memory-based deficits in math fact retrieval. At a younger age, these children may also have problems in counting and often make errors in the application of algorithms. Written problems involving carrying and borrowing are difficult, as is the learning of algorithms necessary to complete complex multiplication and division. There are no studies of which we are aware that link developmentally-immature and error-prone counting strategies in solving simple arithmetic problems in early childhood to later use of developmentally-immature procedures in solving more complex multidigit written arithmetic problems.

To return to our example of children with spina bifida and hydrocephalus who have profound difficulties with math, Barnes et al. (in press) showed that good readers with this form of brain injury made more procedural errors than age-matched controls, but similar numbers of math fact retrieval and visual-spatial errors. Furthermore, their procedural errors were similar to those of younger children who were matched in math ability with these older brain-injured children. In other words, the good readers with hydrocephalus made errors in written computation that were developmentally immature for their age, but not different in kind from younger children with no MD. These data are consistent with the hypothesis that children who are good readers but who are poor at math can have a procedural deficit that involves the application of developmentally immature algorithms for solving written computations.

Figure 7. Profiles of cognitive performance by children with only reading disability (RD), only math disability (MD), both RD and MD (RD-MD), attention-deficit hyperactivity disorder (ADHD) with no RD or MD, and no LD (NL). The profiles show differences in shape and level of performance suggesting that the groups are different with distinct patterns associated with RD, MD, and ADHD as well as areas of overlap suggesting comorbidity of RD, MD, and ADHD. The NL group is clearly different from all three groups with LD in shape and elevation.

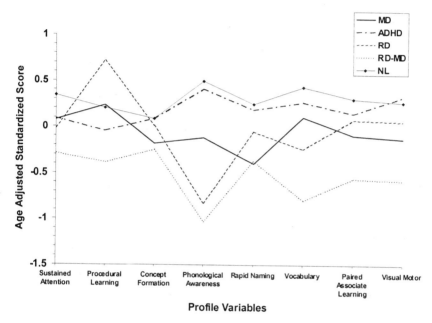

Comparison of specific MD, RD, and RD-MD

Children with word-level RD, computational MD and no RD, and both RD and MD can be differentiated. Figure 7 compares these groups with a contrast group of children who only have problems with behavior, meeting diagnostic criteria for ADHD but with no evidence of LD. The contrast with ADHD is important as some of the hypothesized cognitive correlates of specific MD are also apparent in studies of children with ADHD (Barkley, 1997), though such studies rarely address the issue of comorbidity. A group with no LD (NL) is also included.

These groups are compared on variables that have been related to ADHD (attention, paired associate learning), both ADHD and MD (problem solving, concept formation), and RD (phonological awareness, rapid naming, and vocabulary). Figure 7 demonstrates the pervasive problems experienced by children who have specific or comorbid RD on measures of phonological awareness. In addition, whereas children with MD had the most significant difficulties with concept formation, children with RD and MD, ADHD without LD, and only MD share in common difficulties on a problem solving measure. Finally, it is clear that children with both RD and MD are the most pervasively impaired, whereas children with no LD and only ADHD show much stronger performance in areas that involve language, working memory, and visual-motor integration. The group with only ADHD has problems with sustained attention (continuous performance test) and procedural learning, the latter representing strength in the group with only RD.

If Table 7 broke the three LD groups out by IQ-discrepancy/low achieving or by presence/absence of ADHD, the effect would be only on the level of the profiles, not the patterns. As the RD-MD example demonstrates, whenever a child has a disability in more than one area, their overall performance is lower. While IQ may also be lower, it is knowing that the child is disabled in more than one domain (including ADHD) that is critical. Thus, assessment of the academic (and behavioral) domains, and cognitive correlates, are the keys to understanding the disability—not level of IQ.

The differences in results across studies of LD and ADHD may well reflect variations in whether these domains are assessed. For example, children with only ADHD have small cognitive impairments relative to any child with LD. A study that combined children with only ADHD and both ADHD and RD-MD would show more significant cognitive impairments that may be attributed to ADHD if the comorbidity is not addressed. It is not surprising that studies of children defined as LD without specification of the academic domains that are impaired have not contributed much to research or practice.

What is particularly intriguing about the differences in the three LD subgroups (RD, MD, and RD-MD) comes from the possibility that the neural correlates are different. Functional imaging studies of children with RD and RD-MD reliably demonstrate aberrant activations involving the left temporoparietal areas (see Constitutional Factors below). Although there are presently no functional neuroimaging studies of children with math difficulties, studies of how math is represented in normal adults show that there are different neural correlates of precise calculation versus estimation (Dehaene, Spelke, Pinel, Stanescu, & Tsiukin, 1999). Precise estimation involves the inferior prefrontal cortex in the left hemisphere, as well as the left angular gyrus. These areas overlap substantially with those that mediate language functions. In contrast, estimation tasks showed bilateral activation in the inferior parietal lobes, which represent areas that overlap with spatial cognition. As many children with specific MD have been found to also have spatial cognition difficulties, this overlap in neural representation of estimation and spatial cognition may help explain why the spatial processing difficulties do not seem to bear a strong relationship to math abilities in these children, but are often as profound as the math difficulties themselves. Any cognitive task sensitive to how these areas of the brain function will be deficient in children with specific RD, but this does not mean that the cognitive deficits themselves are tightly linked.

Altogether, there is burgeoning evidence for the existence of a group defined by difficulty in learning and retrieving math facts from memory (RD-MD), and some evidence for the existence of a group that has difficulty learning math calculations because of procedural difficulties (MD only). There is little evidence for a separate subgroup with impairment in math concepts, but this possibility has not really been studied. In a sense, all children with disabilities in math probably have difficulty at some level with math concepts broadly conceived. The meaningfulness of this putative category of LD—math concepts disability— is not clear.

Written Expression

There is also research on disorders that involve written expression (Berninger & Graham, 1998; Graham & Harris, 2000). This is clearly an area of difficulty for many children. In some students, writing difficulties reflect an inability to spell, most closely associated with difficulties in word recognition skills (Rourke, 1993). Even some children with specific MD can have difficulty with handwriting, often because they commonly have impairments in their motor development. Their spelling errors, interestingly, are typically phonetically constrained, in contrast to children who have word recognition difficulties (Rourke, 1993). Once these two difficulties (spelling and motor skills) are taken into account, is there a subgroup of children whose difficulties are restricted to written expression? Here the classification research that is necessary to evaluate this hypothesis has not been completed, but there is some evidence for this possibility. In particular, some children have specific problems with handwriting and respond to prevention interventions (Graham, Harris, & Fink, 2000). Future research should target this possible subgroup in an effort to flush out the heterogeneity hypothesis.

Conclusions: Heterogeneity

There is support for the heterogeneity classification hypothesis. It is clear that there are at least two types of RD (word recognition, comprehension) and probably a third (reading fluency). In addition, there is evidence for a form of specific MD involving calculations. Children with both RD and MD have problems associated with either domain alone, reflecting more pervasive disruptions of language and working memory (Rourke, 1993; Swanson & Siegel, in press). This type of LD should be differentiated from specific RD and specific MD. Research is weakest for disorders of written expression.

Children with disorders in listening and speaking can be differentiated from children who have problems with reading and math. Although there is overlap, only about 50% of those who develop specific language disorders also develop reading and math disorders (Tomblin & Zhang, 1999). When a child with a speech and language disorder develops a reading or math problem, it is for the same reasons that a child with a reading and math problem and no disorder of oral language develops these difficulties. To illustrate in the area of word recognition skills, it is because the child does not develop adequate phonological awareness skills, has problems with rapid naming, and has deficient vocabulary and oral language comprehension skills. There is little evidence for meaningful dissociations of listening and reading comprehension when word recognition skills are adequate. Research in reading comprehension disabilities has largely proceeded from the assumption that the comprehension disability occurs in both reading and listening (with many researchers using oral language tasks to measure components of comprehension), and the data have amply demonstrated that when reading decoding and reading fluency are intact, the comprehension deficit is similar in written and oral language (e.g., Stothard & Hulme, 1992). Thus, many children who have specific problems with reading comprehension have parallel difficulties in listening, i.e., understanding oral language.

Why disorders of listening and speaking are included in the LD category is unclear, as there is a separate category for speech and language disorders and disorders of listening and speaking are not specific academic skills disorders. Dropping them from the LD category would increase the conceptual clarity of the LD category.

Table 2 provides a hypothetical classification of types of LD. Although the evidence for each of these types varies and there is undoubtedly overlap, there is support for each of these six types. Each of the academic domains representing the disorders can be measured and something is known about the cognitive correlates of each domain, except possibly for written expression. As such, a single definition for all these forms of LD seems less useful than a set of inclusionary definitions that specific the domain and its associated cognitive correlates. Such an approach would be more directly related to intervention and would facilitate communication.

Table 2. Comprehension in poor comprehenders with and without known brain pathology (Barnes & Dennis, 1996)

	Brain Pathology	No Known Brain Pathology	
	Average IQ Hydrocephalus	Poor Decoders–Poor Comprehenders	Good Decoders–Poor Comprehenders
Word recognition	Intact	Poor	Intact
Vocabulary knowledge	Intact	Poor	Intact
Reading comprehension	Poorer than word recognition	Poor	Poor
Literal recall of text	Poor	Intact	Intact
Inferencing	Poor	Poor	Poor
Primary source of inferencing failure	Accessing text- & knowledge-based information	Integrating text- & knowledge-based information	Integrating text- & knowledge-based information

Exclusion Hypothesis

Most definitions of LD include an exclusion clause, which simply states that LD is not primarily the result of other conditions that can impede learning. These other conditions include mental deficiency; sensory disorders; emotional disturbance; cultural, social, and economic conditions; and inadequate instructional opportunities. Given the role of the exclusion element within definitions of LD, children identified as LD are often identified on the basis of what they are not, rather than what they are. This is unfortunate for three major reasons. First, by placing an emphasis on exclusion, the development of inclusionary characteristics that are linked to assessment and intervention is difficult. To illustrate, the 1977 operationalization of the federal definition suggests that RD be assessed with IQ and achievement tests; it does not specify the domains of reading and ignores the variation in components of reading that may represent differential treatment emphases. Second, an exclusionary definition is a negative definition that adds little to conceptual clarity and clearly constrains understanding the disorder to its fullest extent. Think of the difference in clarity when we identify a child as LD versus identify the child with a reading comprehension disability. Third, many of the conditions that are excluded as potential influences in LD are themselves possible factors that interfere with the development of those cognitive and linguistic skills that lead to the academic deficits that form the basis for LD (Lyon et al., 2001). Parents with reading problems, for example, may find it difficult to establish adequate home literacy practices because of the cumulative effects of their reading difficulties (Wadsworth et al., 2000).

It is reasonable to stipulate that children with mental deficiency and sensory disorders are excluded from classifications of LD. Separate categories exist and their treatment needs are different. This stipulation begs the question of how to differentiate mild mental deficiency and LD (Gresham, MacMillan, & Bocian, 1996), given the weakness of psychometric definitions. Other exclusions are even more difficult to justify. For example, where is the evidence suggesting that RD and MD are different in children who are anxious, depressed, or even psychotic? Recent longitudinal studies suggest that early achievement is causally related to and often precedes the development of behavioral problems, and the interventions that enhance academic achievement prevent behavioral difficulties (Kellam, Rebok, Mayer, Ialongo, & Kalodner, 1994; Onatsu-Arvilommi & Nurmi, 2000). Thornier are exclusions based on social, economic, and cultural disadvantage, and inadequate instruction. This differentiation is based on the presumption that constitutional factors are more relevant for children with LD than environmental factors. In addition to reviewing evidence for exclusion according to environmental factors, we will also review additional evidence on the role of constitutional factors in LD, raising again the question of how well either environmental or constitutional factors distinguish children with LD from low achievement commonly ascribed to environmental factors.

Social, Economic, and Cultural Disadvantage

A variety of factors related to the literacy environment in which a child develops are clearly related to the acquisition of academic skills. When optimal social and economic conditions are not present, the child is at a much higher risk for the development of an academic problem. In reading, a variety of factors have been studied, including print exposure, parental literacy levels, and reading to the child. All these factors are related to the development of reading skills (Adams, 1990) and probably to other academic skills as well. Recent qualitative studies (Hart & Risley, 1999) have provided graphic documentations of the differences in the language environment experienced by advantaged and disadvantaged children. For example, by the age of 5 years, economically advantaged children have vocabularies of approximately 500,000 words, while economically disadvantaged children have vocabularies of approximately 250,000 words (Hart & Risley, 1999). It is widely believed that these types of differences in language development have some (unspecified) effect on brain development, and they are certainly related to the development of proficiency in academic skills.

These types of factors impede oral language development. When oral language development is affected, a variety of language skills are at risk, including those related to the development of word recognition and reading comprehension skills. In a series of longitudinal studies, Whitehurst and Lonigan (1998) provided excellent documentation of the relationship of different oral language skills and the acquisition of reading ability. In evaluating children entering Head Start programs at age 3, Whitehurst and Lonigan (1998) found that skills related to knowledge of the alphabet and word structures were closely tied to reading success in kindergarten, Grade 1, and Grade 2. More general oral language skills that involved vocabulary, language comprehension, and exposure to language through literature and oral reading were related to the development of reading comprehension skills, particularly in Grades 2 and 3.

These results are particularly striking when national evaluations of Head Start programs are examined (Whitehurst & Massetti, in press). These studies have shown that, on average, children who graduate from Head Start programs enter kindergarten knowing one letter of the alphabet. Interviews with teachers showed that they were often discouraged from engaging in activities that promoted understanding of the alphabetic structure of the language because such activities were not viewed as "developmentally appropriate." Nonetheless, when children in Head Start programs were provided with these sorts of activities, higher literacy levels were apparent (Whitehurst & Lonigan, 1998).

What is important in these examples is the illustration that environmental factors influence the development of oral language skills that are known to affect beginning (and later) reading skills. Interventions that address the early development of these skills seem to promote success in reading. Such findings are also apparent in evaluative studies of Title I Programs as well as intervention studies in which alphabetic forms of instruction have been shown to be advantageous for economically disadvantaged children (Foorman et al., 1998; National Reading Panel, 2000). Thus, the mechanisms and practices that promote reading success in advantaged populations appear to be similar to those that promote reading success and failure in disadvantaged populations. There is little evidence that the phenotypic representation of RD varies according to socioeconomic status. Children at all levels of socioeconomic status appear to have reading problems predominantly (but not exclusively) because of word-level difficulties apparent in the beginning stages of reading development (Foorman et al., 1998; Wood, Flowers, Buchsbaum, & Tallal, 1991).

As Kavale (1988) and Lyon (1996) pointed out, the basis for excluding disadvantaged children from the LD category has more to do with how children are served than with empirical evidence demonstrating that characteristics of reading failure are different in LD in economically disadvantaged groups. Indeed, Kavale (1988) suggested that arguments usually point to the fact that "the culturally disadvantaged child is well served by various federally funded title programs, but these are usually mandated under guidelines and revisions different from special education.

Specifically, the emphasis is on compensatory education while special education programs function as remedial programs" (p. 195). This has the effect of eliminating economically disadvantaged children from special education services, with the exception of categories related to mental deficiency and emotional disturbance; economically disadvantaged children are disproportionably represented in these special education categories. As Kavale stated,

> since culturally disadvantaged children have been shown to exhibit the behavioral characteristics included as primary traits in definitions of LD, it is difficult to determine why the culturally disadvantaged group is categorically excluded from the LD classification. Yet, children from lower SES levels with LD-type behaviors have little chance for receiving LD diagnoses and treatment with an increased likelihood of being labeled retarded in spite of the fact that LD and ED groups are not clearly identifiable as separate entities. (p. 205)

There is little empirical evidence supporting the exclusion of economically disadvantaged children from special education services as a valid classification practice. The exclusion is a policy decision that represents a desire to clearly separate funds dedicated to special education and compensatory education. We have, essentially, a two-tier service delivery system for children with academic difficulties, where advantaged children are designated as LD and served through remedial classes that are questionably effective (Lyon et al., 2001). In contrast, children who qualify for free lunches served under Title I often receive compensatory education programs, which in some studies appear to be effective (Slavin, Karweit, & Madden, 1989). Our concept of LD, however, must not hinge on policy issues. Here there is little basis for distinguishing types of poor achievement according to putative causes, since the phenotypic manifestations seem to be similar across levels of socioeconomic status.

Instruction

Virtually any definition of LD excludes children from consideration if their learning problems are primarily a product of inadequate instruction. Of all the different assumptions in the concept of LD, this assumption is the least frequently examined and perhaps the most important. Some would interpret the exclusion to indicate that children who profit from instruction do not have a biologically based disorder. The functional imaging studies reviewed below suggest that this is hardly the case and that instruction is necessary to establish the neural networks that support reading. Keep in mind that no child is born as a reader; all children are taught to read. Written language is scaffolded upon our natural capacities for developing oral language (Lukatela & Turvey, 1998). It may be that there are differences in brain function that make some children more refractory to intervention than others, but we do not presently have data that would indicate that this is the case.

Another problem with the inadequate instruction exclusion is that it presumes that the field has a good understanding of what constitutes adequate instruction. At the time the federal definition was adopted, this was not case. Recent consensus reports (National Reading Panel, 2000; Snow et al., 1998) make it clear that we do know a lot about teaching children to read. Given what we know, consideration of the students' response to well designed and well implemented early intervention as well as remediation programs may need to become part of the definition of LD. Why should the complex identification criteria and expensive due process procedures of special education be used before an attempt is made to provide a powerful intervention early in the child's development? A child's failure to respond to intervention may be the best way to operationalize the notion of adequate instruction. While a child's failure to respond to appropriate instruction is a very strong indication of a disability, the cognitive problems associated with their LD parallel those exhibited by children who do not respond to inadequate instruction. The two types of children are equally disabled and there is no evidence that there are differences at a neurological level, prior to intervention or in terms of their intervention needs, that would make them different. For children with mental deficiency, sensory disorders, and emotional disturbance, there are other classifications in IDEA that can lead to services. For the child who is deemed culturally, economically, or socially disadvantaged, compensation education programs are available. What is there for the child who develops academic difficulties because of poor instruction? Excluding children on the basis of inadequate instruction does not seem a reasonable practice.

Constitutional Factors

Approaching the exclusion hypothesis from the perspective of classification research shows little evidence supporting exclusions based on emotional disturbance; social, cultural, and economic disadvantage; or inadequate instruction. This reflects the difficulties of differentiating forms of low achievement that are presumably specific or unexpected from those than can be attributed to other causes, where low achievement is expected. Related to this hypothesis is another source of data that is frequently invoked in explaining unexpected low achievement. That is the notion that unexpected LD is due to constitutional factors that are intrinsic to the child. In the current federal definition of LD, the intrinsic/neurological component is implicit in the use of terms like "basic psychological processes." In other contemporary non-federal definitions the concept is explicitly stated. For example, the definition of LD proposed by the National Joint Committee on Learning

Disabilities (1988) states: "these disorders [LD] are intrinsic to the individual, presumed to be due to central nervous system damage, and may occur across the life span" (p.1).

Neurobiological factors do not represent formal classification hypotheses in the sense that they are used to identify students with LD. They do represent components that can be tested for validity purposes. If children with unexpected low achievement differ from children in whom achievement is expected on constitutional factors, then this might support the hypothesis that expected and unexpected low achievement should be differentiated.

It has long been assumed that neurobiological factors were the basis of LD, reflecting its conceptual origins in the notion of organically based behavior disorders (Doris, 1993; Rutter, 1982; Satz & Fletcher, 1980). Neurobiological (constitutional) dysfunction was inferred from what was then known about the linguistic, cognitive, academic, and behavioral characteristics of adults with documented brain injury or lesion. As the field progressed, definitions of LD continued to attribute the disabilities in learning to intrinsic (neurological) rather than extrinsic (e.g., environmental, instructional) causes, even though there was no objective way to adequately assess the presence of putative brain damage or dysfunction. These assumptions of constitutional etiology were buttressed by associations of a variety of indirect indices of neurological dysfunction and LD. These indirect indices included observations of perceptual-motor problems (i.e., difficulty copying geometric figures), paraclassical or "soft" neurological signs (e.g., gross motor clumsiness, fine motor incoordination), and anomalies on electrophysiological measures, such as an electroencephalogram (Taylor & Fletcher, 1983). Even at the time, the lack of specificity of these observations with either LD or neurological integrity was widely acknowledged (Satz & Fletcher, 1980). Nevertheless, the neurobiological deficits were presumed to be selective rather than diffuse, resulting in specific difficulties processing linguistic, visual, and motor information critical to academic learning without concomitant loss of general intellectual functions.

Over the past two decades, some evidence, varying widely in methodological quality, has been obtained from investigations designed to identify, more directly, the neurological basis for LD and particularly RD. For example, data derived from postmortem studies performed on dyslexic adults and structural neuroimaging studies with children and adults have indicated that some individuals with RD are characterized by differences in the size of specific brain structures (e.g., planum temporale) and in the presence of specific neuroanatomical anomalies (e.g., ectopias) (Filipek, 1996; Galaburda, 1993). Structural imaging studies reliably show that people with RD have a smaller left hemisphere, or less asymmetric hemispheres. Both the autopsy and structural imaging studies have been confounded by subject selection problems, failure to account for comorbid neurological disease (e.g., seizures) and other variables (e.g., handedness). Interpretation of the structural imaging studies has been impeded by the use of different neuroimaging methods and data analytic techniques, as well as difficulties replicating the findings of these studies (Filipek, 1996; Shaywitz et al., 2000).

More recently, research using different types of functional neuroimaging methods to measure brain activation in response to visual, linguistic, and reading tasks among skilled and unskilled readers indicates systematic and selective brain activity in several left hemisphere neural systems subserved by the basal surface of the temporal lobe, the middle temporal gyrus, the temporoparietal region, and the inferior frontal region. Converging evidence from a range of functional imaging methods used in studies with both good and poor readers indicate that a network of brain areas is involved in the ability to recognize words accurately, and that adults and children with RD manifest different patterns of activation in these areas when compared with skilled readers (Shaywitz et al., 2000).

A critical question that has been raised by the functional neuroimaging studies of those with LD in reading is whether the patterns seen in these individuals with RD are compensatory in nature ("compensatory hypothesis") or reflect the failure of the environment and/or instruction to impact the brain in a manner necessary to form the neural networks that support word recognition. Thus, the pattern in RD children may be similar to that seen in a young child who has not learned to read and may change by virtue of development, instruction, or even intervention ("normalization hypothesis"). Given this possibility, functional neuroimaging studies may provide an example of how brain and environment interact in forming neural networks for complex behaviors. Such studies are feasible and investigations that combine neuroimaging and reading intervention studies are currently being completed.

Figure 8. Individual activation maps from a 10-year-old child who was experiencing serious difficulties in learning to read, before and after an intense phonologically-based intervention. Activation maps were obtained using a pseudoword rhyme-matching task. The child showed dramatic improvement in phonological decoding skills after 8 weeks (80 hours) of enrollment in the program, analogous to that reported by Torgesen et al. (2001). Note the dramatic increase in the activation of the left temporoparietal regions.

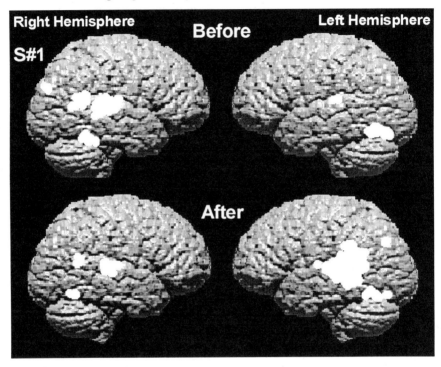

Figure 8 provides an example from a pilot study in which functional neuroimaging studies were performed using magnetic source imaging while a child read words. The imaging studies occurred before and after approximately 60 hours of intense intervention (over 8 weeks) in which the child, who was 10 years old with severe RD, showed significant improvement in word reading ability into the average range. The top part of the figure shows the standard brain activation pattern characterized by activity predominantly in the temporoparietal regions of the right hemisphere. After intervention, the pattern shifts to predominant activation involving the homologous areas of the left hemisphere, an activation pattern typical of nondisabled readers. Thus, these results are more consistent with the normalization hypothesis than the compensatory hypothesis.

The preliminary data from these types of studies suggest different conceptualizations of the role of constitutional factors in LD. The view that is emerging suggests that neural systems develop and are deployed for specific behaviors through the interaction of brain and environment (including instruction) as opposed to representing fixed properties of the nervous system that inherently limit learning potential. As such, the concept of LD retains the optimism that was intended with its inception.

This interaction perspective is also supported by genetic studies of individuals with RD. It has long been known that reading problems reoccur across family generations, with a risk in the offspring of a parent with RD 8 times higher than in the general population. Multiple genes are most likely involved, with similar modes of transmission in dyslexic and non-dyslexic families. Linkage studies implicate markers on chromosomes 1, 2, 6, and 15. However, genetic factors account for only about half of the variability in reading skills, which means that the environment has a significant influence on reading outcomes. This also suggests that what is inherited is a susceptibility for RD that may manifest itself given specific interactions, or lack thereof, with the environment. For example, parents who read poorly may be less likely to read to their children. As such, the quality of reading instruction provided in the school may be more critical for children when there is a family history of poor reading giving rise to limited environmental-instructional interactions in the home (Olson, Forsberg, Gayan, & DeFries, 1999; Pennington, 1999; Wadsworth et al., 2000).

Conclusions: Exclusionary Criteria

There is little evidence that children excluded from LD classifications due to emotional disturbance; social, economic, and cultural disadvantage; or instructional history are meaningfully different from those included as LD. In particular, none of these criteria provide robust differentiations of expected and unexpected low achievement. The notion that expected and unexpected low achievement reflects variation in cognitive and behavioral correlates, prognosis, response to instruction, or even a broad range of neurobiological factors, does not have strong validity. This does not mean that the concept of LD is not valid or that the exclusions should not be used, particularly since many children can be served under other categories in IDEA or other approaches to providing services (e.g., compensatory education). There may well be needs outside the academic area that are better addressed through identification for other categories or programs. Exclusions due to inadequate instruction are not justifiable as lack of instruction can essentially cause LD. The exclusions must be seen as policy-based determinations to facilitate service delivery and avoid commingling of facts, not as classification factors that have strong validity.

FUTURE DIRECTIONS FOR CLASSIFICATIONS OF LD

In this paper, we have reviewed federal and non-federal definitions of LD, pointing out that these definitions embed hypothetical classifications at three levels: IQ discrepancy, heterogeneity, and exclusion. We also evaluated the evidence for the hypothesis that LD can be related to constitutional factors, showing that environmental factors must be accounted for in explaining not only why a child develops LD, but also the role of instruction. Throughout the paper, we highlighted some alternative approaches to classification, reflecting different ways of thinking about LD. We focused specifically on the value of inclusionary definitions that identify specific forms of LD, leading to specific (and less time-consuming) identification practices that we believe are directly linked to intervention. We suggested a hypothetical reorganization of the types of LD identified in the 1977 operationalization of the federal definition of LD. We recognized that exclusions, with the exception of inadequate instruction, largely reflect that there are other ways of serving children including different categories in IDEA and other services, such as compensatory education. There is little evidence that children meeting these exclusionary criteria have different instructional needs or respond differently to intervention.

Kavale and Forness (2000) presented an approach to the classification, definition, and identification of LD that in many respects is the antithesis of what would be recommended based on the research reviewed in this report. It begins with the acceptance of unexpected low achievement at the first level and the notion that discrepancy sets apart a specific form of LD as a necessary but not sufficient criterion at the first level of identification. The approach recognizes the heterogeneity of LD at the second level, tying LD to achievement deficiencies in language, reading, writing, and math. These deficiencies presume the presence of IQ discrepancy. At levels III and IV, issues related to learning processes are added. At level V, children are excluded because of sensory impairment, mental deficiency, emotional disturbance, social and cultural disadvantage, and inadequate instruction.

This approach to classification hinges on the validity of IQ discrepancy as demarcating a specific form of LD that is differentiated from low achievement. The evidence reviewed in this paper shows that IQ-discrepant and low achieving groups overlap substantially in cognitive characteristics and show little difference in response to intervention and long-term outcome. Similar problems affect the use of exclusionary criteria. Consider children who have (a) an IQ discrepancy, (b) problems in reading, (c) processing difficulties, and (d) who do not meet any of the exclusionary criteria. How are they meaningfully different or have different instructional needs from children with (a) through (c), but who meet exclusionary criteria and are therefore not defined as LD? There is little evidence that this would be the case, even if the hypothesis was tested only within IQ-discrepant children.

There is really no hypothesis to test, as there is no basis for imagining how such subgroups could differ if the sorting was based solely on the exclusionary criteria. Even if one argued that exclusion would be infrequent because of all the prior levels of identification, the evidence in this paper does not support the hypothesis that children excluded as non-LD are meaningfully different from those who make the cut.

We do not mean to indicate that federal and non-federal definitions that have been used to the present have not had utility. On the positive side, the evolution of the current federal definition in IDEA has successfully served as a rallying point for special interest groups and for increased funding for special education programs. The current omnibus federal definition has served well as a galvanizing force for advocacy groups in their quest to obtain funding and secured educational services support for children with LD. Current (and historical) classifications and the resultant definitions of LD should be conceptualized as hypotheses that require rigorous, ongoing evaluation. The review of evidence in this paper shows that the classifications have become obsolete and should be revised, especially if the goal is to guide and reform instruction.

A major problem is the notion that low achievement in LD is unexpected, leading to a focus on exclusion. The accumulation of research over the past 30 years shows that low achievement is expected and suggests a focus on identifying the factors responsible for poor achievement in every child. Such a shift would suggest the need to develop inclusionary definitions that build upon the cumulative research base on LD. The move from exclusionary to inclusionary definitions is the first of many steps.

Psychometric Approaches Are Limited

In addition to the need for inclusionary definitions, we must recognize that an approach to identification based solely on test scores is not likely to be reliable and begs the question of where to put the cut-score. Achievement test scores are continuous and largely normally distributed. The tests used to measure these domains have measurement error. Any attempt to set a cut-point will lead to instability around the cut-point as scores fluctuate around the point with repeat testing, even for a decision as straightforward as demarcating low achievement. This fluctuation is not a problem of repeat testing, nor is it a matter of selecting the ideal cut-score. The problem stems from the fact that no single score can perfectly capture a student's ability in a single domain. There is always measurement error. Fluctuation will also vary across tests, depending in part on the cut-score, as tests vary in their precision at various ranges of the ability scale. This problem is more significant as the cut-point moves from the center of the distribution.

A second problem with the typical use of cut-scores concerns their arbitrary nature. A cut-point on a norm-referenced test is an arbitrary, relative standard of performance. The arbitrariness of the standard does not mean that a cut-point does not indicate a problem. Rather, arbitrariness reflects the meaninglessness of distinctions between, for example, the 15th and 20th percentile (or the 20th and 21st percentile). The problem with arbitrariness is not so much with the use of norm-referenced tests for establishing cut-points, but reflects difficulties inherent in any approach that would make critical decisions based on a single indicator. A single assessment at a single point in time is not psychometrically adequate for deciding placement. The flexibility in IDEA that allows interdisciplinary teams to go beyond test scores and encourages clinical judgment is necessary because of these issues. But the basis for clinical judgment should include performance on psychometric tests that involve achievement and cognitive performance. Inclusionary definitions based on patterns on these types of tests may be especially useful.

IQ Tests Are Not Needed

Such an approach would dramatically reduce the reliance on IQ tests for the identification of LD. Although there may be a role for IQ tests in determining mental deficiency, even here the more important concept is adaptive behavior, and there are difficulties establishing the upper range that distinguishes mental deficiency from LD (MacMillan, Siperstein, & Gresham, 1996).

The problems that we observed above in setting cut-points also apply to IQ distributions. There is no natural subdivision that demarcates mental deficiency from LD. Even with the stipulation of mental deficiency, there is no need to give every child referred for special education an IQ test. For LD, the information has limited relevance, particularly for intervention. The concept of IQ as it is applied to LD is outmoded and reflects an obsolete practice. The use of IQ tests reflects a focus on compliance as opposed to results that must shift if placement in special education as LD is to benefit the person so designated. IQ tests do not measure aptitude for learning or provide an index of response to intervention. The processes that contribute to performance on an IQ test may well be an outcome of the same processes that led to the LD. Dropping IQ from the LD definition would shift the focus to achievement/cognitive processes and also result in more efficient, less expensive evaluations.

"Slow Learner" Is Not a Useful Concept

Related to the issue of the obsolete role of IQ for LD is the notion of the *slow learner*, or *garden-variety* poor learner. These terms are also used to refer to children with low achievement at levels consistent with their IQ. There are clearly children who have impairments in multiple cognitive and academic domains who obtain lower scores on IQ tests. Many of these children represent what we described earlier as the comorbid RD-MD group.

Although it is commonly assumed that IQ is an indicator of the slow learner, this does not appear to be the case. It is difficult to identify an IQ cut-point, even in the non-mentally deficient range, that would differentiate specific LD and garden-variety LD. IQ scores do not reliably differentiate children with different types of LD. To illustrate, McFadden (1990) completed a cluster analysis to determine whether level of IQ was associated with different types of LD. McFadden found that (1) children with IQs between 70 and 80 were generally represented in all clusters of children with learning disabilities; (2) many children with low IQs exhibited similar patterns of cognitive difficulties relative to children defined as having learning disabilities by discrepancy criteria; (3) although a WISC full scale IQ cut-off of 80 reduced the number of children with low IQs in learning disabilities clusters, several subtypes still contained children with approximately 20 percent lower IQs; and (4) children with low IQs were apparent in clusters of children with learning disabilities and, within such clusters, differences occurred in level but not shape. These results question the validity of differentiating learning disabilities according to IQ cutoffs of 80 and above, but do not identify appropriate cutoffs (if any).

In another cluster analytic study, Morris et al. (1998) were able to distinguish children with specific RD who had cognitive problems relatively restricted to the phonological domain from those who had more generalized difficulties in multiple cognitive domains (e.g., vocabulary, speech production, attention). On average, children with non-specific RD had lower scores on IQ tests than children with specific RD, but IQ ranged considerably within each subtype. The differences between specific and non-specific subtypes were most reliably indexed by the child's vocabulary development and could be understood as the consequences of the child's poor language development, which in turn produced lowered IQ scores.

The notion that low achievement is expected in garden-variety RD and unexpected in specific RD is also specious. The basis for reading difficulties was associated with phonological processing in all subtypes with word reading problems. Some specific subtypes read as poorly as the non-specific subtypes, but the groups did not differ qualitatively in language characteristics related to reading (i.e., in the phonological domain). The garden-variety group may well have a poorer prognosis and need different types of instruction. The garden-variety group may even show different neurological characteristics. But would we really want to restrict our concept of LD or eligibility for services to children with specific types? Schools are interested in serving the lowest achievers as these are most difficult to teach (MacMillan et al., 1996).

Research on children with LD has not progressed to the point where we can say definitively that children with specific and garden-variety subtypes need different interventions, have different prognoses, or respond differently to treatment. This reflects in part the preoccupation with concepts of LD based on unexpectedness, IQ-discrepancy, and anxiety over the role of underachievement in LD. The consolidating issue is that the concept of underachievement and the linking of LD to an academic deficiency (e.g., reading, math) are *necessary* to the concept of LD. They are not *sufficient* and it is essential to include the concept of process (e.g., language, perceptual skills) as necessary to the concept of LD (Kavale & Forness, 2000). It is also essential to drop notions of "potential," "ability," and their operationalization in measures of IQ and to move towards attributes or components that are measurable and linked to intervention. Thus, we would move the concept of LD from a disorder that is unexpected because of discrepancies between ability potential and achievement to one in which underachievement is expected because of impairment of key cognitive processes. These processes are measurable and can be directly linked to intervention.

Response to Intervention Is Important

It is essential to introduce the student's response to well-designed instruction and remediation programs as a major component of the identification of LD. This introduction should be made in the context of early identification and prevention programs that are seen as fundamental to general and special education. Children who do not benefit from early and intensive interventions will require even more powerful remediation programs as well as educational accommodations as they proceed through their schooling. The information on how well the child responded operationalizes the "inadequate instruction" component and those who do not respond to increasingly intense interventions may indeed be disabled. In addition, continuous monitoring of progress will be helpful not only for instructional planning, but also for identifying those who do not respond to adequate instruction (Fuchs & Fuchs, 1998).

Consensus Process

To do justice to the need for a classification of LD that yields inclusionary defini-tions with the features we have identified as being desirable, we call for the devel-opment of a consensus process. As part of this process, the relevant federal agencies responsible for research and practice involving people with LD should work to-gether to synthesize the available research. The principles and goals of a new overarching classification should be explicitly articulated, with specification of boundaries and overlaps with other classifications of childhood disorders (e.g., mental deficiency, emotional disorders). The possibility of comorbid associations should be incorporated. Working groups could be assembled to formulate defini-tions of different types of LD. Definitions should be formulated only for those types of LD where there is clear evidence of their nature and correlates. The classi-fication and definitions should be treated as hypotheses. Research to evaluate the resultant classifications is desirable and should be supported. Plans to periodically update and revise the definitions should be made. Such a process would hopefully permit the development of specific procedures for identifying different types of LD that are efficient, that do not waste resources, and that lead to specific interven-tions.

Thus, we propose careful assessment of academic skills and their cognitive corre-lates as part of the implementation of inclusionary definitions. These assessments should be completed to address prevention/intervention needs with a goal of evalu-ating the instructional needs of the child. Adding continuous monitoring of progress and response to intervention as considerations in this process may go a long way towards the ultimate goal of helping as many children as possible master academic skills and return to regular education. A consensus process would help ensure that the last available evidence from research and the best available presentations were marked in a re-formulation of the federal classification of LD. Any changes must take into account the need for improved teacher preparation in general and special education, especially if the federal classification is changed.

Learning Disabilities Are Real Phenomena

Some researchers have confused the IQ-discrepancy hypothesis with the concept of LD, which is not appropriate. For example, Aaron (1997) stated that "when the discrepancy formula disappears from the educational science, so will the concept of LD" (p. 489). Similarly, Kavale and Forness (1994) stated that "... the notion of discrepancy ... has led to a confounding ... most clearly seen in the suggestion that there are more similarities than differences between LD and low achieving students. Such a suggestion calls into question the very notion of LD" (p. 43).

This conceptualization could be shown to be unreliable and invalid with no consequences for the validity of the concept of LD. This is clearly indicated in Figure 7, which shows that children with RD, MD, and RD-MD can be differentiated from those with no LD, even when ADHD is involved. Patterns of performance differentiate types of LD, while both level and patterns differentiate those with and without LD. Children identified with either an IQ discrepancy or LD definition *are* disabled, need to be identified, and respond similarly to appropriate educational interventions. What is being questioned is the validity of *classifications* of LD based on the presence or absence of IQ discrepancy and exclusion, not the reality of LD. Both definitions validly identify LD with or without the exclusions. As a classification, coverage, reliability, and validity are not adequate.

When the original federal definition of LD was proposed, there was little research that supported the discrepancy, heterogeneity, and exclusionary components of LD classifications. Since then research has accumulated suggesting that the discrepancy and exclusion components have (at best) weak validity and may be harmful and represent an obstacle to effective intervention. The goal should be to close the achievement gap for students identified as LD relative to their peers. Unfortunately, this happens all too infrequently by virtue of placing students with LD in special education (Lyon et al., 2001). One part of the solution is to revise the federal definition of LD and develop new classifications that are linked to research. New definition and identification practices will emerge, so that those who serve children with LD can focus on early identification, prevention, and effective remedial strategies. Eligibility and compliance presently consume excessive fiscal and emotional resources; this consumption should be redirected to intervention and special education should be re-oriented towards results, which means truly remediating children and returning them to the educational mainstream. These are the ultimate purposes of classifying a student as LD and the reasons that such classifications were developed. Such purposes must guide the reworking of the federal classification of LD essential to ensuring that all children can learn and reach their full potential in our society.

REFERENCES

Aaron, P. G. (1997). The impending demise of the discrepancy formula. *Review of Educational Research, 67*, 461–502.

Ackerman, P. T. & Dykman, R. A. (1995). Reading-disabled students with and without comorbid arithmetic disability. *Developmental Neuropsychology, 11*, 351–371.

Adams, M. J. (1990). *Beginning to read*. Cambridge, MA: MIT Press.

Algozzine, B., Ysseldyke, J. E., & McGue, M. (1995). Differentiating low-achieving students: Thoughts on setting the record straight. *Learning Disabilities Research, 10*, 140–144.

Ashcraft, M. H. (1992). Cognitive arithmetic: A review of data and theory. *Cognition, 44*, 75–106.

Badian, N. A., (1999). Reading disability defined as a discrepancy between listening and reading comprehension: A longitudinal study of stability, gender differences, and prevalence. *Journal of Learning Disabilities, 32*, 138–148.

Barkley, R. A. (1997). Behavioral inhibition, sustained attention, and executive functions: Constructing a unifying theory of ADHD. *Psychological Bulletin, 121*, 65.

Barnes, M. A., & Dennis, M. (1992). Reading in children and adolescents after early onset hydrocephalus and in normally developing age peers: Phonological analysis, word recognition, word comprehension, and passage comprehension skills. *Journal of Pediatric Psychology, 17*, 445–465.

Barnes, M. A., & Dennis, M. (1996). Reading comprehension deficits arise from diverse sources: Evidence from readers with and without developmental brain pathology. In C. Cornoldi and J. Oakhill (Eds.), *Reading comprehension difficulties: Processes and intervention* (pp. 251–278). Mahwah, NJ: Lawrence Erlbaum Assoc.

Barnes, M. A., Dennis, M., & Wilkinson, M. (1999). Reading after closed head injury in childhood: Effects on accuracy, fluency, and comprehension. *Developmental Neuropsychology, 15*, 1–24.

Barnes, M. A., Pengelly, S., Dennis, M., Wilkinson, M., Rogers, T., & Faulkner, H. (in press). Mathematics skills in good readers with hydrocephalus. *Journal of the International Neuropsychological Society*.

Berninger, V., & Graham, S. (1998). Language by hand: A synthesis of a decade of research in handwriting. *Handwriting Review, 12*, 11–25.

Bisanz, J., Morrison, F. J., & Dunn, M. (1995). Effects of age and schooling on the acquisition of elementary quantitative skills. *Developmental Psychology, 31*, 221–236.

Cain, K., & Oakhill, J. V. (1999). Inference making and its relation to comprehension failure in young children. *Reading and Writing: An Interdisciplinary Journal, 11*, 489–503.

Cain, K., Oakhill, J. V., & Bryant, P. (2000). Phonological skills and comprehension failures: A test of the phonological processing deficits hypothesis. *Reading and Writing, 13*, 31–56.

Cataldo, M. G., & Cornoldi, C. (1998). Self-monitoring in poor and good reading comprehenders and their use of strategy. *British Journal of Developmental Psychology, 16*, 155–165.

Clements, S. D. (1966). *Minimal brain dysfunction in children.* NINDB Monograph No. 3. Washington DC: U.S. Department of Health, Education, and Welfare.

Cohen, J. (1983). The cost of dichotomization. *Applied Psychological Measurement, 7*, 249–253.

Cornoldi, C., DeBeni, R., & Pazzaglia, F. (1996). Profiles of reading comprehension difficulties: An analysis of single cases. In C. Cornoldi and J. Oakhill (Eds.), *Reading comprehension difficulties: Processes and intervention* (pp. 113–136). Mahwah, NJ: Lawrence Erlbaum Assoc.

Critchley, M. (1970). *The dyslexic child.* Springfield, IL: Charles C. Thomas.

Cunningham, A. E., & Stanovich, K. E. (1998). What reading does for the mind. *American Educator, 4*, 8–15.

Dehaene, S. (1992). Varieties of numerical abilities. *Cognition, 44*, 1–42.

Dehaene, S. (1999). Fitting two languages into one brain. *Brain, 122*, 2207–2208.

Dehaene, S., Spelke, E., Pinel, P., Stanescu, R., & Tsiukin, S. (1999). Sources of mathematical thinking: Behavioral and brain-injury evidence. *Science, 284*, 970–974.

Doris, J. (1993). Defining learning disabilities: A history of the search for consensus. In G. R. Lyon, D. B. Gray, J. F. Cavanaugh, & N. A. Krasnegor (Eds.), *Better understanding learning disabilities* (pp. 97–116). Baltimore: Paul H. Brookes.

Filipek, P. (1996). Structural variations in measures in the developmental disorders. In R. Thatcher, G. Lyon, J. Rumsey, N. Krasnegor (Eds.), *Developmental neuroimaging: Mapping the development of brain and behavior* (pp. 169–186). San Diego, CA: Academic Press.

Fletcher, J. M. (1985). Memor for verbal and nonverbal stimuli in learning disability subgroups: Analyis by selective reminding. *Journal of Experimental Child Psychology, 40*, 244–259.

Fletcher, J. M., Foorman, B. R., Shaywitz, S. E., & Shaywitz, B. A. (1999). Conceptual and methodological issues in dyslexia research: A lesson for developmental disorders. In H. Tager-Flusberg (Ed.), *Neurodevelopmental disorders* (pp. 271–306). Cambridge, MA: MIT Press.

Fletcher, J. M., Francis, D. J., Rourke, B. P., Shaywitz, B. A., & Shaywitz, S. E. (1993). Classification of learning disabilities: Relationships with other childhood disorders. In G. R. Lyon, D. Gray, J. Kavanagh, & N. Krasnegor (Eds.), *Better understanding learning disabilities* (pp. 27–55). New York: Paul H. Brookes.

Fletcher, J. M., Francis, D. J., Shaywitz, S. E., Lyon, G. R., Foorman, B. R., Stuebing, K. K., et al. (1998). Intelligent testing and the discrepancy model for children with learning disabilities. *Learning Disabilities Research & Practice, 13*, 186–203.

Fletcher, J. M., Francis, D. J., Stuebing, K. K., Shaywitz, B. A., Shaywitz, S. E., Shankweiler, D. P., et al. (1996). Conceptual and methodological issues in construct definition. In G. R. Lyon and N. A. Krasnegor (Eds.), *Attention, memory, and executive functions* (pp. 17–42). Baltimore: Paul H. Brookes.

Foorman, B. R., Francis, D. J., Beeler, T., Winikates, D., & Fletcher, J. M. (1997). Early interventions for children with reading problems: Study designs and preliminary findings. *Learning Disabilities, 8*, 63–71.

Foorman, B. R., Francis, D. J., Fletcher, J. M., Schatschneider, C., & Mehta, P. (1998). The role of instruction in learning to read: Preventing reading failure in at-risk children. *Journal of Educational Psychology, 90*, 37–55.

Francis, D. J., Fletcher, J. M., Shaywitz, B. A., Shaywitz, S. E., & Rourke, B. P. (1996). Defining learning and language disabilities: Conceptual and psychometric issues with the use of IQ tests. *Language, Speech, and Hearing Services in Schools, 27*, 132–143.

Francis, D. J., Shaywitz, S. E., Stuebing, K. K., Shaywitz, B. A., & Fletcher, J. M. (1996). Developmental lag versus deficit models of reading disability: A longitudinal individual growth curves analysis. *Journal of Educational Psychology, 88*, 3–17.

Frankenberger, W., & Fronzaglio, K. (1991). A review of states' criteria for identifying children with learning disabilities. *Journal of Learning Disabilities, 24*, 495–500.

Fuchs, D., Fuchs, L. S., Mathes, P. G., & Lipsey, M. E. (2000a). Reading differences between low-achieving students with and without learning disabilities: A meta-analysis. In R. Gersten, E. P. Schiller, & S. Vaughn, *Contemporary special education research* (pp. 105–136). Mahwah, NJ: Lawrence Erlbaum Assoc.

Fuchs, D., Fuchs, L. S., Mathes, P. G., Lipsey, M. E., & Eaton, S. (2000b). A meta-analysis of reading differences between underachievers with and without the disability label: A brief report. *Learning Disabilities, 10,* 1–4.

Galaburda, A. M. (1993). The planum temporale. *Archives of Neurology, 50,* 457.

Geary, D. C. (1993). Mathematical disabilities: Cognitive, neuropsychological, and genetic components. *Psychological Bulletin, 114,* 345–362.

Geary, D. C. (1994). *Children's mathematical development: Research and practical applications.* Washington, DC: American Psychological Association.

Geary, D. C., Bow-Thomas, C. C., & Yao, Y. (1992). Counting knowledge and skill in cognitive addition: A comparison of normal and mathematically disabled children. *Journal of Experimental Child Psychology, 54,* 362–391.

Geary, D. C., Brown, S. C., & Samaranayake, V. A. (1991). Cognitive addition: A short longitudinal study of strategy choice and speed-of-processing differences in normal and mathematically disabled children. *Developmental Psychology, 27,* 787–797.

Geary, D. C., Fan, L., & Bow-Thomas, C. C. (1992). Numerical cognition: Loci of ability differences comparing children from China and the United States. *Psychological Science, 3,* 180–185.

Geary, D. C., Hoard, M. K., & Hamson, C. O. (1999). Numerical and arithmetical cognition: Patterns of functions and deficits in children at risk for a mathematical disability. *Journal of Experimental Child Psychology, 74,* 213–239.

Gelman, R., & Gallistel, C. R. (1978). *The child's understanding of number.* Cambridge, MA: Harvard University Press.

Ginsburg, H. P., Klein, A., & Starkey, P. (1998). The development of children's mathematical thinking: Connecting research with practice. In W. Damon (Series Ed.), I. E. Siegel, & K. A. Renninger (Vol. Eds.), *Handbook of child psychology: Vol. 4. Child psychology in practice* (5th ed., pp. 401–476). New York: John Wiley & Sons.

Goldman, S. R., Pellegrino, J. W., & Mertz, D. L. (1988). Extended practice of basic addition facts: Strategy changes in learning-disabled students. *Cognition and Instruction, 5,* 223–265.

Graham, S., & Harris, K. R. (2000). Helping children who experience reading difficulties: Prevention and intervention. In L. Baker, J. Dreher, & J. Guthrie (Eds.), *Engaging young readers: Promoting achievement and motivation* (pp. 43–67). New York: Guilford Press.

Graham, S., Harris, K. R., & Fink, B. (2000). Is handwriting causally related to learning to write: Treatment of handwriting problems in beginning writers. *Journal of Educational Psychology, 92,* 620–633.

Gresham, F. M., MacMillan, D. L., & Bocian, K. M. (1996). Learning disabilities, low achievement, and mild mental retardation: More alike than different? *Journal of Learning Disabilities, 29,* 570–581.

Hart, B., & Risley, T. R. (1999). *Meaningful differences in the everyday experience of young American children.* Baltimore: Paul H. Brookes.

Hatcher, P., & Hulme, C. (1999). Phonemes, rhymes, and intelligence as predictors of children's responsiveness to remedial reading instruction. *Journal of Experimental Child Psychology, 72,* 130–153.

Hoskyn, M., & Swanson, H. L (2000). Cognitive processing of low achievers and children with reading disabilities: A selective meta-analytic review of the published literature. *The School Psychology Review, 29,* 102–119.

Jordan, N. C., & Hanich, L. B. (2000). Mathematical thinking in second-grade children with different forms of LD. *Journal of Learning Disabilities, 33,* 567–578.

Jordan, N. C., Levine, S. C., & Huttenlocher, J. (1995). Calculation abilities in young children with different patterns of cognitive functioning. *Journal of Learning Disabilities, 28,* 53–64.

Jorm, A. F., Share, D. L., Matthews, M., & Matthews, R. (1986). Cognitive factors at school entry predictive of specific reading retardation and general reading backwardness: A research note. *Journal of Child Psychology and Psychiatry, 27,* 45–54.

Kavale, K. A. (1988). Learning disability and cultural disadvantage: The case for a relationship. *Learning Disability Quarterly, 11,* 195–210.

Kavale, K. A. (1995). Setting the record straight on learning disability and low achievement: The tortuous path of ideology. *Learning Disabilities Research & Practice, 10,* 145–152.

Kavale, K. A., & Forness, S. R. (1994). Learning disabilities and intelligence: An uneasy alliance. In T. E. Scruggs & M. M. Mastropieri (Eds.), *Advances in learning and behavioral disabilities* (pp. 1–63). Greenwich, CT: Jai Press.

Kavale, K. A., & Forness, S. R. (2000). What definitions of learning disability say and don't say: A critical analysis. *Journal of Learning Disabilities, 33,* 239–256.

Kavale, K. A., Fuchs, D., & Scruggs, T. E. (1994). Setting the record straight on learning disability and low achievement: Implications for policymaking. *Learning Disabilities Research & Practice, 9,* 70–77.

Kavale, K. A., & Reese, J. H. (1992). The character of learning disabilities: An Iowa profile. *Learning Disability Quarterly, 15,* 74–94.

Kellam, S. G., Rebok, G. W., Mayer, L. S., Ialongo, N., & Kalodner, C. R. (1994). Depressive symptoms over first grade and their response to a developmental epidemiologically based preventive trial aimed at improving achievement. *Development and Psychopathology, 6*, 463–481.

Kirk, S. A. (1962). *Educating exceptional children*. Boston: Houghton Mifflin.

LeFevre, J. (2000). Research on the development of academic skills: Introduction to the special issue on early literacy and early numeracy. *Canadian Journal of Experimental Psychology, 54*, 57–60.

Lerner, J. (1989). Educational intervention in learning disabilities. *Journal of the American Academy of Child and Adolescent Psychiatry, 28*, 326–331.

Lukatela, G., & Turvey, M. T. (1998). Reading in two alphabets. *American Psychologist, 53*, 1057–1072.

Lyon, G. R. (1995). Toward a definition of dyslexia. *Annals of Dyslexia, 45*, 3–30.

Lyon, G. R. (1996). The future of children: Special education for students with disabilities. *Learning Disabilities, 6*, 54–76.

Lyon, G. R., Fletcher, J. M., Shaywitz, S. E., Shaywitz, B. A., Wood, F. B., Schulte, A., et al. (2001). Rethinking learning disabilities. In C. E. Finn, Jr., R. A. J. Rotherham, & C. R. O'Hokanson, Jr. (Eds.), *Rethinking special education for a new century*. Washington, DC: Thomas B. Fordham Foundation and Progressive Policy Institute.

MacMillan, D. L., Siperstein, G. N., & Gresham, F. M. (1996). Mild mental retardation: A challenge to its viability as a diagnostic category. *Exceptional Children, 62*, 356–371.

McFadden, G. T. (1990). *Determination of the subtypal composition of several samples of learning disabled children selected on the basis of WISC FSIQ IQ level: A neuropsychological, multivariate approach*. Unpublished doctoral dissertation, University of Windsor, Ontario, Canada.

McLean, J. F., & Hitch, G. J. (1999). Working memory impairments in children with specific arithmetic learning difficulties. *Journal of Experimental Child Psychology, 74*, 240–260.

Mercer, C. D., Jordan, L., Allsop, D. H., & Mercer, A. R. (1996). Learning disabilities definitions and criteria used by state education departments. *Learning Disability Quarterly, 19*, 217–232.

Morris, R., & Fletcher, J. M. (1988) Classification in neuropsychology: A theoretical framework and research paradigm. *Journal of Clinical and Experimental Neuropsychology, 10*, 640–658.

Morris, R. D., Stuebing, K. K., Fletcher, J. M., Shaywitz, S. E., Lyon, G. R., Shankweiler, D. P., et al. (1998). Subtypes of reading disability: Variability around a phonological core. *Journal of Educational Psychology, 90*, 347–373.

Morrison, S. R., & Siegel, L. S. (1991). Arithmetic disability: Theoretical considerations and empirical evidence for this subtype. In L. V. Feagans, E. J. Short, & L. J. Meltzer (Eds.), *Subtypes of learning disabilities: Theoretical perspectives and research.* (pp. 189–208). Hillsdale, NJ: Lawrence Erlbaum Assoc.

Nation, K., Adams, J. W., Bowyer-Crane, A., & Snowling, M. J. (1999). Working memory deficits in poor comprehenders reflect underlying language impairments. *Journal of Experimental Child Psychology, 73*, 139–158.

Nation, K., & Snowling, M. J. (1998). Semantic processing and the development of word-recognition skills: Evidence from children with reading comprehension difficulties. *Journal of Memory and Language, 37*, 85–101.

National Reading Panel (2000). *Teaching children to read: An evidence-based assessment of the scientific research literature on reading and its implications for reading instruction.* Washington, DC: National Institute of Child Health and Human Development.

National Joint Committee on Learning Disabilities (1988). Letter to NJCLD member organizations.

Nunes, T., & Bryant, P. (1996). *Children doing mathematics.* Oxford, England: Blackwell.

Oakhill, J. (1993). Children's difficulties in reading comprehension. *Educational Psychology Review, 5*, 1–15.

Oakhill, J. V., Cain, K., & Bryant, P. E. (in press). The dissociation of single-word and text comprehension: Evidence from component skills. *Language and Cognitive Processes.*

Oakhill, J. V., Yuill, N., & Parkin, A. (1986). On the nature of the difference between skilled and less-skilled comprehenders. *Journal of Research in Reading, 9*, 80–91.

Olson, R. K., Forsberg, H., Gayan, J., & DeFries, J. C. (1999). A behavioral-genetic analysis of reading disabilities and component processes. In R. M. Klein & P. A. McMullen (Eds.), *Converging methods for understanding reading and dyslexia* (pp. 133–153). Cambridge, MA: MIT Press.

Onatsu-Arvilommi, T., & Nurmi, J. E. (2000). The role of task-avoidant and task-focused behaviors in the development of reading and mathematical skills during the first school year: A cross-lagged longitudinal study. *Journal of Educational Psychology, 92*, 478–491.

Pennington, B. F. (1999). Dyslexia as a neurodevelopmental disorder. In H. Tager-Flusberg (Ed.), *Neurodevelopmental disorders* (pp. 307–330). Cambridge, MA: MIT Press.

Pennington, B. F., Gilger, J. W., Olson, R. K., & DeFries, J. C. (1992). External validity of age versus IQ discrepant definitions of reading disability: Lessons from a twin study. *Journal of Learning Disabilities, 25*, 639–654.

Perfetti, C. A. (1985) *Reading ability*. New York: Oxford University Press.

Perfetti, C. A., Marron, M. A., & Folz, P. W. (1996). Sources of comprehension failure: Theoretical perspectives and case studies. In C. Cornoldi and J. Oakhill (Eds.), *Reading comprehension difficulties: Processes and intervention* (pp. 137–166). Mahwah, NJ: Lawrence Erlbaum Assoc.

Rasanen, P. P., & Ahonen, T. (1995). Arithmetic disabilities with and without reading difficulties: A comparison of arithmetic errors. *Developmental Neuropsychology, 11*, 275–295.

Robinson, N. M., Zigler, E., & Gallagher, J. J. (2000). Two tails of the normal curve: Similarities and differences in the study of mental retardation and giftedness. *American Psychologist, 55*, 1413–1424.

Rodgers, B. (1983). The identification and prevalence of specific reading retardation. *British Journal of Educational Psychology, 53*, 369–373.

Rourke, B. P. (1993). Arithmetic disabilities specific and otherwise: A neuropsychological perspective. *Journal of Learning Disabilities, 26*, 214–226.

Rutter, M. (1982). Syndromes attributed to "minimal brain dysfunction" in childhood. *American Journal of Psychiatry, 139*, 21–33.

Rutter, M. (1989). Isle of Wight revisited: Twenty-five years of child psychiatric epidemiology. *Journal of the American Academy of Child and Adolescent Psychiatry, 29*, 633–653.

Rutter, M., & Yule, W. (1975). The concept of specific reading retardation. *Journal of Child Psychology and Psychiatry, 16*, 181–197.

Sattler, J. M. (1993). *Assessment of children's intelligence and special abilities*. New York: Allyn and Bacon.

Satz, P., & Fletcher, J. M. (1980). Minimal brain dysfunctions: An appraisal of research concepts and methods. In H. Rie & E. Rie (Eds.), *Handbook of minimal brain dysfunctions: A critical view* (pp. 669–715). New York: Wiley Interscience Series.

Shankweiler, D., Lundquist, E., Katz, L., Stuebing, K., Fletcher, J., Brady, S., et al. (1999). Comprehension and decoding: Patterns of association in children with reading difficulties. *Scientific Studies of Reading, 3*, 69–94.

Share, D. L., McGee, R., & Silva, P. A. (1989). I.Q. and reading progress: A test of the capacity notion of I.Q. *Journal of the American Academic of Child and Adolescent Psychiatry, 28,* 97–100.

Share, D. L., McGee, R., & Silva, P. A. (1991). The authors reply. *Journal of the American Academy of Child and Adolescent Psychiatry, 30,* 697.

Shaywitz, B. A., Fletcher, J. M., & Shaywitz, S. E. (1997). Attention-Deficit/ Hyperactivity Disorder. In K. F. Swaiman & S. Ashwal (Eds.), *Pediatric neurology: Principles & practice* (pp. 585–597). St. Louis: C.V. Mosby.

Shaywitz, B. A., Holford, T. R., Holahan, J. M., Fletcher, J. M., Stuebing, K. K., Francis, D. J., et al. (1995). A Matthew effect for IQ but not for reading: Results from a longitudinal study. *Reading Research Quarterly, 30,* 894–906.

Shaywitz, S. E. (1996). Dyslexia. *Scientific American, 275,* 98–104.

Shaywitz, S. E., Escobar, M. D., Shaywitz, B. A., & Fletcher, J. M., & Makuch, R. (1992). Distribution and temporal stability of dyslexia in an epidemiological sample of 414 children followed longitudinally. *New England Journal of Medicine, 326,* 145–150.

Shaywitz, S. E., Pugh, K. R., Jenner, A. R., Fulbright, R. K., Fletcher, J. M., Gore, J. C., et al. (2000). The neurobiology of reading and reading disability (dyslexia). In M. L. Kamil, P. B. Mosenthal, P. D. Pearson, & R. Barr (Eds.), *Handbook of reading research* (Vol. III; pp. 229–249). Mahwah, NJ: Lawrence Erlbaum Assoc.

Siegel, L. S. (1992). Dyslexic vs. poor readers: Is there a difference? *Journal of Learning Disabilities, 25,* 618–629.

Siegler, R. S., & Shrager, J. (1984). Strategy choices in addition and subtraction: How do children know what to do? In C. Sophian (Ed.), *Origins of cognitive skills* (pp. 229–293). Hillsdale, NJ: Lawrence Erlbaum Assoc.

Silva, P. A., McGee, R., & Williams, S. (1985). Some characteristics of nine-year-old boys with general reading backwardness or specific reading retardation. *Journal of Child Psychology and Psychiatry, 20,* 407–421.

Skinner, H. A. (1981). Toward the integration of classification theory and methods. *Journal of Abnormal Psychology, 90,* 68–87.

Slavin, R. E., Karweit, N. L., & Madden, N. A. (1989). *Effective programs for students at risk.* Boston: Allyn & Bacon.

Snow, C., Burns, M. S., & Griffin, P. (Eds.) (1998). *Preventing reading difficulties in young children.* Washington, DC: National Academy Press.

Stanovich, K. E. (1991). Discrepancy definitions of reading disability: Has intelligence led us astray? *Reading Research Quarterly, 26,* 1–29.

Stanovich, K. E. (1993). The construct validity of discrepancy definitions of reading disability. In G. R. Lyon, D. B. Gray, J. F. Kavanagh, & N. A. Krasnegor (Eds.), *Better understanding learning disabilities* (pp. 273–308). Baltimore: Paul H. Brooks.

Sternberg, R. J. (1991). Are we reading too much into reading comprehension tests? *Journal of Reading, 34*, 540–545.

Stevenson, J. (1988). Which aspects of reading disability show a "hump" in their distribution? *Applied Cognitive Psychology, 2*, 77–85.

Stothard, S. E., & Hulme, C. (1992). Reading comprehension difficulties in children: The role of language comprehension and working memory skills. *Reading and Writing, 4*, 245–256.

Stothard, S. E., & Hulme, C. (1996). A comparison of reading comprehension and decoding difficulties in children. In C. Cornoldi and J. Oakhill (Eds.), *Reading comprehension difficulties: Processes and intervention* (pp. 93–112). Mahwah, NJ: Lawrence Erlbaum Assoc.

Stuebing, K. K., Fletcher, J. M., LeDoux, J. M., Lyon, G. R., Shaywitz, S. E., & Shaywitz, B. A. (in press). Validity of IQ-discrepancy classifications of reading disabilities: A meta-analysis. *American Educational Research Journal.*

Swanson, H. L. (1999). Reading research for students with LD: A meta-analysis of intervention outcomes. *Journal of Learning Disabilities, 32*, 504–532.

Swanson, H. L., & Siegel, L. (in press). Learning disabilities as a working memory deficit. *Issues in Education.*

Tager-Flusberg, H., & Cooper, J. (1999). Present and future possibilities for defining a phenotype for specific language impairment. *Journal of Speech, Language, and Hearing Research, 42*, 1275–1278.

Tannock, R., Martinussen, R., & Frijters, J. (2000). Naming speed performance and stimulant effects indicate effortful, semantic processing deficits in attention-deficit/hyperactivity disorder. *Journal of Abnormal Child Psychology, 28*, 237–252.

Taylor, H. G., & Fletcher, J. M. (1983) Biological foundations of specific developmental disorders: Methods, findings, and future directions. *Journal of Child Clinical Psychology, 12*, 46–65.

Tomblin, J. B., & Zhang, X. (1999). Language patterns and etiology in children with specific language impairment. In H. Tager-Flusberg (Ed.), *Neurodevelopmental disorders* (pp. 361–382). Cambridge, MA: MIT Press.

Torgesen, J. K., Wagner, R. K., Rashotte, C. A., Rose, E., Lindamood, P., Conway, J., et al. (1999). Preventing reading failure in young children with phonological processing disabilities: Group and individual responses to instruction. *Journal of Educational Psychology, 91*, 579–594.

U.S. Department of Education (1999). 34 CFR Parts 300 and 303, Assistance to the states for the education of children with disabilities and the early intervention program for infants and toddlers with disabilities; final regulations. *Federal Register, 64*(48), 12406–12672.

U.S. Office of Education (1968). *First annual report of the National Advisory Committee on Handicapped Children.* Washington, DC: U.S. Department of Health, Education, and Welfare.

U.S. Office of Education (1977). Assistance to states for education for handicapped children: Procedures for evaluating specific learning disabilities. *Federal Register, 42*, G1082-G1085.

van der Wissell, A., & Zegers, F. E. (1985). Reading retardation revisited. *British Journal of Developmental Psychology, 3*, 3–9.

Vellutino, F. R. (1979). *Dyslexia: Theory and research.* Cambridge, MA: MIT Press.

Vellutino, F. R., Scanlon, D. M., & Lyon, G. R. (2000). Differentiating between difficult-to-remediate and readily remediated poor readers: More evidence against the IQ-achievement discrepancy definition for reading disability. *Journal of Learning Disabilities, 33*, 223–238.

Waber, D. P., Wolff, P. H., Forbes, P. W., & Weiler, M. D. (in press). Rapid automatized naming in children referred for evaluation of heterogeneous learning problems: How specific are naming speed deficits to reading disability? *Child Neuropsychology.*

Wadsworth, S. J., Olson, R. K., Pennington, B. F., & DeFries, J. C. (2000). Differential genetic etiology of reading disability as a function of IQ. *Journal of Learning Disabilities, 33*, 192–199.

White, J. L., Moffitt, T. E., & Silva, P. A. (1992). Neuropsychological and socio-emotional correlates of specific-arithmetic disability. *Archives of Clinical Neuropsychology, 7*, 1–16.

Wechsler, D. (1974). *Manual for the Wechsler Intelligence Scale for Children–Revised.* San Antonio, TX: Psychological Corp.

Whitehurst, G., & Lonigan, C. (1998). Child development and emergent literacy. *Child Development, 69*, 848–872.

Whitehurst, G. J., & Massetti, G. (in press). How well does Head Start prepare children to learn to read. In E. Zigler & S. J. Styfco (Eds.), *The Head Start Debates (Friendly and Otherwise).* New Haven: Yale University Press.

Wise, B. W., Ring, J., & Olson, R. K. (1999). Training phonological awareness with and without attention to articulation. *Journal of Experimental Child Psychology, 72*, 271–304.

Wolf, M., & Bowers, P. G. (1999). The double deficit hypothesis for the developmental dyslexias. *Journal of Educational Psychology, 91*, 415–438.

Wolf, M., Bowers, P. G., & Biddle, K. (2001). Naming-speed processes, timing, and reading: A conceptual review. *Journal of Learning Disabilities, 33*, 387–407.

Wood, F. B., Flowers, L., Buchsbaum, M., & Tallal, P. (1991). Investigation of abnormal left temporal functioning in dyslexia through rCBF, auditory evoked potentials, and positron emission tomography. *Reading and Writing: An Interdisciplinary Journal, 3*, 379–393.

Woodcock, R. W., & Johnson, M. B. (1979). *Woodcock-Johnson Psycho-Educational Test Battery*. Boston: Teaching Resources.

Ysseldyke, J. E., Algozzine, B., Shinn, M. R., & McGue, M. (1982). Similarities and differences between low achievers and students classified learning disabled. *The Journal of Special Education, 16*, 73–85.

REDEFINING LD IS NOT THE ANSWER: A RESPONSE TO FLETCHER, LYON, BARNES, STUEBING, FRANCIS, OLSON, SHAYWITZ, AND SHAYWITZ

Linda K. Elksnin, The Citadel

In their paper, "Classification of Learning Disabilities: An Evidence-Based Evaluation," Fletcher and his colleagues propose that the federal definition of learning disabilities (LD) be changed. Specifically, they argue that little difference exists between poor readers with no demonstrated discrepancy between ability and achievement (i.e., low achieving group) and poor readers who demonstrate a discrepancy (i.e., LD group). Based on this argument, Fletcher et al. conclude that the discrepancy and exclusion components of the current federal definition be abolished and that school districts begin offering special education services to the low achieving group. The authors' conclusions are largely based on results of research sponsored by the National Institute for Child Health and Human Development (NICHD) that focused on early reading acquisition (Fletcher, Francis, Rourke, Shaywitz, & Shaywitz, 1992; Fletcher et al., 1998; Shaywitz, Fletcher, Holahan, & Shaywitz, 1992). At present, Fletcher et al.'s arguments to radically alter the federal definition of LD and accompanying identification criteria are unpersuasive.

THE REALITY

Under the current definition, close to three million students with LD are served by the public schools (U.S. Department of Education, 2000). Many agree that these students represent the lowest performing of low achievers (Algozzine & Ysseldyke, 1983; Algozzine, Ysseldyke, & McGue, 1995; Kavale, 1995; Kavale, Fuchs, & Scruggs, 1994), not just in the area of basic reading skills (the area addressed by NICHD-sponsored studies), but in reading comprehension, mathematics calculation, mathematics reasoning, and/or written expression. This group of students with

LD likely represents what Torgesen (2000) refers to as "treatment resisters" who require intensive intervention. Therefore, although reading interventions implemented by NICHD researchers may reduce the numbers of children who are casualties of the general education curriculum, a group of children will remain who will require intensive special education services. According to Torgesen (2000), approximately 2% to 6% of children would remain poor readers despite receiving NICHD-funded prevention interventions.

Interventions required by these lowest of low achievers are not restricted to beginning reading instruction. The greatest increases in the number of students with disabilities served in the last 10 years are in the 12–17 age group (U.S. Department of Education, 1999). In order to acquire content literacy, many of these older students require learning strategies instruction (Deshler et al., 2001) and teachers who provide advanced organization and explicit practice opportunities (Swanson & Hoskyn, 2001).

THE CONCEPT OF LD VS. ITS OPERATIONAL DEFINITION

Experts and novices alike demonstrate an implicit understanding of the characteristics of LD (Swanson & Christie, 1994). Thus, problems with LD classification stem not from how LD is conceptualized, but from how LD has been operationally defined by practitioners (Shaw, Cullen, McGuire, & Brinckerhoff, 1995).

Currently, school districts use a variety of quantitative procedures, or discrepancy formulas, to determine if a discrepancy exists between the student's ability as measured by an intelligence test and achievement as measured by a standardized measure of achievement. These approaches include simple contrast of standard scores (probably the most widespread and least psychometrically defensible procedure), a variety of procedures that correct for measurement error, and regression procedures that take into consideration the correlation between IQ and achievement tests (see Elksnin, 1984; Loper & Reeve, undated). Despite many deserved criticisms of the use of discrepancy formulas (e.g., Aaron, 1997; Bateman, 1994), the pitfalls of discrepancy formulas do not negate the construct of discrepancy as it applies to students with LD:

> A criticism of discrepancy formulas and procedures does not imply that the concept of intelligence or general abilities is unrelated to the diagnosis of reading or learning disabilities. One salient characteristic of individuals with learning disabilities and reading disabilities is that they do not achieve at a level of expected performance based on their other abilities. (Mather & Roberts, 1994, p. 53)

IMPLICATIONS FOR PRACTICE

Rather than rely on discrepancy formulas to determine presence of LD, eligibility teams should be given the flexibility to use the collective professional judgment of team members after considering information from a variety of sources (Bateman, 1994; Bocian, Beebe, MacMillan, & Gresham, 1999). Qualitative information (i.e., error analysis, task analysis, observation) from norm-referenced tests can provide needed information (Mather & Roberts, 1994). Focusing on assessment of cognitive skills and how these skills contribute to reading, writing, and mathematics will move assessment beyond using formulas and cut-off scores to determine LD eligibility (Mather & Roberts, 1994; Reid, Hresko, & Swanson, 1996; Swanson, 2000). A system that seeks to identify information-processing conditions or deficits as part of the LD eligibility process developed by the Minnesota Department of Children, Families & Learning (Ayers et al., 1977) shows particular promise in operationalizing the federal LD definition and identification criteria beyond ability-achievement discrepancy. The Minnesota process requires eligibility teams to use interviews, observations, questionnaires, informal inventories, and item analysis in order to determine that

1. The pupil has an information processing condition that is manifested by such behaviors as: inadequate or lack of organizational skills (such as following directions, written and oral; spatial arrangements; correct use of developmental order in relating events; transfer of information onto paper), memory (visual and auditory), expression (verbal and nonverbal), and motor control for written tasks such as pencil and paper assignments, drawing, and copying;
2. The disabling effects of the pupil's information processing condition occur in a variety of settings. (Ayers et al., 1977, p. II-4)

In addition, education professionals must acknowledge the importance of clinical judgment in the LD classification process just as mental health professionals acknowledge its importance in the diagnosis and classification of mental disorders. For example, the preface to the *Diagnostic and Statistical Manual of Mental Disorders* (DSM–IV; American Psychiatric Association, 1994) clearly states the importance of professional judgment:

The diagnostic categories, criteria, and textual descriptions are meant to be employed by individuals with appropriate clinical training and experience in diagnosis. It is important that DSM–IV not be applied mechanically by untrained individuals. The specific diagnostic criteria included in DSM–IV are meant to serve as guidelines to be informed by clinical judgment and are not meant to be used in a cookbook fashion.

For example, the exercise of clinical judgment may justify giving a certain diagnosis to an individual even though the clinical presentation falls just short of meeting the full criteria for the diagnosis as long as the symptoms that are present are persistent and severe. (American Psychiatric Association, 1994, p. xxiii)

CLASSIFICATION OF LD AND RESPONSE TO TREATMENT

Fletcher et al. suggest that definitions of LD be treatment oriented. Specifically, they argue that alternative definitions "provide specific criteria indicating that the child has a particular type of LD [and that they] point towards a set of potential interventions" (this volume). However, the fact that the federal definition of LD fails to prescribe treatment is irrelevant. Few definitions or classification systems include treatment recommendations, including the other Individuals with Disabilities Education Act definitions. Likewise, noneducational classification systems such as the DSM–IV are used to classify, not to treat, mental disorders.

The federal definition of LD is used to make entitlement decisions, including the presence of disability and eligibility for special education services, rather than for treatment or intervention. Different assessment information is required for post-entitlement decisions such as intervention planning (Salvia & Ysseldyke, 2001). Unexpected low achievement is a symptom of a learning disability, not a cause. The cause of the LD, such as an inability to store, organize, acquire, retrieve, express, or manipulate information, will help determine the intervention approach. To expect a definition of LD to prescribe treatment is akin to treating a headache without considering its many possible causes (i.e., muscle tension, high blood pressure, glaucoma, sinus problems, syphilis, brain tumors). Few physicians would advocate brain surgery for a headache caused by muscle tension. Similarly, few educators would advocate implementing the same social skills intervention with all children, for example, without considering if the social skills deficit is due to lack of knowledge, lack of opportunity, lack of feedback, lack of sensitivity to environmental cues, or lack of reinforcement (Elksnin & Elksnin, 1995).

Although they fail to make a strong case for LD definitions to prescribe treatment, Fletcher et al. rightly emphasize the importance of effective instruction for all students. Teachers, whether special or general, need to use empirically validated practices. At present we have substantial evidence regarding instructional practices that are effective with students with LD. For example, results of the most comprehensive meta-analysis of LD intervention studies to date indicate that direct instruction and cognitive strategies training have the largest treatment effect sizes (Swanson & Hoskyn, 1998; Swanson, Hoskyn, Sachee-Lee, & O'Shaughnessy, 1997). Similarly, direct instruction, cognitive strategies training, behavior modification, and cognitive behavior modification have been found to have the greatest impact upon student achievement (Lloyd, Forness, & Kavale, 1998). With respect to reading, it appears that direct instruction improves reading recognition, whereas improvements in comprehension require combining strategy and direct instruction (Swanson, 1999). NICHD-sponsored research findings support those of earlier intervention research, which noted that many students benefit from explicit instruction in phonics (Adams & Engelmann, 1996; Chall, 1967), but that ability to decode words may be insufficient to comprehend what is read.

IMPLICATIONS FOR RESEARCH

Efforts to determine the validity of discrepancy formulas for differentiating LD from low achievement have been restricted to the discrepancy between cognitive ability and reading. Thus, the validity of discriminating between groups in mathematics, writing, and problem-solving performance is unknown (Swanson, 2000). However, whether valid or invalid, quantitative methods for determining ability-achievement discrepancy are unlikely to lead to specification of recognizable LD behaviors. When achievement-ability discrepancy is the primary (or in some cases, the only) basis for classifying children, it is not surprising that some researchers differentiated LD groups from low achievement groups (Badian, 1999; Fuchs, Fuchs, Mathes, & Lipsey, 2000; Jorm, Share, Matthews, & MacLean, 1986; Kavale, 1995; Kavale et al., 1994; Kavale & Forness, 2000; Kavale & Reese, 1992; Share & Silva, 1986; Silva, McGee, & Williams, 1985), whereas others did not (Algozzine et al., 1995; Fletcher et al., 1989; Fletcher et al., 1998; Fletcher et al., 1992; Shaywitz, Escobar, Shaywitz, Fletcher, & Makuch, 1992; Shaywitz et al., 1992; Siegel, 1992; Stanovich, 1991; Stuebing et al., 2001).

A more productive line of inquiry than determining whether low achieving and LD students exhibit a discrepancy between achievement and ability would be to identify the cognitive processes mediating discrepancies and nondiscrepancies among poorly performing students (Swanson, 2000). Few researchers have examined this question (Swanson, 2000).

A second productive area of research that has received little attention is students' responsiveness to intervention (Swanson, 2000). Consideration of how LD and low achieving, and discrepant and nondiscrepant, groups respond to specific interventions may help identify group similarities and differences. For example, based on a review of prevention interventions, Torgesen (2000) estimated that from 2% to 6% of children resisted treatment (i.e., they continued to demonstrate inadequate reading skills following intervention). As a result of these findings, Torgesen suggested that differentiated treatment might be indicated for two groups of children at risk for reading failure, those who have generalized language deficits and those with specific phonological awareness difficulties.

At present we have an arsenal of interventions proven effective with LD and other low-performing students (see Lloyd et al., 1998; Swanson, 1999; Swanson & Hoskyn, 1998, 2001; Swanson et al., 1997). Of course, getting teachers to implement effective practices remains a challenge. As Ball and Cohen (1996) note

> All of the reform rhetoric and ambitious plans discussed in the governors' conferences and in so many policy papers will be of little value unless they lead to changes in the day-to-day instructional practices of teachers in our nation's schools. (p. 7)

Therefore, a third productive line of research would be to examine ways to implement, support, and sustain effective instructional practices in schools (Gersten & Dimino, 2001; Slavin & Fashiola, 1998). This is critical to prevention and intervention efforts.

Finally, one of the difficulties in interpreting LD research is that subjects are inconsistently and/or inadequately described. If LD subjects are selected strictly on the basis of public school identification criteria, the result is a post hoc interpretation of subject characteristics and task performance. Federal agencies could address this issue by requiring minimum standards and a universal protocol for describing participants in federally funded LD research. This recommendation has been made on numerous occasions over the years (Morris et al., 1994; Rosenberg et al., 1992), beginning with Keogh's call for using a system of marker variables (Keogh, Major-Kingsley, Omori-Gordon, & Reid, 1982).

Summary and Conclusions

By refocusing national attention on the importance of early reading instruction, NICHD-sponsored research has helped to emphasize that "reading is not a natural process" for some children (Lyon, 2000), who require explicit instruction in order to become proficient readers. In addition, NICHD-sponsored research has refocused attention on the importance of early intervention through use of effective instructional practice to prevent educational failure of large groups of children. However, drawing heavily upon NICHD-sponsored research results, Fletcher et al. fail to make a compelling case for abandoning the current federal LD definition and accompanying identification for several reasons:

1. Examination of the validity of the construct of unexpected underachievement as it relates to LD undertaken by NICHD researchers and others has been restricted to cognitive ability and beginning reading, and these results are equivocal. The validity of discrepancy as applied to other areas such as written expression, mathematics calculation and reasoning, and general problem solving remains to be investigated.

2. Students with LD remain the lowest performing of low achievers who require intensive intervention not typically available in general education settings.

3. Problems with the LD classification are not due to the current federal definition but stem from how it has been operationalized.

Radical changes in policy regarding how students with LD are identified and served are unwarranted at this time. That is not to say that practices cannot be improved. Specifically, personnel should be discouraged from over-reliance upon formulas and cutoff scores to determine LD eligibility.

Rather than continuing to focus on symptoms of LD such as discrepancy, research needs to focus on the cognitive processes that mediate discrepancies and nondiscrepancies among students who perform poorly in school. Similarly, LD will be better understood by examining LD and low achieving students' responses to interventions and better treated by identifying ways to implement, support, and sustain effective interventions in classrooms.

Researchers and practitioners must acknowledge that, although measurement problems continue to plague the field, the concept of LD remains valid. As Keogh (1987) eloquently notes:

> Differences in assessment techniques and in selection criteria and procedures will lead to differences in who and how many individuals are identified as LD. Do these differences imply that there is no such thing as LD? I think not. Fishermen using different nets collect different sizes and numbers of fish. We have made a serious logical error in equating the concept of LD with the ways in which it is operationalized and measured. It is rather like saying that there is no such thing as intelligence because our measures of IQ are imprecise, or that anxiety is not real because it is not reliably quantified. (p. 6)

REFERENCES

Aaron, P. B. (1997). The impending demise of the discrepancy formula. *Review of Educational Research, 67,* 461–502.

Adams, G., & Engelmann, S. (1996). *Research on direct instruction: 25 years beyond DISTAR.* Seattle: Educational Achievement Systems.

Algozzine, B., & Ysseldyke, J. E. (1983). Learning disabilities as a subset of school failure: The oversophistication of a concept. *Exceptional Children, 50,* 242–246.

Algozzine, B., Ysseldyke, J. E., & McGue, M. (1995). Differentiating low-achieving students: Thoughts on setting the record straight. *Learning Disabilities Research & Practice, 10,* 140–144.

American Psychiatric Association. (1994). *Diagnostic and statistical manual of mental disorders* (4th ed.). Washington, DC: Author.

Ayers, L., Brumbaugh, C., Carlson, B., Gustafson, L., Larson, N., Murphree, J., et al. (1977). *Information processing: Definition, assessment, instruction.* Minneapolis: Minnesota Department of Children, Families, & Learning.

Badian, N. A. (1999). Reading disability defined as a discrepancy between listening and reading comprehension: A longitudinal study of stability, gender differences, and prevalence. *Journal of Learning Disabilities, 32,* 138–148.

Ball, D. L., & Cohen, D. K. (1996). Reform by the book: What is—or might be—the role of curriculum materials in teacher learning and instructional reform. *Educational Researcher, 25,* 6–8.

Bateman, B. D. (1994). Toward a better identification of learning disabilities. *Learning Disabilities: A Multidisciplinary Journal, 5*(2), 95–99.

Bocian, K. M., Beebe, M. E., MacMillan, D. L., & Gresham, F. M. (1999). Competing paradigms in learning disabilities classification by schools and the variations in the meaning of discrepant achievement. *Learning Disabilities Research & Practice, 14,* 1–14.

Chall, J. (1967). *Learning to read: The great debate.* New York: McGraw-Hill.

Deshler, D. D., Schumaker, J. B., Lenz, B. K., Bulgren, J. A., Hock, M. F., Knight, J., et al. (2001). Ensuring content-area learning by secondary students with learning disabilities. *Learning Disabilities Research & Practice, 16,* 96–108.

Elksnin, L. K. (1984). A comparison of four quantitative methods for determining severe discrepancy and school LD placement decisions. (Doctoral dissertation, University of Virginia, 1984). *Dissertation Abstracts International, 46,* 2994.

Elksnin, L. K., & Elksnin, H. N. (1995). *Assessment and instruction of social skills.* San Diego, CA: Singular Publishing Group.

Fletcher, J. M., Espy, K. A., Francis, D. J., Davidson, K. C., Rourke, B. P., & Shaywitz, S. E. (1989). Comparisons of cutoff and regression-based definitions of reading disabilities. *Journal of Learning Disabilities, 22,* 334–338.

Fletcher, J. M., Francis, D. J., Rourke, B. P., Shaywitz, S. E., & Shaywitz, B. A. (1992). The validity of discrepancy-based definitions of reading disabilities. *Journal of Learning Disabilities, 25,* 555–561.

Fletcher, J. M., Francis, D. J., Shaywitz, S. E., Lyon, G. R., Foorman, B. R., Stuebing, K. K., et al. (1998). Intelligent testing and the discrepancy model for children with learning disabilities. *Learning Disabilities Research & Practice, 13,* 186–203.

Fuchs, D., Fuchs, L. S., Mathes, P. G., & Lipsey, M. W. (2000). Reading differences between low-achieving students with and without learning disabilities: A meta-analysis. In R. Gersten, E. P. Schiller, & S. Vaughn, *Contemporary special education research* (pp. 105–136). Mahwah, NJ: Lawrence Erlbaum Assoc.

Gersten, R., & Dimino, J. (2001). The realities of translating research into classroom practice. *Learning Disabilities Research & Practice, 16,* 120–130.

Jorm, A. F., Share, D. L., Matthews, R., & MacLean, R. (1986). Behavior problems in specific reading retarded and general reading backward children: A longitudinal study. *Journal of Child Psychology and Psychiatry and Allied Disciplines, 27,* 33–43.

Kavale, K. A. (1995). Setting the record straight on learning disability and low achievement: The tortuous path of ideology. *Learning Disabilities Research & Practice, 10,* 145–152.

Kavale, K. A., Fuchs, D., & Scruggs, T. E. (1994). Setting the record straight on learning disability and low achievement: Implications for policymaking. *Learning Disabilities Research & Practice, 9,* 70–77.

Kavale, K. A., & Forness, S. R. (2000). What definitions of learning disability say and don't say: A critical analysis. *Journal of Learning Disabilities, 33,* 239–256.

Kavale, K. A., & Reese, J. H. (1992). The character of learning disabilities: An Iowa profile. *Learning Disability Quarterly, 15,* 74–94.

Keogh, B. K. (1987). Learning disabilities: In defense of a construct. *Learning Disabilities Research & Practice, 3,* 4–9.

Keogh, B. K., Major-Kingsley, S., Omori-Gordon, H., & Reid, H. P. (1982). *A system of marker variables for the field of learning disabilities.* Syracuse, NY: Syracuse University Press.

Lloyd, J. W., Forness, S. R., & Kavale, K. A. (1998). Some methods are more effective than others. *Intervention in School and Clinic, 33*, 195–200.

Loper, A. B., & Reeve, R. E. (undated). *Quantitative procedures to estimate underachievement.* University of Virginia, Charlottesville, VA.

Lyon, G. R. (2000, January/February). Why reading is not a natural process. *LDA Newsbriefs*, 12–14, 17–18,

Mather, N., & Roberts, R. (1994). Learning disabilities: A field in danger of extinction? *Learning Disabilities Research & Practice, 9*, 49–58.

Morris, R., Lyon, G. R., Alexander, D., Gray, D. B., Kavanagh, J., Rourke, B. P., et al. (1994). Proposed guidelines and criteria for describing samples of persons with learning disabilities. *Learning Disability Quarterly, 17*, 106–109.

Reid, D. K., Hresko, W. P., & Swanson, H. L. (1996). *Cognitive approaches to learning disabilities* (3rd ed.). Austin, TX: PRO-ED.

Rosenberg, M., Bott, D., Majsterek, D., Chiang, B., Simmons, D., Gartland, D., et al. (1992). Minimum standards for the description of participants in learning disabilities research. *Learning Disabilities Quarterly, 15*, 65–70.

Salvia, J., & Ysseldyke, J. E. (2001). *Assessment* (8th ed.). Boston: Houghton Mifflin.

Share, D. L., & Silva, P. A. (1986). The stability and classification of specific reading retardation: A longitudinal study from 7 to 11. *British Journal of Educational Psychology, 56*, 32–39.

Shaw, S. F., Cullen, J. P., McGuire, J. M., & Brinckerhoff, L. C. (1995). Operationalizing a definition of learning disabilities. *Journal of Learning Disabilities, 28*, 586–597.

Shaywitz, B. A., Escobar, M. D., Shaywitz, B. A., Fletcher, J. M., & Makuch, R. (1992). Distribution and temporal stability of dyslexia in an epidemiological sample of 414 children followed longitudinally. *New England Journal of Medicine, 326*, 145–150.

Shaywitz, B. A., Fletcher, J. M., Holahan, J. M., & Shaywitz, S. E. (1992). Discrepancy compared to low achievement definitions of reading disability: Results from the Connecticut longitudinal study. *Journal of Learning Disabilities, 25*, 639–648.

Siegel, L. S. (1992). An evaluation of the discrepancy definition of dyslexia. *Journal of Learning Disabilities, 25*(10), 618–629.

Silva, P. A., McGee, R., & Williams, S. (1985). Some characteristics of 9-year-old boys with general reading backwardness or specific reading retardation. *Journal of Child Psychology and Psychiatry and Allied Disciplines, 28*, 407–421.

Slavin, R. E., & Fashiola, O. S. (1998). *Show me the evidence! Proven and promising programs for America's schools.* Thousand Oaks, CA: Corwin Press.

Stanovich, K. E. (1991). Discrepancy definitions of reading disability: Has intelligence led us astray? *Reading Research Quarterly, 26,* 1–29.

Stuebing, K. K., Fletcher, J. M., LeDoux, J. M., Lyon, G. R., Shaywitz, S. E., & Shaywitz, B. A. (2001). Validity of IQ-discrepancy classifications of reading disabilities: A meta-analysis.

Swanson, H. L. (1999). Instructional components that predict treatment outcomes for students with learning disabilities: Support for a combined strategy and direct instruction model. *Learning Disabilities Research & Practice, 14,* 129–140.

Swanson, H. L. (2000). Issues facing the field of learning disabilities. *Learning Disabilities Quarterly, 23,* 37–49.

Swanson, H. L., & Christie, L. (1994). Implicit notions about learning disabilities: Some directions for definitions. *Learning Disabilities Research & Practice, 9,* 244–254.

Swanson, H. L., & Hoskyn, M. (1998). A comprehensive synthesis of experimental intervention for students with learning disabilities. *Review of Educational Research, 68,* 276–321.

Swanson, H. L., & Hoskyn, M. (2001). Instructing adolescents with learning disabilities: Component and composite analysis. *Learning Disabilities Research & Practice, 16,* 109–119.

Swanson, H. L., Hoskyn, M., Sachee-Lee, C., & O'Shaughnessy, T. (1997). *Intervention research for students with learning disabilities: A meta-analysis of treatment outcomes.* (Final Report HO23E400114). Washington, DC: U.S. Department of Education.

Torgesen, J. J. (2000). Individual differences in response to early interventions in reading: The lingering problem of treatment resisters. *Learning Disabilities Research & Practice, 15*(1), 55–64.

U.S. Department of Education (1999). *Twenty-first annual report to Congress on the Implementation of the Individuals with Disabilities Education Act.* Washington, DC: Author.

U.S. Department of Education (2000). *Twenty-second annual report to Congress on the Implementation of the Individuals with Disabilities Education Act.* Washington, DC: Author.

A RESPONSE TO CLASSIFICATION OF LEARNING DISABILITIES: AN EVIDENCE-BASED EVALUATION

Nancy W. Larson,
Minnesota Department of Children, Families and Learning

Fletcher and his distinguished colleagues, Lyon, Barnes, Stuebing, Francis, Olson, Shaywitz, & Shaywitz, have authored a complicated paper and an exhaustive argument for a new classification of children with learning disabilities (LD). It would be difficult to critique the research base on which their proposal is developed, for their evidence is cited from very noted researchers in the LD field. Instead, this response to their paper identifies field-based and legal issues such as entitlement, heterogeneity, terminology, field application, and teacher shortage as they relate to a potential change in LD classification. As difficult as it is to develop a conceptual model and reach consensus with research peers, it is even more challenging to uniformly apply both a new definition and the eligibility criteria essential to the implementation of a law or rule. LD is unusual in that it is the only categorical disability with a federal definition, specific criteria, and requirements for report writing.

ENTITLEMENT

The most critical and least emphasized political issue in altering the definition of LD is that of the potential for a change in entitlement. A change in the federal definition of LD would result in many students currently identified with LD no longer being entitled to a free and appropriate public education (FAPE) under the Individuals with Disabilities Education Act (IDEA). When theorists and researchers undertake a discussion of the basis of the definition of LD, they may forget that the most volatile political issue in this discussion is entitlement. Whatever the new definition of LD, it will have the potential to alter if not eliminate the entitlement of children currently identified with LD.

A few of the changes proposed by the authors and other researchers (Fletcher et al., 1998; Fletcher et al., this volume; Swanson, 2000) include a student's response to interventions, the elimination of cut-off scores, and a different structure for service delivery. These proposed definitional changes are about evaluation processes and should be included in criteria or left to state policy development, not included in the federal definition of LD. They do not contribute much to increasing the clarity of the concept of LD.

Also, there exists some confusion between the concepts included in the LD definition, LD eligibility criteria, and required evaluation components. Criteria are typically developed by state education agencies. Using the public law and rulemaking process, not all states developed a "lowest common denominator" or overly simplified definition of LD or of LD eligibility criteria. Some states retained the notion that the etiology of LD presumes central nervous system dysfunction or includes identifiable basic psychological processing issues (e.g., short-term memory, fluency, as identified in the Fletcher article). Some states defined "severe" from a psychometric perspective and set the level of severe discrepancy between ability and achievement for LD eligibility at 1.75 to 2.0 standard deviations, adopting regression formulas rather than relying on the more common but less valid subtraction of standard scores discrepancy calculation. This subtraction of standard scores is a procedure criticized by Fletcher and his colleagues.

The responsibility for rule implementation, whether at the best practice or the lowest common denominator level, rests with states, not with researchers. Fletcher et al., in combining elements of both criteria and definition, hope to create a definition that mistakenly includes criteria. Definition should inform criteria. Criteria should then be correlated with specific elements of definition and may contain direction for evaluation. Criteria are best left to states to develop. Researchers need to trust the process at the state level with its charge to entitle children with LD and other disabilities with an educational effect at a level considered to be disabling.

HETEROGENEITY TO SPECIFICITY

Any definition of a categorical disability should stand alone as a concept. Current definitions of categorical disabilities under IDEA are not related to specific teaching areas such as reading or math; rather, they convey a global sense of what the disability is. The concept of "LDness" seems still confused by some and expressed in terms of curriculum. Thankfully, the special education field is not nearly as confused by the notions of mild to moderate mental impairment, speech/language disorder, or physical disability. Care needs to be taken in the area of LD that in embracing the lure of research results that focus on a narrow, carefully defined population, the essential concept of specific learning disability is still retained. As

Fletcher et al. acknowledge, there is nothing mild about LD in terms of its academic, social, emotional, and behavioral effects. Fletcher and his colleagues argue for a massive early intervention program that excludes no child. The right to FAPE and specially designed instruction is well established in special education and whether a massive early intervention approach denies or delays FAPE to students with LD will need examination.

Most researchers and practitioners agree that the definition of LD needs tweaking in light of current research findings (Kavale & Forness, 2000; MacMillan, Gresham & Bocian, 1998; Swanson, 2000; Tomasi & Weinberg, 1999). The white paper by Fletcher et al. proposes an LD model based on selected research evidence that actually confuses the definitional issue by moving from a heterogeneous concept of LD to a very specific classification system, and at the same time introducing the concept of subtypes of LD not currently in federal law or rule (IDEA 97). It may be more appropriate to identify subtypes in criteria. However, the entire idea of limiting the field to certain subtypes seems precipitous.

A definition of a disability should not contain references to specific criteria issues, to evaluation methods, or to the success of interventions. Given its controversial history, specific learning disability as a disability stands alone as a target for endless revision by researchers, psychologists, theorists, and clinicians, indeed everyone but practitioners. This constant revision plays out to the detriment of teachers, parents, and students with specific learning disabilities. Despite trying to stem a steady stream of controversy regarding the definition of LD, practitioners are now faced with Fletcher et al. crafting an LD model in which professionals are made to be apologists for not anticipating the findings of current research. The premise of Fletcher et al. is that the definition (maybe the criteria too) of specific learning disabilities must change to "be consistent with changes in the knowledge base, which always evolves" (this volume). Is this the case for all categorical disabilities or is the push to revise and reconceptualize really a matter of economics?

According to Fletcher et al. and others (Lyon, 1996; Padget, 1998; Raskind et al., 1999; Swanson, 2000; Vaughn, Gersten, & Chard, 2000), researchers have identified clusters of symptoms of individuals who experience problems in specific academic areas. They have suggested the use of *specific reading disability, math disability,* and various other terms related to academic problems. While certain academic problems might be characteristic of individuals with specific learning disabilities, defining a disability in terms of a deficit curricular area alone is contrary to the notion of disability. To carry the "curricular disability" thinking one step further, if the field is to contend with new categories of curricular disabilities (reading disability and math disability), why not also propose science and social studies disabilities? How about having a research skills disability? The fallacy in this discussion is the failure to identify the disability as intrinsic to the individual, not intrinsic to the curriculum. LD may manifest in a specific curricular area, but the rationale for providing special education service to a child is the concept of disability itself. The disability and its effects on school performance are the basis of the child's entitlement to special education.

TEACHER COMPETENCIES

Recruitment and retention of special education teachers is an acute national crisis. In response to the teacher shortage and to the complaints of administrators, some states have streamlined their special education licensure and no longer require disability-specific competencies. As a consequence, there are now many special education teachers without the competencies necessary to perform evaluations using current criteria, which contributes to the already questionable identification of some students with LD. "Watered-down" licensure requirements will result in less qualified teachers and create the need to develop easy-to-understand and less technical eligibility criteria.

While most evaluators are not advocates for the notion of basing eligibility decisions solely on a severe discrepancy between ability and achievement, discrepancy criteria are relatively easy to understand. In order to move from the current discrepancy-based federal definition to a definition based on specific research-based indicators, the entire workforce in LD would need to acquire many competencies in evaluation. This may not be an adequate reason for maintaining the status quo with the current federal definition of LD, but still a lack of technical competencies in the emerging special education workforce is a reality.

TERMINOLOGY PITFALLS

The use of terms such as reading retardation, reading disability, math disability, mental deficiency, and dyslexia is not helpful for the field. Some of these terms are offensive to teachers, parents, and students; some are merely befuddling. *Reading retardation* and *mental deficiency* are particularly odious terms. Moreover, using the terms *reading disability* and *dyslexia* interchangeably and then equating them with the eligibility criteria for LD is simply adding a further confounding layer of jargon to the top of the LD definitional and criteria cake.

The three components of LD classification according to Fletcher et al. are discrepancy, heterogeneity, and exclusion. The practitioner's three components might be conceptualized very differently as underachievement, discrepancy, and psychological processing problems, all of which are more easily operationalized in an evaluation. LD is a disability of exclusion, but the factors listed in federal rule are not meant to define what is meant by the term *specific learning disability*. Rather, the exclusionary factors speak to the etiology of a student's underachievement, not to the etiology of a student's LD. It follows that if another reason exists (other than LD) for a student's underachievement, whether expected or not, then the appropriate eligibility determination would be made and special education services would follow. Researchers and evaluators may directly link only some of the underachievement of individuals with LD to specific cognitive patterns or factors, but the effort may ultimately result in confirming Fletcher et al.'s model of specific learning disabilities.

Another confounding and confusing issue in terminology is the labeling of curriculum-oriented disabilities (i.e., reading disability or math disability), a problem from a school perspective. Instead of labeling specific learning disabilities by curriculum deficit, a charge to researchers to conceive of an improved gestalt for LD that is recognizable to the field might be more practical. The field is in the business of providing FAPE to children and youth with disabilities, not to children and youth who can't read or can't do math. LD teachers are left to explain a team's eligibility determination based on LD criteria to parents, general education teachers, and advocates. If the definition of LD keeps shifting to curriculum, then every child in school could potentially be identified as having curricular needs and therefore as eligible for special education services.

Furthermore, the shifting LD definition could create a sort of Matthew effect for teachers. Hypothetically, a teacher may be 2 years behind in acquiring the competencies necessary to implement the current LD criteria. As the criteria change, the teacher will then be lacking necessary additional competencies to either evaluate students or implement new interventions, resulting in an ever-increasing gap between what a teacher knows and what is necessary to operate effectively in the field.

FIELD REALITIES

It takes years to implement relatively minor changes in federal or state rule. According to federal monitoring reports, many states have not yet fully implemented the changes in IDEA 97. It is impossible to project the difficulties with implementing the changes in the LD definition suggested by Fletcher et al. Moreover, a significant departure in conceptualization and implementation of a disability category affects the entire spectrum of teacher preparation, including staff development. In order to implement a new change, teacher preparation programs must begin to define and teach the new concept. Effective tools and interventions must be validated and recommended. Information about the new definition must be communicated to special education administrators, who in turn, must communicate this information to their district level administrators, who must further communicate this information to practitioners. Workshops must be developed. A cadre of expert trainers must be identified, and suddenly there will be a market for user-friendly short-term memory devices or whatever is included in the definition, whether research-based or not. The good news presented by Fletcher et al. is that researchers have begun to identify the characteristics specific to individuals with LD. The bad news is that the field is light years away from the uniform implementation of effective practice.

Still, it is important to note that there have been variations in definitions of LD in different studies since the 1960s. Some of the definitional differences are attributable to selection criteria such as whether the study groups were part of a clinical population, whether the researchers established their own criteria, whether state and federal eligibility criteria were used, and whether groups were defined by underachievement alone. Another selection issue is whether researchers used screening tools, instruments that are not commonly used in eligibility determination. Researchers may also be so focused on describing specific characteristics of LD that they lose track of a conceptual model or framework for LD. It is very easy in this sort of discussion to lose the big picture. The challenge to researchers is to continue the search for identifiable characteristics and to place them in an understandable framework.

POLITICS

A major player in the politics of LD is the special education team, a political entity within a larger political system. At any level, political systems may act expediently by advocating for defining all underachievers as LD or as low achievers, to reduce the time required to analyze individual student learning patterns. Special education teams may do the same. Making eligibility decisions by analyzing a set of complex data rather than through expedience requires high levels of expertise. A dramatic increase in evaluation competencies on the part of current and new special education teachers is unlikely, given the teacher shortage and the trends toward generic special education licensure. To illustrate this problem, the different characteristics of students with LD compared to low achievers who may be discrepant or nondiscrepant is difficult for teachers to analyze in a knowledgeable manner. Fletcher et al., in an effort to clarify characteristics of LD, actually contribute to the current definitional fuzziness in their more technical and complex discussion of an LD classification system. The proposed classification system raises even more questions than it answers.

Here are just a few of the definitional questions generated by my reading of the Fletcher paper. What are the criteria for low achievement? What is salient about knowing that low achievers have a lower vocabulary or have lower IQs? Why is the

25th percentile used in some studies as a cut-off for identifying severe underachievement (needing special education service) for LD or any other disability? (One of the distinguishing markers of a disability is that it is not common and the bottom 25% is too broad a range to be helpful in identifying students with disabilities.) What are the criteria for a reading disability? Who are IQ-discrepant students? How discrepant are they? Why are discrepant students identified by a subtraction of standard scores when this is considered poor practice? How does specific language impairment interface with LD from a definitional standpoint? What is a "general delay" in language? Why not use general intellectual ability, emphasizing those components loading on general intellectual ability? Why is the cut-off score for any other disability not considered equally arbitrary? Why wouldn't the definition of LD be driven by psychometric characteristics to some extent? Clearly, when specific research-based elements are introduced into the LD definition discussion, many more definitional issues reveal themselves.

In direct contrast to their expressed concerns with the severe discrepancy criteria, Fletcher et al. say that "children identified with either an IQ discrepancy or LD definition *are* disabled, need to be identified, and respond similarly to appropriate educational interventions" (this volume). If, as Fletcher et al. contend, specific learning disabilities exist and individuals with LD have a disability to the extent that entitlement, accommodations, due process, special education, and programming are required, then the treatment should relate to the disability and to the needs of the individual, not the other way around.

UNDERACHIEVEMENT

It is easy to subsume children with LD into federally mandated programs such as Title I and Head Start, which already exist for underachieving students. If Fletcher and his colleagues can simplify the number and type of characteristics of LD and relate them to a meaningful concept of LD, then perhaps there will be measurable attributes of LD other than simple underachievement. If underachievement levels alone are the sole criteria of specific learning disabilities, then LD no longer has a foundation as a disability and funding entitlements will fade, marking the end of special education service to this population. Shifting definitions of a categorical disability serve as an alarm to the public. While there seems to be an interest in fully funding special education, such inconsistencies in the educational message alarm politicians.

It is important to debate the complexities of LD among stakeholders, but there is a spillover effect on the public. LD teachers and administrators have to approach the education community at large and the general public "hat in hand," apologizing for the fuzziness of the ever-changing definition of LD. It is no wonder that public financial support for LD is sometimes lessened and special educators are labeled "coddlers" of students who should simply "pull themselves up by the bootstraps."

SUMMARY

Deriving or altering state and federal definitions of learning disabilities on the basis of research findings is extremely difficult. The goals of researchers and the goals of public policy are different. Special education rules and regulations are developed to ensure the entitlement of FAPE to entitled individuals with learning and other disabilities. Researchers are engaged in a discovery process of accurately identifying the characteristics of LD to facilitate the comparison of populations of students with LD across studies. Definitions of other categorical disabilities such as hearing and vision impairments seem immune to the demand to reflect research findings. Perhaps the current debate over the definition of LD is the wave of the future and the special education field as a whole will craft more flexible disability definitions that are more inclusive and responsive to research findings.

REFERENCES

Fletcher, J. M., Francis, D. J., Shaywitz, S. E., Lyon, G. R., Foorman, B. R., Stuebing, K. K., & Shaywitz, B. A. (1998). Intelligent testing and the discrepancy model for children with learning disabilities. *Learning Disabilities Research & Practice, 13*(4), 186–203.

Gregg, N., & Scott, S. (2000). Definition and documentation: Theory, measurement, and the courts. *Journal of Learning Disabilities, 33*(1), 5–20.

Kauffman, J. M., Hallahan, D. P., & Lloyd, J. W. (1998). Politics, science and the future of learning disabilities. *Learning Disability Quarterly, 21,* 276–281.

Kavale, K. A., & Forness, S. R. (1995). *The nature of learning disabilities.* Mahwah, NJ: Lawrence Erlbaum Assoc.

Kavale, K. A., & Forness, S. R. (2000). What definitions of learning disability say and don't say: A critical analysis. *Journal of Learning Disabilities, 33*(3), 239–256.

Lyon, G. R. (1996). Learning disabilities. *The Future of Children: Special Education for Students with Disabilities, 6*(1), 54–75.

MacMillan, D. L., Gresham, F., & Bocian, K. M. (1998). Discrepancy between definitions of learning disabilities and school practices empirical investigation. *Journal of Learning Disabilities, 31*(4), 314–322.

National Joint Commission on Learning Disabilities. (1998). Learning disabilities: Preservice preparation of general and special education teachers. *Learning Disability Quarterly, 21,* 182–193.

Padget, S. Y. (1998). Lessons from research on dyslexia: Implications for a classification system for learning disabilities. *Learning Disability Quarterly, 21,* 167–176.

Raskind, M. H., Goldberg, R. J., Higgins, E. L., & Herman, K. L. (1999). Patterns of change and predictors of success in individuals with learning disabilities: Results from a twenty-year longitudinal study. *Learning Disabilities Research and Practice, 14*(1), 35–49.

Swanson, H. L. (2000). Issues facing the field of learning disabilities. *Learning Disability Quarterly, 23,* 37–49.

Tomasi, S. F., & Weinberg, S. L. (1999). Classifying children as LD: An analysis of current practice in an urban setting. *Learning Disability Quarterly, 22,* 31–42.

Vaughn, S., Gersten, R., & Chard, D. J. (2000). The underlying message in LD intervention research: Findings from research syntheses. *Exceptional Children, 67*(1), 99–114.

THE SOCIOPOLITICAL PROCESS OF CLASSIFICATION RESEARCH: MAKING THE IMPLICIT EXPLICIT IN LEARNING DISABILITIES

Robin Morris, Georgia State University

The consequences of deciding whether or not a child meets the criteria to be classified as learning disabled (LD) are broad. Such decisions impact a child's educational program, which, depending upon its success, can impact their socioemotional functioning, their motivation regarding learning, and their self-esteem, not to mention their ability to read, write, and do arithmetic at the levels they will need to be successful in the future. Such decisions therefore cannot be taken lightly, and understanding the foundations on which such decisions are made should be of significant interest to all those with an investment in the future of these children. Fletcher, Lyon, Barnes, Stuebing, Francis, Olson, Shaywitz and Shaywitz (this volume) have provided the most explicit and comprehensive analysis to date of the key components of this process: the underlying classification system and diagnostic criteria used. Unfortunately, their findings and conclusions will not be easily accepted by the LD establishment, as they represent fundamental changes in how we would decide whether a child should be provided with special education services for LD or not. Of more concern is that similar recommendations, although not as well articulated and supported by recent data, have been voiced for almost 30 years (Applebee, 1971) without any impact on a policy and system set into place in the 1960s. Clearly historical precedence and inertia have taken hold of an area even though we have made significant advances in our knowledge and understanding of these children and their needs.

We should be explicit in our acknowledgement that our current classification criteria for LD are not based in data or our scientific knowledge, but are more impacted by sociopolitical processes. Such processes are well known in the development and modification of classification systems and reflect the ongoing struggle between the dual purposes of most classification systems: communication and prediction. On one hand, everyone wants classification systems to help them communicate with others about the phenomena of interest, in this case, children with LD. The goal of the classification system in this framework is to improve the consistency and ease of communication between professionals who use it. The simpler it is to use and understand, the better it is. On the other hand, if one wants a classification system whose primary purpose is to predict the best treatment options and/or outcomes, then the use of all available data is required, and an increasingly complex system will result. The struggle between improving a classification system's communicative precision, versus its predictive accuracy, is one that will always exist. Only when a system is able to balance both attributes, or is explicit in its bias in one direction that meets the need of its users, will it be widely accepted. Clearly understanding the goals of its users, whether they are primarily communicative, predictive, or both, is critical in understanding the debates around any classification system.

Fletcher et al., clearly interested in predictive classification systems, provide such an extensive review of the issues and data involved that one might easily miss the forest for the trees. What are the important discussion points? First is that all classifications and identification criteria are hypotheses about how best to organize and separate children with different characteristics into educationally distinct programs that should be of maximal benefit to them. Decisions about what child characteristics will be used for such decisions, how they will be assessed, and what level of functioning is required to be placed into any group are all critical decisions that should be based on our best knowledge base. Any such hypothesis will always require ongoing, systematic evaluation of its validity. Based on such a framework, all such LD criteria and decisions should always be open to question. That Fletcher et al. question the validity of the current discrepancy criteria for LD should therefore not be taken as an attack on the validity of LD, but as questioning the validity of the IQ-achievement discrepancy criteria that is used to identify LD children. This point is not well made in their paper, and it would be easy for readers to interpret their findings as suggesting that they do not believe that LD is a valid entity. A careful review, though, of the literature they present and a review of the broader literature show strong support and validity for the diagnosis of LD children. There is significant data to show that they differ on a wide variety of characteristics compared to typical, non-LD children and compared to children who are classified into other special education groups.

Second, Fletcher et al., after presenting the history of the discrepancy criteria (unexpected underachievement) that is used as the basis for identifying LD children in almost all states, clearly present data that call into question its validity, particularly when comparing IQ-achievement discrepant to low achieving children who are also poor readers. It is probably this issue that is most central to their thesis, but there are many angles to it. Probably the one of most concern, and the one that has historically been of most controversy, is that of using standardized IQ tests as the index of a child's aptitude. We now know that most widely used IQ tests primarily are good at measuring the semantic aspects of language functioning but little else in the language domain, although phonological aspects of language are most predictive in understanding early reading development. The IQ test does not measure many of the critical cognitive or linguistic attributes known to be involved in early reading. At the same time, we know that vocabulary development is critically linked to a child's reading activities, particularly after about the 3rd grade, which will directly impact a child's IQ score. Therefore, a child who is not reading at the expected levels will be expected to show decreases in their verbal intelligence over time. We also know that IQ has limited predictive value regarding treatment outcomes, while at the same time the current LD classification system is founded on its predictive validity for impacting outcomes. Therefore, there are conceptual, psychometric, developmental, logical, and predictive problems with using IQ tests as a valid index of a child's potential related to their early reading or other related academic skills. Fletcher et al. imply that IQ tests shouldn't be used in discrepancy criteria for children with LD, and it is hard to argue with the data or their logic.

At the same time, there is acknowledgement that there also may be more basic problems conceptually with any two-dimensional discrepancy definition. Reading is not easily measured by any single measure; there are different types of reading behaviors (single word identification, reading comprehension, reading fluency, oral reading), and the cognitive and language abilities that best predict this range of reading abilities are also multidimensional. Therefore, one cannot expect simplistic two-dimensional discrepancy definitions to help us address the underlying complexities and multidimensional nature of reading or any other academic behavior. There is clearly a need for expanding the number of different types of children with LD, but this will increase the complexity of this endeavor. Unfortunately, there is also a tendency in some educational and political arenas to want to dummy down the complexities and complications of real children and related educational phenomena, and the use of two-dimensional discrepancy definitions is a good example of that trend.

Their discussion of the discrepancy criteria also raises the many limitations of the traditional exclusionary components of such definitions (cultural disadvantage, emotional disturbance, inadequate instruction), and the appropriate call for more positive, inclusion definitions. Although their discussion is not as explicit as it might be in these areas, it still must be clear that many children have been, and are, being excluded from educational programs that may be advantageous to them because they are minorities, come from poor schools with inadequate teaching, or have a history of behavioral or emotional problems. As an aside, the idea that many of these children are well served by Title I programs is open to debate, but more importantly, could raise the issue of whether children with LD might also be well served by the same programs. Related to the use of exclusionary definitions is the question of what is the "primary" disabling condition. This is another classification question that must be asked by those who classify these children, even though there is almost no data on which to justify such a differentiation. Overall, the current criteria for LD are clearly conceptually and logically limited, and anyone who has had to identify children for special education services has known this for years. Fletcher et al. have provided the field a service in clearly articulating the many limitations of these widely used criteria and definitions. The real problem that such analysis raises is what to replace the current model with?

Fletcher et al. do try to provide some ideas regarding how to transform the current classification system into one that is more consistent with our current knowledge base and concepts of LD. One of their most important points is that a child's LD is not an "unexpected underachievement" but is actually expected, in that we can explain it based on the cognitive processing deficits that the child has that we know are related to reading. The only reason in the past that this looked like it was unexpected was because we were not assessing those components that we now know are critically important (i.e., phonological awareness) in understanding these children's reading problems. A second point, and one that was not made as directly as it might have been, is that the etiology of these cognitive processing deficits is not a critical consideration, as there may be many different routes to the same underlying cognitive processing problems. We do not have to make unfounded inferences regarding the etiology or the primacy of the condition to include or exclude children from it. In fact, Fletcher et al. makes a strong case that it may be necessary to include a child's response to good instruction as a necessary component to any future definition of LD because of this, as their response would provide more information regarding the potential differential or interactive effect of biological and environmental influences on academic outcomes.

The outcome of Fletcher et al.'s review strongly suggests the need to make definitions of LD more specific (get rid of generic, one-size-fits-all definitions); to reflect the complexity of the academic areas of interest (maybe having a definition of decoding deficits or reading comprehension deficits, not just "reading"); and to include evidence-based definitions of domain-specific abilities. It may be even possible to identify such children just based on their pattern of academic strengths and weaknesses, once the critical, specific academic domains are clearly delineated, or the relationships between specific cognitive processing abilities and related academic domains are identified. The key argument here is that whatever new classification criteria are developed should be based on the characteristics the child has that makes them LD, the developmental pattern of the child with an LD, and based on this model, the best treatment for this specific type of child with an LD. In the best of all worlds, such criteria would allow the early identification of such children so that interventions could begin before they experience extended academic failure. Probably the best example of such a definition is the current definition of dyslexia developed by the International Dyslexia Society, although it does not provide an explicit developmental framework that would easily allow for early identification and intervention.

Policy, such as that represented in the current federal and state definitions and operationalization of LD, appears to have its foundation in the consensus of stakeholders and the need to ensure compliance. But as most know who work in schools, there is a basic conflict in trying to work within the current problematic criteria and trying to meet the educational needs of the diverse children being referred for special education services under the LD criteria. Because of this, the current model has created a distribution of users and educators: At one end are those who only care about the definitions and criteria for LD and compliance, in an almost mechanistic manner, while those at the other end of the distribution don't care at all about the LD definitions or criteria, but only care about the treatments required to address an individual child's educational needs. Science has had little influence on either end of this continuum, and to date has had almost no influence on the classification system used for LD.

Many aspects of our language system, particularly the nouns we use, represent a shared and agreed-upon classification system of the objects of interest in the world around us. Classification is a basic human neurocognitive activity. A young child develops this capacity as they gain experience from the world around them, and with the help of new information from those around them. They move from calling all things *birds*, to understanding that airplanes and mosquitoes are not birds, and that there are different kinds of birds (i.e., crows, eagles) as they begin to understand the necessary, sufficient, and inclusive attributes of *birds*. They also learn that there are always some unusual exceptions (i.e., penguins, ostriches) to all the rules. This natural developmental process is not unlike the current examination of the criteria for LD. As we learn more about the phenomena of interest, in this case the characteristics of children with LD and the limitations of our current classification and identification system, our sophistication regarding the criteria for LD needs to change to keep up with our knowledge base. This developmental process will lead us to better educational programs and outcomes for such students. It's only natural.

REFERENCES

Applebee, A. N. (1971). Research in reading retardation: Two critical problems. *Journal of Child Psychology and Psychiatry, 12*, 91–113.

CLASSIFICATION OF LEARNING DISABILITIES: CONVERGENCE, EXPANSION, AND CAUTION

Deborah L. Speece, University of Maryland

My response to the Fletcher et al. paper will emphasize points of agreement between their conclusions and other viewpoints on the classification of learning disabilities (LD), will present suggestions that expand their perspective, and will sound a note of caution. Before discussing these points, it is important to be clear on the nature of the evidence reviewed by Fletcher and his colleagues: Most of our knowledge on LD classification is located in the domain of reading defined by word-level skills of primary-aged children. That is, the knowledge base on classification of learning problems in academic domains other than reading (mathematics, spelling, writing) is sparse, we have little research on classifying older children in any domain, and our knowledge of reading disability classification does not include reading comprehension difficulties. On one hand, what we don't know is sobering and discouraging. On the other hand, the review by Fletcher and his colleagues shows there is progress and promise in efforts to define and classify LD.

CONVERGENCE

It is serendipitous that I received the Fletcher paper as I finished data analysis for a study on experts' opinions of the definition of reading disability (Speece & Shekitka, in press). Hedges and Washington (1993) noted that convergence of evidence between research and expert opinion provides validation for both sources. Thus, it is instructive to compare the conclusions of Fletcher et al. and the opinions of experts who were members of editorial boards for journals in learning disabilities and reading. We asked these professionals, among other things, to select components of a definition of reading disability for practice, to select the most important component, and to indicate whether exclusion criteria should be part of a definition.

Fletcher et al. concluded that (a) IQ-achievement discrepancy is not a valid criterion for LD classification, (b) exclusionary clauses are not positive indicators of LD, and (c) the classification of LD will likely include responsiveness to instruction. Only 30% of our experts believed IQ-achievement discrepancies should be part of a definition, thereby supporting the first assertion. However, 75% of the respondents believed exclusion criteria should be used, specifically mental retardation, inadequate instruction, and sensory deficits. Although this finding contradicts Fletcher et al., the exclusion criteria that Fletcher et al. found least supportable (emotional and behavioral disability, cultural differences, and economic disadvantage) were selected by fewer than 30% of the respondents, thereby lending some support to the view that exclusion criteria are not useful. With respect to the third conclusion on response to instruction, two-thirds of our experts agreed that treatment validity, defined in part as response to instruction, should be a component of a reading disability definition. This is a surprising finding given the recent appearance of treatment validity in discussions of identification (Fuchs, 1995; Fuchs & Fuchs, 1998). I will return to this point in the consideration of expanded approaches to identifying LD.

A particularly thorny issue for both Fletcher et al. and our experts is what to do with intelligence. Agreeing that the discrepancy criterion is not valid is not the same thing as declaring intelligence irrelevant. Less than half of our respondents agreed that intelligence should be a criterion and none selected intelligence as the most important component. Yet of those respondents who believed exclusion clauses should be used in a definition, the most frequently selected criterion was mental retardation, which is largely defined by subaverage intelligence. A similar ambivalence was evident in the Fletcher et al. paper. Evidence was cited that suggested IQ was irrelevant, but a conclusion on this issue was not drawn clearly. I point this out not because I believe the authors should have an answer to this question but rather to highlight the point that the role of IQ will continue to be problematic in efforts to identify LD. To summarize, there appears to be a convergence of data and thought that IQ-achievement discrepancy formula and exclusion criteria that specify emotional and behavioral disability, cultural differences, and economic disadvantage are not valid criteria for the identification of learning disabilities.

EXPANSION

Responsiveness to instruction. There also is agreement that responsiveness to instruction can play an important role in the identification of LD. Responsiveness to treatment represents a critically important expansion of criteria to define LD. Definitions and classification of LD focus exclusively on intrinsic (within-child) causes to the exclusion of the role of contextual factors including instruction (Keogh & Speece, 1996; Speece, 1993). That it took decades to begin to acknowledge the role of context in LD puts our field in the company of most social sciences. Duncan and Raudenbush (1999) commented that "social science research is far from definitive about whether 'context matters'" despite the fact that contexts such as families, neighborhoods, and schools "are essential to making the child fully human" (p. 29). Fletcher et al. provide a coherent explanation of the problems associated with a view of learning disabilities that neglects the effects of context generally and instruction specifically. What is missing in their discussion is reference to an existing model developed by Fuchs and Fuchs (Fuchs, 1995; Fuchs & Fuchs, 1998) that provides conceptual specificity to the link between LD and lack of responsiveness to instruction. Undoubtedly this model will be reviewed in Gresham's paper. However, it requires mention here because of its potential to address several points raised by Fletcher et al. including the point that responsiveness to instruction should be considered a classification criterion for LD.

Briefly, the treatment validation model requires continual monitoring of the academic progress of all children in a classroom, identifying children who fail to respond given a generally effective instructional program, and intervening within the general education classroom with the identified children. Children who fail to demonstrate progress after well designed and implemented general education intervention would be candidates for more intensive instruction in special education and may be considered learning disabled or at risk for LD. Fuchs and Fuchs (1998) provided a complete analysis of this process including preliminary data. What is of interest to the present discussion is how this model supports points raised by Fletcher et al. These points include reunion of research and practice, retirement of IQ, focus on behaviors relevant to instruction, acknowledgment that LD may be best indexed within academic domains, and focus on inclusion criteria rather than exclusion criteria. This seems to me to represent a substantial convergence of ideas in an area that has created more anxiety than agreement. The treatment validity model is limited by some of the same weaknesses mentioned at the beginning of this essay, specifically that the underlying measurement model only is appropriate for children in elementary school. Other methods of conceptualizing response to treatment (e.g., benchmarks, dynamic assessment) are plausible and should be studied. The primary point, however, is that we can use the points of agreement to guide a reconceptualization of LD that recognizes that classification is a dynamic process (Gould, 1989) and that LD is a developmental phenomenon.

Values, beliefs, and validity. In their discussion of validity, Fletcher et al. located their arguments in the realm of construct validity. This is appropriate because construct validity is the cornerstone of any discussion on validity. However, analysis of classification validity needs to be expanded to include other facets of validity as defined by Messick (1980, 1989, 1995). Messick proposed that assessment of validity (which may be content, criterion-related, or construct) depends not only on this traditional psychometric evidence but also on the consequences of test use or, in the present context, the consequences of applying a particular method of LD classification. In Messick's (1995) terms, this would mean analysis of the values implications of LD classification and the social consequences of LD classification.

For example, the validity of IQ-achievement discrepancy formulas as a classification criterion should be assessed not only with hypotheses related to low achievement (construct validity) but also in terms of the consequences of applying the criterion. Specifically, we know that it is difficult for young children to qualify for special education under the discrepancy criterion. This outcome violates what many would hold as an important value: the ability of a classification system to identify children for services before they experience repeated failure. In terms of social consequences, the discrepancy formula as applied in schools results in over-representation of males and minority children. However, studies that used researcher-defined samples did not find these biases (Shaywitz et al., 1990; Speece & Case, 2001) suggesting that over-representation of males and minorities is an unintended and negative consequence of school identification. These examples illustrate that the discrepancy criterion may not pass muster on several facets of validation and provide important evidence with which to evaluate the validity of the classification criteria. The examples also emphasize the requirement that both intended and unintended consequences be evaluated (Messick, 1989, 1995).

I suggest the adoption of an expanded view of validity, because Messick's views emphasize that both data and logic are required, because consequences of a classification need careful consideration, and because the LD enterprise brings with it a host of values and beliefs that are often unstated and unexamined. Analysis of validity via Messick's framework requires that values and beliefs be examined as carefully as data. Hypothesis testing is critical but a view of validity that encompasses and extends traditional approaches will result in a classification system that is more comprehensive and acceptable to the many interested audiences. Admittedly, there has been little work on construct validity, but if we are to begin anew with consensus committees, let's be sure to incorporate a comprehensive and contemporary view of what is required to establish validity.

CAUTION

Finally, Fletcher et al. recommended that the IQ-discrepancy criterion be dropped from federal policy but do not offer a replacement strategy. On the face of it, dropping discrepancy may seem a reasonable suggestion given the conclusion that discrepancy is not a valid identification criterion. It is important to consider the implications of this suggestion in the absence of an alternative. One plausible outcome of a moratorium on discrepancy is that professionals will conclude that since criteria are not offered to guide selection of students, LD really is low achievement; thus, LD does not exist. Fletcher et al. are clear that they believe LD to be a real phenomenon but their recommendation may work against this belief. They also are clear that children identified by discrepancy experience learning difficulty. The invalidity of discrepancy from their perspective lies in coverage: Not all children who experience problems are identified. Thus, under the (faulty) assumption that schools use regression-based discrepancy as a primary means of identifying children as LD, children so identified *are* disabled and should receive special education services. To increase coverage perhaps the recommendation should be to drop the exclusion criteria rather than the discrepancy requirement, to provide a placeholder for the construct of LD until a valid classification is determined.

If a moratorium on discrepancy is declared, then a reasonable alternative must be offered. In light of evidence that many children identified by schools as LD do not exhibit a discrepancy, Shepard (1983) recommended that schools limit the number of children identified by capping the percentage eligible. Schools are capable of identifying which children are neediest; finer discriminations at this point may be unwarranted. Although this is not a satisfactory solution to the classification dilemma, it may offer a short-term solution as classification research proceeds. However it may lead professionals to the same conclusion as eliminating the discrepancy requirement: LD is not legitimate.

In conclusion, there is convergence of data and opinion on salient aspects of LD classification. Although this convergence is broad rather than detailed, it does offer a starting point for serious analysis and discussion. Perhaps most remarkable is the agreement that identification of LD be expanded to include consideration of context. I suggested that Messick's unified view of validity be used as a guide for future research and discussion, especially given the current limited empirical base for LD classification. Also, schools need some guidance if the requirement of meeting a discrepancy criterion is dropped. We need to be clear that while instructional improvement and intensive remediation efforts are reasonable recommendations, they do not replace the need to define clearly the phenomenon of LD or the requirements of early identification. Although we would hope that general education instructional efforts would be enough to meet the needs of all children, this hope does not conform to the reality that some children will not respond (Torgesen, 2000). As noted by Fletcher et al., LD is a real phenomenon. As scientists and practitioners it is our job to find methods of identification and remediation.

REFERENCES

Duncan, G. J., & Raudenbush, S. W. (1999). Assessing the effects of context in studies of child and youth development. *Educational Psychologist, 34,* 29–41.

Fuchs, L. S. (1995, May). *Incorporating curriculum-based measurement into the eligibility decision-making process: A focus on treatment validity and student growth.* Paper prepared for the National Academy of Sciences Workshop on Alternatives to IQ Testing, Washington, DC.

Fuchs, L. S., & Fuchs, D. (1998). Treatment validity: A unifying concept for reconceptualizing the identification of learning disabilities. *Learning Disabilities Research & Practice, 13,* 204–219.

Gould, S. J. (1989). *Wonderful life: The Burgess shale and the nature of history.* New York: Norton.

Hedges, L. V., & Washington, T. (1993). From evidence to knowledge to policy: Research synthesis for policy formation. *Review of Educational Research, 63,* 345–352.

Keogh, B. K., & Speece, D. L. (1996). Learning disabilities within the context of schooling. In D. L. Speece & B. K. Keogh (Eds.), *Research on classroom ecologies: Implications for inclusion of children with learning disabilities* (pp. 1–14). Mahwah, NJ: Lawrence Erlbaum Assoc.

Messick, S. (1980). Test validity and the ethics of assessment. *American Psychologist, 35,* 1012–1027.

Messick, S. (1989). Validity. In R. L. Linn (Ed.), *Educational measurement* (3rd ed.; pp. 13–103). New York: MacMillan.

Messick, S. (1995). Validity of psychological assessment: Validation of inferences from persons' responses and performances as scientific inquiry into score meaning. *American Psychologist, 50,* 741–749.

Shaywitz, S. E., Shaywitz, B., Fletcher, J. M., & Escobar, M. D. (1990). Prevalence of reading disability in girls and boys: Results from the Connecticut Longitudinal Study. *Journal of the American Medical Association, 264,* 998–1002.

Shepard, L. (1983, Fall). The role of measurement in educational policy: Lessons from the identification of learning disabilities. *Educational Measurement: Issues and Practices,* 4–8.

Speece, D. L. (1993). Broadening the scope of classification research: Conceptual and ecological perspectives. In G. R. Lyon, D. B. Gray, J. F. Kavanaugh, & N. A. Krasnegor (Eds.), *Better understanding learning disabilities: New views from research and their implications for education and public policy* (pp. 57–72). Baltimore: Brooks.

Speece, D. L., & Case, L. P. (2001). Classification in context: An alternative approach to identifying early reading disability. *Journal of Educational Psychology, 93,* 735–749.

Speece, D. L., & Shekitka, L. (2001). How should reading disabilities be operationalized? A survey of experts. *Learning Disabilities Research & Practice.*

Torgesen, J. K. (2000). Individual differences in response to early intervention in reading: The lingering problem of treatment resisters. *Learning Disabilities Research & Practice, 15,* 55–64.

CHAPTER IV: LEARNING DISABILITIES AS
OPERATIONALLY DEFINED BY SCHOOLS

Donald L. MacMillan, University of California, Riverside, &
Gary N. Siperstein, University of Massachusetts, Boston

The Individuals With Disabilities Education Act (IDEA; Public Law 105-17) stipulates regulations that guide the public schools in identifying students eligible for special education and related services. Moreover, it provides compliance reviews that ensure that the public schools in a given state act in accordance with the regulations. It is our position in this paper that the schools follow the letter of the law, albeit somewhat reluctantly at times, in establishing eligibility of children for special education by virtue of meeting criteria for learning disabilities (LDs). Furthermore, we contend that the public schools attempt to implement this process in compliance with IDEA stipulations and, in so doing, yield a population of LD students that

- Includes a substantial proportion who fail to meet criteria specified in the state education code and authoritative definitions (false positive LD cases).

- Fails to include a segment of students, of unknown magnitude, who do in fact meet criteria specified in the state education code and authoritative definitions (false negative LD cases).

- Varies considerably in the severity of the achievement deficits and other characteristics salient to the educational process from state to state, district to district, and school building to school building.

- Reflects the perceptions of school building personnel in terms of the students at that site most in need of, and likely to benefit from, the services available at that site.

The population of LD students has also changed over the years as our public schools have responded to societal and policy changes and the ways in which these have affected both general and special education.

Between 1976–77 and 1992–93, the number of children served as LD nationwide increased by 198% (U.S. Department of Education, 1995). Commenting on the magnitude of the increase in LD, MacMillan, Gresham, Siperstein, and Bocian (1996) wrote: "Were these epidemic-like figures interpreted by the Center for Disease Control one might reasonably expect to find a quarantine imposed on the public schools of America" (p. 169). There have been many debates over the reasons for this dramatic rise in the prevalence of LD. There are those who contend that LD has "matured" and detection methods improved, resulting in the identification of cases that would have been overlooked in the early years of the LD field (Hallahan, 1992). In addition, Hallahan noted increased threats to developing children (e.g., prenatal substance abuse, environmental toxins) that, when extreme, result in mental retardation, but when only moderate may be expressed as a more modest disability— LD. In contrast, there are those who believe that despite all of the debates over the true definition of LD, the disability category reflects the changing culture and process of our schools. In fact, as Reid Lyon was recently quoted in the *Los Angeles Times* (Colvin & Helfand, 2000), "Learning disabilities has become a sociological sponge to wipe up the spills of general education…It's where children who weren't taught well go in many respects" (p. 1). This operational definition hearkens back to the prophetic words of Evelyn Deno (1970) who noted that special education accepts regular education's "fallout." We believe that regardless of one's perspective on this issue, it is time to ask whether LD, as originally conceived (e.g., Bateman, 1965), is no longer recognizable in our schools. This paper will explore what we believe are the reasons for the significant increase in the prevalence of LD and by so doing, cast doubt on the continued utility of the present approach to defining LD.

To begin, let us turn our attention to the definition guiding school identification and then the evidence bearing on the extent to which school-identified LD meets the definitional criteria.

AUTHORITATIVE DEFINITIONS OF LEARNING DISABILITIES

Before reviewing the stages in the identification process that emerge when the regulations in IDEA are implemented, let us turn our attention to the authoritative definition ostensibly guiding school identification of LD. Then we will examine the evidence bearing on the extent to which *subjectivity* in schools' decision-making process departs from the definition. The authoritative definition produced by the National Advisory Committee on Handicapped Children (1968) was adopted in the federal regulations authored by the U.S. Office of Education (1977) defining LD (Mercer, Jordan, Allsopp, & Mercer, 1996). The definition reads:

"Specific learning disability" means a disorder in one or more of the basic psychological processes involved in understanding or in using language, spoken or written, which may manifest itself in an imperfect ability to listen, think, speak, read, write, spell, or to do mathematical calculations. The term includes such conditions as perceptual handicaps, brain injury, minimal brain dysfunction, dyslexia, and developmental aphasia. The term does not include children who have learning problems which are primarily the result of visual, hearing, or motor handicaps, of mental retardation, or emotional disturbance, or of environmental, cultural, or economic disadvantage. (USOE, 1977, p. 65083)

Of importance to the present paper is what is included in the definition and what is excluded. For example, included in the definition are the following three elements: (a) the conditions of brain injury and minimal brain dysfunction, (b) evidence of in-child, presumably causal, neurological condition(s), and (c) exclusionary criteria specifying that these learning problems are not the result of mental retardation or of environmental, cultural, or economic disadvantage (Keogh, 1994). We point out the exclusionary criteria, particularly, for it is here that we will see the differences between research-identified (RI) and school-identified (SI) perspectives.

THE PROCESS PRESCRIBED IN IDEA GUIDING SCHOOL IDENTIFICATION

To best understand the actual prevalence of LD, we must first make salient the two different perspectives on "who is LD." Specifically, we distinguish between SI and RI samples of students with LD (MacMillan, Gresham, & Bocian, 1998). The reason for this distinction is that the two approaches typically identify overlapping, but substantially different, groups of students. Stated differently, the compendium of research findings comparing the two approaches suggests that over half of the SI LD children fail to meet the criteria employed in RI LD sampling and specified in federal regulations or state education codes (MacMillan, Gresham, & Bocian, 1998; MacMillan & Speece, 1999; Shepard, 1983; Shepard, Smith, & Vojir, 1983). This is a paradoxical finding in light of the fact that the public schools are presumably required to establish a child as eligible for special education and related services by virtue of that child meeting the specified criteria for eligibility.

Since LD was recognized as an educational disability category, an ongoing discussion of the definition and the criteria adopted in implementing the definition has failed to result in consensus (see Doris, 1993; Kavale & Forness, 1985; Keogh, 1986), as also attested to in the other chapters in this volume. Maybe as a result of this failure to achieve consensus, the field has engaged in extensive and ongoing debate regarding the definition and criteria for establishing eligibility. However, that exchange has occurred almost exclusively in the context of RI cases of LD; that is, discussing "what ought to be" rather than "what is." The urgency in public school settings to provide assistance and support to children encountering academic difficulties has necessitated labeling some children as LD despite the fact that the debate over definition and criteria continues. Let us be clear that we are not suggesting that the debate over definition and criteria be terminated.

Because academics author most of the papers addressing these issues, a clear preference for RI over SI emerges. Academics tend to interpret the failure of the SI population of LD to perfectly match the RI population as an error by the schools. Gerber (1999–2000) described this state of affairs as follows: "Demonstration that schools identify problem learners with markedly different characteristics than those proposed by formal models…too often has led to premature conclusion that the models must be right and the schools wrong" (p. 40). Our message here is that we cannot, and should not, disregard the SI LD population, because it is that SI LD population over which public policy issues have been raised. It is the SI LD population, with all its imprecision, that is counted in the *Annual Reports to Congress*. It is the SI LD population that is examined in efforts by the Office of Civil Rights (OCR) to monitor the representation of the various racial/ethnic groups in the LD category in its surveys. It is the SI LD population that raises concerns over the dramatic increase in identification rates which is being described as an epidemic. Therefore, the only way to understand the SI LD population is to understand how public schools function and to acknowledge the various reasons schools have for identifying individuals with LD.

Of the five reasons that educators have for identifying LD listed by Keogh (1994) (eligibility, planning for services, assessing outcomes, research, and advocacy), "planning for services" drives schools' diagnostic identification process, with only secondary concerns for "eligibility." In contrast, "eligibility" and "research" drive researchers as they seek to protect against threats to the internal validity of their research. Furthermore, we suspect that the schools approach eligibility with a different set of concerns than those faced by researchers (Bocian, Beebe, MacMillan, & Gresham, 1999).

In the present paper we take an educational perspective in exploring who the schools serve as LD and attempt to describe the decision-making process that has resulted in the dramatic increases in LD students. The sorting of students ultimately resulting in some students being found eligible for special education services by virtue of qualifying as LD proceeds through several steps required under provisions of IDEA. The "protections" provided prohibit eligibility decisions being reached on the basis of single tests, particularly tests considered inappropriate for use with particular groups of children. In addition, parental consent is required prior to assessments, and parental roles in the process were strengthened under the reauthorization of IDEA. At the risk of oversimplifying the sorting process, let us suggest that several stages are apparent: referral by general education teacher, prereferral intervention efforts implemented in the general education setting, formal assessment of the student, and finally, eligibility and development of an individualized education plan (IEP) by a team.[1] As we describe these stages, the reader is asked to recognize a recurrent theme: at each stage, clinical judgment introduces a degree of subjectivity which affects the ultimate eligibility decision. Furthermore, the subjectivity present at each successive stage is additive.

STAGE 1: THE IMPORTANCE OF TEACHER REFERRAL

Ysseldyke and Algozzine (1983) noted years ago that the most important decision in the assignment of children to LD programs is the decision by the regular classroom teacher to refer. Zigmond (1993) echoed this sentiment when she wrote: "The referral is a signal that the teacher has reached the limits of his or her tolerance of individual differences, is no longer optimistic about his or her capacity to deal effectively with a particular student in the context of the larger group, and no longer perceives that the student is teachable by him- or herself" (pp. 262–263). Any understanding of the population of SI LD students begins with a consideration of those students that general education teachers consider "difficult to teach." Given the process prescribed in IDEA, different perspectives are dominant at different stages of the referral-assessment-placement process that contribute to false positive and false negative identifications. Decisions to refer made by a general education teacher are influenced by factors beyond child characteristics. That is, two hypothetical children with identical reading deficits enrolled in different districts are not equally at risk for being referred by their classroom teacher. The extent to which respective teachers are optimistic about their ability to successfully teach the child (i.e., the teacher's self-efficacy) enters into the decision. Zigmond (1993) reported on one of her projects that explored the extreme differences in rates of special education services. Fiscal and demographic variables failed to explain why some districts served large proportions of their students (11–15%) while others served small percentages (2–4%); neither did the availability or use of prereferral options at the school building level explain the disproportion. Teachers in schools serving small proportions of their students in special education did, however, express greater optimism about the likelihood of success of non-special-education strategies and interventions than did teachers in the schools serving high proportions of students in special education.

A teacher's decision to refer is also influenced by a comparison of a given child's academic performance to that of classmates or some absolute standard held by the teacher regarding "how well a second-grade student should be reading." The modal level of achievement in a given classroom is the baseline against which teachers judge the adequacy of specific children's performance. The two hypothetical students with the same level of reading performance are differentially at risk for referral if enrolled in two different classes where the modal level of achievement in one is 2 years below grade level and the other is 2 years above grade level. Presently, judgment by the general education classroom teacher that a child's performance is inadequate and unresponsive to materials and methods available in that teacher's classroom prompts referral, a necessary but insufficient step in becoming SI as LD. A parent less frequently initiates referral; however, even in such cases it is prompted by a perception that the child's progress in general education is inadequate and treatments provided are ineffective. These judgments are, by their very nature, subjective because they are made in the context of a specific teacher's classroom or a parent's experience with other children, neighborhood peers, and family relatives and friends.

General education teachers do not refer all students who have, if tested, a psychometric profile that meets state education code criteria. As noted above, referral is necessary for SI as LD. Cases meeting criteria that are not referred will not be available for sampling as SI LD, but would be included in a RI population of LD. However, the only way one could "catch" unreferred students meeting RI LD criteria would be by doing massive screenings of all schoolchildren with nationally standardized scales and then rigidly applying criteria. In subsequent discussion we will refer to this group of students (psychometrically eligible but not SI as LD) as "false negative" cases of LD. Students who are SI as LD but do not meet eligibility criteria will be referred to as "false positive" cases of LD.

The false negatives first emerge at the referral stage. If students are not referred, they will not be SI as LD. We can't begin to estimate the magnitude of this group, although we will subsequently describe situations in which students are referred by their teacher and found to be psychometrically eligible as LD, yet they elude being identified by the schools as LD.

The general education teacher serves as an "imperfect test" (Gerber & Semmel, 1984; Gresham, MacMillan, & Bocian, 1997), thereby determining which children get referred and which do not. The imperfections include the optimism discussed above, but could also result from other factors independent of the specific academic deficiencies noted as a concern. One line of research has examined whether general education teachers are racially and/or gender biased in their referrals, with somewhat mixed findings. Zucker and his colleagues (Prieto & Zucker, 1981; Zucker & Prieto, 1977; Zucker, Prieto, & Rutherford, 1979) used vignettes and manipulated the ethnicity and gender of the child when presenting the vignettes to teachers. Their findings suggested that teachers were more inclined to judge a child as appropriate for special education placement if he or she were described as Black or Hispanic; however, no effects for gender were found. Shinn, Tindal, and Spira (1987), however, found that both racial and gender biases were plausible for the referral behavior of elementary school students with severe reading deficits.

Two other investigations (Bahr, Fuchs, Stecker, & Fuchs, 1991; Tobias, Zibrin, & Menell, 1983) extended the design to consider the race of both the referring teacher and the child being considered for referral. In the Tobias et al. study, neither the race of the teacher nor that of the student exerted a significant effect on the referral recommendation. However, Bahr et al. found a significant effect for the race of the student (i.e., with Black students being judged as more appropriate for placement) but not for the effect of the race of the teacher or the interaction.

Similarly, MacMillan, Gresham, Lopez, and Bocian (1996) examined a sample, stratified on the basis of ethnic group, of primary-grade students who had actually been referred by their teachers for prereferral interventions. They concluded that these teachers defined "difficult to teach" (i.e., the reasons for their referral) in terms of absolute low achievement and problem behaviors, primarily externalizing behaviors. In essence, those students whose academic performance deviates significantly from that of classmates and those whose behavior is disruptive and threatening to the smooth running of the classroom are at heightened risk for referral. Several findings from that study bear directly on the issue of potential bias. Comparisons on the basis of ethnic group (White, Black, Hispanic) and gender resulted in the following significant differences: (a) referred White students had significantly higher verbal IQ scores and reading achievement scores than did referred students from the other two ethnic groups, (b) referred Black students were more likely to have a higher incidence of behavior problems than were Hispanic students, and (c) gender differences were evident in the problem behaviors exhibited (males having more) but did not emerge on cognitive or achievement measures. Contrary to some of the previously summarized studies, these data suggest that teachers were more reluctant to refer Black students. That is, Black students who were referred exhibited achievement deficits more severe than those prompting the referral of White students and behavior problems more serious than those prompting referral of Hispanic students.

We call attention to the fact that when teachers make decisions about a child's academic progress, it is *teacher judgment* that is employed, using *local norms* as the child's performance is compared to that of classmates and grade peers (Bocian et al., 1999). When teachers refer a child they do not know if that child is LD or mildly mentally retarded (MMR). Instead, they know that the child's progress is unacceptable in comparison to local norms. We know of precious little evidence that addresses the magnitude of the population of children who would psychometrically qualify as LD but who are never referred by their general education teacher. These would be the "false negative" cases (if one assumes the RI LD are the "real LD"). Ironically, the limited evidence forthcoming from MacMillan, Gresham, and Bocian (1998) reveal that among *referred* students, the traditional LD student with above-average intelligence and discrepant achievement was among those *not placed in special education.*

Referral by general education teachers then initiates a process that can ultimately lead to a child being SI as LD. We have noted that the teacher employs local norms in deciding that a child's academic performance is deficient. The achievement of the child's classmates or the teacher's subjective standards for acceptable achievement provide the basis for comparison. While the evidence is somewhat conflicting, it would appear that teachers *might* employ slightly different standards when evaluating the achievement of children of different racial or ethnic groups. Moreover, the referral decision is grounded in the child's absolute level of achievement rather than comparing it to an expected level of achievement based on the individual child's aptitude or achievement in other subjects. As a result, subjectivity is introduced into the process in this initial stage that precludes any possibility of yielding the population of LD children defined in education codes and authoritative definitions. The false negative cases, where teachers fail to refer, are of unknown magnitude but will not be SI as LD. Already some students who meet RI LD criteria have been eliminated from possible identification. The cases moving to the next stage (assessment) also include students who do not meet criteria for LD, but whose exclusion will depend on being detected and eliminated from possible classification during one of the two following stages in the process. As we will see, however, subjectivity is present at these stages as well, making the ultimate decision contaminated by additive subjectivity.

Stage 2: Assessment

For those students who are resistant to interventions provided in general education, something has to be done, be it retention in grade or consideration for special education services. In order to qualify for special education services, the child must qualify for one of the disability categories, determination of which requires psychological evaluation. MacMillan and Speece (1999) characterized this gate, the psychological assessment, as representing a cognitive paradigm intended to detect or document the existence of a within-child problem. In the case of LD, a common definitional criterion for eligibility is a severe discrepancy between aptitude and achievement; 98% of the states include a discrepancy of some magnitude in either the definition or criteria for LD (Mercer, Jordan, Allsopp, & Mercer, 1996). Bocian et al. (1999) expanded on this characterization of the assessment gate by suggesting that the psychometric data on aptitude and achievement permit determining whether the child's level of achievement is *acceptable*. If achievement is far below predicted levels (based on aptitude), then the placement team would probably conclude that it is unacceptable—the student should be doing much better. On the other hand, if the measures of intelligence and achievement are consistent (i.e., both very low), then one would reluctantly conclude that achievement is "acceptable" (if not desirable) and presumably consider "exclusionary" criteria that might prevent eligibility as LD.

In comparison to the referral stage, the assessment stage employs national norms. The use of "objective" evidence is a cornerstone of psychological assessment, and information from standardized tests is used—administration protocols scripted, the scoring carefully prescribed, and comparisons of a child's performance made to norms established on nationally representative samples. While teacher judgment was employed in decisions concerning referral, the assessment stage is devoid of such factors.

When one considers the process prescribed under IDEA, these two "competing paradigms"—teacher referral employing local norms and the assessment employing national norms—the tension between "those whom teachers perceive as needing help" and "those whom psychometric profiles indicate are entitled to receive help"—result in overlapping populations. Were the psychometric template applied to all public school students, a segment of children who, for whatever reason, are not referred by their teachers (referred to previously as "false negatives") would emerge. Moreover, of those referred by their teachers, some number are found ineligible when the psychometric template is applied. The psychometric data suggest that either the level of achievement is not sufficiently discrepant from aptitude to warrant eligibility as LD or the IQ score may be below the criterion for mental retardation. In other words, the assessment stage serves to screen the referrals made by the teacher and has historically been used to make a differential diagnosis, differentiating between cases of LD, mental retardation, emotional disturbance, and speech and language.

In previous writings (MacMillan, Gresham, Siperstein, & Bocian, 1996; MacMillan et al., 1997, 1998) we have described the difference between what is supposed to be and what really is in the use of assessment in qualifying children for special education services. The compendium of results from studies examining the degree of congruence between criteria specified in authoritative definitions or state education codes and the characteristics of students actually served under a given disability rubric is not very high. For example, when we examined the group of children that the public schools ultimately qualified as LD, less than half (29 of a total 61) evidenced the required discrepancy using the Wechsler Intelligence Scale for Children III (WISC-III) and Wide Range Achievement Test–Revised (WRAT-R) scores. MacMillan et al. (1998) wrote, "...public school practices for diagnosing children with LD bear little resemblance to what is prescribed in federal and state regulations...defining LD..."(p. 323). The models suggested in the federal and state regulations, particularly concerning criteria, are "measurement bound," specifying cutoff scores, requisite discrepancies, and various other psychometric profiles on tests and rating scales that are to be applied "objectively" in establishing eligibility. Below we argue that despite the appearance of "objectivity" at the assessment stage, considerable subjectivity is introduced which serves to further distance SI cases of LD from RI cases of LD.

What do the public schools do? On the basis of our findings and rather extensive discussions with school personnel in several states, we conclude that the *concept* of LD used in the schools is not defined by psychometric profiles prescribed in legislation or employed by researchers. First, school personnel knowingly classify children with very low cognitive skills (mentally retarded?) as LD, despite exclusionary criteria and a lack of required discrepancies. Moreover, they express particular disrespect for tests of intelligence, which they perceive to be unfair and totally lacking in instructional validity. In addition, placement committee members and special education directors believe that the label "mentally retarded" is extremely pessimistic in its prognosis and are reluctant to use it. As one administrator put it, there is no upside to classifying a child as mentally retarded—the child is stigmatized, the parents resent the label, and we can develop an appropriate program for the child through the IEP process regardless of what we call the child.

These conclusions are consistent with those of Gottlieb, Alter, Gottlieb, and Wishner (1994) who also noted the fact that the discrepancy component is ignored by school professionals. They concluded that one reason is that urban practitioners knowingly ignore the absence of the required IQ-achievement discrepancy in "an effort to marshal scant resources for low-achieving students" (p. 459). The same sentiment is reflected in Shepard's (1983) comments: "Specialists would be more willing to make tough decisions about whether a child was really LD if rejecting the label was not tantamount to denying help" (p. 8).

A second observation about the assessment process and how school personnel use the results is in order. Placement committee members are painfully aware that certain assessments are mandated by state regulations. Moreover, school personnel dutifully, if unenthusiastically, comply with these regulations, although seeing them as "necessary evils" because that is the mandated process required *in order to get services to children.* As MacMillan, Gresham, Siperstein, & Bocian (1996) expressed it, school personnel are more concerned with "what to do" than with "what kind of kid this is." In this same spirit, one also encounters "creative testing" employed in order to record a combination of numbers that justifies the classification as LD. For instance, if the aptitude estimate using the WISC-III is "too low," then a nonverbal test of intelligence or an older version of the WISC (e.g., WISC-R) with outdated norms might be employed in order to secure a higher aptitude score and thereby the requisite discrepancy. Once convinced that this child needs and will benefit from services available in special education placement, school personnel seek ways to justify the action. School personnel repeatedly note the lack of instructional validity of intelligence tests for teachers' instructional planning and object to the cost of performing these assessments merely for qualifying the eligibility of children. We reiterate a point made in the early portion of this chapter: The schools' reason for classifying students LD is primarily for planning for services. In order to plan for services, the process prescribed under IDEA first requires that a child be qualified as eligible and in most states that requires the right combination of numbers (Mercer et al., 1996).

The subjectivity noted at the referral stage is exacerbated by additional subjectivity being introduced during the assessment stage. While objectivity is the hallmark of psychometric assessment, the selection of specific tests to be used (and the combination thereof) in order to justify the decision to serve this child results in most cases in false positive identifications. That is, a child who would not display the requisite discrepancy if one combination of tests is used is assessed with another combination of tests. Increasingly, the discrepancy between SI LD and RI LD is increased even further. As will be discussed in the next section, there is also the potential for increasing the number of false negatives, but it occurs in the deliberations of the committee assigned responsibility for placement. That committee may attend to the perceived need of a child and choose to disregard an IQ-achievement discrepancy when the absolute level of achievement is considerably higher for a nondiscrepant profile with very low reading achievement, for example. Let us now turn our attention to the third stage in the referral-assessment-placement process: the committee decision making that serves as the final arbitrator in the SI process prescribed in IDEA.

STAGE 3: PLACEMENT COMMITTEE DELIBERATIONS

The recommendation of the placement committee (we use this term here recognizing that various other terms are used to describe it) ultimately determines if a given child will be classified as LD after considering *all of the evidence brought to its attention*. IDEA specifically prescribes that a multidisciplinary team decision must be made, and specifies the role of the parent in this decision. These specifications make it clear that the psychometric profile alone cannot be used to determine eligibility—to do so would be out of compliance. This interdisciplinary team is responsible for determining eligibility and, when appropriate, crafting the IEP and determining least restrictive environment (LRE) for a given case. Like the teacher at the referral stage, the team is permitted to exercise professional judgement, but it is "collective judgement" rather than individual judgment, as was the case at the referral stage.

Bocian et al. (1999) reasoned that the team decision regarding eligibility and "placement" is guided by the concept of *profitability*, which reflects the collective judgment on whether *the specific special education services provided by the special education staff at that school site* will or will not be beneficial to the child. At this stage, the information and perceptions that prompted the general education teacher to refer the child, the results of the formal psychological assessment comparing that child to norms based on national samples, and sociocultural and contextual factors that inform the decision are all considered by the placement team. The team must weigh evidence coming from the competing paradigms described above (e.g., local vs. national norms). Bocian et al. noted that a number of contextual factors are considered prior to making its decision:

> Ideally, this team decision will weigh evidence provided by the general education teacher, the school psychologist, the parents, and all members regarding the perceived efficacy of the services that accompany alternative decisions. In addition, very practical considerations enter into the decision: openings in a special day class, caseload of resource teachers, second language issues, and the stridency of the parents when they oppose a course of action. (p. 3)

It was also noted that the relative forcefulness and competence of participants in specific team meetings play a role in the course of action ultimately taken. For example, a forceful general education teacher pressing for placement and a school psychologist with borderline discrepancy evidence may arrive at a different decision than a team with an ambivalent teacher and an articulate and forceful school psychologist.

When one examines the decisions made by a multidisciplinary team in light of the evidence available from the teacher's perspective and the school psychologist's perspective, the process prescribed by IDEA apparently does yield rational decisions. Bocian et al. (1999) examined the team recommendations to certify students as LD. In certain cases the teacher rated the child as having very severe achievement deficits, while in other cases the teacher ratings indicated only modest deficits— these cases reflected "local norms" as we've used the term. National norms were reflected in these cases by the presence or absence of the required IQ-achievement discrepancy. When there was congruence between these conflicting paradigms (i.e., either [a] the teacher rated the achievement deficit as very severe and the discrepancy was present, *or* [b] the teacher rated the achievement deficit as only modest and the discrepancy was not present), the decisions reached were consistent: 78% of [a] were classified as LD; 100% of the cases in situation [b] were not classified as LD. However, when the teacher rating of the severity of the achievement deficit and the presence or absence of a discrepancy were misaligned (i.e., achievement rated relatively high-discrepancy *or* achievement rated low-nondiscrepant), the rate at which the LD label was appended was much lower—45% and 39%, respectively.

Payette and Clarizio (1994) also examined team decisions on LD eligibility and found that three fourths of the children classified as LD did meet the severe discrepancy. In this investigation, the authors went on to examine factors related to "two kinds of misclassification observed: ineligibility with a severe discrepancy, and eligibility without a severe discrepancy" (p. 43). We have referred to these two situations elsewhere in the paper as "false negatives" and "false positives." In false negative cases, which constituted 16.57% of the referred sample, these investigators found that this group had significantly higher IQ scores than did students with a severe discrepancy found eligible by the placement team. In addition, they were significantly more likely to be White and older and have higher achievement scores. In the false positive cases, which constituted 9.59% of the sample, when compared to those found not eligible, findings indicated that they had lower Full-Scale IQ (FSIQ), were more likely to be girls, and were significantly lower in achievement. It is worth noting that the rate of false positive cases reported by Payette and Clarizio is considerably smaller than noted earlier for other investigations. However, the mean FSIQ for their ineligible cases was 102.30 and for the eligible children it was 95.03. In MacMillan, Gresham, Lopez, & Bocian (1996) study on students referred to prereferral intervention, the mean Verbal IQ scores were as follows: 87.42 (White), 79.93 (Black), and 78.17 (Hispanic). Such variability in characteristics across school districts attests to the "relativity" of LD and, in the MacMillan et al. study, the difficulty in demonstrating a discrepancy is evident.

DEVELOPMENTS FURTHER EXPANDING THE CONCEPT OF LD IN THE PUBLIC SCHOOLS

In this paper we have described the process followed by school personnel primarily to explain that there is subjectivity at each of the three stages considered and that this subjectivity is additive. We believe this subjectivity explains, in part, the lack of congruence between those whom the schools identify as LD and the criteria specified in education codes and authoritative definitions. Since LD emerged as a formally recognized disability category, there have been changes in the definition of mental retardation which, in turn, affected the definition of LD and extended boundaries of SI LD (MacMillan, 1993). Increasingly schools have opted to ignore the "exclusionary criteria" (mental retardation and cultural impoverishment) in order to serve students in need. This has been particularly true since changes in the definition of mental retardation have put more and more children into a gray area: those who do not meet the criteria either for mental retardation or for LD. Moreover, provisions of P.L. 94-142 diminished the importance of differential diagnosis and, in fact, provided the schools with the means to minimize the extent to which they used the diagnosis of mental retardation. Both the eligibility decision-making process employed by the public schools and the characteristics of children served as LD were altered markedly by these developments despite little or no change in authoritative definitions of LD or criteria specified in state education codes.

DELETION OF "BORDERLINE MENTAL RETARDATION"

When Kirk introduced the term "LD" in 1963 he referred to a segment of students who encountered academic difficulties but were not eligible for special education services under already existing categories (e.g., mental retardation, emotional disturbance). In other words, mental retardation and emotional disturbance had "territorial rights" to groups of children already defined. The LD category was crafted to make eligible those children who were not heretofore eligible. In recognition of the preexisting categories, certain "exclusionary" criteria were employed, acknowledging, in certain instances, that children with already recognized disabilities were not subsumed under the umbrella of this new category. "Children assigned to this new category were defined primarily by what they were not: They were not learning, and they did not have visual, hearing, or motor disabilities, mental retardation, emotional disturbance, or environmental, cultural, or economic disadvantage that restricted their learning" (Raymond, 2000, p. 97). In the reauthorization of IDEA in 1997, the notion of exclusionary criteria is further expanded to include children who have not had the opportunity to learn—they are not to be identified as having a learning disability under these more recent guidelines (Council for Exceptional Children, 1998).

Consider the changes in the definition of mental retardation, specified as one reason for precluding eligibility as LD, and the impact it had on criteria for identifying students as eligible as LD. When LD came into existence, the authoritative definition of mental retardation was the 1961 American Association on Mental Deficiency (AAMD) (Heber, 1961) definition. Mental retardation constituted the largest disability in special education at that time. It continued to be the category with the largest enrollments when President Ford signed P.L. 94-142 into law in 1975. The Heber definition specified an upper IQ boundary of −1 SD (roughly IQ 85) and represented the most liberal or inclusive definition of mental retardation ever seen (Clausen, 1967). In 1973, AAMD (Grossman, 1973) reversed the trend toward inclusiveness, and shifted the upper IQ boundary to −2 SDs (or IQ 70). If eligibility as LD required excluding students who qualified as mentally retarded, then the segment of children with IQ scores between 70 and 85 (roughly 13% of the general population) was suddenly disenfranchised. The definition of LD and the criteria for establishing eligibility were intimately linked to the definition of mental retardation, and "changes in the LD definition" in fact occurred when mental retardation was redefined in 1973; suddenly 13 percent of the general population was cured of mental retardation. Were any of these children, described by Forness as being in a demilitarized zone, now eligible as LD? Academics might debate whether this disenfranchised group should be eligible for services as LD if they exhibit the requisite discrepancy (standard score or regressed?), but the public schools could not await resolution of that debate. State education codes revised criteria for mental retardation to be consistent with the Grossman (1973) definition and, in effect, directed school districts to cease identifying children in the IQ range of 70–85 as mentally retarded. However, school districts had to do something about a segment of children exhibiting severe and chronic low achievement accompanied by low cognitive skills. As we will describe below, it appears that the schools chose to serve them in substantial numbers in special education and did so by expanding the LD category.

How This Expanded the LD Category

Faced with the practical problem of low cognitive students with chronic and persistent academic problems and the increased exclusiveness of the mental retardation criteria, schools had to decide a course of action. It is our position that the decision the schools reached was to expand the boundaries of LD to include these low cognitive children and serve them where they appeared. Doing so dramatically increased the heterogeneity of the SI LD population and widened the discrepancy between definitions of LD and characteristics of children served in public schools as LD. The essence of the reason for widening the gap was captured by Gerber (1999–2000) in the following passage: "In 1973 we stopped teachers from nominating students with IQs between 75 and 85, simply removed the categorical label that once defined these students, simply defined educable mental or familial retardation out of existence. Did these students or their difficulties in learning go away?" (p. 38). No, they did not. In fact, they continued to present a significant challenge to teachers in whose classes they were enrolled. In turn, these teachers continued to refer them. Confronted with this situation many public schools chose to continue to serve them, but did so as LD.

It is important to note that evidence on the prevalence of former "borderline" and mild cases of mental retardation clearly shows that the condition is intimately related to poverty (see Richardson, 1981). An extensive research base documented that cases of "borderline" or MMR were a phenomenon arising from factors linked to poverty (Haskins, 1986). A series of investigations was undertaken to explore the extent to which the adverse effects of sociolinguistic/economic disadvantage could be reversed with early intervention programs targeting areas in which disadvantage was believed to affect academic performance (e.g., Garber, 1988; Ramey & Finkelstein, 1981). While the LD field has since its inception attributed the learning difficulties to intrinsic factors, the presence of many children of poverty with low cognitive skills in school populations of LD students certainly challenges the attributions dominant in the "LD literature" and requires a reconsideration of these assumptions at least as they pertain to SI LD.

The ignoring of exclusionary criteria is not restricted to MMR. Reluctance to classify children as emotionally disturbed (ED) is also evident, and is illustrated by a study conducted by Duncan, Forness, and Hartsough (1995). They examined 85 cases of students served as severely emotionally disturbed (SED) in two counties of California. At the time these students were *initially* certified as eligible for special education, 53% were identified as LD, 31% as SED, 11% as speech and language impaired, and 5% in other categories. The authors reported the age of the child when a problem was first noticed, the age at which the first intervention was initiated, the age at which the first special-education IEP was developed, and the age at which the first SED placement was made. SED placement was found to occur some 4 to 6 years after the problem was first noticed. The following passage illustrates the point made herein that LD is being used as a nonspecific diagnosis:

> His problem first came to the attention of someone outside the family when he was about 5 years old. Formal intervention for these problems was initiated when he was about 6½, and his first special education placement occurred when he was about 8....There was a likelihood that his initial special education diagnosis was in the learning disability category, but he was ultimately found to be eligible as SED. (p. 17)

Either the schools are reluctant to use the ED designation or the schools are using LD as an initial nonspecific category, appending an acceptable label because it is less stigmatizing and pessimistic in its prognosis, to be used until the treatments provided are deemed ineffective and inappropriate. Nevertheless, the presence of children classified as LD whose achievement deficiencies are primarily due to low cognitive functioning or behavioral excesses that impair learning serves only to contaminate the LD category.

VARIATIONS IN LD CHARACTERISTICS ACROSS SITES

As we have alluded to, it is our contention that the dramatic increase in the number of children identified as LD is in large part due to the fact that public schools violate the most fundamental exclusionary criteria for LD by enrolling children as LD who in fact qualify as mentally retarded or even ED. In addition, the schools' categorical approach to establishing eligibility tends to obscure cases of comorbidity (the presence of characteristics defining two or more disability categories simultaneously). That is, a child is to be placed in one, and only one, disability category when found eligible for special education. For schools, LD has become the "disability of choice" because it is less stigmatizing, more acceptable to parents, and more optimistic in the prognosis it conveys. The result is that classification of children as LD does not constitute a diagnosis; rather, it has become a catchall designation for eligibility and planning for services.

MacMillan et al. (1998) provide an example of the generalized use of LD as a catchall designation for eligibility for services when they described their referred sample of children who were ultimately classified as LD by the public schools. Their research was conducted in California, which reported that 5.93% of its students were classified as LD. These investigators had classified all referred children using research criteria as being mentally retarded, learning disabled, having attention deficit–hyperactivity disorder (ADHD), emotionally/behaviorally disordered (EBD), or ineligible for special education by virtue of not qualifying on research criteria for any of the four categories. Of the first cohort of 150 referred children, 61 were ultimately classified as LD by the schools. When the research categories into which these students were placed were examined using research criteria, the heterogeneity of these 61 cases was apparent. Table 1 shows the 61 cases cast by either the single category suggested by applying research criteria or the comorbid cases (e.g., child met criteria for LD and EBD; or mentally retarded [MR] and EBD). Approximately a third of the cases did meet the LD criteria only; however, almost the same percentage ($n = 18$) did not qualify as LD but did qualify as mentally retarded (either solely or comorbidly with ADHD, EBD, or ADHD × EBD × MR), in which case they achieved a FSIQ on the WISC-III of 75 or less. Ten cases were classified as LD by the schools but failed to meet research criteria for any of the four possible designations.

Table 1. School-identified students as LD and classifications based on research diagnostic criteria.

RDC Classifications	No. of Cases	Percentage
LD only	20	32.8
ADHD only	3	4.9
MR only	10	18.0
EBD only	0	0.0
LD × ADHD	6	9.8
LD× MR*	–	–
LD × EBD	0	0.0
ADHD × MR	6	9.8
ADHD × EBD	0	0.0
MR × EBD	1	1.6
LD × ADHD × MR*	–	–
LD ×ADHD × EBD	3	4.9
ADHD × MR × EBD	1	1.6
None of the 4	10	16.4
Total	61	100.0

Note: RDC = research diagnostic criteria; LD = learning disabilities; ADHD = attention deficit/hyperactivity disorder; MR = mental retardation; EBD = emotional and behavioral disorders; * = This combination was not possible, as the IQ for LD had to be above 82 and the IQ for MR had to be 75 or below.

Source: Raw data provided by Peter McCabe at Office of Civil Rights.

The evidence clearly documents that the public schools similarly disregarded the "exclusionary criteria" specified in the authoritative definitions of LD. By focusing on absolute low achievement and forgoing the requisite discrepancy, schools knowingly include children with subaverage general intellectual functioning in eligibility classifications of students with LD. In other words, with regard to absolute low achievement being the basis for LD placement, actual school practices mirror the concern with low achievement definitions of learning disabilities articulated by Fletcher et al. (1998) who wrote:

This approach treats IQ as a measure of cognitive capacity that functions much like a threshold ability, using IQ to determine whether the child has sufficient cognitive ability to be successful at a complex cognitive skill such as reading. In essence, it integrates the classification of mental retardation and learning disabilities into a unified system, whereby deficiencies in complex skills below an IQ of 80 are ascribed to the child's cognitive capacity, but deficiencies in children with IQs of 80 or higher are ascribed to failures in the specific component skills, behaviors, experiences, and attitudes that determine successful performance of that skill. The validity of this distinction has not been established and the cut point of 80 is completely arbitrary. (p. 199)

Gottlieb et al. (1994) reported on data collected over a 10-year span in a large urban school district, and their findings bear directly on our concerns that the exclusionary criteria are patently ignored in current placement situations. The current LD population in many settings includes substantial numbers of children who fit the criteria for mental retardation more closely than those for LD; furthermore, the failure to rule out sociocultural disadvantage as a contributor/cause of the learning difficulties is evident. These authors noted that in the 1960s and 1970s the IQ band for placement in educable mentally retarded (EMR) programs was between 55 and 85, varying somewhat by year and the most current definition. Gottlieb et al. found that the mean IQ for children classified as mentally retarded in their districts was 54 in urban districts and 55 in suburban districts—highly similar, to say the least. In marked contrast, they found the mean IQ for children classified as LD in urban districts to be one and one-half standard deviations lower than was found with their suburban LD students. They wrote: "In our 1992 research, for example, the mean for the urban learning disability sample ($N = 175$) was 81.4 ($SD = 13.9$) and the mean for the suburban sample ($N = 55$) was 102.8 ($SD = 13.4$)" (p. 455). In another sample of 320 children classified as LD collected in 1984, they found 41% achieving IQ scores between 70 and 85 with an additional 7.5% with IQ scores of below 70. In yet another more recent survey of 175 students classified LD, approximately one quarter had IQ scores of 90 or above, while 16.6% had IQ scores of less than 70. The findings of Gottlieb et al. regarding substantial proportions of the SI LD cases being low cognitive students are consistent with our own findings (MacMillan, Gresham, Siperstein, & Bocian, 1996); however, they also reported data illustrating the failure to rule out poverty and disadvantage.

THE NEED TO ACKNOWLEDGE URBAN SPECIAL EDUCATION

Earlier we discussed the difference between RI and SI; however, it is equally important to acknowledge that among SI LD students there is a dramatic difference between urban and suburban LD students. Data reported above by Gottlieb et al. attests to this situation simply on the basis of mean IQ of LD students in urban and suburban districts.

Cultural, environmental, and economic factors, rather than serving as a cause for rejecting the diagnosis of LD, often weigh heavily in the school's decision to classify a child as LD. Nowhere is this more evident than in studies that contrast the decision-making process in urban and suburban school districts. Differences in populations classified as LD are obviously a function of the social class of the families served in a school. Stated differently, the meaning of LD is quite different in a poor urban school district than it is in an affluent suburban school district. The large urban district in which Gottlieb et al. (1994) collected their 1992 data (N = 139,780; 165 urban public schools) enrolled a majority of poor children. More than 80% of the children in that district live in poverty. These authors demonstrated that for the general education population of that urban district, a "poverty index" (based on average class size, percentage of Hispanic enrollment; percentage of teachers with fewer than 5 years of teaching experience, number of children qualifying for free meals or other forms of welfare, and the extent of overcrowding) accounted for 65% of the variance in schoolwide reading scores. On average, only 34% of the children in the general education population read at or above grade level. When they looked at the LD students specifically, they found that 90% were on some form of public assistance and 95% were members of a minority group (note: 93% of the entire school population was minority). They also characterized these LD students as "an immigrant population" with 19% being foreign born and 44% coming from homes where English was not the primary language spoken by parents. What then is LD in a large urban district? Gottlieb et al. described the operational definition of LD as "[l]ow-achieving, low-ability children who do not exhibit aggressive or bizarre behavior and whom teachers cannot accommodate in their general education classrooms" (pp. 458–459).

CHANGES IN THE IMPORTANCE OF DIFFERENTIAL DIAGNOSIS

In the 1960s and early 1970s, the assessment/classification process was a "high stakes enterprise" in the sense that the disability classification made in the case of a given child had profound consequences for that child's educational experience (MacMillan, Gresham, Bocian, & Siperstein, 1997). The classification decision whether a child was EMR or LD carried with it consequences in terms of the administrative arrangement into which a child would be served and the curriculum/services that would be provided. Figure 1 schematically represents the shift in consequences for differential diagnosis discussed in the following paragraphs. Recall that the earlier time frame in this schematic predates passage of P.L. 94-142 (Education for All Handicapped Children Act of 1975) and the requirements for a free appropriate public education (FAPE), LRE, and IEPs.

If a diagnosis of EMR was made, the question of "where," or the administrative arrangement in which the child would receive services, was essentially automatic. Robinson and Robinson (1965) described educational services for EMR students in that era, explaining that "The consensus of special educators today definitely favors special class placement for the mildly retarded" (p. 466). So, a specific placement (self-contained special class) was linked to the diagnosis of EMR. Moreover, an alternative curriculum—that is, a functional curriculum—that differed markedly from the general education curriculum was taught to EMR students. It is important to note that special education for virtually all disabilities *except mental retardation* consisted of modification in how a child was taught. In the case of mental retardation, however, special education consisted of modifications in both how and what the child was taught. The curriculum for EMR students typically emphasized the promotion of prevocational skills in the elementary grades along with social and interpersonal skills and functional academics. In the secondary programs vocational training received considerable attention.

Diagnosis of LD, on the other hand, resulted most commonly in service delivery in resource settings, and yet *what* was taught was the standard general education curriculum. Special education for LD consisted of assistance provided by a resource teacher in order to enable the LD child to succeed in the general education curriculum. Unlike what the EMR student at that time was taught, there was seldom any consideration of an alternative curriculum for LD students.

School personnel responsible for diagnosis in the 1960s and 1970s did agonize over what "type" of child they were considering. The diagnostic decision they would make had profound consequences for the child under consideration. One diagnosis conveyed the belief that the general curriculum was appropriate (i.e., LD), and the other diagnosis (EMR) reflected the belief that an alternative curriculum was needed. To convey the significance of that decision, one of the major and most telling criticisms of the "EMR program" was that the decision was irreversible— once the child was put into the alternative curriculum for any period, the possibility of returning that child to the general curriculum was effectively blocked.

Figure 1. Importance of differential diagnosis at two points in time.

Time	Placement	Curriculum
1965		
LD	Resource room	Remediation of skills
MMR	Self-contained class	Functional curriculum

2000		
LD	Negotiated as LRE	Negotiated as IEP
MMR	Negotiated as LRE	Negotiated as IEP

Note: LD = learning disabled; MMR = mildly mentally retarded; LRE = least restrictive environment; IEP = individualized education plan

Passage of P.L. 94-142 almost imperceptibly reduced the stakes in making differential diagnoses; it took the pressure off public school personnel in their classification efforts. We believe this is why today school personnel tell us that they know the child is mentally retarded but classify him or her as LD because there is no upside to calling a child mentally retarded. Apparently they don't believe there is a downside to making an "erroneous" classification. Why? While a diagnosis of one of the disabling conditions recognized under IDEA establishes *eligibility for special education and related services,* other provisions of the law call for the IEP to be individually negotiated for a child. No longer does the diagnostic category under which a child's eligibility is established carry with it any consequences for the curriculum; those are negotiated. Similarly, the LRE provision of the law precludes placement of all children in a given category in a given administrative arrangement (e.g., a special class). Placement also must be individually determined on a case-by-case basis. One consequence is that a very low cognitive child being diagnosed as LD could conceivably get a functional curriculum delivered in a special day class if that is the result of the IEP process considering LRE on an individual basis. In other words, the diagnostic category is not determinative of the placement or the treatment a child will experience, making diagnosis no longer a high-stakes venture.

Table 2. OSEP child count data for LD.

STATE	OSEP	STATE	OSEP
Alabama	5.52%	Montana	5.93%
Alaska	7.09%	Nebraska	5.68%
Arizona	5.76%	Nevada	6.40%
Arkansas	4.91%	New Hampshire	6.24%
California	5.93%	New Jersey	8.72%
Colorado	4.90%	New Mexico	8.60%
Connecticut	6.41%	New York	7.32%
Delaware	8.11%	North Carolina	5.17%
District of Columbia	5.79%	North Dakota	4.73%
Florida	6.67%	Ohio	4.41%
Georgia	3.28%	Oklahoma	6.69%
Hawaii	4.99%	Oregon	6.15%
Idaho	5.81%	Pennsylvania	6.12%
Illinois	6.49%	Rhode Island	9.62%
Indiana	5.74%	South Carolina	5.98%
Iowa	6.43%	South Dakota	4.91%
Kansas	4.77%	Tennessee	6.40%
Kentucky	3.40%	Texas	6.86%
Louisiana	4.86%	Utah	5.97%
Maine	6.17%	Vermont	4.35%
Maryland	5.52%	Virginia	6.09%
Massachusetts	9.90%	Washington	4.96%
Michigan	5.32%	West Virginia	6.59%
Minnesota	4.64%	Wisconsin	5.52%
Mississippi	5.53%	Wyoming	6.21%
Missouri	7.11%		

Note: OSEP = Office of Special Education Programs
Source: Raw data provided by Peter McCabe at Office of Civil Rights.

VARIABILITY WITHIN THE SI LD POPULATION

A teacher hired to teach LD students is likely to encounter a very heterogeneous group of students identified as LD by the three-stage process described. However, the degree of heterogeneity and the nature of the LD students they encounter will vary as a function of the state in which they live and the school building in which they are employed. Simply looking at the prevalence rates for LD in the public schools across states reveals considerable variability in the percentage of children identified as LD. The *Twentieth Annual Report to Congress on the Implementation of the Individuals With Disabilities Education Act* (U.S. Department of Education, 1998) reported that 3.28% of the children in Georgia and 3.40% of those in Kentucky are classified as LD, while 9.62% in Rhode Island and 9.90% in Massachusetts are so classified. While the variability in LD rates across states is less pronounced than is found for MR or ED (Hallahan, Keller, & Ball, 1986), it is far greater than one would expect for a clinical entity reliably assessed. Table 2 shows the percentage for all states. In all probability, the children served as LD in Georgia and Kentucky do differ in important ways from those served in Rhode Island and Massachusetts. The key here is that there is variability in LD prevalence across states attributable to a number of factors such as different criteria for eligibility and different perspectives on classifying children as MMR. It is also important to keep in mind that data aggregated at the state level tend to obscure variations within states at the district level.

In addition to differences in the rate of LD identification, it is important to factor in the point raised earlier that the nature of the SI LD child varies for urban and suburban school districts. Evidence has been presented herein clearly documenting that LD students in urban settings represent very different learning problems that do those in suburban districts. They score lower on measures of intelligence and require that we consider sociocultural factors as contributors, if not causes, of their learning difficulties. They frequently come from families living in poverty. Thus, factors such as low birthweight, exposure to lead, exposure to prenatal substance abuse, living in crowded residences, being raised by parents with less formal education, and various other conditions associated in the past with the condition of MMR are clearly salient to the current urban LD population.

Variability is also evident in the breakdown of SI LD by gender. For example, national projection data from the 1997 Office of Civil Rights survey reveals that 68.35 percent of LD are male, with 31.65 percent being female. While this gender disproportion has been widely accepted in most of the mild disability categories, it is not as apparent when surveys employ RI LD samples. For example, in the Connecticut Longitudinal Study (Shaywitz, Fletcher, Holahan, & Shaywitz, 1992; Shaywitz, Shaywitz, Fletcher, & Escobar, 1990), a two-stage probability sample used RI LD criteria of two types: (a) an IQ-based regressed discrepancy of 1.5 SD and (b) low reading achievement (using an age-adjusted standard score £25% on the Reading Cluster of the Woodcock-Johnson). Neither the discrepancy criteria nor the low reading achievement criterion yielded differential rates by gender. It seems reasonable to speculate that the gender difference so apparent in SI LD populations arises from differential expectations and/or concomitant externalizing behaviors accompanying reading difficulties for males and factors associated with teacher referral behavior. MacMillan, Gresham, Lopez, & Bocian (1996) found gender differences in referral rates of teachers for White and Black students, but not for Hispanic students.

When rates of SI LD by racial or ethnic group are aggregated at the national level and examined, the issue of overrepresentation of Black students found in the mental retardation category is not found for LD (MacMillan & Reschly, 1998). However, it is noteworthy that the percentages of White, Black, and Hispanic children served in the LD category have also increased dramatically. Yet, because the increase has been "proportionate" (at approximately the same rate for all three ethnic groups), it is not viewed as a problem. In 1978 the projected national figures showed that 2.23% of Black students were being served in LD; in the 1997 survey 6.15% of Black students were being served in LD. For White students the change in the same period was from 2.23% to 5.53%. Using the 1997 survey data, there are considerable variations across ethnic groups. For example, the percentage of Asian/Pacific Island students served as LD is only 1.90% in contrast to the following percentages for other ethnic groups: American Indian/Alaskan, 6.41%; Hispanic, 5.99%; Black, 6.15%, and White, 5.53%. Hence, comparing the rates to that of White students suggests no overrepresentation for Black and Hispanic students; however, if one uses the rate for Asian/Pacific Island students, there are considerably higher rates for all other ethnic groups.

ISSUES RAISED ABOUT THE CURRENT PROCESS

Inherent in the current process is the apparent belief that differentiation of the broad band of children presenting with low achievement is essential in order to match treatment to individual need. Federal and state regulations promote such distinctions, providing criteria to be used in the identification of, and distinction between, children with LD, mental retardation, speech and language impairments, and emotional disturbance. On the other hand, evidence has been presented herein suggesting that the public schools give lip service to this process but have increasingly used the LD category in a manner quite different from that suggested in these regulations—as a cross-categorical designation. As we have argued elsewhere (MacMillan, Gresham, Siperstein, & Bocian, 1996; MacMillan et al., 1997, 1998), the time has come to consider the limitations of current policy and to examine the consequences of current practices. Let us turn to the issues we believe need to be addressed in the identification process and then turn to the consequences that we anticipate will result from the failure to resolve these issues.

ELIGIBILITY USING A ONE-TIME-ONLY ASSESSMENT

The current process establishes a child as eligible based on assessments conducted at one point in time (i.e., after referral and failure to respond to prereferral interventions). We see this as problematic in two ways. First, there is a problem with assessing a child, let's say in third grade, and finding a psychometric profile permitting eligibility as LD. One of the benchmarks currently employed is low academic achievement (usually in reading) discrepant from expected level of achievement (based on IQ). Assessing current level of functioning, however, is unable to inform us as to "why" the child's academic performance is low. Among the low scorers in third grade are some children who, in fact, do have problems processing information despite good instruction in first and second grade. Others who score low have no serious problems processing information yet score low because they have not been instructed well in first and/or second grade. The current process, which uses a "one-time-only" assessment, fails to differentiate between these two possibilities. Hence, it is difficult to refute the contention of those who argue that a child identified as LD in third grade is not simply a failure of general education. This issue is independent of the debate over discrepant versus nondiscrepant low achievement, and rather derives from the provision regarding exclusion in the reauthorization of IDEA 1997 to include children who have not had the opportunity to learn—they are not to be identified as having a learning disability.

Given the previous data provided on children in urban districts identified as LD, this distinction becomes even more important. We know that inner-city schools are staffed more often by new teachers (currently in some districts, the majority of which lack credentials) and teachers who are unable to secure transfers to more affluent schools. Urban districts often have older school buildings with poorer equipment, fewer amenities such as adequate computer facilities, and student bodies often coming from more disadvantaged backgrounds. The likelihood of confusing "disability" with "disadvantage" in such settings is great, yet the current process provides little direction for distinguishing between the two. How is one to establish that the low reading achievement exhibited by a child in third grade is not due to "a lack of opportunity to learn"? Currently, this requirement is met in a cavalier fashion—at best by attesting to the prereferral intervention efforts. However, prereferral interventions are a nonspecific, often very weak intervention seldom targeted to the problem prompting referral and seldom, if ever, implemented with fidelity.

Elsewhere in this volume (see work of Torgesen) is presented converging evidence that in the area of reading, there are validated procedures which if implemented are successful in promoting significant improvement in reading skills in children presenting with reading disabilities (see, for example, Foorman, Francis, Winikates, Mehta, Schatschneider, & Fletcher, 1997; Torgesen, Alexander, Wagner, Rashotte, Voeller, & Conway, 2001). Less systematic work has been done in the area of mathematics. However, the benefit of structured instruction in mathematics has been demonstrated to reduce the gap evident upon entry to school for low socioeconomic status (SES) students in comparison with high SES students (Case, Griffin, & Kelly, 1999; Griffin & Case, 2000). The Number Knowledge Test (see Griffin & Case, 2000, Appendix A) provides a quick reliable assessment of the child's developmental stage in elementary math. Moreover, 6-year-old children who attended school in low-income areas and were ready to enter first grade performed at the 3- to 4-year-old level on the Number Knowledge Test. A program called Rightstart was developed (the name changed to Number Worlds later) and appears successful for many children in promoting number facility in initially low-scoring, low SES students, enabling them to perform at a level comparable to that of high SES children. Empirically validated procedures are in place that could be used to ensure "the opportunity to learn" reading and math. Before using a one-time-only assessment to establish the presence of a disability, it seems reasonable to ask that validated interventions implemented with integrity are provided and that the child's responsiveness to these interventions is examined prior to labeling.

A second concern with the current process derives from the mere fact that whether a child will exhibit the requisite "severe discrepancy" is, in part, a function of the age/grade level at which the assessment occurs. Requiring a discrepancy between achievement and intelligence has been characterized as a "wait and fail" method of classification because several years of schooling are usually required in order to obtain a sufficiently large discrepancy to qualify as LD. Failure to target reading problems early, as one waits for the discrepancy to be achieved, has been a concern of many (e.g., Fletcher & Foorman, 1994; Speece & Case, submitted). Delays in targeting treatment permit the child to flounder, experience additional failure, and reduce the probability that treatments will be effective once they are finally introduced.

An alternative to using one-time assessments to document a severe discrepancy has been described by Lynn and Doug Fuchs (Fuchs, 1995; Fuchs & Fuchs, 1998). Their approach, based on tenets of treatment validity, uses curriculum-based measurement (CBM) that provides for repeated measurement and is sensitive to change or growth. The approach contrasts the entry-level skills to those of classmates (level) *and* rate of progress over time (slope) in comparison to classmates receiving the same quality of instruction delivered by the same teacher. Fuchs and Fuchs (1998) used the term "dual discrepancy" to capture the criteria employed by their approach to LD eligibility: *both* level and rate of progress have to differ from that of peers to be eligible. In a recently reported study, Speece and Case (submitted) compared children identified as dually discrepant (level and slope using CBM measures) with others exhibiting an IQ-reading achievement discrepancy. The dually discrepant group was lower in IQ and younger than the IQ-reading achievement discrepant group; however, the two groups did not differ on reading, phonological awareness, social skills, or SES measures. Interestingly, neither approach identified a gender disproportion, while the dual discrepancy approach did identify a larger proportion of younger children. Obviously, we do not know which approach identified the "real LD" cases; however, the use of repeated measurements tracking growth strikes us as an attractive feature. The downside of this approach is its labor-intensiveness, thereby reducing the likelihood of it being adopted widely in the public schools.

Going beyond the "opportunity to learn," there is the possibility that really poor instructional programs may not only prevent optimal development, but may actually have a deleterious effect on the child. Consider the work of Kellam, Ling, Merisca, Brown, and Ialongo (1998), albeit dealing primarily with aggressive behavior, as it bears on the influences of classroom context on the course of behavior. In this study, involving 19 public elementary schools, schools and teachers were randomly assigned to intervention or control conditions and children within each school were assigned sequentially to classrooms from alphabetized lists. Despite these efforts to randomize, "…classroom differences in levels of aggressive behavior emerged as early as the first quarter of first grade, suggesting that the very origins of variation in classroom aggression levels came from the classroom teacher and/or the mix of students and the teachers" (p. 181). That is, classrooms (as opposed to poverty, school building) were associated with levels of aggression, and the levels of aggression evident in classrooms were bimodally distributed—either high or low levels of aggression being evident. When these students were followed into middle school, aggressive males from these "chaotic classrooms" were at increased risk for serious conduct disorders. The authors summarized the importance of first-grade classroom contextual factors as follows:

> We suggest the following hypothetical model to better understand the classroom effect on the more aggressive males. The skills of the teachers in highly aggressive, disruptive classrooms were not sufficient to promote an integrative prosocial classroom social system. Effective classroom behavior management appears to be essential in the socialization of young children, and for boys whose initial behavior response is aggressive, disruptive, the lack of providing teachers [with] sufficient background training is critical. Teacher training does not provide effective methods and

experience in classroom management. This, coupled with the lack of staff support for the classroom, places such children at greater risk of later conduct disorder and related academic problems. (p. 182)

In their conclusions, Kellam et al. stated, "The implications of these findings are that the first grade classroom has a critical impact on the developmental course of aggressive behavior for the boys whose initial responses to classrooms are aggressive, disruptive" (p. 184).

What is the likelihood that a first-grade teacher who has difficulty controlling behavior also has difficulty teaching reading? If the students do not attend to instruction, that instruction is unlikely to have an effect. Moreover, if the inability to control behavior is an indicator of a poor or inexperienced teacher, then we would likely see similar weaknesses in the instructional program provided to students in the class. Where do we tend to find more inexperienced or ineffective teachers? We submit it is in the same schools where we find "at risk" students because of the presence of poverty, second-language issues, deteriorating classrooms, higher mobility rates for students, and so forth. When one conducts a one-time assessment in third grade and finds a discrepancy between aptitude and achievement, how risky is a conclusion that it reflects a within-child problem? When an IEP team excludes inadequate prior instruction as a contributor to the child's learning deficiency, on what basis is that determination made? The need for consideration of such contextual factors is paramount, but heretofore too often ignored in the LD field (Keogh & Speece, 1996).

In contrast to the field's willingness to consider environmental factors to explain or understand mild mental retardation, the field *assumes* that achievement deficits exhibited by students labeled LD are due to within-child, neurological factors. The denial evident in the exclusive focus on intrinsic factors will not serve the field well. The population of students served as LD includes substantial numbers of children whose academic performance deficits are clearly linked to environmental influences and contextual factors, traditionally excluded from consideration by the LD field.

ASSUMED INTRINSIC/NEUROBIOLOGICAL ETIOLOGY OF LD

During the late 1970s increased attention was devoted to refining the definition of LD. Zigmond (1993) noted that an improved understanding of the condition emerged from research, in terms of "the psychological, cognitive, neurological, and neuropsychological characteristics of students with learning disabilities…" (p. 256). An alternative definition resulted after years of discussion by the National Joint Committee on Learning Disabilities (NJCLD; McLoughlin & Netick, 1983)—a definition characterized by Zigmond as reflecting "a growing consensus regarding the intrinsic nature of the disorder" (p. 256). The wording in the definition certainly reflected this perspective: "These disorders are intrinsic to the individual and presumed to be due to central nervous system dysfunction" (McLaughlin & Netick, 1983, p. 22). This preoccupation with intrinsic/neurological factors explains in part why so little is known about the contextual influences on the expression of learning disabilities (Keogh & Speece, 1996). Although LD is "intrinsic to the individual, *presumed* to be due to central nervous system dysfunction" (Kavanagh & Truss, 1988, p. 1), acceptance of this hypothesis does not negate the powerful role of environmental features in either the amelioration or exacerbation of a learning disability. The bias in the scientific study of LD toward intrinsic explanations of the disorder has led to virtual disregard of the contextual factors that either coexist with or are causal to learning disabilities (Speece, 1993). If the problem resides "within the child," then it logically follows that one would not examine experiential factors, home and neighborhood, or parent educational level, as these would be of interest only if they somehow contributed to central nervous system (CNS) dysfunction.

The combination, however, of one-time assessment and the inability to rule out prior instruction and experiential factors as contributors to a child's deficiencies in academics, particularly reading, leads to serious questions about the presumption of a neurological basis for the problem. The more recent research on reading interventions based on phonological awareness noted previously (see Foorman et al., 1997; Torgesen, this volume; Torgesen et al., 2001) suggests that a substantial proportion of young children presenting at one point in time as deficient in reading skills can be taught using moderately intensive interventions. Interestingly, after exposure to these treatments, small percentages (usually 4–10%) of these disabled readers are "nonresponders" who appear to resist even these intensive instructional efforts. Are these (the nonresponders) the cases of "neurologically based" learning problems, while the rest (over 90%) are simply "instructionally underserved"? We suspect that children coming from the most poverty-stricken circumstances not only enter school behind on readiness skills, but also are most likely to be exposed to primary elementary teachers with the least experience or the least success in promoting reading achievement. As long as the schools identify children as LD on the basis of one-time assessments without truly examining response to "good instruction," the practice of classifying them as "learning disabled" (suggesting in-child problems) and presuming a neurological basis for the deficiencies is an inferential leap that is risky at best.

It is also noteworthy that the program of research on reading disability (e.g., Fletcher, et al., 1998; Shaywitz et al., 1990; Shaywitz et al., 1992; Shaywitz, et al., 1995) fails to identify any processing differences between discrepant low readers and nondiscrepant low readers, calling into question the salience of an IQ-achievement discrepancy as a "marker" for reading disabilities. This topic is addressed in detail elsewhere in this volume (see Fletcher et al., this volume) and we raise it here only to further challenge the neurological basis for LD. If nondiscrepant poor readers and discrepant poor readers do not differ on processing variables, apparently either absolute low achievement is indicative of neurological dysfunction or IQ-achievement discrepancy is not a "marker" of such neurologically based learning difficulties presumed to define LD.

CURRICULAR CONSEQUENCES OF THE HETEROGENEITY OF SI LD POPULATIONS

As long as special education and related services for LD students in our public schools absorb students with IQ scores of 70–85 as well as those with scores below 70 there are serious issues to be addressed in the area of curriculum modification. It is clearly evident that the public schools are not willing to identify children in this IQ range as mentally retarded (MacMillan, Siperstein, & Gresham, 1996). Nevertheless, it is equally evident that this group of children is perceived by teachers as among the most difficult to teach and a group that they are going to refer to, and qualify for, special education services regardless of authoritative definitions and eligibility criteria. Third, they are identifying this group as eligible by "certifying" their eligibility as LD students. As indicated previously, we see this neither as a temporary state of affairs nor as one that will be changing in the foreseeable future. As such, LD is currently operationally defined in the public schools as absolute low achievement, not necessarily discrepant from aptitude and not necessarily excluding cases ostensibly due to mental retardation or circumstances suggesting disadvantage of either a sociolinguistic or instructional nature.

To the extent that treatment is linked to labels we must be concerned—that is, if the treatment provided to all children classified as LD assumes homogeneity among those so labeled, and further assumes similar characteristics and needs, we anticipate inappropriate or, at the very least, untested treatments being applied to a segment of the SI LD students. Take, for example, the intervention treatments evaluated on reading disabled students promoting phonemic awareness. As noted above, one finds a nonresponse rate somewhere between 4 and 10% in samples of reading disabled children studied. However, most of those studies set selection criteria for participating at IQ of 80 or above. As such, we have precious little evidence on the usefulness of these treatments with children scoring below IQ 80, yet we find such children in substantial numbers classified as LD. Which of the SI LD students are likely to profit from training in phonemic awareness? Should acquisition of phonemic awareness be a goal on the IEP for all SI LD students or only for some subset with IQ scores of 80 or above?

Last, and possibly most important, the "treatments" provided to SI LD students have been validated on samples absent the low cognitive students. Consider, for example, that the mean IQ of the urban SI LD students in Gottlieb et al. (1994) was 81.4 while the mean IQ scores reported in MacMillan, Gresham, Lopez, & Bocian (1996) for students referred for prereferral intervention were 87.42 for White, 79.93 for Black, and 78.17 for Hispanic students. Yet, in a meta-analysis published by Swanson, Carson, and Saches-Lee (1996) of intervention studies with LD students conducted between 1967 and 1993, they reported a mean IQ across studies for the treatment groups of 95.79 (with a range of 85–106). If the effectiveness of interventions recommended for "LD students" is based on evaluations implemented with mean IQ scores approximating the national average, and the SI LD population in urban districts contains substantial proportions of students with IQ scores a full standard deviation or more lower, then we really don't know how effective such interventions are with SI LD in urban public schools.

Furthermore, we recognize that two second-grade students reading at a standard score of 75, regardless of their IQs, resemble one another and may be taught identically by their teacher. However, if one of these children has an IQ of 98 and the other 65, would one predict the same developmental trajectory for these two children? In other words, would one expect these two students to be reading at the same level in sixth grade assuming they are exposed to the "same treatment"? Assuming the efficacy of a certain reading program documented for children with "normal" intelligence (say IQ 80 and above), is there an IQ threshold below which a beneficial result cannot be predicted? That research, we believe, has yet to be done but is crucial to answering the above questions.

Consequences of this failure to recognize that low cognitive students are being identified as LD and whether intensive reading instruction is the "appropriate" (as in FAPE) treatment for such cases are captured in the following passage. In an article published in the *Los Angeles Times* describing the differing perspectives of an experienced teacher and of the district director of special education, who is committed to the primacy of reading, one can see the faith of an administrator that *all* students labeled LD can profit from reading instruction and the belief of a teacher that a functional curriculum would best serve her LD students:

> Royalstine Bowman, a 33-year veteran teacher at San Bernardino High School, favors teaching students life skills with a home-grown curriculum that district officials have dubbed "Bowman's Way."
>
> She has little patience with current research that focuses on daily doses of phonics instruction for special education students.

Her approach is based on three decades of experience, salvaging teaching manuals dating to 1942, and a belief that even the most impaired learners can be taught to become independent.

For her students, ranging from ninth- to 12th graders, Bowman's Way means getting drilled on the importance of a firm handshake, a confident introduction and legible handwriting. It means learning how to tell time and how to make change, how to cook and how to fill out job applications borrowed from local fast-food stands and Cadillac dealerships.

For a few students, it also means patient individual help in learning to memorize their home addresses and to spell their last names.

District officials make it clear that they believe Bowman's Way is outmoded. They plan to replace her curriculum with one that makes expert reading instruction a priority.

"I don't care what kind of situation a student is in, being in special education is no excuse for not learning to read," said Joan Roberts, hired a year ago to upgrade the district's special education program. "I want our students learning to read right up to the last second of their senior year."

Bowman counters that "the experts don't know my students."

"The truth is, not every student goes to college," she said. "And nobody asks applicants for jobs as custodians and stock boys what their reading level is." (Colvin & Helfand, 2000, p. 8)

WHERE ARE WE NOW AND WHERE MIGHT WE GO?

It is evident that the "concept" of LD used by the schools deviates markedly from the original concept of LD articulated in authoritative definitions. We have no doubt that the SI LD population reflects a group of children who do, in fact, need assistance; however, among the children identified as LD by the schools are subsets never considered in previous descriptions of LD that acknowledged the heterogeneity present in the original conception of LD (problems in reading, writing, mathematics, verbal expression, etc.). Today, we find children classified as LD who would more appropriately be classified as MR or ED if diagnostic criteria were applied rigorously. As long as the LD category absorbs children with IQ scores in the 70–85 range, as well as those with scores below 70, we will never clean up the LD category. It is of paramount importance that those advocating for a cleansing of LD acknowledge the special needs of these low cognitive children, encourage research that clarifies whether their needs differ in degree or kind from those of the traditional LD child, and advocate for appropriate services for these children. Why? We are convinced that the children whom research criteria would designate as mildly retarded or borderline retarded are far more difficult to teach than a traditional LD child. They require modifications by general education teachers in virtually every curricular area—not just reading. As such, they will continue to be among the first referred and will fill "the special education slots" available at a school site or in a district.

TITRATION OF INTENSITY OF TREATMENTS IN DECISION MAKING

Currently, the LD category appears to be used by the schools as a general, nonspecific category embracing students who can best be characterized as exhibiting *absolute low achievement*. In some ways, its use by the schools negates the need for the "developmental delay" category permitted for younger students under IDEA guidelines. Elsewhere we (MacMillan, Gresham, Bocian, & Siperstein, 1997) have described the decision-making process in the public schools as one that uses resistance to treatments as its guiding principle. Figure 2 is a schematic representing how treatments are titrated and how a child resistant to one treatment is subsequently moved to a treatment that is more intense until the child ultimately receives effective instruction or is reclassified. We characterized the application of increasingly more "intensive" treatments as a titration process. Resources available in the general education classroom are rather weak treatments and a child failing to make adequate progress might receive Chapter I services. However, if inadequate progress persists, the child is referred for prereferral interventions, individually tailored interventions are implemented, and the impact is evaluated. If these prereferral interventions are judged to be ineffective, the child is typically referred by a team for formal evaluation and assessment (described in detail elsewhere in this paper).

The initial diagnosis is commonly LD, often despite a failure to exhibit criteria specified, and the IEP calls for an initial treatment of pullout resource service for a limited duration (e.g., 2 to 4 hours per week). If this action fails to remediate the academic weaknesses, the duration of resource help is increased (e.g., to 6 to 8 hours per week) or a child is placed into a special day class—in some way providing for more intensive academic and remedial treatments. For a segment of the SI LD population receiving the most intensive LD services available, a failure to respond is still noted. In Figure 2 these cases are sometimes reclassified as MR or ED. Recall the experiences of ED students described by Duncan et al. (1995) who were initially classified as LD only to be reclassified as ED later in their school careers.

In the titration model described herein, the data coming from formal assessments contribute little to the decision-making process; instead, they are necessarily collected in order to comply with regulations. IQ data are ignored when they point to mental retardation as a diagnosis and also when establishing "expected" levels of reading or arithmetic achievement for purposes of LD eligibility. This raises the issue of how, if at all, intelligence testing should be used in the process.

ISSUE OF INTELLIGENCE TESTING

Few things have been as hotly debated as the role of IQ, and we do not intend to rehash that history here. Instead, we urge some focused discussion of the usefulness of IQ in classification and informing intervention efforts. Our reading of the literature on discrepant versus nondiscrepant low achievement (see Fletcher et al., 1998) in students with IQ scores of 80 or above seems to conclude that intelligence tests have limited usefulness for the identification of students with LD. Yet administration of such tests is currently mandated for establishing eligibility in most states for students as LD or MR—at what cost? Gresham and Witt (1997) wrote:

> Estimates suggest that between 1 and 1.8 million intelligence tests are administered individually to children each year in the United States. Recent survey data suggest that two-thirds of a school psychologist's time is spent in special education eligibility determination and the typical school psychologist administers over 100 individual tests of intelligence each year. (p. 249)

Evidence presented throughout this paper points to the fact that the IQ data are *not used in making differential diagnoses.* Moreover, even the most ardent defendant of intelligence testing would probably concede that given the omnibus nature of the test, it has no "curricular relevance" (i.e., does not inform us as to what instructional strategies will work). If IQ scores are not used in a consistent fashion for purposes of classification *and* they are not instructionally relevant, does it make sense to mandate their continued use on a wholesale basis merely to establish eligibility? We find little evidence to support their continued use on a wholesale basis.

Figure 2. Titration of intensity of treatments.

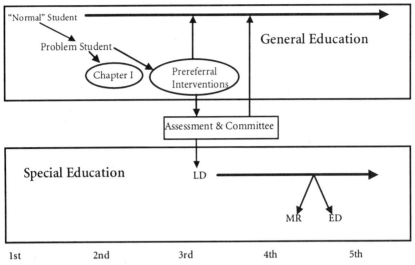

Note: LD = learning disabled; MR = mentally retarded; ED = emotionally disturbed

The one issue that must be considered, however, if the routine administration of IQ tests is discontinued, is the importance of exclusionary criteria. That is, if a reconceptualization of LD continues to exclude conditions like mental retardation, then the grounds on which to make the exclusionary decision warrants consideration. If a defining characteristic of mental retardation is "low general intelligence," then there will have to be some basis on which to make that determination. Abundant evidence has been presented (e.g., MacMillan, Gresham, Siperstein, & Bocian, 1996) showing that even when IQ data are presented to document mental retardation and permit the exclusion, the schools ignore it in most instances and do not enforce the exclusionary criteria. Another reasonable position is to adopt a domain-specific approach to what is now LD (e.g., reading disability, math disability) and, without establishing the presence of mental retardation, use an approach consistent with that proposed by Lynn Fuchs in which students with a reading disability, for example, are exposed to best-practice treatments implemented with integrity. For those cases who fail to respond favorably to a validated intervention implemented with integrity, consider the consequences of persisting in pursuing achievement in reading (and side effects of continued failure) and consider providing that child with a more functional curriculum. Does it matter for educational decision making whether a nonresponder has a low IQ or such a severe problem independent of low IQ?

The ultimate decision regarding the use of IQ in classification for school purposes ought to be made after careful consideration of the consequences of the alternatives.

EFFORTS TO "FIX" LD: THE NEED FOR A BROADER PERSPECTIVE

We have seen an ongoing debate over the definition of LD for more than a quarter of a century. During this same time, special education has become more "specialized" in the sense that the generalists have become fewer and fewer and those in our field identify themselves in terms of subspecialties within a disability category (e.g., my area is memory within the LD field). However, as we saw in 1973, a change in the definition of mental retardation was undertaken without consideration of the consequences of this change on the LD population. From the perspective of the schools, the "judgmental categories" (including LD, MMR, ED, speech and language impaired; other health impaired) are being used in idiosyncratic ways in order to serve children the schools believe need special education services. Any attempt to "fix" the LD definition and criteria that fails to consider the criteria for other judgmental categories and issues of comorbidity is, in our opinion, doomed. Furthermore, it is crucial to acknowledge the differences between urban and suburban schools and the implications of these differences for the educational process.

Students served currently as LD, MMR, and ED overlap considerably along certain behavioral dimensions. In terms of reading, students served in all three groups tend to exhibit reading disabilities. Moreover, within a given disability group, the degree of reading disability varies considerably. Another behavioral dimension that is salient to all three categories is externalizing behavior problems. It is a defining characteristic for many ED students, but the frustration experienced by LD students appears to give rise to externalizing behavior problems for many LD and ADHD students (see review by Hinshaw, 1992). Viewed as a Venn diagram, the overlap between members of these disability groups is considerable. A third dimension relevant to all three is the relative weakness in social skills and peer relationships and the frequency with which children in these categories experience social rejection (see Asher & Coie, 1990). As suggested above, the relevance of intelligence is debatable, but might warrant consideration. At present, a categorical approach is used in which children are placed into one, and only one, of the extant disability categories. Yet, a child categorized as LD may, in addition to problems in reading, exhibit significant externalizing behavior problems. Current criteria for ED require that the behavior problems or emotional problems must adversely affect the child's academic performance. Hence, ED students require effective treatments for behavior and academics.

Our point here is that a multidimensional approach to assessing behavioral dimensions salient to all three current disability categories might provide assessments directly relevant to the treatment program. It may further gauge the severity of a given child's problem on a given dimension that would inform those crafting the IEP about the extent to which a given behavior dimension should be addressed in programming. The current assessments measuring static variables often unrelated to treatment protocols fail to capture opportunity to learn as a competing explanation for the low achievement. To the extent that the LD category has embraced students whose low achievement appears linked to experiences of poverty, the issue of sociocultural factors as causes or contributors to the poor achievement simply cannot be ignored. We must recognize that factors of impoverished learners contribute to *both* learning problems in children and how the eligibility process is compromised in schools serving children of poverty.

LD AND SOCIAL CLASS

As noted previously, urban and suburban schools serve LD populations that differ distinctly from one another. The work of Gottlieb et al. (1994) on urban LD students led to the following conclusion: "Data we have collected over a 10-year period indicate that today's child with learning disabilities functions very similarly to the way students with educable mental retardation performed 25 years ago" (p. 453). This finding raises a number of questions for the special education delivery system and those interested in students with LD. Consider that the condition of mild mental retardation is almost exclusively a phenomenon of poverty. Richardson's (1981) research, conducted in Aberdeen, Scotland, where all subjects were White, provided clear evidence that the form of mental retardation with IQ scores above 50 and no evidence of CNS involvement was simply not found in the highest social class strata. Richardson plotted the prevalence of this form of mild mental retardation against the prevalence of two other forms (IQ < 50, evidence of CNS involvement; IQ > 50 and evidence of CNS involvement). In the two lowest social class strata, this form of mental retardation (IQ > 50 and no CNS involvement) constituted the single largest proportion of cases.

In this paper we have provided evidence that children resembling the Richardson cases of mild mental retardation are among the most frequently referred students (MacMillan, Gresham, Siperstein, & Bocian, 1996) and that in urban settings, children with IQ < 85 constitute more than half of the LD population in urban districts. These findings raise a couple of questions in our minds, and we do not know of any data set that provides any answers to the questions. First, in urban districts in which low cognitive children constitute the most visible form of learning problems, are students with the traditional LD profile of low achievement despite average or above-average IQ not being served by special education? We hypothesize that the low cognitive students require the most accommodations in a general education class and therefore deviate most markedly from the model student profile. Teachers in these settings refer these students but do not refer the "traditional LD" cases, or if they do, the committee charged with establishing eligibility uses the available slots in LD programs to serve the low cognitive children. As we discussed previously, this form of false negative case has not been studied and the magnitude of this group is unknown. It would be interesting to know whether fewer cases of false negative LD cases are to be found in affluent suburban districts than in urban districts, given that one would not expect to find the old EMR and borderline children in suburban districts. A second question concerns the proportion of a district's student body that one would expect in the overall special education program. If urban and suburban districts serve roughly the same proportion of their students in the nonjudgmental categories (e.g., visually impaired, orthopedically impaired), but urban districts also serve low cognitive cases associated with poverty *and* traditional LD students, one might hypothesize that a higher proportion of an urban district's student bodies are in need of special education services than is true for suburban districts.

The process prescribed under IDEA plays itself out in very different ways in different school districts. A failure to recognize this leads to false assumptions about the nature of LD students. Moreover, we must come to grips with the realities that school districts serve different populations of children, have differing resources to address problem learners, and make eligibility decisions in light of these different circumstances. At present, schools do not identify cases that consistently fit the idealized models described in authoritative definitions or state education codes. This situation may frustrate the research community and others removed from the front lines of education. At the same time, we know of precious little evidence suggesting that the children who are served as LD in these diverse districts are not in need of help. Any resolution of this state of affairs, in our opinion, must begin with consideration of all judgmental disability categories, not just LD.

CONCLUDING REMARKS

We urge recognition of one reality driving the public schools' focus on planning for services: They are going to continue serving those students they perceive to be the most in need of help. At present, the way they are serving those most in need is by using the LD category as the vehicle for providing the help they perceive as needed. Doing so has resulted in increasingly less and less overlap between the population of children the schools serve as LD and that described in authoritative definitions and state education codes of LD, particularly in urban schools. We must acknowledge the existence of a large segment of *marginalized* students, many of whom encounter learning difficulties for reasons other than intrinsic, neurologically based causes. Moreover, the public schools recognize this large un-differentiated group of students with achievement deficits, use the LD category to justify serving them, and do so on the basis of absolute low achievement, not "discrepant low achievement." Those whose professional interests reside with the traditional LD student would be well advised to acknowledge the educational needs of the nontraditional LD, join forces with those who advocate for serving these "false positive" LD children, advocate for their being served, and engage in a discussion with advocates for these nontraditional LD students in order to secure appropriate services for them while recognizing and acknowledging differing etiologies and presumably differing educational needs. A failure to do so will, in our opinion, result in a continuation of the current state of affairs, clouding the parameters of the LD category, because many of these nontraditional LD children are among the "most difficult to teach" and will be a priority among public school teachers.

There exists an unhealthy schism between research and practice fueled, in part, by the discrepancy between SI and RI students with learning disabilities. Public school personnel perceive the research community as out-of-touch while the research community often views those in the public schools as uninformed. In truth, the research does not inform practice as the data base derives from a population of "LD" students only vaguely resembling SI "LD" students. An analogy to medicine may clarify our point. Research on the treatment of diabetes informs physicians treating diabetics because the researchers and the practitioners agree on who is diabetic. Researchers studying subjects with LD and the practitioners serving students with LD do not agree on who is LD and, as a result, research does not inform practice.

It is our probably naïve belief that efforts to revise definitions of judgmental disability categories should begin with "low achievement due to…" and then acknowledge that in our best clinical judgment the low achievement is apparent due to one of several factors. Among the factors currently confusing the LD category are (a) low general intelligence, (b) emotional/behavioral conditions, (c) specific processing difficulties, (d) environmental disadvantage, and/or (e) lack of opportunity to learn, particularly because of inadequate instruction. This position obviously favors increased refinement, or differentiation of, categories as opposed to "noncategorical categories." To that end we would argue that one-time assessments cannot make such distinctions as they tap static variables that are insensitive to such distinctions. Instead we would argue for multiple assessments of progress, using measures/scales sensitive to change in response to interventions implemented with integrity. In essence, progress monitoring of achievement after exposure to best-practice treatments intimately linked to the very achievement deficits prompting referral would provide the basis for eligibility decision making. Doing so would require revisions in eligibility criteria aligning the new assessments with the primary concerns of the public schools and tapping those achievement deficits targeted in the reading disability and math disability research. We believe that response to known treatments would begin to further clarify the varied etiologies of learning difficulties and create categories with greater validity (i.e., what one knows about cases falling into each of the categories specified above). In turn, cleaning up the "aptitudes" in the equation would enhance examination of aptitude × treatment interactions. One thing is certain; you will never escape the "hall of mirrors that extends to infinity" noted by Cronbach (1975, p. 119) as one studies interactions if the aptitudes are ill-defined. At present LD is ill-defined.

REFERENCES

Asher, S. R., & Coie, J. D. (Eds.) (1990). *Peer rejection in childhood.* New York: Cambridge University Press.

Bahr, M. W., Fuchs, D., Stecker, P. M., & Fuchs, L. S. (1991). Are teachers' perceptions of difficult-to-teach students racially biased? *School Psychology Review, 20,* 599–608.

Bateman, B. (1965). An educator's view of a diagnostic approach to learning disorders. In J. Hellmuth (Ed.), *Learning disorders* (Vol. 1, pp. 219–239). Seattle: Special Child Publications.

Bocian, K. M, Beebe, M. E., MacMillan, D. L., & Gresham, F. M. (1999). Competing paradigms in learning disabilities classification by schools and the variations in meaning of discrepant achievement. *Learning Disabilities Research and Practice, 14,* 1–14.

Case, R., Griffin, S., & Kelly, W. M. (1999). Socioeconomic gradients in mathematical ability and their responsiveness to intervention during early childhood. In D. P. Keating & C. Hertzman, (Eds.), *Developmental health and the wealth of nations: Social, biological, and educational dynamics* (pp. 125–149). New York: The Guilford Press.

Clausen, J. (1967). Mental deficiency: Development of a concept. *American Journal of Mental Deficiency, 71,* 727–745.

Colvin, R. L., & Helfand, D. (2000, December 13). Special education a failure on many fronts. *The Los Angeles Times* (www.latimes.com/news/state/reports/specialeduc/)

Council for Exceptional Children. (1998). *IDEA 1997: Let's make it work.* Reston, VA: Author.

Cronbach, L. J. (1975). Beyond the two disciplines of scientific psychology. *American Psychologist, 30,* 116–127.

Deno, E. (1970). Special education as developmental capital. *Exceptional Children, 37,* 229–237.

Doris, J. L. (1993). Defining learning disabilities: A history of the search for consensus. In G. R. Lyon, D. B. Gray, J. F. Kavanagh, & N. A. Krasnegor (Eds.), *Better understanding learning disabilities: New views from research and their implications for education and public policies* (pp. 97–115). Baltimore: Paul H. Brookes.

Duncan, B. B., Forness, S. R., & Hartsough, C. (1995). Students identified as seriously emotionally disturbed in day treatment: Cognitive, psychiatric, and special education characteristics. *Behavioral Disorders, 20,* 238–252.

Fletcher, J. M., Lyon, G. R., Barnes, M., Stuebing, K. K., Francis, D. J., Olson, R. K., & Shaywitz, S. E. (this volume). Classification of learning disabilities: An evidence-based evaluation.

Fletcher, J. M., & Foorman, B. R. (1994). Issues in definition and measurement of learning disabilities. In G. R. Lyon, D. B. Gray, J. F. Kavanagh, & N. A. Krasnegor (Eds.), *Better understanding learning disabilities: New views from research and their implications for education and public policies* (pp. 185–200). Baltimore: Paul H. Brookes.

Fletcher, J. M., Francis, D. J., Shaywitz, S. E., Lyon, G. R., Foorman, B. R., Stuebing, K. K., & Shaywitz, B. A. (1998). Intelligent testing with the discrepancy model for children with learning disabilities. *Learning Disabilities Research and Practice, 13,* 186–203.

Foorman, B. R., Francis, D. J., Winikates, D., Mehta, P., Schatschneider, C., & Fletcher, J. M. (1997). Early interventions for children with reading disabilities. *Scientific Studies of Reading, 1,* 255–276.

Fuchs, L. S. (1995, May). *Incorporating curriculum-based measurement into the eligibility decision-making process: A focus on treatment validity and student growth.* Paper presented at the Workshop on IQ Testing and Educational Decision Making, National Research Council, National Academy of Sciences, Washington, DC.

Fuchs, L. S., & Fuchs, D. (1998). Treatment validity: A unifying concept for reconceptualizing the identification of learning disabilities. *Learning Disabilities Research and Practice, 13,* 204–219.

Garber, H. L. (1988). *The Milwaukee Project: Preventing mental retardation in children at risk.* Washington, DC: American Association on Mental Retardation.

Gerber, M. M. (1999–2000). An appreciation of learning disabilities: The value of blue-green algae. *Exceptionality, 8,* 29–42.

Gerber, M., & Semmel, M. (1984). Teacher as imperfect test: Reconceptualizing the referral process. *Educational Psychologist, 19,* 137–146.

Gottlieb, J., Alter, M., Gottlieb, B. W., & Wishner, J. (1994). Special education in urban America: It's not justifiable for many. *The Journal of Special Education, 27,* 453–465.

Gresham, F. M., MacMillan, D. L., & Bocian, K. M. (1997). Teachers as "tests": Differential validity of teacher judgments in identifying students at-risk for learning difficulties. *School Psychology Review, 26,* 47–60.

Gresham, F. M., & Witt, J. C. (1997). Utility of intelligence tests for treatment planning, classification, and placement decision: Recent empirical finding and future directions. *School Psychology Quarterly, 12,* 249–267.

Griffin, S., & Case, R. (2000). Rethinking the primary school math curriculum: An approach based on cognitive science. http://oise.utoronto.ca/ICS/issues.htm

Grossman, H. (Ed.) (1973). *Manual on terminology and classification in mental retardation.* Washington, DC: American Association on Mental Deficiency.

Hallahan, D. P. (1992). Some thoughts on why the prevalence of learning disabilities has increased. *Journal of Learning Disabilities, 25,* 523–528.

Hallahan, D. P., Keller, C. E., & Ball, J. (1986). A comparison of prevalence rate variability from state to state for each of the categories of special education. *Remedial and Special Education, 7,* 8–14.

Haskins, R. (1986). Social and cultural factors in risk assessment and mild mental retardation. In D. C. Farran & J. D. McKinney (Eds.), *Risk in intellectual and psychosocial development.* (pp. 29–69). Orlando, FL.: Academic Press.

Heber, R. (1961). Modifications in the manual on terminology and classification in mental retardation. *American Journal of Mental Deficiency, 65,* 499–500.

Hinshaw, S. P. (1992). Externalizing behavior problems and academic underachievement in childhood and adolescence: Causal relationships and underlying mechanisms. *Psychological Bulletin, 111,* 127–155.

Kavale, K., & Forness, S. (1985). *The science of learning disabilities.* Boston: College Hill Press.

Kavanagh, J. F., & Truss, T. J., Jr. (Eds.). (1988). *Learning disabilities: Proceedings of the national conference.* Parkton, MD: York

Kellam, S. G., Ling, X., Merisca, R., Brown, C. H., & Ialongo, N. (1998). The effect of the level of aggression in the first grade classroom on the course and malleability of aggressive behavior into middle school. *Development and Psychopathology, 10,* 165–185.

Keogh, B. K. (1986). Learning disability: Diversity in search of order. In M. C. Wang, M. C. Reynolds, & H. J. Walberg (Eds.), *Handbook of special education research and practice* (pp. 221–251). Oxford England: Pergamon Press.

Keogh, B. K. (1994). A matrix of decision points in the measurement of learning disabilities. In G. R. Lyon (Ed.), *Frames of reference for the assessment of learning disabilities.* (pp. 15–26).

Keogh, B. K., & Speece, D. L. (1996). Learning disabilities within the context of schooling. In D. L. Speece & B. K. Keogh (Eds.), *Research on classroom ecologies: Implications for inclusion of children with learning disabilities* (pp. 1–14). Mahwah, NJ: Lawrence Erlbaum Associates.

MacMillan, D. L. (1993). Development of operational definitions in mental retardation: Similarities and differences with the field of learning disabilities. In G. R. Lyon, D. B. Gray, J. F. Kavanagh, & N. A. Krasnegor (Eds.), *Better understanding learning disabilities.* (pp. 117–152). Baltimore: Paul H. Brookes.

MacMillan, D. L., Gresham, F. M., & Bocian, K. M. (1998). Discrepancy between definitions of learning disabilities and school practices: An empirical investigation. *Journal of Learning Disabilities, 31,* 314–326.

MacMillan, D. L., Gresham, F. M., Bocian, K. M, & Siperstein, G. N. (1997). The role of assessment in qualifying students as eligible for special education: What is and what's supposed to be? *Focus on Exceptional Children, 30(2),* 1–18.

MacMillan, D. L., Gresham, F. M., Lopez, M. F., & Bocian, K. M. (1996). Comparison of students nominated for prereferral interventions by ethnicity and gender. *The Journal of Special Education, 30,* 133–151.

MacMillan, D. L., Gresham, F. M., Siperstein, G. N., & Bocian, K. M. (1996). The labyrinth of I.D.E.A.: School decisions on referred students with subaverage general intelligence. *American Journal on Mental Retardation, 101,* 161–174.

MacMillan, D. L., & Reschly, D. J. (1998). Overrepresentation of minority students: The case for greater specificity or reconsideration of variables examined. *The Journal of Special Education, 32,* 15–24.

MacMillan, D. L., Siperstein, G. N., & Gresham, F. M. (1996). Mild mental retardation: A challenge to its viability as a diagnostic category. *Exceptional Children, 62,* 356–371.

MacMillan, D.L., & Speece, D. (1999). Utility of current diagnostic categories for research and practice. In R. Gallimore, C. Bernheimer, D. MacMillan, D. Speece, & S. Vaughn (Eds.), *Developmental perspectives on children with high incidence disabilities* (pp. 111–133). Lawrence Erlbaum and Associates.

McLoughlin, J. A., & Netick, A. (1983). Defining learning disabilities: A new and cooperative direction. *Journal of Learning Disabilities, 16,* 21–23.

Mercer, C. D., Jordan, L., Allsopp, D. H., & Mercer, A. R. (1996). Learning disabilities definitions and criteria used by state education departments. *Learning Disability Quarterly, 19*, 217–232.

National Advisory Committee on Handicapped Children. (1968). *Special education for handicapped children: First annual report.* Washington, DC: U.S. Department of Health, Education, and Welfare.

Payette, K. A., & Clarizio, H. F. (1994). Discrepant team decisions: The effects of race, gender, achievement, and IQ on LD eligibility. *Psychology in the Schools, 31,* 40–48.

Prieto, A. G., & Zucker, S. H. (1981). Teacher perception of race as a factor in the placement of behaviorally disordered children. *Behavioral Disorders, 7,* 34–38.

Ramey, C. T., & Finkelstein, N. W. (1981). Psychosocial mental retardation: A biological and social coalescence. In M. J. Begab, H. C. Haywood, & H. L. Garber (Eds.), *Psychosocial influences in retarded performance* (Vol. I). Baltimore, MD: University Park Press.

Raymond, E. B. (2000). *Learners with mild disabilities.* Boston: Allyn and Bacon.

Richardson, S. A. (1981). Family characteristics associated with mild mental retardation. In M. J. Begab, H. C. Haywood, & H. L. Garber (Eds.), *Psychosocial influences in retarded performance: Vol. II. Strategies for improving competence* (pp. 29–43). Baltimore: University Park Press.

Robinson, H. B., & Robinson, N. M. (1965). *The mentally retarded child.* New York: McGraw-Hill.

Shaywitz, B. A., Fletcher, J. M., Holahan, J. M., & Shaywitz, S. E. (1992). Discrepancy compared to low achievement definitions of reading disability: Results from the Connecticut longitudinal study. *Journal of Learning Disabilities, 25,* 639–648.

Shaywitz, B. A., Holford, T. R., Holahan, J. M., Fletcher, J. M., Stuebing, K. K., Francis, D. J., & Shaywitz, S. E. (1995). A Matthew effect for IQ but not for reading: Results from a longitudinal study. *Reading Research Quarterly, 30,* 894–906.

Shaywitz, S. E., Shaywitz, B., Fletcher, J. M., & Escobar, M. D. (1990). Prevalence of reading disability in boys and girls: Results from the Connecticut Longitudinal Study. *Journal of the American Medical Association, 264,* 998–1002.

Shepard, L. (1983). The role of measurement in educational policy: Lessons from the identification of learning disabilities. *Educational Measurement: Issues and Practices,* Fall, 4–8.

Shepard, L. A., Smith, M. L., & Vojir, C. P. (1983). Characteristics of pupils identified as learning disabled. *American Educational Research Journal, 20,* 309–331.

Shinn, M. R., Tindal, G. A., & Spira, D. A. (1987). Special education referrals as an index of teacher tolerance: Are teachers imperfect tests? *Exceptional Children, 54,* 32–40.

Speece, D. L. (1993). Broadening the scope of classification research: Conceptual and ecological perspectives. In G. R. Lyon, D. B. Gray, J. F. Kavanaugh, & N. A. Krasnegor (Eds.), *Better understanding learning disabilities: New views from research and their implications for education and public policies* (pp. 57–72). Baltimore, MD: Brookes.

Speece, D. L., & Case, L. P. (submitted). Classification in context: An alternative approach to identifying early reading difficulty.

Swanson, H. L., Carson, C., & Saches-Lee, C. M. (1996). A selective synthesis of intervention research for students with learning disabilities. *School Psychology Review, 25,* 370–391.

Tobias, S., Zibrin, M., & Menell, C. (1983). Special education referrals: Failure to replicate student-teacher ethnicity interaction. *Journal of Educational Psychology, 75,* 705–707.

Torgesen, J. K. (this volume). Empirical and theoretical support for direct diagnosis of learning disabilities.

Torgesen, J. K., Alexander, A. W., Wagner, R. K., Rashotte, C. A., Voeller, K. K., & Conway, T. (2001). Intensive remedial instruction for children with severe reading disabilities: Immediate and long-term outcomes from two instructional approaches. *Journal of Learning Disabilities, 34,* 33–58, 78.

U. S. Department of Education. (1995). *Seventeenth annual report to Congress on the implementation of the Individuals With Disabilities Education Act.* Washington, DC: Author.

U.S. Department of Education. (1998). *Twentieth annual report to Congress on the implementation of the Individuals With Disabilities Education Act.* Washington, DC: Author.

U.S. Office of Education. (1977). Assistance to states for education for handicapped children: Procedures for evaluating specific learning disabilities. *Federal Register, 42,* 65082–65085.

Ysseldyke, J., & Algozzine, B. (1983). LD or not LD: That's not the question! *Journal of Learning Disabilities, 16,* 29–31.

Zigmond, N. (1993). Learning disabilities from an educational perspective. In G. R. Lyon, D. B. Gray, J. F. Kavanaugh, & N. A. Krasnegor (Eds.). *Better understanding learning disabilities: New views from research and their implications for education and public policies* (pp. 251–272). Baltimore, MD: Paul H. Brookes Publishing Co.

Zucker, S. H., & Prieto, A. G. (1977). Ethnicity and teacher bias in educational decisions. *Instructional Psychology, 4,* 2–5.

Zucker, S. H., Prieto, A. G., & Rutherford, R. B. (1979). Racial determinants of teachers' perceptions of placement of the educable mentally retarded. *Exceptional Child Education Resources, 11,* 1.

ENDNOTE

[1] We recognize that another step exists, that of prereferral intervention. In the past, referral led to formal assessment; however, current practices typically involve an intermediate step in the process—prereferral intervention. This step entails a variety of modifications designed to keep the student in general education, and only after a child fails to respond to the prereferral intervention is he or she referred for formal assessment to establish eligibility. However, our experience in the schools suggests that in some schools this step is pro forma, and the child will almost inevitably be referred for formal assessment. Gottlieb et al. (1994) reported this to be the case in large urban districts. In other school districts a legitimate effort is made to maintain the child in general education. We decided to exclude this step because we felt it would cloud the discussion. We note the extent to which clinical judgment enters into decisions regarding what intervention will be tried, where and for what period it will be implemented, and judgments about its perceived effects.

ACKNOWLEDGMENTS

The authors wish to thank Martha Brooks, Michael Gerber, Russell Gersten, and Daniel Reschly for their thoughtful reviews of the original version of this paper and suggestions for modifications.

A LOOK AT CURRENT PRACTICE

Martha Brooks, Delaware Department of Education

Doctors Donald MacMillan and Gary Siperstein have prepared a thoughtful discussion of the differences between *school-identified* (SI) children with learning disability (LD) and *research-identified* (RI) children with LD. They provide a review of the rationales that schools have used, which is best summed up by the statement: "We urge recognition of one reality driving the public schools' focus on planning for services: they are going to continue to serve those students they perceive to be the most in need of help." The understanding of this basic reality of public schools by researchers, parents, advocates, and others will help to clarify and facilitate the discussion about how best to improve public school services for all children.

A number of points made in this paper help to clarify the reality of current practice and provide rational explanations for these practices in the nation's public schools. The first section of this response highlights several points that have particular relevance to the discussion this series of white papers is designed to stimulate.

DECIDING WHICH CHILDREN TO SERVE

The first issue discussed is the critical role of the teacher referral as the initial step in the eligibility process. The authors are correct in their assumptions about the subjectivity of teacher referrals. Children are referred because teachers do not feel the children are meeting the expectations of the "norm" of their class and/or school. Teachers are concerned they, themselves, are not meeting the needs of the child, and the further the child is from the "norm" of the class, the more likely a referral will be made. Teachers care about the students they teach and if the only way they feel they can get additional help for a child who is struggling is to refer them to "special education," then that is what most will do.

A second initial referral issue that the authors discuss is the failure to refer children who may actually have a "learning disability" but who have managed to stay within the performance range of their peer group. This "false negative" group is a concern to researchers as well as advocates and educators because these children do have a disability and yet, because they are able to keep up, are not identified for special education services. Increasingly, these young people are being identified under Section 504 of the Rehabilitation Act and have accommodation plans. They meet the first criteria for eligibility under the Individuals With Disabilities Education Act (IDEA)—that is, they have a disability. They do not meet the second criteria of requiring special education services in order to make meaningful progress in their educational program. This is one of the enduring debates in education concerning who are the children who require "special education services."

The second stage in the eligibility process is assessment. For access to the LD category, this raises issues related to the use of discrepancy between achievement and aptitude. This issue is well discussed in this and other articles in this series. From a practitioner's perspective, the use of the discrepancy as a basis for LD determination is a contentious one, and school psychologists are divided on the role it should play, if any. I have yet to find a psychologist who cannot find a discrepancy somewhere if he or she really needs to, and, for the most part, recommendations for eligibility center on whether or not the student will benefit from services that eligibility will make available to them.

The authors do not discuss early childhood issues related to eligibility as a student with LD, but this is a component of the issue that must be addressed. The discrepancy model makes it difficult to qualify young children because it is limited to the language domain. Everything we know about early childhood indicates we should be ensuring access to high-quality programs for all children and providing more intensive services to any child experiencing a delay in a major life-skills area. Now that the developmental delay category is available under IDEA, it may be appropriate to eliminate the "judgmental categories" including LD for young children up to ages 7 or 8.

Another critical assessment issue that this article helped to clarify is the significance of the change in the American Association of Mental Deficiency definition for mental retardation, which is the basis for eligibility under the mental disability category in most states. When the eligibility criterion was lowered in 1973 to an IQ of 70, a significant population of children was no longer eligible for special education, but their need for supports and services had not gone away. Again, school personnel make decisions based on what they think will help the child, and the expanded use of the LD classification was one way to make sure these children continued to receive special education services.

Many children in this population live in poverty and historically have not had strong advocates. The authors do an excellent job of discussing the impact the current decision-making process has on children living in poverty and/or attending poor urban schools. They also confront the issue of disproportionality of minorities in special education in terms of both the poverty link and racial and cultural bias. Although this has long been an issue in the mild mental retardation classification, it is increasingly one in the LD category. Again, I do not need to add to what is a very thoughtful analysis, but I do want to emphasize the importance of this issue, and the need to keep it in the forefront of our discussion and any proposed changes.

A final background issue is an obvious one, but one we tend to overlook in terms of importance in these discussions. In our society today it is "OK" to be identified as having an LD. It is a label that parents, teachers, and society at large do not object to and it opens the door to services, including accommodations and modifications, that have increased importance in today's high-stakes world. It also keeps children in the general education curriculum, although many children get stuck at the elementary levels of that curriculum. The passage of the IDEA amendments of 1997 with the added focus on access to the general education curriculum is helping to move beyond that limitation, but we are not there yet. As the authors state, eligibility determination requires identification under one of the IDEA categories, but beyond that it has little meaning in terms of developing and implementing the Individualized Education Program (IEP). Consequently, we have a very heterogeneous group of children being identified by schools as LD and yet we are imposing more of an RI expectation on what they should be able to accomplish with the appropriate supports and services.

All states are now involved in standards-based school reform initiatives. Most states use language that talks about *all* children, and President Bush's national agenda for education is entitled *No Child Left Behind*. Accountability is implicit in the reform efforts at both the national and state levels, and increasingly we are seeing high stakes for students, educators, and schools. The impact of these activities on the current discussion of how we determine eligibility for children under the LD category is central. We may already be seeing an increase in referrals to special education, as high stakes become reality in more schools and districts. If you go back to the underlying theme in this article, that schools are already identifying students who need help the most under the LD category, you can begin to see that unless we develop ways to ensure supports and services for all children who need them in order to be effective learners, we will continue to serve those most in need within special education. With the continued focus on high standards and accountability for all students, the numbers of children being referred for special education will continue to grow.

A PROPOSED MODEL

This section of the paper comments on the model briefly proposed by the authors and offers some suggestions for further discussion. The authors conclude their report with a recommendation that the definition be changed so that children are identified with "low achievement due to" one of the following factors:

A. low general intelligence
B. emotional/behavioral conditions
C. specific processing difficulties
D. environmental disadvantage, or
E. lack of opportunity to learn, particularly because of inadequate instruction."

They further advocate for "...progress monitoring of achievement after exposure to best-practice treatments intimately linked to the very achievement deficits prompting referral...." (MacMillan et al., this volume) They feel that this new eligibility process would address the needs of public schools, while helping to clarify the etiologies of learning difficulties.

IEP team members including parents are not going to be any more accepting of the labels of "low general intelligence" or "environmental disadvantage" than they are of mental retardation or emotional disturbance. We need to ask ourselves if we can meet the needs of children in public schools and those of researchers wishing to study specific processing difficulties within the same eligibility process. Do we even want to? Although we understand and appreciate the value of research in terms of improving education for children with disabilities, we may be better served by adding some additional research dollars to provide assessment at the discrimination level researchers need, and allow assessment for access to services to be driven by the needs of the child and the instructional process. We do have other forms of accountability within IDEA and within state accountability legislation. Focusing our efforts on improved results for all children may be a better investment of our assessment energies.

In Delaware we are attempting to institute a process that is based on instructional problem-solving models and would lead eventually to the identification of those students most in need of special education supports and services. Because it is a model operating in the context of the general education system, it would ensure that any (and every) child who was not being a successful learner received the help he or she needed. The model currently being piloted is based on the Maryland Instructional Support Teams (ISTs) and is very similar to those found in Pennsylvania and Iowa. The "formative assessment" process is designed to rely on an instructional problem-solving team at the building level that would look at every child who is not performing at grade level. Interventions are planned with the child's teacher and are based on research-based best practice. Plans are implemented with integrity, and data are gathered on an ongoing basis to measure the effectiveness of the intervention strategies. This curriculum-based assessment and intervention process continues until the right combination of services and supports is found for the individual child. If the level required for the child to be successful reaches the level of special education services, then the child would move into the formal referral process and be found eligible for special education services.

As this is a needs-based system, finances could be a major driver in the actual process of identifying which children require special education supports and services. If we begin with the general education system with no accommodations and/or extra services and supports and then move to accommodations, then finally extra services and supports, the financial resources can be tied to the level of need of the child—that is, how much help does the child need in order to be an effective learner? For example, if a school has a number of children with similar needs (i.e., as in the high-poverty schools discussed in the MacMillan paper), then these more intensive levels of services may be available within general education. This would mean that teacher expertise and funding levels sufficient to ensure small instructional groupings were available. As the authors point out, this is seldom the case, but there are enough good examples of highly successful high-poverty schools to know that it is possible. This model can also be expanded to early care and education programs with a minimum of labeling.

The IST/problem-solving model is not that different from what the authors describe as the "titration of intensity of treatments in decision making." The IST process is designed to drive and improve instruction as well as get supports to children as early as possible, with the hope of preventing the added problems that accumulate when children have to fail before they receive help. The impact of implementing this change in our schools is significant. Several issues are relevant to the larger discussion these papers are designed to generate.

First, the involvement of parents and families in this process must be a reality. Many parents and advocates view this prolonged "prereferral process" as a delaying tactic. However, if they are part of the problem-solving process right from the beginning, they will recognize that the needs of their children are being addressed, and the process will not stop until the right supports and services are identified. We also need to clarify the role of the parent's procedural safeguards in the process.

General education is not accustomed to formally involving parents as partners in their child's education as special education does through the IEP process. Educators are often skeptical of the special education level of parent involvement, because they have all heard the stories of the "one parent" that tied up the system. They are also very concerned about the "paperwork" and we would need to make sure that any paperwork is relevant to the instructional and/or problem-solving process.

In addition, a model such as this has significant ramifications for professional development and the roles of teachers and specialists in our schools. It is a collaborative model that requires time. It requires ready access to specialists like educational diagnosticians, reading specialists, speech and language pathologists, school psychologists, and so on. Currently these people dedicate most of their time to children in the special education system and/or in the referral process. This is the expertise that must be available to the classroom teachers if this model is to be effective.

Finally, we need to look at different ways of addressing the funding issues, including increased flexibility in using funds currently targeted to special education. One would hope for a decrease in the number of children who eventually require more intensive special education services, and that this approach would help to stem the increasing numbers of children being referred to special education. However, the need for collaborative problem-solving teams at the building level is time- and staff-intensive, and additional resources may be needed.

If a model such as this is implemented, children who meet the RI definition of LD will be found. Their learning needs will be addressed and those needing a level of supports and services that may include accommodations and/or special education will be identified. However, *all* of the other students who need help in order to access their education and be effective learners will also receive it.

A META-RESEARCH COMMENTARY ON MACMILLAN AND SIPERSTEIN'S "LEARNING DISABILITIES AS OPERATIONALLY DEFINED BY SCHOOLS"

Michael M. Gerber, University of California Santa Barbara

The paper by MacMillan and Siperstein (this volume) is an excellent, culminating contribution to a line of scholarship initiated by the senior author and his colleagues more than two decades ago. In 1980, MacMillan, Meyers, and Morrison wrote what now must be considered a modern classic in the history of special education scholarship. In highly simplified reduction, that paper argued cogently and forcefully why school-identified samples of students with mild disabilities should be distrusted for purposes of research.[1] Viewed from the standpoint of the research community, awakening to the new, policy-dominated era of special education, MacMillan et al.'s paper was a serious warning of the bumpy road ahead. I direct my comments first to MacMillan and Siperstein's main points. Then I address some meta-research considerations to which MacMillan and Siperstein have only alluded. Finally, I discuss some theoretical ideas about the nature of learning disabilities (LDs) and its identification in schools that have been passed over in this and most other discussions of the issue.

THE MAIN POINTS

MacMillan and Siperstein's main line of argument commences with the distinction between research-identified (RI) and school-identified (SI) samples of students with LD.

- Evidence exists to show that SI samples overlap with but are not identical to RI samples for reasons that can be found in the operation of schools.
- Much of our research base, particularly regarding effective intervention and classroom integration, may not apply.
- SI students with LD represent a broad response by schools to students who experience significant learning problems.

- Membership in SI LD is influenced by failure of schools to identify—or have any motivation to identify—students with mild mental retardation.
- Policy should permit a process of "titration" of "intensity of treatment."

META-RESEARCH COMMENTARY

While I find little to disagree with in this exposition, it represents a view of decision making in schools from some distance; that is, through no fault of the authors, there are few extant data that serve to explain, rather than describe, how people in schools actually decide to allocate scarce resources for all types of specialized instruction. It is insufficient to view this process as if the logic for all teacher cognition, choice, problem solving, planning, and decision making is perfectly captured within the context of behaviors related to the Individuals With Disabilities Education Act (IDEA), or that IDEA-related decisions reflect some special, compartmentalized type of decision making fundamentally different from all other instances. This is not likely. In fact, it is highly unlikely that working teachers think very much about IDEA and its specific mandates at all.

In the years that followed the paper by MacMillan et al. (1980), Ysseldyke and his colleagues at the University of Minnesota's Institute for Research on Learning Disabilities unleashed a torrent of studies that further raised the level of alarm. In sum, the Minnesota researchers showed that special education in the schools, specifically regarding LD, bore only passing resemblance to special education as envisioned in the political and professional compromises that constituted federal policy.

More cries of alarm, too many to cite here, followed. It was a cottage research industry of the 1980s to "discover" that special education in the flesh didn't look as good as in its policy advertisements. For anyone who had read Wetherly and Lipsky's (1977) tutorial on how and why policy looks different at street level from what is suggested by the language of legislation, the barrage of criticism leveled at schools and all who occupy them now seems a little over the top. In retrospect, it was analogous to Captain Renault picking up his winnings at Rick's Café Americain while declaring that he was "shocked, shocked to learn that gambling is going on here!"

If special education policy faced serious problems in those years, special education *researchers* faced a legitimate crisis. What were they to make of the empirical discrepancy between the operation of schools and the high purpose and intent of policy? At least three explanations were offered for what was deemed almost universally as "misidentification" of students with LD. One possibility, a study reported in the *Fifth Annual Report to Congress* (Office of Special Education Programs, 1982) suggested, was that teachers, despite seven years of intensive work to inform practice, still didn't understand what students with LD looked like. A second suggestion, no less denigrating of their intelligence and professionalism, was that perhaps the technical aspects of LD identification simply were beyond the typical teacher. A third, darker conjecture was that teachers might be consciously undermining the intent of policy by purposely ignoring the mandated definitions and criteria.

RESEARCH STRATEGIES

Given the necessity of locating students with LD for research purposes despite what apparently were serious inadequacies in school practice, what strategies could researchers adopt? At least four possibilities seemed to evolve.

One might be characterized as the "damn the torpedos, full speed ahead" approach, essentially ignoring the evidence that practice was at best a fraternal, not identical, twin to policy. This approach represents a radical, if ingenuous, belief that by itself the accumulation of data must ultimately yield truth.

A second approach to the crisis in research on LD was to continue to harangue the schools. "If only they'd do it right, we could get on with the business of generating new knowledge" seemed to be the argument. Research following this approach tried to eliminate, avoid, or disregard the unexplained variance associated with the unhappy fact that special education occurred in the context of schooling. This is like finding and documenting archeological artifacts in excruciating detail with no reference to the geographical location, geology, or spatial organization of the hole from which they are extracted.

Those whose doubts about LD had been raised to a fever by an onslaught of research that used school-based data to criticize fundamental constructs raised a third approach. This approach is interesting because it seems to be only an intellectual half-step away from considering that maybe schools and LD are conceptually bound in some way to one another. However, rather than take seriously the idea that half the available information is in the child and half is in the formally organized systems of education themselves, the "doubters" converted into general education reformers and advocated furiously for inclusion of students with disabilities, whoever they were regardless of circumstance. That is, they acknowledged the hard, material reality of schools, but slipped into believing that disabilities were a mirage.

The fourth approach, still barely explored, sees a harder problem then those we thought we faced. Schools and students with LD are equally real, but are realized only in the transaction that dynamically occurs between them. This approach is analogous to that argued by Sameroff (e.g., Sameroff & Chandler, 1975) with respect to child development. In Sameroff's formulation, child development (and maldevelopment) does not occur as a simple unfolding of behavioral propensities that emanate from univariate (or even multivariate) perinatal factors. Instead, children's behavior is resisted or facilitated by a local caregiving environment in ways that lead to the mutual modification of both child and environment.

Research on LD that follows this approach similarly would treat schools—an extension of the ecology of development—and children with disabilities as mutually determining and mutually modifying. That is, the students with LD express their differential response to instructional arrangements differently at age 9, compared to, say, age 5 or age 13. The current interest in identifying these children earlier for prevention raises questions precisely because the specific behaviors typically used to identify them in late primary and early intermediate grades are not yet available for observation in preschool or early primary grades. Similarly, the classroom and school environments are reshaped by their ongoing encounter with such children at age 5, 9, 13, and so on. That is, teachers' choices and decisions are locally and differentially sensitive across teachers, grade levels, and schools to the presenting characteristics of students with LD. On the other hand, Sameroff points out (Sameroff, 2001) the disturbing fact that caregiving environments for children at high risk for disabilities tend to be very stable over time. That is, part of the cumulating risk experienced by some children is a direct result of the failure of local environments to adapt supportively to individual differences. Again, classrooms and schools can be seen as having analogous impact on students whose individual differences emerge eventually as LD. It is, in fact, special education that intends to provide and improve the support potential of the extant school environment.

In quantitative terms, this characterization suggests a recursive system of nonlinear equations that must be solved simultaneously. Conceptually, this approach has been difficult for special education researchers to embrace, partly because it implies methods that are less well known, or perhaps nonexistent, but also because it doesn't yield in any simple way to an experimentalist paradigm. Also, as a field, we know more about how variations in students predict outcomes than how variations in the organized effort that provides them education—i.e., schools—produce variations in students.

NEED FOR TOLERANCE

It is to this fourth approach that I direct the remainder of my comments on the paper by MacMillan and Siperstein (this volume).

In a series of theoretical papers beginning in 1979 (Gerber, 1988; Gerber & Kauffman, 1979; Gerber & Semmel, 1984, 1985), I have tried to reconceptualize the problem of student identification in a way that would not only take into account classrooms and schools as sources of variation, but also take seriously the idea that learning disabilities are jointly produced by individual differences in students as well as the school environments in which they are schooled. In pursuing these ideas, I have drawn from behavioral sciences other than psychology, particularly economics, as a source of potential insight into the problem of LD. The policy context of special education for students with LD made such an approach reasonable and there is a significant body of theory (e.g., Simon, 1997) in economics suitable for addressing many relevant behaviors (e.g., choices, decisions) of school personnel in their organizational (i.e., classroom and school) contexts.

One example of a theoretical analysis of these problems is based on pioneer work conducted by Brown and Saks (1978). Reconceptualizing teacher behavior in organizational (i.e., economic) terms, Gerber and Semmel (1985) proposed that a key to understanding referral and reintegration (inclusion) decisions was to realize that teachers made choices, under significant resource constraints and with imperfect information, about how to allocate their effort across all the students in their class. Given significant individual differences among children and given resource constraints, teachers could neither avoid this choice nor nullify resource scarcity by an act of will. The choice could be a conscious decision to weigh decisions toward self or externally imposed goal states, such as equality of outcomes, high mean achievement, opportunity for the most capable students, remediation of the slowest, inclusion of students with disabilities, and so on. However, the choice could simply be the cumulative, dynamical consequence of a thousand moment-to-moment value-judged, contingent, or even impulsive decisions. Gerber and Semmel (1985) argued that these circumstances arose as a function of the structure of classroom teaching, and only as an indirect consequence of the characteristics of individuals.

The range of individual differences in a classroom that any given teacher could address with roughly equivalent effect was dubbed the "tolerance" by Gerber and Semmel. The term was used in its engineering sense of a permissible boundary of error around a measurement. Students who fell within the tolerance represent the degree of variation of students that teachers perceive as functionally similar, tolerably alike. The teacher's permanent conundrum, therefore, is how to increase his or her tolerance for any given class. However, with given talents, knowledge, motivation, and skills, the tolerance is relatively inelastic. One way to cope, therefore, is to disinvest in students who present unusual instructional problems. Referral is one way but not the only way to accomplish this end. Conversely, successful inclusion of difficult-to-teach students requires additional resources—hence the increase in instructional aides assigned and managed by special education teachers in inclusion programs. While this theoretical formulation awaits further empirical verification, it seems to fit the observed facts as we know them, including the discrepancy between MacMillan and Siperstein's RI and SI.

LESSONS WE SHOULD HAVE LEARNED

Our first lesson: Schools stand unavoidably between clinical intent and child outcome. Schools are, for all intents and purposes, the treatment milieu. If you want to compose and implement "treatment" interventions for children with disabilities, these must be realized through the complex organizational medium of public schooling.

Special education takes place in schools. This is more than a truism. Schools are not merely the locus of special education; they are also the functional creators of special education. The second lesson, therefore, has been that neither policy nor law can reliably command outcomes (Wetherly & Lipsky, 1977) from complex, hierarchical, and deeply embedded social arrangements. For special education, policy and law establish public values and procedural parameters that hopefully channel the relevant behaviors of parents and professionals alike toward some desirable array of outcomes for children with disabilities. But, the channel is variably wide and deep, and this fact both assaults and burdens researchers who wish it were otherwise.

This arrangement gives the collection of events and actions that constitute special education—the decisions made, the resources employed, the effort organized, the achievement or development attained—an uncomfortably contingent and consensual quality for those trained in the philosophy of experimental science. To these scientists, such phenomena, those for which point prediction must yield to error modeling, are often set aside as too messy, too ambiguous, or simply too complex. For these colleagues, special education phenomena divide neatly into either those clearly seen objects that the lock-picks of experimental psychology can fruitfully disassemble or "just" policy, that sullied and stained collection of uncontrolled and uncontrollable variables that stretch out to the edge of the known world. Or, conversely, researchers blithely proceed as if the stringent conditions for true experiment exist after all, and that our senses are simply mistaken in perceiving a layered, dynamical, and multivariate universe. In the thousands of studies of students with LD that have been conducted or summarized in meta-analyses, how many employ random selection of students from the true, rather than the local, population? Our intuition wants to persuade us that each of these samples are tolerably alike and related to the actual, still unknown population.

That actual, as opposed to theoretical, special education should display this unkempt, stochastic quality is regrettable to many researchers, who often complain in print as if there is something here to be fixed before "science" can occur, as if phenomena that are not experimentally tractable must necessarily belong to some other realm than science. Of course, it is precisely on these issues that special education can be seen to emerge as a *nonexperimental* social science, just like economics, political science, anthropology, or sociology. Not that these sciences cannot be informed by experiment; they can and are. But neither are they fatally constrained from testing theory against empirical observation, nor are they prohibited from deriving tentative conclusions and proposing solutions to problems because the variables at play in the social world cannot be cleanly manipulated.

It is not that either of these responses—ignore complexity or pretend it doesn't matter—is somehow, in some unredeemable sense, wrong. However, to move forward, we will need to confess as well that neither response ultimately serves the interests of science or of students with disabilities particularly well. More and better are necessary. Invention and innovation and imagination are now required more than ever before.

WHERE WE (CONTINUE TO) GO WRONG

When educational and clinical psychologists study students with LD in situ—that is, embedded in complex organizational environments, such as schools—it should surprise no one that they gain little traction and can offer few demonstrably effective remedies. While we steadfastly adhere to empiricism, our evaluation of units of analysis larger than students or student-teacher dyads is often embarrassingly dependent on unexamined assumptions about how policy, teachers, and schools work. Formulating interventions above the level of student, they rely on experience, consensus, intuition, speculation, conjecture, and "common sense." Interventions at the level of classroom, school, district, state, and nation are approached with a strident but decidedly decontextualized and atheoretical pragmatism. This brute-force empiricism yields relationships among measures, but tends to reify rather than explore the phenomena that lie beneath the measures. We work hard to demonstrate internal validity and virtually ignore external validity. We know the main effects, but not the nature of the contextual interactions. How does any research we have accumulated really inform policy?

We just do not understand how instructional variables rise and fall and transact in the natural rhythms of classroom and school life. In fact, our knowledge about cognition in children with LD is far better and more extensive than our knowledge about the organization, content, and influences on cognition of teachers. Beyond this unfortunate impoverishment of knowledge, we also have little understanding of how teachers as a coordinated *body*, as a staff of a school, behave with respect to children with LD. This is not a trivial matter.

One consequence of our confusion about the embeddedness of phenomena such as identification of students with LD is that we have little understanding of how to scale and sustain at scale simple experimental effects over long stretches of time. The data we do have on changing teachers' behaviors suffer from a host of limitations: selection bias, inadequate specification of critical attributes, lack of controls, and most of all, little knowledge of the effects of school organization on individual teacher's behaviors. Ultimately, if we care about the success of policies for identification of students with LD (or any other special education policy for that matter), we must be concerned about how whole schools of teachers act. It is, after all, the aggregate and serial effects of teachers' decisions and resultant behaviors in an entire school that produce outcomes for students—both learning disabled and non-learning disabled. Even if we think we have a handle on how to retrain or motivate individual teachers, is it not the aggregate and additive effects that policy must address? Otherwise, is it reasonable that we should formulate and implement policies that aim at school change, one teacher at a time?

THE REAL PROBLEM

We are confused in our purposes and studying the wrong variables. Are we trying to procure from schools better research samples, or are we trying to improve the implementation of policies that will result in better outcomes for students? If the former, then our interest should be in finding ways for SI samples to better approximate RI samples. If the latter, though, our interest should be focused on studying instrumental variables that policy can manipulate and that hold some promise of positively influencing outcomes. Furthermore, if our intent is to improve outcomes though improvement of policy, we are not required to abandon the goal of improving conformity of school with RI samples of students with LD as long as there is some compelling reason to assert such a goal.

Recently, there has been a general throwing up of the hands while declaring that, since schools won't cooperate and can't simply be commanded in using research criteria, national policy should abandon LD as an eligibility category altogether. These proposals are defeatist, unethical, and illogical. If researchers believe they have sufficient evidence to support the construct of a learning disability, why would we want schools to cease trying to identify and serve students with LD? The fact that teachers in schools also prefer to identify learning needs defined more broadly, more variably, and for reasons not always well understood, does not make continued efforts to identify students with LD any less important. It does mean, however, that the policy, as codified in IDEA, may be wrong.

Eligibility standards in IDEA represent attempts to accomplish too many policy goals simultaneously, only one of which is a correct matching of educational and related resources to categories of disabilities. Clearly, another not-always-compatible goal in current eligibility standards is to control costs. That is, in the legislative history of IDEA's predecessor, Education for all Handicapped Children Act (EHA), Congress clearly wanted to know how many students with disabilities they could expect schools to identify so that resources attached to the new national policy would match the projected need.

However, there is ample evidence that even in 1975, professional estimates of incidence and prevalence not only varied but varied significantly from what Congress was willing to spend. Professional opinion about the prevalence of severe emotional disturbance was many times the expectation (i.e., 2%) ultimately established by the legislation. Testimony about prevalence of LD varied between 1% and 30%; no compelling scientific evidence then (or now) unequivocally established a true prevalence of 1%. It should not be forgotten as well that Congress never funded EHA (or IDEA) at a level anywhere close to the original 40% proposal. The point is, long before schools began to wrestle with discrepancies between federal definitions and local realities, eligibility criteria bore no clear relationship to either science or real, less differentiated need.

REFERENCES

Brown, B., & Saks, D. H. (1978). *An economic perspective on classroom reading instruction* (Research series No. 22). Institute for Research on Teaching, Michigan State University, East Lansing, MI.

Gerber, M. M. (1988). Tolerance and technology of instruction: Implications of the NAS Report for special Education. *Exceptional Children, 54,* 309–314.

Gerber, M. M., & Kauffman, J. M. (1979). Production functions in special education: Microanalysis and behavioral technology. *Journal of Special Education Technology, 3,* 25–28.

Gerber, M. M., & Semmel, M. I. (1984). Teacher as imperfect test: Reconceptualizing the referral process. *Educational Psychologist, 19,* 1–12.

Gerber, M. M., & Semmel, M. I. (1985). The microeconomics of referral and reintegration: A paradigm for evaluation of special education. *Studies in Educational Evaluation, 11,* 13–29.

MacMillan, D. L., Meyers, C. E., & Morrison, G. M. (1980). System-identification of mildly mentally retarded children: Implications for interpreting and conducting research. *American Journal of Mental Deficiency, 85,* 108–115.

MacMillan, D. L., & Siperstein, G. N. (this volume). Learning disabilities as operationally defined by schools.

Norman, C. A., Jr., & Zigmond, N. (1980). Characteristics of children labeled and served as learning disabled in school systems affiliated with child service demonstration centers. *Journal of Learning Disabilities; 13,* 542–547.

Office of Special Education Programs (OSEP). (1982). *Fifth Annual Report to Congress.* Washington, DC: U.S. Government Printing Office.

Sameroff, A. (2001). *Risk and resilience from infancy to adolescence: Is it better to change the child or the context?* Presentation at the OSEP Research Project Directors' Meeting, Washington, DC.

Sameroff, A. J., & Chandler, M. J. (1975). Reproductive risk and the continuum of caretaking casualty. In F. D. Horowitz, M. Hetherington, S. Scarr-Salapatek, & E. G. Siegel (Eds.), *Review of Child Development Research* (Vol. 4). Chicago: University of Chicago Press.

Shapiro, J. Z. (1984). On the application of econometric methodology to educational research: a meta-theoretical analysis. *Educational Researcher, 13,* 12–19.

Shinn, M. R., Tindal, G A., & Spira, D. A. (1987). Special education referrals as an index of teacher tolerance: Are teachers imperfect tests? *Exceptional Children, 54,* 32–40.

Simon, H. (1997). *Models of bounded rationality* (Vol. 3). Cambridge, MA: MIT Press.

Wetherly, R., & Lipsky, M. (1977). Street-level bureaucrats and institutional innovation: Implementing special education reform. *Harvard Educational Review, 47,* 171–197.

ENDNOTE

[1] To be sure, MacMillan and his colleagues were not alone in recognizing discrepancy between "scientific" characterizations of learning disabilities and characteristics observed in applied settings (see Norman & Zigmond, 1980). However, MacMillan et al. (1980) were the first to examine and conjecture about why and how school identifications might systematically differ from researchers' expectations.

LEVELING THE PLAYING FIELD: COMMENTARY ON "LEARNING DISABILITIES AS OPERATIONALLY DEFINED BY SCHOOLS"

Russell Gersten, ERI & University of Oregon

MacMillan and Siperstein provide a compelling analysis of how and why schools identify students as learning disabled, and they compare this to the differences in the manner in which researchers identify learning disability (LD). The richness of their perspective, which incorporates historical trends in the fields of learning disabilities and mental retardation, helps us understand how the seemingly imprecise definition of LD used by the schools evolved and developed and how it differs from researchers' definition of LD, and offers a suggestion for resolving this incongruity. Throughout the text, the authors adopt a dispassionate yet thoughtful tone as they discuss the complexities, confounds, and discrepancies of the diagnosis and education of students with LD faced by educators and researchers today.

This commentary will address the two most tantalizing and critical points made by the authors:

1. Should the field of special education move to redefine LD as the "inability to respond to quality early intervention" in reading, as many are currently arguing?
2. How do teachers effectively teach students who not only possess serious reading disabilities but also have low IQ scores (i.e., students who should definitely not be classified as LD since they demonstrate no discrepancy between IQ and achievement), yet definitely need intensive support?

I will argue that in discussing the first issue, we need to proceed with deliberate caution, waiting until we truly know what we are doing before rapidly "scaling up." Regarding the latter issue, which MacMillan and Siperstein refer to as providing services to learners "disenfranchised" by the Grossman (1973) redefinition of mental retardation, we urge that researchers and educators pay serious attention.

THE PSEUDO-OBJECTIVE PROCESS OF IDENTIFICATION AND REFERRAL FOR SERVICES

In diagnosing children with LD, according to MacMillan and Siperstein, "…schools follow the letter of the law, albeit somewhat reluctantly at times…" (this volume). The authors artfully convey how the process of identification and referral of a student for special education services is essentially subjective and idiosyncratic, and often merely a formalization of a classroom teacher's sense that a given child needs serious help. Research suggests that referrals for LD virtually always stem from a teacher's concern regarding low academic performance or externalizing behaviors by a student. "Any understanding of the population of SI [school-identified] LD students begins with a consideration of those students that general education teachers consider 'difficult to teach…'"(this volume). They cite Zigmond (1993) who concluded, "…referral is a signal that the teacher has reached the limits of his or her tolerance…is no longer optimistic about his or her capacity to deal effectively with a particular student in the context of the larger group, and no longer perceives that the student is teachable [by that particular teacher]" (pp. 262–263).

Thus, the initiation of the referral process is based on teachers' expected level of achievement and sense of grade-level norms. This identification can result from a somewhat subjective or idiosyncratic sense of local norms dependent on the abilities of the peers in the classroom, as well as the values and skills embraced and possessed by the teacher.

MacMillan and Siperstein elegantly describe the pseudo-scientific aspects of the process, which continues through assessment and into the placement committee's final round of decision making. While assessment tools themselves are "objective" measures, the authors suggest that in some cases, subjectivity reenters this scenario when school psychologists select a particular IQ or achievement test that would be more likely to qualify a student for services. The placement committee decision weighs various factors above and beyond the IQ and achievement test scores, including parental preferences and teacher judgment. Practical considerations such as availability of classes, level of parental support, and caseload size also play into the decision-making process. Last, the concept of a discrepancy between IQ and actual achievement rarely enters into the picture. MacMillan and Siperstein affirm that the balance of objective (i.e., standardized tests) and subjective appraisals leads, ultimately, to what must be called a subjective—or pseudo-scientific—process.

TOWARD THE FUTURE: INSTRUCTIONAL STRATEGIES FOR THE DISENFRANCHISED

MacMillan and Siperstein foreshadow an important theme in their early discussion of how and why teachers consider special education referral. They introduce the idea of teachers' efficacy and teachers' capability to teach low performing students as a critical facet in the identification process. In this manner, they raise the relevance of appropriate, high-quality instructional strategies for disenfranchised learners.

And what of the quality and efficacy of teacher instruction? MacMillan and Siperstein (this volume) note this dilemma: ". . .two hypothetical children with identical reading deficits enrolled in different districts are not equally at risk for being referred by their classroom teacher. The extent to which respective teachers are optimistic about their ability to successfully teach the child (i.e., the teacher's self-efficacy) enters into the decision." Thus, judgment (which is based on local norms that compare the child's performance to that of classmates and peers) and teacher self-efficacy (which varies greatly from teacher to teacher) guide the referral to LD.

Teaching groups of LD students has become a more challenging endeavor because of the level of heterogeneity in a classroom LD population. For example, the authors note how virtually all children diagnosed with behavior disorders or severe emotional disturbance were initially diagnosed as learning disabled, with the LD diagnosis seemingly accepted as the polite "first step." The population of students diagnosed with LD almost quadrupled in a 7-year period. MacMillan and Siperstein remind us that there exists a group of disenfranchised students whose diagnosis previously would have been educable mentally retarded (EMR), but is now LD. (Grossman's redefinition in 1973 readjusted the IQ range for an EMR diagnosis from 85 down to 70.) Therefore, these children—who no longer "fit" the definition of mental retardation—are expected to forgo intensive support services for students with low IQs, and partake instead of services that originally were developed for LD students who demonstrated "average" intelligence.

EDUCATING THE DISENFRANCHISED

The authors build a strong, passionate argument for the need to provide better means of instruction for students with low IQs and low achievement levels. I have argued for years that a major emphasis of special education services should be the improvement of teachers' general competence to teach students with academic problems (Gersten & Dimino, 2001; Gersten, Morvant, & Brengelman, 1995; Gersten & Woodward, 1990). However, it behooves us to recognize that the tasks of simultaneously building classroom teachers' capacities to reach students with disabilities and then serving these students effectively are formidable challenges.

I concur with MacMillan and Siperstein, who advocate high-quality, effective, and appropriate instruction as one way to meet the needs of students with LD. This is especially critical for children scoring low on both achievement and intelligence tests, many of whom would have been considered EMR in the 1970s. With the notable exception of O'Connor and colleagues (O'Connor, Notari-Syverson, & Vadasy, 1998), little research has been focused on these students who continuously score low in both achievement and intelligence. We need much more extensive knowledge on how to teach students who, in addition to demonstrating reading disabilities, have significant problems in their knowledge of key vocabulary words and concepts and low abilities in analogue reasoning and other abstract cognitive abilities tested in conventional IQ tests. For example, in developing instruction for these students, it is imperative to include oral language and development activities that are not part of the typical curriculum.

Another critical piece is instructionally relevant assessment, particularly assessment of growth in vocabulary. These assessments could be along a curriculum-based measurement model (Carnine, Caros, Crawford, Hollenbeck, & Harniss, 1996) or could look like the reading vocabulary section of Woodcock Reading Mastery Tests or the vocabulary in the Wechsler Intelligence Scale for Children III (WISC-III). The purpose of such assessment is to evaluate whether or not a child needs work in building knowledge of vocabulary concepts. If this skill is identified as an area of weakness, interventions like that of Beck, Stahl, and Echevarria (for second language) (Beck, Perfetti, & McKeown, 1982; Echevarria, Vogt, & Short, 2000; Stahl, 1983) can be used to address the specific deficiency. This approach is much more sensible for both special education and general education teachers. In addition, the research of Wong, William, Englert and Deshler (Deshler, Ellis, & Lenz, 1996; Englert, Raphael, Anderson, Anthony, & Stevens, 1991; Williams, Brown, Silverstein, & deCani, 1994; Wong, Butler, Ficzere, & Kuperis, 1997) is not often promoted, but when infused in curriculum and used with a wide and relevant group of children, it can also be very effective.

I believe we need to do a lot more for this group of school-identified LD students who are also weak in oral language and vocabulary knowledge. This would be an excellent focus for future programmatic research.

ABILITY TO BENEFIT FROM TREATMENT: VALID ALTERNATIVE, OR YET ANOTHER PIPE DREAM?

The tendency in any historical analysis of a problem is to conclude with a catalogue of promising alternatives. MacMillan and Siperstein do not claim that there is any easy answer to the problems they have identified. They note, " We have no doubt that the SI LD population represents a group of children who do, in fact, need assistance..." (MacMillan & Siperstein, this volume). They go on to state that this is a large group of students, much larger and more heterogeneous than envisioned by Kirk, Bateman, and other pioneers who originally developed a concept of learning disabilities: This is a population so large and ill-defined that members share little in common. They correctly note that schools now serve as "LD" those students who previously would have been considered students with mental retardation or emotional and behavioral disorders, and even those "...whose low achievement appears linked to experiences of poverty..." (MacMillan & Siperstein, this volume).

Like many others in the profession, they note the problem, discuss its deleterious effects on the profession, and grasp for solutions. Clearly, the complex array of societal trends that led to this problem, so artfully described by MacMillan and Siperstein in their paper, is unlikely to get a quick fix. One model they propose is to operationally define LD, or a child in need of specially designed alternative intervention, as a student who fails to benefit from well-designed instruction.

MacMillan and Siperstein note that this concept of inability to respond to quality instruction has been discussed and studied on a small scale by a host of researchers in the past 5 years. On its face, it has merits as a viable alternative to the current definition of LD. For example, if a student beginning in kindergarten or first grade is taught according to our best contemporary knowledge on reading instruction and still is unable to make adequate progress, this student, surely, would seem to be a student in need of special assistance.

The advantages of such a definition are several: There is no need for costly IQ testing; the assessment team does not prematurely conclude there is something inherently wrong with the child; and, as a data-based organization (with a well-conceptualized reading program), the school determines that data strongly suggest that a given set of children require extra, more intensive, and perhaps more expert assistance.

We have seen several examples of this type of idea succeeding in small-scale studies. Kame'enui, Simmons, and Coyne (Kame'enui, Simmons, & Coyne, 2000) are currently engaged in a reading intervention program with the lowest scoring 25% of kindergarten and first-grade students in several schools (Fuchs & Fuchs, 1998; Speece & Case, submitted; Vaughn, Thompson, Kouzekanani, Bryant, & Dickson, in review)

SOME CONSIDERATIONS AS WE BEGIN TO LEVEL THE PLAYING FIELD

Operationally defining LD or reading disability as "inability" to benefit from well-designed instruction is intellectually appealing. Yet I am troubled by the inherent subjectivity and problems in operationalizing that the definition that evokes. This concept is in harmony with the zeitgeist of the times, in which schools are considered data-based, accountable organizations that use data and research to improve the quality of services they provide and that use data to assess which clients require extra assistance.

However, as MacMillan and Siperstein point out, the current LD process is prone to subjective or "pseudo-scientific" judgments, despite seeming objective. The amount of teacher, committee, and psychological discretion can be immense in virtually any operation schools engage in.

The notion of redefining LD is fraught with other tensions as well. At what point will we draw the line? Isn't the commonly used term "treatment resister" a troubling label to pin on a child?

Critical components in operationalizing responsiveness to treatment include (a) quality of curricula used in instruction, (b) quality of implementation, and (c) feasibility of the model. Yet these points bring up other issues. To date, there is a growing consensus as to what quality kindergarten and first-grade instruction looks like. As one progresses into other academic areas and grade levels, defining "quality of instruction" becomes nebulous and difficult to evaluate. Even to operationalize the quality of beginning reading instruction is not easy. There are now several beginning reading programs that are based on contemporary research on phoneme awareness, knowledge of alphabetic understanding, and explicit teaching of strategies. These programs are, obviously, potentially good "tests" of responsiveness treatment. However, implementation varies widely (Baker & Gersten, 2001; Foorman, Fletcher, Francis, & Schatschneider, 2000)

The various components of the treatment itself and a student's response to it need to be carefully evaluated. Who precisely determines when implementation is so unsatisfactory that it cannot be used as a basis for determining nonresponsiveness?

Historically, national policy has distorted good intentions and resulted in ineffective practice in the schools. Nationwide requirements to complete functional assessments are one example of this phenomenon.

Should the field of special education move to redefine LD to be "the ability to benefit from quality instruction," I propose this concept be seriously and rigorously field-tested before it becomes considered as national policy. I confess to finding the proposal both compelling and frightening. Aside from the need to establish clear definitions and measures of "quality instruction," something else is disturbing about this conceptual framework: It has not been rigorously field-tested.

The initial small-scale experimental research that Fuchs and Fuchs (1998) and Simmons and colleagues (2000) have conducted is merely a solid first step in the process. But we must remain cautious, as much of this small-scale experimental work has been conducted only in kindergarten and first grade, and has yet to be generalized to larger, more complex contexts.

Currently, the U.S. Department of Education is planning to support four large centers, each of which will work with seven schools to implement radically different ways of identifying and serving students in the early grades with reading problems. As a field, we can and should learn a great deal from this type of rigorous, controlled field research. However, we cannot assume that what works under these auspices—projects that are well-funded, are managed by experts and trained graduate students, and have access to state-of-the-art educational innovations—will quickly and painlessly "scale up" to all schools.

I suggest we exercise discretion before we decide to "scale up" this concept. We need to clearly define and field-test this proposal on a larger scale, and ensure that it works on the real-world "playing field" of schools. Field-testing before scaling up is typical practice in business (be it the airline or yogurt business—or in this case, the business of educating children). It allows us to get a feel of what happens in relatively uncontrolled settings, those settings that are not monitored for implementation by graduate students and that remain impervious to researchers' desire for control over all variables.

Our field has witnessed the implementation of too many intellectually compelling concepts (such as prereferral intervention and intelligence-achievement discrepancy) that have suddenly been mandated into law. It is true that the landscape of LD has shifted dramatically. MacMillan and Siperstein astutely and wisely draw our attention to these changes. The idea of redefining LD holds promise, but like any promise, it can become broken and destructive. The reality is that moving too quickly can be detrimental to the field, to schools and teachers, and, most important, to the children we want to serve and support.

REFERENCES

Baker, S., & Gersten, R. (2001, April). *Teaching history to students with learning disabilities: Experimental research involving innovative instruction.* Paper presented at the Council for Exceptional Children Annual Conference, Kansas City, MO.

Beck, I. L., Perfetti, C. A., & McKeown, M. G. (1982). Effects of long-term vocabulary instruction on lexical access and reading comprehension. *Journal of Educational Psychology, 74,* 506–521.

Carnine, D., Caros, J., Crawford, D., Hollenbeck, K., & Harniss, M. (1996). Designing effective United States history curricula for all students. In J. Brophy (Ed.), *Advances in research on teaching, Vol. 6, History teaching and learning* (pp. 207–256). Greenwich, CT: JAI Press.

Deshler, D. D., Ellis, E. S., & Lenz, B. K. (1996). *Teaching adolescents with learning disabilities: Strategies and methods* (2nd ed.). Denver, CO: Love Publishing Company.

Echevarria, J., Vogt, M., & Short, D. J. (2000). *Making content comprehensible for English language learners: The SIOP model.* Boston: Allyn and Bacon.

Englert, C. S., Raphael, T. E., Anderson, L. M., Anthony, H. M., & Stevens, D. D. (1991). Making writing strategies and self-talk visible: Cognitive strategy instruction in regular and special education classrooms. *American Educational Research Journal, 28,* 337–372.

Foorman, B. R., Fletcher, J. M., Francis, D. J., & Schatschneider, C. (2000). Response: Misrepresentation of research by other researchers. *Educational Researcher, 29*(6), 27–37.

Fuchs, L. S., & Fuchs, D. (1998). Treatment validity: A unifying concept for reconceptualizating the identification of learning disabilities. *Learning Disabilities Research and Practice, 13,* 204–219.

Gersten, R., & Dimino, J. (2001). The realities of translating research into classroom practice. *Learning Disabilities Research & Practice, 16,* 113–122.

Gersten, R., Morvant, M., & Brengelman, S. (1995). Close to the classroom is close to the bone: Coaching as a means to translate research into classroom practice. *Exceptional Children, 62*(1), 52–66.

Gersten, R., & Woodward, J. (1990). Rethinking the regular education initiative: Focus on the classroom teacher. *Remedial and Special Education, 11*(3), 7–16.

Grossman, H. (Ed.) (1973). *Manual on terminology and classification in mental retardation.* Washington, DC: American Association on Mental Deficiency.

Kame'enui, E., Simmons, D. C., & Coyne, M. D. (2000). Schools as host environments: Toward a schoolwide reading improvement model. *Annals of Dyslexia, 50,* 33–51.

MacMillan, D. L., & Siperstein, G. N. (this volume). Learning disabilities as operationally defined by schools.

O'Connor, R. E., Notari-Syverson, A., & Vadasy, P. F. (1998). First-grade effects of teacher-led phonological activities in kindergarten for children with mild disabilities: A follow-up study. *Learning Disabilities Research & Practice, 13*(1), 43–52.

Simmons, D. C., Kame'enui, E. J., Harn, B. A., Edwards, L. L., Coyne, M. D., Thomas-Back, C., Kauffman, N., Peterson, K., & Smith, S. B. (2000). The effects of instructional emphasis and specificity on early reading and vocabulary development of kindergarten children. Manuscript submitted for publication.

Speece, D. L., & Case, L. P. (submitted). Classification in context: An alternative approach to identifying early reading difficulty.

Stahl, S. A. (1983). Differential word knowledge and reading comprehension. *Journal of Reading Behavior, 15*(4), 33–50.

Vaughn, S., Thompson, S. L., Kouzekanani, K., Bryant, D. P., & Dickson, S. (in review). The effects of three grouping formats on the reading performance of monolingual and English Language Learners with reading problems. *Journal of Educational Psychology.*

Williams, J. P., Brown, L. G., Silverstein, A. K., & deCani, J. S. (1994). An instructional program in comprehension of narrative themes for adolescents with learning disabilities. *Learning Disability Quarterly, 17*, 205–221.

Wong, B. Y. L., Butler, D. L., Ficzere, S. A., & Kuperis, S. (1997). Teaching adolescents with learning disabilities and low achievers to plan, write, and revise compare-contrast essays. *Learning Disabilities Research & Practice, 12*, 2–15.

Zigmond, N. (1993). Learning disabilities from an educational perspective. In G. R. Lyon, D. B. Gray, J. F. Kavanaugh, & N. A. Krasnegor (Eds.), *Better understanding learning disabilities: New views from research and their implications for education and public policies* (pp. 251–272). Baltimore, MD: Paul H. Brookes Publishing Co.

ACKNOWLEDGMENTS

The author wishes to thank Rachell Katz and Michelle Jensen for their assistance in the preparation of this manuscript.

MINORITY OVERREPRESENTATION: THE SILENT
CONTRIBUTOR TO LD PREVALENCE AND DIAGNOSTIC CONFUSION

Daniel J. Reschly, Vanderbilt University

Minority overrepresentation in special education is a significant but largely silent contributor to a quarter century of increasing learning disability (LD) prevalence and to the current diagnostic confusion about what LD is and how it should be identified. The sharp decline in mild mental retardation (MMR) prevalence is part of the story of increasing LD prevalence and diagnostic confusion. From 1976–77 when prevalence data were first collected by the Office of Special Education Programs (OSEP) to 1998–99, mental retardation (MR) declined from 969,547 to 613,207 students, or 36%. LD increased from 797,213 to 2,064,120 students, or 260%. These changes are even more impressive because they occurred during a period when children and youth with moderate, severe, and profound MR gained access to the public schools for the first time. Although the OSEP child count data do not differentiate between levels of MR, it is highly likely that the decline in MMR has been even greater than the overall MR decline.

STATE VARIATIONS

Before going too far with prevalence analysis, it is important to acknowledge that the OSEP prevalence results published in its *Annual Report to Congress* depend on annual reports from the states, which exercise wide discretion in how categories are used, including the names for disabilities, conceptual definitions, and classification criteria (NASDE, 1999). In addition to the rising national LD prevalence, there are enormous variations in the prevalence of high-incidence disabilities reported by the states (Reschly, 2000). MR prevalence varies by a factor of 9, LD by a factor of 3, and emotional disturbance (ED) by a factor of 33; that is, the ED prevalence in the highest and lowest states varies by 33 times. Clearly, the states use these categories differently, with varying conceptual definitions and classification criteria (Denning, Chamberlain, & Polloway, 2000; Mercer, Jordan, Allsopp, & Mercer,

1996). Analysis of disability prevalence has to take a state-by-state as well as national perspective. MR prevalence in some states (such as Alabama, Iowa, Ohio, and Nebraska) has not declined substantially over the past 25 years, while in other states (such as California and Mississippi) MR rates have declined by large amounts. In 1998–99, 17 states reported overall MR prevalence of <0.6% and 28 reported <1.0%. These results support the conclusion that many students likely eligible for the MMR diagnosis are served in special education using other categories such as LD or are not being served.

REASONS FOR MMR DECLINE

The reasons for the declining MMR prevalence have been discussed extensively elsewhere (Reschly, 1988). Some critical factors were the increasing availability of the LD category which has less negative connotation and less stigma, increasingly stringent MR classification criteria, dissatisfaction with the results of self-contained special classes, and litigation regarding overrepresentation. Of these factors, perhaps the greatest influence was overrepresentation litigation.

Overrepresentation litigation had direct and indirect influences (Reschly, Kicklighter, & McKee, 1988). Massive declassification generally followed consent decrees or court opinions (e.g., *Diana v. State Board of Education,* 1970), producing markedly lower MR prevalence and contributing significantly to increased LD prevalence. One current effect of the overrepresentation litigation is the continuing reluctance to use the MMR category (MacMillan, Gresham, & Bocian, 1998). In many instances it appears that teams ignore evidence of other disabilities such as ED and MMR and simply confer the LD diagnosis in order to place the child in special education where much-needed services can be obtained (Bocian, Beebe, MacMillan, & Gresham, 1999).

The kind of declassification experienced in California, Mississippi, and Arizona in the 1970s and 1980s after consent decrees occurs less frequently today. An exception to this trend is under way in Alabama as a result of the *Lee v. Macon* (2000) consent decree that requires markedly more stringent criteria for MMR classification. The nearly inevitable result will be a dramatic decline in the Alabama MR prevalence that is likely to be accompanied by a sharp increase in LD. Declassification pressures also come from Office of Civil Rights (OCR) investigations of districts which often focus on MMR overrepresentation. OCR compliance agreements such as those implemented in Davenport, Iowa, Minneapolis, Minnesota, and many other places are likely to further diminish MR and increase LD prevalence.

OVERREPRESENTATION

LD generally is not implicated in current discussions of minority overrepresentation. It is crucial to clarify the meaning of the statistics used to analyze overrepresentation. The *composition statistic* indicates the proportion of a special education category by group. For example, enrollment in MR programs is approximately 9% Hispanic and 34% Black. Another example of a composition statistic is the observation that 70% of public school educators are women. The *risk statistic* is the percentage of a group that is placed in a program; for example, approximately 0.78% of Hispanic and 2.63% of Black students are in MR programs. Continuing the above example, the "risk" of being a teacher is about 1.5% for women; that is, of all women, about 1.5% are teachers. Risk statistics are the most understandable to most audiences and should be used more frequently because the group composition statistics are easily misunderstood as indicating that a high proportion of minority students are in special education.

As shown in Table 1, only a small proportion of minority students are in special education, and the overall differences between the risk of special education enrollment are only slightly greater for some minority groups. Asian-Pacific Islander (API) students are markedly underrepresented, and Hispanic students are slightly underrepresented compared to white students. In contrast, American Indian/Alaskan Native (AI) students are slightly overrepresented in LD and Black students are overrepresented in MR and ED. The current enrollment pattern in LD involves slight overrepresentation of AI students, but nearly equal rates for Hispanic, Black, and White students, and marked underrepresentation for API students. From these data it would be easy to conclude that overrepresentation in LD will not be an issue in the future. That impression may be incorrect.

A recent analysis of OCR data since 1974 yielded two interesting results: First, the rate of LD increase has been higher for AI, Hispanic, and Black students. If that trend continues, overrepresentation of these groups relative to White students could emerge in the next 5 to 10 years. Furthermore, several states were identified in which Black students were significantly overrepresented in LD, suggesting that OCR challenges at the state level, like those in MR, could lead to unpredictable changes in LD.

SUMMARY

The overall effect of the overrepresentation litigation and OCR investigations has been to reduce MMR and increase LD. Furthermore, staffing teams in many states appear to be reluctant to use the MMR category in special education eligibility, choosing instead to use LD or ED even when the individual evaluation is more

Table 1. OCR 1998 data for three categories.

	Native American Indian		Asian Pacific Islander		Hispanic		African American		White	
	CI	RI	CI	RI	CI	RI	CI	RI	CI	RI
MR	1.04%	1.28%	1.90%	0.64%	10.04%	0.92%	33.04%	2.64%	53.97%	1.18%
ED	1.23%	1.03%	1.16%	0.26%	8.87%	0.55%	26.92%	1.45%	61.82%	0.91%
LD	1.38%	7.45%	1.51%	2.23%	16.04%	6.44%	18.48%	6.49%	62.59%	6.02%
TOTAL: MR + ED + LD Risk	9.76%		3.13%		7.81%		10.58%		8.11%	
Composition of General Ed. Pop.	1.11%		4.08%		15.01%		17.14%		62.66%	

Notes: C I = composition index; R I = risk index; M R = mentally retarded; E D = emotionally disturbed; L D = learning disabled

Read the CI columns as the proportion of a particular category by group. For example, of the students in MR special education programs, 33.04% are African American. Read the RI columns as indicating the proportion of some group in a special education category. That is, 2.63% of all African American students are classified as MR and placed in special education.

consistent with MMR. These issues are complicated further by recent attacks on the ability-achievement discrepancy criterion used by most states along with the exclusion factors and low achievement to determine LD eligibility.

NICHD Dyslexia Studies

Scholars associated with the National Institute of Child Health and Human Development (NICHD) Dyslexia Program concluded that IQ testing and ability-achievement discrepancy determination contribute little to identifying appropriate groups for reading interventions or to designing effective treatments (Lyon et al., 2001). Moreover, use of the discrepancy model to identify LD produces a "wait to fail" effect that delays treatment until third grade or beyond. Criticism of the ability-achievement discrepancy part of LD classification is not new. What is new is the concerted attack by scholars associated with a large-scale federally funded research program. A critical issue is determining the continued viability of the discrepancy method, as well as evaluating alternatives. Little information exists on the latter, although a number of intriguing possibilities have been suggested.

Universal Screening and Early Intervention

One possible outcome of the NICHD research is universal early screening of all students for phonological awareness and early intervention for students likely to develop reading disabilities. One likely effect of early screening is identification of a relatively high proportion of students as needing early intervention (25% or more) and many more females as having very low reading achievement, perhaps eliminating the current LD male-to-female ratio of 2:1 (Shaywitz, Shaywitz, Fletcher, & Escobar, 1990).

An unanticipated effect of universal early screening not discussed to date is the virtually inevitable outcome of identifying a markedly disproportionate number of minority students as needing early reading interventions. If the early interventions prevent reading disabilities in a high proportion of the current LD population *and* are differentially even more effective for currently overrepresented minority students, current patterns of overrepresentation could diminish. If, however, the early interventions have the effect of raising reading achievement generally, but at the same time preserving the current achievement variability with the same *relative* minority achievement levels, the likely result is exacerbated degrees of overrepresentation that most likely will occur in LD.

The higher minority identification rates are likely to occur with universal screening because the current system identifies fewer minority students as disabled than those eligible according to a universal screening measure such as IQ or achievement (Heller, Holtzman, & Messick, 1982, p. 42). To put it differently, if universal screening were applied now, minority overrepresentation likely would be more pronounced. Imperfect current screening procedures that depend in large part on teacher referral miss many low achieving students who are eligible according to eligibility criteria. The degree to which early screening is likely to increase overrepresentation will also depend on whether national or local norms are used in identifying students at risk for academic failure. National norms applied to current disadvantaged, low achieving students would identify high proportions as needing special interventions (West, Denton, & Reaney, 2000). The acceptability of these effects will depend on the outcomes of the interventions.

Special education outcomes were the principal issue in the overrepresentation litigation, although most commentators focused on IQ tests and other aspects of assessment. This point was made clear by the *Larry P. v. Riles* trial judge in a later commentary on the case where he said the ban on IQ tests was "...clearly limited to the use of IQ tests in the assessment and placement of African-American students in dead end programs such as MMR" (*Crawford et al. v. Honig*, 1992, p. 15). Further, the decision was largely concerned with "...the harm to African-American children resulting from improper placement in dead-end educational programs" (*Crawford et al. v. Honig*, 1992, p. 23).

Outcomes Criteria

The greatest challenge today is showing that special education programs are effective in producing better results than continued placement in general education for students with the high-incidence disabilities of LD, MMR, and ED. Thinking in special education must change from excessive emphasis on eligibility determination to a greater focus on what can be changed in instruction, classroom organization, and behavior management schemes in both general and special education that will produce better results. System reform efforts that emphasize noncategorical eligibility, functional assessment with formative evaluation, and student performance outcomes as the basis for all special education decisions have the potential for improving outcomes across disability categories (Reschly, Tilly, & Grimes, 1999).

The essential features of these reform efforts are improved problem solving at all levels of service, markedly enhanced support in general education, direct measures of performance in natural settings, functional analysis of instruction/environments, graphing results with frequent progress monitoring, formative evaluation, and evaluation of results in terms of goals in the general education curriculum. These approaches involve reallocating resources from expensive and time-consuming eligibility evaluations that yield little useful information for interventions to equally expensive and time-consuming but intervention-related functional assessment activities. The results of the intervention determine special education eligibility and continue to be used in designing further interventions and evaluating outcomes if special education is warranted (Reschly et al., 1999).

Much is yet to be learned about the most appropriate ways to determine LD eligibility and to ensure positive outcomes for students. Newer models have promise, but need careful scrutiny to determine if they can be implemented with good fidelity and whether initially promising results persist in subsequent replications.

SUMMARY

There are significant parallels as well as differences in the recent history of the MMR and LD fields. Both are high-incidence disability categories that are rarely identified before school entrance. LD is the current dominant category in special education, a position held by MMR until the late 1970s. Overrepresentation litigation based on concerns about stigma and program effectiveness led to a sharp decline in MMR. Current LD practices and identification trends have problems similar to those of the MMR programs of the 1960s and 1970s—specifically, problems with demonstrating outcomes and increasing stigma. Reforms to address these trends, especially improving outcomes, will determine whether LD follows the path of MMR.

REFERENCES

Bocian, K. M., Beebe, M. E., MacMillan, D. L., & Gresham, F. M. (1999). Competing paradigms in learning disabilities classification by schools and the variations in meaning of discrepant achievement. *Learning Disabilities Research and Practice, 14,* 1–14.

Crawford et al. v. Honig. No. C-89-0014 RFP U.S. District Court, Northern District of California, Complaint for Declaratory Judgment, May 1988; Order, September 29, 1989; Memorandum and Order, August 31, 1992. (also see *Larry P. v. Riles,* 1979, 1986, 1992, 1994)

Denning, C. B., Chamberlain, J. A., & Polloway, E. A. (2000). An evaluation of state guidelines for mental retardation: Focus on definition and classification practices. *Education and Training in Mental Retardation and Developmental Disabilities, 35,* 226–232.

Diana v. State Board of Education. No. C-70-37 RFP U.S. District Court, Northern District of California, Consent Decree, February 3, 1970.

Heller, K., Holtzman, W., & Messick, S., (Eds.). (1982). *Placing children in special education: A strategy for equity.* Washington, DC: National Academy Press.

Lee v. Macon, No. 2455-N, U.S. District Court, Middle District, Northern Division, Alabama, August 24, 2000 (consent decree).

Lyon, G. R, Fletcher, J. M., Shaywitz, S. E., Shaywitz, B. A., Wood, F. B., Schulte, A., & Olson, R. (2001). Rethinking learning disabilities. In C. E. Finn, Jr., A. J. Rotherham, & C. R. Hokanson, Jr. (Eds.). *Rethinking special education for a new century* (pp. 259–287). Washington, DC: Thomas B. Fordham Foundation and Progressive Policy Institute.

MacMillan, D. L., Gresham, F. L., & Bocian, K. M. (1998). Discrepancy between definitions of learning disabilities and school practices: An empirical investigation. *Journal of Learning Disabilities, 31,* 314–326.

Mercer, C. D., Jordan, L., Allsopp, D. H., & Mercer, A. R. (1996). Learning disabilities definitions and criteria used by state education departments. *Learning Disability Quarterly, 19,* 217–232.

National Association of State Directors of Special Education (NASDE). (1999). *Child count variations and anomalies across states.* Washington, DC: Author.

Reschly, D. J. (1988). Assessment issues, placement litigation, and the future of mild mental retardation classification and programming. *Education and Training of the Mentally Retarded, 23,* 285–301.

Reschly, D. J., (2000). Assessment and eligibility determination in the Individuals With Disabilities Act of 1997. In C. F. Telzrow & M. Tankersley, (Eds.) *IDEA amendments of 1997: Practice guidelines for school-based teams* (pp. 65–104). Bethesda, MD: National Association of School Psychologists.

Reschly, D. J., Kicklighter, R. H., & McKee, P. (1988). Recent placement litigation Part II, Minority EMR overrepresentation: Comparison of *Larry P.* (1979, 1984, 1986) with *Marshall* (1984, 1985) and *S-1* (1986). *School Psychology Review, 17,* 20–36.

Reschly, D. J., Tilly, W. D., III., & Grimes, J. P. (Eds.) (1999). *Special education in transition: Functional assessment and noncategorical programming.* Longmont, CO: Sopris West.

Shaywitz, S. E., Shaywitz, B. A., Fletcher, J. M., & Escobar, M. D. (1990). Prevalence of reading disability in boys and girls: Results of the Connecticut longitudinal study. *Journal of the American Medical Association, 264,* 998–1002.

West, J., Denton, K., & Reaney, L. M. (2000). The kindergarten year: Findings from the early childhood longitudinal study, kindergarten class of 1998–1999 (NCES-2000). Washington, DC: National Center for Educational Statistics.

CHAPTER V: DISCREPANCY MODELS IN THE IDENTIFICATION OF LEARNING DISABILITY

Kenneth A. Kavale, University of Iowa

On April 6, 1963, Samuel A. Kirk told a parent advocacy group that "Recently, I have used the term 'learning disability' to describe a group of children who have disorders in development, in language, speech, reading, and associated communication skills needed for social interaction" (Kirk, 1975, p. 9). By 1968, "specific learning disability" (LD) became a federally designated category of special education (U.S. Office of Education, 1968). The formal definition offered at the time has not changed substantively and was reaffirmed in the 1997 reauthorization of the Individuals With Disabilities Education Act [IDEA] (Public Law 105-17) as follows:

> The term "specific learning disability" means a disorder in one or more of the basic psychological processes involved in understanding or in using language, spoken or written, which may manifest itself in imperfect ability to listen, think, speak, read, write, spell or do mathematical calculation. The term includes such conditions as perceptual disabilities, brain injury, minimal brain dysfunction, dyslexia, and developmental aphasia. Such term does not include a learning problem that is primarily the result of visual, hearing or motor disabilities, of mental retardation, of emotional disturbance, or of environmental, cultural, or economic disadvantage (IDEA Amendments of 1997, PL105-17, 11 Stat. 37 [20 USC 1401(26)]).

DISCREPANCY AND INTRA-INDIVIDUAL DIFFERENCES

The federal definition does not stipulate procedural guidelines for LD identification. In fact, the definition is primarily exclusive, describing what LD is not rather than identifying what LD is. Consequently, operational definitions necessary for practice have usually considered factors that may not have been articulated in the formal definition. One such factor that originated in the Kirk (1962) LD definition was the notion of intra-individual differences, the possibility of subaverage functioning in only a few areas with average or above functioning in other areas. Gallagher (1966) termed these "developmental imbalances" that were represented by discrepancies in psychoeducational functioning. One of the first such discrepancies investigated was related to the cognitive abilities of students with LD. Using subtest scores from cognitive assessments like the Wechsler Intelligence Scale for Children (WISC), patterns of strengths and weaknesses were examined to determine whether the resulting scatter ("profile") differentiated students with LD from other average or low achieving populations.

COGNITIVE DISCREPANCIES

The clinical use of scatter-analysis methods has precipitated debate about its relationship to the nature of LD (e.g., Miller, 1980; Wallbrown, Blaha, & Vance, 1980; Wallbrown, Vance, & Blaha, 1979). For example, hypotheses about uniqueness assume that the profile for samples of students with LD is characteristic of the entire LD population or that the LD subtest profile varies significantly from the average population. The empirical evidence, however, has not supported any assumptions about LD profile uniqueness (e.g., Dudley-Marling, Kaufman, & Tarver, 1981; Gutkin, 1979; Kaufman, 1981).

In a comprehensive quantitative synthesis, Kavale and Forness (1984) found no WISC profile for students with LD. For example, a discrepancy between Verbal IQ and Performance IQ (VIQ-PIQ) has been assumed to be a primary LD characteristic. The difference (PIQ > VIQ) was, on average, only 3½ IQ points, which was well below the requisite 11 IQ points necessary for significance. In addition, although students with LD generally performed more poorly on Verbal subtests, no Verbal or Performance subtest score fell below the *average* level. Any measure of WISC inter-subtest variability ("scatter") was not significant and indicated no subtest strength or weakness that distinguished LD performance.

On the basis of hypotheses about cognitive performance, a number of different subtest score groupings have been proposed to reveal discrepant abilities. One method involves recategorizing subtest scores exemplified in the proposal by Bannatyne (1968) that included a Spatial, Conceptual and Sequential category, each based on three WISC subtests. An LD sample was presumed to show a Spatial > Conceptual > Sequential pattern, but, although exhibiting the required pattern, the magnitude of the score differences was well below required significance values. A second primary method was to seek a profile that either specifies particular subtest scores as high or low or identifies subtests where students with LD might score low. For example, Ackerman, Peters, and Dykman (1971) studied the ACID profile (low scores on the Arithmetic, Coding, Information, and Digit Span subtests) but, again, LD performance did not reach the required level of significant suppression. Similarly, WISC factor scores (e.g., Naglieri, 1981) and WISC patterns (e.g., Myklebust, Bannochie, & Killen, 1971) have also been investigated, but in no instance was discrepant LD performance at a level that could be termed significant.

The longstanding criticism (e.g., Bijou, 1942) of examining discrepancies in cognitive performance to identify LD appears justified. In summarizing the available research, Kavale and Forness (1984) concluded that "Regardless of the manner in which WISC subtests were grouped and regrouped, no recategorization, profile, pattern, or factor cluster emerged as a 'clinically' significant indicator of LD. In fact, when compared to average levels, the LD group was found to exhibit no significant deviations, and on average, revealed less variability than normal populations" (p. 150).

ORIGINS OF ABILITY-ACHIEVEMENT DISCREPANCY

The failure to find significant cognitive (IQ) discrepancies in LD populations and the desire to reinforce notions about the academic achievement deficits associated with LD directed attention to the possibility of conceptualizing IQ-achievement discrepancies as a feature of LD. The IQ-achievement discrepancy notion was introduced by Bateman (1965) in a definition of LD that included the description of "an educationally significant discrepancy between estimated intellectual potential and actual level of performance related to basic disorders in the learning processes" (p. 220).

The idea of IQ-achievement discrepancy was introduced by Franzen (1920) in the "Accomplishment Quotient" (AQ). The AQ is the ratio of Educational Quotient (EQ) to Intelligence Quotient (IQ). The importance of IQ "lies in its diagnosis of power of adaptation, and it has a high correlation with maximum possible school progress" (p. 434) while the EQ "is the quotient resulting from the division of the age level reached on the test in question by the chronological age of the pupil" (p. 435). "[T]he ratio of EQ to IQ [the AQ] gives the percentage of what that child could do, that he has actually done" (p. 436).

In cases where the AQ is less than 90, there is potential "underachievement." A number of analyses appeared to show that, in general, AQs were typically less than unity (1.00) (e.g., McPhail, 1922; Pintner & Marshall, 1921; Ruch, 1923). The resulting discrepancy demonstrated by the "laggards" was often attributed to "laziness (i.e., lack of effort) and if pupils are pushed to the extreme limit of their ability, the correlation between their educational achievement and their intelligence is not only high but actually reaches unity" (Whipple, 1922, p. 600). In general, there was a belief that "bright" students were achieving less than expected, relative to ability, than were "dull" students whose lagging performance was presumed to indicate limited effort. Interestingly, with the 1920s view of intelligence as a fixed entity, IQ was regarded as an index of the upper limit for academic attainment which meant AQs really could not exceed unity. As suggested by Franzen (1920), "One's differences when EQ is subtracted from IQ are always positive when they are large enough to be significant and small enough to seem spurious when they are negative....It is safe, therefore, for practical use to assume that the optimum accomplishment is 1.00" (p. 436).

In reality, findings surrounding the AQ were unreliable because of a number of psychometric and statistical problems. In a comprehensive analysis, Toops and Symonds (1922) discussed a number of flaws with the AQ that were a presage of many later analyses of ability-achievement discrepancy. Many other critiques appeared; for example, J. C. Chapman (1923) pointed out the unreliability of using difference scores based on intelligence and achievement test scores. W. R. Wilson (1928) suggested that "Conclusions based on the use of the accomplishment quotient are misleading unless they take into account the reliability of the measures employed, the validity of the measures employed, and the part played by factors determining the intelligence quotient in school achievement under conditions of maximum maturation" (p. 10).

The major statistical criticism of AQ surrounded the operation of the "regression effect" (Crane, 1959; Cureton, 1937). The calculation of AQ assumed an almost perfect correlation between IQ and EQ, whereas the value is closer to 0.60. With less than perfect correlation between measures, scores well above average on one measure will be less superior on the second measure, and at the other end of the continuum, those scores well below average on the first measure will be less inferior on the second. Consequently, if AQ does not account for the effects of statistical regression, then there will be an overrepresentation of "bright" students and an underrepresentation of "dull" students. This result was demonstrated by Popenoe (1927) who found that "Instead of each pupil having an equal chance to get a favorable accomplishment quotient, it appears that out of almost five hundred pupils, in no case did an individual having a high intelligence quotient get a favorable accomplishment quotient, and that individuals having a low intelligence quotient obtained accomplishment quotients far above the average. So an AQ of 100 means an entirely different thing in a part of the range from what it does in another" (p. 45). The many difficulties with AQ led to the conclusion that "the administrative use of the accomplishment quotient is open to serious criticism" (p. 47) and foreshadowed many later issues about the use of ability-achievement discrepancy for LD classification.

DISCREPANCY AND LD IDENTIFICATION: RULES AND REGULATIONS

The Bateman (1965) notion of discrepancy was not formally incorporated into the federal LD definition. In fact, there was no modification of the LD definition in the 1975 Education for All Handicapped Children Act (Public Law 94-142), indicating that an inherent vagueness and imprecision remained, as well as difficulties in using the definition in actual practice (Kavale & Forness, 2000). In an attempt to remedy the situation, the then Bureau of Education for the Handicapped issued regulations outlining procedures for LD identification. The U.S. Office of Education (USOE; 1976) regulations read as follows:

> A specific learning disability may be found if a child has a severe discrepancy between achievement and intellectual ability in one or more of several areas: oral expression, written expression, listening comprehension or reading comprehension, basic reading skills, mathematics calculation, mathematics reasoning, or spelling. A "severe discrepancy" is defined to exist when achievement in one or more of the areas falls at or below 50% of the child's expected achievement level, when age and previous educational experiences are taken into consideration (p. 52405).

FORMULA-BASED DISCREPANCY

To assist the process, a formula to determine the presence of a severe discrepancy level (SDL) was proposed, but comments and testimonies about its usefulness were decidedly negative. For example, Lloyd, Sabatino, Miller, and Miller (1977) objected to the use of general intelligence measures and the negative effects of measurement error on accuracy, while Sulzbacher and Kenowitz (1977) objected to the standard 50% discrepancy across academic areas. In an empirical analysis of the SDL, Algozzine, Forgnone, Mercer, and Trifiletti (1979) cast doubt on the 50% discrepancy level "except for children whose measured intelligence falls exactly at 100" (p. 30). Danielson and Bauer (1978) reviewed the issues surrounding formula-based classification procedures and concluded by questioning whether "a technically adequate solution to the problem of LD identification exists" (p. 175).

By 1977, the SDL formula was dropped but not the concept of discrepancy as stipulated in regulations indicating the following:

> A team may determine that a child has a specific learning disability if: (1) The child does not achieve commensurate with his or her age and ability in one or more of the areas listed in paragraph (2) of this section, when provided with learning experiences appropriate for the child's age and ability levels; and (2) The team finds that a child has a severe discrepancy

between achievement and intellectual ability in one or more of the following areas: (i) oral expression, (ii) listening comprehension, (iii) written expression, (iv) basic reading skill, (v) reading comprehension, (vi)
mathematics calculation, or (vii) mathematics reasoning. (USOE, 1977,
p. 65083)

Thus, discrepancy was reinforced as the primary criterion for LD identification
(see Chalfant & King, 1976) and, although not given precise specification in a particular formula, became over time almost the exclusive variable used for LD eligibility determination (Frankenberger & Fronzaglio, 1991; Mercer, Jordan, Allsopp,
& Mercer, 1996).

QUANTIFYING DISCREPANCY: METHODS

With the idea that a severe discrepancy must be demonstrated, individual states
were free to choose their own methodology, but wide variation in procedures introduced a substantial element of arbitrariness to LD identification (Divoky, 1974;
Shepard, 1983). Nevertheless, an *in numeris veritas* [in numbers there is truth]
mentally developed, and different means of quantifying the presence of a severe
discrepancy were attempted even though "there is little reason to believe and much
empirical reason to disbelieve the contention that some arbitrarily weighted function of two variables will properly define a construct" (Cronbach & Furby, 1970, p.
79). A significant question arose: Can two variables (ability and achievement) be
combined to determine the presence or absence of a construct (LD)? The theoretical problems were exacerbated by practical difficulties surrounding the notion of
prediction. As pointed out by Thorndike (1963), prediction is almost always imperfect because of (1) errors of measurement, (2) heterogeneity of the criterion
(i.e., achievement), (3) limited scope of the predictors, and (4) impact of varied
experiences upon the individual.

GRADE-LEVEL DEVIATION

The simplest but least sophisticated discrepancy method examines grade level deviations where an expected grade level (EGL) score is compared to an actual grade
level (AGL) score and the discrepancy is calculated from the EGL-AGL difference.
For example, expected grade level might be based on chronological age (CA), and
then discrepancy calculated in terms of "years behind" (CA − 5). The 5 represents
the 6 years of informal activity before school entry, with one year subtracted because the real AGL is 1.0, not 0. When the difference is "significant" (usually 1 to 2
years below grade level), a discrepancy exists. The most fundamental problem is
the lack of consideration for the level and degree of instruction received. In place of
CA, mental age (MA) was substituted because of the presumed closer relationship

between intellectual ability and school achievement (Harris, 1961). The search for increased accuracy led to formulas with additional factors and differential weighing of variables (Harris, 1971; Monroe, 1932). Although no formula proved entirely satisfactory, the grade level deviation method was at one time a relatively common procedure for LD identification in research studies (e.g., J. S. Chapman & Boersma, 1979; Gottesman, 1979; Selz & Reitan, 1979).

EXPECTANCY FORMULAS

The next type of discrepancy calculation involves more comprehensive expectancy formulas including some combination of variables (usually IQ and perhaps CA, MA, years in school [YS], or grade age [GA]). The USOE (1976) SDL formula provides an example:

$$SDL = CA\left(\tfrac{IQ}{300} + 0.17\right) - 2.5$$

Earlier examples were provided by Bond and Tinker (1973), Harris (1975), and Johnson and Myklebust (1967) .The Bond and Tinker formula is

$$\left(YSx\tfrac{IQ}{100} + 1.0\right) - AGL$$

The underlying logic for the Bond and Tinker formula seems confounded; an IQ score was included to account for unequal learning rates, but the included constant (1.0) makes this point moot because it negates the differential effects of IQ during the first 6 years of life (Dore-Boyce, Misner, & McGuire, 1975). To remedy this confounding, one set of proposed formulas (Horn, 1941) assigned different weights to MA and CA so formulas may be applied at four different age ranges and the problem of unequal learning rates presumably negated. Without some modification of this sort, the Bond and Tinker (as well as the Harris) formulas are poor predictors that over- and underidentify students with low and high IQs, respectively (Alspaugh & Burge, 1972; Rodenborn, 1974; Simmons & Shapiro, 1968).

PROBLEMS AND ISSUES

The formula proposed by Johnson and Myklebust (1967) introduced the problem of interpreting ratio scores in determining discrepancy level. The Johnson and Myklebust formula calculates an expectancy level (MA + CA + GA / 3), but instead of a direct comparison (EGL – AGL), discrepancy is calculated from a ratio score (AGL / EGL × 100) with a value less than 90 considered significant.

Because of the absence of an absolute zero and equal intervals, ratio scores do not possess inherent meaning. Only extreme scores are meaningful on what is really an ordinal scale, and a value such as 90 cannot be interpreted to mean 90% of average, for example. The situation is further complicated by the variable standard deviations (SDs) across age levels which means that the significance of a given discrepancy ratio will vary from one grade to another. The difficulties such SD variability causes were demonstrated by Macy, Baker, and Kosinski (1979) where the Johnson and Myklebust (1967) discrepancy quotients were quite variable across different combinations of age, grade, and content areas.

The expectancy formula approach to discrepancy calculation has been roundly criticized. McLeod (1979) discussed the negative influence of measurement errors and regression: "Regression means that if scores on two tests are positively correlated, as are intelligence, reading, arithmetic, and spelling scores, then individuals who obtain a particular score on one test will on the average obtain a score nearer to the population average, i.e., regress toward the mean on the other test" (p. 324). Hoffman (1980) suggested that the theoretical problems surrounding regression were not well understood, which led to "considerable uncertainty and possibly confusion among many professionals as to what the data mean at an applied level" (p. 11). If not considered, regression effects lead to increased possibility of misclassification, as pointed out by Thorndike (1963):

If a simple difference between aptitude and achievement standard scores, or a ratio of achievement to aptitude measure, is completed, the high aptitude group will appear primarily to be "underachievers" and the low aptitude group to be "overachievers." For this reason it is necessary to define "underachievement" as discrepancy of actual achievement from the *predicted* value, predicted upon the basis of the regression equation between aptitude and achievement. A failure to recognize this regression effect has rendered questionable, if not meaningless, much of the research in "underachievement" (p. 13).

The questionable reliability associated with some tests used in determining discrepancy almost ensures the presence of regression effects (Coles, 1978; Thurlow & Ysseldyke, 1979). The test validity question is captured in what Kelley (1927) long ago labeled the "jingle and jangle" fallacy—the assumption that tests with the same names measure similar functions, or that tests with different names measure different functions. Hanna, Dyck, and Holen (1979) focused their criticism on the psychometric difficulties associated with age- and grade-equivalent scores. The many associated problems made the expectancy approach a less than optimal means of determining and interpreting a "significant" discrepancy (Davis & Shepard, 1983). L. R. Wilson, Cone, Busch, and Allee (1983) discussed the incorrect assumption that achievement follows a linear growth pattern which results in an inherent bias when discrepancy is defined as a fraction of some expected achievement value because of different slopes in the patterns.

When used in practice, the expectancy formula approach to discrepancy "yielded strikingly disparate results in terms of the number of children identified as learning disabled by each" (Forness, Sinclair, & Guthrie, 1983, p. 111). In actuality, the resulting prevalence rates ranged from 1% to 37% (Sinclair, Guthrie, & Forness, 1984). Confounding this variability was the additional finding that in a sample of students deemed eligible for LD programs, 64% were not identified by any expectancy formula (Sinclair & Alexson, 1986). Finally, O'Donnell (1980) found that a discrepancy derived from an expectancy formula was not a distinctive characteristic of LD and was equally likely to be found among other students with disabilities.

DISCREPANCY SCORE COMPONENTS

Although discrepancy methods were the object of contentious debate, discrepancy continued to be reinforced as a primary criterion for LD identification (e.g., Chalfant, 1985) mainly because of a desire to reduce the reliance on clinical judgment in LD diagnosis (see Meehl, 1954). Thus, the continued use of discrepancy in the LD diagnostic process required improved methodology.

The first problem requiring attention was related to the types of test scores included in discrepancy formulas. Age-equivalent scores (e.g., MA), for example, lack a consistent unit of measurement. More problematic are grade-equivalent (GE) scores that possess difficulties related to the fact that they ignore both the dispersion of scores about the mean and the nonequivalent regression lines between grade and test scores across both grade levels and content areas (Gullicksen, 1950). Consequently, exact values are difficult to achieve, and GEs, therefore, usually involve an excess of extrapolation, especially at the upper and lower ends of a scale. The difficulties are compounded because scores calculated between testing periods (often 1 year) must be interpolated, but such a calculation is based on the invalid assumption of a constant learning rate. What this means is that achievement tests do not exhibit identical GEs. For example, a seventh grade student who is 2 years below grade level in reading will receive quite different percentile rankings (a possible range of 12 percentile ranks) depending on the reading achievement measure used (Reynolds, 1981). When included in discrepancy formulas, GEs from different tests assessing different academic areas may distort scores that may exaggerate small performance differences (Berk, 1981). The problem of GE comparability is thus significant and, by grade 8, GE scores may possess essentially no meaning (Hoover, 1984).

The problems associated with GEs may be partially remedied by the use of standard scores that hold the advantage of being scaled to a constant mean (M) and SD which permits more accurate and precise interpretation. Nevertheless, Clarizio and Phillips (1986) pointed out the potential limitations with standard scores: (a) no basis for comparisons across grade levels, (b) possible distortions in profile comparisons, and (c) inconsistency of unit size caused by within-grade variability. Although their use provides advantages over GEs, standard scores also need to be interpreted cautiously.

STANDARD SCORE METHODS

Standard score (SS) discrepancy methods typically involve a direct comparison between common metrics for intellectual ability and academic achievement (Elliot, 1981; Erickson, 1975; Hanna et al., 1979). For LD determination, the standard scores for ability (IQ) and achievement most often have an M = 100 and SD = 15 with the SDL criterion usually being a minimum of 15-point IQ-achievement difference.

Although advancing discrepancy calculation, the SS procedure is not without limitation. One problem surrounds the invalid assumption that, on average, IQ and achievement scores should be identical (e.g., a child with an IQ of 115 should have a reading or math achievement score of 115). This assumption would be true only if IQ and achievement were perfectly correlated ($r = 1.00$). The actual correlation is about 0.60, which means that the expected achievement for an IQ of 130 is actually 122, not 130. With below-average IQs, an opposite effect occurs (i.e., an IQ of 85 actually has an expected achievement level of about 88). Thus, the SS approach to discrepancy will always possess a systematic bias (Thorndike, 1963). For LD identification, this means the overidentification of high-ability underachievers and the underidentification of low-ability achievers who may in fact be LD.

The less-than-perfect correlation between ability and achievement measures also produces measurement errors that may influence the resulting difference scores. When different IQ and achievement tests are used in calculating discrepancy, the use of particular test combinations will identify more students as LD than will other test combinations (Bishop & Butterworth, 1980; Jenkins & Pany, 1978). The measurement errors also affect the inherent meaning of score comparisons because of the possibility that unique elements may not be measured. Hopkins and Stanley (1981) illustrated the substantial overlapping variance possible between ability and achievement tests. Across grade levels on average, 47% of the variance overlaps, which means that almost half the time the same skills are being measured, making it questionable whether or not "true" differences are being revealed.

DIFFERENCE SCORES

The SS approach produces a difference score that is presumably an index of discrepancy. The difference score, however, often lacks adequate reliability, resulting in uncertainty as to whether or not the difference may have really occurred by chance (Feldt, 1967; Payne & Jones, 1957). For example, the acceptable individual reliabilities of most IQ and achievement tests (about 0.90) produce a difference score with a reliability of only about 0.75. Measurement error is again the primary factor producing this unreliability (see Cronbach, Gleser, Nanda, & Rajaratnam, 1972) which ultimately may distort the discrepancy score as discussed by Thorndike (1963), who concluded that

> if *nothing* but the errors of measurement in the predictor and criterion were operating, we could *still* expect to get a spread of discrepancy scores represented by a standard deviation of half a grade-unit. We would *still* occasionally get discrepancies between predicted and actual reading level of as much as a grade and a half. This degree of "underachievement" would be possible as a result of nothing more than measurement error (p. 9).

Algozzine and Ysseldyke (1981a), using various IQ-achievement test correlations, demonstrated the significantly lower reliabilities of difference scores compared with both of the reliabilities of the tests on which they were based. Using the standard error of measurement (SEM) (a theoretical range around the presumed true score), Schulte and Borich (1984) also demonstrated the unreliability of difference scores. The calculated SEMs of difference scores were substantial and would significantly influence the type and rate of errors made in LD identification. In an empirical analysis, Salvia and Clark (1973) showed how "the standard error of measurement for deficit scores is sufficiently large to preclude rigid adherence to deficits as a criterion for learning disabilities" (p. 308). Reynolds (1981) showed how it is possible to determine the significance of the difference between two scores, but it is a time-consuming process and does not fully answer the question about where to set the cut-off (i.e., criterion) score for LD identification (Schulte & Borich, 1984).

REGRESSION METHODS

With SS methods being problematic, alternative means of calculating discrepancy were considered. Shepard (1980) suggested a regression discrepancy method to remedy many of the existing problems. The measurement error associated with IQ and achievement measures ensures that statistical regression will occur, especially when dealing with IQ levels outside of a 95–105 range. The regression method involves calculating equations for IQ and achievement where "The anticipated [expected] achievement score is the norm for children of the same ability, grade level, and sex" (Shepard 1980, p. 80). Measurement error makes a "true" score indeterminate, and its value may be expressed through the SEM, a range surrounding the obtained score. The formula includes the SD of the test and its reliability estimate and is computed from

$$SEM = SD\sqrt{\left(1 - r_x\right)}$$

The SEM is then used to calculate a CI that reflects a range within which the "true" score might be found. The formula is

$$CI = x \pm z(SEM)$$

where x is the obtained score and z is the normal curve value corresponding to confidence level (e.g., 95% level = 1.96).

The standard error of estimate (SEE) is a statistic similar to the SEM that is used in the case of two independent scores when one is used to predict the second. Essentially, the SEE places a CI around the predicted score. The formula is

$$SEE = SD\sqrt{\left(1 - r_{xy}^{\,2}\right)}$$

where SD is the standard deviation of the achievement test and $\left(r_{xy}^{\,2}\right)$ is the squared correlation between IQ and achievement.

Because the correlation between IQ and achievement is not perfect, regression effects will operate (i.e., individuals who obtain an extreme score on one test will, on average, obtain a score closer to the population mean on the second test). The predicted achievement score $\left(\hat{y}\right)$ may be adjusted for regression effects if both IQ and achievement test scores are expressed as SS with M = 100 and SD = 15, and the IQ-achievement correlation $\left(r_{xy}\right)$ is multiplied by the obtained IQ minus the mean of the IQ test, which is then added to the mean of the achievement test (100) as follows:

$$\hat{y} = r_{xy}(IQ - 100) + 100$$

The actual value is computed from the following equation:

$$(\hat{y} - y) > 15z\sqrt{\left(1 - \underline{r}_{xy}\right)}$$

which includes (a) measuring IQ, (b) predicting achievement level, (c) measuring actual achievement (y), (d) establishing confidence intervals (CIs) around the predicted achievement score using the SEE, and (e) comparing the predicted and actual achievement scores $(\hat{y} - y)$ using the SEE to determine significant differences. For both IQ and achievement, standard scores $(M = 100; SD = 15)$ are typically used in the formula.

An example of the regression method shows how it is used to determine the presence of a discrepancy. To illustrate, assume a student with a measured IQ of 115. Next, assume an r_{xy} of 0.54 (usually derived from the available research literature). With these values, a predicted achievement score is calculated $\left(\hat{y} = .54(115 - 100) + 100\right)$ and found to be 108.1. At the 95% level, the z-value is 1.96, which is used in the equation $15(1.96)\sqrt{1 - .54}$ to obtain a value of 19.93. Using this value, a CI is constructed by adding and subtracting 19.93 from the predicted achievement score of 108.1 to create a CI of 88.17–128.03. If the student's actual achievement score (y) was 85, then it falls below the lower end of the CI (88.17) and a significant discrepancy is said to exist.

The actual calculations may be aided by computer programs that compute significant IQ-achievement discrepancies using a regression approach (e.g., McDermott & Watkins, 1985; Reynolds & Snow, 1985; Watkins & Kush, 1988). The computer programs reduce mathematical error and may be used to create tables for various combinations of IQ and achievement tests as exemplified in the Iowa Regression Discrepancy Tables (Iowa Department of Public Instruction, 1981).

EVALUATION OF REGRESSION METHODS

L. R. Wilson and Cone (1984) argued that the regression discrepancy method provides a "best fit" line for empirically establishing expected achievement values at various IQ levels, and "because regression is a real-world phenomenon, the equation automatically adjusts expected academic scores so that they are less extreme" (p. 99). Evans (1990) discussed six advantages of the regression discrepancy method including (a) determining whether IQ-achievement score differences are due to random error or real, nonchance differences, (b) determining expected achievement score based on individual IQ scores and the correlation between intelligence and achievement, (c) defining discrepancy as the difference between expected and actual achievement score, (d) measuring discrepancy in terms of the SD of the discrepancy difference score, (e) taking into account the SEM of the discrepancy by considering measurement error of IQ and achievement tests, and (f) determining if the discrepancy falls in a predetermined critical ("severe") range when measurement error is considered.

The regression discrepancy method still possesses some practical difficulties, however. Ideally, the regression equation calculated would be based on IQ and achievement scores obtained from large-scale random sampling from the population of interest. Because this is not usually feasible, population statistics for the correlations between individual IQ scores and specific achievement scores, the M and SD of the population IQ, and the M and SD for each specific achievement score must be estimated. With estimated values, the resulting equations may possess errors that limit generalizability [see methods proposed by Woodbury (1963) and McLeod (1979)], but with best estimates and noncontroversial assumptions about linear relationships and normal distributions, "[t]he regression equation approach provides the *best method* for determining academic discrepancy because unlike other approaches, it considers regression, measurement errors, and evidence" (L. R. Wilson & Cone, 1984, p. 107, emphasis added).

Although the regression discrepancy method provides the best answer to the question, "Is there a severe discrepancy between this child's score on the achievement measure and the average achievement score of all other children with the same IQ as this child?" (Reynolds, 1985, p. 40), another practical difficulty remains. A regression equation requires the choice of a value to denote "severity level" but the vagaries surrounding LD make this choice uncertain. The most usual value chosen is two SDs (gleaned from the historical two SDs below the mean IQ level used for the diagnosis of mental retardation [MR]), but while presumably meeting a criterion of "relative infrequency" in the population, the value remains uncertain because of the lack of a true prevalence rate for LD. The uncertainty may produce classification errors of two types: false positive (i.e., identifying a student as LD when he or she is not, in fact, LD) and false negative (i.e., failing to detect real LD). Shepard (1980) suggested that "it is likely that the Regression Discrepancy Method falsely labels more normal children as LD than it correctly identifies children who really have a disorder. At the same time, errors of overidentification do not assume that all real instances of LD will be detected" (p. 88).

EVALUATION OF DISCREPANCY METHODS

Cone and Wilson (1981) analyzed the four basic methods of quantifying a discrepancy and concluded that SS and regression equation methods are preferred. This conclusion has been affirmed in other comparative analyses of discrepancy methods (e.g., Bennett & Clarizio, 1988; Braden & Weiss, 1988; Clarizio & Phillips, 1989).

The primary difficulty with regression equation methods is the numerous and complex empirical calculations required that may be further exacerbated by assessment instruments which may not meet acceptable psychometric standards as well as other technical problems (e.g., calculating the correlation between measures or choosing a proper incidence figure). Berk (1984), in an analysis of discrepancy methods, urged caution because of questions surrounding reliability and validity of outcomes. In a similar analysis, Reynolds (1984–1985) validated the use of regression equation models but noted possible confusion in choosing one type of regression equation over another:

> Case *a* will be far too restrictive and is conceptually illogical in several regards: It will create a more homogeneous group of children; however, LD is characterized by the individuality of the learner, not traits or characteristics held in common with other children. Objections to application of case *b* are less conceptual than mathematical. Routinely applying both models and accepting qualification by either introduces a significantly greater probability of finding a severe discrepancy when none actually exists than does the application of either model....Using both models with all children will then not aid in reducing the conceptual confusion in the field as might application of a uniform model (p. 465).

Even the most defensible method of discrepancy calculation (i.e., SS and regression equation) remains less than perfect with respect to optimal psychometric and statistical considerations. The problems are exacerbated by the many different measurement models that might be employed (see Willson & Reynolds, 1984–1985) and the curious situation involving the fact that as these models become more defensible statistically, they become more complicated to use in practice (Boodoo, 1984–1985). Consequently, actual diagnostic practice in the LD field lags behind state-of-the-art statistical models, which almost makes discrepancy "an atheoretical, psychologically uninformed solution to the problem of LD classification" (Willson, 1987, p. 28).

PRACTICAL DIFFICULTIES

The technical problems create real-world difficulties. Ross (1992a, b), in a survey of school psychologists, found that fewer than 10% were able to correctly evaluate whether four sets of ability-achievement scores reflected chance measurement differences or reliable, nonchance differences. Barnett and Macmann (1992) attributed much of the inaccuracy in discrepancy interpretation to basic misunderstandings surrounding test interpretation; statistical significance, confidence intervals, and measurement error. For example, Macmann, Barnett, Lombard, Belton-Kocher, and Sharpe (1989) found classification agreement rates ranging from 0.57 to 0.86 with different discrepancy calculation methods. When different achievement measures were used in the same calculations, however, the classification agreement rates fell to a range of 0.19 to 0.47. When both ability and achievement measures varied, agreement rates were consistently below 0.25 (Clarizio & Bennett, 1987). Thus, on average, only about 1 in 4 students deemed to possess a "severe" discrepancy would be identified as such with different sets of ability and achievement test scores. Macmann and Barnett (1985) affirmed this finding in a computer simulation study that concluded that "the identification of a severe discrepancy between predicted and actual achievement was disproportionately related to chance and instrument selection" (p. 371). The consequences become even more problematic in cases where more than one achievement test was administered, and the lowest score among them was used in discrepancy calculation. Sobel and Kelemen (1984) showed how this situation will likely result in a difference between the proportion of students actually classified LD and the proportion originally expected. For example, in the case of three achievement measures administered and the lowest score selected, the original criterion value of 6.68% LD cases identified would increase to 12.2%.

INSTABILITY OF DISCREPANCY SCORES

The inherent variability associated with discrepancy calculation is made more unsure by findings showing instability in discrepancy scores over time. O'Shea and Valcante (1986) found that SDL comparisons between groups of students with LD and low achieving students without LD differed significantly from grade 2 to grade 5. The groups appeared to develop diverging SDLs over time with increasingly larger differences for students with LD in language and mathematics compared to reading but, nevertheless, the SDL for reading doubled from grade 2 to grade 5. White and Wigle (1986), in a large-scale evaluation of school-identified students with LD, found four different patterns of discrepancy over time. The largest group (40%) revealed no ability-achievement discrepancy at initial placement or at reevaluation. The next largest groups demonstrated either a pattern of being discrepant at placement but not at reevaluation or, conversely, a pattern of not being discrepant at initial placement but discrepant at reevaluation. The smallest group showed a discrepancy at both placement and reevaluation. Considering that discrepancy is a primary identification criterion for LD, its instability over time is a source of concern, but the problem appears endemic. For example, Shepard and Smith (1983) reported that only 43% of a statewide sample of school-identified students with LD met strict identification criteria, with discrepancy being the primary criterion.

An early survey of 3,000 students with LD in Child Service Demonstration Centers showed that the average discrepancy was only about 1 year, leading to the conclusion that "[t]his discrepancy can be interpreted as a moderate retardation, rather than a severe disability" (Kirk & Elkins, 1975, p. 34). In a later similar analysis, Norman and Zigmond (1980) applied the federal (1976) SDL formula and found that, on average, 47% of students met the SDL criterion. For children aged 6 to 10 years (the likely age range of identification), less than 40% met the SDL criterion while the percentage for students aged 15 to 17 was 68%. Although providing greater confidence in the LD classification of the older children, the smaller percentage of younger children meeting the SDL criterion raises questions about the validity of their LD classification.

DISCREPANCY AND THE IDENTIFICATION OF LEARNING DISABILITY

Shepard and Smith (1983) suggested that "the validity of LD identification cannot be reduced to simplistic statistical rules" (p. 125), but the inconsistent application of existing criteria creates significant difficulties in the LD diagnostic process. Shepard, Smith, & Vojir (1983), using a "discrepancy criterion," found that 26% of identified students with LD in Colorado revealed no discrepancy while 30% revealed a significant discrepancy with the use of any reading or math test. When validated with a second achievement measure, 5% of all students with LD had a significant discrepancy on two math tests while 27% revealed a significant discrepancy on two reading tests. Thus, not only was the discrepancy criterion not validated, but a "below grade level" criterion was not affirmed either; "Many LD pupils were not achieving below grade level as measured by standardized tests" (p. 317).

In contrast, Cone, Wilson, Bradley, and Reese (1985) found that 75% of a school-identified LD population in Iowa met the required discrepancy criterion. As this LD population continued in school, achievement levels became increasingly discrepant. In a later analysis, L. R. Wilson, Cone, Bradley, and Reese (1986) found that the identified students with LD were clearly different from other students with mild disabilities in Iowa (e.g., MR and behavior disorders [BDs]): "The main factor providing differentiations was discrepancy between achievement and ability" (p. 556). They concluded that students with LD were primarily underachievers, not simply low achievers.

In a later analysis, Valus (1986a) found 64% of identified students with LD to be significantly underachieving. In a large-scale analysis of Iowa's LD population, Kavale and Reese (1992) found that 55% met the discrepancy criterion. In different locales, the percentage of students with LD meeting the discrepancy criterion ranged from 32% to 75%. Thus, in any LD population, there will be a significant proportion who do not meet a significant discrepancy criterion, and, because of possible differences in interpretation, considerable variability in the proportions that do meet the discrepancy criterion across settings.

The finding of significant inconsistencies about the percentage of students meeting the discrepancy criterion is common among studies analyzing identified LD populations. For example, McLeskey (1989) found that 64% of an Indiana LD population met the discrepancy criterion, but this figure was achieved only after more rigorous and stringent state guidelines for LD identification were implemented. The 64% figure was almost double the 33% found in an earlier study (McLeskey & Waldron, 1991). In general, about one third of identified LD samples have been found not to meet the stipulated discrepancy criterion (e.g., Bennett & Clarizio, 1988; Dangel & Ensminger, 1988; Furlong, 1988).

Statistical Classification vs. Clinical Judgment

Shepard and Smith (1983) referred to the approximately one third of identified students with LD as "clinical cases," meaning that their eligibility was a discretionary judgment made by a multidisciplinary team (MDT) which was at variance with the statistical (i.e., discrepancy) information. This situation may occur because (a) the LD may have caused ability level (i.e., IQ) to decline, and if achievement remained at a comparatively low level, then a discrepancy would not exist; (b) intact skills permitted the student to "compensate" for the effects of LD which means that achievement test scores may reveal an increase while ability level remained constant; or (c) a "mild" discrepancy was present but not unexplained because of factors such as limited school experience, poor instructional history, behavior problems, or second-language considerations. The essential question: Are such students "truly" LD, or is the inconsistency between team decisions and statistical status "truly" misclassification?

The many vagaries associated with "system identification" (Morrison, MacMillan, & Kavale, 1985) are the primary reason for the difficulty in decisions about the presence or absence of LD (Frame, Clarizio, Porter, & Vinsonhaler, 1982). In analyses of MDT decisions, it appears that LD identification criteria, especially the primary criterion of severe discrepancy, were neither rigorously or consistently applied (Epps, McGue, & Ysseldyke, 1982; Furlong & Yanagida, 1985; Furlong & Feldman, 1992). The difficulties begin with the lack of uniformity across educational agencies in setting "severe" discrepancy criterion levels (Perlmutter & Parus, 1983; Thurlow & Ysseldyke, 1979) which are then often exacerbated by differences in interpreting existing guidelines (Thurlow, Ysseldyke, & Casey, 1984; Valus, 1986b). The misapplication of criteria in LD identification procedures is further complicated by external pressures that might include the desire of MDTs to provide special education services, the request of general education teachers to remove difficult-to-teach students, and parental demands for LD placement (e.g., Algozzine & Ysseldyke, 1981b; Sabatino & Miller, 1980; Ysseldyke, Christenson, Pianta, & Algozzine, 1983).

When LD is viewed as primarily a socially constructed disability (Gelzheiser, 1987), the many external pressures often become primary considerations because a criterion like SDL is viewed as too child-centered in a medical model sense and does not permit examination of complex contextual interactions presumed relevant for valid diagnosis (Algozzine & Ysseldyke, 1987). Gerber and Semmel (1984) even argued that an instructional perspective rather than a statistical one should be the basis for determining LD eligibility. They suggested that the teacher become the "test" for determining whether a student has a "real" learning problem. Under such circumstances, it is not surprising to find that MDTs often do not "bother with the data" (Ysseldyke, Algozzine, Richey, & Graden, 1982).

The "clinical cases" of LD represent, at best, a "functional" LD because even though deemed eligible, the students in question really did not meet stipulated identification criteria with discrepancy often being the most tangible. The failure to meet stipulated criteria, however, raised serious questions about the reliability and validity of "clinical diagnoses" of LD (Shepard, 1983). It was, therefore, not surprising to find that judges were not able to differentiate students with LD based solely on an examination of test scores (Epps, Ysseldyke, & McGue, 1984).

VAGARIES OF IDENTIFICATION AND PREVALENCE

When LD determination is not based on the application of strict criteria, the diagnostic process may be likened to the U.S. Supreme Court's definition of pornography: "I know it when I see it." The lack of rigor in the diagnostic process has led to an accelerated rate of LD identification and LD becoming, by a wide margin, the largest category in special education. Presently, LD accounts for more than 50% of all students with disabilities and more than 5% of all students in school (U.S. Department of Education, 1999). In commenting on the magnitude of the increase in LD prevalence, MacMillan, Gresham, Siperstein, and Bocian (1996) suggested that "Were these epidemic-like figures interpreted by the Center for Disease Control, one might reasonably expect to find a quarantine imposed on the public schools of America" (p. 169). There is little justification for such numbers, and the problem is compounded by the lack of consistency in the way the LD population is distributed across settings (Kavale & Forness, 1995). Clearly, fewer students are identified as LD when a strict discrepancy criterion is implemented rigorously (e.g., Finlan, 1992), but external factors (e.g., financial resources) may significantly influence (and increase) the number of students identified as LD (Noel & Fuller, 1985). Forness (1985) showed how state special education policy changes in California significantly affected the number of students identified in the high-incidence mild disability categories. LD saw a 156% gain compared to the 104% gain nationally, and a comparison with concomitant losses for MR and BD led Forness to the conclusion "that California's relatively dramatic increase in children identified as learning disabled may be at the expense of two other related categories" (p. 41). Such state disparities were not uncommon and led to the conclusion that "Our results suggest that variation in LD diagnostic levels across states is significantly related to distinctions in diagnostic practice as well as or instead of actual disease prevalence" (Lester & Kelman, 1997, p. 605). In contrast, far greater consistency in classification rates has been found for hearing impairment and physical/multiple disability compared to LD (Singer, Palfrey, Butter, & Walker, 1989).

CONFOUNDING AMONG HIGH-INCIDENCE MILD DISABILITIES

The confounding among high-incidence mild disabilities appears to be primarily between LD and MR. MacMillan et al. (1996) found among 150 referred students 43 with IQ levels at 75 or below. Of the 43, only 6 were classified MR even though they met the requisite eligibility cut-off score, while 18 were classified LD primarily because the LD label was viewed as a more acceptable designation. Similarly, Gottlieb, Alter, Gottlieb, and Wishner (1994) found that an urban LD sample possessed a mean IQ level that was 1½ SD lower than a suburban comparison sample. They concluded that "These children today are classified as learning disabled when in fact most are not" (p. 463). This view was affirmed by MacMillan, Gresham, and Bocian (1998) who found that out of 61 students classified LD by schools, only 29 met the required discrepancy criterion. In analyzing the results, they remarked that "We did not anticipate the extent to which the process would yield children certified as LD who failed to meet the discrepancy required by the education code" (p. 322). Thus, even though discrepancy remains the primary (and sometimes sole) criterion for LD identification, it was often ignored in actual practice. Gottlieb et al. (1994) suggested "the discrepancy that should be studied most intensively is between the definition of learning disability mandated by regulation and the definition employed on a day-to-day basis in urban schools" (p. 455).

Because "public school practices for diagnosing children with LD bear little resemblance to what is prescribed in federal and state regulations (i.e., administrative definitions) defining LD" (MacMillan et al., 1998, p. 323), the LD population has become increasingly heterogeneous and the longstanding "problem of heterogeneity" firmly entrenched (Gallagher, 1986). For example, Gordon, Lewandowski, and Keiser (1999) analyzed the problems associated with the LD label for "relatively well functioning" students. By failing to rigorously adhere to a SDL criterion, students with LD may not demonstrate underachievement, a primary LD feature (Algozzine, Ysseldyke, & Shinn, 1982) which then makes the utility of the LD category open to question (Epps et al., 1984).

CONFOUNDING BETWEEN LEARNING DISABILITY AND LOW ACHIEVEMENT

The vagaries of LD classification, especially the inability to differentiate LD and low achievement (LA), have been demonstrated in studies conducted by the University of Minnesota Institute for Research on Learning Disabilities (Minnesota studies). Ysseldyke, Algozzine, and Epps (1983) analyzed psychometric data obtained from students without LD using 17 operational definitions of LD. For 248 cases, 85% met the requirements for one operational definition of LD, while 68% qualified with two or more operational definitions. Only 37% of the non-LD sample did not meet the criteria specified in any of the 17 operational definitions of LD. A second analysis examined data for students with LD and students with LA to determine how many would qualify with each of the 17 operational definitions of LD used earlier. For the LD group, 1% to 78% were classified LD with each definition while the LA group was also classified LD from 0% to 71% of the time using each operational definition. Further analysis showed that 4% of the LD group was not classified by any of the 17 operational definitions while 88% of the LA group qualified as LD by using at least one operational definition. In a similar investigation, Epps, Ysseldyke, and Algozzine (1983) examined the number of students identified as LD with each of 14 operational definitions that emphasized the discrepancy criterion. The definitions classified from 7% to 81% of students as LD, whereas 5% to 70% of a non-LD group were also classified LD using at least one of these 14 operational definitions. To determine the congruence among the 14 operational definitions, Epps, Ysseldyke, and Algozzine (1985) performed a factor analysis and found two factors. The first factor (I) emphasized LA whereas the second factor (II) was represented by discrepancy. In terms of their respective weights, Factor I accounted for 70% of the variance compared to 16% for Factor II. The difference in explained variance led to the conclusion that LD might be properly conceptualized as a category reflecting LA, rather than discrepancy.

Epps et al. (1985) also found that knowing how many LD definitions qualified a student provided little assistance in correctly predicting group membership (LD vs. LA). Algozzine and Ysseldyke (1983) also found considerable inaccuracy in decisions about group membership (LD vs. LA) and concluded that "To make classification dependent on these discrepancies seems somehow arbitrary and capricious" (p. 245). Consequently, discrepancy appeared to possess limited value, and suggestions about its worth as a criterion for LD identification possessed little merit because "there may be an equally large number of children exhibiting similar degrees of school achievement not commensurate with their measured ability who are not categorized and therefore are *not* receiving special education services even though they are eligible for them under the current conceptual scheme represented by the category of learning disabilities" (p. 246). Thus, the failure to make LD a classification predicated on discrepancy suggests that it has not been possible to unequivocally define a category different from LA, and it might be more appropriate to recognize LA as the major problem.

The Minnesota studies appeared to support the view that reliance upon a discrepancy criterion for LD identification may not be defensible because it does not provide a clear distinction between LD and LA. L. R. Wilson (1985), however, challenged the idea that the LD category should be eliminated in favor of a more general classification like LA because a more general category will do little to eliminate the ambiguities and inconsistencies associated with LD. In fact, the Minnesota studies may themselves possess ambiguities and inconsistencies that limit the findings. For example, the Minnesota studies used only a discrepancy criterion for LD identification, and failed to include other components of the federal definition such as the exclusion which "states that the academic deficit cannot be the result of other possible causes such as emotional and personality factors, cultural deprivation, impaired sensory acuity, or educational deprivation" (p. 45). Since this aspect of the federal definition was not applied, the identification process was necessarily incomplete and restricted.

The other major problem area was related to sampling, specifically the possibility of bias in the Minnesota samples. The final sample used in the Minnesota studies was selected from a much larger population, which raised the question, "Is there evidence to suggest that the selection was random or is there reason to believe that bias may have distorted the findings?" (L. R. Wilson, 1985, p. 45). With respect to the LA group, L. R. Wilson suggested that "there is good reason to suspect that selection factors may have produced a disproportionately large number of discrepant achievers in the group of low achievers who were not formally labeled as learning disabled" (p. 46). Finally, the restricted nature of the selected samples raised questions about the generalizibility of the Minnesota findings.

In an analysis of a large-scale Iowa sample, L. R. Wilson (1985) demonstrated "that the federal definition of learning disabilities can be successfully used, that it can be consistently applied by a large group of special education professionals, that the various components of currently accepted learning disability definitions can provide the basis for discriminating a reasonably unique group of children, and that the exceptions found in this study, and other similar ones, do not automatically invalidate the previous conclusions" (pp. 49–50). The application of both a discrepancy *and* exclusion criterion resulted in a sound foundation for LD classification. As a result, the LD concept was quite defensible, and it would be "premature to eliminate it in favor of other concepts that probably have the very same weaknesses" (p. 51). In response, Algozzine (1985) suggested that there was really no reprieve for the LD concept and again LD was suggested to be a less than viable special education category because "creating the *new* concept of learning disabilities has not reduced the ambiguities, inconsistencies, and inadequacies that existed when low achievement was not a separate diagnostic category" (p. 75).

LEARNING DISABILITY VS. LOW ACHIEVEMENT DEBATE

The continuing debate about the LD-LA distinction began to erode the integrity of LD. Longstanding critiques of the LD definition (e.g., Reger, 1979; Senf, 1977; E. Siegel, 1968) evolved into suggestions that LD really did not exist as an independent entity as well as its depiction as myth (McKnight, 1982), questionable construct (Klatt, 1991), or imaginary disease (Finlan, 1994). The assumption that LD and LA could not be reliably distinguished became conventional wisdom. The primary evidence came from a study by Ysseldyke, Algozzine, Shinn, and McGue (1982) showing a substantial degree of overlap between the test scores of LD and LA groups and a conclusion raising "serious concerns regarding the differential classification of poorly achieving students as either LD or non-LD" (p. 82). Further confirmation was found in a study by B. A. Shaywitz, Fletcher, Holahan, and Shaywitz (1992) who concluded that "Our findings suggest more similarities than differences between the reading disabled groups" (p. 646). Group membership in this case was defined with a discrepancy criterion (LD) or low achievement (LA) criterion (scoring below 25th percentile in reading). When the LD and LA groups were compared across a number of child-, teacher-, and parent-based measures, few differences were found, with the major exception being in the ability (i.e., IQ) area. Nearly all the variance between groups was accounted for by IQ, but this may only be a reflection of the way groups were defined.

The findings from these studies have had significant impact and have been reported with remarkable consistency. For example, the Ysseldyke, Algozzine, Shinn, & McGue (1982) study has been used to conclude that limited LD-LA differences existed as exemplified in the following statements gleaned from the literature:

a. Certain researchers have suggested that LD is largely a category for low-achieving children.

b. [Ysseldyke et al.] found few psychometric differences between groups of students identified as learning disabled (LD) and low achievers who did not carry the label.

c. Recent studies of children diagnosed as learning disabled have shown that many such children...are virtually indistinguishable from low-achieving non-handicapped peers.

The difficulties in differentiating LD and LA groups were based on the Ysseldyke, Algozzine, Shinn, & McGue (1982) findings of a large number of identical scores between LD and LA subjects as well as a high percentage of overlap between scores. For example, on the Woodcock-Johnson Psychoeducational Battery, LD and LA groups showed identical scores 33 out of 49 times and an average overlap percentage of 95%. On five other psychoeducational measures, in better than half the cases there were identical scores and a 96% percentage of overlap. These metrics appeared, however, to be at variance with the reported statistical analyses. A comparison of Woodcock-Johnson scores revealed "that on average the LD group performed significantly poorer on 10 of the subtests" (p. 98), while statistical comparison of the five other psychoeducational measures showed "that the mean level performance of the LD children was lower on many of the measures, particularly the PIAT [Peabody Individual Achievement Test], and at times was significantly less than the mean level of their low-achieving peers" (p. 79).

REANALYSIS OF THE MINNESOTA STUDIES

Kavale, Fuchs, and Scruggs (1994) reexamined the Minnesota studies using quantitative synthesis methods (meta-analysis) and demonstrated how the percentage of overlap metric used by Ysseldyke, Algozzine, Shinn, & McGue (1982) may have masked real performance differences. The overlap metric used in the Minnesota studies was calculated by using the range of scores found for one group and then comparing how many cases from the second group fell within that same range, but with such a methodology, "[t]he potential bias toward overlap is high because the comparison is based on the variability demonstrated by only one group with the other being forced into that distribution without regard to the characteristics of its own variability" (Kavale et al., 1994, p. 74). The effect size (ES) statistic used in meta-analysis, because it is a standard score (z-score), eliminates potential bias by representing the extent to which groups can be differentiated, or, conversely, the degree of group overlap. For example, an ES of 1.00 indicates that the two compared groups differed by 1 SD and that 84% of one group can be clearly differentiated from the other group with a 16% group overlap.

Using the data from the Ysseldyke, Algozzine, Shinn, & McGue (1982) study, Kavale et al. (1994) calculated ES's for 44 comparisons and found an average ES of 0.338. This means that, on average, it would be possible to reliably differentiate 63% of the LD group. Conversely, 37% could not be differentiated, and this represented the degree of overlap that was substantially less than the average 95% reported by Ysseldyke, Algozzine, Shinn, & McGue (1982). For the Woodcock-Johnson Cognitive Ability subtests, an average ES of 0.304 was found, while the Achievement subtests provided an average ES of 0.763. With little reason to expect cognitive (IQ) differences between LD and LA groups, the modest group differentiation was not surprising. On the other hand, almost 8 out of 10 members of the LD group scored at a level that made it possible to discern clear achievement differences when compared with the LA group members. Similar findings emerged with other cognitive and achievement tests. For example, Wechsler Intelligence Scale for Children–Revised (WISC-R) comparisons revealed an average ES of 0.141 (56% level of group differentiation) while PIAT comparisons showed an average ES of 1.14, indicating that in almost 9 out of 10 cases (87%), the LD group performance was substantially below the LA group. Consequently, "it appears that the lower achievement scores of the LD group are of a magnitude that distinguishes them from their LA counterparts" (Kavale et al., 1994, pp. 74–75).

Algozzine, Ysseldyke, and McGue (1995) contested the meta-analytic findings but agreed that students with LD may be the lowest of the low achievers. They suggested that the difficulty was in interpreting the meaning of that status: "Where we part company is in the inference that because students with LD may be the lowest of a school's low achievers, they necessarily represent a group of people with qualitatively different needs who require qualitatively different instruction" (pp. 143–144). What Algozzine et al. (1995) failed to consider, however, were the findings showing minimal group differentiation in the cognitive domain. With essentially no difference in ability but large differences in achievement, the LD group demonstrated "significant discrepancy" that was not shown by the LA group. Consequently, Kavale (1995) suggested that the LD and LA groups "represent two distinct populations. Because the LD group are lower on achievement dimensions but not on ability, they are, in addition to being the lowest of the low achievers, a different population defined by an ability-achievement distinction represented in a different achievement distribution but not in a different ability distribution" (p. 146).

EXAMINING LEARNING DISABILITY AND LOW ACHIEVEMENT SAMPLES

In a similar comparison of LD and LA groups that also included comparisons with an MR group defined as IQ < 75, Gresham, Macmillan, and Bocian (1996) found an average LD-LA level of differentiation of 61% $\left(\overline{ES} = .28\right)$ (compare with the 63% reported by Kavale et al. 1994). The differentiation levels for LD-MR and LA-MR averaged 68.5% and 67.5%, respectively. On achievement measures, LD-LA group comparisons revealed an average ES of 0.39 indicating a 65% level of differentiation and confirmation of the finding that "LD children performed more poorly in academic achievement than LA children" (p. 579). The LD group performed most poorly in reading, where almost 3 out of 4 students with LD could be reliably differentiated from LA students. The large achievement differences in reading between LD and LA groups were affirmed by Fuchs, Fuchs, Mathes, and Lipsey (2000) who found that 72% of the LA group performed better in reading than the LD group $\left(\overline{ES} = .61\right)$. Even larger ES differences were found with more rigorous measures, "suggest[ing] that researchers and school personnel in fact do identify as LD those children who have appreciably more severe reading problems compared to other low-performing students who go unidentified" (p. 95).

Gresham, MacMillan & Bocian (1996) also investigated cognitive ability (IQ) differences among the three groups. As expected, 94% of the LD group could be reliably differentiated from the MR group. The percentage fell to 73% in differentiating LD and LA groups, suggesting greater cognitive ability overlap between these two groups. Gresham et al., however, included an LA group defined differently from both the Ysseldyke, Algozzine, Shinn, & McGue (1982) and B. A. Shaywitz et al. (1992) studies: "Our LA group was closer to what might be considered a 'slow learner' group on the basis of their average-level intellectual functioning relative to the LA groups in [the other] studies" (p. 579). The result was that even though achievement was depressed, it was not discrepant when compared to IQ level. In contrast, the LD group revealed significant discrepancies and was thus properly classified because "Children with LD perform more poorly in reading than LA children, even when the former group has higher cognitive ability" (p. 580). This finding has been confirmed by Short, Feagans, McKinney, and Appelbaum (1986) in an analysis of LD subtypes. In examining reading achievement across five groups, they found that "the joint application of IQ- and age-discrepancy criteria appeared to be useful for distinguishing between seriously disabled students and those who might be more appropriately classified as slow learners or underachievers" (p. 223). In summary, Gresham, MacMillan, & Bocian (1996) concluded that LD, LA, and MR groups "could be reliably differentiated using measures of cognitive ability and tested academic achievement" (p. 580). When LD is defined with an ability-achievement difference criterion, the resulting discrepancy appears to be an appropriate metric that permits reliable differentiation between LD and LA groups.

LEARNING DISABILITY AND INTELLIGENCE

Although empirical evidence appeared to indicate that LD and LA could be reliably differentiated with a discrepancy criterion, questions about its use continued. One form of questioning focused on IQ and whether it was necessary in defining LD. Beginning with the finding that IQ was not useful in locating students with reading disability (L. S. Siegel, 1988), questions arose about whether or not IQ was a necessary component in definitions of LD (L. S. Siegel, 1989, 1990). A major problem surrounded IQ tests and what they presumably measure. Stanovich (1991b) concluded that "an IQ test score is not properly interpreted as a measure of a person's potential" (p. 10). Yet, "the LD field has displayed a remarkable propensity to latch onto concepts that are tenuous and controversial....The LD field seems addicted to living dangerously" (Stanovich, 1989, p. 487). At a practical level, for example, there was controversy about what type of IQ score should be used in discrepancy calculation. Although it was commonly recommended that performance or nonverbal IQ be used (e.g., Stanovich, 1986a; Thomson, 1982), an equally compelling case could be made for the use of verbal IQ (e.g., Hessler, 1987). Without resolution about what IQ tests actually measure, "IQ is a superordinate construct for classifying a child as reading disabled. Without clear conception of the construct of intelligence, the notion of a reading disability, as currently defined, dissolves into incoherence" (Stanovich, 1991a, p. 272).

The ability-achievement discrepancy criterion treats intelligence and achievement as separate and independent variables, but L. S. Siegel (1989) suggested that this may not be valid because "A lower IQ score may be a consequence of the learning disability, and IQ scores may underestimate the real intelligence of the individual with LD" (p. 471). Further confounding was introduced by findings that the IQ of students with LD may actually decline over time (Share & Silva, 1987; Van den Bos, 1989). If this is a valid finding and also assuming that students remain close to their original reading levels over time (see Juel, 1988), then discrepancies should increase over time, but McLeskey (1992) found a negative association between discrepancy level and CA where "students in the elementary grades were most likely to manifest a severe discrepancy between expected and actual achievement, while high school students were least likely to have such a discrepancy" (p. 18).

A partial explanation may be found in what Stanovich (1986b) termed the "Matthew effect," referring to the Biblical statement (Matthew 13:12) that suggests that each advantage leads to further advantage, or conversely, initial disadvantage multiplies into even more disadvantage. For reading, this means that the poor get poorer: "Children with inadequate vocabularies—who read slowly and without enjoyment—read less, and as a result have slower development of vocabulary knowledge, which inhibits further growth in reading ability" (p. 381). B. A. Shaywitz et al. (1995), however, found no evidence of a Matthew effect in reading but a modest Matthew effect for IQ in a large-scale LD sample. For both IQ and reading, however, "the influence of the regression-to-the-mean effect tends to mask the relatively small Matthew effect" (p. 902) which suggests that the presumed cumulative disadvantage (Matthew effect) really refers to the rate of gain or loss in reading ability compared to initial level (see Walberg & Tsai, 1983). There are thus complex reciprocal relationships between reading ability and cognitive skills that are seen to confound the discrepancy notion because "the logic of the learning disabilities field has incorrectly assigned all the causal power to IQ. That is, it is reading that is considered discrepant from IQ rather than IQ that is discrepant from reading" (Stanovich, 1991b, p. 275).

THE ROLE OF INTELLIGENCE IN DEFINITIONS

The problem of confounding is most likely to arise in situations where concepts are defined with dual criteria. For example, although the psychometric characteristic IQ has long defined MR (e.g., Hollingworth, 1926), there was a later decision to include a second criterion in the form of adaptive behavior: the effectiveness and degree to which individuals meet standards of self-sufficiency and social responsibility (Heber, 1959). There was, however, concern over the inclusion of adaptive behavior in the MR definition primarily because of measurement issues (Clausen, 1972; MacMillan & Jones, 1972). Specifically, there were no adequate instruments to evaluate adaptive behavior that made it a psychometric characteristic comparable to IQ. [Of course, this situation was remedied with instruments like the American Association on Mental Retardation (AAMD) Adaptive Behavior Scale and the Vineland Social Maturity Scale]. With only one measure acceptable, there would be no means to evaluate *both* criteria, and this situation would create the possibility of students identified as MR who did not meet the dual criteria definition as well as students not identified who would meet the definition if appropriate assessments for *both* criteria were available.

When reliable and valid assessments are not available, clinical judgment was likely substituted but was often equally unreliable, especially in the "milder" regions of MR. With significant impairment in intellectual ability (IQ < 50), the corresponding adaptive behavior was probably equally impaired and not difficult to judge. As the upper limit of the IQ criterion was approached (IQ 70–75), however, the probability that adaptive behavior would correspond similarly decreased and clinical judgment became more problematic.

In defining LD, Kavale and Forness (1985) recommended a dual criteria definition similar to MR that included (a) significant subaverage academic impairment and (b) IQ in the average range. The advantage would be that both criteria can be reliably measured and little clinical judgment would be necessary. The two criteria can be readily compared and decision rules adopted to determine when the obtained difference ("discrepancy") was significant. If an additional exclusion criterion was added, then the identification process would avoid the myriad difficulties surrounding attempts to include other definitional parameters (e.g., psychological process deficits, central nervous system dysfunction) that cannot be reliably assessed. For this reason, IQ remains an important component in LD definition.

DEFINING LEARNING DISABILITY WITHOUT INTELLIGENCE

Even though IQ should be considered a necessary criterion, L. S. Siegel (1989) suggested that the LD field "abandon the use of the IQ test in the definition of learning disabilities.... [T]he IQ-achievement deviation definition should be abandoned because of its illogical nature" (p. 477). Stanovich (1989) suggested, however, that such a position might be "too extreme" (p. 489) and "perhaps ends up saying too little about too much" (p. 490). Lyon (1989) concluded that "Siegel has raised some interesting and compelling issues but has confounded her position by taking a narrow conceptual and methodological stance in addressing the relationship between intelligence and the LD definition" (p. 506). Baldwin and Vaughn (1989) suggested that "Siegel's position might be illogical because the reasoning was convoluted and misleading" (p. 513).

Meyen (1989) objected to the suggestion that IQ should be eliminated in the LD definition because "challenging the use of intelligence measures in defining learning disabilities, in essence, questions the efficacy of the category of learning disabilities itself as a means to identify students who warrant special education services" (p. 482). By eliminating IQ, a situation would be created where "we would largely serve low achievers and have no basis for determining whether or not a student is achieving at a reasonable level given his or her ability" (p. 482). The result would be an even more contentious LD-LA differentiation debate. The situation would not be remedied with a different IQ cut-off score which L. S. Siegel (1989) suggested as an alternative solution. In applying the discrepancy criterion in LD identification, there has long been the implicit assumption that IQ is at an average or above level in order to "discriminate between poor achievement that is expected (that is, on the basis of intellectual ability or sensory handicaps) and poor achievement that is not expected (that is, the probable presence of LD)" (Scruggs, 1987, p. 22). With an IQ cutoff of, for example, 75 (a level closer to the MR criterion) less than average academic achievement would be neither unexpected nor unexplained. There may be a need for special education, but such a student would not be properly classified as LD.

The primary difficulty with a lower IQ cutoff score in defining LD would be the potential confounding with MR. The AAMD (see Grossman, 1973) shifted the upper cutoff score for MR from −1 to −2 SD, that is, an IQ level of 70 instead of 85. Grossman (1983) later suggested the IQ cutoff could be as high as 75 since IQ should be viewed as only a rough guideline. Thus, cutoff scores really represent arbitrary statistical decisions rather than being based on scientific classification procedures (Zigler & Hodapp, 1986). Such arbitrary decisions create real dilemmas because they cause widely varying prevalence rates. For example, Reschly (1992) demonstrated that the use of an IQ cutoff of 75 and below results in twice as many individuals potentially eligible than would using IQ 70 and below. In addition, more cases fall in the interval 71–75 than in the entire range associated with mild MR (IQ 55–70). For LD with a 75 IQ cutoff, an additional 22.5% of the population would be eligible (given an "average" IQ level arbitrarily defined at 92.5) with perhaps 3% of this group potentially eligible for either MR or LD. With a discrepancy criterion, eligibility for LD can also be defined in SD units similar to MR (−1 to −2 SD depression) (see Mercer et al., 1996). As with MR, however, the choice of criterion level remains arbitrary and will also affect prevalence: the smaller the required discrepancy, the larger the prevalence. The current high prevalence rate for LD suggests a decision including smaller discrepancy levels, but the resulting LD classifications also suggest an increased probability of confounding with MR.

The consequences of the confounding between LD and MR are seen in large variations across states in prevalence rates with the typical outcome being more LD and less MR than expected (U.S. Department of Education, 1999). Gresham et al. (1996) showed that the percentage of students classified as MR was inversely related to the percentage of students classified as LD (r = −0.24). Thus, states serving a small percentage of students with MR classify a larger percentage of students as LD, and vice versa. It is entirely possible then that students with similar cognitive abilities and disabilities are served in one state as LD and in another as MR (MacMillan, Siperstein, & Gresham, 1996).

Although average or above IQ has been considered a prerequisite for LD, a longstanding view holds that average or above intelligence is not a necessary or desirable criterion (e.g., Ames, 1968; Belmont & Belmont, 1980; Cruickshank, 1977). Support for this view was found in large-scale evaluations of LD populations that have found mean IQ levels in both the low average (IQ 80–90) range (e.g., Koppitz, 1971; Smith, Coleman, Dokecki, & Davis, 1977; J. D. Wilson & Spangler, 1974) and the lower regions of the average (IQ 90–100) range (e.g., Kirk & Elkins, 1975;

McLeskey & Waldron, 1990; Norman & Zigmond, 1980). In addition, IQ levels of students with LD tended to be quite variable, and anywhere from 10% to 40% of LD samples were found to have IQ scores falling below 85 (e.g., Gajar, 1980; Kavale & Reese, 1992; Shepard et al., 1983).

To explain why the actual IQ level of students with LD might be below average, Burns (1984) used the bivariate normal distribution to show how LD samples can have average IQ scores well below 100. With the known relationship between IQ and achievement, the average IQ of LD samples will decrease as the correlation between IQ and achievement increases. For example, if cases below a given cutoff for achievement (e.g., $z < -1.0$) and above a given IQ cutoff (e.g., IQ > 80) are considered while postulating a correlation of 0.50 between IQ and achievement, then the average IQ of a sample on the bivariate normal distribution will be about 93. Piotrowski and Siegel (1986), however, suggested that using the bivariate normal distribution to explain mean IQ levels less than 100 for LD samples may not be appropriate. The primary difficulty was found in the use of *fixed* achievement cutoff scores regardless of IQ score, as achievement is likely to vary as a function of both MA and CA. For example, a student with an IQ of 80 and achievement z-score of –0.05 would meet the LD discrepancy criterion under the bivariate normal distribution, but, in reality, demonstrate almost no underachievement. Conversely, a student with an IQ of 130 and achievement z-score of –0.95 would in fact be underachieving significantly but would not meet the discrepancy criterion for LD. These problems are compounded further as the correlation between IQ and achievement increases. Finally, the bivariate model requires IQ scores to be normally distributed, but this is unlikely given the finding that the IQ of students with LD reveals less stability over time (Kaye & Baron, 1987; Lally, Lloyd, & Kulberg, 1987).

With a proportion of the LD population showing IQ levels falling more than 1 SD below the mean, this group would, at one time, be considered as having borderline MR (see Heber, 1961). As such, this group would qualify under the rubric "slow learners" and likely manifest *generalized* academic deficiencies. The essential question: Is this group also LD? In some instances the answer might be affirmative, but the majority of this group would probably exhibit academic deficits across *all* achievement domains that would run counter to the assumption that students with LD exhibit achievement deficits in one or more (but not all) academic areas. When all academic achievement areas are equally depressed, the notion of *specificity*, in the sense of the presence of intra-individual differences, would not be achieved, even though the idea that LD results from a circumscribed set of problems that interfere selectively with academic performance has received support (Stanovich, 1986a). Thus, instead of specific LD (as defined in the federal definition), there is a more generalized LD, a concept closer to that defined by MR particularly at the borderline levels.

The "unexpected" failure idea often associated with LD has been the source of other concerns about IQ and LD. When identified as LD, a student presumably possesses average or above IQ and meets the discrepancy criterion which then suggests that the cause of the academic problems cannot be attributed to low intelligence. On the other hand, the academic deficiencies of slow learners should not be surprising because the demonstrated achievement problems are consistent with the lower than average intellectual ability. These differences suggest that the etiology of the two conditions is really not the same, and consequently, LD and LA groups appear to possess quantitative and qualitative differences.

LEARNING DISABILITY AND LOW ACHIEVEMENT: QUANTITATIVE OR QUALITATIVE DIFFERENCES?

The origins of assumptions about possible qualitative differences between LD and LA can be found in the Isle of Wight epidemiological studies (Rutter & Yule, 1975; see also Rutter & Yule, 1973; Yule, Rutter, Berger, & Thompson, 1974). Essentially, the LA sample of poor readers was differentiated into two groups: general reading backwardness (GRB) and specific reading retardation (SRR). The GRB group was defined as reading below expected CA (i.e., no discrepancy between IQ and achievement) while SRR was defined as reading below grade level predicted from IQ (i.e., the presence of an IQ-achievement discrepancy).

In analyzing the population, Rutter and Yule (1975) found that while IQ scores were approximately normally distributed, reading achievement scores did not show the same normal distribution because, at the lower end of the distribution, there was a "hump" indicating the presence of a greater proportion than the 2.3% expected in a normal distribution. This "hump" contained the SRR group whose problems were viewed as "specific" to the reading process. As Yule et al. (1974) suggested, "*Extreme* underachievement in reading occurs at appreciably above the rate expected on the basis of a normal distribution and so constitutes a hump at the lower end of the Gaussian curve....There are no grounds for believing that the hump is anything but a true finding, and the finding implies that there is a group of children with severe and specific reading retardation which is *not* just the lower end of a normal continuum" (p. 10, emphasis in original).

Rutter and Yule (1975) concluded that, in addition to IQ differences, "Reading retardation is shown to differ significantly from reading backwardness in terms of sex ratio, neurological disorder, pattern of neurodevelopmental deficits and educational prognosis. It is concluded that the concept of specific reading retardation is valid" (p. 195). Rutter (1978) later affirmed the GRB-SRR distinction and the possibility of etiological differences particularly as manifested in the minimal brain dysfunction syndrome (Clements, 1966).

QUALITATIVE DISTINCTIONS IN MENTAL RETARDATION

The idea of distributional and etiological differences in a population was first proposed in the MR field. At IQ 50, it becomes possible to distinguish between mild and severe MR. Severe MR (about 25% of the MR population) typically represents "clinical" MR in the sense of probably possessing, besides limited cognitive ability, central nervous system pathology and associated disabilities. The larger mild MR group typically shows no neurological signs or associated clinical signs, and represents what is termed "familial" MR (Zigler, 1967). In the severe cases, the pathological factors significantly interfere with intellectual development (see Tarjan, Wright, Eyman, & Keeran, 1973) to such an extent that they distort the IQ score distribution as shown by Dingman and Tarjan (1960). In comparing the IQ distributions of low IQ populations (mild and severe) with those of the general population, there was an indication of an excess of cases ("hump") at the lower end of the distribution. Above IQ 50, there were few discrepancies between expected and actual percentages in the distribution but an excess of cases in the 0–19 IQ and 20–49 IQ ranges. This excess population formed a hump: an additional normal distribution of IQs with a mean IQ of 32 and an SD of 16. Clearly, when compared with IQ levels, the two groups appeared to differ with respect to etiology and clinical manifestations (Jastak, 1967; Weir, 1967).

The qualitative differences between the two MR "populations" became a source of debate and evolved into what was termed the "developmental-difference controversy" (Zigler & Balla, 1982). Generally, "this controversy centers around the question of whether the behavior of those retarded persons with no evidence of central nervous system dysfunction is best understood by those principles in developmental psychology that have been found to be generally applicable in explaining the behavior and development of non-retarded persons, or whether it is necessary to involve specific differences over and above a generally lower rate and asymptote of cognitive development" (p. 3).

QUALITATIVE DISTINCTIONS IN LEARNING DISABILITY

Because of the developmental-difference controversy, the related GRB-SRR distinction also became contentious. For example, many studies have failed to find a GRB-SRR bimodal distribution (e.g., Rodgers, 1983; Share, McGee, McKenzie, Williams, & Silva, 1987; Stevenson, 1988). Van der Wissel and Zegers (1985) suggested that no hump was found because it may, in reality, be an artifact resulting from floor and ceiling effects associated with the reading measures used. Using designs where students differed in reading level but were comparable in age (CA design) or comparable in reading level but varied in age (reading-level match design), a number of studies failed to demonstrate that SRR groups (achievement scores below levels predicted by IQ, i.e., discrepant) could be differentiated from a GRB group (depressed achievement not discrepant from IQ) (Fletcher et al., 1989; Fletcher, Francis, Rourke, Shaywitz, & Shaywitz, 1992; Foorman, Francis, Fletcher, & Lynn, 1996; Rispens, van Yperen, & van Duijn, 1991; Share & Silva, 1986; B. A. Shaywitz et al., 1992; L. S. Siegel, 1992; Vellutino, Scanlon, & Lyon, 2000). Consequently, IQ was not a major factor associated with SRR, which was interpreted to mean that SRR was not a discrete entity, but rather

> ...occurs along a continuum that blends imperceptibly with normal reading ability. These results indicate that no distinct cut-off exists to distinguish children with dyslexia clearly from children with normal reading ability; rather, the dyslexic children simply represent a lower portion of a continuum of reading capabilities (S. E. Shaywitz, Escobar, Shaywitz, Fletcher, & Makuch, 1992, p. 148).

Rutter (1990) suggested that "the crucial test of the SRR hypothesis, however, does not depend on the presence or absence of a hump in the distribution but whether the correlates and outcomes of SRR serve to differentiate the syndrome from GBR" (p. 637). A number of studies have failed to differentiate GRB and SRR groups, however. For example, GRB groups (i.e., no I.Q.-achievement discrepancy) performed no differently on independent measures of reading achievement or on assessments of the cognitive abilities presumed to underlie the ability to learn to read (Fletcher et al., 1994; Francis, Shaywitz, Stuebing, Shaywitz, & Fletcher, 1996; Morris et al., 1998; Share, McGee, & Silva, 1989; Stanovich & Siegel, 1994). With respect to gender differences, the presumption of a disproportionately greater number of boys than girls in SRR groups has not received support (Pennington, Gilger, Olson, & DeFries, 1992; Share et al., 1987; S. E. Shaywitz, Shaywitz, Fletcher, & Escobar, 1990). Finally, SRR groups were presumed to have a poorer educational prognosis than GRB groups (Yule, 1973), but no evidence supports the validity of this assumption (Francis et al., 1996; Share et al., 1989; B. A. Shaywitz et al., 1992; Vellutino et al., 1996).

In a summary of the available evidence, Fletcher et al. (1998) concluded that

> Under no circumstances is wholesale use of IQ test for learning disabilities justified. We have shown numerous problems with the discrepancy model, regardless of whether IQ tests or some other measures are used to operationalize the aptitude index. It is not the use of the IQ test that creates the problems with discrepancy. Classifications of children as discrepant versus low achievement lack discriminative validity (p. 200).

It was then suggested that the discrepancy criterion not be part of the LD identification process primarily because "it is not the score on the IQ test that identifies the child as having learning disabilities, but rather the score on the test of academic achievement that identifies the child with LD" (p. 201). Similarly, Aaron (1997) concluded that "a review of research in the area of reading disabilities indicates that classifying poor readers on the basis of a discrepancy formula into LD and non-LD categories lacks validity on both theoretical and empirical grounds" (p. 488). As an alternative, Aaron suggested a more pragmatic approach based on the Reading Component Model that identifies the source of the reading problem for all students and then focuses remedial efforts on that particular source.

THE STATUS OF DISCREPANCY IN THE IDENTIFICATION OF LEARNING DISABILITY

The discrepancy criterion for LD identification has thus been seriously challenged, with some anticipating its "impending demise" (Aaron, 1997). One difficulty, however, is in interpreting what that means for LD. The many analyses investigating discrepancy focused attention on the GRB-SRR distinction where, in both cases, the primary problem was an inability to read. Consequently, there was little question about the presence of reading disability (RD), but the presence or absence of LD was not really considered except by implication. Although students with LD are quite likely to manifest reading difficulties, they may not, and this fact makes any generalization from a GRB-SRR comparison suspect. The primary difficulty is conceptual and relates to the fact that if RD and LD are considered equivalent, then the law of parsimony is violated (Swanson, 1991). There appears, however, to be a decided tendency to view LD and RD as the same thing as evidenced by statements such as, "It is time to abandon the discrepancy-based classification of poor readers into LD and non-LD categories and expand the boundaries of LD to include all children who experience difficulties in learning to read" (Aaron, 1997, p. 488). Instead of providing conceptual clarity, such a suggestion would result in even greater confounding between concepts.

The same possible confounding is found with RD itself. The focus on GRB and SRR as discrete groups tends to obscure the fact that almost all students with SRR could be classified as GRB, while half of students with GRB can be classified as SRR (Hinshaw, 1992). Even when considering SRR itself, there are questions about its proper relationship with dyslexia, an RD equally difficult to define with precision (Benton & Pearl, 1978). The many similarities between the conditions raise the question as to whether SRR and dyslexia are the same thing (Yule & Rutter, 1976). Regardless of the answer, discussion about LD seems inappropriate as it is a different (and distinct) phenomenon that may or may not include students with these types of reading problems.

Thus, both LD and RD are complex entities, and eliminating the discrepancy criterion does not appear to be a sensible solution for resolving these complexities. Any suggested alternative, as, for example, in the Reading Component Model proposed by Aaron (1997), does not appear to be a viable solution in any significant sense unless it is also accompanied by a belief that LD is not a legitimate construct. When LD is not considered legitimate, there is a general theme that calls for a cessation of the illegitimate and unnecessary LD labeling, and a focusing instead on the difficulties of some students in learning to read by providing them with effective and responsive interventions (e.g., Christensen, 1992; McGill-Franzen & Allington, 1993; Swerling & Sternberg, 1996). As suggested by Aaron (1997), "When the discrepancy formula disappears from the educational scene, so will the concept of LD. After 40 years of wandering in the wilderness of learning disabilities, we are beginning to get a glimpse of the promised land" (p. 489). Whether or not the disappearance of the discrepancy formula leads to a promised land is certainly moot and would do little to resolve the complex and vexing problems associated with defining LD.

A major roadblock to problem resolution is the lack of a precise description of LD (Kavale & Forness, 2000). Although the description of LD is far from complete, the field has witnessed unprecedented growth and has accomplished this expansion not by using formal, albeit limited, definitions but rather by using a number of singular operational definitions stipulating rules about how a term is to apply in a particular case if specified actions yield characteristic results. Thus, a concept like LD may have a set of operations that define it, and knowing these operations presumably provides complete understanding of the concept (Benjamin, 1955).

For LD, the primary (and often sole) operation has been the application of a discrepancy criterion. Beginning with the USOE (1976) regulations and reaffirmed in proposed operational definitions (e.g., Chalfant & King, 1976; Shaw, Cullen, McGuire, & Brinckerhoff, 1995), discrepancy has emerged as the major means of LD identification. The LD identification process, however, may be more difficult and complicated than it appears to be with the use of a discrepancy criterion. For example, a problem surrounds the theoretical validity of operations. In a scientific sense, an operational definition must bear a logical and rational relationship with the verified theoretical constructs stipulated in the formal definition (Bergmann, 1961). For LD, a problem is created because the formal definition includes no mention of discrepancy (or underachievement) (Kavale, 1993). The resulting lack of congruence between definitions means that essentially two distinct views of LD are being presented: a formal representation and an operational representation.

The lack of correspondence creates a consequential problem: an increased probability that the operational definition may not be justified and may lead to potentially meaningless and insignificant operations that do not meet formal criteria (Deese, 1972). The operations specified may not actually "define" anything but merely state procedures required to test for the presence of the phenomenon to which the operations refer (Kavale, Forness, & Lorsbach, 1991). For example, assume an operational definition of LD that is based on the Learning Disability Coefficient (LDC) whose procedures require a calculation including an individual's white blood cell count multiplied by body weight in ounces, divided by head circumference in centimeters. Although possible to calculate, the LDC would possess little meaning or significance because the available validated knowledge about LD clearly indicates that the LDC does not "fit" any of it.

A less obvious example surrounds the different meanings that may be conveyed when different operational indicators are chosen. For example, discrepancy is defined as the difference between ability and achievement, but any number of ability (i.e., IQ) measures and probably even a greater number of achievement measures might be chosen for comparison. The problem is that when different combinations of measures are used to define discrepancy, it is not at all clear that the assessments are operationally, and thus, definitionally equivalent (Deese, 1972). It may, therefore, be difficult to "make sense" of the calculated discrepancy.

The use of operational definitions is thus neither a simple nor straightforward process but one that requires significant theoretical verification. Unfortunately, the LD field has not achieved the necessary verification primarily because discrepancy was so quickly embraced: "The debate that rages over what LD might be and the lack of consensus over the importance of any given variable is in sharp contrast to the relative unanimity regarding discrepancy. The consensus regarding discrepancy as the primary identification variable for LD has entrenched discrepancy to the point where it now represents the foundation concept for LD diagnosis" (Kavale & Forness, 1994, p. 23). In fact, discrepancy has become a deified concept as evidenced in its ascension to the status of "imperial criterion" (Mather & Healey, 1990) and a reified concept as seen in its elevation to an almost tangible property of students with LD (Kavale, 1987). Such deification and reification do not appear justified given the fact discrepancy itself is a hypothetical construct defined by hypothetical constructs (see Messick, 1981) resulting in the possibility that, in a theoretical sense, discrepancy may be a "fictitious concept" (Hempel, 1952).

The wide embrace of discrepancy has obscured some fundamental considerations. One such consideration surrounds the relationship between discrepancy and LD. With discrepancy often the only criterion used for LD identification, there has been an accompanying assumption that discrepancy represents the operational definition of LD. In reality, "Discrepancy is best associated with the concept of underachievement. This is true now and has historically been the case" (Kavale, 1987, p. 18). In a theoretical context, Shepard (1983, 1989) argued that discrepancy is the operational definition of underachievement. Thus, when a student meets the discrepancy criterion, what is being affirmed is underachievement, not LD. The scientific law of parsimony would suggest that underachievement and LD are not the same thing. To avoid confounding, the proper conclusion when the discrepancy criterion is met is that underachievement has been identified. If it is believed that underachievement is associated with LD (certainly a valid assumption), then discrepancy becomes a necessary but not sufficient criterion for LD identification (Kavale, 1987; Reynolds, 1984–1985).

Within the context of LD identification, discrepancy and the documentation of underachievement should represent only the first step in diagnosis (Kavale & Forness, 1994). Discrepancy is important in the identification process because it establishes a sound theoretical foundation for later LD determination. Although the discrepancy concept possesses psychometric and statistical problems, they have been satisfactorily addressed, and a technically defensible procedure to indicate the presence or absence of underachievement has been achieved. The findings from large-scale investigations appear to have affirmed the relationship between discrepancy and underachievement, and the possibility of reliably differentiating LD (i.e., students who meet the discrepancy criterion) from LA (i.e., students who do not meet the discrepancy criterion). Although critical as the initial step in LD determination, discrepancy should not be elevated to the status of being LD but rather viewed simply as the most useful means for defining underachievement, a necessary part of LD.

With discrepancy placed in proper perspective, attention needs to be directed at what else should be considered in the identification process in order to capture the complex and multivariate nature of LD (Kavale & Nye, 1991). Kavale and Forness (1995) suggested a way the process might proceed. The initial step is the formulation of foundation principles aimed at developing a theoretical framework for elucidating the basic nature of LD. Kavale and Forness (2000) elucidated the process further by proposing an operational definition in the form of a hierarchical scheme where each level depicts a decision point in the determination of LD. The scheme includes five levels where the first includes an ability (IQ)-achievement discrepancy to document the presence or absence of underachievement. The next levels focus on other stipulated criteria (e.g., psychological process deficits, exclusion), and a final LD designation is predicated on a student proceeding through each level. The process ceases if a student cannot meet the requisite criterion at any level. With its initial position, discrepancy provides the foundation and would be further strengthened if the difference score were based on the most reliable *total* IQ score and *total* achievement test score. In this way, a too narrowly focused discrepancy, as in, for example, a comparison between a Performance IQ and a Social Studies achievement subtest, would be eliminated. With such a scheme, a more comprehensive view of LD is achieved along with greater confidence in declaring that a student is "truly" LD.

CONCLUSION

Discrepancy is an important and legitimate concept applied to LD. Beginning with its status as a measure of educational progress, discrepancy evolved into an index of underachievement. Because LD has always been viewed as a construct associated with underachievement, discrepancy became a necessary component of LD. Although subject to debate about statistical and psychometric properties, discrepancy calculation can be made adequate and defensible for use in LD identification. Because of pragmatic reasons, discrepancy has become the primary LD identification criterion, and this emphasis has led to a number of difficulties, most noticeably the failure to appropriately differentiate LD and LA. When viewed properly, discrepancy is a useful component for LD identification and any presumed problems can be resolved satisfactorily. The most important point is that discrepancy not be used alone for LD identification. Discrepancy is the operational definition of underachievement and, when present, reliably and appropriately documents the presence of underachievement, not LD. With the valid assumption that LD and underachievement are not equivalent, the task becomes one of deciding what other factors need to be considered before there is confidence that LD has been determined. When placed in proper context, any arguments about the use of discrepancy for LD determination would cease. It would, therefore, be an error to eliminate discrepancy when considering the best means of defining the LD construct. The task is one of using discrepancy so that it is not LD itself but rather only part of a more comprehensive identification process.

REFERENCES

Aaron, P. G. (1997). The impending demise of the discrepancy formula. *Review of Educational Research, 67,* 461–502.

Ackerman, P., Peters, J., & Dykman, P. (1971). Children with learning disabilities: WISC profiles. *Journal of Learning Disabilities, 4,* 150–166.

Algozzine, B. (1985). Low achiever differentiation: Where's the beef? *Exceptional Children, 52,* 72–75.

Algozzine, B., Forgnone, C., Mercer, C., & Trifiletti, J. (1979). Toward defining discrepancies for specific learning disabilities: An analysis and alternatives. *Learning Disability Quarterly, 2,* 25–31.

Algozzine, B., & Ysseldyke, J. E. (1981a). An analysis of difference score reliabilities on three measures with a sample of low-achieving youngsters. *Psychology in the Schools, 18*, 133–138.

Algozzine, B., & Ysseldyke, J. E. (1981b). Special education services for normal children: Better safe than sorry. *Exceptional Children, 48*, 238–243.

Algozzine, B., & Ysseldyke, J. (1983). Learning disabilities as a subset of school failure: The oversophistication of a concept. *Exceptional Children, 50*, 242–246.

Algozzine, B., & Ysseldyke, J. E. (1987). Questioning discrepancies: Retaking the first step 20 years later. *Learning Disability Quarterly, 10*, 301–312.

Algozzine, B., Ysseldyke, J. E., & McGue, M. (1995). Differentiating low-achieving students: Thoughts on setting the record straight. *Learning Disabilities Research and Practice, 10*, 140–144.

Algozzine, B., Ysseldyke, J. E., & Shinn, M. R. (1982). Identifying children with learning disabilities: When is a discrepancy severe? *Journal of School Psychology, 20*, 299–305.

Alspaugh, J., & Burge, P. (1972). Determination of reading expectancy. *The Journal of Experimental Education, 40*, 1–5.

Ames, L. B. (1968). A low intelligence quotient often not recognized as the chief cause of many learning difficulties. *Journal of Learning Disabilities, 1*, 735–738.

Baldwin, R. S., & Vaughn, S. (1989). Why Siegel's arguments are irrelevant to the definition of learning disabilities. *Journal of Learning Disabilities, 22*, 513, 520.

Bannatyne, A. (1968). Diagnosing learning disabilities and writing remedial prescriptions. *Journal of Learning Disabilities, 1*, 242–249.

Barnett, D. W., & Macmann, G. M. (1992). Aptitude-achievement discrepancy scores: Accuracy in analysis misdirected. *School Psychology Review, 21*, 494–508.

Bateman, B. D. (1965). An educational view of a diagnostic approach to learning disabilities. In J. Hellmuth (Ed.), *Learning disorders* (Vol. 1, pp. 219–239). Seattle, WA: Special Child Publications.

Belmont, I., & Belmont, L. (1980). Is the slow learner in the classroom learning disabled? *Journal of Learning Disabilities, 13*, 496–499.

Benjamin, A. C. (1955). *Operationism*. Springfield, IL: C. C. Thomas.

Bennett, D., & Clarizio, H. (1988). A comparison of methods for calculating a severe discrepancy. *Journal of School Psychology, 20*, 359–369.

Benton, A. L., & Pearl, D. (Eds.). (1978). *Dyslexia: An appraisal of current knowledge.* New York: Oxford University Press.

Bergmann, G. (1961). Sense and nonsense in operationism. In P. G. Frank (Ed.), *The validation of scientific theories* (pp. 45–56). New York: Collier.

Berk, R. A. (1981). What's wrong with using grade-equivalent scores to identify learning disabled children? *Academic Therapy, 17,*(2), 133–140.

Berk, R. A. (1984). An evaluation of procedures for computing an ability-achievement discrepancy score. *Journal of Learning Disabilities, 17,* 262–266.

Bijou, S. W. (1942). The psychometric pattern approach as an aid to clinical analysis—a review. *American Journal of Mental Deficiency, 46,* 354–362.

Bishop, D. V., & Butterworth, G. E. (1980). Verbal-performance discrepancies: Relationship to birth risk and specific reading retardation. *Cortex, 16,* 375–389.

Bond, G. L., & Tinker, M. (1973). *Reading difficulties: Their diagnosis and correction (3rd ed.).* New York: Appleton-Century-Crofts.

Boodoo, G. (1984–1985). A multivariate perspective for aptitude-achievement discrepancy in learning disability assessment. *Journal of Special Education, 18,* 489–494.

Braden, J. P., & Weiss, L. (1988). Effects of simple difference versus regression discrepancy methods: An empirical study. *Journal of School Psychology, 26,* 133–142.

Burns, E. (1984). The bivariate normal distribution and the I.Q. of learning disability samples. *Journal of Learning Disabilities, 17,* 294–295.

Chalfant, J. C. (1985). Identifying learning disabled students: A summary of the National Task Force Report. *Learning Disabilities Focus, 1,* 9–20.

Chalfant, J. C., & King, F. S. (1976). An approach to operationalizing the definition of learning disabilities. *Journal of Learning Disabilities, 9,* 228–243.

Chapman, J. C. (1923). The unreliability of the difference between intelligence and educational ratings. *Journal of Educational Psychology, 14,* 103–108.

Chapman, J. S., & Boersma, F. J. (1979). Learning disabilities, locus of control, and mother attitudes. *Journal of Educational Psychology, 71,* 250–258.

Christensen, C. A. (1992). Discrepancy definitions of reading disability: Has the quest led us astray? A response to Stanovich. *Reading Research Quarterly, 27,* 276–278.

Clarizio, H. F., & Bennett, D. E. (1987). Diagnostic utility of the K-ABC and WISC-R/PIAT in determining severe discrepancy. *Psychology in the Schools, 24,* 309–315.

Clarizio, H. F., & Phillips, S. E. (1986). The use of standard scores in diagnosing learning disabilities: A critique. *Psychology in the Schools, 23,* 380–387.

Clarizio, H. F., & Phillips, S. E. (1989). Defining severe discrepancy in the diagnosis of learning disabilities: A comparison of methods. *Journal of School Psychology, 27,* 383–391.

Clausen, J. (1972). Quo vadis, AAMD? *Journal of Special Education, 6,* 51–60.

Clements, S. D. (1966). *Minimal brain dysfunction in children: Terminology and identification.* (NINDS Monograph No. 3, U.S. Public Health Service Publication No. 1415). Washington, DC: Department of Health, Education, and Welfare.

Coles, G. S. (1978). The learning-disabilities test battery: Empirical and social issues. *Harvard Educational Review, 48,* 313–340.

Cone, T. E., & Wilson, L. R. (1981). Quantifying a severe discrepancy: A critical analysis. *Learning Disability Quarterly, 4,* 359–371.

Cone, T. E., Wilson, L. R., Bradley, C. M., & Reese, J. H. (1985). Characteristics of LD students in Iowa: An empirical investigation. *Learning Disability Quarterly, 8,* 211–220.

Crane, A. R. (1959). An historical critical account of the accomplishment quotient idea. *British Journal of Educational Psychology, 29,* 252–259.

Cronbach, L. J., & Furby, L. (1970). How we should measure "change"—or should we? *Psychological Bulletin, 74,* 68–80.

Cronbach, L. J., Gleser, G. C., Nanda, H., & Rajaratnam, N. (1972). *The dependability of behavioral measurements: Theory of generalizability for scores and profiles.* New York: Wiley.

Cruickshank, W. M. (1977). Myths and realities in learning disabilities. *Journal of Learning Disabilities, 10,* 51–58.

Cureton, E. E. (1937). The accomplishment quotient technique. *Journal of Experimental Education, 5,* 315–326.

Dangel, H. L., & Ensminger, E. E. (1988). The use of discrepancy formulas with LD students. *Learning Disabilities Focus, 4,* 24–31.

Danielson, L. C., & Bauer, J. N. (1978). A formula-based classification of learning disabled children: An examination of the issues. *Journal of Learning Disabilities, 11,* 163–176.

Davis, W. A., & Shepard, L. A. (1983). Specialists' use of tests and clinical judgment in the diagnosis of learning disabilities. *Learning Disability Quarterly, 6,* 128–138.

Deese, J. (1972). *Psychology as science and art.* New York: Harcourt Brace Jovanovich.

Dingman, H. F., & Tarjan, G. (1960). Mental retardation and the normal distribution curve. *American Journal of Mental Deficiency, 64,* 991–994.

Divoky, D. (1974). Education's latest victim: The "LD" kid. *Learning, 3,* 4–8.

Dore-Boyce, K., Misner, M., & McGuire, D. (1975). Comparing reading expectancy formulas. *The Reading Teacher, 29*, 8–14.

Dudley-Marling, C., Kaufman, N., & Tarver, S. (1981). WISC and WISC-R profiles of learning disabled children: A review. *Learning Disability Quarterly, 4*, 307–319.

Elliot, M. (1981). Quantitative evaluation procedures for learning disabilities. *Journal of Learning Disabilities, 14*, 84–87.

Epps, S., McGue, M., & Ysseldyke, J. E. (1982). Inter-judge agreement in classifying students as learning disabled. *Psychology in the Schools, 19*, 209–220.

Epps, S., Ysseldyke, J. E., & Algozzine, B. (1983). Impact of different definitions of learning disabilities on the number of students identified. *Journal of Psychoeducational Assessment, 1*, 341–352.

Epps, S., Ysseldyke, J. E., & Algozzine, B. (1985). An analysis of the conceptual framework underlying definitions of learning disabilities. *Journal of School Psychology, 23*, 133–144.

Epps, S., Ysseldyke, J. E., & McGue, M. (1984). "I know one when I see one"— Differentiating LD and non-LD students. *Learning Disability Quarterly, 7*, 89–101.

Erickson, M. T. (1975). The z-score discrepancy method for identifying reading-disabled children. *Journal of Learning Disabilities, 8*, 308–312.

Evans, L. D. (1990). A conceptual overview of the regression discrepancy model for evaluating severe discrepancy between I.Q. and achievement scores. *Journal of Learning Disabilities, 23*, 406–412.

Feldt, L. A. (1967). Reliability of differences between scores. *American Educational Research Journal, 4*, 139–145.

Finlan, T. G. (1992). Do state methods of quantifying a severe discrepancy result in fewer students with learning disabilities? *Learning Disability Quarterly, 15*, 129–134.

Finlan, T. G. (1994). *Learning disability: The imaginary disease.* Westport, CT: Bergin & Garvey.

Fletcher, J. M., Espy, K. A., Francis, P. J., Davidson, K. C., Rourke, B. P., & Shaywitz, S. E. (1989). Comparisons of cutoff and regression-based definitions of reading disabilities. *Journal of Learning Disabilities, 22*, 334–338.

Fletcher, J. M., Francis, D. J., Rourke, B. P., Shaywitz, S. E., & Shaywitz, B. A. (1992). The validity of discrepancy-based definitions of reading disabilities. *Journal of Learning Disabilities, 25*, 555–561, 573.

Fletcher, J. M., Francis, D. J., Shaywitz, S. E., Lyon, G. R., Foorman, B. R., Stuebing, K. K., & Shaywitz, B. A. (1998). Intelligent testing and the discrepancy model for children with learning disabilities. *Learning Disabilities Research and Practice, 13,* 186–203.

Fletcher, J. M., Shaywitz, S. E., Shankweiler, D. P., Katz, L., Liberman, I. Y., Stuebing, K. K., Francis, D. J., Fowler, A. E., & Shaywitz, B. A. (1994). Cognitive profiles of reading disability: Comparisons of discrepancy and low achievement definitions. *Journal of Educational Psychology, 86,* 6–23.

Foorman, B. R., Francis, D. J., Fletcher, J. M., & Lynn, A. (1996). Relation of phonological and orthographic processing to early reading: Comparing two approaches to regression-based, reading-level-match design. *Journal of Educational Psychology, 88,* 639–652.

Forness, S. R. (1985). Effects of public policy at the state level: California's impact on MR, LD, and ED categories. *Remedial and Special Education, 6,* 36–43.

Forness, S. R., Sinclair, E., & Guthrie, D. (1983). Learning disability discrepancy formulas: Their use in actual practice. *Learning Disability Quarterly, 6,* 107–114.

Frame, R. E., Clarizio, H. F., Porter, A. F., & Vinsonhaler, J. R. (1982). Inter-clinician agreement and bias in school psychologists' diagnostic and treatment recommendations for a learning disabled child. *Psychology in the Schools, 19,* 319–327.

Francis, D. J., Shaywitz, S. E., Stuebing, K. K., Shaywitz, B. A., & Fletcher, J. M. (1996). Developmental lag versus deficit models of reading disability: A longitudinal, individual growth curves analysis. *Journal of Educational Psychology, 88,* 3–17.

Frankenberger, W., & Fronzaglio, K. (1991). A review of states' criteria and procedures for identifying children with learning disabilities. *Journal of Learning Disabilities, 24,* 495–500.

Franzen, R. (1920). The accomplishment quotient: A school mark in terms of individual capacity. *Teachers College Record, 21,* 432–440.

Fuchs, D., Fuchs, L. S., Mathes, P. G., & Lipsey, M. W. (2000). Reading differences between low-achieving students with and without learning disabilities: A meta-analysis. In R. Gersten, E. P. Schiller, & S. Vaughn (Eds.), *Contemporary special education research: Syntheses of the knowledge base on critical instructional issues* (pp. 81–104). Mahwah, NJ: Lawrence Erlbaum.

Furlong, M. J. (1988). An examination of an implementation of simple difference score distribution model in learning disability identification. *Psychology in the Schools, 25,* 132–145.

Furlong, M. J., & Feldman, M. G. (1992). Can ability-achievement regression to the mean account for MDT discretionary decisions? *Psychology in the Schools, 29*, 205–212.

Furlong, M. J., & Yanagida, E. H. (1985). Psychometric factors affecting multidisciplinary team identification of learning disabled children. *Learning Disability Quarterly, 8*, 37–46.

Gajar, A. H. (1980). Characteristics across exceptional categories: EMR, LD, and ED. *Journal of Special Education, 14*, 165–173.

Gallagher, J. J. (1966). Children with developmental imbalances: A psychoeducational definition. In W. M. Cruickshank (Ed.), *The teacher of brain-injured children* (pp. 20–34). Syracuse, NY: Syracuse University Press.

Gallagher, J. J. (1986). Learning disabilities and special education: A critique. *Journal of Learning Disabilities, 19*, 595–601.

Gelzheiser, L. M. (1987). Reducing the number of students identified as learning disabled: A question of practice, philosophy, or policy? *Exceptional Children, 54*, 145–150.

Gerber, M. M., & Semmel, M. I. (1984). Teacher as imperfect test: Reconceptualizing the referral process. *Educational Psychologist, 19*, 137–148.

Gordon, M., Lewandowski, L., & Keiser, S. (1999). The LD label for relatively well-functioning students: A critical analysis. *Journal of Learning Disabilities, 32*, 485–490.

Gottesman, R. C. (1979). Follow-up of learning disabled children. *Learning Disability Quarterly, 2*, 60–69.

Gottlieb, J., Alter, M., Gottlieb, B. M., & Wishner, J. (1994). Special education in urban America: It's not justifiable for many. *Journal of Special Education, 27*, 453–465.

Gresham, F. M., MacMillan, D. L., & Bocian, K. M. (1996). Learning disabilities, low achievement, and mild mental retardation: More alike than different? *Journal of Learning Disabilities, 29*, 570–581.

Grossman, H. J. (Ed.). (1973). *Manual on terminology and classification in mental retardation.* Washington, DC: American Association on Mental Deficiency.

Grossman, H. J. (Ed.). (1983). *Classification in mental retardation* (3rd rev.). Washington, DC: American Association on Mental Deficiency.

Gullicksen, H. (1950). *Theory of mental tests.* New York: Wiley.

Gutkin, T. B. (1979). WISC-R scatter indices: Useful information for differential diagnosis? *Journal of School Psychology, 17*, 368–371.

Hanna, G. S., Dyck, N. A., & Holen, M. C. (1979). Objective analysis of achievement-aptitude discrepancies in LD classification. *Learning Disability Quarterly, 2*, 32–38.

Harris, A. J. (1961). *How to increase reading ability* (4th ed.). New York: McKay.

Harris, A. J. (1971). *How to increase reading ability* (5th ed.). New York: McKay.

Harris, A. J. (1975). *How to increase reading ability* (6th ed.). New York: McKay.

Heber, R. F. (1959). A manual on terminology and classification in mental retardation. *American Journal of Mental Deficiency Monograph (Supp. 64).*

Heber, R. (1961). Modifications in the manual on terminology and classification in mental retardation. *American Journal of Mental Deficiency, 65*, 499–500.

Hempel, C. (1952). Fundamentals of concept formation in empirical science. *International Encyclopedia of Unified Science (Vol. II, No. 7).* Chicago: University of Chicago Press.

Hessler, G. L. (1987). Educational issues surrounding severe discrepancy. *Learning Disabilities Research, 3*, 43–49.

Hinshaw, S. (1992). Externalizing behavior problems and academic underachievement in childhood and adolescence: Causal relationships and underlying mechanisms. *Psychological Bulletin, 111*, 127–155.

Hoffman, J. V. (1980). The disabled reader: Forgive us our regressions and lead us not into expectations. *Journal of Learning Disabilities, 13*, 7–11.

Hollingworth, L. S. (1926). *The psychology of subnormal children.* New York: Macmillan.

Hoover, H. D. (1984). The most appropriate scores for measuring educational development in the elementary schools: GEs. *Educational Measurement: Issues and Practice, 3*, 8–14.

Hopkins, K. D., & Stanley, J. C. (1981). *Educational and psychological measurement and evaluation* (6th ed.). Englewood Cliffs, NJ: Prentice-Hall.

Horn, A. (1941). *The uneven distribution of the effects of special factors.* Southern California Education Monographs, No. 12.

Iowa Department of Public Instruction. (1981). *The identification of pupils with learning disabilities.* Des Moines, IA: Author.

Jastak, J. F. (1967). Mental Retardation. *Science, 155*, 577–578.

Jenkins, J. R., & Pany, D. (1978). Standardized achievement tests: How useful for special education? *Exceptional Children, 44*, 448–453.

Johnson, D. J., & Myklebust, H. R. (1967). *Learning disabilities: Educational principles and practices.* New York: Grune & Stratton.

Juel, C. (1988). Learning to read and write: A longitudinal study of 54 children from first through fourth grades. *Journal of Educational Psychology, 78,* 243–245.

Kaufman, A. S. (1981). The WISC-R and learning disabilities assessment: State of the art. *Journal of Learning Disabilities, 14,* 520–526.

Kavale, K. A. (1987). Theoretical issues surrounding severe discrepancy. *Learning Disabilities Research, 3,* 12–20.

Kavale, K. A. (1993). A science and theory of learning disabilities. In G. R. Lyon, D. B. Gray, J. F. Kavanagh, & N. A. Krasnegor (Eds.), *Better understanding of learning disabilities: New views from research and their implications for education and public policies* (pp. 171–195). Baltimore: Brookes.

Kavale, K. A. (1995). Setting the record straight on learning disability and low achievement: The tortuous path of ideology. *Learning Disabilities Research and Practice, 10,* 145–152.

Kavale, K. A., & Forness, S. R. (1984). A meta-analysis of the validity of Wechsler Scale profiles and recategorizations: Patterns or parodies? *Learning Disability Quarterly, 7,* 136–156.

Kavale, K. A., & Forness, S. R. (1985). *The science of learning disabilities.* San Diego, CA: College-Hill Press.

Kavale, K. A., & Forness, S. R. (1994). Learning disabilities and intelligence: An uneasy alliance. In T. E. Scruggs & M. A. Mastropieri (Eds.), *Advances in learning and behavioral disabilities* (Vol. 8, pp. 1–63). Greenwich, CT: JAI Press.

Kavale, K. A., & Forness, S. R. (1995). *The nature of learning disabilities: Critical elements of diagnosis and classification.* Mahwah, NJ: Lawrence Erlbaum.

Kavale, K. A., & Forness, S. R. (2000). What definitions of learning disability say and don't say: A critical analysis. *Journal of Learning Disabilities, 33,* 239–256.

Kavale, K. A., Forness, S. R., & Lorsbach, T. C. (1991). Definition for definitions of learning disabilities. *Learning Disability Quarterly, 14,* 257–266.

Kavale, K. A., Fuchs, D., & Scruggs, T. E. (1994). Setting the record straight on learning disability and low achievement: Implications for policymaking. *Learning Disabilities Research and Practice, 9,* 70–77.

Kavale, K. A., & Reese, J. H. (1992). The character of learning disabilities: An Iowa profile. *Learning Disability Quarterly, 15,* 74–94.

Kaye, D. B., & Baron, M. B. (1987). Long-term stability of intelligence and achievement scores in specific-learning-disabilities samples. *Journal of Psychoeducational Assessment, 3,* 257–266.

Kelley, T. L. (1927). *Interpretation of educational measurements.* New York: World Book.

Kirk, S. A. (1962). *Educating exceptional children.* Boston: Houghton Mifflin.

Kirk, S. A. (1975). Behavioral diagnosis and remediation of learning disabilities. In S. A. Kirk & J. M. McCarthy (Eds.), *Learning disabilities: Selected ACLD papers.* Boston: Houghton Mifflin.

Kirk, S. A., & Elkins, J. (1975). Characteristics of children enrolled in the child service demonstration centers. *Journal of Learning Disabilities, 8,* 630–637.

Klatt, H. J. (1991). Learning disabilities: A questionable construct. *Educational Theory, 41,* 47–60.

Koppitz, E. M. (1971). *Children with learning disabilities: A five year follow-up study.* New York: Grune & Stratton.

Lally, M. J., Lloyd, R. D., & Kulberg, J. M. (1987). Is intelligence stable in learning-disabled children? *Journal of Psychoeducational Assessment, 3,* 411–416.

Lester, G., & Kelman, M. (1997). State disparities in the diagnosis and placement of pupils with learning disabilities. *Journal of Learning Disabilities, 30,* 599–607.

Lloyd, J., Sabatino, D., Miller, T., & Miller, S. (1977). Proposed federal guidelines: Some open questions. *Journal of Learning Disabilities, 10,* 69–71.

Lyon, G. R. (1989). I.Q. is irrelevant to the definition of learning disabilities: A position in search of logic and data. *Journal of Learning Disabilities, 22,* 504–506, 512.

Macmann, G. M., & Barnett, D. W. (1985). Discrepancy score analysis: A computer simulation of classification stability. *Journal of Psychoeducational Assessment, 4,* 363–375.

Macmann, G. M., Barnett, D. W., Lombard, T. J., Belton-Kocher, E., & Sharpe, M. N. (1989). On the actuarial classification of children: Fundamental studies of classification agreement. *Journal of Special Education, 23,* 127–143.

MacMillan, D. L., Gresham, F. M., & Bocian, K. M. (1998). Discrepancy between definitions of learning disabilities and school practices: An empirical investigation. *Journal of Learning Disabilities, 31,* 314–326.

MacMillan, D. L., Gresham, F. M., Siperstein, G. N., & Bocian, K. M. (1996). The labyrinth of IDEA: School decisions on referred students with subaverage general intelligence. *American Journal on Mental Retardation, 101,* 161–174.

MacMillan, D. L., & Jones, R. L. (1972). Lions in search of more Christians. *Journal of Special Education, 6,* 81–91.

MacMillan, D., Siperstein, G., & Gresham, F. (1996). A challenge to the viability of mild mental retardation as a diagnostic category. *Exceptional Children, 62,* 356–371.

Macy, M., Baker, J., & Kosinski, S. (1979). An empirical study of the Myklebust learning quotient. *Journal of Learning Disabilities, 12,* 93–96.

Mather, N., & Healey, W. C. (1990). Deposing aptitude-achievement discrepancy as the imperial criterion for learning disabilities. *Learning Disabilities: A Multidisciplinary Journal, 1,* 40–48.

McDermott, P. A., & Watkins, M. (1985). McDermott Multidimensional Assessment of Children. [Computer program]. New York: Psychological Corporation.

McGill-Franzen, S., & Allington, R. L. (1993). Flunk 'em or get them classified: The contamination of primary grade accountability data. *Educational Researcher, 22,* 19–22.

McKnight, P. T. (1982). The learning disability myth in American education. *Journal of Education, 164,* 351–359.

McLeod, J. (1979). Educational underachievement: Toward a defensible psychometric definition. *Journal of Learning Disabilities, 12,* 322–330.

McLeskey, J. (1989). The influence of level of discrepancy on the identification of students with learning disabilities. *Journal of Learning Disabilities, 22,* 435–438, 443.

McLeskey, J. (1992). Students with learning disabilities at primary, intermediate, and secondary grade levels: Identification and characteristics. *Learning Disability Quarterly, 15,* 13–19.

McLeskey, J., & Waldron, N. L. (1990). The identification and characteristics of students with learning disabilities in Indiana. *Learning Disabilities Research, 5,* 72–78.

McLeskey, J., & Waldron, N. L. (1991). Identifying students with learning disabilities: The effect of implementing statewide guidelines. *Journal of Learning Disabilities, 24,* 501–506.

McPhail, A. H. (1922). The correlation between the I.Q. and the A.Q. *School and Society, 16,* 586–588.

Meehl, P. E. (1954). *Clinical versus statistical prediction.* Minneapolis: University of Minnesota Press.

Mercer, C. D., Jordan, L., Allsopp, D. H., & Mercer, A. R. (1996). Learning disabilities definitions and criteria used by state education departments. *Journal of Learning Disabilities, 19,* 217–232.

Messick, S. (1981). Constructs and their vicissitudes in educational and psychological measurement. *Psychological Bulletin, 89,* 575–588.

Meyen, E. (1989). Let's not confuse test scores with the substance of the discrepancy model. *Journal of Learning Disabilities, 22,* 482–483.

Miller, M. (1980). On the attempt to find WISC-R profiles for learning and reading disabilities: A response to Vance, Wallbrown, and Blaha. *Journal of Learning Disabilities, 13,* 338–340.

Monroe, M. (1932). *Children who cannot read.* Chicago: University of Chicago Press.

Morris, R. D., Stuebing, K. K., Fletcher, J. M., Shaywitz, S. E., Lyon, G. R., Shankweiler, D. P., Katz, L., Francis, D. J., & Shaywitz, B. A. (1998). Subtypes of reading disability: Variability around a phonological core. *Journal of Educational Psychology, 90,* 347–373.

Morrison, G. M., MacMillan, D. L., & Kavale, K. A. (1985). System identification of learning disabled children: Implications for research sampling. *Learning Disability Quarterly, 8,* 2–10.

Myklebust, H. R., Bannochie, M. N., & Killen, J. R. (1971). Learning disabilities and cognitive processes. In H. R. Myklebust (Ed.), *Progress in learning disabilities* (Vol. II, pp. 213–251). New York: Grune & Stratton.

Naglieri, J. A. (1981). Factor structure of the WISC-R for children identified as learning disabled. *Psychological Reports, 49,* 891–895.

Noel, M. M., & Fuller, B. C. (1985). The social policy construction of special education: The impact of state characteristics on identification and integration of handicapped children. *Remedial and Special Education, 6,* 27–35.

Norman, C. A., & Zigmond, N. (1980). Characteristics of children labeled and served as learning disabled in school systems affiliated with Child Service Demonstration Centers. *Journal of Learning Disabilities, 13,* 542–547.

O'Donnell, L. E. (1980). Intra-individual discrepancy in diagnosing specific learning disabilities. *Learning Disability Quarterly, 3,* 10–18.

O'Shea, L. J., & Valcante, G. (1986). A comparison over time of relative discrepancy scores of low achievers. *Exceptional Children, 53,* 253–259.

Payne, R. W., & Jones, H. G. (1957). Statistics for the investigation of individual cases. *Journal of Clinical Psychology, 13,* 115–121.

Pennington, B. F., Gilger, J. W., Olson, R. K., & DeFries, J. C. (1992). The external validity of age- versus I.Q.-discrepancy definitions of reading disability: Lessons from a twin study. *Journal of Learning Disabilities, 25,* 562–573.

Perlmutter, B., & Parus, M. (1983). Identifying children with learning disabilities: A comparison of diagnostic procedures across school districts. *Learning Disability Quarterly, 6,* 321–328.

Pintner, R., & Marshall, H. (1921). A combined mental-educational survey. *Journal of Educational Psychology, 12*, 32–43.

Piotrowski, R. J., & Siegel, D. J. (1986). The I.Q. of learning disability samples: A reexamination. *Journal of Learning Disabilities, 19*, 492–493.

Popenoe, H. (1927). A report of certain significant deficiencies of the accomplishment quotient. *Journal of Educational Research, 16*, 40–47.

Reger, R. (1979). Learning disabilities: Futile attempts at a simplistic definition. *Journal of Learning Disabilities, 12*, 31–34.

Reschly, D. J. (1992). Mental retardation: Conceptual foundation, definitional criteria, and diagnostic operations. In S. R. Hooper, G. W. Hynd, & R. E. Mattison (Eds.), *Developmental disorders: Diagnostic criteria and clinical assessment* (pp. 23–67). Hillsdale, NJ: Lawrence Erlbaum.

Reynolds, C. R. (1981). The fallacy of "two years below grade level for age" as a diagnostic criterion for reading disorders. *Journal of School Psychology, 19*, 350–358.

Reynolds, C. R. (1984–1985). Critical measurement issues in learning disabilities. *Journal of Special Education, 18*, 451–476.

Reynolds, C. R. (1985). Measuring the aptitude-achievement discrepancy in learning disability diagnosis. *Remedial and Special Education, 6*, 37–55.

Reynolds, C. R., & Snow, M. (1985). Severe discrepancy analysis. [Computer program]. College Station, TX: TRAIN.

Rispens, J., van Yperen, T. A., & van Duijn, G. A. (1991). The irrelevance of I.Q. to the definition of learning disabilities: Some empirical evidence. *Journal of Learning Disabilities, 24*, 434–438.

Rodenborn, L. V. (1974). Determining and using expectancy formulas. *The Reading Teacher, 28*, 286–291.

Rodgers, B. (1983). The identification and prevalence of specific reading retardation. *British Journal of Educational Psychology, 53*, 369–373.

Ross, R. P. (1992a). Accuracy in analysis of discrepancy scores: A nationwide study of school psychologists. *School Psychology Review, 21*, 480–493.

Ross, R. P. (1992b). Aptitude-achievement discrepancy scores: Accuracy in analysis ignored. *School Psychology Review, 21*, 509–514.

Ruch, G. M. (1923). The achievement quotient technique. *Journal of Educational Psychology, 14*, 334–343.

Rutter, M. (1978). Prevalence and types of dyslexia. In A. L. Benton, & D. Pearl (Eds.), *Dyslexia: An appraisal of current knowledge* (pp. 5–28). New York: Oxford University Press.

Rutter, M. (1990). Isle of Wight revisited: Twenty-five years of child psychiatric epidemiology. *Journal of American Academy of Child and Adolescent Psychiatry, 29,* 633–653.

Rutter, M., & Yule, W. (1973). Specific reading retardation. In L. Mann, & D. Sabatino (Eds.), *The first review of special education* (pp. 49–62). Philadelphia: JSE Press.

Rutter, M., & Yule, W. (1975). The concept of specific reading retardation. *Journal of Child Psychology and Psychiatry, 16,* 181–197.

Sabatino, D. A., & Miller, T. L. (1980). The dilemma of diagnosis in learning disabilities: Problems and potential directions. *Psychology in the Schools, 17,* 76–86.

Salvia, J., & Clark, J. (1973). Use of deficits to identify the learning disabled. *Exceptional Children, 39,* 305–308.

Schulte, A., & Borich, G. D. (1984). Considerations in the use of difference scores to identify learning-disabled children. *Journal of School Psychology, 22,* 381–390.

Scruggs, T. E. (1987). Theoretical issues surrounding severe discrepancy: A discussion. *Learning Disabilities Research, 3,* 21–23.

Selz, M., & Reitan, R. (1979). Rules for neuropsychological diagnosis: Classification of brain function in older children. *Journal of Consulting and Clinical Psychology, 47,* 258–264.

Senf, G. M. (1977). A perspective on the definition of LD. *Journal of Learning Disabilities, 10,* 537–539.

Share, D. L., McGee, R., McKenzie, D., Williams, S., & Silva, P. A. (1987). Further evidence relating to the distinction between specific reading retardation and general reading backwardness. *British Journal of Developmental Psychology, 5,* 34–44.

Share, D. L., McGee, R., & Silva, P. D. (1989). I.Q. and reading progress: A test of the capacity notion of I.Q. *Journal of American Academy of Child and Adolescent Psychiatry, 28,* 97–100.

Share, D. L., & Silva, P. A. (1986). The stability and classification of specific reading retardation: A longitudinal study from age 7 to 11. *British Journal of Educational Psychology, 56,* 32–39.

Share, D. L., & Silva, P. A. (1987). Language deficits and specific reading retardation: Cause or effect? *British Journal of Disorders of Communication, 22,* 219–226.

Shaw, S. F., Cullen, J. P., McGuire, J. M., & Brinckerhoff, L. C. (1995). Operationalizing a definition of learning disabilities. *Journal of Learning Disabilities, 28,* 586–597.

Shaywitz, S. E., Escobar, M. D., Shaywitz, B. A., Fletcher, J. M., & Makuch, R. (1992). Evidence that dyslexia may represent the lower tail of a normal distribution of reading ability. *New England Journal of Medicine, 326,* 145–150.

Shaywitz, B. A., Fletcher, J. M., Holahan, J. M., & Shaywitz, S. E. (1992). Discrepancy compared to low achievement definitions of reading disability: Results from the Connecticut Longitudinal Study. *Journal of Learning Disabilities, 25,* 639–648.

Shaywitz, B. A., Holford, T. R., Holohan, J. M., Fletcher, J. M., Stuebing, K. K., Francis, D. J., & Shaywitz, S. E. (1995). A Matthew effect for I.Q. but not for reading: Results from a longitudinal study. *Reading Research Quarterly, 30,* 894–906.

Shaywitz, S. E., Shaywitz, B. A., Fletcher, J. M., & Escobar, M. D. (1990). Prevalence of reading disability in boys and girls: Results of the Connecticut Longitudinal Study. *Journal of the American Medical Association, 264,* 998–1002.

Shepard, L. (1980). An evaluation of the regression discrepancy method for identifying children with learning disabilities. *Journal of Special Education, 14,* 79–91.

Shepard, L. A. (1983). The role of measurement in educational policy: Lessons from the identification of learning disabilities. *Educational Measurement: Issues and Practices, 2,* 4–8.

Shepard, L. A. (1989). Identification of mild handicaps. In. R. Linn (Ed.), *Educational measurement* (3rd ed., pp. 545–572). New York: Macmillan.

Shepard, L. A., & Smith, M. L. (1983). An evaluation of the identification of learning disabled students in Colorado. *Learning Disability Quarterly, 6,* 115–127.

Shepard, L. A., Smith, M. L., & Vojir, C. P. (1983). Characteristics of pupils identified as learning disabled. *American Educational Research Journal, 20,* 309–331.

Short, E. J., Feagans, L., McKinney, J. D., & Appelbaum, M. I. (1986). Longitudinal stability of LD subtypes based on age-and I.Q.-achievement discrepancies. *Learning Disability Quarterly, 9,* 214–225.

Siegel, E. (1968). Learning disabilities: Substance or shadow. *Exceptional Children, 35,* 433–437.

Siegel, L. S. (1988). Evidence that I.Q. scores are irrelevant to the definition and analysis of reading disability. *Canadian Journal of Psychology, 42,* 201–215.

Siegel, L. S. (1989). I.Q. is irrelevant to the definition of learning disabilities. *Journal of Learning Disabilities, 22*, 469–478, 486.

Siegel, L. S. (1990). IQ and learning disabilities: R.I.P. In H. L. Swanson & B. Keogh (Eds.), *Learning disabilities: Theoretical and research issues* (pp. 111–128). Hillsdale, NJ: Erlbaum.

Siegel, L. S. (1992). An evaluation of the discrepancy definition of dyslexia. *Journal of Learning Disabilities, 25*, 618–629.

Simmons, G. A., & Shapiro, B. J. (1968). Reading expectancy formulas: A warning note. *Journal of Reading, 2*, 625–629.

Sinclair, E., & Alexson, J. (1986). Learning disability discrepancy formulas: Similarities and differences among them. *Learning Disabilities Research, 1*, 112–118.

Sinclair, E., Guthrie, D., & Forness, S. R. (1984). Establishing a connection between severity of learning disabilities and classroom attention problems. *Journal of Educational Research, 78*, 18–21.

Singer, J., Palfrey, J., Butter, J., & Walker, D. (1989). Variation in special education classification across school districts: How does where you live affect what you are labeled? *American Educational Research Journal, 26*, 261–281.

Smith, M. D., Coleman, J. M., Dokecki, P. R., & Davis, E. E. (1977). Intellectual characteristics of school labeled learning disabled children. *Exceptional Children, 43*, 352–357.

Sobel, M., & Kelemen, E. (1984). On an application of statistical ranking and selection tables to the identification of the learning disabled. *Journal of Educational Statistics, 9*, 215–226.

Stanovich, K. E. (1986a). Cognitive processes and the reading problems of learning disabled children: Evaluating the assumption of specificity. In J. K. Torgesen, & B .Y. L. Wong (Eds.), *Psychological and educational perspectives on learning disabilities* (pp. 87–131). Orlando, FL: Academic Press.

Stanovich, K. E. (1986b). Matthew effects in reading: Some consequences of individual differences in the acquisition of literacy. *Reading Research Quarterly, 21*, 360–407.

Stanovich, K. E. (1989). Has the learning disabilities field lost its intelligence? *Journal of Learning Disabilities, 22*, 487–492.

Stanovich, K. E. (1991a). Conceptual and empirical problems with discrepancy definitions of reading disability. *Learning Disability Quarterly, 14*, 269–280.

Stanovich, K. E. (1991b). Discrepancy definitions of reading disability: Has intelligence led us astray? *Reading Research Quarterly, 26*, 7–29.

Stanovich, K. E., & Siegel, L. S. (1994). Phenotypic performance profile of children with reading disabilities: A regression-based test of the phonological-core variable-difference model. *Journal of Educational Psychology, 86,* 24–53.

Stevenson, J. (1988). Which aspects of reading disability show a "hump" in their distribution? *Applied Cognitive Psychology, 2,* 77–85.

Sulzbacher, S., & Kenowitz, L. A. (1977). At last, a definition of learning disabilities we can live with? *Journal of Learning Disabilities, 10,* 67–69.

Swanson, H. L. (1991). Operational definitions and learning disabilities: An overview. *Learning Disability Quarterly, 14,* 242–254.

Swerling, S. L., & Sternberg, R. J. (1996). *Off track: When poor readers become learning disabled.* Boulder, CO: Westview Press.

Tarjan, G., Wright, S. W., Eyman, R. K., & Keeran, C. V. (1973). Natural history of mental retardation: Some aspects of epidemiology. *American Journal of Mental Deficiency, 77,* 369–379.

Thomson, M. (1982). Assessing the intelligence of dyslexic children. *Bulletin of the British Psychological Society, 35,* 94–96.

Thorndike, R. L. (1963). *The concepts of over- and underachievement.* New York: Teachers College, Columbia University Press.

Thurlow, M. L., & Ysseldyke, J. E. (1979). Current assessment and decision-making practices in model LD programs. *Learning Disability Quarterly, 2,* 15–24.

Thurlow, M. L., Ysseldyke, J. E., & Casey, A. (1984). Teachers' perceptions of criteria for identifying learning disabled students. *Psychology in the Schools, 21,* 349–355.

Toops, H. A., & Symonds, P. M. (1922). What shall be expected of the AQ? *Journal of Educational Psychology, 13,* 513–528.

U.S. Department of Education. (1999). *To assure the free appropriate public education of all children with disabilities: Twenty-first annual report to the Congress on the implementation of the Individuals With Disabilities Education Act.* Washington, DC: Author.

U.S. Office of Education. (1968). *First annual report of the National Advisory Committee for Handicapped Children.* Washington, DC: U.S. Department of Health, Education, and Welfare.

U.S. Office of Education (1976, December 29). Proposed rule-making. *Federal Register, 41,* (230), 52404–52407. Washington, DC: U.S. Government Printing Office.

U.S. Office of Education (1977, December 29). Assistance to states for education of handicapped children: Procedures for evaluating specific learning disabilities. *Federal Register, 42,* (250), 65082–65085. Washington, DC: U.S. Government Printing Office.

Valus, A. (1986a). Achievement-potential discrepancy status of students in LD programs. *Learning Disability Quarterly, 9,* 200–205.

Valus, A. (1986b). Teacher perceptions of identification criteria emphasized in initial learning disabilities placement. *Learning Disabilities Research, 2,* 21–25.

Van den Bos, K. P. (1989). Relationship between cognitive development, decoding skill, and reading comprehension in learning disabled Dutch children. In P. Aaron & M. Josh (Eds.), *Reading and writing disorders in different orthographic systems* (pp. 75–86). Dordrecht, The Netherlands: Kluwer.

Van der Wissel, A., & Zegers, F. E. (1985). Reading retardation revisited. *British Journal of Developmental Psychology, 3,* 3–9.

Vellutino, F. R., Scanlon, D. M., & Lyon, G. R. (2000). Differentiating between difficult-to-remediate and readily remediated poor readers: More evidence against the I.Q.-achievement discrepancy definition of reading disability. *Journal of Learning Disabilities, 33,* 223–238.

Vellutino, F. R., Scanlon, D. M., Sipay, E. R., Small, S. G., Pratt, A., Chen, R., & Denckla, M. B. (1996). Cognitive profiles of difficult-to-remediate and readily remediated poor readers: Early intervention as a vehicle for distinguishing between cognitive and experiential deficits as basic causes of specific reading disability. *Journal of Educational Psychology, 88,* 601–638.

Walberg, H. J., & Tsai, S. (1983). Matthew effects in education. *American Educational Research Journal, 20,* 359–373.

Wallbrown, F. H., Blaha, J., & Vance, H. B. (1980). A reply to Miller's concerns about WISC-R profile analysis. *Journal of Learning Disabilities, 13,* 340–345.

Wallbrown, F. H., Vance, H. B., & Blaha, J. (1979). Developing remedial hypotheses from ability profiles. *Journal of Learning Disabilities, 12,* 557–561.

Watkins, M., & Kush, J. (1988). The research assistant. [Computer program]. Phoenix, AZ: South West Ed Psych.

Weir, M. (1967). Mental Retardation. *Science, 155,* 576–577.

Whipple, G. M. (1922). Educational determinism: A discussion of Professor Bagley's address at Chicago. *School and Society, 15,* 599–602.

White, W. J., & Wigle, S. E. (1986). Patterns of discrepancy over time as revealed by a standard-score comparison formula. *Learning Disabilities Research, 2,* 14–20.

Willson, V. L. (1987). Statistical and psychometric issues surrounding severe discrepancy. *Learning Disabilities Research, 3*, 24–28.

Willson, V. L., & Reynolds, C. R. (1984–1985). Another look at evaluating aptitude-achievement discrepancies in the diagnosis of learning disabilities. *Journal of Special Education, 18*, 477–487.

Wilson, J. D., & Spangler, P. F. (1974). The Peabody Individual Achievement Test as a clinical tool. *Journal of Learning Disabilities, 7*, 384–387.

Wilson, L. R. (1985). Large-scale learning disability identification: The reprieve of a concept. *Exceptional Children, 52*, 44–51.

Wilson, L. R., & Cone, T. (1984). The regression equation method of determining academic discrepancy. *Journal of School Psychology, 22*, 95–110.

Wilson, L. R., Cone, T., Bradley, C., & Reese, J. (1986). The characteristics of learning disabled and other handicapped students referred for evaluation in the state of Iowa. *Journal of Learning Disabilities, 19*, 553–557.

Wilson, L. R., Cone, T. E., Busch, R., & Allee, T. (1983). A critique of the expectancy formula approach: Beating a dead horse? *Psychology in the Schools, 20*, 241–249.

Wilson, W. R. (1928). The misleading accomplishment quotient. *Journal of Educational Research, 17*, 1–10.

Woodbury, C. (1963). The identification of underachieving readers. *The Reading Teacher, 16*, 218–223.

Ysseldyke, J., Algozzine, B., & Epps, S. (1983). A logical and empirical analysis of current practice in classifying students as handicapped. *Exceptional Children, 50*, 160–166.

Ysseldyke, J. E., Algozzine, B., Richey, L., & Graden, J. L. (1982). Declaring students eligible for learning disability service: Why bother with the data? *Learning Disability Quarterly, 5*, 37–44.

Ysseldyke, J. E., Algozzine, B., Shinn, M. R., & McGue, M. (1982). Similarities and differences between low achievers and students classified learning disabled. *Journal of Special Education, 16*, 73–85.

Ysseldyke, J. E., Christenson, S., Pianta, B., & Algozzine, B. (1983). An analysis of teachers' reasons and desired outcomes for students referred for psychoeducational assessment. *Journal of Psychoeducational Assessment, 1*, 73–83.

Yule, W. (1973). Differential prognosis of reading backwardness and specific retardation. *British Journal of Educational Psychology, 43*, 244–248.

Yule, W., & Rutter, M. (1976). Epidemiology and social implications of specific reading retardation. In R. M. Knights & D. J. Bakker (Eds.), *The neuropsychology of learning disorders: Theoretical approaches* (pp. 25–39). Baltimore: University Park Press.

Yule, W., Rutter, M., Berger, M., & Thompson, J. (1974). Over- and under-achievement in reading: Distribution in the general population. *British Journal of Educational Psychology, 44,* 1–12.

Zigler, E. (1967). Familial mental retardation: A continuing dilemma. *Science, 155,* 292–298.

Zigler, E., & Balla, D. (Eds.). (1982). *Mental retardation: The developmental-difference controversy.* Hillsdale, NJ: Lawrence Erlbaum.

Zigler, E., & Hodapp, R. (1986). *Understanding mental retardation.* New York: Cambridge University Press.

THERE'S MORE TO IDENTIFYING
LEARNING DISABILITY THAN DISCREPANCY

John Wills Lloyd, Curry School of Education, University of Virginia

Unsurprisingly, problems in defining learning disability have been a topic of concern throughout the brief history of the field. As Kavale's (this volume) discussion of Franzen's 1920s work on accomplishment quotient shows, some of the underlying concepts predate the field by 40 years! In light of such longstanding and continued interest in discrepancy between expected and actual achievement, one should predict that controversy about ability-achievement discrepancy in learning disabilities will be the topic of academic debates another 40 years hence.

Kavale's treatment of the topic of discrepancy represents first-order scholarship. He examined the arguments and evidence so fully and elucidated the concepts in such a well-connected way that there is little to add to his treatment of discrepancy. I am reduced to providing elaborations—recommendations about landscaping, paint, and chintz after the architect and builder have constructed a solid house. However, I consider it important to emphasize some points Kavale made and to add some contextual factors so that readers can place the details of his analysis into a larger perspective. I assert several foundational concepts in the next section before addressing general issues and then turning to additional concerns.

FOUNDATIONAL CONCEPTS ABOUT LEARNING DISABILITY

Problems in defining learning disability are products of several factors and those factors provide an important context for the thorough and well-integrated treatment of the topic of discrepancy that Kavale provided. Among these contextual variables are some enduring themes that my colleagues and I have presented in greater detail elsewhere (Hallahan, Kauffman, & Lloyd, 1999) and that I consider worthy of consideration in this symposium. In this section, I present them.

First among these is that learning disability is not a unitary condition; it is a heterogeneous complex of multiple attributes. Many students with learning disabilities have difficulties with the decoding aspect of reading, but not all do. Some students with learning disabilities have difficulty with attention, but not all do. Some students with learning disabilities have difficulties with planning algorithms for solving mathematical problems, but not all do. There is no student so typical of all students with learning disabilities that we can safely refer to "the learning-disabled child." (For this reason alone, it is sensible to adhere to so-called people-first language.)

Efforts to stipulate that discrepancy is the distinguishing mark of learning disabilities violate this assumption. Advocates who rely on findings that the distribution of learning disabilities is a continuous part of the normal distribution (e.g., Shaywitz, Escobar, Shaywitz, Fletcher, & Makugh, 1992) are failing to acknowledge that those distributions must, per force, describe a single measure. The distributions are not multivariate. Given that heterogeneity is expected among students with learning disabilities, the distributions must be multivariate. Discrepancy cannot be the sine qua non of learning disability. An important corollary of this rule is that identification requires subtle human judgment, as envisioned in laws promulgated in the United States over the last 25 years of the 20th century. Furthermore, relying on a single factor such as discrepancy readily leads to assumptions about other, often undocumented factors, such as the presence of process disorders (Kavale & Forness, 1997).

Second, focusing on discrepancy between ability and achievement in identification overemphasizes the classification of learning disability in the face of need for emphasis on primary, secondary, and tertiary prevention. Indeed, this same concern led Bateman, in the very publication often cited as the source for focusing on discrepancy, to argue that the field must

> Reformulate [its] concept of diagnosis so that its primary emphasis is on *what to do* with the child—i.e., on preventive or remedial planning. In retrospect it is fairly easy to see that in past reliance upon the medical precedent...we failed to realize that while the medical concept of diagnosis did, in most cases, lead directly to treatment our labeling did *not*. (1965, p. 221, emphasis in original)

Third, as a category of special education rather than a diagnostic entity, learning disability provides a gateway through which pass students who need extra help during their school years. In asserting this, I do not mean that learning disability is a product of schooling; to be sure, most students with learning disabilities may have attributes recognizable in the pre- or postschool years that distinguish them from their peers (from some more easily than others). I am simply asserting that from an educational perspective, the purpose of identifying students as having learning disabilities is to make them eligible for special education services. Once the students are identified, the laws governing special education provide for the development of an individualized education plan for that student, not a "0.86 discrepancy plan" or even a "learning disability plan."

Fourth, learning disability is at least in part socially constructed. Educators, psychologists, physicians, speech-language clinicians, and others agree that the children and youth who have the difficulties labeled as "learning disabilities" differ from their peers. In most cases, the problems are quite apparent, even to untrained observers. But the boundaries between learning disability and *not* learning disability are not set by nature in the way that the boundaries between eye colors or sexes are. They are not even set as well as the boundaries for visual impairment. (Note that the cut points for levels of visual impairment are socially constructed, too; people can set them wherever they wish.) By advancing this argument, I do not mean to go as far as some (e.g., Coles, 1987; Finlan, 1994) and contend that, because there are elements of social construction in learning disability, the category is bogus. I simply want to make clear that the decisions about what is within the perimeter of learning disabilities is a decision we make, not a fact of nature awaiting scientific discovery.

Fifth, Keogh (1987) got things right when she discussed the importance of thinking about learning disabilities as a construct. If we think of learning disability as a heterogeneous cluster of problems that is not captured in any one metric and that is primarily a socially constructed gateway to services for students whose problems are so severe that they need extra help, then we have a useful construct for education.

Hoping the reader can hold these points in working memory, I turn to more esoteric concerns. Identification requires consideration of the fallibility of classification and the consequences of policy decisions.

IDENTIFICATION ISSUES: GENERAL

Determining whether a condition exists, predicting it, and exercising control over it are hallmarks of scientific knowledge of the phenomenon. However, all three features of scientific knowledge are subject to error. No one of them can be achieved with perfection and the consequence is that, while science seeks to minimize error by continually refining measurement, policy must be based on balancing false positives and false negatives. Identification of students with learning disabilities is no exception.

Fallibility

Even seemingly perfect rules are fallible. For example, given that one is out of doors in the dark when the sky begins to lighten and birds begin to sing, one would presume that it is morning. Such a presumption will be correct most of the time, but it is not absolutely accurate. The same set of circumstances obtains toward the end of a total solar eclipse. Diagnostic assessment for human immunodeficiency virus (HIV) is also fallible, giving rise to untold anxiousness.

Because identification of learning disabilities is based on measuring attributes of individuals and because measurement is not perfect, it follows that identification of learning disabilities will not be perfect. Unfortunately, this imperfection has led some to the generalization that "there currently is no defensible system for declaring students eligible for LD services" and, fortunately, to express suspicion about "efforts to increasingly sophisticate the assessment process (development of 'new' formulas, neuropsychological assessment, etc.)" (Ysseldyke et al., 1983, p. 79). That the assessment of learning disability depends on measurement of multiple attributes (heterogeneity) compounds the problem of fallibility. To be sure, experts in measurement can mitigate the problem using increasingly sophisticated statistical methods, but they will be unable to make it disappear. Kavale's (this volume) discussion of standard error of estimate (SEE) shows clearly that the error in measurement expected from instruments used in assessing attributes of learning disability predicts fallible identification. Even if the SEE for discrepancy could be infallible, basing identification on it would overlook other attributes that are relevant to identification of learning disability, some of which may best be assessed by another imperfect test—teachers (Gerber & Semmel, 1984).

Researchers in measurement and learning disabilities are responsible for continued efforts to reduce the fallibility in identification by refining measures and criteria in the future, but parents, practitioners, and policy makers cannot wait for a perfect system. People concerned about the academic and social development of today's students with learning disabilities must work within contemporary constraints and balance the consequences of error. For those children and youth experiencing learning disabilities, the most pressing need is not for certainty about whether they have true learning disabilities, but for effective services.

Balance

In the case of determining whether a condition exists, the consequences of error come in two forms: false positives and false negatives. False positives and false negatives refer to the probability that a case is incorrectly identified as having a condition or incorrectly identified as not having a condition. These errors in diagnostic specificity are a source of concern in most areas concerned with identification, as reflection on testing for HIV illustrates.

In an oversimplified way, Figure 1 portrays how diagnostic procedures produce false positive and negative results. The shaded ovals represent the true population of students with learning disabilities and the unshaded ovals represent the population identified incorrectly as either not having learning disability (upper half of the oval) or having learning disability (lower half).[1] In an ideal diagnostic situation (not shown in the figure), the predicted category overlaps with the actual category perfectly. However, the ideal is seldom (if ever) real. Usually, there are more errors of one or the other type; for example, more false negatives than false positives. The policy question that arises is whether one prefers to err on the side of missing students who actually should receive services (minimize false negatives) or on the side of making sure students who do not require service do not get them (minimize false positives).

Figure 1. Relationship between false-positive and false-negative identification errors.

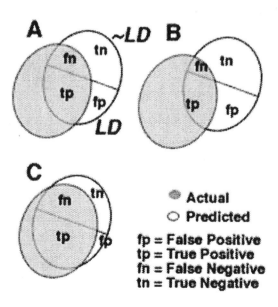

Assertions that "there is no such thing as a learning disability" (Finlan, 1994, p. 1) and questions about whether special education benefits learners (e.g., Brantlinger, 1997) encourage educators to reduce positive identifications. This position argues that we have too many false positives (represented by Panel B in Figure 1). Others are concerned that there are too many students who have learning disabilities but are not officially identified (see Panel C). The important idea is that there is a roughly reciprocal relationship between false positives and false negatives; increases in one often (not always) are associated with decreases in the other.

False-positive and false-negative rates are influenced by the reliability of the system used for classification and the integrity of the underlying actual condition. Given that—barring divine consultation—educators will never perfectly classify students, the decision about the relative balance between false negatives and positives becomes one of policy. Educators and others concerned about services for students with learning disabilities must set limits. The decision about the level of error that educators should entertain is not a statistical matter, but one of public policy.

WHO'S WHO?

Concerns about the technical aspects of classification are usually the domain of researchers, and concerns about the practical effects of classification are usually the domain of practitioners. As my colleagues and I developed in greater detail elsewhere (Lloyd, Hallahan, & Kauffman, 1980), these differing areas of concern align with different perspectives on defining learning disabilities. In this section, I examine several different perspectives on defining learning disability.

Researchers are concerned about the representivity of the samples they study, that is, whether results from studies of those samples can be expected to apply to the population. When the population under study is not precisely defined, as is admittedly the case with learning disability, generalization from sample to population is problematic. So, researchers will benefit from having clear and defensible cut points that define the boundaries between learning disability and no disability. For researchers, the contingencies encourage balancing false positives and false negatives, that is, minimizing both and approximating accuracy.

In contrast, people concerned with the well-being of individual children and youth—namely, parents and teachers—would not benefit as readily as researchers from having a carefully codified definition. In the murky world of providing services, there is not a lot of difference between a student with a discrepancy of 1.49 units and another student with a discrepancy of 1.51 units. From the perspective of teachers, both students probably need help. So, practitioners and parents will benefit from having the authority to exercise judgment in determining who is eligible for services using a flexible standard—essentially what has been in place throughout the brief history of learning disabilities. The contingency here favors minimizing false negatives.

In yet further contrast, educational administrators and policy makers have different constraints on their views of defining learning disability. They live in a world where budgets have very high, if not paramount, importance and so must look for ways to constrain expenditures. When one notes the increasing number of students classified as having learning disability by U.S. schools and adds the debate about defining the ill-defined nature of learning disability, it only makes sense to assume that budgets are going to burst. So, for administrators and policy makers, the pressure is toward an objectively determinable classification system. Further, it is perhaps important that the criteria for classification be tightened—minimizing false positives and inevitably increasing false negatives.

SUMMARY

Efforts to cast discrepancy as the defining feature of learning disability are misguided, as Kavale has clearly shown. In my view, we have to realize that learning disability is, in fact, a construct we created. Unlike a disease for which there are highly specified criteria (e.g., the presence of antibodies for HIV or Lyme disease), learning disability is a concept and one should not expect the criteria to be specified. Indeed, even with high-specificity diseases such as HIV, the chance of error in identification (false positive or negative) is greater than zero. Educators must accept the responsibility for making policies about to whom education will deliver special services rather than searching for one distinguishing characteristic of learning disabilities.

Those who conduct research are capable of identifying and describing the nature of their samples without having to identify a unique distinguishing feature for the population. Researchers do not need a precisely delineated syndrome. It is incumbent on those who study human groups to describe their samples in sufficient detail and with sufficient rigor so that others can determine whether the samples are similar or different from those they are studying or to which they hope to apply the findings. Given the heterogeneity of learning disabilities, studies of the nature, causes, evaluation, or treatment of students who have difficulty calculating sums would not be thought to generalize to students who have difficulty comprehending written language. There may be common characteristics between the two groups, but that is for researchers to establish.

Instead of devoting our greatest efforts to refining the definition of learning disability and the means by which we determine whether individuals do or do not have a true disability, I recommend that we turn our focus to ascertaining how to determine the unique needs of individuals with these problems and how to prevent the problems. The definitional controversy does not advance our ability to determine need and provide effective service.

Gerber (2000) argued that the controversial nature of learning disability has been valuable because it has encouraged research that has benefited not only students identified as having learning disabilities, but also others who have low achievement. Indeed, much of the earliest work on two important areas of instruction—phonemic awareness and teaching cognitive strategies—was associated with learning disabilities. That work has influenced general education in beneficial ways. Those innovations arose from conditions in which learning disability was defined and classified much as it has been since the 1960s. Having a precise definition of learning disabilities probably would not have affected whether they arose. What probably mattered more than the criteria by which the students were identified was the fact that those working with learning disabilities sought ways to promote the achievement of the students with whom they were working.

REFERENCES

Bateman, B. (1965). An educator's view of a diagnostic approach to learning disabilities. In J. Hellmuth (Ed.), *Learning disorders* (Vol. 1, pp. 217–239). Seattle: Special Child.

Brantlinger, E. (1997). Using ideology: Cases of nonrecognition of the politics of research and practice in special education. *Review of Educational Research, 67,* 425–459.

Coles, G. (1987). *The learning mystique: A critical look at "learning disabilities."* New York: Pantheon.

Finlan, M. (1994). *Learning disability: The imaginary disease.* Westport, CT: Bergin & Garvey.

Gerber, M. M. (2000). An appreciation of learning disabilities: The value of blue-green algae. *Exceptionality, 8,* 29–42.

Gerber, M. M., & Semmel, M. I. (1984). Teacher as imperfect test: Reconceptualizing the referral process. *Educational Psychologist, 19,* 137–148.

Hallahan, D. P., Kauffman, J. M., & Lloyd, J. W. (1999). *Introduction to learning disabilities.* Needham Heights, MA: Allyn & Bacon.

Kavale, K. A., & Forness, S. R. (1997). Defining learning disabilities: Consonance and dissonance. In J. W. Lloyd, E. J. Kameenui, & D. Chard (Eds.), *Issues in educating students with disabilities* (pp. 3–25). Mahwah, NJ: Erlbaum.

Keogh, B. K. (1987). Learning disabilities: In defense of a construct. *Learning Disabilities Research, 3*(1), 4–9.

Lloyd, J., Hallahan, D. P., & Kauffman, J. M. (1980). Learning disabilities: A review of selected topics. In L. Mann & D. A. Sabatino (Eds.), *Third review of special education* (pp. 35–60). Philadelphia: JSE Press.

Shaywitz, S. E., Escobar, M. E., Shaywitz, B. A., Fletcher, J. M., & Makugh, R. (1992). Evidence that dyslexia may represent the lower tail of a normal distribution of reading ability. *New England Journal of Medicine, 326,* 145–150.

Ysseldyke, J. E., Thurlow, M., Graden, J., Wesson, C., Algozzine, B., & Deno, S. (1983). Generalizations from five years of research on assessment and decision making: the University of Minnesota Institute. *Exceptionality, 4*(1), 75–93.

ENDNOTE

[1] I used a 50-50 split to make the illustration easier to label. I recognize that the prevalence of LD is not 0.5.

A FUNCTIONAL AND INTERVENTION-BASED ASSESSMENT APPROACH TO ESTABLISHING DISCREPANCY FOR STUDENTS WITH LEARNING DISABILITIES

Douglas Marston, Minneapolis Public Schools

Kenneth Kavale's examination of the role of discrepancy in the identification of learning disabilities (LDs) is both thorough and insightful. It is thorough in its description of the many discrepancy models that have been developed over the years and the issues that have surfaced as these models have been implemented. The joining of these many issues is insightful to this reader because it highlights the need for finding an alternative approach to establishing discrepancy.

In his paper Kavale identifies a range of difficulties that include problems with quantification of the discrepancy, questions regarding the necessity of IQ tests and their usefulness as a measure of potential, confounding among high-incidence disabilities, and definition of learning disabilities. In the Minneapolis Public Schools (MPS), many special education staff members share the concerns that Kavale raises.

Historically, in MPS, IQ test scores were not a major part of our LD assessment because school psychologists questioned their technical adequacy (Canter, 1991). Psychologists spent only approximately 30% of their time testing. This practice ended in 1992 when our State Board of Education approved new eligibility criteria for learning disabilities and mild to moderate mental impairment (MMMI). These criteria required the use of IQ tests.

After implementing the new IQ test requirement, several trends emerged. In the area of learning disabilities assessment we discovered that while White American and African American referred students had similar levels of low reading achievement, the IQ scores of the African American students were significantly lower than those of White Americans (Heistad, 1993). Using a discrepancy model for LD determination would underidentify students of color. Conversely, in the area of mental impairment, our district saw an increase in African American students placed in classes for the mentally impaired (Ysseldyke & Marston, 1999). In the area of psychological testing, Canter (1995) established that between 1979 and 1992 MPS psychologists spent on average 30% of their time in testing and the remainder in consultation and direct intervention with students. After the use of IQ tests was required, testing time of psychologists increased to 58%. Finally, community organizations representing students of color asked why special educators were emphasizing the use of IQ tests.

Fortunately, in Minnesota, school districts may pursue waivers of state rules. Given our district data and the increase in research questioning the use of IQ tests and the discrepancy model (Fletcher, 1992; *Larry P. v. Riles*, 1984; Macmann and Barnett, 1985; Siegal, 1989), we felt empowered to approach our State Board of Education for a waiver. At the time we were particularly encouraged by Reschly, Kicklighter, and McKee's (1988) review of *Marshall et al. v. Georgia* (1985), in which they wrote "...assessment procedures focusing on correlated traits like general intellectual functioning are not as clearly related to interventions and are therefore more difficult to justify, particularly if used as the sole or the primary basis for significant classification/placement decisions" (p. 9).

Given this backdrop, the Minneapolis special education staff began building on previous department philosophy to develop an alternative model for nondiscriminatory assessment and noncategorical labeling of students with high-incidence disabilities. The proposal included a multidisciplinary team approach to functional assessment that includes special and general education staff and leads to more interventions for students who need support (Deno, 1985; National Association of State Boards of Education, 1990; Tilly, Grimes, & Reschly, 1993). Our district applied for a waiver in November 1993 which was unanimously approved by the State Board of Education. In our waiver we asked for permission to use a Problem Solving Model as an alternative to the IQ-achievement discrepancy score. In addition, we asked for permission to not use the labels LD and MMMI and instead use the term "SNAP": students needing alternative programming.

THE PROBLEM SOLVING MODEL

The traditional assessment approach to discrepancy results in IQ tests being used to determine student potential and eligibility for service. An alternative is a systematic process emphasizing (a) problem identification and analysis; (b) intervention design and implementation; and (c) ongoing monitoring and evaluation of intervention effects (Deno, 1995; Tilly, Grimes, & Reschly, 1993). We refer to this intervention-based approach as the Problem Solving Model (PSM). The process is data-based, includes specific decision-making points, and emphasizes the use of functional and multidimensional assessment procedures. Functional assessment procedures are used that provide information specific to the areas of concern. A variety of assessments are used that provide data on instruction, curriculum, classroom environment, motivation, and engaged time. Particular attention is paid to using nondiscriminatory assessments (U.S. Office for Civil Rights, 2000).

The decision-making flow, which utilizes problem identification, intervention design, and systematic progress monitoring across three stages of implementation, is illustrated below in Figure 1.

Figure 1. The Problem Solving Model.

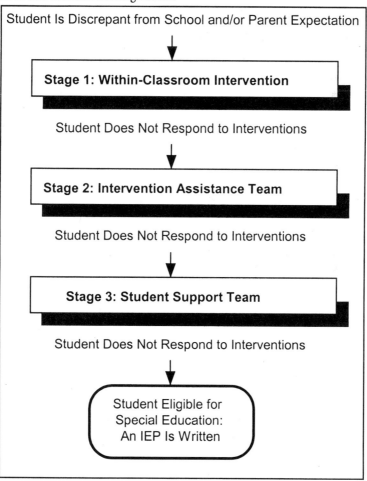

At **Stage 1** the general education classroom teacher is trained to specifically identify the problem, deliver modified instruction, and systematically evaluate the impact of instruction. If these interventions do not work within the classroom, a building intervention assistance team addresses the needs of this student at Stage 2. This team, which may or may not include building special education staff, opens up access to more resources in developing interventions, which may include remediation from building specialists or educational assistants, Title I support, and/or help from English Language Learner (ELL) staff (Self, Benning, Marston, & Magnusson, 1991). If interventions are not effective at Stage 2, the student moves to Stage 3 where the Student Support Team, which includes special education staff, school social worker, and building psychologist, examines the student's difficulties. At this point due process begins and more intensive interventions are attempted. At each stage in the PSM, school staff repeat the three-step process of identifying the problem, developing an appropriate instructional strategy, and then systematically evaluating the effectiveness of that intervention.

An important part of the PSM is the ability to measure student response to instruction. MPS staff has trained regular and special education teachers to use curriculum-based measurement (CBM) as one approach to assessing the effects of different instructional strategies used within the PSM. In this model (Deno, 1985; Marston & Magnusson, 1988; Self, Benning, Marston, & Magnusson, 1991), staff are trained to collect academic performance data on a weekly basis, graph the results, and examine the effectiveness of the interventions tried by the teacher. Below in Figure 2 is an example of how CBM is an intervention-based assessment approach that assists in the evaluation of instruction in the PSM. On the graph the effectiveness of two reading interventions for a second-grade regular education student with reading difficulties is compared. Because Intervention B, which is a general education intervention, is effective, the student is not referred to special education for service.

When determining eligibility for special education under the PSM, the evaluation team must consider whether a severe discrepancy exists between the student's level of performance and the expected performance of same-age peers with similar educational experiences. The data gathered from all sources and through all stages of the PSM should be considered in order to summarize how the student's performance compares to that of typical peers or identified standards. If a student does not respond to interventions at each of the stages and has received appropriate general education instruction, and the team has ruled out exclusionary factors, he or she is declared eligible by the Student Support Team for special education service. The student is called a "Student Needing Alternative Programming," and an individualized education plan (IEP) is written. The main point here is that the student is not declared eligible for special education because of a discrepancy score

Figure 2. An example of how curriculum-based measurement is used to evaluate the effectiveness of instruction.

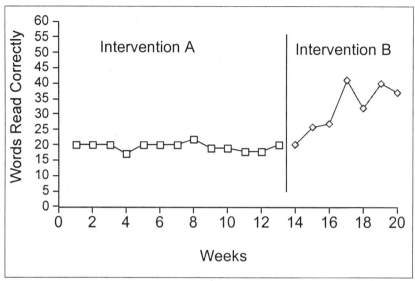

between IQ and achievement, but because his or her expected academic performance did not improve as the result of trying a continuum of progressively more intensive regular education interventions.

Evaluation Results

We formulated five evaluation questions for examining the effectiveness of our model. Those questions were:

1. Does the Problem Solving Model increase the rates of students with high-incidence disabilities?
2. Does the Problem Solving Model increase the effectiveness of prereferral strategies?
3. Do the students identified with the Problem Solving Model look significantly different than traditional LD students?
4. Does the Problem Solving Model affect the number of students of color referred and identified for special education?
5. Are parents satisfied with the Problem Solving Model?

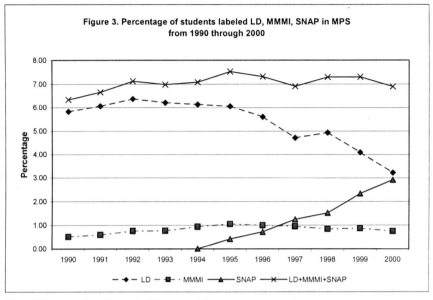

Figure 3. Percentage of students labeled LD, MMMI, SNAP in MPS from 1990 through 2000

Notes: LD = learning disabled; MMMI = mild to moderate mental impairment; SNAP = student needing alternative programming; MPS = Minneapolis Public Schools

DOES THE PROBLEM SOLVING MODEL INCREASE THE RATES OF STUDENTS WITH HIGH-INCIDENCE DISABILITIES?

Critics of PSM have speculated the model would lead to increases in special education population. We investigated this question by examining child count rates in MPS for LD, MMMI, and SNAP for the past 10 years (SNAP identification began in 1994). As can be seen in Figure 3, the number of SNAP students increased with the phased-in implementation of PSM while the number of traditional LD students decreased. Overall rates for MMMI declined slightly after 1995. Under the PSM, the total child count rate for students with high-incidence disabilities increased only slightly. This slight increase occurred at a time that the ELL population more than doubled and free and reduced lunch numbers increased by almost 20%. One could conclude the PSM did not significantly add students to the special education population.

DOES THE PROBLEM SOLVING MODEL INCREASE THE EFFECTIVENESS OF PREREFERRAL STRATEGIES?

In 1995 Reschly and Starkweather conducted an independent, state-funded evaluation of the Minneapolis PSM. In their investigation they studied a sample of 128 waiver (PSM) students and 56 special education students identified through the traditional system of discrepancy formulas and IQ test administration. They reported that prereferral interventions under the waiver services were superior to those under the traditional system. They concluded that the effect of the waiver program appeared to "identify students as needing special education at earlier grades and to allow students to receive special education services without being classified as mentally impaired or specific learning disabled."

DO THE STUDENTS IDENTIFIED WITH THE PROBLEM SOLVING MODEL LOOK SIGNIFICANTLY DIFFERENT THAN TRADITIONAL LD STUDENTS?

In the Reschly and Starkweather (1995) study, special education students identified from waiver and traditional systems performed at about the same levels on academic achievement measures and received highly similar special education programs. In addition, these investigators found that all students in both samples exhibited significant learning and/or behavioral problems and that a few students in each of the samples were not eligible according to criteria from either system for special education classification and placement.

Over a 4-year period, Heistad (2001) followed 87 traditionally identified LD students and 34 SNAP students from the PSM on the Northwest Achievement Levels Test for reading and math. These students did not significantly vary on their levels of performance or their rate of growth during this time.

DOES THE PROBLEM SOLVING MODEL AFFECT THE NUMBER OF STUDENTS OF COLOR REFERRED AND IDENTIFIED FOR SPECIAL EDUCATION?

On the basis of the results from extensive comparisons of African American and White American students, Reschly & Starkweather (1995) concluded that the waiver program achieved "an equal treatment conception of non-discrimination." With regard to disproportionate numbers of minority students in special education, internal district evaluation data indicated the probability of an African American student being identified as needing special education was 46% at a "PSM" school versus 59% at a "traditional criteria" school.

We have since followed up these analyses by using the odds ratio analysis (Parrish, 2000). An *odds analysis* describes the chances of being placed in a particular disability category, such as SNAP, for a particular ethnic group, such as African American. An *odds ratio* extends this analysis by comparing the odds for a target ethnic group to the odds for White Americans. In Figure 4, the odds ratios for students with either LD, MMMI, or SNAP in Minneapolis Public Schools from 1994 through 2000 are presented. In general, the odds ratio to be labeled LD, MMMI, or SNAP ranged from 1.90 for African American students in 2000 to 2.04 in 1995.

Compared to statewide data from the Harvard Civil Rights project (Parrish, 2000), MPS appears to be below the Minnesota average. According to that report the odds ratios for being labeled LD was about 2.72 for African American students in Minnesota.

ARE PARENTS SATISFIED WITH THE PROBLEM SOLVING MODEL?

A random sample of parents ($n = 91$) of students identified as SNAP were interviewed by telephone in February 2001. All of these students had participated in the PSM. Parents were asked to respond to three questions:

1. Do you think your child's assessment for determining eligibility for special education was useful?
2. Your child is attending a school that does not use labels such as "Learning Disabled" or "Mentally Impaired." Are you satisfied with this approach?
3. Are you satisfied with the special education services your child is receiving?

Of the 91 parents interviewed, 76% believed that their child's assessment was useful, 91% were satisfied with not using labels such as learning disabled and mentally impaired, and 87% were satisfied with their child's special education services.

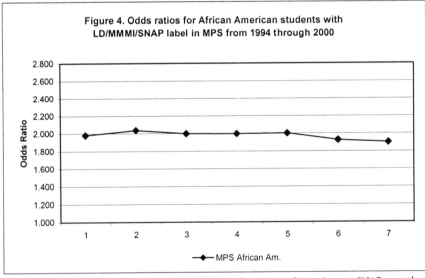

Figure 4. Odds ratios for African American students with LD/MMMI/SNAP label in MPS from 1994 through 2000

Notes: LD = learning disabled; MMMI = mild to moderate mental impairment; SNAP = student needing alternative programming; MPS = Minneapolis Public Schools

CONCLUSION

Kavale delineates many of the problems that occur when the IQ-achievement discrepancy model is implemented, yet concludes "discrepancy is an important and legitimate concept associated with LD." I would agree, but would maintain that students and educators would be better served by revising the concept as it currently exists in the field of learning disabilities. The PSM described here provides an alternative approach to interpreting student discrepancy. Just as we would do in other disability areas, such as vision, behavior, and autism, the PSM is used to examine the extent to which students are discrepant from typical levels of performance. For example, students who have severe visual difficulties and do not see as well as typical peers are identified as disabled and receive special education services. Special educators do not assess "visual potential" for all students, and then serve only those students who are most discrepant from their individual "visual potential."

The PSM combines functional assessment of relevant academic skills with measuring response to instruction to give the educator a broad base of information for decision-making. The model has worked well in Minneapolis and other sites as well, such as the state of Iowa (Tilly, Reschly, & Grimes, 1999). In Minneapolis we have shown that the PSM

- Improves the quality of prereferral interventions
- Does not increase child count
- Identifies "high incidence" students whose performance is similar to traditional LD students
- Addresses issue of disproportion and students of color
- Has a high degree of parent satisfaction

Schrag's (2000) survey of state directors of education regarding use of discrepancy approaches is also encouraging: "SEA respondents indicated that the 1997 amendments to IDEA [Individuals With Disabilities Education Act] support a shift away from the use of discrepancy approaches that rely on standardized achievement and ability tests" (p. 6). Many in the survey favor incorporating functional measures of student performance into the eligibility process. The PSM, which emphasizes functional assessment, moves eligibility decision-making for high-incidence disabilities in this direction.

REFERENCES

Canter, A. (1991). Effective psychological services for all students: A data based model of service delivery. In G. Stoner, M. Shinn, & H. Walker (Eds.), *Interventions for achievement and behavior problems* (pp. 49–78). Washington, DC: National Association of School Psychologists.

Canter, A. (1995). School psychology department annual report. Minneapolis, MN: Minneapolis Public Schools.

Deno, S. L. (1985). Curriculum-based measurement: The emerging alternative. *Exceptional Children, 52*(3), 219–232.

Deno, S. L. (1995). School Psychologist as problem solver. In A. Thomas & J. Grimes, *Best practices in school psychology.* Washington, DC: National Association of School Psychologists.

Fletcher, J. M. (1992). The validity of distinguishing children with language and learning disabilities according to discrepancies with IQ: Introduction to the special series. *Journal of Learning Disabilities, 25*(4), 546–548.

Heistad, D. (1993). Personal note on African American and White American student enrollment in classes for mentally impaired. Minneapolis, MN: Minneapolis Public Schools, district evaluation activities.

Heistad, D. (2001, March). *MPS 1997–2000 NALT reading growth compared to MPBST equated standard by special education group.* Minneapolis, MN: Minneapolis Public Schools Research, Evaluation, & Assessment.

Larry P. v. Riles. (1984). Supra, 495 F. Supp. at 951-52, aff'd 83-84 EHLR 555: 304, 307 (CA9 1984).

Macmann, G. & Barnett, D. (1985). The technical adequacy of LD formulas. *Journal of Psychoeducational Assessment, 4,* 363–375.

Marston, D., & Magnusson, D. (1988). Curriculum-based assessment: District level implementation. In J. Graden, J. Zins, & M. Curtis (Eds.), *Alternative educational delivery systems: Enhancing instructional options for all students* (pp. 137–172). Washington, DC: National Association of School Psychologists.

National Association of State Boards of Education. (1990). *Winners all: A call for inclusive schools.* The report of the NASBE Study Group on Special Education. Alexandria, VA: Author.

Parrish, T. (2000, November 17). *Disparities in the identification, funding, and provision of special education.* Paper presented at the conference of The Civil Rights Project on Minority Issues in Special Education, Cambridge, MA.

Reschly, D. J., Kicklighter, R., & McKee, P. (1988). Recent placement litigation part II, minority EMR overrepresentation: Comparison of Larry P. with Marshall and S-1. *School Psychology Review, 17,* 22–38.

Reschly, D. & Starkweather, A. (1995). *Evaluation of an alternative special education assessment and classification program in the Minneapolis Public Schools.* Ames, IA: Iowa State University.

Schrag, J. A. (2000, October). *Discrepancy approaches for identifying learning disabilities.* Alexandria, VA: National Association of State Directors of Special Education, Project Forum, Quick Turn Around.

Self, H., Benning, A., Marston, D., & Magnusson, D. (1991). Cooperative teaching project: A model for students at risk. *Exceptional Children, 58*(1), 26–34.

Siegal, L. S. (1989). IQ is irrelevant to the definition of learning disabilities. *Journal of Learning Disabilities, 22*(8), 469–486.

Tilly, W. D., Grimes, J., & Reschly, D. (1993). Special education system reform: The Iowa story. *Communique* (insert).

Tilly, W.D., Reschly, D. J., & Grimes, J. (1999). Disability determination in problem-solving systems: Conceptual foundations and critical components. In D. Reschly, W. Tilly, & J. Grimes (Eds.), *Special Education in Transition* (Chapter 12). Longmont, CO: Sopris West.

U.S. Office for Civil Rights (2000). *The use of tests when making high-stakes decisions for students: A resource guide for educators and policy-makers.* Washington, DC: U.S. Office for Civil Rights.

Ysseldyke, J. E., & Marston, D. (1999). Origins of categorical special education services in schools and a rationale for changing them. In D. Reschly, W. Tilly, & J. Grimes (Eds.), *Special Education in Transition* (Chapter 1). Longmont, CO: Sopris West.

ACKNOWLEDGMENTS

I would like to thank the following Minneapolis staff for their contributions to this paper: Andrea Canter, David Heistad, Mathew Lau, Paul Muyskens, and Cheryl Reid.

DISCREPANCY MODELS IN THE IDENTIFICATION
OF LEARNING DISABILITY: A RESPONSE TO KAVALE

Margo A. Mastropieri & Thomas E. Scruggs, George Mason University

In our university special education teacher preparation courses, we have frequently referred to the case of "Andrew." Andrew was a third grader in a middle-class suburban school who had received the same instruction in school as his peers. It has been informative to note the expressions on the faces of the university students as they hear a tape of Andrew's reading: presented with a familiar story in his middle third-grade-level text, this bright, articulate third-grader stumbles, repeats, hesitates, self-corrects, sighs, tries to sound out, and reveals himself to be completely inadequate to this task. His reading rate is an excruciating six words per minute, an average of one word every 10 seconds. Half of these words are read correctly only because of teacher prompting. He is next presented with a reading selection from a beginning second-grade-level reader, and reads this selection at eight words per minute. Throughout, Andrew's demeanor is polite and cooperative, if somewhat resigned. His free writing sample includes a drawing of what appears to be a meteor falling from the sky, with a single sentence printed below: "It vush the oue wun." While the university students cringe in empathy with Andrew's unsuccessful efforts, they also feel the same fascination that brought many of us to the field of special education: What is the nature of Andrew's failure to learn, and what can we do to help him?

The psychological data are presented next, but they really just confirm objectively much of what we have already observed. Andrew has a Full Scale IQ of 104 and a reading standard score of 82, or 74, depending on the test used (his math and spelling scores are similarly low). His perceptual-motor functioning is average; his vocabulary is above average; his listening comprehension and verbal expression scores are almost exactly average. Behavior rating scales are average for his age. The test data, and our observations, describe a boy of average abilities and positive demeanor who nevertheless shows a surprising inability to cope with literacy tasks. Although we feel satisfied with what Andrew's learning problems are probably *not* caused by (sensory, physical, intellectual, emotional, environmental, cultural, economic factors), we are much less certain of what the cause actually is.

In his paper on discrepancy models, Kavale discusses the attempts over the years to provide an objective foundation to describe cases such as that of Andrew. He provides an analysis of an overwhelming amount of previous research and conceptual analysis, most of which has been undertaken over the past few decades. Interestingly, in spite of the near universal acceptance of discrepancy models by states and local school districts, most of the literature that exists today is critical of discrepancy as one component of the procedure for identifying learning disabilities (LDs). Correspondingly, Kavale's paper frequently—and appropriately, in our view—provides a defense of discrepancy models against arguments that such models be abandoned in favor of some often unspecified alternative. In some cases, it is argued that abandoning discrepancy models will lead to the demise of the LD category: "When the discrepancy formula disappears from the educational scene, so will the concept of LD" (Aaron, 1997, p. 489). This enactment, according to Aaron, will take us out of the "wilderness" and into the "promised land" (p. 489).

Kavale begins his paper with a detailed history of different models of discrepancy, and how different formulas have evolved over time into present standard score methods. As noted by Kavale, numerous difficulties are associated with standard score discrepancy score formulas. Formulas have been proposed, and are frequently used, to address the problem of regression in using two correlated measures. Other difficulties include measurement issues, such as meeting acceptable psychometric standards and calculating correlations between measures, as well as practical difficulties associated with the application of discrepancies in real-world situations. Authors such as Shepard and Smith (1983) and MacMillan, Gresham, and Bocian (1998) have provided evidence that many school-identified students with learning disabilities do not meet the presumably more rigorous standards of these university researchers. Although there is little doubt that students sometimes are inappropriately identified as having learning disabilities without meeting strict discrepancy criteria, it is also true that schools and university researchers may disagree for other reasons. These reasons may include time of testing, type of test used, skill area assessed, and the nature of the discrepancy formula employed. It is also true that, in many cases, discrepancy formulas are appropriately employed (McLeskey & Waldron, 1990).

In fact, schools typically begin not with test data, but with referral by a teacher who has noticed that individual students are not learning adequately in a particular educational setting. Multidisciplinary teams meet and consider test data as well as the characteristics of the student within the context of available school resources, and decisions are made that are thought to be in the best interest of the student. Often considered also are the disadvantages of labeling as compared with the advantages of special educational services. If such decisions are not always identical to researcher analysis of a specified set of test scores, perhaps that is not surprising. At any rate, deviations from "true" identification procedures can be viewed as problems of implementation, rather than problems of definition.

A point commonly made by opponents of discrepancy formulas is that they do not clearly discriminate between students with learning disabilities and more generic low-achieving (LA) students. Kavale discusses a number of individual investigations of LD-LA differences who concluded either that there was considerable overlap (e.g., Ysseldyke, Algozzine, Shinn, & McGue, 1982) or that there was no reason to provide qualitatively different treatment to these two groups of students (Algozzine, Ysseldyke, & McGue, 1995). In fact, as pointed out by Kavale, differences between performances between students with learning disabilities and students with general low achievement have been frequently identified and found to be substantial, in both academic and social functioning (see also, e.g., Bursuck, 1989; Cleaver, Bear, & Juvonen, 1992; Donahoe & Zigmond, 1990; Fuchs, 1998; Kavale, Fuchs, & Scruggs, 1994; Merrill, 1990; Tur-Kaspa & Bryan, 1994).

In fact, when LD-LA score distributions do overlap, this fact should not be particularly surprising, especially when considering that low achievement, such as in reading, is a common characteristic of both populations. Further, low achievement is a common characteristic of most students referred for special education, and substantial overlap should be expected on this dimension (e.g., Scruggs & Mastropieri, 1986). The conclusions of researchers such as Francis, Shaywitz, Stuebing, Shaywitz, and Fletcher (1994) that reading disability represents "extreme cases in an otherwise normal distribution of reading achievement and aptitude" (p. 51) may not be particularly troubling (or surprising), and do not necessarily mean that identification approaches are "arbitrary" (p. 51). The fact that their data suggest that students with reading disability represent extreme cases hints that there is something systematic about the selection process.

What seems interesting to us about this debate is how infrequently identification of learning disabilities is compared with identification in other categories of special education, such as severe emotional disturbance or hearing impairments. Virtually every area of disability has experienced challenges in developing clear and objective identification criteria (e.g., Smith, 1985). In fact, identification for educationally relevant purposes is problematic in all areas, requires judgment and group decision-making, and can result in seemingly arbitrary or subjective decisions. Further, different categories of exceptionality have also wrestled with identification criteria. For example, in 1921 the American Association for the Study of the

Feebleminded (which itself would go through two additional name changes to become the American Association on Mental Retardation, or AAMR), developed a definition of mental retardation that would be revised in 1933, 1941, 1957, 1959, 1961, 1973, 1977, 1983, and 1992 (Beirne-Smith, Ittenbach, & Patton, 1998). Some of these definitions varied substantially. Under the 1961 definition, up to about 16 percent of the population could be classified as having mental retardation, while the criteria in 1973 included less than 3 percent of the population. The difference between these two populations, essentially those scoring between 70 and 85 on IQ tests, represents about 13 percent of the school population. While these students are not mentally retarded by current guidelines, they may very well have learning problems yet not be eligible for special education services under this category. The number of individuals in this IQ range is substantially higher than the 4.4% of students presently classified as having learning disabilities (U.S. Department of Education, 1998). In fact, students from this lower IQ population may frequently be identified as having learning disabilities in order to provide educational assistance to them. But is this problem primarily the result of the LD definition being employed in an overly inclusive manner, or the result of the definition of "mental retardation" being overly restrictive?

Kavale also described those who argued (e.g., Algozzine, Ysseldyke, & McGue, 1995) that LA students and students with learning disabilities (i.e., with or without discrepancies) do not require qualitatively different methods of instruction. Aaron (1997) also maintained that this premise "cannot be empirically validated" (p. 475). In fact, for years most special educators have acknowledged that a variety of poorly achieving students can be taught with similar methods, if "methods" means a general approach to instruction. Nevertheless, students may differ very substantially in their requirements for intensity, pace, and duration of instruction, or the specific skills being taught, even when the overall method or approach is similar. Such features could clearly result in students being placed in different instructional environments or groupings. The argument that "qualitatively different" instruction must be performed to justify identification is reminiscent of the thinking of decades past, when ineffective approaches such as gross motor and perceptual motor training were recommended (Kavale & Mattson, 1983).

Kavale also describes potential problems with the use of the intelligence quotient in identifying learning disabilities. However, the consequences of suggestions that IQ be eliminated in identification of learning disabilities (e.g., Siegel, 1989) can be evaluated by examining procedures in schools in the state of California that in many instances have eliminated the use of IQ scores. Unfortunately, the result has been to further confuse rather than clarify identification (Forness, 1985).

Kavale concludes by suggesting that "it would be an error to eliminate discrepancy as a factor in LD determination," given that it is not used as the sole criterion. Discrepancy is then simply a factor in the identification process. We can add some more thoughts on the positive value of discrepancy formulas. First, discrepancy is not specific to grade level or age, and can be useful at all grade and age levels. Discrepancy sets a necessary but not sufficient basis for identification; though there can be other reasons than learning disabilities for exhibiting discrepancy, these other reasons are eliminated in the identification process. Further, discrepancy is not limited to one subject or skill area, but can be used to support a learning disability in a variety of areas. Finally, if elimination of discrepancy criteria does not result in the elimination of learning disabilities as a special education category, it must be replaced with a standard that is found to be more useful. It would then be necessary to demonstrate the utility of the new standard. To date, the superiority of other possible identification procedures has yet to be demonstrated.

Kavale's analysis of discrepancy models is both thorough and relevant. In the case of Andrew, failure of this alert, cooperative third grader to perform adequately in academic areas was painfully obvious, as was his need for special help. Analysis of his test scores revealed that he exhibited discrepancies in reading of 22 or 30 points, depending on which measure is used, 15 points in spelling, and 31 points in math. His mental ability was normal, as were his vision, hearing, and motor abilities. He was not deprived of necessary cultural exposure, and had received normal educational experiences. Are such considerations inadequate or misguided in identifying Andrew as having a learning disability? We think not, and recommend that Kavale's important recommendations be carefully considered.

REFERENCES

Aaron, P. G. (1997). The impending demise of the discrepancy formula. *Review of Educational Research, 67,* 461–502.

Algozzine, B., Ysseldyke, J. E., & McGue, M. (1995). Differentiating low-achieving students: Thoughts on setting the record straight. *Learning Disabilities Research and Practice, 10,* 140–144.

Beirne-Smith, M., Ittenbach, R. F., & Patton, J. R. (1998). *Mental retardation* (5th ed.). Columbus, OH: Merrill.

Bursuck, W. (1989). A comparison of students with learning disabilities to low achieving students on three dimensions of social competence. *Journal of Learning Disabilities, 22,* 188–194.

Cleaver, A., Bear, B., & Juvonen, J. (1992). Discrepancies between competence and importance in self-perceptions of children in integrated classes. *The Journal of Special Education, 26,* 125–138.

Donahoe, K., & Zigmond, N. (1990). Academic grades of ninth-grade urban learning-disabled students and low-achieving peers. *Exceptionality, 1,* 17–27.

Forness, S. R. (1985). Effects of public policy at the state level: California's impact on MR, LD, and ED categories. *Remedial and Special Education, 6*(3), 36–43.

Francis, D. J., Shaywitz, S. E., Stuebing, K. K., Shaywitz, B. A., & Fletcher, J. M. (1994). Measurement of change: Assessing behavior over time and within a developmental context. In R. Lyon (Ed.), *Frames of reference for the assessment of learning disabilities: New views on measurement issues* (pp. 29–58). Baltimore: Brookes.

Fuchs, D. (1998). *Is "LD" just a fancy term for "underachievement"?* Paper presented at the annual meeting of the Council for Exceptional Children, Minneapolis.

Kavale, K. A., Fuchs, D., & Scruggs, T. E. (1994). Setting the record straight on learning disabilities and low achievement. *Learning Disabilities Research & Practice, 9,* 70–77.

Kavale, K. A., & Mattson, M. P. (1983). One jumped off the balance beam: A meta-analysis of perceptual-motor training. *Journal of Learning Disabilities, 16,* 165–173.

MacMillan, D. L., Gresham, F. M., & Bocian, K. M. (1998). Discrepancy between definitions of learning disabilities and school practices: An empirical investigation. *Journal of Learning Disabilities, 31,* 314–326.

McLeskey, J., & Waldron, N. L. (1990). The identification and characteristics of students with learning disabilities in Indiana. *Learning Disabilities Research, 5,* 72–78.

Merrill, K. W. (1990). Differentiating low achieving students and students with learning disabilities: An examination of performances on the Woodcock-Johnson Psycho-Educational Battery. *The Journal of Special Education, 24,* 296–305.

Scruggs, T. E., & Mastropieri, M. A. (1986). Academic characteristics of behaviorally disordered and learning disabled children. *Behavioral Disorders, 11,* 184–190.

Shepard, L. A., & Smith, M. L. (1983). An evaluation of the identification of learning disabled students in Colorado. *Learning Disability Quarterly, 6,* 115–127.

Siegel, L. S. (1989). I.Q. is irrelevant to the definition of learning disabilities. *Journal of Learning Disabilities, 25,* 618–629.

Smith, C. R. (1985). Identification of handicapped children and youth: A state agency perspective on behavioral disorders. *Remedial and Special Education, 6*(4), 34–41.

Tur-Kaspa, H., & Bryan, T. (1994). Social information-processing skills of students with learning disabilities. *Learning Disabilities Research and Practice, 9,* 12–23.

U.S. Department of Education (1998). *Twentieth annual report to Congress on the implementation of the Individuals With Disabilities Education Act.* Washington, DC: Author.

Ysseldyke, J. E., Algozzine, B., Shinn, M. R., & McGue, M. (1982). Similarities and differences between low achievers and students classified learning disabled. *Journal of Special Education, 16,* 73–85.

DO DISCREPANCY MODELS SATISFY
EITHER THE LETTER OR THE SPIRIT OF IDEA?

Diane J. Sawyer & Stuart E. Bernstein,
Department of Psychology, Middle Tennessee State University

The concept of a learning disability is rooted in the premise that neurological anomalies can cause uneven development of cognitive capabilities. The resulting pattern of strengths and weaknesses is captured in an operational definition. The modal version of the definition is a significant discrepancy between ability and achievement. Despite widespread use of this definition, its adequacy has been questioned. We argue that a satisfactory operational definition must meet three criteria. The first two criteria are customary for any definition in science: validity and reliability. The third criterion is unique to the learning disability (LD) initiative—the definition must meet the letter and spirit of special education laws. Kavale's review of nearly 40 years of legislation and research (Kavale, this volume) supports the idea that a version of an IQ-achievement discrepancy definition can be statistically reliable (e.g., Kavale, Fuchs, & Scruggs, 1994) but the review fails to establish that the other two criteria have been satisfied.

The most serious problem with the discrepancy definition is a lack of validity. *Concurrent validity* is challenged by the fact that measurements used to document an IQ/achievement discrepancy are not clearly independent of the assessments used to describe the nature of the learning disability. There is also a lack of *predictive validity*. An identified discrepancy does not predict future performance any more accurately than low achievement does. The discrepancy definition, as it is now applied, does not satisfy the intent of special education legislation—to identify and help children at risk for failure.

CONCURRENT VALIDITY

The validity of the discrepancy definition has been examined in several large-scale studies. Fletcher et al. (1998) reviewed four of these studies. In each case, children were identified as displaying low achievement or a discrepancy between ability and achievement. In general, there were no meaningful or systematic differences in tests of cognitive abilities and reading skills that were independent of the tests used for the initial assessment. For example, Fletcher et al. (1994) identified readers displaying an aptitude-achievement discrepancy using a regression formula. A comparison group of readers displaying low achievement was identified using a standard score cutoff. Concurrent validity was assessed with eight general cognitive measures taken from a model of language and reading development (Liberman, Shankweiler, & Liberman, 1989). Despite an 18-point advantage in performance IQ when compared to the low achievement group, the discrepancy group did not display the predicted advantage in independently measured cognitive abilities. Scores for both groups were nearly identical for phonological awareness, verbal memory, nonverbal memory, rapid naming, speech production, and visual attention. This finding is contrary to the prediction that the discrepancy group is qualitatively different than the low achievement group because of relatively high cognitive function. In other words, the findings did not demonstrate concurrent validity for the discrepancy model.

PREDICTIVE VALIDITY

The predictive validity of a discrepancy classification has been tested in a longitudinal study (Francis, Shaywitz, Stuebing, Shaywitz, & Fletcher, 1996). According to the discrepancy model, children with high ability but low achievement are more capable of benefiting from future instruction than lower ability individuals. Francis et al. (1996) tested this prediction by following the development of reading skills among 403 children. Their sample included normally developing children, low achieving children, and a discrepancy group. Reading abilities were measured annually for 9 years. It was found that the improvement in reading achievement from age 7 through 15 was identical for the low achievement and discrepancy groups. This finding is contrary to the discrepancy model's prediction that children with higher ability should show a greater benefit from instruction. Predictive validity for the discrepancy model was not demonstrated.

FAILURE OF THE DISCREPANCY DEFINITION

The Kavale and Forness (2000) operational definition of a specific learning disability suggests that a general deficit in the process of learning can result in limited responsiveness to instruction within a specific cognitive skill area. These areas include language, reading, writing, and math. This general deficit in learning is operationally defined as underachievement which, in turn, can be manifested as a discrepancy between cognitive ability and achievement. However, this definition is compromised by repeated failures to establish the concurrent and predictive validity of the discrepancy.

Failure to establish validity for operational definitions of discrepancy has led to a search for definitions of developmental imbalances that are based on other models. One such alternative is a skill-based approach, such as Aaron's (1997) reading component model or the application of Frith's (1985) stage model of development by Sawyer, Kim, and Lipa-Wade (2000; Sawyer & Kim, 2000). Kavale expresses two concerns related to this type of approach. The first is that adopting this approach undermines the concept of a general learning disability. However, the concept of a general learning disability is actually compromised by an operational definition that makes it impossible to establish the presence of a learning disability independently of the measurement of the consequences of that disability.

Kavale's second concern involves the potential for confounding LD and reading disability (RD). However, the confounding is worse in the discrepancy approach than in the alternatives. A specific reading disability is most prevalent among those who are now diagnosed as having a learning disability—about 75–80% of those with an LD label (Ellis & Cramer, 1994). It is unclear why Kavale argues that general achievement is the best measure of what has not been learned when children's deficiencies are most often manifested as specific problems with reading. The confounding of LD and RD can be avoided by addressing more restricted questions of how to accurately identify children at risk in a particular skill domain. The adequacy of any alternative operational definition of a developmental imbalance can be analyzed with the same three standards that were applied to the discrepancy definition: The alternative definition must demonstrate statistical reliability and validity and should satisfy the intent of special education legislation.

THE LOW ACHIEVEMENT DEFINITION

Low achievement in skills that are specific to reading is an alternative operational definition of a developmental imbalance. The low achievement model is based on the idea that reading skills follow a continuous distribution. Children who fall in the lower tail of the curve are at risk for failure. Unlike the discrepancy model, in the low achievement model there is no assumption of qualitative differences among children at risk for failure (Stanovich, 1988). Research has identified three areas of deficits displayed by children at risk for reading failure. One is a deficit in *analytic abilities,* including *phonemic awareness.* This is the ability to isolate and order individual sounds (phonemes) in spoken words. The second is a deficit in *production abilities,* including *phonics,* which is knowledge of letter sounds and how the alphabet works to code spoken words. The third is a deficit in *recognition abilities* including *orthographic knowledge.* This is the ability to automatically respond to spelling patterns that do not follow the rules of phonics for translation from print to speech.

Correlational studies have shown that phonemic awareness, orthographic knowledge, and phonics are relatively distinct from general cognitive abilities (e.g., Scarborough, 1998). This distinctiveness explains why general intelligence is of limited usefulness when assessing the ability to learn reading skills. Low achievement in the skills themselves is the best predictor of future performance. Deficits in phonemic awareness, orthographic knowledge, and phonics can be identified in kindergarten and are reliable predictors of low reading achievement in later grades (Manis, Seidenberg, & Doi, 1999; Scarborough, 1998; Torgesen et al., 1999). These findings support the predictive validity of a low achievement definition.

The construct validity of grouping early reading skills into three areas is supported by factor analytic studies. For example, Sawyer et al. (2000) performed a factor-analytic study of reading abilities among low-performing kindergarten students. Low-performing students in kindergarten classes were identified using a sentence dictation task. These children were subsequently tested with a battery of nine screening tasks that were independent of the sentence dictation task used for the initial identification. Performance on the nine screening tasks loaded on three separate clusters of abilities in a factor analysis. The three factors that were identified support the construct validity of the low achievement model. One factor was *analytic abilities,* which included sentence segmentation, syllable segmentation, and knowledge of letter sounds. A second factor was *production abilities,* which included rhyme production, sound blending, and a logo-naming task. The third factor was *recognition tasks,* including word rhyme recognition, letter rhyme recognition, and letter name recognition. Concurrent validity was established because performance on the initial screening task, sentence dictation, was significantly correlated with each of the three factors. The most important feature of the study's design was that the three factors were based on measurements of ability that were independent of the initial screening task.

Intervention studies support the predictive validity of the low achievement model. For instance, Torgesen et al. (1999) identified children in kindergarten classes who displayed low scores on two tasks: letter name knowledge and phoneme elision.

The selected children participated in a 2½-year study examining the effectiveness of various types of training. Children in the control group received no training while other children received four 20-minute lessons per week. When tested at the end of the study, over 50% of the control group performed significantly below average on three measures of reading: word attack (53% below average), word identification (53% below average), and passage comprehension (56% below average). Children who received comprehensive training in early literacy skills (Lindamood & Lindamood, 1994) showed significant improvement. Children improved in word attack (24% below average), word identification (21% below average), and passage comprehension (36% below average). Blachman, Tangel, Ball, Black, and McGraw (1999) obtained similar results in a study involving a sample of kindergarten students from an inner-city school.

The intervention studies establish that a low achievement operational definition has predictive validity in two respects. First, children with low achievement in phonics, phonemic awareness, and orthographic knowledge will show later deficits in reading performance if untreated. Second, if these children are helped in kindergarten and/or first grade, they will display significant gains in reading performance. In many cases these children were scoring in the average range following intervention.

Spirit vs. Letter of the Law

It seems reasonable, now, to consider the original intent of Public Law 94-142 (Education for All Handicapped Children Act of 1975). The specification of learning disabilities as a categorical designation within special education opened the door to targeted services for a population of students who had not previously been recognized as possessing special needs. The intent was *inclusion,* within the framework of special education services, of students who exhibited various manifestations of the psychological processing deficits presumed to be at the core of low achievement. Implicit in the definition is the expectation that such processing deficits are not themselves observable. However, low achievement, not otherwise accounted for by obvious physical or environmental factors, could be accepted as evidence that such processing deficits might be present. Unfortunately, this clear intent to include has been confounded, through the years, by attempts to establish a scientific means for determining who may be included. The pursuit of increasingly more stringent mathematical approaches to identification too frequently superseded the necessity of obtaining a reliable clinical diagnosis to guide personalized interventions. This divergence of emphasis is analogous to a sports team that scrupulously dedicates its efforts to perfecting the rules of the game rather perfecting its performance in the game itself.

The proportion of students served under the LD label varies from state to state, presumably as a function, at least in part, of differences in the application of the severe discrepancy criterion (Reynolds, 1984). However, Lester and Kelman (1997) report that demographic and sociopolitical factors are also in play. Lester and Kelman analyzed the relationship among 13 variables that were independent of the actual incidence of learning disabilities in the population. These variables included the proportion of a state's population living in poverty, the proportion of the adult population with bachelor's degrees, and the abortion rate. They concluded that these variables did influence the diagnosis of a learning disability but not of sensory and physical disabilities. The discretionary diagnosis of a learning disability was more prevalent in more affluent states. We must conclude that exclusion is less of a concern when states and school systems have the resources to address unexpectedly low achievers as a class of learners.

Does the discretionary diagnosis of a learning disability represent failure to adhere to scientific rigor, as Kavale suggests in his review? Alternatively, a discretionary diagnosis could be seen as acknowledgment of the imprecision inherent in the identification of a process deficit. We suggest that affluent states, because they can afford to do so, are pursuing identification in ways that are actually more consistent with the spirit of P.L. 94-142. Affluent states give more weight to manifestations of imperfect abilities to listen, think, speak, read, write, and do math than to test scores. One might assume that the goal in these settings is tilted more toward diagnosis of a learning problem than to categorization of a learner.

Pennington (1991) likens the process of making a diagnosis to that of hypothesis testing in scientific research: "...a good hypothesis or diagnosis should be more than just a descriptive relabeling of the data..." (p. 33). Yet, this seems to precisely describe the ability/achievement model of identification now in place—a relabeling of test data using the LD label. Pennington describes diagnoses as "fuzzy sets" in which membership is determined only after multiple sources of data have been collected, drawn together, and interpreted. These data sources include (a) referring symptoms; (b) history; (c) behavioral observations; and (d) tests (p. 36).

In practice, the identification process is the task of school multidisciplinary teams (MDTs). It is their responsibility to go beyond test data in determining eligibility for services. However, in Kavale's review the validity and reliability of these clinical diagnoses are called into question specifically because "...school personnel could not differentiate students with LD based solely on an examination of test scores" (p. 20). Given the text of the discrepancy-based regulations for identification, established by the U.S. Office of Education (1977), this thinking appears to be circuitous. The regulations authorize a school-based team to make a determination of LD after drawing together information regarding (a) achievement over time;

(b) response to instruction that is appropriate to age and ability; and (c) a severe discrepancy between current achievement and intellectual ability. Because the requisite magnitude of the discrepancy is not specified, the regulations provide an implicit sanction for clinical judgment to prevail. What is considered a "severe discrepancy" must reasonably be tied to age and educational opportunity as well as to measured intelligence and academic achievement. However, the determination of LD must also consider health history, emotional status, motivation, and receptive and expressive language. Typically, these factors are addressed only superficially in the testing reports prepared by school psychologists. Effective MDT meetings place all of these factors into the mix in arriving at a determination of eligibility.

IDENTIFICATION AS A MEANS TO AN END

Given the current regulations that guide identification, Kavale concludes that the discrepancy criterion may be necessary but not sufficient for LD identification (p. 39). If the discrepancy criterion is retained, we suggest that the magnitude of the discrepancy should not be tied to a fixed standard. Demanding a discrepancy of one or more standard deviations before certifying eligibility is contrary to all we now know about the importance of *early* intervention (e.g., Sawyer & Butler, 1991; Torgesen, Wagner, & Rashotte, 1997). Furthermore, the use of a discrepancy as a necessary first step in diagnosis (e.g., Kavale & Forness, 2000) denies the significant body of international research on valid early predictors of school failure (see, for example, Badian, 2000). It is neither reasonable nor just to withhold supportive services until a student demonstrates a degree of academic failure that is deemed to be sufficiently "severe." Yet, this is the situation in American schools today. Identification was not intended to be the goal of current federal legislation (IDEA). Rather, IDEA is a means by which supportive services are made available to those who will not flourish without such services. The diagnostic process, which runs parallel to the identification process, is intended to serve the true goal—an individualized education plan designed to maximize educational progress.

An alternative interpretation of the data we have presented is that current regulations cannot guide reasonable and just decisions regarding eligibility for early supportive services. Research has failed to establish the validity of the current standard, which is the discrepancy definition of learning disabilities. An alternative operational definition, low achievement, has been proven to be valid and statistically reliable. Furthermore, low achievement allows early identification of children who are at risk for failure and would benefit from special education services, which satisfies the intent of special education legislation. It may be time for a new definition of developmental imbalances, along with associated guidelines that can be applied earlier and with greater accuracy.

Berninger and Abott (1994) suggested a dynamic assessment model for identification which would take into account multiple developmental domains and document "failure to respond, over time, to validated intervention protocols" (p. 165). The National Institute of Child Health and Human Development has adopted a definition of dyslexia (Lyon, 1995) which, as Dickman (2001) points out, might be viewed as the definition of a specific or unique disability within a broader system of classification. Within this conceptual framework of a hierarchical system for classification, Dickman (2001) proposed the following general definition of learning disabilities:

> Learning disabilities are a class of distinct disorders of constitutional origin that predict anomalies in the adaptive development of skills having consequences across the life span, are unexpected in relation to age and other cognitive and academic abilities, and are not the result of sensory impairment or instructional inadequacy.

Such a definition might open the door to specifying related but independent operational definitions of a reading disability, a math disability, a language disability, and so on. We believe that the term "predict" is the key element within Dickman's definition, having the power to shift the focus of the field from failure to that of prevention of failure. Only in this way can our society ensure that there is *No Child Left Behind* (Bush, 2001).

REFERENCES

Aaron, P. G. (1997). The impending demise of the discrepancy formula. *Review of Educational Research, 67,* 461–502.

Badian, N. A. (Ed.). (2000). *Prediction and prevention of reading failure.* Baltimore, MD: York Press.

Berninger, V. W., & Abott, R. D. (1994). Redefining learning disabilities: Moving beyond the aptitude-achievement discrepancies to failure to respond to validated treatment protocol. In G. Reid Lyon (Ed.), *Frames of reference for the assessment of learning disabilities: New views on measurement issues* (pp. 163–184). Baltimore, MD: P. H. Brookes.

Blachman, B. A., Tangel, D. M., Ball, E. W., Black, R., & McGraw, C. K. (1999). Developing phonological awareness and word recognition skills: A two-year intervention with low-income, inner-city children. *Reading and Writing: An Interdisciplinary Journal, 11,* 239–273.

Bush, G. W. (2001). *No child left behind.* Washington, DC: U. S. Department of Education.

Dickman, G. E. (2001). Dyslexia and the aptitude-achievement discrepancy controversy. *Perspectives, 27*(1), 23–27.

Ellis, W., & Cramer, S. C. (1994). Learning disabilities: A national responsibility. Report of the Summit on Learning Disabilities in Washington, DC. September 20–21. New York: National Center for Learning Disabilities.

Fletcher, J. M., Francis, D. J., Shaywitz, S. E., Lyon, G. R., Foorman, B. R., Stuebing, K. K., & Shaywitz, B. A. (1998). Intelligent testing and the discrepancy model for children with learning disabilities. *Learning Disabilities Research & Practice, 13*(4), 186–203.

Fletcher, J. M., Shaywitz, S. E., Shankweiler, D. P., Katz, L., Liberman, I. Y., Fowler, A., Francis, D. J., Stuebing, K. K., & Shaywitz, B. A. (1994). Cognitive profiles of reading disability: Comparisons of discrepancy and low achievement definitions. *Journal of Educational Psychology, 86*(1), 1–18.

Francis, D. J., Shaywitz, S. E., Stuebing, K. K., Shaywitz, B. A., & Fletcher, J. M. (1996). Developmental lag versus deficit models of reading disability: A longitudinal individual growth curves analysis. *Journal of Educational Psychology, 88*(1), 3–17.

Frith, U. (1985). Beneath the surface of developmental dyslexia. In K. Patterson, M. Coltheart, & J. Marshall (Eds.), *Surface dyslexia.* Mahwah, NJ: Lawrence Erlbaum Associates.

Kavale, K. A. (this volume). Discrepancy models in the identification of learning disability.

Kavale, K. A., & Forness, S. R. (2000). What definitions of learning disability say and don't say: A critical analysis. *Journal of Learning Disabilities, 33*(3), 239–256.

Kavale, K. A., Fuchs, D., & Scruggs, T. E. (1994). Setting the record straight on learning disability and low achievement: Implications for policymaking. *Learning Disabilities Research and Practice, 9,* 70–77.

Lester, G., & Kelman, M. (1997). State disparities in the diagnosis and placement of pupils with learning disabilities. *Journal of Learning Disabilities 30*(6), 599–607.

Liberman, I. Y., Shankweiler, D. P., & Liberman, A. M. (1989). The alphabetic principle and learning to read. In D. P. Shankweiler & I. Y. Liberman (Eds.), *Phonology and reading disability: Solving the reading puzzle* (pp. 1–33). Ann Arbor, MI: University of Michigan Press.

Lindamood, C. H., & Lindamood, P. C. (1994). *Auditory discrimination in depth.* Austin, TX: Pro-Ed.

Lyon, G. R. (1995). Toward a definition of dyslexia. *Annals of Dyslexia, 45,* 3–27.

Manis, F. R., Seidenberg, M. S., & Doi, L. M. (1999). See Dick RAN: Rapid naming and the longitudinal prediction of reading subskills in first and second graders. *Scientific Studies of Reading, 3*(2), 129–157.

Pennington, B. F. (1991). *Diagnosing learning disorders: A neuropsychological framework*. New York: Guilford Press.

Reynolds, C. R. (1984). Critical measurement issues in learning disabilities. *Journal of Special Education 18,* 451–475.

Sawyer, D. J., & Butler, K. (1991). Early language intervention: A deterrent to reading disability. *Annals of Dyslexia, 41,* 55–79.

Sawyer, D. J., & Kim, J. K. (2000). Variation in the development of decoding and encoding skills among students with phonological dyslexia. *Thalamus, 18*(2), 1–16.

Sawyer, D. J., Kim, J. K., & Lipa-Wade, S. (2000). Application of Frith's developmental phase model to the process of identifying at-risk beginning readers. In A. Badian (Ed.), *Prediction and prevention of reading failure* (pp. 87–103). Baltimore, MD: York Press.

Scarborough, H. S. (1998). Predicting the future achievement of second graders with reading disabilities: Contributions of phonemic awareness, verbal memory, rapid naming, and IQ. *Annals of Dyslexia, 48,* 115–136.

Stanovich, K. E. (1988). Explaining the differences between the dyslexic and the garden-variety poor reader: The phonological-core-variable-difference model. *Journal of Learning Disabilities, 21*(10), 590–604.

Torgesen, J. K., Wagner, R. K., & Rashotte, C. A. (1997). Prevention and remediation of severe reading disabilities: Keeping the end in mind. *Scientific Studies of Reading, 1*(3), 217–234.

Torgesen, J. K., Wagner, R. K., Rashotte, C. A., Rose, E., Lindamood, P., Conway, T., & Garvan, C. (1999). Preventing reading failure in young children with phonological processing disabilities: Group and individual responses to instruction. *Journal of Educational Psychology, 91*(4), 579–593.

U.S. Office of Education. (1977). Assistance to states for education of all handicapped children: Procedures for evaluating specific learning disabilities. *Federal Register, 42* (250), 65082–65085. Washington, DC: U. S. Government Printing Office.

CHAPTER VI: RESPONSIVENESS TO INTERVENTION: AN ALTERNATIVE APPROACH TO THE IDENTIFICATION OF LEARNING DISABILITIES

Frank M. Gresham, University of California-Riverside

The process by which public schools identify students as learning disabled often appears to be confusing, unfair, and logically inconsistent. In fact, G. Reid Lyon of the National Institute of Child Health and Human Development has suggested that the field of learning disabilities is a sociological sponge whose purpose has been and is to clean up the spills of general education. Research indicates that substantial proportions of school-identified students with learning disability (LD) fail to meet state or federal eligibility criteria (Lyon, 1996; MacMillan, Gresham, & Bocian, 1998; Shaywitz, Shaywitz, Fletcher, & Escobar, 1990; Shepard, Smith, & Vojir, 1983). In discussing this situation, MacMillan and Speece (1999) noted that although this finding is not in and of itself surprising, the *magnitude* of the percentage of school-identified LD students who fail to meet eligibility criteria ranged from 52 to 70%.

It may be tempting to interpret such findings as a reflection of the failure on the part of school personnel to comply with state special education codes governing eligibility determination. Keogh (1994), however, suggested that classification has three purposes: advocacy, services, and scientific study. "Error rates" in school identification of LD students can be estimated by validating cases of schools for purposes of service delivery against criteria specified in state education codes that are relevant for scientific study.

Unlike diagnosing children with physical or sensory disabilities or those with more severe forms of mental retardation, efforts to detect students exhibiting milder disabilities such as LD or mild mental retardation (MMR) are fraught with much "error" in the sense that children meeting criteria often go undetected. Because diagnosis of these milder disabilities primarily occurs in public schools, only those children referred for assessment are at risk for formal labeling. Previous work examining students whom general education teachers referred has shown that almost half of those referred had IQ scores between 71 and 85 and an additional 16% scored below an IQ of 70 (MacMillan, Gresham, Bocian, & Lambros, 1998). Clearly, teachers perceive low aptitude students as among the most difficult to teach. When MacMillan et al. applied the current IQ cut scores recommended by the American Association on Mental Retardation (IQ < 75), they found that approximately 30% of all referred children scored below that level.

Despite the abundance of children psychometrically eligible for labeling as mildly mentally retarded, only 14% of the 43 children with IQ < 75 were classified by schools as such (MacMillan, Gresham, Siperstein, & Bocian, 1996). More germane to the current topic, 44% of these cases were labeled as LD by the schools, a finding consistent with that of Gottlieb, Alter, Gottlieb, and Wishner (1994) who found school-identified urban LD students to have a mean IQ that was substantially lower than that of suburban LD students and to resemble mildly mentally retarded students of the 1970s.

The LD category now accounts for 52% of all students with disabilities served in special education under the Individuals with Disabilities Education Act (IDEA). Between 1976–77 and 1996–97, the number of students served as LD increased from 797,213 to 2,259,000—a 283% increase. During this same period, the number of students served as MR decreased from 967,567 to 584,000, representing a 60% decrease (U.S. Department of Education, 1998). In commenting on the dramatic increase in LD, MacMillan and colleagues suggested, "Were these epidemic-like figures interpreted by the Center [sic] for Disease Control, one might reasonably expect to find a quarantine imposed on the public schools of America" (MacMillan, Gresham, Siperstein, & Bocian, 1996, p. 169).

Frankly, there is neither a completely accurate nor universally accepted explanation for these data. However, the increase in LD, in part, is attributable to school practices of classifying LD on the basis of absolute low achievement regardless of IQ level or a discrepancy between IQ and achievement—and including in substantial numbers children who meet criteria for MMR (MacMillan et al., 1998). In fact, an analysis of current classification practices suggested the following: (a) a small minority of such children are classified as mildly mentally retarded, (b) a substantial proportion of these children are served (erroneously) in special education as LD, and (c) some unknown proportion avoid detection, are overlooked by teachers, or are not referred by teachers despite concerns about the child's academic performance (MacMillan, Gresham, Bocian, & Siperstein, 1997; MacMillan, Siperstein, & Gresham, 1996).

PARADIGMS OF LD CLASSIFICATION

The process employed by public schools can be conceptualized as consisting of three steps: (a) the decision to refer by a child's general education teacher, (b) the psychological evaluation of the child, which yields a combination of psychometric scores corresponding to criteria specified in the state as a prerequisite for eligibility, and (c) the team placement decision arrived at after review and discussion of all evidence by a school placement team. It is significant that these three steps occur in a set sequence as presented above. As a result, a student who is not referred by his or her general education teacher is not at risk for being identified as LD. Only those students passing through this first gate—referral—are even considered for psychological evaluation. In addition to the steps in the above sequence, consideration must be given to the fact that at each gate there are differences in the weighting given to various factors that result in three competing paradigms for the identification process. These factors are (a) the nature and role of professional judgment permitted at a specific gate, (b) the concept or question addressed by those involved in the decision making at a particular gate, (c) the use of local versus national norms employed at various gates, and (d) the extent to which sociocultural and contextual factors are considered (Bocian, Beebe, MacMillan, & Gresham, 1999).

Viewing the identification process through the lens of competing paradigms may serve to clarify the process by which schools identify children as LD and why there is often a gap between who is identified by schools and research criteria. The following sections expand on how each of the four factors just noted operate in concert or in competition with each of the three paradigms or gates in the identification process.

Referral

Being referred by a general education teacher is a necessary but insufficient requirement for being school-identified as LD. Although teachers refer students to prereferral teams for academic and/or behavioral difficulties, the referral issue with LD is almost always academic deficiencies. The child's academic performance relative to the modal performance of the class or the gap between the target child's reading level and that of members of the lowest reading group is more salient in reaching the referral decision than are standardized test scores. This perspective reflects what has been referred to in the literature as "teachers as imperfect tests" (Bahr, Fuchs, Stecker, & Fuchs, 1991; Gerber & Semmel, 1984; Gresham, MacMillan, & Bocian, 1997; Gresham, Reschly, & Carey, 1987). The principle guiding the teacher at this step is one of *relativity*—that is, what is the likelihood that this teacher will be able to close the gap in achievement relative to the target child's peers in both the classroom and grade level, given class size, past responsiveness of the child to intervention, and the resources available in the classroom? When the teacher concludes that this relative gap cannot be substantially narrowed without assistance, the decision to refer is highly probable.

Although the referral decision is almost never influenced by information from nationally normed scales, the decision can be and sometimes is tempered by sociocultural and contextual factors. Even in cases where the teacher judges a child's academic performance to be deficient, he or she might refrain from referring because of circumstances involving the home, the facility of both regular and special education teachers with the child's native language, or health concerns. The point here is that although local norms are employed to determine academic performance at the referral step, sociocultural and contextual factors are considerations that sometimes influence the referral decision.

Testing

It is likely that children who were referred and fail to respond to prereferral efforts will ultimately be subjected to the second gate in the referral process—psychoeducational evaluation. MacMillan and Speece (1999) characterized this gate as representing a cognitive paradigm intended to detect or document the existence of a within-child problem. It is through psychoeducational assessment that the referred child's eligibility for special education as LD is established as 98% of the states include a discrepancy in either their definition of or criteria for identifying students with LD (Mercer, Jordan, Allsopp, & Mercer, 1996).

The concept guiding the decision to pass the child through this gate and on to the school-placement team is one of *acceptability*. Through the assessment with standardized tests, one can determine whether the referred child's low level of academic performance is acceptable. If it is severely discrepant from the aptitude score, a low performance in reading is unacceptable (i.e., the child should be doing better). This situation reflects the concept of LD as unexpected underachievement. Conversely, if a child with a very low reading score performs equally low on an individually administered measure of intelligence, he or she is doing about as well as can be expected. This situation reflects the notion of expected underachievement. Finally, although teachers weigh sociocultural and contextual factors in deciding whether to refer the child, the testing step is devoid of such factors.

Team Recommendation

Multidisciplinary teams (MDTs) are responsible for determining eligibility and recommending placement. These teams are permitted to exercise judgment, but unlike the teacher in the referral step, it is a "team judgment," not an individual one. It brings together the two major players involved in referral and testing—that is, the general education teacher who referred the child and the school psychologist or educational diagnostician who performed the psychoeducational assessment.

The decision reached by the MDT reflects a considerable amount of team judgment, as opposed to individual judgment which is reflected in the referral process. The general education teacher assesses the child's academic performance relative to local norms and the school psychologist assesses the child's academic performance discrepancy relative to aptitude and national norms. However, although local norms predominate at the referral step and national norms predominate at the testing step, all three perspectives are considered by the MDT in arriving at a placement decision: local norms, national norms, and sociocultural and contextual factors.

The concept guiding the team decision regarding placement is *profitability*, which reflects the collective perception that the specific special education services provided at that school site will or will not benefit the child. As such, the anticipated profitability gauges the interaction between child characteristics (derived from the comparisons of this child's level of performance to both local and national norms) and the quality of special education services on site. Parental wishes and concerns also will factor into the ultimate decision regarding placement.

The dynamics of specific MDTs will result in assignment of differential weighting to local norms, national norms, and sociocultural and contextual factors in arriving at placement decisions. Thus, team decisions are likely to vary, even in the face of hypothetically identical information, because of the relative forcefulness of particular players serving on the team. Any effort to understand school-identified LD students must consider the importance of these three steps (referral, testing, and team recommendation) and the relative weighting given to available data at each step.

Implications of Competing Paradigms in LD Identification

Presently, research on LD students often examines a group of students who are screened according to criteria for only one of the gates. For example, a "sample" will sometimes be selected from children with a certain psychological profile reflective of the testing gate even though a referring teacher did not initially screen the sample. Such sampling results in a group that overlaps with but is not identical with children who will be school-identified as LD. Findings over the past 15 years have pointed out the lack of consistent definition in policy or practice in the identification of LD students, a circumstance that has been a major stumbling block to effective research and practice (Lyon, 1996). Response to this challenge has ranged from impugning the concept of LD as neither valid nor instructionally relevant, to criticizing teachers and schools for failing to implement criteria correctly. Some researchers have suggested that schools seek flexibility and the opportunity to exercise professional judgment rather than being held to a rigid code of precise formulas (Keogh & Speece, 1996; MacMillan et al., 1997; McLeskey & Waldron, 1991).

A second implication of the competing paradigm model is the accuracy with which teachers identify within-child variables relevant to the classroom that are later validated by psychoeducational assessments. Teachers' accurate evaluations of students' abilities should be sought after rather than continually challenged. Teachers may be "imperfect tests," but in terms of classroom relevance, their perceptions often outrank students' performances on psychoeducational assessments on isolated tasks conducted under ideal, pristine conditions.

A third implication is recognizing the severe limitations and the ability of the discrepancy concept of LD to both plan instruction and identify students for early intervention. The recent national downward trend in reading achievement and the public pressure for student outcomes and accountability have led to an enhanced focus in the field on reading disabilities (Lyon, 1996). This approach surely holds more promise for students and teachers alike, particularly given the ability of teachers to identify reading disabilities based on curriculum-achievement discrepancy or an achievement discrepancy relative to peers. Perhaps of greater import is the need to train and encourage teachers to exercise their judgment at even earlier points in a student's career. The research field should work to validate that judgment with operationalized criteria, particularly with reading problems.

Although the competing paradigm multiple-gate system now in place does work to identify students in need of services, the competition between expensive, time-consuming assessments at three different steps could be streamlined and articulated in a fashion more respectful of both teacher and school professional judgment to meet students' need for immediate intervention services. The most serious flaw in the current process is the absence of a direct link between assessment procedures used for identification and subsequent interventions that might be prescribed based on these assessment procedures (i.e., treatment validity). In fact, it is clear that most reading difficulties exhibited by students now classified as LD are caused by inadequate literacy experiences, inadequate instruction, or some combination of both (Clay, 1987; Vellutino, Scanlon, & Tanzman, 1998). This being the case, an alternative approach to the identification of students with LD is justified. Therefore, the focus of the current paper is to describe how such an assessment process can be developed and used in identifying and instructing students with LD.

Definitions of LD and the Discrepancy Approach

The purpose of this section is to provide a very brief overview of the history of and difficulties in defining LD and some of the issues inherent in using a discrepancy approach to operationalize the LD construct. Other chapters in this book provide a much more detailed analysis of the issues involved in the definition of LD. This overview is intended to provide a context for discussing a different approach to LD definition: *responsiveness to validated intervention procedures.*

Brief Recent History of LD

Kirk (1962) first used "learning disabled" to describe a group of children who have retardation, disorder, or delayed development in one of more of the processes of speech, language, reading, writing, arithmetic, or other school subjects. This definition was the first to introduce the concept of psychological process disorders and how these processing deficits adversely affect academic achievement (Kavale & Forness, 2000). Shortly thereafter, Bateman (1965) proposed the notion of underachievement as a fundamental aspect of LD. In Bateman's definition, the idea of an "educationally significant discrepancy" between intellectual potential and actual level of academic performance was emphasized. This definition did not specify what constituted an "educationally significant discrepancy" and did not provide information on how to measure intellectual potential and actual level of performance (Kavale & Forness, 2000). More than three decades later, the field of LD still has not arrived at a consensus in terms of resolving these definitional and measurement issues.

Rutter and Yule (1975) defined two types of reading underachievement difficulties: general reading backwardness (GRB) and specific reading retardation (SRR). GRB is defined as reading below the level expected of a child's chronological age, whereas SRR is defined as reading below the level predicted from a child's intelligence. Rutter and Yule estimated the prevalence of GRB in the school-age population to be 7% and 20% (rural and inner-city settings, respectively), whereas the prevalence rate of SRR was 4% and 10%, respectively. It should be noted that, according to Hinshaw (1992), almost all children with SRR could be classified as GRB, but only half of children with GRB are classifiable as SRR.

Children such as those described by Rutter and Yule (1975) as having SRR may be considered as having LD in most states using a discrepancy-based definition of LD (Mercer et al., 1996). In fact, the prevalence rate of SRR of 4–10% in Great Britain is consistent with the 5% prevalence rate of children served as LD in the United

States. Moreover, children who might be described as low achievers might meet the definition of GRB. SRR and GRB capture the concepts of unexpected and expected reading underachievement, respectively.

Issues in Defining LD: The LD/LA Disputes

Differentiation among groups of children having mild disabilities such as LD and MMR as well as low achievement (LA) has always been problematic. Children functioning around the margin of what might be considered a disability group create special problems in assessment, measurement, and eligibility determination for special education programs. At what point, for instance, is low academic achievement considered to be due to MMR and not to LD? How is MMR different from LA? Is LD different from LA, and if so, how is it different? Are LD and LA primarily reflective of differences in degree or kind of academic underachievement? Although these questions remain fundamental to the identification of students having difficulties in school, definitive answers to these questions have not been forthcoming.

Researchers have debated the similarities and differences between students classified as LD (discrepant low achievers) and those classified as LA. The heart of these debates centers on the degree to which LD can be differentiated from LA and the extent to which distributions of these groups' intellectual, academic achievement, and social behavior functioning overlap (Epps, Ysseldyke, & McGue, 1984; Fuchs, Mathes, Fuchs, & Lipsey, 2001; Kavale, Fuchs, & Scruggs, 1994; Ysseldyke, Algozzine, Shinn, & McGue, 1982). Perhaps the most widely cited study in this debate was reported by Ysseldyke et al. (1982) in which school-identified children with LD were compared to a group of LA children on a variety of psychoeducational measures. This study suggested that LD could not be differentiated from LA, with 96% of the scores on psychoeducational measures being in a common range. Ysseldyke et al. argued that LD and LA are essentially identical constructs, and they questioned the diagnostic validity of the term "learning disabilities."

Kavale et al. (1994) criticized the interpretation and analyses of Ysseldyke et al. (1982), indicating that the data had been misused to support policies from the Regular Education Initiative. Kavale et al. reanalyzed Ysseldyke et al.'s original data, using a meta-analytic statistic (Cohen's d) that compares the means of each group relative to the groups' variability (pooled standard deviation [SD]). On the basis of 44 comparisons, Kavale et al. showed that 63% of the LD group could be differentiated from the LA group (effect size = 0.338), with 37% overlap between the groups. This 37% overlap figure is substantially less than the 96% overlap reported by Ysseldyke et al. With respect to academic achievement, almost 80% of the LD group could be differentiated from the LA group, with LD children scoring lower than the LA group.

The results of the Connecticut Longitudinal Study added further fuel to the debate concerning the differentiation of LD and LA (Shaywitz, Fletcher, Holahan, & Shaywitz, 1992). This investigation compared children with LD (defined as a 22-point discrepancy between aptitude and reading achievement) with low achievers (defined as children scoring below the 25th percentile in reading, but who did not show a severe discrepancy). Using a variety of child-, teacher-, and parent-based measures, these authors found more similarities than differences between LD and LA groups, suggesting that both groups could be considered eligible for special education services.

The separate analyses and interpretations of the same data set by Ysseldyke et al. (1982) and Kavale et al. (1994), coupled with the longitudinal study by Shaywitz et al. (1992), leave a fundamental question unresolved: Are LD and LA quantitatively or qualitatively different? The studies and analyses by Ysseldyke et al. and Shaywitz et al. suggest that LD and LA groups are more alike than different. The analyses by Kavale et al. suggest these groups are more different than alike, particularly in the area of academic achievement. Researchers and practitioners are left with the decision of deciding which group's analyses and conclusions to believe. This distinction is important, given that important educational decisions are made for children with these characteristics and that these decisions have rather substantial economic and legal consequences for school districts.

Recently, a meta-analysis of 79 studies on this topic was completed by Fuchs et al. (2001), the purpose of which was to determine whether LD and LA reflect differences in *degree* of underachievement or differences in *kind* of underachievement. That is, is LD *quantitatively* different or *qualitatively* different from LA in terms of reading achievement? On the basis of 112 effect sizes, the mean weighted effect size was 0.61 (95% CI: 0.56 to 0.65); however, there was considerable heterogeneity among studies concerning the magnitude of differences in reading between LD and LA groups.

Fuchs et al. (2001) interpreted the 0.61 effect size as being large, thereby suggesting that LD could be differentiated from LA (LD < LA in reading achievement). However, this 0.61 effect size translates into only a 9-point ($M = 100$, $SD = 15$) standard score difference between LD and LA groups. In fact, Cohen and Cohen (1983) would define a 0.61 effect size as moderate and a large effect size as being 0.80 or greater. Assuming a median reliability coefficient of 0.90 for reading domain measures used in calculating effect sizes and a standard error of measurement of 4.74 ($SD = 15$), a 95% confidence interval calculates to +9.48 standard score points. Clearly, this difference is not large, particularly when taking into account measurement error of the dependent measures.

It is difficult to make the case that a standard score difference which is within the range of measurement error represents a substantial difference in kind rather than degree and therefore somehow validates the LD construct. Certainly, these data do not support a two-groups approach to LA like that found in the field of mental retardation (Zigler, Balla, & Hodapp, 1984). For the sake of argument, the average IQ scores of students with MMR is around 70 and the average IQ score of students with profound mental retardation is about 25. Few would argue that these two groups do not differ in *kind* on a number of variables such as identification prior to school entry, severe deficits in independent functioning, and frequent comorbid biomedical conditions (MacMillan, Gresham, & Siperstein, 1993).

The Fuchs et al. (2001) meta-analysis suggested that a standard-score point difference of 9 (0.61 SD) was sufficient to conclude that LD students differ in kind from LA students, particularly on timed reading tasks reflecting deficits primarily in automaticity of reading skills. By comparison, in the area of sensory disabilities, there are clear distinctions between hearing impaired and deaf as well as visually impaired and blind based on rather substantial differences in the magnitude of hearing and visual loss, respectively. Clearly, the field of LD must be able to present more convincing evidence to conclude that LD students differ in kind from LA students and thus legitimately deserve special education and related services based on this minimal difference.

IQ-Achievement Discrepancy and LD Definition

There have been a variety of ways of operationalizing the LD construct using some variation of a discrepancy-based notion. Berninger and Abbott (1994) suggested that four major methods have been used to compute discrepancy; all of which have measurement difficulties: (a) deviation from grade level, (b) expectancy formulas, (c) simple standard-score difference, and (d) standard regression analysis. A *deviation from grade-level* approach makes the fallacious assumption that all students should be functioning on grade level. Of course, this assumption ignores the most fundamental principle of standardized achievement tests: In a normal distribution of test scores, half the students will be above level and half will be below grade level. How far below grade level one must be to qualify for LD using this approach is influenced by a variety of factors such as level of intelligence, socioeconomic status of the school, and measurement problems with grade-equivalent scores.

Another approach is to compare a child's expected and observed grade level in an academic area controlling for IQ (*expectancy approach*). To determine this discrepancy, this approach uses grade-equivalent scores which vary greatly across grade levels in terms of the raw scores underlying these scores and are not comparable across test instruments (Berninger & Abbott, 1994). A third approach uses standard-score differences between IQ and achievement measures (sometimes called the *simple difference method*) to quantify LD. This approach, however, does not account for measurement error in IQ and achievement measures, the unreliability of difference scores, and the attendant effects of regression toward the mean. In a final method, the *regression discrepancy approach*, the measurement errors using the simple difference method are accounted for by calculating aptitude-achievement discrepancies using the parameters of reliability of aptitude, reliability of achievement, and reliability of aptitude-achievement difference scores (Reynolds, 1984). This approach, like the standard-score difference approach, assumes that IQ is the exclusive and self-limiting determinant of achievement.

The aforementioned approaches to quantifying LD have been used to qualify students for special education and related services. Each method, as briefly reviewed, has a number of conceptual and statistical drawbacks. A major controversy in discrepancy-based notions of defining LD is the central importance assigned to IQ tests in this process (Gresham & Witt, 1997; Kavale & Forness, 2000; Siegel, 1989). Perhaps the most important criticism of IQ tests is that they contribute little reliable information to the planning, implementation, and evaluation of instructional interventions for children and youth. Moreover, according to the research contrasting LD and LA populations, IQ tests are not particularly useful in diagnostic and classification purposes for students with mild learning problems. What appears to be needed is an approach to defining LD based on how students respond to instructional interventions rather than some arbitrarily defined discrepancy between ability and achievement.

RESPONSIVENESS TO INTERVENTION

Historical Background: Aptitude × Treatment Interaction

The notion of alternative responsiveness to intervention is not a new concept in the field of education and psychology. In his presidential address to the American Psychological Association, Cronbach (1957) called for the integration of correlational and experimental disciplines of scientific psychology by using the concept of aptitude × treatment interactions (Atis). ATI research focuses on the measurement of valid aptitudes (characteristics or traits) and how these aptitudes interact with various treatments (instructional methods or types of therapy). ATI research originally attempted to provide a hybrid science spliced from the study of individual differences (aptitudes) and experimental psychology (treatments). Interactions occur when treatments or instructional methods have different effects on persons known to differ in measured aptitudes or characteristics.

Cronbach and Snow (1977) defined an aptitude as any characteristic of a person that predicts the probability of success under a particular treatment condition. These characteristics or aptitudes theoretically can be anything ranging from test-derived aptitudes (verbal-spatial, fluid-crystallized, field dependent-independent) to physical variables (right versus left hemispheric functioning, temporal versus frontal lobe damage). Treatments are defined as any manipulable variable such as instructional method, type of psychotherapy, classroom climate, and so on.

The fundamental logic of ATIs is the matching of instructional treatments to aptitudes. The basic rationale for this matching is based on the belief that learners having strengths in some aptitudes will respond better to treatments capitalizing on these aptitude strengths. Whereas Cronbach and Snow (1977) suggested that aptitudes and treatments could be matched in several ways (capitalization, compensation, and remediation), most ATI matching studies have been based on capitalization, which adapts instruction to the abilities of the student. For example, students high in verbal comprehension might be expected to learn more under verbal instruction rather than visual instruction.

At its most basic level, an ATI study must have at least two aptitudes and two treatments and thus four data points. For example, one could use scores from the Wechsler Intelligence Scale for Children III (WISC-III) Verbal (Verbal Comprehension) and Performance (Perceptual Organization) scales to define Verbal and Visual learners, respectively. These scores would represent two aptitudes. One could also use phonics and whole-word approaches to reading instruction to define two treatments. To demonstrate an ATI, one could show that Verbal learners respond better to phonics instruction than Visual learners and Visual learners respond better to whole-word instruction than Verbal learners. This example is a *disordinal ATI* and this logic is employed most frequently by school psychologists and special educators to make instructional recommendations based on cognitive ability or aptitude measures (Gresham & Witt, 1997; Reschly & Ysseldyke, 1995). In an ordinal ATI, there is a larger effect on one treatment for one aptitude, but no differences between the two aptitude groups for the other treatment. For instance, phonics may be more effective for Verbal learners with no differences between Verbal and Visual learners using the whole-word treatment.

From a logical perspective, we have every reason to expect that many ATIs exist in teaching students with LD. Ostensibly, "verbal" learners should learn more efficiently and effectively under verbal instruction and "visual" learners should learn more efficiently and effectively under visual instruction. Unfortunately, there is little empirical support for the differential prescription of treatments based on different abilities or aptitudes like these and others found in the literature. This lack of support continues to surprise many professionals who interpret test results and recommend treatments based on the presumption of largely mythical ATIs (Gresham & Witt, 1997; Reschly & Ysseldyke, 1995).

Brief Overview of ATI Research

A comprehensive review of the ATI research literature is far beyond the scope of the current paper; however, a number of reviews of this literature support the unfeasibility of matching aptitudes to treatments for children with LD or other learning difficulties. Comprehensive reviews of the modality matching literature (Arter & Jenkins, 1979; Kavale & Forness, 1987, 1995; Ysseldyke & Mirkin, 1982) fail to consistently show significant ATIs. Studies and reviews conducted within the cognitive style/processing literature fail to consistently demonstrate ATIs (Ayres & Cooley, 1986; Ayres, Cooley, & Severson, 1988; Das, 1995; Das, Naglieri, & Kirby, 1995; Good, Vollmer, Creek, Katz, & Chowdhri, 1993).

Finally, the use of a neuropsychological model within ATI research focuses on inferred brain strengths or functioning. For instance, a child having left hemispheric strength might be presumed to learn more efficiently using methods that capitalize on this strength (e.g., phonics, verbally presented material) whereas children with right hemispheric strengths might perform better using other methods (e.g., holistic, visually presented material). Despite the proliferation of this ATI logic in the neuropsychological literature (see D'Amato, Rothlisberg, & Work, 1999; Hynd, 1989; Reynolds & Fletcher-Jantzen, 1989), I was unable to locate a single, methodologically sound empirical study demonstrating a significant ATI based on neuropsychological assessment, interpretation, and treatment with children having mild learning problems. In fact, reviews by Reschly and Gresham (1989) and Teeter (1987, 1989) question the entire enterprise of applying ATI logic in neuropsychological assessment practices to children with mild learning problems.

Considering the disappointing results of ATI studies using modality matching, cognitive style/processing, and neuropsychological assessment, there is little, if any, empirical support for prescribing different treatments based on the assessment of different aptitudes. Cronbach (1975) expressed his frustration with ATI research by stating: "Once we attend to interactions, we enter a hall of mirrors that extends to infinity" (p. 119). Abandoning the quest for ATIs, Cronbach (1975) suggested context-specific evaluation and short-run empiricism: "One monitors responses to treatment and adjusts it" (p. 126). The approach recommended by Cronbach forms the conceptual basis for *responsiveness to treatment* as the criterion in making LD eligibility determinations. Yet before describing specific research using this approach for students with LD, I provide a conceptual basis for responsiveness to intervention in the following section.

Responsiveness to Intervention Defined

Responsiveness to intervention can be defined as the change in behavior or performance as a function of an intervention (Gresham, 1991). The concept of responsiveness to intervention uses a discrepancy-based approach; however, the discrepancy is between pre- and postintervention levels of performance rather than between ability and achievement scores. Given that a goal of all interventions is to produce a discrepancy between baseline and postintervention levels of performance, the failure to produce such a discrepancy within a reasonable period (an inadequate response to *intervention*) might be taken as partial evidence for the presence of an LD. Responsiveness to intervention has received a great deal of attention over the past 25 years in the experimental analysis of behavior literature (see Nevin, 1988, 1996 for comprehensive reviews).

In an analogy to Newtonian physics, Nevin (1988) used the term *behavioral momentum* to explain a behavior's resistance to change. That is, a moving body possesses both mass and velocity and will maintain constant velocity under constant conditions. The velocity of an object will change only in proportion to an external force and in inverse proportion to its mass. Considering the momentum metaphor, an effective intervention ("force") results in a high level of momentum ("responsiveness") for the behavior in question (e.g., learning to read).

For example, a reading intervention designed to produce oral reading fluency would be considered successful if it produced reading fluency rapidly and reliably during intervention and if reading fluency persisted after the intervention is withdrawn. In contrast, if oral reading fluency deteriorated after the intervention is withdrawn, teachers would not be satisfied with the rate of oral reading fluency no matter how well a student read during intervention. Also, if oral reading performances occurred at low rates with numerous errors (omissions, substitutions) during intervention, teachers would likely conclude that the student had not established automaticity in oral reading and would seek to extend, intensify, or change the reading instruction.

In the field of LD, the goal for all students is to facilitate the momentum of academic performances, primarily in reading. One can conceptualize *response to intervention* as being determined by response strength ("momentum") in relation to an intervention implemented to change behavior ("external force"). Most children at risk for LD exhibit poor performances in the area of reading (e.g., poor fluency, lack of phonological awareness). That is, their reading behavior has low velocity, which does not change when they are exposed to typical reading instruction in the general education classroom. A *response to intervention* approach to eligibility determination identifies students as having an LD if their academic performances in relevant areas do not change in response to a validated intervention implemented with integrity.

As we shall see later, much sound empirical work has been done on the idea of identifying treatment-adequate and -inadequate responders to intervention in the field of reading disabilities (Fuchs, Fuchs, & Hamlett, 1989a; Vellutino et al., 1996, 1998). The following section describes the concept of treatment validity and how it can be incorporated into the notion of responsiveness to intervention.

Treatment Validity

Treatment validity (sometimes referred to as treatment or instructional utility) is the degree to which any assessment procedure contributes to beneficial outcomes for individuals (Cone, 1989; Hayes, Nelson, & Jarrett, 1987). Although the concept of treatment validity evolved from the behavioral assessment camp, it shares several characteristics and concepts found in the traditional psychometric literature: (a) Treatment validity contains an aspect of Sechrest's (1963) notion of *incremental validity* in that it requires an assessment procedure to improve prediction over and above existing procedures; (2) treatment validity contains the idea of utility and cost-benefit analysis that is common in the personnel selection literature (Mischel, 1968; Wiggins, 1973); and (c) treatment validity is related to Messick's (1995) evidential basis for test interpretation and use, particularly as it relates to construct validity, relevance/utility, and social consequences. It is possible for a particular test interpretation to have construct validity, but have little or no relevance or utility for a particular use of that test (e.g., recommendations for treatments based on the test). Finally, as previously noted, the whole idea behind ATI research is based on the notion of treatment validity, the matching of instructional treatments to aptitudes.

The ATI literature on modality matching, cognitive style/processing, and neuropsychological assessment provides little evidence that the information gathered about aptitudes results in "incremental advance information" that helps in recommending instructional interventions for students with learning difficulties. More than 15 years ago in a review in the *Buros Mental Measurement Yearbook* of the Wechsler Intelligence Scale for Children-Revised (WISC-R), Witt and Gresham (1985) wrote: "The WISC-R lacks treatment validity in that its use does not enhance remedial interventions for children who show specific academic skill deficiencies... For a test to have treatment validity, it must lead to better treatments (i.e., better educational programs, teaching strategies, etc.)" (p. 1717). This statement could be extended to *all* cognitive ability measures based primarily on their inability to inform or guide instructional interventions (Gresham & Witt, 1997; Reschly & Grimes, 1995). Voicing a similar sentiment regarding using IQ tests in the diagnosis of reading disability, Share, McGee, and Silva (1989) argued:

> It may be timely to formulate a concept of reading disability that is independent of IQ. Unless it can be shown to have some *predictive value for the nature of treatment outcomes*, consideration of IQ should be discarded in discussions of reading difficulties. (p. 100, emphasis added)

In describing the value of using a treatment validity criterion in the field of LD, Fuchs and Fuchs (1998) suggested that this approach focuses on maximizing regular education's potential effectiveness for *all* students. Judgment about the need for special education is reserved until the effects of instructional adaptations have been assessed in the regular classroom *and* data verify that a special education program would enhance learning. One promising assessment approach that meets the treatment validity criterion and can be used to make eligibility decisions is *curriculum-based measurement* (CBM) (Fuchs & Fuchs, 1997, 1998; Reschly & Grimes, 1995; Shinn, 1995).

Support for a Treatment Validity Approach

There is a great deal of empirical support for adopting a treatment validity approach rather than a discrepancy-based approach to defining LD (Clay, 1987; Foorman, Francis, Fletcher, Schatschneider, & Mehta, 1998; Fuchs & Fuchs, 1997, 1998; Torgesen et al., 2001; Vellutino, Scanlon, & Lyon, 2000; Vellutino et al., 1996, 1998). Vellutino et al. (1996) noted that the discrepancy approach to defining LD does not screen out those children whose reading difficulties might be due to either inadequate schooling or limited exposure to effective reading instruction. Instead, Vellutino et al. argued for using exposure to intensive reading instruction as a "first-cut" diagnostic aid in distinguishing between reading problems caused by cognitive deficits versus those caused by experiential deficits (poor or inadequate reading instruction).

Vellutino et al. (1996) conducted a longitudinal study of 183 kindergarten children composed of poor readers (*n* =118) and normal reader controls (*n* = 65). Poor readers were selected on the basis of scoring below the 15th percentile on measures of word identification or letter-sound correspondences using nonsense words. Children in the poor reader group (a subsample of 74 children) were given daily one-to-one tutoring (30 minutes per day) for a total of 15 weeks over 70–80 sessions (35–40 hours of tutoring). Using hierarchical linear regression analyses, Vellutino et al. calculated growth rates for each child from kindergarten to second grade. Slopes from these analyses were rank-ordered and used to place children into 1 of 4 groups: Very Limited Growth (VLG), Limited Growth (LG), Good Growth (GG), and Very Good Growth (VGG). Approximately half of the sample showed VLG (26%) or LG (24%).

If one accepts the proposition that "difficult to remediate" children can be considered LD and easily remediated children are not LD, then the entire questionable process of calculating ability-achievement discrepancies can be summarily abandoned. Vellutino et al. (1996, 2000) showed that IQ-achievement discrepancy scores did not reliably distinguish between disabled and nondisabled readers, did not distinguish between difficult-to-remediate (VLG and LG) and readily-remediated (VGG and GG) students, and did not predict response to remediation. In short, IQ-achievement discrepancy scores did not have treatment validity.

Requirements for Adopting a Treatment Validity Approach

Adopting a treatment validity approach to the identification of students with LD has several technical requirements. These requirements include (a) ability of measures to model academic growth (Burchinal, Bailey, & Synder, 1994; Fuchs & Fuchs, 1997, 1998; Vellutino, Scanlon, & Tanzman, 1998; Vellutino et al., 1996), (b) availability of validated treatment protocols (Berninger & Abbott, 1994; Torgesen et al., 2001), (c) capability of distinguishing between ineffective instruction and unacceptable individual learning (Fuchs & Fuchs, 1997, 1998), (d) suitability in informing instructional decisions (Fuchs & Fuchs, 1997, 1998; Vellutino et al., 1996, 1998; Witt & Gresham, 1997), and (e) sensitivity to detection of treatment effects (Fuchs & Fuchs, 1997; Marston, Fuchs, & Deno, 1986; Marston, 1987–88; Vellutino et al., 1996, 1998). Each of these requirements for treatment validity will be described in the following sections.

Ability to Model Academic Growth

All intervention investigations attempt to determine whether a change in a dependent variable is due to systematic and controlled changes in an independent (treatment) variable. Traditionally, this question has been addressed using a pretest/posttest design in which an experimental (treatment) and a control group are measured before and immediately after intervention. The effects of treatment in such designs are evaluated by comparing pretest and posttest scores using either repeated measures analysis of variance (ANOVA) or analysis of covariance (ANCOVA, using pretest scores as covariates), or by computing simple differences for groups between pretest and posttest scores (Kirk, 1994). Although these types of analyses can tell us whether or not a given treatment produced mean differences on a dependent variable relative to a control group, these analyses do not supply enough data to model individual change adequately (Burchinal et al., 1994).

A viable alternative to traditional pretest/posttest design comparisons is the use of growth curve analysis (GCA) using hierarchical linear models as a means of modeling academic growth. GCA is used to address three fundamental research questions (Bryk & Raudenbush, 1987; Burchinal et al., 1994). First, GCA is used to determine patterns of change for both individuals and groups. A common example is physicians charting height and weight of children to assess whether or not a child is displaying adequate growth compared to a matched reference group. Second, GCA is used to determine if certain groups show different patterns of change over time. For example, children exposed to a reading intervention emphasizing phonological awareness might be compared to a similar group of children receiving a reading program focusing on orthographic skills. Comparisons between these two groups would be expressed in terms of differences in rate (slopes) and level (intercepts) of change. Third, GCA is often used to study the correlates of change. For instance, a researcher might be interested in contrasting the patterns of change for LD and LA groups who receive the same reading intervention. In addition, the researcher may want to assess whether background characteristics (e.g., gender, ethnicity, socioeconomic status, IQ) moderate these patterns of change over time.

Several assumptions must be met in using GCA to model academic growth (Bryk & Raudenbush, 1987; Burchinal et al., 1994): (1) Growth parameters are assumed to be normally distributed and measured on either an interval or ratio scale; (2) dependent measures are expressed in the same units of measurement over time; (3) structure of the dependent variable does not change over time; (4) each group being compared has homogeneous variances (homogeneity of variance), and (5) an adequate model of change, whether it be linear, quadratic, or cubic, has been selected and fit to the data to model patterns of growth. It should be noted that GCA does not require the same data collection design for each participant in a study; that is, some individuals may be measured 4 times, others 6 times, and still others 8 times. Moreover, spacing between data collection points for each individual does not need to be equal. In short, GCA allows for a broader representation of the effects of an intervention on growth and is extremely flexible with respect to the number and timing of observations across research participants (Bryk & Raudenbush, 1987; Burchinal et al., 1994).

Fuchs and Fuchs (1998) describe the use of CBM as a promising measurement tool for modeling academic growth within the special education eligibility determination process. CBM meets many of the assumptions of GCA in that it provides equal scaling of the dependent variable for individuals over time, it measures the dependent variable on an interval scale, and the structure of the dependent variable remains constant over time. Use of the CBM model in LD eligibility determination will be described in detail in a subsequent section of this paper.

Validated Treatment Protocols

In order to adopt a responsiveness-to-intervention approach, validated treatment protocols must be implemented for students who might be considered learning disabled. Within both the general education and special education classroom, this may be a daunting task. For example, general education teachers often are not prepared to deal with the normal variation among students in the acquisition of reading and writing skills (Berninger, Hart, Abbott, & Karovsky, 1992). Moreover, a survey of state departments of education revealed that only 29 states require elementary teachers to take academic coursework in reading and no states require coursework in writing (Nolen, McCutchen, & Berninger, 1990). Many students classified as LD may fail to acquire basic academic skills *not* because of some underlying processing disorder, but rather because they have not been given adequate opportunities to learn. There is ample reason to believe that most reading difficulties (and children subsequently labeled as LD) are caused by woefully inadequate preliteracy experience, inadequate instruction, or some combination of both (Vellutino et al., 1996, 1998).

A number of validated treatment protocols can be used to differentiate *adequate* from *inadequate* treatment responders. Recently, Torgesen et al. (2001) compared two carefully designed instructional approaches to facilitate academic growth in reading for 8- to 10-year-old children. One intervention was the Auditory Discrimination in Depth (ADD) program that emphasized discriminations among phonemes, monitoring/representation of sound sequences in spoken syllables, and self-monitoring skills (Lindamood & Lindamood, 1998). The second intervention was Embedded Phonics (EP), which provided direct, explicit instruction in word-level reading skills and providing extensive opportunities to read and write meaningful text (Torgesen et al., 2001). The ADD and EP programs differed in depth and extent of instruction in phonemic awareness and phonemic decoding skills. Both the ADD and EP programs were provided to students on a 1:1 basis, in two 50-minute sessions, 5 days per week for 8–9 weeks and students were assessed at 1- and 2-year followups. Hours of intensive reading instruction for the ADD and EP groups totaled 67.5. Following training, all students received 8 weeks of generalization training consisting of a single 50-minute session each week.

The results of the Torgesen et al. study showed that the ADD and EP programs were equally effective in remediating reading difficulties based on the Woodcock-Johnson Broad Reading Cluster score (slope effect sizes = 4.4 and 3.9, respectively). In fact, these interventions "normalized" the reading skills of approximately one half to two thirds of the students, depending on the outcome measure used. Scores on reading comprehension (Woodcock-Johnson Passage Comprehension) were even better with 80–85% of students performing in the average range. About 40%

of the students in this investigation were returned full-time to the general education classroom and were no longer considered in need of special education. Torgesen et al. concluded:

> ...the similarities in growth rate of the ADD and EP conditions in our study suggest that given the right level of intensity and teacher skill, it is possible to obtain these rates of growth via a variety of approaches to direct instruction in reading. We might even suggest that these rates could serve as a benchmark for "reasonable progress" in reading for students receiving remedial instruction in both public and private settings... [T]hey are clearly much higher than is typically achieved in most current special education settings. (p. 52)

The Torgesen et al. investigation provides insight into how we might define *inadequate responders* based on the responsiveness-to-intervention concept. Approximately 25% of students in this investigation were nonresponders to the intensive reading interventions with mean standard scores of about 70 on Word Attack, Word Identification, and Comprehension. Similarly, the Vellutino et al. (1996) study described earlier suggested that approximately 25% of students exposed to an intensive reading intervention of 37.5 hours showed VLG on measures of word identification and phonological skills. In using this resistance-to-intervention notion to diagnose reading disabilities, Vellutino et al. stated:

> ...to render a diagnosis of specific reading disabilities in the absence of early and labor-intensive remedial reading that has been tailored to the child's individual needs is, at best, a hazardous and dubious enterprise, given all of the stereotypes attached to this diagnosis... [O]ne can increase the probability of validating the diagnosis if one combines impressions and outcomes derived from early, labor-intensive, and individualized remediation with results of relevant psychological and educational testing in evaluating the etiology of a child's difficulties in learning to read. (p. 632)

Additional information on what constitutes a *validated treatment protocol* can be found in a recent meta-analysis by Swanson and Hoskyn (1999) who summarized 180 intervention studies for students with LD. Interventions were classified into one of four categories: (a) Direct Instruction (DI), (b) Strategy Instruction (SI), (c) Combined DI+SI, and (d) non-DI/non-SI. Swanson and Hoskyn (1999) defined DI as interventions that used fast-paced instruction in small groups; presented well-sequenced, highly focused lessons; provided numerous opportunities to respond; gave frequent performance feedback on accuracy and responses; and used frequent on-topic questions regarding academic material (Englemann & Carnine, 1991; Kame'enui, Jitendra, & Darch, 1995; Lovett, Borden, DeLuca, Lacerenza, Benson, & Brackstone, 1994; Slavin, 1987).

Studies were categorized as SI if they met the following three criteria: (a) They provided elaborate explanations of material (e.g., explanations, elaborations, and plans directing task performance), (b) they used modeling from teachers which included verbal modeling, questioning, and demonstration, and (c) they incorporated prompts or reminders or multiprocess instructions and dialogue between teachers and students (Borkowski & Turner, 1990; Graham & Harris, 1996; Levin, 1986; Pressley & Ghatala, 1990; Rosenshine, 1995). Finally, studies meeting both DI and SI criteria were categorized as Combined DI+SI and studies meeting neither of these criteria were classified as non-DI/non-SI.

On the basis of these 180 studies, a total of 1,537 effect sizes were calculated comparing LD students in the treatment groups with LD students in control groups. Overall, the mean effect size was 0.79 (*SD* = 0.52). Swanson and Hoskyn (1999) described the typical intervention study as including 22.47 minutes of daily instruction, 3.58 times per week, over 35.72 sessions. On average, students received 80 minutes per week over almost 10 weeks of intervention, or approximately 13.3 hours of instruction. With respect to the type of intervention, the Combined DI+SI group had greater effect sizes (*M* = 0.81) than the DI alone (*M* = 0.77), SI alone (*M* =0.67), and non-DI/non-SI (*M* = 0.62) interventions. There were no significant differences among these latter three intervention groups. Interestingly, studies producing the largest effect sizes reported only minimal discrepancies between IQ and reading achievement (*M* = 0.95) supporting the questionable use of the IQ-achievement discrepancy in predicting responsiveness to intervention described by Vellutino et al. (1998). Also, interventions were less effective with students having reading scores slightly higher than their IQ scores (reading scores > 90 and IQ 85–90).

Swanson and Hoskyn's (1999) meta-analysis suggests that there are several validated intervention approaches in reading for students with LD with effect sizes from 0.58 to 0.81. The Combined DI+SI interventions produced a large effect size (0.81) which indicates that 80% of students in the intervention groups had reading scores equal to or greater than students in control groups. This effect size, however, is substantially lower than those reported by Torgesen et al. (2001) and Vellutino et al. (1996). The lower effect sizes reported by Swanson and Hoskyn may be due, in part, to differences in the intensity of treatment. Torgesen et al. provided 67.5 hours of instruction over 8 weeks and Vellutino et al. provided 35–40 hours of instruction over 15 weeks. The prototypical intervention in the Swanson and Hoskyn meta-analysis provided only 13.3 hours of instruction over approximately 10 weeks.

Regardless of these effect size differences, a substantial body of empirical research supports the validity of treatment protocols for remediating reading deficiencies of students with LD.

Distinguishing Between Acquisition and Performance Deficits

An important decision in using a responsiveness-to-intervention approach to defining LD is the differentiation of skill (acquisition) deficits from performance (motivational) deficits. *Skill deficits* refer to the absence of an academic skill in a student's repertoire ("can't do" problems) and performance *deficits* describe a lack of motivation to perform a given academic skill ("won't do" problems). Skill deficits most often result from inadequate, insufficient, or inappropriate instruction whereas performance deficits result from inadequate, insufficient, or inappropriate arrangement for contingencies for academic performance (Gresham, 1986; Lentz, 1988).

To determine an existing deficit for a particular child, Noell and Witt (1999) have suggested a straightforward process. First, a "test" for a performance deficit is conducted using CBM reading probes (i.e., 100–200-word passages) selected from a child's basal reader as well as two basal readers that immediately precede the current reader. The reading probes are administered under standard (nonreinforced) conditions and under conditions where a preferred reinforcer is given for reading above a prespecified criterion. If performance increases markedly under the reinforcement conditions, then the student is assumed to have a performance deficit rather than a skill deficit. If reinforcement does not markedly improve performance, the student is assumed to have a skills deficit because even under conditions of high motivation, the student still cannot perform the requisite reading skills.

A number of examples in the applied behavior analysis literature have addressed the issue of skill versus performance deficits (Ayllon & Roberts, 1974; Daly & Martens, 1994; Daly, Martens, Dool, & Hintze, 1998; Daly, Martens, Hamler, Dool, & Eckert, 1999; Lovitt, Eaton, Kirkwood, & Pelander, 1971). For instance, Lovitt et al. (1971) gave incentives to improve students' oral reading fluency and to encourage them to read faster. A similar procedure was used by Daly et al. (1998, 1999). Another approach to assess academic performance deficits is to offer students a *choice* among reading materials or a *choice* in the order in which they will complete assignments (silent reading first, followed by vocabulary drill) (Daly, Witt, Martens, & Dool, 1997; Dunlap et al., 1994; Kern, Childs, Dunlap, Clarke, & Falk, 1994). If performance improves dramatically under choice conditions relative to no-choice conditions, then one can assume the student has a performance rather than a skill deficit.

MODELS OF RESPONSIVENESS TO INTERVENTION

Several models of intervention might be considered in adopting the responsiveness-to-intervention approach in defining LD. These models include (a) predictor-criterion models that use and teach those skills that best predict reading competency; (b) a dual-discrepancy model based on children's failure to respond to well-planned and implemented general education interventions, and (c) applied behavior analytic models which focus on manipulation of antecedent and consequent environmental events to improve reading competence.

Predictor-Criterion Models

These models of intervention focus on component skills or processes that represent the best predictors of skill in learning to read. Berninger and Abbott (1994) suggested that oral language skills (e.g., phonemic awareness, phonetic segmentation, rime) and orthographic skills (letter coding, letter cluster, word recognition) are among the best predictors of reading. Criteria used to evaluate reading competence include reading accuracy, reading rate, and reading comprehension. Similarly, direct instruction models (e.g., Englemann & Carnine, 1992; Kame'enui et al., 1995) and strategy training models (e.g., Graham & Harris, 1996; Levin, 1986; Pressley & Ghatala, 1990) focus on teaching those skills and strategies that best predict reading performances.

As reviewed previously, reading intervention programs having the most empirical support are those using a combination of direct instruction and strategy training (Swanson & Hoskyn, 1999). In addition, the work of Torgesen et al. (2001) showed strong and equal effects of reading programs focusing primarily on phonemic awareness and phonemic decoding versus programs emphasizing application of these skills in reading meaningful text. The intensity of this treatment may have influenced treatment outcome as well. Recall that these interventions were implemented for 67.5 hours over 8 weeks. Vellutino et al. (1996) used a similar intervention program that included a large component of strategy training. This intervention lasted 30–40 hours over 15 weeks. Swanson and Hoskyn's (1999) meta-analysis showed that the prototypical reading intervention lasted 13.3 hours over approximately 7 weeks.

Clearly, these models of intervention in the literature have produced rather strong effects in the literature with disabled readers. However, a key and unresolved question concerns how these models might be adopted within the LD eligibility process. The purpose of LD identification is to identify students who are *inadequately responding* to a validated intervention after a reasonable period, not to remediate or "normalize" reading skills. What must be determined is what constitutes a "reasonable period" and how to determine inadequate responsiveness. These issues are addressed in the final section of this paper.

Dual-Discrepancy Model

Fuchs and Fuchs (1997, 1998) have suggested using a CBM approach that measures a student's responsiveness (or lack thereof) to intervention delivered in the general education classroom. The logic behind the CBM approach to measure responsiveness to intervention is similar to that in endocrinology in which a child's growth over time is compared to that of a same-age group (Fuchs, 1995). A child who shows a large discrepancy between his or her height and that of a normative comparison group may be considered a candidate for certain types of medical intervention. In education, if a child is showing a discrepancy between the current level of academic performance and that of same-age peers, then that child may be a candidate for special education. It should be noted, however, that a low-performing child who shows growth rates similar to that of peers in the same classroom would not be a candidate for special education because the child is deriving similar education benefits (low though they may be) from that classroom (Fuchs, 1995).

Fuchs and Fuchs (1998) proposed a reconceptualization of the LD identification process based on a *treatment validity* notion. In this approach, students are not classified as LD unless and until it has been demonstrated empirically that they are not benefiting from the general education curriculum. Unlike traditional LD assessment, which assesses a student's status on ability and achievement measures at one point in time, the treatment validity approach repeatedly assesses the student's progress in the general education curriculum using CBM. Fuchs and Fuchs indicate that special education should be considered only when a child's performance shows a *dual discrepancy*—that is, the student *both* performs below the level evidenced by classroom peers and shows a learning rate substantially below that of classroom peers.

Fuchs and Fuchs (1998) state that the dual-discrepancy model is based on three related propositions. First, it assumes that because student ability varies widely, different students will experience different educational outcomes. Second, low academic performance is relative to the classroom in which the student is placed. If a student's growth rate is similar to peers, then that student would not be considered discrepant from peers' learning rates and would not be a candidate for special education placement. Conversely, a student whose growth rate is low relative to classroom peers would be considered a candidate for either an alternative intervention or special education placement. Third, if the majority of students in a general education classroom are demonstrating inadequate growth relative to local or national norms, then one must consider enhancing the educational program for the entire classroom before considering a student's unresponsiveness to intervention.

Use of this CBM dual-discrepancy approach to determine eligibility is a two-stage process: *problem identification* and *problem certification* (Fuchs & Fuchs, 1997; Marston & Magnusson, 1988; Shinn, 1989). *Problem identification* attempts to determine if a student's academic performance is sufficiently deficient to justify further assessment. Shinn (1989) recommended that three to five CBM tests in each academic area of concern be administered on consecutive days using the student's curriculum materials. On the basis of these brief assessments, the student's median score is used as an estimate of performance level. This performance level is then compared to the same assessment data collected from typical peers in the same classroom.

Fuchs and Fuchs (1997) suggest that procedures for sampling "typical peers" vary in completeness, elaboration, and time. Some districts routinely collect local CBM normative data and use this information to gauge progress in the curriculum and/ or to determine special education eligibility (Shinn, 1989, 1995; Shinn, Tindal, & Stein, 1988). For districts not collecting normative CBM data, one can assess three same-gender peers selected randomly from students a teacher nominates as having adequate academic achievement in the classroom. With large-scale normative data, a referred student would be identified for further assessment if his/her median score fell at or below the 10th percentile or between 1 and 2 standard deviations below the mean. With data available only at the classroom level, discrepancies between actual and expected performance would be calculated by dividing the expected performance (based on the mean CBM performances of selected peers) divided by the referred student's median CBM score. A ratio of 2.0 or greater would suggest that further assessment is needed.

The *problem certification* phase is designed to determine whether or not the magnitude and severity of the student's academic deficiencies justify special education and related services (Shinn, 1995). In making this determination, three CBM probes are administered at successively lower levels of the student's curriculum. On the basis of these assessments, the highest level at which the student demonstrates successful performance is that student's grade placement. Fuchs and Fuchs (1997) suggest that "success" can be operationalized in two ways. First, if a large CBM normative data base is unavailable, success can be defined relative to fixed standards such as 40–60 words read correctly per minute in second-grade text. Second, if one has access to a large CBM data base, success is based on percentile ranks relative to the student's grade placement. If a student's median score falls between the 25th and 75th percentile for typical students at that grade level, then the student is demonstrating successful performance (Fuchs & Fuchs, 1997).

The longstanding and impressive research program using CBM by Lynn and Doug Fuchs of Peabody College at Vanderbilt University provides empirical support for the dual-discrepancy approach as a decision-making guide in LD eligibility determination (Fuchs, 1995; Fuchs et al., 1989a; Fuchs, Fuchs, & Fernstrom, 1993; Fuchs, Fuchs, Hamlett, Phillips, & Karns, 1995). Similarly, Douglas Marston of Minneapolis Public Schools has successfully used CBM to make eligibility determinations for students with LD (Marston et al., 1986; Marston & Magnusson, 1988; Marston, Mirkin, & Deno, 1984).

A recent investigation by Speece and Case (in press) provided additional data supporting the dual-discrepancy approach to defining LD. These authors identified children as at risk for reading failure if their mean performance on CBM reading probes placed them in the lowest quartile of their class. A contrast group was identified that was composed of five students from each classroom based on scores at the median (2 students) and the 30th, 75th, and 90th percentiles (1 student at each level). At-risk children were placed into one of three groups: CBM dual discrepancy (CBM-DD), regression-based IQ-reading achievement (IQ-DS), and low achievement (LA). Students in the CBM-DD group were given 10 CBM oral reading probes administered across the school year. Slopes (based on ordinary least squares regression) for each child and classroom were calculated, and each student's performance level was based on the mean of the last two data points. Children were placed in the CBM-DD group ($n = 47$) if their slope across the year and level of performance at the end of the year were >1 standard deviation below that of classmates. Students were placed in the IQ-DS group ($n = 17$) if their IQ-reading achievement discrepancy was 1.5 or more standard errors of prediction (approximately a 20-point discrepancy). Children were placed in the LA group ($n = 28$) if their total reading score was <90.

Results of this investigation showed that the CBM-DD group was more deficient on measures of phonological processing and was rated by teachers as having lower academic competence and social skills and more problem behaviors than the IQ-DS and LA groups However, the CBM-DD and IQ-DS groups were *not* different on a standardized measure of reading achievement demonstrating the specificity of the CBM-DD model. These data provided additional support for using the CBM-DD model to identify students with LD, specifically those with a phonological deficit. In summarizing their findings, Speece and Case (in press) suggested:

Most research on reading disability proceeds from the assumption of failure to learn despite adequate instruction, a tenet of most definitions of learning disability, but this assumption is rarely tested. The dual discrepancy method does not reject the importance of individual differences to reading disability, but, in our view, expands the conceptualization to include the importance of instruction in the expression of the disability. (p. 36)

Fuchs and Fuchs (1997) proposed a three-phase model for determining LD eligibility using the CBM-DD approach. Phase I involves the documentation of adequate classroom instruction and dual discrepancies. It begins with weekly CBM assessments for *all students* in each school. An assessment team composed of a principal, school psychologist, special education teacher, and social worker review these data after 6 weeks to reach two decisions. First, the team decides if the overall classroom performance is adequate relative to other classrooms and district norms. Second, if classroom performance is acceptable, the team reviews individual student data to determine which students meet the dual-discrepancy criteria defined as (a) a difference of 1 standard deviation between a student's CBM median score and that of classmates *and* (b) a difference of 1 standard deviation between the student's CBM slope of improvement (growth) and that of classmates. Assuming students meeting these criteria do not have accompanying low-incidence conditions (e.g., mental retardation, sensory disabilities, autism), they proceed to Phase II of the process.

Phase II involves a prereferral intervention in which one member of the assessment team works with the general education teacher to design an intervention to remediate the student's dual discrepancy. CBM data are collected to judge the effectiveness of the intervention with the provision that the teacher implement a minimum of two interventions over a 6-week period. If students do not show adequate progress, they enter Phase III of the process.

Phase III of this process involves the design and implementation of an extended intervention plan. Essentially, this phase represents a special-education diagnostic trial period in which the student's responsiveness to a more intense intervention is measured. This phase lasts approximately 8 weeks, after which the team reconvenes and makes decisions concerning the child's placement. The team could decide that the intervention was successful and an individualized education plan (IEP) would be developed and the plan continued. Or, the team could decide that the intervention was unsuccessful in eliminating the dual discrepancy and consider alternative decisions such as changing the nature and intensity of the intervention, collecting additional assessment information, considering a more restrictive placement, or changing to a school having additional resources that better address the student's needs.

In summary, Fuchs and Fuchs (1997) propose that in order to qualify a student for special education, a three-pronged test must be passed: (a) a dual-discrepancy between the student's performance level and growth (1 standard deviation for each) and that of peers must be documented, (b) the student's rate of learning with adaptations made in the general education classroom is inadequate, and (c) the provision of special education must result in improved growth.

Functional Assessment Models

Another approach to identifying students on the basis of responsiveness to intervention comes from the applied behavior analysis (ABA) camp (Daly, Lentz, & Boyer, 1996; Daly & Martens, 1994; Daly et al., 1997; Haring, Lovitt, Eaton, & Hansen, 1978; Howell, Fox, & Morehead, 1993). This approach attempts to offer a *functional* rather than a *structural* explanation for children's academic difficulties. I also include within the ABA approach the Direct Instruction (Englemann & Carnine, 1991; Gersten et al., 1986) as well as the Precision Teaching models of intervention (Lindsley, 1991). The field of LD has traditionally offered structural explanations in the form of labels or traits to explain academic problems (e.g., LD, dyslexia, processing disorders). Structural explanations are not particularly useful from an intervention perspective because student traits (inferred from performances) cannot be directly manipulated and because the explanations do not identify environmental factors that might be contributing to academic failure (Daly et al., 1997).

Alternatively, a functional approach to understanding academic failure attempts to relate academic performance to environmental events that precede and follow student performance (e.g., opportunities to respond, reinforcement for accurate responding, time allocated for instruction, modeling and feedback of academic behaviors). From a functional perspective, the job of the interventionist is to analyze those factors that may explain poor performance and implement an instructional intervention to improve academic responding. In a functional approach, academic responding is operationalized using curriculum-based measures of oral reading, mathematics computation, written expression, and spelling such as those recommended in the dual-discrepancy approach of Fuchs and Fuchs (1997, 1998).

Daly et al. (1997) identified five common reasons why students fail and provided rather straightforward methods for testing these hypotheses quickly and efficiently so as to lead to interventions. The reasons are as follows: (a) they do not want to do it ("won't do" problems), (b) they have not spent enough time doing it (lack of practice and feedback), (c) they have not had enough help to do it (insufficient prompting or poor fluency), (d) the student has not had to do it that way before (instructional demands do not promote mastery), and (e) it is too hard (poor match between student skill level and instructional materials).

An extremely important concept in a functional approach to remediating academic difficulties is the instructional hierarchy (Haring et al., 1978). The instructional hierarchy describes the relationship between intervention components and stages of skill mastery. In the instructional hierarchy, students move through states of *acquisition, fluency, generalization,* and *adaptation.* Strategies that use modeling, prompting, and error correction can be expected to improve acquisition (accuracy), and strategies including practice and reinforcement are expected to improve fluency. Generalization training involves discrimination training across stimuli and maintenance activities over time (Daly et al., 1996; Martens, Witt, Daly, & Vollmer, 1999).

There is an extensive research base supporting the ABA model for improving academic performances (Daly et al., 1997, 1999; Elliott, Busse, & Shapiro, 1999; Englemann & Carnine, 1991; Greenwood, 1991; Skinner, 1998). Swanson and Sachs-Lee (2000) summarized 85 studies using single-subject designs across the academic domains of reading, mathematics, writing, and language using direct instruction (DI), strategy training (SI), Combined DI+SI, and non-DI/non-SI described earlier in this paper (see Swanson & Hoskyn, 1999). Based on an analysis of 793 effect sizes, the mean effect size was 0.87 ($SD = 0.32$), suggesting a strong effect. The average age of participants was almost 11 years and the mean IQ and achievement levels of participants were 95 and 77, respectively ($M = 100$, $SD = 15$). Results of this meta-analysis showed that DI and SI were effective in remediating academic deficits (except handwriting) and all interventions were more effective with lower IQ students than higher IQ students in reading.

The use of the ABA approach for eligibility determination creates some measurement challenges because this model relies almost exclusively on single-case experimental design data. Both the predictor-criterion and CBM-DD models use well-established and straightforward quantitative approaches to determine treatment nonresponders. An unresolved issue in the ABA approach concerns the most appropriate way of quantifying the effects of intervention. Gresham and Lambros (1998) identified several methods for quantifying the effects of interventions using single-case experimental design data that are described below. Time-series analysis is not included here because fitting these regression models with relatively few data points often yields inaccurate results and it is often impossible to meet the statistical assumptions of these models in educational practice (Kazdin, 1984).

Visual Inspection

Visual inspection of graphed data is by far the most common way of analyzing data from single-case designs (Johnston & Pennypacker, 1993). Effects of intervention are determined by comparing baseline levels of performance to postintervention levels of performance to detect treatment effects. Unlike statistical analyses, this method uses the "interocular" test of significance. There is a considerable body of research, however, suggesting that even highly trained behavior analysts cannot obtain consensus in evaluating single case data using visual inspection (Center, Skiba, & Casey, 1985–86; DeProspero & Cohen, 1979; Knapp, 1983; Matyas & Greenwood, 1990, 1991; Ottenbacher, 1990). It would appear that visual inspection of graphed data often results in erroneous conclusions regarding the presence or absence of treatment effects, particularly given that the data points are serially dependent or autocorrelated.

A study by Matyas and Greenwood (1990) showed that Type I error rates ranged from 16 to 84% for autocorrelated data, suggesting that researchers often judge the presence of treatment effects where none exist. Given the interpretative problems with graphed data in determining treatment effects and unacceptably high Type I error rates, other procedures should be used to supplement or corroborate interpreta⁺ on of graphed data (Fisch, 1998). These are described in the following sections.

Reliable Changes in Behavior

Another method of quantifying effects in single-case designs is to calculate the extent to which changes in academic performance are reliable. Nunnally and Kotsche (1983) first proposed a reliable change index (RCI) to determine the effectiveness of an intervention for individuals. The RCI is defined as the difference between a posttest score and a pretest score divided by the standard error of difference between posttest and pretest scores (Christensen & Mendoza, 1986; Jacobson, Follette, & Revenstorf, 1984). The standard error of difference is the spread or variation of the distribution of change scores that would be expected if no actual change had occurred. An RCI of $+1.96$ ($p < 0.05$) would be considered a reliable change in behavior.

With single-case data, RCIs must be computed for baseline (pretest) and intervention (posttest) phases of the design. For example, in an ABAB withdrawal design, pretest scores would be calculated from the initial baseline (A) and posttest scores from the mean of the two intervention phases $(B_1 + B_2)$. Similarly, in a multiple baseline design, pretest scores would be calculated from the baselines of each subject (setting or behavior) and posttest scores from the means of the respective intervention phases. The standard error of difference would be based on the autocorrelation and variation of baseline and intervention phases. Although the RCI approach can be used to detect reliable changes in academic performance (relative to baseline) for a single student, it does not provide specific decision rules that might be used in making an LD eligibility determination. Moreover, RCIs are influenced by the reliability of the dependent measures used. If a measure is highly reliable (0.90 or higher), then small changes in behavior could be considered statistically reliable. Conversely, if a measure has low reliability, then large changes in behavior might not be statistically reliable, but could be important.

Effect sizes. Another way of quantifying single-case data is through the use of effect sizes. Although effect sizes typically are used to integrate group design research studies, Busk and Serlin (1992) have proposed two methods for calculating effect sizes in single-case studies. The first approach makes no distributional assumptions and calculates effect sizes by subtracting the treatment mean from the baseline mean and dividing by the standard deviation of the baseline mean. The second approach, based on the homogeneity of variance assumption, is the same, except that it uses the pooled within-phase variances as the error term. Effect sizes calculated in this way are interpreted the same way as traditional effect-size estimates. They can be used to estimate the effects of one or more treatments for an individual or to summarize a body of single-case intervention.

Swanson and Sachs-Lee (2000) used an alternative approach to calculate effect size by using the last three data points in baseline and treatment phases to calculate the means. This difference was then divided by the correlation between baseline and treatment data points, taking into account the average standard deviation for repeated measures. These authors argue that the number of sessions may inflate or deflate effect sizes and are subject to fluctuations in the dependent variable that are not a result of the treatment (cyclicity).

Effect sizes also can be calculated by computing the percentage of nonoverlapping data points (PNOL) between baseline and treatment phases (Mastropieri & Scruggs, 1985–86). PNOL is computed by indicating the number of treatment data points that exceed the highest baseline data point and dividing by the total number of data points in the treatment phase. For example, if 8 of 10 treatment data points exceed the highest baseline data point, then PNOL is 80%. This method provides for quantitative synthesis of single-case data that is relatively easy. However, the method would be inappropriate in some situations, including unusual baseline trends, floor and ceiling effects, and students in the initial stages of skill acquisition (Strain, Kohler, & Gresham, 1998).

Yet another approach in quantifying the effects of interventions in single-subject designs is to analyze trends over time by using time-structured Markov chains (Fisch, 1998). Markov chains involve the analysis of two-dimensional matrices containing the probabilities of changing from one set of conditions (e.g., preintervention performances) to another set of conditions (postintervention performances). Haccou and Meelis (1992) indicate that Markov chains are used frequently in naturalistic settings to assess changes in "states" of behavior from one time period to the next.

Social Validation

Social validity deals with three fundamental questions faced by professionals in the field of LD: What should we change? How should we change it? How will we know it was effective? There are sometimes disagreements among professionals as well as between professionals and consumers on these three fundamental questions. Wolf (1978) described the social validation process as the assessment of the *social significance* of the goals of intervention, the *social acceptability* of the intervention procedures to attain these goals, and the *social importance* of the effects of the intervention. This last component of the social validation process is most relevant to quantifying a student's responsiveness to intervention in the LD eligibility determination process.

The social importance of the effects produced by an intervention established the practical or educational significance of changes in academic performance. Do the quantity and quality of the change in academic performance make a difference in the student's academic functioning? Does the change in academic performance have habilitative validity (Hawkins, 1991)? Is the student's academic performance now in the "functional" range? All of these questions capture the essence of establishing the social importance of intervention effects.

One means of establishing the social importance of intervention effects is to conceptualize academic functioning as belonging to either a functional or dysfunctional distribution. For example, we could socially validate a reading intervention by demonstrating that a student moved from a dysfunctional to a functional range of reading performance. This result could be established by calculating the probability that the student's reading score belonged to a functional rather than a dysfunctional distribution. We could base these calculations on norm-referenced achievement tests or locally normed CBM measures.

Fawcett (1991) suggested that in evaluating the social importance of effects, we should specify various levels of performance. For example, one could specify *ideal* (the best performance available), *normative* (typical or commonly occurring performance), or *deficient* (the worst performance available). Interventions moving a student from a deficient level of performance to normative or ideal levels of performance could be considered socially important.

Conclusion

This paper argues that a child's inadequate responsiveness to an empirically validated intervention can be taken as evidence of LD and should be used to classify children as such. Some might argue that diagnoses in medicine, for example, are not confirmed or disconfirmed on the basis of whether a patient responds to treatment. However, one should always keep in mind that medical diagnoses often have direct treatment implications and that the causes of many physical diseases (unlike mild disabilities such as LD) are known. Moreover, treatment intensity in medicine is typically matched to the nature and severity of whatever physical malady is present. Obviously, a physician's first choice of treatment for most medical problems is not hospitalization. The point here is that not all children will require the most intense form of treatment of academic difficulties, and treatment intensity, strength, and/ or duration should increase only after the child fails to show an adequate response to intervention.

In the current paper, I argue that children who fail to respond to empirically validated treatments implemented with integrity might be identified as LD. The concept of *responsiveness to intervention* appears to be a viable alternative approach to defining LD, particularly in light of the myriad difficulties with discrepancy-based models. This paper defines *responsiveness to intervention* as a change in academic performance as a function of an intervention. In order to employ treatment responsiveness as a criterion for identifying students as LD, assessment procedures should have treatment validity; that is, the assessment should contribute to the planning and implementation of more effective treatments to remediate academic deficits (Fuchs & Fuchs, 1998; Gresham & Witt, 1997; Nelson et al., 1987). Several issues in adopting the responsiveness-to-intervention approach appear to have been resolved, including (a) modeling academic growth, (b) sensitivity of measures to reflect growth, and (c) validated treatment protocols. These were discussed at length in this paper and will not be reiterated here except to say that the validated treatment protocols represent different intensities and durations of treatment. Depending on a student's response to treatment, these treatments may have to be titrated until an acceptable level of academic functioning is achieved. More important, several unresolved issues await further investigation and deliberation before the field can adopt responsiveness to intervention in eligibility determination.

Unresolved Issues in the Alternative Responsiveness-to-Intervention Approach

Five important issues appear to be most important at this time in adopting responsiveness to intervention as the criterion for LD eligibility determination: (a) selecting the "best" intervention available, (b) determining the optimal length and intensity of the intervention, (c) ensuring the integrity of interventions, and (d) conducting cost-benefit analyses. These issues are discussed in the following sections.

Selecting the "best" intervention available. According to available research, there appears to be a consensus on the core components a reading intervention should address for students with reading disabilities. Reading research over the past 20 years indicates that the reading difficulties of these students are caused by weaknesses in the ability to process the phonological aspects of language (Liberman, Shankweiler, & Liberman, 1989; Stanovich & Siegel, 1994; Torgesen, 1996). In fact, reading growth is best predicted by initial levels of phonological skill rather than verbal ability or discrepancy between IQ and reading achievement (Torgesen et al., 2001; Vellutino et al., 1996, 1998). Torgesen et al. (2001) suggested that these phonological weaknesses require reading instruction that is more phonemically explicit and systematic than that provided to other children and there are many ways in which this might be accomplished in designing instructional activities.

Given the above consensus regarding the most important skills to target in intervention, what is the "best" intervention to accomplish this end? The meta-analysis by Swanson and Hoskyn (1999) suggested that interventions using a combination of direct instruction and strategy instruction produced the largest effect sizes, with 80% of the treatment groups having mean reading scores equal to or greater than those of control group students. Recall that the typical intervention in this meta-analysis was 13.3 hours over 10 weeks. Vellutino et al.'s (1996) intervention provided 35–40 hours of instruction over 15 weeks whereas the recent study by Torgesen et al. (2001) involved 67.5 hours over 8–9 weeks.

Comparisons among these studies are difficult given the large variability in the intensity and length of interventions (to be discussed below). Interventions based on applied behavior analysis, while effective, typically are of shorter duration, and outcome measures typically are more narrowly defined (Daly et al., 1996; Daly & Martens, 1994; Haring et al., 1978). Given the various effective intervention options available, practitioners must determine what "best practices" will be at the local level in terms of selecting and implementing a given strategy.

Determining the optimal length and intensity of intervention. Determining the length and intensity of intervention that is implemented is a crucial decision when using responsiveness to intervention as the criterion for identifying LD. Keep in mind a fundamental principle: The length and intensity of intervention will depend entirely on a student's responsiveness to it, which is individually based. Fuchs and Fuchs (1997, 1998) indicated that a general educator should attempt two interventions lasting no longer than 6 weeks before placing the student in a special education trial period. This special education trial period should last no longer than 8 weeks, after which time the assessment team reconvenes to continue and/or enhance the intervention program. Fuchs and Fuchs (1997) suggested that any assessment method must provide adequate data for evaluating treatment effectiveness and should answer the following questions. Is the nonadapted regular education classroom producing adequate academic growth? Have adaptations to the general education classroom produced improved growth? Has the provision of special education interventions improved student learning?

Another insight into this issue of length and intensity of interventions can be found in the meta-analysis of Swanson and Hoskyn (1999). As stated earlier, the typical intervention consisted of 22.47 minutes of daily instruction delivered 3.58 times per week for 35.72 sessions. Thus, the prototypical intervention consisted of about 13.3 hours of instruction distributed over approximately 10 weeks. It should be noted, however, that there was a huge degree of variability in terms of minutes of daily instruction ($SD = 29.71$ minutes), times per week ($SD = 1.58$), and number of sessions ($SD = 21.72$ sessions). Moreover, the samples used in these studies varied greatly regarding criteria used for participant selection, thereby introducing a confounding factor when evaluating responsiveness to intervention.

The prototypical study using (a) direct instruction, (b) strategy training, and (c) combined direct instruction + strategy training produced effect sizes of 0.77, 0.67, and 0.81, respectively. Also, students having the most severe reading deficits (<85) responded better to treatments ($M = 0.71$) than students with less severe reading difficulties (>84 and <91; $M = 0.51$). If one were to use the length and intensity of the prototypical reading study in this meta-analysis with a combination of direct instruction and strategy training, one could expect to produce a standard score point difference of 12 ($M = 100$, $SD = 15$) between pretest and posttest scores. For example, a student entering the intervention with a standard score of 78 could be expected to improve to a score of 90 at posttest, thereby indicating near-normal performance.

Another approach to determining optimal length and intensity of intervention can be found in the Vellutino et al. (1996) investigation. Recall that this study selected children who scored at or below the 15th percentile in reading (Word

Identification and Word Attack) and were given 35–40 weeks of intensive one-to-one tutoring in reading. Each session lasted for 30 minutes, and 80 sessions were spread over 15 weeks for a total of 35–40 hours of reading instruction. At posttest, about half of the children showed either Good Growth or Very Good Growth in reading with posttest percentile ranks in the 44th and 64th percentiles, respectively, by the end of second grade. This study suggested that an intensive one-to-one reading intervention could be used to normalize reading performances of poor readers selected in the first grade. It is unknown at this time, however, how much one might change or otherwise deviate from this effective treatment protocol and produce similar results.

Finally, the study by Torgesen et al. (2001) compared two interventions with fourth graders implemented in two, 50-minute daily sessions, 5 days per week over 8–9 weeks (67.5 hours of intervention). The 19 children who were returned to general education subsequent to intervention moved from pretest scores of about 70 (average of Word Attack and Word Identification) to 2-year follow-up scores of approximately 95. In contrast, the students remaining in special education moved from pretest scores of about 67 to posttest scores of 83. Relative to growth made in the regular resource room, the average effect size was approximately 4.15 for the two treatment groups (difference between pretreatment and posttreatment slopes divided by pooled variability of pretreatment slopes). As with the Vellutino et al. (1996) study, we do not know how much this intervention can be modified or diluted and still obtain relatively large treatment effects.

One means of determining the optimal length and intensity of interventions based on the extant literature is to employ a multiple gating procedure similar to that used in the Heartland Area Education Agency (AEA) in Iowa to make special education entitlement decisions (Reschly & Tilly, 1999; Reschly & Ysseldyke, 1995). Figure 1 shows the problem-solving model used in the Heartland AEA for making special education eligibility determinations. Note that I have superimposed examples of interventions varying in intensity (that were reviewed in the current paper) within the Heartland AEA model. The responsiveness-to-intervention approach in this model makes the following assumptions:

1. The intensity (and costs) of intervention is matched to the degree of unresponsiveness to the intervention.

2. Movement through levels of intervention intensity is based on inadequate response to interventions implemented with integrity.

3. Decisions regarding movement through levels are based on an ongoing collection of empirical data collected from a variety of sources.

4. An increasing body of knowledge (data) is collected to inform decision making as a student moves through the levels.

5. Special education and IEP determination should be considered only after a student shows inadequate responsiveness to interventions at the previous levels.

Figure 1. Degree of unresponsiveness and intensity of treatment.

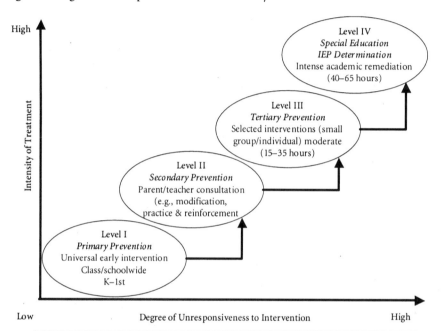

Five Fundamental Principles

1. Intensity of intervention is matched to the degree of unresponsiveness to the intervention.
2. Movement through levels is based on inadequate response to intervention.
3. Decisions regarding movement through levels are based on empirical data collected from a variety of sources.
4. An increasing body of data is collected to inform decision making as a student moves through the levels.
5. Special education and IEP determination should be considered only after a student shows inadequate responsiveness to intervention.

Ensuring the integrity of interventions. Treatment integrity (sometimes called treatment fidelity or procedural reliability) refers to the degree to which a treatment is implemented as intended (Gresham, 1989; Yeaton & Sechrest, 1981). Establishing and maintaining the integrity of treatments is one of the most important aspects of both the scientific and practical application of instructional procedures. It is likely that the ineffectiveness of many instructional interventions can be attributed, in part, to the poor integrity with which these procedures were implemented (i.e., deviations from an established treatment protocol). Adopting a responsiveness-to-intervention approach to identifying LD makes treatment integrity (the reliability of treatment implementation) a central feature of the entire process. In contrast, the entire practice of determining the most appropriate IQ-achievement discrepancy model is based on the reliability of difference scores (e.g., simple difference, predicted difference). In order to determine the degree of responsiveness to intervention, a treatment must be reliably and accurately implemented.

Recently, Gresham, MacMillan, Beebe-Frankenberger, and Bocian (2000) sought to determine the extent to which integrity was assessed in the LD intervention literature by analyzing articles in the three major LD journals from January 1995 to August 1999 (*Journal of Learning Disabilities, Learning Disability Quarterly,* and *Learning Disabilities: Research & Practice*). Of the 479 articles published in these journals, 65 articles (13.6%) were intervention articles. Of these 65 articles, only 12 articles (18.5%) actually measured and reported data on treatment integrity. In their synthesis of the LD intervention literature, Swanson, Carson, and Saches-Lee (1996) reported that less than 2% of the studies provided *any* information about treatment integrity. In spite of the methodological and statistical rigor used in this and other meta-analyses of the LD literature, none of these methodological considerations can answer two fundamental questions: (a) How are treatments implemented, and (b) What is the relation between treatment integrity and treatment outcomes in LD intervention research?

Swanson and Sachs-Lee (2000), in their review of the single-case intervention research with LD, found that only 28% of the studies ($N = 24$ studies) provided any measure of treatment integrity. Of these 28 studies, only 8 studies specified steps used to measure the integrity of the intervention. There appears to be a curious double standard in the LD intervention literature with respect to the measurement and reporting of reliability for the independent and dependent variables. That is, it is almost always the case that reliability data for the dependent variable are presented in published treatment-outcome research. In contrast, this same type of information rarely is required for the independent (treatment) variable.

Given the central importance of assessing treatment integrity in the responsiveness-to-intervention model of LD identification, the following recommendations are offered concerning how researchers and practitioners might conduct integrity assessments:

- Specific components of an intervention should be operationally defined and measured much like the operational definition and measurement of dependent measures.

- Each component of a treatment should be measured by either direct observation or videotaping using an occurrence-nonoccurrence method. Levels of treatment integrity should be obtained by summing the number of components correctly implemented and dividing this number by the total number of components to yield percentage integrity.

- Two estimates of treatment integrity should be calculated. One, the integrity of each component across days or sessions of treatment should be computed to yield *component integrity*. Two, the integrity of all treatment components within days or sessions of treatment should be calculated to yield *daily or session integrity*. Given these two estimates of integrity, failure to find significant treatment effects might be explained by poor component integrity over time, by poor daily or session integrity, or both.

- Indirect methods of assessing treatment integrity such as instructional manuals, permanent products, self-reports, interviews, and behavior rating scales should be used to supplement direct measures of integrity, but they must be interpreted cautiously. There is often low agreement between direct and indirect methods of integrity assessment (Gresham, 1997; Noell & Witt, 1999; Wickstrom, Jones, LaFleur, & Witt, 1998).

Cost-benefit analysis. An important aspect of using the responsiveness-to-intervention approach to LD identification is determining the financial costs to school districts. As mentioned earlier, the average cost of a traditional eligibility determination for a student with a mild disability is around $2,500 per case (Reschly, personal communication, 2001). What costs are incurred by using the CBM–dual-discrepancy model in which local normative data are collected over 20 weeks? What costs are associated with adopting any of the functional assessment models? Currently, we have no published data to assist us in calculating these costs.

Torgesen (personal communication, 2001), however, provided some data regarding the costs of his intensive intervention program described earlier (Torgesen et al., 2001). Torgesen states that a teacher who was doing this kind of intervention with children (two 50-minute sessions per day) could probably work with two children at a time for 8 weeks and the rest of the time could be spent following up on children taught earlier, or working as a teacher consultant, or planning. Given the normal interruptions in schools (assemblies, absences) it takes about 10 weeks of teacher time to deliver the full 80 sessions.

A teacher could work with about six severely LD children a day for 10 weeks. On the basis of a 37-week school year, a teacher could probably go through about three treatment cycles with six students per cycle and thus provide intensive reading intervention services to approximately 18 children per year (6 students × 3 treatment cycles). Remember, however, that Torgesen et al.'s (2001) data suggest that about half of these children will no longer need special education after the intervention. One way Torgesen calculates the cost is to take the cost per session at $50 (more or less depending on local costs for private tutoring) and multiply this figure by 80 sessions of instruction; the cost per student is approximately $2,000. Thus, for a teacher working with 18 students per year, the total cost of an intensive, treatment-oriented approach to LD would be about $36,000 per year. The mere cost of simply identifying, but not treating, 18 LD students using traditional IQ-achievement discrepancies is estimated to be $45,000 (18 × $2500).

One should consider these costs in light of the fact that the cost of educating a student in a resource room placement is 1.7 to 2.0 times the cost of educating a general education student in a regular classroom. In addition, remember that in the Torgesen et al. (2001) study, 40% of the students in the study no longer needed special education. Moreover, one should also note that the efficacy of traditional special-education-delivered interventions, according to meta-analyses, have been somewhat less than impressive (Kavale & Forness, 1999).

Another consideration in calculating these cost-benefits is the cost of LD eligibility determination using the traditional competing paradigm model described in concert with special education costs. Assuming the cost of a typical eligibility process is approximately $2,500 and also remembering that all LD students must undergo 3-year reevaluations, the cost of identifying and providing special education for LD students is almost twice that of educating general education students. As such, there may be long-term cost-benefits in adopting the responsiveness-to-intervention model, particularly in light of the following: (a) The average effect size of special education placement for LD students is about 0.30 (Kavale & Forness, 1999), (b) relatively few students get decertified as LD during their school careers, (c) early intensive reading interventions for poor readers (kindergarten-first grade) leads to GG or VGG in reading for about 50% of this population, and (d) intensive intervention may lead to a decertification of about 40% of children receiving this type of intervention.

The question for the LD field remains: How long do we implement an intervention before we determine that a child is an inadequate responder and thus eligible for more intensive special education services? Further, what is the cost of this intervention-based model relative to the traditional eligibility approach? Is the responsiveness-to-intervention approach more expedient in identifying students as LD so that intervention takes place earlier? How intense should this intervention be and how long should it last? Who should implement the intervention (teachers, paraprofessionals, reading specialists)? These questions must be addressed first when adopting a responsiveness-to-intervention approach to the identification of LD.

One must realize that some individuals have political, personal, financial, and/or other reasons in wanting to maintain the status quo in the classification of students as LD. This position is indefensible in light of the overwhelming evidence in the field that the IQ-discrepancy approach to LD identification is simply not valid and, most important, does not inform treatment decisions. These individuals may argue that a treatment-responsiveness model is analogous to confirming the accuracy of a cancer diagnosis by determining whether or not a treatment regimen of chemotherapy and radiation leads to remission. They might also argue that this approach does not improve the identification of students as LD, that it has some insurmountable measurement problems, that it leads to late identifications, and that it will be extremely expensive. However, it always should be remembered that these arguments are simply red herrings in the sea of abyss of what we now call LD.

It is incumbent upon the LD field to focus on answering the critical questions using empirical findings for assessment and interventions provided in this paper as a foundation. Establishing an effective method for determining eligibility for LD that can be linked to intervention can go a long way toward decreasing, if not eliminating, the probability that learning disabilities will continue to be the sociological sponge that wipes up the spills of general education.

REFERENCES

Arter, J., & Jenkins, J. (1979). Differential-diagnosis-prescriptive teaching: A critical appraisal. *Review of Educational Research, 49,* 517–555.

Ayllon, T., & Roberts, M. (1974). Eliminating discipline problems by strengthening academic performance. *Journal of Applied Behavior Analysis, 7,* 71–76.

Ayres, R., & Cooley, E. (1986). Sequential versus simultaneous processing on the K-ABC: Validity in predicting learning success. *Journal of Psychoeducational Assessment, 4,* 211–220.

Ayres, R., Cooley, E., & Severson, H. (1988). Educational translation of the Kaufman Assessment Battery for Children: A construct validity study. *Journal of Psychoeducational Assessment, 4,* 113–124.

Bahr, M., Fuchs, D., Stecker, P., & Fuchs, L. (1991). Are teachers' perceptions of difficult-to-teach students racially biased? *School Psychology Review, 20,* 599–608.

Bateman, B. (1965). An educational view of a diagnostic approach to learning disorders. In J. Hellmuth (Ed.), *Learning disorders* (Vol. 1, pp. 219–239). Seattle, WA: Special Child.

Berninger, V. W., & Abbott, R. D. (1994). Redefining learning disabilities: Moving beyond aptitude-achievement discrepancies to failure to respond to validated treatment protocols. In G. Reid Lyon (Ed.), *Frames of reference for the assessment of learning disabilities* (pp. 163–183). Baltimore, MD: Paul H. Brookes.

Berninger, V., Hart, T., Abbott, R., & Karovsky, P. (1992). Defining reading and writing disabilities with and without IQ: A flexible developmental perspective. *Learning Disability Quarterly,* 103–118.

Bocian, K., Beebe, M., MacMillan, D., & Gresham, F. M. (1999). Competing paradigms in learning disabilities classification by schools and variations in the meaning of discrepant achievement. *Learning Disabilities Research & Practice, 14,* 1–14.

Borkowski, J., & Turner, L. (1990). Transsituational characteristics of metacognition. IN W. Schneider & F. Weinert (Eds.), *Interactions among aptitudes, strategies, and knowledge in cognitive performance* (pp. 159–176). New York: Springer-Verlag.

Bryk, A., & Raudenbush, S. (1987). Application of hierarchical linear models to assessing change. *Psychological Bulletin, 101,* 147–158.

Burchinal, M., Bailey, D., & Snyder, P. (1994). Using growth curve analysis to evaluate child change in longitudinal investigations. *Journal of Early Intervention, 18,* 403–423.

Busk, P., & Serlin, R. (1992). Meta-analysis for single-case research. In T. Kratochwill & J. Levin (Eds.), *Single-case research design and analysis* (pp. 187–212). Hillsdale, NJ: Erlbaum.

Center, B., Skiba, R., & Casey, A. (1985–1986). A methodology for the quantitative synthesis of intra-subject design research. *The Journal of Special Education, 19,* 387–400.

Christensen, L., & Mendoza, J. (1986). A method of assessing change in a single subject: An alteration of the RC index. *Behavior Therapy, 17,* 305–308.

Clay, M. (1987). Learning to be learning disabled. *New Zealand Journal of Educational Studies, 22,* 155–173.

Cohen, J., & Cohen, P. (1983). *Applied multiple regression/correlation analysis for the behavioral sciences.* Hillsdale, NJ: Lawrence Erlbaum Inc.

Cone, J.D. (1989). Is there utility for treatment utility? *American Psychologist, 44,* 1241–1242.

Cronbach, L. (1957). The two disciplines of scientific psychology. *American Psychologist, 12,* 671–684.

Cronbach, L. (1975). Beyond the two disciplines of scientific psychology. *American Psychologist, 30, 116*–127.

Cronbach, L., & Snow, R. (1977). *Aptitudes and instructional methods.* New York: Wiley (Halstead Press).

Daly, E., & Martens, B. (1994). A comparison of three interventions for increasing oral reading performance: Application of the instructional hierarchy. *Journal of Applied Behavior Analysis, 27,* 459–469.

Daly, E., Lentz, F. E., & Boyer, J. (1996). The instructional hierarchy: A conceptual model for understanding the effective components of reading interventions. *School Psychology Quarterly, 11,* 369–386.

Daly, E., Martens, B. K., Dool, E., & Hintze, J. (1998). Using brief functional analysis to select interventions for oral reading. *Journal of Behavioral Education, 8,* 203–218.

Daly, E., Martens, B. K., Hamler, K., Dool, E., & Eckert, T. (1999). A brief experimental analysis for identifying instructional components needed to improve oral reading fluency. *Journal of Applied Behavior Analysis, 32,* 83–94.

Daly, E., Witt, J. C., Martens, B. K., & Dool, E. (1997). A model for conducting functional analysis of academic performance problems. *School Psychology Review, 26,* 554–574.

D'Amato, R. C., Rothlisberg, B., & Work, P. (1999). Neuropsychological assessment for intervention. In C. Reynolds & T. Gutkin (Eds.), *Handbook of school psychology* (3rd ed., pp. 452–475). New York: Wiley.

Das, J. P. (1995). Neurocognitive approach to remediation: The PREP Model. *Canadian Journal of School Psychology, 9,* 157–173.

Das, J. P., Naglieri, J., & Kirby, J. (1995). *Assessment of cognitive processes.* Needham, MA: Allyn & Bacon.

DeProspero, A., & Cohen, S. (1979). Inconsistent visual analyses of intrasubject data. *Journal of Applied Behavior Analysis, 12,* 573–579.

Dunlap, G., DePerczel, M., Clarke, S., Wilson, D., Wright, S., White, R., & Gomez, A. (1994). Choice making to promote adaptive behavior for students with emotional and behavior challenges. *Journal of Applied Behavior Analysis, 27,* 505–518.

Elliott, S., Busse, R., & Shapiro, E. (1999). Intervention techniques for academic performance problems. In C. R. Reynolds & T. B. Gutkin (Eds.), *Handbook of school psychology* (3rd ed., pp. 664–685). New York: Wiley.

Englemann, S., & Carnine, D. (1991). *Theory of instruction: Principles and application.* Eugene, OR: ADI.

Epps, S., Ysseldyke, J., & McGue, M. (1984). Differentiating LD and non-LD students: "I know one when I see one." *Learning Disability Quarterly, 7,* 89–101.

Fawcett, S. (1991). Social validity: A note on methodology. *Journal of Applied Behavior Analysis, 24,* 235–239.

Fisch, G. (1998). Visual inspection of data revisited: Do the eyes still have it? *The Behavior Analyst, 21,* 111–123.

Foorman, B., Francis, D., Fletcher J., Schatschneider, C., & Mehta, P. (1998). The role of instruction in learning to read: Preventing reading failure in at-risk children. *Journal of Educational Psychology, 90,* 37–55.

Fuchs, D., Fuchs, L., & Fernstrom, P. (1993). A conservative approach to special education reform: Mainstreaming through transenvironmental programming and curriculum-based measurement. *American Education Research Journal, 30,* 149–178.

Fuchs, L., & Fuchs, D. (1997). Use of curriculum-based measurement in identifying students with disabilities. *Focus on Exceptional Children, 30,* 1–16.

Fuchs, L., & Fuchs, D. (1998). Treatment validity: A unifying concept for reconceptualizing the identification of learning disabilities. *Learning Disabilities Research & Practice, 13,* 204–219.

Fuchs, L., Fuchs, D., & Hamlett, C. (1989a). Effects of alternative goal structures within curriculum-based measurement. *Exceptional Children, 55,* 429–438.

Fuchs, L., Fuchs, D., & Hamlett, C. (1989b). Effects of instructional use of curriculum-based measurement to enhance instructional programs. *Remedial and Special Education, 10,* 43–52.

Fuchs, L., Fuchs, D., & Hamlett, C. (1989c). Monitoring reading growth using student recalls: Effects of two teacher feedback systems. *Journal of Educational Research, 83,* 103–111.

Fuchs, L., Fuchs, D., Hamlett, C., Phillips, N., & Karns, K. (1995). General educators' specialized adaptation for students with learning disabilities. *Exceptional Children, 61,* 440–459.

Fuchs, D., Mathes, P., Fuchs, L., & Lipsey, M. (2001). *Is LD just a fancy term for underachievement? A meta-analysis of reading differences between underachievers with and without the label.* Nashville, TN: Vanderbilt University.

Gerber, M., & Semmel, M. (1984). Teacher as imperfect test: Reconceptualizing the referral process. *Educational Psychologist, 14,* 137–146.

Gersten, R., Woodward, J., & Darch, J. (1986). Direct Instruction: A research-based approach to curriculum and teaching. *Exceptional Children, 53,* 17–31.

Good, R., Vollmer, M., Creek, R., Katz, L., & Chowdhri, S. (1993). Treatment utility of the Kaufman Assessment Battery for Children: Effects of matching instruction and student processing strength. *School Psychology Review, 22,* 8–26.

Gottlieb, J., Alter, M., Gottlieb, B., & Wishner, J. (1994). Special education in urban America: It's not justifiable for many. *The Journal of Special Education, 27,* 453–465.

Graham, S., & Harris, K. (1996). Self-regulation and strategy instruction for students who find writing and learning challenging. In C. Levy & S. Ransdell (Eds.), *The science of writing: Theories, methods, individual differences, and applications* (pp. 347–360). Mahwah, NJ: Erlbaum.

Greenwood, C. (1991). A longitudinal analysis of time, engagement, and achievement in at-risk versus non-risk students. *Exceptional Children, 57,* 521–535.

Gresham, F. M. (1986). Conceptual issues in the assessment of social competence in children. In P. Strain, M. Guralnick, & H. Walker (Eds.), *Children's social behavior: Development, assessment, and modification* (pp. 143–179). New York: Academic Press.

Gresham, F. M. (1989). Assessment of treatment integrity in school consultation and prereferral intervention. *School Psychology Review, 18,* 37–50.

Gresham, F. M. (1991). Conceptualizing behavior disorders in terms of resistance to intervention. *School Psychology Review, 20,* 23–36.

Gresham, F. M. (1997). Treatment integrity in single-subject research. In R. Franklin, D. Allison, & B. Gorman (Eds.), *Design and analysis of single case research* (pp. 93–117). Mahwah, NJ: Lawrence Erlbaum.

Gresham, F. M., & Lambros, K. (1998). Behavioral and functional assessment. In T. S. Watson & F. M. Gresham (Eds.), *Handbook of child behavior therapy* (pp. 3–22). New York: Plenum.

Gresham, F. M., MacMillan, D. L., Beebe-Frankenberger, M., & Bocian, K. (2000). Treatment integrity in learning disabilities intervention research: Do we really know how treatments are implemented? *Learning Disabilities Research & Practice, 15,* 198–205.

Gresham, F. M., MacMillan, D. L., & Bocian, K. (1997). Teachers as "tests": Differential validity of teacher judgments in identifying students at-risk for learning difficulties. *School Psychology Review, 26,* 47–60.

Gresham, F. M., Reschly, D. J., & Carey, M. (1987). Teachers as "tests": Classification accuracy and concurrent validation in the identification of learning disabled children. *School Psychology Review, 16,* 543–563.

Gresham, F. M., & Witt, J. C. (1997). Utility of intelligence tests for treatment planning, classification, and placement decisions: Recent empirical findings and future directions. *School Psychology Quarterly, 12,* 249–267.

Haccou, P., & Meelis, E. (1992). *Statistical analysis of behavioural data: An approach based on time-structured models.* Oxford, England: Oxford University Press.

Haring, N., Lovitt, T., Eaton, M., & Hansen, C. (1978). *The fourth R: Research in the classroom.* Columbus, OH: Merrill.

Hawkins, R. (1991). Is social validity what we are interested in? Argument for a functional approach. *Journal of Applied Behavior Analysis, 24,* 205–213.

Hayes, S., Nelson, R., & Jarrett, R. (1987). The treatment utility of assessment: A functional approach to evaluating assessment quality. *American Psychologist, 42,* 963–974.

Hinshaw, S. (1992). Externalizing behavior problems and academic underachievement in childhood and adolescence: Causal relationships and underlying mechanisms. *Psychological Bulletin, 111,* 127–155.

Howell, K., Fox, S., & Morehead, M. (1993). *Curriculum-based evaluation: Teaching and decision making* (2nd ed.). Belmont, CA: Brooks-Cole.

Hynd, G. (1989). Learning disabilities and neuropsychological correlates: Relationship to neurobiological theory. In D. Bakker & H. Van der Vlugt (Eds.), *Learning disabilities: Neuropsychological correlates and treatment* (Vol. 1, pp. 123–147). Amsterdam: Swets & Zeitlinger.

Jacobson, N., Follette, W., & Revenstorf, D. (1984). Psychotherapy outcome research: Methods for reporting variability and evaluating clinical significance. *Behavior Therapy, 15,* 336–352.

Johnston, J., & Pennypacker, H. (1993). *Strategies for human behavioral research* (2nd ed.). Hillsdale, NJ: Lawrence Erlbaum.

Kame'enui, E., Jitendra, A., & Darch, C. (1995). Direct instruction in reading as contronym and eonomine. *Reading & Writing Quarterly: Overcoming Learning Difficulties, 11,* 3–17.

Kavale, K., & Forness, S. (1987). How not to specify learning disability: A rejoinder to Koss. *Remedial and Special Education, 8,* 60–62.

Kavale, K., & Forness, S. (1995). *The science of learning disabilities.* San Diego: College-Hill Press.

Kavale, K., & Forness, S. (1999). Effectiveness of special education. In C. R. Reynolds & T. B. Gutkin (Eds.), *Handbook of school psychology* (3rd ed., pp. 984–1024). New York: Wiley.

Kavale, K., & Forness, S. (2000). What definitions of learning disability do and don't say: A critical analysis. *Journal of Learning Disabilities, 33,* 239–256.

Kavale, K., Fuchs, D., & Scruggs, T. (1994). Setting the record straight on learning disability and low achievement: Implications for policy making. *Learning Disabilities Research & Practice, 9,* 70–77.

Kazdin, A. (1984). Statistical analysis for single-case experimental designs. In D. Barlow & M. Hersen (Eds.), *Single case experimental designs: Strategies for studying behavior change* (pp. 285–324). New York: Pergamon.

Keogh, B. (1994). A matrix of decision points in the measurement of learning disabilities. In G. R. Lyon (Ed.), *Frames of reference for the assessment of learning disabilities* (pp. 15–26). Baltimore: Paul H. Brookes.

Keogh, B., & Speece, D. (1996). Learning disabilities within the context of schooling. In D. Speece & B. Keogh (Eds.), *Research on classroom ecologies: Implications for inclusion of children with learning disabilities* (pp. 1–14). Mahwah, NJ: Lawrence Erlbaum.

Kern, L., Childs, K., Dunlap, G., Clarke, S., & Falk, G. (1994). Using assessment-based curricular intervention to improve the classroom behavior of a student with emotional and behavioral challenges. *Journal of Applied Behavior Analysis, 27,* 293–323.

Kirk, R. E. (1994). *Experimental design: Procedures for the behavioral sciences* (3rd ed.). Pacific Grove, CA: Brooks-Cole.

Kirk, S. (1962). *Educating exceptional children.* Boston: Houghton Mifflin.

Knapp, T. (1983). Behavior analysts' visual appraisal of behavior change in graphic display. *Behavioral Assessment, 5,* 155–164.

Levin, J. (1986). Four cognitive principles of learning strategy instruction. *Educational Psychologist, 21,* 3–17.

Lentz, E. (1988). Effective reading interventions in the regular classroom. In J. Graden, J. Zins, & M. Curtis (Eds.), *Alternative educational delivery systems: Enhancing instructional options for all students* (pp. 351–370). Washington, DC: National Association of School Psychologists.

Liberman, I., Shankweiler, D., & Liberman, A. (1989). The alphabetic principle and learning to read. In D. Shankweiler & I. Liberman (Eds.), *Phonology and reading disability: solving the reading puzzle* (pp. 1–33). Ann Arbor: University of Michigan Press.

Lindamood, P., & Lindamood, P. (1998). *The Lindamood phoneme sequencing program for reading, spelling, and speech.* Austin, TX: PRO-ED.

Lindsley, O.R. (1991). Precision teaching's unique legacy from B.F. Skinner. *Journal of Behavioral Education, 1,* 253–266.

Lovett, M., Borden, S., DeLuca, T., Lacerenza, L., Benson, N., & Brackstone, D. (1994). Treating the core deficits of developmental dyslexia: Evidence of transfer of learning after phonologically and strategy-based reading programs. *Developmental Psychology, 30,* 805–822.

Lovitt, T., Eaton, M., Kirkwood, M., & Pelander, J. (1971). Effects of various reinforcement contingencies on oral reading rate. In E. Ramp & B. Hopkins (Eds.), *A new direction for education: Behavior analysis* (pp. 54–71). Lawrence KS: University of Kansas.

Lyon, G. R. (1996). Learning disabilities. *The Future of Children, 6,* 54–76.

MacMillan, D. L., Gresham, F. M., & Bocian, K. (1998). Discrepancy between definitions of learning disabilities and what schools use: An empirical investigation. *Journal of Learning Disabilities, 31,* 314–326.

MacMillan, D. L., Gresham, F. M., Bocian, K., & Lambros, K. (1998). Current plight of borderline students: Where do they belong? *Education and Treatment of Children, 33,* 83–94.

MacMillan, D. L., Gresham, F. M., Bocian, K., & Siperstein, G. (1997). The role of assessment in qualifying students as eligible for special education: What is and what's supposed to be. *Focus on Exceptional Children, 30,* 1–20.

MacMillan, D. L., Gresham, F. M., Siperstein, G., & Bocian, K. (1996). The labyrinth of IDEA: School decisions on referred students with subaverage general intelligence. *American Journal on Mental Retardation, 101,* 161–174.

MacMillan, D. L., Gresham, F. M., & Siperstein, G. (1993). Conceptual and psychometric concerns over the 1992 AAMR definition of mental retardation. *American Journal on Mental Retardation, 98,* 325–335.

MacMillan, D. L., Siperstein, G., & Gresham, F. M. (1996). Mild mental retardation: A challenge to its viability as a diagnostic category. *Exceptional Children, 62,* 356–371.

MacMillan, D. L., & Speece, D. (1999). Utility of current diagnostic categories for research and practice. In R. Gallimore, L. Hernheimer, D. MacMillan, D. Speece, & S. Vaughn (Eds.), *Developmental perspectives on children with high-incidence disabilities* (pp. 111–133). Mahwah, NJ: Lawrence Erlbaum.

Marston, D. (1987–88). The effectiveness of special education: A time-series analysis of reading performance in regular and special education settings. *The Journal of Special Education, 21,* 13–26.

Marston, D., Fuchs, L., & Deno, S. (1986). Measuring pupil progress: A comparison of standardized achievement tests and curriculum-based measures. *Diagnostique, 11,* 71–90.

Marston, D., & Magnusson, D. (1988). Curriculum-based assessment: District-level implementation. In J. Graden, J. Zins, & M. Curtis (Eds.), *Alternative educational delivery systems: Enhancing instructional options for all children* (pp. 137–172). Washington, DC: National Association of School Psychologists.

Marston, D., Mirkin, P., & Deno, S. (1984). Curriculum-based measurement: An alternative to traditional screening, referral, and identification. *The Journal of Special Education, 18,* 109–117.

Martens, B., Witt, J., Daly, E., & Vollmer, T. (1999). Behavior analysis: Theory and practice in educational settings. In C. R. Reynolds & T.B. Gutkin (Eds.), *Handbook of school pyschology* (3rd ed., pp. 638–663). New York: Wiley.

Mastropieri, M., & Scruggs, T. (1985–86). Early intervention for socially withdrawn children. *The Journal of Special Education, 19,* 429–441.

Matyas, T., & Greenwood, K. (1990). Visual analysis of single-case time series: Effects of variability, cerial dependence, and magnitude of intervention effects. *Journal of Applied Behavior Analysis, 23,* 341–351.

Matyas, T., & Greenwood, K. (1991). Problems in the estimation of autocorrelation in brief time series and some implications for behavioral data. *Behavior Assessment, 13,* 137–157.

McCleskey, J., & Waldron, N. (1991). Identifying students with learning disabilities: The effect of implementing state guidelines. *Journal of Learning Disabilities, 24,* 501–506.

Mercer, C., Jordan, L., Allsopp, D., & Mercer, A. (1996). Learning disabilities definitions and criteria used by state education departments. *Learning Disability Quarterly, 19,* 217–232.

Messick, S. (1995). Validity of psychological assessment: Validation of inferences from persons' responses and performances as scientific inquiry into score meaning. *American Psychologist, 50,* 741–749.

Mischel, W. (1968). *Personality and assessment.* New York: Wiley.

Nevin, J. (1988). Behavioral momentum and the partial reinforcement effect. *Psychological Bulletin, 103*, 44–56.

Nevin, J. (1996). The momentum of compliance. *Journal of Applied Behavior Analysis, 29*, 535–547.

Noell, G. H., & Witt, J. C. (1999). When does consultation lead to intervention implementation? *The Journal of Special Education, 33*, 29–35.

Nolen, P., McCutchen, D., & Berninger, V. (1990). Ensuring tomorrow's literacy: A shared responsibility. *Journal of Teacher Education, 41*, 63–72.

Nunnally, J., & Kotsche, W. (1983). Studies of individual subjects: Logic and methods of analysis. *Journal of Clinical Psychology, 22*, 83–93.

Ottenbacher, K. J. (1990). When is a picture worth a thousand p values? A comparison of visual and quantitative methods to analyze single case data. *The Journal of Special Education, 23*, 436–449.

Pressley, M., & Ghatala, E. (1990). Self-regulated learning: Monitoring learning from text. *Educational Psychologist, 25*, 19–34.

Reschly, D. J., & Gresham, F. M. (1989). Current neuropsychological diagnosis of learning problems: A leap of faith. *Handbook of clinical neuropsychology* (pp. 503–519). New York: Plenum.

Reschly, D. J., & Grimes, J. (1995). Intellectual assessment. *Best practices in school psychology III* (pp. 763–774). Washington, DC: National Association of School Psychologists.

Reschly, D., & Tilly, W. D. (1999). Reform trends and system design alternatives. In D. Reschly, W. D. Tilly, & J. Grimes (Eds.), *Special education in transition: Functional assessment and noncategorical programming* (pp. 19–48). Longmont, CO: Sopris West.

Reschly, D. J., & Ysseldyke, J. (1995). School psychology paradigm shift. In A. Thomas & J. Grimes (Eds.), *Best practices in school psychology III* (pp. 17–32). Washington, DC: National Association of School Psychologists.

Reynolds, C. (1984). Critical issues in learning disabilities. *The Journal of Special Education, 18*, 451–476.

Reynolds, C. R., & Fletcher-Janzen, E. (Eds.) (1989). *Handbook of clinical child neuropsychology.* New York: Plenum.

Rosenshine, B. (1995). Advances in research on instruction. *Journal of Educational Research, 88*, 262–268.

Rutter, M., & Yule, W. (1975). The concept of specific reading retardation. *Journal of Child Psychology and Psychiatry, 16*, 181–197.

Sechrest, L. (1963). Incremental validity: A recommendation. *Educational and Psychological Measurement, 23*, 153–158.

Share, D., McGee, R., & Silva, P. (1989). IQ and reading progress: A test of the capacity notion. *Journal of the American Academy of Child and Adolescent Psychiatry, 28,* 97–100.

Shaywitz, B., Fletcher, J., Holahan, J., & Shaywitz, S. (1992). Discrepancy compared to low achievement definitions of reading disability: Results from the Connecticut Longitudinal Study. *Journal of Learning Disabilities, 25,* 639–648.

Shaywitz, S., Shaywitz, B., Fletcher, J., & Escobar, M. (1990). Prevalence of reading disability in boys and girls: Results of the Connecticut longitudinal study. *Journal of the American Medical Association, 264,* 998–1002.

Shepard, L., Smith, M., & Vojir, C. (1983). Characteristics of pupils identified as learning disabled. *American Educational Research Journal, 20,* 309–331.

Shinn, M. (1989). *Curriculum-based measurement: Assessing special children.* New York: Guilford.

Shinn, M. (1995). Best practices in curriculum-based measurement and its use in a problem-solving model. In A. Thomas & J. Grimes (Eds.), *Best practices in school psychology III* (pp. 547–567). Washington, DC: National Association of School Psychologists.

Shinn, M., Tindal, G., & Stein, S. (1988). Curriculum-based assessment and the identification of mildly handicapped students: A research review. *Professional School Psychology, 3,* 69–85.

Siegel, L. (1989). IQ is irrelevant in the definition of learning disabilities. *Journal of Learning Disabilities, 22, 469–478.*

Skinner, C. (1998). Prevention of academic skill deficits. In T. S. Watson & F. M. Gresham (Eds.), *Handbook of child behavior therapy* (pp. 61–82). New York: Plenum Press.

Slavin, R. (1987). Grouping for instruction in the elementary school. *Educational Psychologist, 22, 109–122.*

Speece, D., & Case, L. (in press). Classification in context: An alternative to identifying early reading disability. *Journal of Educational Psychology.*

Stanovich, K., & Siegel, L. (1994). The phenotypic performance profile of reading-disabled children: A regression-based test of the phonological-core variable-difference model. *Journal of Educational Psychology, 86,* 24–53.

Strain, P., Kohler, F., & Gresham, F. M. (1998). Problems in logic and interpretation with quantitative syntheses of single-case research: Mathur and colleagues (1998) as a case in point. *Behavioral Disorders, 24,* 74–85.

Swanson, H. L., Carson, C., & Saches-Lee, C. (1996). A selective synthesis of intervention research for students with learning disabilities. *School Psychology Review, 25*, 370–391.

Swanson, H. L., & Hoskyn, M. (1999). Definition X treatment interaction for students with learning disabilities. *School Psychology Review, 28*, 644–658.

Swanson, H. L., & Sachs-Lee, C. (2000). A meta-analysis of single-subject intervention research for students with LD. *Journal of Learning Disabilities, 33*, 114–136.

Teeter, P. A. (1987) Review of neuropsychological assessment and intervention with children and adolescents. *School Psychology Review, 16*, 582–593.

Teeter, P. A. (1989). Neuropsychological approaches to the remediation of educational deficits. In C. Reynolds & E. Fletcher-Jantzen (Eds.), *Handbook of clinical child neuropsychology* (pp. 357–376). New York: Plenum Press.

Torgesen, J. (1996). A model of memory from an information processing perspective: The special case of phonological memory. In G. Reid Lyon (Ed.), *Attention, memory, and executive function: Issues in conceptualization and measurement* (pp. 157–184). Baltimore: Brookes.

Torgesen, J., Alexander, A., Wagner, R., Rashotte, C., Voeller, K., & Conway, T. (2001). Intensive remedial instruction for children with severe reading disabilities: Immediate and long-term outcomes from two instructional approaches. *Journal of Learning Disabilities, 34*, 33–58.

United States Department of Education. (1998). *Twentieth annual report to Congress on implementation of the Individuals With Disabilities Education Act.* Washington, DC: Author.

Vellutino, F., Scanlon, D., & Lyon, G. R. (2000). Differentiating between difficult-to-remediate and readily remediated poor readers: More evidence against the IQ-achievement discrepancy definition of reading disability. *Journal of Learning Disabilities, 33*, 223–238.

Vellutino, F., Scanlon, D., Sipay, E., Small, S., Pratt, A., Chen, R., & Denckla, M. (1996). Cognitive profiles of difficult-to-remediate and readily remediated poor readers: Early intervention as a vehicle for distinguishing between cognitive and experiential deficits as basic causes of specific reading disability. *Journal of Educational Psychology, 88*, 601–638.

Vellutino, F., Scanlon, D., & Tanzman, M. (1998). The case for early intervention in diagnosing reading disability. *Journal of School Psychology, 36*, 367–397.

Wickstrom, K., Jones, K., LaFleur, L., & Witt, J. (1998). An analysis of treatment integrity in school-based behavioral consultation. *School Psychology Quarterly, 13*, 141–154.

Wiggins, J. (1973). *Personality and prediction: Principles of personality assessment.* Reading, MA: Addison-Wesley.

Witt, J. C., & Gresham, F. M. (1985). Review of the Wechsler Intelligence Scale for Children-Revised. In J. Mitchell (Ed.), *Ninth mental measurements yearbook* (pp. 1716–1719). Lincoln, NE: Buros Institute.

Witt, J. C., & Gresham, F. M. (1997). Utility of intelligence test for treatment planning, classification, and placement decisions: Recent empirical findings and future directions. *School Psychology Quarterly, 12,* 249–267.

Wolf, M. (1978). Social validity: The case for subjective measurement or how applied behavior analysis is finding its heart. *Journal of Applied Behavior Analysis, 11,* 203–214.

Yeaton, W., & Sechrest, L. (1981). Critical dimensions in the choice and maintenance of successful treatments: Strength, integrity, and effectiveness. *Journal of Consulting and Clinical Psychology, 49,* 156–167.

Ysseldyke, J., Algozzine, B., Shinn, M., & McGue, M. (1982). Similarities and differences between low achievers and students classified as learning disabled. *The Journal of Special Education, 16,* 73–85.

Ysseldyke, J., & Mirkin, P. (1982). The use of assessment information to plan instructional interventions: A review of the research. In C. Reynolds & T. Gutkin (Eds.), *Handbook of school psychology* (pp. 395–435). New York: Wiley.

Zigler, E., Balla, D., & Hodapp, R. (1984). On the definition and classification of mental retardation. *American Journal of Mental Retardation, 89,* 215–230.

NOTES

Portions of this paper previously appeared in Bocian, K., Beebe, M., MacMillan, D., & Gresham, F. M. (1999). Competing paradigms in learning disabilities classification by schools and the variations in the meaning of discrepant achievement. *Learning Disabilities Research & Practice, 14,* 1–14.

THREE CONCEPTUALIZATIONS OF "TREATMENT" IN A RESPONSIVENESS-TO-TREATMENT FRAMEWORK FOR LD IDENTIFICATION

Lynn S. Fuchs, Peabody College of Vanderbilt University

Treatment responsiveness as a framework for identifying students with learning disability (LD) was originally conceptualized by Heller, Holtzman, and Messick (1982) and subsequently operationalized by others (e.g., Fuchs, 1995; Fuchs & Fuchs, 1998; Vellutino et al., 1996). The premise is that students are identified as learning disabled when their response to educational treatment is dramatically inferior to that of peers. The inference is that children who respond poorly to otherwise effective treatments have some critical constellation of deficits that require specialized intervention to effect the important schooling outcomes associated with successful adult life. A central assumption is that responsiveness to treatment can differentiate between two explanations for low achievement: poor instruction versus disability.

Assessing treatment responsiveness requires three major activities: (a) implementing a generally effective treatment, (b) measuring students' response to that treatment, and (c) applying a responsiveness criterion below which students are identified as learning disabled. If treatment responsiveness is to provide a viable framework for LD identification, then these three components of the assessment process must be specified with sufficient clarity so that school personnel can implement treatment-responsiveness assessment in a manner that lends conceptual, if not procedural, standardization across districts and states.

In his paper, Dr. Gresham provided a broad overview of treatment responsiveness for identifying LD. Space limitations preclude a point-by-point critique of that paper. Instead, I focus on one critical problem in Gresham's overview: his failure to consider how alternative treatments, with different levels of intensity, timing, and criteria for demarcating disability, can fundamentally alter the notion of treatment responsiveness for the purpose of identifying LD. Dr. Gresham's implicit belief in the interchangeability of alternative forms of treatment introduces conceptual and procedural confusion about the treatment responsiveness framework for LD identification. So, in this essay, I explore how alternative approaches to treatment are distinctive in ways that fundamentally alter conceptualizations of treatment responsiveness for LD identification. I borrow three of Dr. Gresham's examples to illustrate this point; I propose a scheme for classifying treatment; and I argue that the field needs to be deliberate in selecting among possible forms of treatment for the purpose of assessing treatment responsiveness.

THREE APPROACHES TO CONCEPTUALIZING TREATMENT

My three categories for conceptualizing treatment are intensive remediation, intensive prevention, and general education prevention. For each category, I summarize an example from Gresham and evaluate the approach against three considerations: (1) how early in a child's educational career identification occurs, (2) the intensity of the required intervention and the corresponding resources necessary to implement the approach, and (3) the criterion used to judge responsiveness and to demarcate disability.

Intensive Remediation

With intensive remediation, children with severe deficits are provided with individual tutoring by specially trained personnel using validated treatment protocols. Dr. Gresham illustrated this approach using Torgesen et al.'s (2001) work, where 8- to 10-year-old children received 1:1 tutoring during two 50-minute sessions each day. Over an 8- to 9-week period, treatment accumulated to 67.5 hours of instruction, and for each of the following 8 weeks, students received a 50-minute generalization session. This intensive remedial effort "normalized" the reading skills of the approximately one half of participants who achieved a posttreatment word-reading standard score of 90 or better. Within the context of a treatment-responsiveness assessment paradigm, the implication of Torgesen's study is that responsiveness to 67 hours of individual tutoring delivered in a 2-month period may be used to differentiate false positive learning disabilities (i.e., students whose posttreatment standard scores exceed 89) from true learning disabilities.

So, how does such an intensive remedial treatment fare against the three criteria posed for considering "treatment" within a treatment-responsiveness model for LD identification? With respect to the timing of identification, an intensive remedial approach precludes early identification. Rather, before students become the target for treatment responsiveness assessment, they must demonstrate a severe achievement deficit, as illustrated by Torgesen's subjects, who began the study with word-reading standard scores at least 1.5 standard deviations below the mean. Because a substantial period of failure is required to manifest such deficits, this approach produces identifications timed in a similar way to those required for an IQ-achievement discrepancy model of identification. In fact, Torgesen's students were already in fourth grade.

In terms of the intensity of intervention and the corresponding resources required for implementation, an intensive remedial treatment approach falls at the high end of the continuum: Torgesen's intervention required nearly 2 hours of individual attention each day. Response to this extreme form of remediation seems to validate the appropriateness of specialized instruction, rather than providing the basis for deeming an individual disability-free and supposing that a normalized education will be effective.

This level of intensity, moreover, is extremely expensive for schools to implement because it requires a skilled teacher to work with no more than six children per year. Gresham used two arguments to support the cost feasibility of this intensive remedial approach to LD identification. I question the tenability of both arguments. First, he contended that traditional assessment costs of $2,500 per child exceed the $1,688 required for the individual tutoring associated with intensive remediation. When multiplied by the six students each teacher serves over an entire school year, however, this estimate translates into an annual teacher salary of only $10,128. Obviously, something is amiss here.

Gresham's second claim is that a treatment-responsiveness approach to identification would yield savings by decreasing the number of children served in special education. This point, however, must be weighed against prevalence estimates based on state-of-the-art reading instruction, which suggest that demand for LD services, currently at approximately 5% of the school-age population, is unlikely to decrease. This fact is clear from Torgesen's (2000) analysis of the National Institute of Child Health and Human Development intervention studies, from which estimates of the incidence of word-reading disabilities fall between 4 and 6%. If we add another 1% of the population to account for students with mathematical disabilities without comorbid reading disabilities (McLeod & Armstrong, 1982), and consider the likelihood that some additional proportion of the population manifests later comprehension difficulties without having experienced earlier word-reading problems, then the incidence of LD is unlikely to decrease.

The fact that intensive remedial tutoring for LD identification is at least as expensive as traditional assessment, and that a treatment-responsiveness model of identification is unlikely to decrease the incidence of LD, argues for a more cost-effective means of operationalizing "treatment" within treatment-responsiveness assessment.

Schools are unlikely to muster the resources necessary to provide intensive remedial treatment for the purpose of identifying LD while continuing to serve 5% of the population as learning disabled. A more likely use for the Torgesen model is to remediate the reading problems of students already identified as learning disabled with the hope that they may exit special education.

A third consideration for analyzing alternative approaches to treatment is the criterion used to judge responsiveness and to demarcate disability. Within the context of Torgesen's intensive remedial approach, the criterion for responsiveness is a return to normalcy, that is, achieving a posttreatment standard score of 90 or better. The normative framework for establishing this criterion for disability, therefore, is the general population, but measurement is limited to posttreatment assessment. Of course, some children whose posttreatment status falls below 90 will have manifested better growth than counterparts who meet the normalcy criterion and are deemed free of LD. Because responsiveness therefore is not directly indexed using posttreatment status, it is interesting to consider why Torgesen chose to reference his criterion for treatment responsiveness in this way.

One possibility is the difficulty associated with legitimizing a criterion for intensive remediation when the normative framework for growth is necessarily restricted to very poor readers. After all, there is no circumstance imaginable where the full range of students might be provided with 100 minutes of individual daily tutoring for the purpose of establishing growth norms. And disability cut-points, of course, are traditionally referenced to the general population (as in mental retardation where 2 standard deviations below the mean signifies deviance). Because (a) an intensive approach to treatment precludes the traditional normative framework and (b) a normative framework limited to very poor readers creates conceptual challenges to setting cut-points, an alternative framework for judging responsiveness to intensive remediation may be required. A criterion-referenced framework, for example, would provide growth cut-points, below which meaningful long-term functional reading competence is severely jeopardized. Unfortunately, the systematic, longitudinal research program required to identify such criterion-referenced cut-points is yet to be conceptualized.

In sum, Torgesen's work represents an impressive method for remediating the achievement deficits of many children with severe reading disabilities. As an approach to assessing treatment responsiveness for the purpose of LD identification, however, remedial treatment is problematic. It precludes early identification. It rests on the questionable assumption that success in response to heroic remediation constitutes evidence that severe academic deficits resulted from poor instruction rather than from disability. It is very costly for schools to implement. And it fails to offer persuasive cut-points for demarcating disability.

Intensive Prevention

An alternative approach to "treatment," as illustrated by Vellutino and colleagues (1996), is intensive prevention. These researchers identified children who manifested early signs of reading problems, as judged by first-grade teachers in November and as verified by word-reading performance in the bottom 15th percentile. Certified teachers, who had at least 2 years of experience and had completed a 30-hour seminar in reading theory and practice, provided the poor readers with 30 minutes of individual daily tutoring for 15 weeks, for a total of 35–40 hours. Vellutino rank-ordered slopes representing children's growth in response to tutoring; children whose slopes fell in the bottom half were deemed "difficult to remediate." Vellutino et al. argued that such treatment provided a "first-cut diagnostic" in distinguishing between disabled and nondisabled learners.

This intensive preventive approach offers at least two advantages over the intensive remedial approach for operationalizing "treatment" in a treatment-responsiveness model for LD identification. First, intensive prevention permits early identification, before severe achievement deficits accrue. Second, the costs are lower than those associated with intensive remediation because prevention precludes the accumulation of severe performance deficits. The intensity of the tutoring required to effect growth, therefore, is typically less than what can be expected with remediation. Of course, even 30 minutes per day of skilled, individual tutoring, as illustrated in the Vellutino study, will require considerable investment by schools.

Unfortunately, intensive prevention shares two substantial problems with intensive remediation. First, assessing disability via responsiveness to intensive prevention requires the tenuous assumption that good progress in response to intensive tutoring constitutes evidence that initial difficulties were caused by poor instruction, rather than by child deficits, which may render future learning within the normalized general education environment problematic. If intensive tutoring is needed to effect growth (when most children make adequate growth in general education), then a safer assumption might be that the child has some deficit requiring the intensive tutoring that special education, with additional resources, might provide.

The second problem involves the criterion used to judge responsiveness and demarcate disability. As with an intensive remedial approach, the costs associated with implementing 20–30 minutes of daily individual tutoring prohibit sampling growth among the full range of the achievement continuum. Thus, intensive prevention again requires the normative framework to be limited to poor readers. In confronting this challenge, Vellutino and colleagues simply designated their lower half as disabled. The validity of such a method for establishing a cut-point for identification is, of course, questionable. As with an intensive remedial approach, what is required instead is a criterion-referenced cut-point for growth, below which meaningful long-term functional reading competence is jeopardized. Until such data are available, however, framing appropriate cut-points for growth to intensive tutoring will remain a challenge to a treatment-responsiveness framework for LD identification.

General Education Prevention

With general education prevention, the distribution of student responsiveness to effective general education instruction is estimated for the general population; children whose growth rates are dramatically below those of peers are identified for prereferral intervention, and LD classification is considered for children whose responsiveness to prereferral intervention does not improve in relation to general education norms. The notion is that failure to thrive in an educational environment from which most children derive benefit reveals some underlying deficit, which requires special instruction to effect adequate learning. In classrooms where effective prevention is conducted, most children's growth rates will be strong, thus highlighting children whose response to the same environment is inadequate. By contrast, ineffective classrooms will reveal low growth rates across many students, making detection of unresponsiveness difficult but signaling school personnel to intervene at the classroom level.

Dr. Gresham illustrated this approach with a study by Speece and Case (in press), who sampled the curriculum-based measurement (CBM) performance of five students per first- and second-grade class in a way that approximated the class distribution. After collecting 10 data points per child across 6 months, the researchers classified children who manifested a CBM "dual discrepancy" (i.e., low performance level at end of the 10 weeks as well as poor growth across the 10 weeks) as treatment nonresponders. In my work (Fuchs, 1995; Fuchs & Fuchs, 1998), I have conducted CBM on a weekly basis to identify dually discrepant children earlier in the year and in response to general education as well as to prereferral intervention.

The question is how general education prevention fares against the three criteria posed for considering "treatment" within a treatment-responsiveness model of identification. With respect to timing, a general education prevention treatment approach satisfies the need for early identification. In terms of the resources required to implement treatment, general education prevention compares favorably against intensive prevention as well as intensive remediation. After all, general education remains responsible for delivering the instruction against which responsiveness is indexed. Of course, the efficacy of general education classroom instruction in most schools is far from optimal, and an infusion of resources is clearly required to enhance the general effectiveness of practice. This situation is true, however, with or without a treatment-responsiveness model for LD identification. An added financial burden more specifically tied to a general education prevention approach is that the performance of classroom peers must be sampled to provide a normative framework for judging responsiveness. Even with ongoing assessment of classroom peers to provide a normative framework for judging responsiveness, however, a general education approach should be less costly than daily, individual tutoring.

Beyond cost-effectiveness, however, the level of intensity associated with general education prevention provides conceptual advantages over individual tutoring. By defining "treatment" as the generally effective instruction all children receive, the general education prevention approach assumes that disability should be assessed as it occurs under normalized conditions: in the general education classroom. This context parallels the one within which other psychological conditions are diagnosed, where costly intervention is reserved for intervening with, not assessing the existence of, conditions. To assess disability by determining whether heroic effort ameliorates a condition seems analogous to assessing the accuracy of a cancer diagnosis by judging whether a bone-marrow transplant restores the patient to a state of health.

So, if treatment is not a conventional part of the diagnostic protocol for identifying other conditions, why might a treatment-responsiveness paradigm be appropriate for LD identification? Because education, by definition, involves treatment. That treatment, however, is of the intensity represented by effective general education, not intensive tutoring. When a student fails to respond as do his peers to effective general education, then the conclusion is that some critical constellation of deficits makes learning in response to typical instruction difficult. This conclusion creates the basis for determining that some special form of education, such as the intensive tutoring that should be available with special education, is needed to effect adequate growth. In a related way, general education prevention fares best with respect to my third criterion because it permits a normative framework referenced to a typical population. This framework parallels other methods for disability identification and offers established cut-points for demarcating disability.

CONCLUSIONS

Gresham's description of "treatment" within a treatment-responsiveness framework to LD identification incorrectly mixes different approaches. In this essay, I described critical differences among three approaches to treatment and highlighted their advantages and disadvantages. An intensive remedial approach does not lend conceptual or logistical strength to a treatment-responsiveness model of identification. It produces late identifications; it is prohibitively expensive; it is conceptually flawed as an approach to classification; and it requires a normative framework based exclusively on very poor readers, making growth cut-points difficult to establish. Intensive prevention and general education prevention fare better in my analysis. Both permit early identification and require fewer resources than intensive remediation. General education prevention does, however, offer three distinctive advantages over intensive remediation or intensive prevention. First, general education prevention is most affordable. Second, it offers the conceptual advantage of locating "treatment" in the normalized environment, from which conclusions about disability and the need for intensive forms of instruction (as might be offered via special education) are best drawn. And third, it permits normative comparisons referenced to the general population, which provide the basis for well-established guidelines for setting disability cut-points.

It is interesting to note that, in terms of resource demands, regardless of which approach to treatment is adopted, treatment-responsiveness assessment can be expected to add expense to the current system. Intensive remediation and intensive prevention require a wealth of skilled tutors; general education prevention demands an infusion of dollars to sample responsiveness among classroom peers. Given that each treatment approach is likely to require more resources than the traditional mode, cost-effectiveness is not a persuasive rationale for adopting treatment validity for LD identification. More compelling arguments in favor of treatment-responsiveness assessment include early identification, identification of children for whom poor instruction has been excluded as a viable explanation for failure, and an emphasis on growth that provides a uniform framework for identification, for enhancing individual programs, and for evaluating general and special education efficacy.

Regardless of which approach to treatment is adopted, I hope that my analysis clarifies the importance of defining "treatment" within treatment-responsiveness assessment in ways that provide conceptual and procedural standardization. Without clear definition, a revised focus on treatment responsiveness for LD identification is unlikely to lend the classificatory clarity and integrity we all seek in considering definitional alternatives to IQ discrepancy.

References

Fuchs, L. S. (1995, May). *Incorporating curriculum-based measurement into the eligibility decision-making process: A focus on treatment validity and student growth.* Paper prepared for the National Academy of Sciences Workshop on Alternatives to IQ Testing, Washington, DC.

Fuchs, L. S., & Fuchs, D. (1998). Treatment validity: A unifying concept for reconceptualizing the identification of learning disabilities. *Learning Disabilities Research and Practice, 13,* 204–219.

Heller, K. A., Holtzman, W. H., & Messick, S. (Eds.). (1982). *Placing children in special education: A strategy for equity.* Washington, DC: National Academy Press.

McLeod, T., & Armstrong, S. (1982). Learning disabilities in mathematics-skill deficits and remedial approaches at the intermediate and secondary level. *Learning Disability Quarterly, 5,* 305–311.

Speece, D. L., & Case, L. (in press). Classification in context: An alternative to identifying early reading disability. *Journal of Educational Psychology.*

Torgesen, J. K. (2000). Individual differences in response to early interventions in reading: The lingering problem of treatment resisters. *Learning Disabilities Research and Practice, 15,* 55–64.

Torgesen, J. K., Alexander, A., Wagner, R., Rashotte, C., Voeller, K., & Conway, T. (2001). Intensive remedial instruction for children with severe reading disabilities: Immediate and long-term outcomes from two instructional approaches. *Journal of Learning Disabilities, 34,* 33–58.

Vellutino, F., Scanlon, D., Sipay, E., Small, S., Pratt, A., Chen, R., & Denckla, M. (1996). Cognitive profiles of difficult-to-remediate and readily remediated poor readers: Early intervention as a vehicle for distinguishing between cognitive and experiential deficits as basic causes of specific reading disability. *Journal of Educational Psychology, 88,* 601–638.

RESPONSIVENESS TO INTERVENTIONS: THE NEXT STEP IN SPECIAL EDUCATION IDENTIFICATION, SERVICE, AND EXITING DECISION MAKING

Jeff Grimes, Heartland Area Education Agency

Mark Twain said, "Everyone complains about the weather but nobody does anything about it." Learning disability (LD) identification has been like that—until now. Gresham identifies the rationale for changing the way in which students with learning disabilities are identified and proposes a viable alternative for turning that idea into responsible actions that are supported by research. Gresham's proposal to systematically focus attention on intervention effects has far-reaching positive implications for the quality of services provided to students with disabilities at the points of identification, design of educational services, and exiting special education services. The focus on interventions affects special education as a system.

Over the past three decades the Education for all Handicapped Children Act of 1975 (EHA; Education for all Handicapped Children Act, 1975) and the Individuals with Disabilities Education Act Amendments of 1997 and 1999 (IDEA; Individuals with Disabilities Education Act, 1999) have represented an enduring national commitment to protect and promote the educational well-being of children with disabilities. Across the same period there have been ongoing adjustments in federal regulations and improvements in professional practices in order to enhance educational results for students with disabilities. The distinction between unchanging philosophical commitments and changing professional practices is critical to our continued progress toward positive results for students with disabilities. Gresham proposes the use of responsiveness-to-intervention data for the identification of students with disabilities. In addition, intervention data informs the decision-making process within an individualized education plan (IEP). Using responsiveness-to-intervention data is a reasonable and responsible action that is in accord with the four purposes of IDEA (§300.01). When implementing this proposal, professional practices change, yet the commitment to students with disabilities remains an unwavering constant.

Concerns have been expressed over three decades about the definition and identification processes for LD (Epps, Ysseldyke, & McGue, 1984; Gottlieb, Alter, & Gottlieb, 1999; Kavale & Forness, 2000; Ysseldyke, Algozzine, & Epps, 1983). The prevailing framework for LD identification includes an intelligence and achievement discrepancy, a process that represents an ongoing source of concern within special education (Fletcher et al., 1994; Lyon, 1996; Reschly & Ysseldyke, 1995). The number of LD students has continued to rise since 1975 (EHA, IDEA) and currently the LD category is 52% of all students with disabilities (U.S. Department of Education, 2000). Effectiveness of current special education programs is an area for enhancement (Kavale & Forness, 1999). These issues support consideration for improving the process for making special education decisions.

The application of a responsiveness-to-intervention approach represents an important paradigm shift for special education (Reschly, 1988; Reschly & Ysseldyke, 1995). Tilly and Flugum (1995) define interventions as a "planned modification of the environment made for the purpose of altering behavior in a prespecified way." Intervention-oriented systems take a proactive approach to student instruction and adjust plans based on whether results lead to improved student performance. These actions are shown in Figure 1 as a four-step problem-solving process (Heartland Area Education Agency, 2001). First, the magnitude of the problem is determined and there is an analysis of why the problem is happening. Second, a goal-directed intervention plan is devised to improve the student's performance. Third, the intervention is implemented as planned, data collected to monitor progress, and instruction modified based on the student's responsiveness to the intervention. Last, the results are evaluated to determine the intervention's impact on the student's behavior and make decisions about future actions. In the problem-solving process, the data about a student's responsiveness to intervention becomes the driving force in determining the design of future interventions. From an analysis of a student's responsiveness to interventions, it can be determined which environmental factors enable learning and which factors do not. This paper supports the concept proposed by Gresham to use intervention outcome data to improve educational decision making.

ISSUES WITH THE CURRENT SYSTEM

Existing technologies make it feasible to effectively address educational issues in ways that were impossible a few decades ago. Professionals, guided by scientific experimentation, determine which practices are effective for individual students

Figure 1.

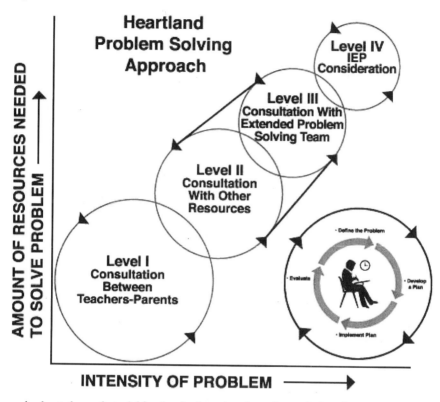

and adopt those that yield valued educational results and abandon unsupported practices, regardless of past acceptance. This section considers commonplace practices that are unsupported by research, incompatible with an intervention center approach, and worthy of planned abandonment.

Abandoning ATI-Based Processes

Gresham asserts with clarity and convincing documentation that the aptitude by treatment interaction (ATI) approach has been unsuccessful in demonstrating positive results (Cronbach, 1975; Cronbach & Snow, 1977). Differential diagnosis of LD subtypes (Gresham & Witt, 1997; Reschly & Ysseldyke, 1995) is an equally unproductive pursuit. Simple alignment of students classified as LD based on intelligence-achievement discrepancy and placed in LD programs have not yielded convincing educational outcomes (Good, Vollmer, Creek, Katz & Chowdhri, 1993; Kavale & Forness, 1999). As psychiatrist Thomas Szasz (1970) said, "Insanity is continuing to do the same thing and expecting different results." To promote better outcomes for LD students, actions designed to implement processes based on ATI logic need to be replaced by better alternatives. The responsiveness-to-intervention approach is a viable foundation for improving future services to students with LD.

Intelligence-Achievement Discrepancy

The intelligence and achievement discrepancy measures is an application of ATI logic (Reschly & Grimes, 1995). Intelligence tests were originally designed to distinguish between those individuals who would benefit from instruction in general educational environments and those who would not. That purpose remains an application of these instruments, a practice that is inconsistent with IDEA ideals. The process of making eligibility decisions for LD students based on intelligence and achievement discrepancy is, at best, minimally related to the design of instructional interventions (Fletcher et al., 1998; Gresham & Witt, 1997). Categorical diagnoses that result simply in the classification of children fall short of the need to support educators who provide ongoing instruction for students with disabilities (Vellutino, Scanlon, & Lyon, 2000). The important challenge is to diagnose conditions that enable learning, not the presence of an achievement-intelligence discrepancy that is considered to represent evidence of LD. Gresham proposes better practices to meaningfully link intervention assessment data with educational decisions.

RESPONSIVENESS TO INTERVENTION—PROPOSAL AND REACTIONS

Gresham proposes the use of a responsiveness-to-intervention approach in lieu of the aptitude-achievement discrepancy framework. The responsiveness-to-intervention practice offers distinct advantages; most important, it links student assessments directly to individualized instructional decisions while making discriminating judgments about those individuals requiring special education assistance. Interventions begin in general education.

Early Intervention and Prevention

Early identification and the provision of general education interventions are critical to preventing the rising tide of students with reading difficulties who may later be determined to qualify for special education services as students with learning disabilities. Juel (1988) found that poor readers at the end of first grade had the probability of 0.88 of being poor readers in fourth grade; likewise, the probability of an average reader at the end of first grade being an average reader in fourth grade was 0.87. Early intervention has long-term implications, as does the lack of intervention, on the prevalence of learning disabilities and students' reading performance (Vellutino, Scanlon & Tanzman, 1998).

The means to reading success is found in early instruction focused on skills that are foundational to reading proficiency (National Reading Panel, 2000; National Research Council 1998; Simmons & Kame'enui, 1998). Students' acquisition of essential early literacy skills can be assessed with precision using a schoolwide model involving all learners in general education (Kaminski & Good, 1996, 1998). For example, Dynamic Indicators of Basic Early Literacy Skills (DIBELS) measures all kindergarten and first-grade students' performance in critical early reading skills. These measures can be repeated throughout kindergarten and first grade to determine whether a student is responsive to instruction. On the basis of students' performance data, instruction is adjusted by general education teachers to match educational needs. Student results are considered as the index of instructional need rather than a within-student deficiency about which nothing can be done. The logic is to teach often, measure growth often, and adjust instruction based on intervention data. (For further discussion of the schoolwide model, see Kame'enui and Simmons, 1998; Simmons et al., 2000.)

Early intervention and prevention cannot be efficiently accomplished on a case-by-case basis. The magnitude of students' educational needs is too great. Schoolwide models that provide formative assessment of student performance in reading and math instruction are currently in use (Fuchs, Fuchs, Hamlett, Phillips & Bentz, 1994). Schoolwide assessment assists in identifying individuals who need intensive instruction. The results of instruction can be systematically monitored for all students in general education. This technology supports a broad-based application of the responsiveness-to-intervention approach advocated by Gresham. Students who are not responding to instruction receive additional assistance to prevent educational failure. General education data lead to additional intervention and monitoring results with the intent of achieving improved student outcomes. Prevention of school failure through effective and timely intervention is the purpose of the schoolwide model.

Diagnosing Solutions

When students are resistant to early intervention effort, more intensive instruction is warranted. One depiction of a system designed to provide intervention tailored to student needs is shown in Figure 2 (Heartland Area Education Agency, 2001). In this model, educational resources are matched with the magnitude of student need across four levels of educational support, from general classroom at level I to specially designed instruction at level IV. As the magnitude of students' needs increases, the amount of educational resources increases proportionally to provide interventions required to support students' continuing educational growth. The intention of interventions at Levels I, II, and III is to (a) provide educational assistance in a timely manner, (b) determine the effectiveness of environmental adjustments on student performance and modify instruction when warranted, and (c) improve student performance and thereby avoid behaviors that could be considered as requiring specially designed instruction. Vellutino et al. (1996) advocates intensive instruction as the "first cut" in the referral process. This four-level approach provides a mechanism for implementing a systematic intervention-oriented process to meet the instructional needs of students in general and special education. A byproduct of this service delivery model is the development of a progression of interventions, all of which yield student data. These data are evidence of a student's responsiveness to interventions. These data can define educational needs and the instructional supports that are necessary to enable continued improvement in student learning.

Barker (1993) states that a paradigm defines boundaries and tells what constitutes success within those boundaries. The indicators of success in a responsiveness-to-intervention approach are seen when assessment is linked to intervention decisions. Based on student performance data, intervention plans are developed and implemented and the results analyzed to shape future interventions. The intent of this process is to demonstrate useful solutions to students' learning problems, not simply describe the behavior or develop a plan. These results may be used to determine which individuals are resistant to interventions, but the goal of the intervention is to find factors that are successful in producing educational progress—that is, to determine what factors enable learning.

Clearly, intervention quality is central to the decision-making process. Quality standards to guide professional practice have been developed for intervention design and implementation steps (Flugum & Reschly, 1994; Telzrow, 2002; Upah & Tilly, 2002). Judging treatment integrity and effects are at the crux of the responsiveness-to-intervention approach. Comprehensive models are developed to assist professionals in diagnosing students' educational needs and translating those needs into intervention plans. Examples of such models are curriculum-based evaluation (Howell, Fox, & Morehead, 1993), instructional consultation (Rosenfield & Gravois, 1996), and behavioral consultation (Gutkin & Curtis, 1990; Kratochwill & Bergan, 1990). All of these models are applications of a response-to-intervention approach and each systematically uses intervention data for educational decision making. Within specific areas of student performance, technology is available for monitoring students' responsiveness to academic growth using academic

Figure 2.

PROBLEM SOLVING PROCESS

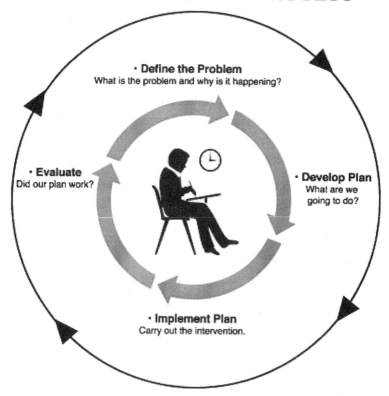

- **Define the Problem**
What is the problem and why is it happening?

- **Evaluate**
Did our plan work?

- **Develop Plan**
What are we going to do?

- **Implement Plan**
Carry out the intervention.

indicators such as curriculum-based measurement (Fuchs & Fuchs, 1986; Shinn, 1989, 1995) and indicators of social improvement (Gresham, 1999; Hintze, Volpe, & Shapiro, 2002).

Application of Responsiveness to Intervention Approaches

Various states and local educational agencies are currently supporting efforts to implement intervention-focused service-delivery systems that align with IDEA concepts. These system reform efforts are often identified as problem-solving models. This type of systemic intervention-based services is occurring in states and agencies such as Florida (School Board of St. Lucie County), Illinois (Flexible Service Delivery System applied in local agencies), Iowa (Heartland Area Education Agencies), Kansas (Northeast Kansas Educational Service Center), Minnesota

(Minneapolis Public Schools), Ohio (Southwestern Ohio Special Education Resource Center), South Carolina (Horry County Schools), and Wisconsin (Milwaukee Public Schools). The common elements among these special education service delivery systems, consistent with Figure 1, include (a) a focus on direct assessment of student behavior, (b) linking assessments to individualized educational interventions, (c) providing ongoing progress monitoring of intervention effects on student performance, (d) judging outcomes based on student data, and (e) involvement of parents at all levels of the decision-making process. Typically these interventions begin in general education environments and may continue with special education assistance when warranted. When special education eligibility decisions are made, data-based judgments include student responsiveness to interventions. These educational systems determine students' responsiveness to individualized interventions and let those data guide decisions about identification, service, and exiting.

Some agencies are using responsiveness to intervention as part of the decision-making process for determining special education eligibility (Heartland AEA, 2001; Ikeda, Tilly, Stumme, Volmer & Allison, 1996, Ikeda et al., in press). The example shown in Figure 3, developed by Kurns, Allison, Ikeda, Gruba, Grimes, and colleagues, illustrates an eligibility decision-making framework (Heartland Area Education Agency, 2000). This model uses multiple sources of data that converge to support responsible decision making for special education eligibility. Problem-solving data are collected to address questions in three areas: educational progress, student discrepancy from expected performance, and instructional need. The substantive questions corresponding to these three areas are shown in Figure 2. When making an entitlement decision, the multidisciplinary IEP team relies on convergent data from multiple sources to support conclusions. Multiple sources of data are drawn from record reviews, interviews, observations, and direct assessments of student performance, including intervention results. The central issue is to determine what interventions will ensure ongoing educational progress for the student. Such a determination involves analysis of the student's learning in relationship to setting demands, instruction, curriculum, and the environment. Conceptually sound frameworks are used for making special education eligibility decisions that incorporate responsiveness-to-intervention data.

Successful Exit of Special Education

IDEA requires that state and local education agencies develop and apply robust child-find procedures. There is no equally rigorous effort for the process of successfully exiting students from special education services. The lack of attention to exiting procedures contributes to the total number of students classified as LD (Shinn, 1986). Torgesen et al. (2001) found that 40% of students receiving services could be, but were not, exited from special education programs. When there is

Figure 3.

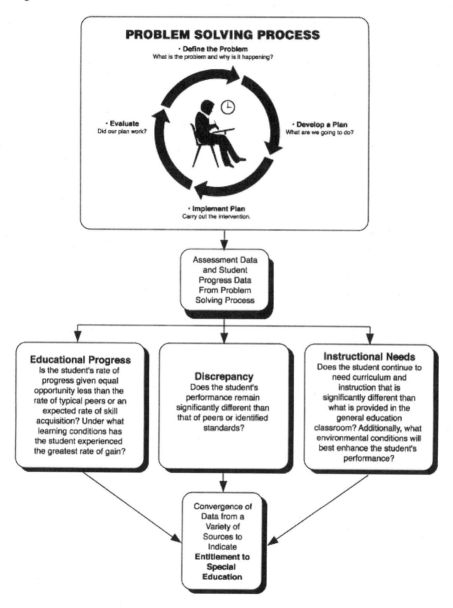

ongoing attention to the evaluation of intervention effects, teachers are more likely to make decisions about adjustments in instruction (Fuchs, Fuchs, & Fernstrom, 1992; Fuchs, Roberts, Fuchs, & Bowers, 1996). Availability of ongoing student performance data facilitates comparison to standards relevant in the general education classroom. When an IEP student's performance is comparable to general education expectations, the student can be considered for reintegration into full-time general education support (Powell-Smith & Stewart, 1998). Responsiveness-to-intervention data facilitate comparison with expected performance in the general education environment and support appropriate exiting decision making. One indicator of a successful special education system could be rate of reintegration of some students into general education.

OSEP Support for Enhancing Outcomes for Students With Disabilities

The philosophy of IDEA is a bedrock commitment to the education of children with disabilities. The Office of Special Education Programs (OSEP) has a responsibility to champion this cause, as do state departments of education, local education agencies, professional associations, parents, and individual professionals. It is the common cause that binds all parties together in a unified direction. Gresham's proposal strengthens and activates IDEA's philosophy by placing increased emphasis on the results of special education interventions. This emphasis represents an important change in professional thinking and practice (Tilly, 2002). Leadership is required for successful transformation as a new paradigm emerges (Barker, 1993). OSEP has a crucial role in ensuring that responsiveness-to-intervention practices become the next step in our national commitment to improved services for children with disabilities.

Alignment of Responsiveness-to-Intervention Practices With IDEA Philosophy

The responsiveness-to-intervention approach supports IDEA regulations. The following are illustrations of the alignment between IDEA and responsiveness-to-interventions practices by IEP teams engaged in special education decisions. Frequent monitoring of academic interventions provides evidence of individual growth rates (Fuchs, 1989; Fuchs & Fuchs, 1986; Shinn, 1989). Such data assist IEP teams in setting measurable goals as required in IDEA §300.347. With responsiveness-to-intervention data available, parents and teachers can consider ambitious growth rates as targets for student improvement across an annual goal period (§300.347).

IDEA (§300.550) supports decisions to provide instruction in the least restrictive environment (LRE). Educational services occur outside of the regular education classroom only when instruction cannot be supported with supplementary aids and services. LRE decisions should be based on trial experiences with and without supplementary aids and services, and data should be collected to allow comparison of an individual's performance under varied classroom conditions. Such decisions are consistent with the responsiveness-to-intervention methodology.

Responsiveness-to-intervention methodology matches the IDEA expectation that evaluation procedures include a variety of assessment tools and strategies to gather relevant, functional, and developmental information about the student's functioning (§300.532).

Disability Services With or Without Categorical Designations

The IDEA explicitly supports the identification of students without disability labels (§300.125): "Nothing in this Act requires that children be classified by their disability...." At the same time, OSEP requires state education agencies to report data by categories (§300.751). The inconsistency is problematic.

Professional associations have long supported students' rights without label and have adopted formal position papers promoting this policy (NASP, 1985, 1986). The response-to-intervention approach is a responsible methodology for documenting student need and supporting effective educational interventions without reliance on categories (Gresham, 1999; Reschly & Tilly, 1999; Reschly, Tilly, & Grimes, 1999). OSEP's leadership is essential in assisting educational agencies in operationalizing systems that focus on student outcomes rather than categorical diagnosis.

OSEP Support for Improvements in Professional Practices

OSEP interprets acceptable legal practices and establishes funding incentives that influence the direction of research priorities. OSEP can promote improved services for students with learning disabilities in four ways. First, it can support an aggressive research agenda to address implementation issues in a response-to-intervention methodology. Gresham's article identifies some questions that require attention. In addition, funding model sites implementing intervention-based eligibility decision-making procedures would be highly desirable. Second, as state eligibility documents are amended, OSEP can support state education agencies in defining practices that include a responsiveness-to-intervention approach. Third, it can assist states through the federal compliance monitoring processes by supporting continuous improvement process that includes due process and an emphasis on data-based approaches to the identification, service, and successful exiting of students from special education assistance. Last, OSEP's leadership is critical in setting a national agenda supporting the exchange of information about policy, procedures, practices, and research related to responsiveness-to-intervention services.

CONCLUSION

Responsiveness to intervention is the next step in the ongoing evolution of professional practices to enhance educational outcomes for students with disabilities in America. To become a reality, it requires leadership, commitment, and flexibility by national leaders at all levels in the system. In pursuing a responsiveness-to-intervention approach, the commitment to the ideals of IDEA remains unchanged. However, professional standards and practices must adapt to new technologies and be responsive to current research. A solid research base is in place to (a) support schoolwide efforts for early intervention in general education, (b) design high-quality interventions based on direct assessment of students' educational performance, (c) develop interventions that meet quality standards, (d) support general and special educators in implementing interventions, and (e) use intervention information for educational decision making. Progress is always a matter of change, refinement, and innovation. The next step is to support an intervention-oriented, data-based approach for identification, service delivery, and, when appropriate, successful exiting of students from special education.

REFERENCES

Barker, J. A. (1993). *Future edge: Discovering the new paradigms of success.* New York: Willam Morrow & Company.

Cronbach, L. (1975). Beyond the two disciplines of scientific psychology. *American Psychologist, 30,* 116–127.

Cronbach, L., & Snow, R. (1977). *Aptitudes and instructional methods.* New York: Wiley (Halstead Press).

Education for All Handicapped Children Act of 1975, 20 U.S.C. §1400 *et seq.* (statute); 34 CFR 300 (regulations published in 1977).

Epps, S., Ysseldyke, J., & McGue, M. (1984). Differentiating LD and non-LD students: "I know one when I see one." *Learning Disability Quarterly, 7,* 89–101.

Fletcher, J. M., Francis, D. J, Shaywitz, S. E., Lyon, G. R., Foorman, B. R., Stuebing, K. K, & Shaywitz, B. A. (1998). Intelligent testing and the discrepancy model for children with learning disabilities. *Learning Disabilities Research and Practice, 13,* 186–203.

Fletcher, J. M., Shaywitz, S. E., Shankweiler, D. P., Katz, L., Liberman, I. Y., Fowler, A., Francis, D. J., Stuebing, K. K., & Shaywitz, B. A. (1994). Cognitive profiles of reading disability: Comparisons of discrepancy and low achievement definitions. *Journal of Educational Psychology, 85,* 1–23.

Flugum, K. R., & Reschly, D. J. (1994). Pre-referral interventions: Quality indices and outcomes. *Journal of School Psychology, 32,* 1–14.

Fuchs, L. S. (1989). Evaluating solutions: Monitoring progress and revising intervention plans. In M. Shinn (Ed.), *Curriculum-based measurement: Assessing special children.* New York: Guilford.

Fuchs, L. S., & Fuchs, D. (1986). Effects of systematic formative evaluation: A meta-analysis. *Exceptional Children, 53,* 199–208.

Fuchs, D., Fuchs, L. S., & Fernstrom, P. (1992). Case-by-case reintegration of students with learning disabilities. *Elementary School Journal, 92,* 261–281.

Fuchs, L. S., Fuchs, D., Hamlett, C. L., Phillips, N. B., & Bentz, J. (1994). Classwide curriculum-based measurement: Helping general educators meet the challenge of student diversity. *Exceptional Children, 60,* 518–537.

Fuchs, D., Roberts, P. H., Fuchs, L. S., & Bowers, J. (1996). Reintegrating students with learning disabilities into the mainstream: A two-year study. *Learning Disabilities Research and Practice, 11*(4), 214–229.

Good, R. H., Vollmer, M., Creek, R. J., Katz, L., & Chowdhri, S. (1993). Treatment utility of the Kaufman Assessment Battery for Children: Effects of matching instruction and student processing strength. *School Psychology Review, 22,* 8–26.

Gottlieb, J., Alter, M., & Gottlieb, B. W. (1999). General education placement for special education students in urban schools. In M. J. Coutinho & A. C. Repp (Eds.), *Inclusion: The integration of students with disabilities.* Belmont, CA: Wadsworth Publishing Co.

Gresham, F. M. (1999). Noncategorical approaches to K–12 emotional and behavioral difficulties. In D. J. Reschly, W. D. Tilly III, & J. P. Grimes (Eds.), *Special education in transition: Functional assessment and noncategorical programming* (pp. 107–138). Longmont, CO: Sopris West.

Gresham, F. M., & Witt, J. C. (1997). Utility of intelligence tests for treatment planning, classification, and placement decisions: Recent empirical findings and future directions. *School Psychology Quarterly, 12,* 249–267.

Gutkin, T. B., & Curtis, M. J. (1990). School-based consultation: Theory, techniques, and research. In C. R. Reynolds & T. B. Gutkin (Eds.), *The handbook of school psychology* (pp. 577–611). New York: Wiley.

Heartland Area Education Agency (2000). *Improving children's educational results through data-based decision making.* Johnston, IA: Author

Heartland Area Education Agency (2001). *Procedures Manual for Special Education.* Johnston, IA: Author

Hintze, J. M., Volpe, R. J., & Shapiro, E. S. (2002). Best practices in systematic direct observation of student behavior. In A. Thomas & J. Grimes (Eds.), *Best practices in school psychology IV* (pp. 993–1006). Bethesda, MD: National Association of School Psychologists.

Howell, K. W., Fox, S. L., & Morehead, M. K. (1993). *Curriculum-based evaluation: Teaching and decision-making* (2nd ed.). Pacific Grove, CA: Brooks/Cole.

Ikeda, M. J., Grimes, J. P., Tilly, D. W., III, Allison, R. H., Kurns, S. J., & Stumme, J. M. (in press). Implement an intervention-based approach to service delivery: A case example. In M. Shinn, G. Stoner, & H. Walker (Eds.), *Intervention-based service delivery system.* Washington, DC: National Association of School Psychologists.

Ikeda, M. J., Tilly, W. D., III., Stumme, J., Volmer, L., & Allison, R. (1996). Agency-wide implementation of problem solving consultation: Foundations, current implementation, and future directions. *School Psychology Quarterly, 11,* 228–243.

Individuals With Disabilities Education Act, 1999. 34 C.F.R. 300 (Regulations), Regulations Implementing IDEA (1997), *Federal Register,* March 12, 1999, vol. 64, no. 48.

Juel, C. (1988). Learning to read and write: A longitudinal study of 54 children from first through fourth grades. *Journal of Educational Psychology, 80,* 437–447.

Kame'enui, E. J., & Simmons, D. C. (1998). Beyond effective practice to schools as host environments: Building and sustaining a school-wide intervention model in beginning reading. *Oregon School Study Council (OSSC) Bulletin, 41*(3).

Kaminski, R. A., & Good, R. H. (1996). Toward a technology for assessing basic early literacy skills. *School Psychology Review, 25,* 215–227.

Kaminski, R. A., & Good, R. H. (1998). Assessing early literacy skills in a problem-solving model: Dynamic Indicators of Basic Early Literacy Skills. In M. R. Shinn (Ed.), *Advanced applications of curriculum-based measurement* (pp. 113–142). New York: Guilford.

Kavale, K. A., & Forness, S. R. (1999). Effectiveness of special education. In C. R. Reynolds & T. B. Gutkin (Eds.), *The handbook of school psychology* (3rd ed., pp. 984–1024). New York: Wiley.

Kavale, K., & Forness, S. (2000). What definitions of learning disability do and don't say: A critical analysis. *Journal of Learning Disabilities, 33,* 239–256.

Kratochwill, T. R., & Bergan, J. R. (1990). *Behavioral consultation in applied settings: An individual guide*. New York: Plenum Press.

Lyon, G. R. (1996). Learning disabilities. *The Future of Children: Special Education for Students with Disabilities, 6*, 56–76.

National Association of School Psychologists (NASP). (1985). *Position statement on advocacy for appropriate educational services for all children*. Bethesda, MD: Author. http://www.nasponline.org/pdf/pospaper_aaes.pdf

National Association of School Psychologists (NASP). (1986). *Position statement on rights without labels*. Bethesda, MD: Author. http://www.nasponline.org/pdf/pospaper_rwl.pdf

National Reading Panel. (2000). *Teaching children to read: An evidence-based assessment of the scientific research literature on reading and its implications for reading instruction: Reports of the subgroups*. Bethesda, MD: National Institute of Child Health and Human Development.

National Research Council. (1998). *Preventing reading difficulties in young children*. Washington, DC: National Academy Press.

Powell-Smith, K. A., & Stewart, L. H. (1998). The use of curriculum-based measurement in the reintegration of students with mild disabilities. In M. R. Shinn (Ed.), *Advanced applications of curriculum-based measurement* (pp. 254–307). New York: Guilford.

Reschly, D. J. (1988). Obstacles, starting points, and doldrums notwithstanding: Reform/revolution from outcomes criteria. *School Psychology Review, 17*, 495–501.

Reschly, D. J., & Grimes, J. (1995). Intellectual assessment. *Best practices in school psychology III* (pp. 763–774). Washington, DC: National Association of School Psychologists.

Reschly, D. J., & Tilly, W. D., III. (1999). Reform trends and system design alternatives. In D. J. Reschly, W. D. Tilly III, & J. P. Grimes (Eds.), *Special education in transition: Functional assessment and noncategorical programming* (pp. 19–48). Longmont, CO: Sopris West.

Reschly, D. J., Tilly, W. D., III, & Grimes, J. P. (Eds.) (1999). *Special education in transition: Functional assessment and noncategorical programming*. Longmont, CO: Sopris West.

Reschly, D. J., & Ysseldyke, J. (1995). School psychology paradigm shift. In A. Thomas & J. Grimes (Eds.), *Best practices in school psychology III* (pp. 17–32). Washington, DC: National Association of School Psychologists.

Rosenfield, S. A., & Gravois, T. A. (1996). *Instructional consultation teams: Collaborating for change*. New York: Guilford Press.

Shinn, M. R. (1986). Does anyone care what happens after the referral-test-placement process? The systematic evaluation of special education effectiveness. *School Psychology Review, 15,* 49–58.

Shinn, M. R. (Ed.). (1989). *Curriculum-based measurement: Assessing special children.* New York: Guilford.

Shinn, M. R. (1995). Best practices in curriculum-based measurement and its use in a problem-solving model. In A. Thomas & J. Grimes (Eds.), *Best practices in school psychology III* (pp. 547–567). Washington, DC: National Association of School Psychologists.

Simmons, D. C., & Kame'enui, E. J. (Eds.). (1998). *What reading research tells us about children with diverse learning needs: Bases and basics.* Mahwah, NJ: Lawrence Erlbaum Associates.

Simmons, D. C., Kame'enui, E. J., Good, R. H., III, Harn, B. A., Cole, C., & Braun, D. (2000). Building, implementing, and sustaining a beginning reading model: School by school and lessons learned. *Oregon School Study Council (OSSC) Bulletin, 43*(3), 3–30.

Szasz, T. (1970). *Etiology of insanity.* Garden City, NJ: Anchor Books.

Telzrow, K. S. (2002). Best practice in facilitating intervention adherence and integrity. In A. Thomas & J. Grimes (Eds.), *Best practices in school psychology IV* (pp. 503–516). Bethesda, MD: National Association of School Psychologists.

Tilly, D. W., III. (2002). School psychology as a problem solving enterprise. In A. Thomas & J. Grimes (Eds.), *Best practices in school psychology IV* (pp. 21–36). Bethesda, MD: National Association of School Psychologists.

Tilly, D. W., III., & Flugum, K. (1995). Best practices in ensuring quality interventions. In A. Thomas & J. Grimes (Eds.), *Best practices in school psychology IV* (pp. 485–500). Washington, DC: National Association of School Psychologists.

Torgesen, J., Alexander, A., Wagner, R., Rashotte, C., Voeller, K., & Conway, T. (2001). Intensive remedial instruction for children with severe reading disabilities: Immediate and long-term outcomes from two instructional approaches. *Journal of Learning Disabilities, 34,* 33–58.

Upah, K. F., & Tilly, D. W., III. (2002). Designing, implementing and evaluating quality interventions. In A. Thomas & J. Grimes (Eds.), *Best practices in school psychology IV* (pp. 483–502). Bethesda, MD: National Association of School Psychologists.

U.S. Department of Education, Office of Special Education Programs. (2000). *To assure the free appropriate public education of all children with disabilities: Twenty-second annual report to Congress on the implementation of the Individuals with Disabilities Education Act* (Ed Pubs Publication No. EH 0116P). Jessup, MD: Author.

Vellutino, F., Scanlon, D., & Lyon, G.R. (2000). Differentiating between difficult-to-remediate and readily remediated poor readers: More evidence against the IQ-achievement discrepancy definition of reading disability. *Journal of Learning Disabilities, 33,* 223–238.

Vellutino, F., Scanlon, D., Sipay, E., Small, S., Pratt, A., Chen, R., & Denckla, M. (1996). Cognitive profiles of difficult-to-remediate and readily remediated poor readers: Early intervention as a vehicle for distinguishing between cognitive and experiential deficits as basic causes of specific reading disability. *Journal of Educational Psychology, 88,* 601–638.

Vellutino, F., Scanlon, D., & Tanzman, M. (1998). The case for early intervention in diagnosing reading disability. *Journal of School Psychology, 36,* 367–397.

Ysseldyke, J. E., Algozzine, B., & Epps, S. (1983). A logical and empirical analysis of current practice in classifying students as handicapped. *Exceptional Children, 50,* 160–166.

USING RESPONSE TO TREATMENT FOR
IDENTIFYING STUDENTS WITH LEARNING DISABILITIES

Sharon Vaughn, University of Texas

There is much to like in the Gresham review on responsiveness to treatment as an alternative approach to identification of learning disability (LD). The paper is well written, provides a comprehensive examination of the issue, and very carefully and thoughtfully builds an argument for the use of responsiveness to treatment as an approach for identification of students with LD. Gresham defines response to treatment as a "change in academic performance as a function of an intervention" (Gresham, this volume). Thus, at the essence of implementing a response-to-treatment model is an understanding that we have intervention approaches that are validated and measures that are appropriate for evaluating the progress of these interventions over time.

Though never posed directly in the form of questions, Gresham asks and answers the most pressing issues related to identification of learning disabilities. In this commentary, I have identified what I consider to be the questions addressed by Gresham and my interpretation of the answers.

Is LD Real?

Gresham presents a review of the literature that documents the overlap between students identified as having learning disabilities, mental retardation, and general low achievement. Though not presented in his paper, the overlap between learning disabilities and attention problems as well as speech and language problems is also quite large. Gresham reminds us that there is compelling and convincing data that students with learning disabilities are distinct from other low achievers in that they are often the lowest performing students. He wonders whether these data are persuasive enough to warrant identifying selected students as learning disabled. He comments, "the field of LD must be able to present more convincing evidence to conclude that LD students differ in kind from LA students and thus legitimately deserve special education and related services based on this minimal difference" (Gresham, this volume).

I think that the answer to whether there is compelling evidence to conclude that students with LD can and should be identified, and that their needs warrant special education services, is a resounding "yes." I support this statement in several ways. First, the field of LD is not unique in its challenge to establish that students identified are more than the extreme end of the distribution. Students with emotional and behavior disorders who are identified as disabled are on the extreme end of the behavioral continuum as well. With respect to vision and hearing problems, professionals decide where on the continuum of poor vision and hearing students must perform to be identified as requiring special education. Even in medicine there are no tight categories for most risk indicators. The blood pressure scores that warrant significant intervention (medication) are also points on the continuum of blood pressure scores. What all of these risk categories have in common is that at some point the risk is sufficient to require significant interventions. In education we refer to these significant interventions as special education.

Second, LD is far from unique in its struggle with a consistent and reliable definition. Even disabilities that are more widely accepted than LD, such as autism, mental retardation, and Asperger syndrome, are not consistently identified and agreed upon by professionals in the field.

The life stories of parents of youngsters with LD, youngsters themselves, and their teachers provide compelling evidence about how "real" LD is. The recognition that individuals with LD have significant learning problems that are unexpected considering their performance and abilities in selected areas has been consistently reported. Furthermore, the lifelong nature of their learning disabilities is well described (Gerber, 2001).

HOW ACCURATELY CAN WE IDENTIFY STUDENTS WITH LD?

The identification process for LD, as it is currently implemented, is an inconsistent, imperfect, expensive, and time-consuming one that does not serve the parent, teacher, or child well. There is a disconnect between the assessment measures used and the intervention or treatment needed. This gap prevents the assessment data from having adequate value to educators or parents. In other words, the assessment measures provide little or no helpful information for designing an effective treatment program for the student.

The gap between the assessment measures typically used to identify LD and treatment is reason enough to rethink how we identify students with LD. The most compelling reason, though, is the lack of support for the use of IQ-discrepancy practices as a means of identifying LD.

Gresham has a ready answer to the most obvious next question: How should we identify students with LD if we do not rely on IQ-discrepancy practices? He describes a procedure in which curriculum-based measurement can be used to identify and monitor the progress of students who are provided with an appropriate intervention. On the basis of their progress, students who make minimal gains can be identified as learning disabled.

CAN RESPONSE TO TREATMENT BE USED AS A MEANS TO IDENTIFY STUDENTS WITH LD?

Yes, response to treatment can and should be used as one of several means to identify students with LD—provided the following requirements can be met:

- *Ability to model academic growth.* Essential to the effective implementation of a response-to-treatment model is the ability to have reliable and valid measures that are sensitive to treatment and can be administered multiple times. Fuchs and Fuchs (1998) indicate that curriculum-based measurement is a promising tool for determining academic growth over time.

- *Validated treatment protocols.* For response to treatment to be an effective model for identifying students with LD, we must have systematic and validated approaches to enhancing specific target outcomes (e.g., reading decoding, reading comprehension, expressive writing, math computation, math problem solving). Furthermore, these treatment protocols need to be designed and validated in multiple settings (general and special education) and across the life span since not all students with learning disabilities are identified in the very early grades. As Gresham indicates, this is a daunting task. At this time we are furthest along in verifying validated treatment protocols in early reading and have considerable work to do in other areas.

- *Distinguishing between skill and performance deficits.* Gresham summarizes the considerable research on the importance of distinguishing between what students have not learned or are unable to learn (skill) and what they are not doing but could do. This distinction may be particularly relevant for students with behavior problems or attention problems and older learners.

■ *Detecting treatment effects/establishing cutoff criterion.* If response to treatment is going to be a measure of how and who we identify as learning disabled, then we need to have a metric for deciding whether a student has or has not responded adequately to the treatment provided. As we know, students often respond differentially to selected measures; thus, we need to determine which measure will be used to determine outcome. Furthermore, few students do not respond at all to treatment; however, many students respond to the treatment at what might be considered low or minimal effects. Thus, a criterion for what would be considered minimal response to treatment needs to be established. Finally, many students who respond to treatment initially do not sustain gains. The treatment effects may fade over time and will need to be monitored to ensure that they are not in the risk group.

In summary, while there is every reason to believe that response to treatment is a valuable procedure for identifying students with LD, it is unlikely, at least in the short run, to effectively serve as a sole procedure. The requirements needed to implement response to treatment can possibly be met for reading but few other areas. Though reading problems account for more than 80% of the primary needs of students with LD, they are presently unable to account for the learning problems of all students with LD including (a) students whose LD is in an area other than reading, (b) late-onset LD, and (c) students with recurring LD.

WHAT ARE THE POTENTIAL CONCERNS REGARDING THE EFFECTIVE USE OF RESPONSE TO TREATMENT AS A MEANS OF IDENTIFYING STUDENTS WITH LD?

There are several potential concerns relative to the effective use of a response-to-treatment model as a means of identifying students with LD. Considering these concerns can assist us in thinking about further work needed to effectively implement a response-to-treatment model.

Do we have the measurement in place to effectively implement a response-to-treatment model? As a matter of fact, we are much better prepared to implement a response-to-treatment model in early reading than in any other area. Thus, a first step might be to determine the effectiveness of the implementation of a response-to-treatment model for early reading as one of many procedures for identifying students with LD.

Do we have the treatment validity practices readily identified and verified for implementing a response-to-treatment model? Similar to the previous answer, we are much further along in the area of early reading than in any other area. Establishing models across the country to determine the extent to which these practices can be effectively implemented is an essential first-step.

Do we have the personnel and physical resources to implement a response-to-treatment model? We presently have only very small numbers of professionals who have sufficient knowledge and skills to implement a response-to-treatment model. A seemingly overwhelming number of personnel will need to be trained to implement a response-to-treatment model. Procedures and plans need to be in place to ensure that personnel are adequately trained to implement a response-to-treatment model as a means to identification. This job is substantial but can be accomplished with systematic and extensive professional development training.

Can we implement a response-to-treatment model on a large scale? If a response to treatment model is going to be implemented at a national level, the number of appropriately trained personnel needed to implement the model is staggering. This problem would be of less concern if there were high numbers of existing personnel with the knowledge, skills, and training to implement the measurement and treatment protocols and to interpret the results. Though these procedures have been implemented on a small scale with highly trained personnel in research settings, large-scale implementation is yet to be tested. This is a large hurdle to overcome.

Can we implement a response-to-treatment model across the age span? Presently, we do not have the knowledge base to implement a response-to-treatment model across the age span. Considerable work with students in fourth grade and older will be needed to establish a response-to-treatment model for these learners.

SHOULD A RESPONSE-TO-TREATMENT MODEL BE USED FOR IDENTIFYING STUDENTS AS LEARNING DISABLED?

Despite my previous reservations about our level of "readiness" for a response-to-treatment model, I am optimistic about its use as one of several procedures for identifying students with LD for the following reasons.

First, the procedures we are presently using for identifying students with LD are inadequate in many ways, and they are certainly too distantly linked to instruction. There is a pressing need to find better ways to identify students as learning disabled.

Second, the model of using treatment as a means of identifying students with LD has the highly desirable benefit of early identification and early treatment.

Third, a response-to-treatment model increases the likelihood that students who are identified as learning disabled and provided with special education are truly students who have the greatest academic needs.

Fourth, a model for response to treatment could potentially reduce the bias inherent in the present referral and identification process for students with disabilities. In particular, it is likely that a significantly higher percentage of girls will be identified as needing special education, because girls are presently referred for LD by their teachers at a significantly lower rate than boys but are not less likely to have reading disabilities (Shaywitz, Shaywitz, Fletcher, & Escobar, 1990).

REFERENCES

Fuchs, L., & Fuchs, D. (1998). Treatment validity: A unifying concept for reconceptualizing the identification of learning disabilities. *Learning Disabilities Research & Practice, 13,* 204–219.

Gerber, P. J. (2001). Learning disabilities: A life-span approach. In D. P. Hallahan and B. K. Keogh (Eds.). *Research and global perspectives in learning disabilities* (pp. 167–180). Mahwah, NJ: Lawrence Erlbaum.

Gresham, F. M. (this volume). Responsiveness to intervention: an alternative approach to the identification of learning disabilities.

Shaywitz, S. E., Shaywitz, B. A., Fletcher, J. M., & Escobar, M. D. (1990). Prevalence of reading disability in boys and girls: Results of the Connecticut Longitudinal Study. *Journal of the American Medical Association, 264,* 998–1002.

ON THE ROLE OF INTERVENTION
IN IDENTIFYING LEARNING DISABILITIES

Frank R. Vellutino, The University at Albany,
State University of New York

Gresham's white paper is an excellent document that will serve to set the stage for necessary and important dialogue concerning the role of responsiveness to intervention as an alternative to traditional psychometric/exclusionary approaches to identifying learning disabilities. It quite clearly defines the major problems associated with traditional approaches to identification as well as the important issues that need to be addressed for a full airing of his proposal that intervention-based approaches be substituted for currently used psychometric/exclusionary approaches to identifying learning disabilities. The exposition throughout is based on a comprehensive and, indeed, impressive review of the relevant literature, and Gresham uses this literature quite articulately in supporting the proposals he makes for changing current classification practices. I am acquainted with much of this literature, but not all of it, and the paper provided me with some new perspectives that I'm sure will have singularly positive effects on my own work in this area. For this I am grateful. It is clear that Gresham was the right person to ask to prepare this document and the topics I discuss in this commentary are intended only to amplify, embellish, and reinforce the excellent points he makes and the powerful arguments he forwards in this paper.

THE IQ-ACHIEVEMENT DISCREPANCY REVISITED

As pointed out in Gresham's paper, the central defining criterion of traditional approaches to identifying learning disabilities has been the IQ-achievement discrepancy, but it is clear from the research he reviewed that this criterion has little empirical justification. For example, we have found, in our own research (Vellutino, Scanlon, & Lyon, 2000), that measures of IQ are not highly correlated with measures of basic reading subskills such as word identification and letter-sound decoding, which are typically used to define reading disability. We have also found that IQ tests do not distinguish between impaired readers and normally developing readers of average intelligence, nor do they predict response to remediation or growth in reading following remediation. Gresham reviews a number of studies that have obtained similar results and he points out that the combined results make a strong case for abandoning this practice. I strongly agree. Indeed, as demonstrated by work done elsewhere (Fletcher et al., 1994; Siegel, 1988, 1989; Stanovich & Siegel, 1994), and confirmed by our own research and clinical experience, the IQ-achievement discrepancy far too often overclassifies or underclassifies children as learning disabled. But, an even more important consideration, as Gresham points out in his paper, is the fact that the IQ-achievement discrepancy provides no direction for remedial intervention and, thus, from a practical as well as from a psychometric standpoint, it has not been very useful.

However, I would like to add yet another reason for abandoning the IQ-achievement discrepancy as a criterion for defining learning disability, as alluded to but not specifically discussed by Gresham: It discriminates against disadvantaged and minority children. It has been reasonably well established that most intelligence tests are not "culture fair" and that, because of this, an untoward proportion of such children is inaccurately classified as having low intelligence. Far too many minority and disadvantaged children are not identified as learning disabled when they might very well be learning disabled. Indeed, socioeconomic status is one of the exclusionary criteria that has typically been used to define learning disability, and it is one of the least defensible. Moreover, this criterion, coupled with the IQ-achievement discrepancy, has come to define children who are classified as learning disabled as something of an "elite corps" of impaired learners who, because of the presumption that they have more learning potential than most minority and disadvantaged children, are expected to profit more from remedial instruction and education in general than minority and disadvantaged children. This point was made quite forcefully by McGill-Franzen (1994) in a penetrating paper discussing what she views as the relative ineffectiveness of compensatory and special education, especially for disadvantaged children. In this paper, McGill-Franzen argues that classification practices tied to federal funding have served to lower expectations for disadvantaged and minority children, on the part of teachers and administrators responsible for educating these children, and have also served to reinforce long-held beliefs that poverty inevitably leads to low achievement (Coleman et al, 1966). In addition, she contends that such classification practices have created institutional apathy as to the ability of public schools to effectively educate disadvantaged and minority children, and further have resulted in limited accountability of school districts serving these children. Finally, McGill-Franzen (1994) contends that current classification practices often result in a fracturing of responsibility for the child's educational program, leading to incompatibility between classroom and remedial instruction (Allington, 1993), and that such fracturing has an especially deleterious effect on minority and disadvantaged children. I think that McGill-Franzen's (1994) concerns are quite valid and have elsewhere argued forcefully against continued use of the IQ-achievement discrepancy and socioeconomic status as criteria for defining learning disability (Vellutino et al., 2000). Conversely, the use of response to intervention as the chief criterion for defining learning disability would be a far more equitable approach and serve this population of children far more effectively than these other criteria, at least in my opinion. I base this conclusion on results of intervention research discussed by Gresham, including my own (e.g., Scanlon, Vellutino, Small, & Fanuele, 2000; Torgesen, Wagner, & Rashotte, 1999; Torgesen et al. 2001; Vellutino et al., 1996), as well as on my own clinical experience with children in local schools.

MODELS OF RESPONSIVENESS TO REMEDIATION

McGill-Franzen's (1994) contention that current classification practices often result in a fracturing of responsibility for the child's educational program, leading to incompatibility between classroom and remedial instruction, brings into focus another strong feature of Gresham's paper: his discussion of various models of responsiveness to intervention. Many of the models he discusses are quite promising and are certainly worth further exploration, especially because they may ultimately provide the means by which to ensure greater compatibility between classroom and remedial instruction. For example, the three-phase model proposed by Fuchs and Fuchs (1997), as discussed by Gresham, targets classroom instruction as a possible source of the child's learning difficulties even before targeting ineptitude in the child as the source of such difficulties, and includes a trial period of diagnostic teaching to help ascertain the best approach to remediation. This model makes a great deal of sense to me, not only because it holds promise for facilitating greater precision in identifying the source(s) of a given child's learning difficulties and thereby greater precision in classifying these difficulties as experientially or biologically based, but more important, because it holds promise for preventing long-term learning difficulties in that child by (1) helping to fashion the most effective approach to remediating these learning difficulties tailored to his/her individual needs, (2) facilitating greater compatibility between classroom and remedial instruction, and (3) improving classroom instruction by requiring collaboration between the classroom teacher and the diagnostic team in identifying the source(s) of the child's learning difficulties and devising an intervention to correct them.

The contrast between response-to-intervention approaches to classification and educational planning such as that proposed by Fuchs and Fuchs (1997) and current psychometric/exclusionary approaches should be clear. Whereas the response-to-intervention approaches cast a broader net for identifying the source(s) of the child's learning difficulties by taking into account the child's educational history and home background, as well as his/her academic skills and cognitive abilities in the diagnostic process, current psychometric/exclusionary approaches typically assess only academic skills and cognitive abilities in diagnosing the problem. As a result, in evaluating the source(s) of the child's difficulties, they typically ignore classroom and other school-based and home background influences, including such factors as peer relationships, classroom culture, and early exposure to foundational educational concepts (i.e., "readiness for learning"), all of which could positively or negatively affect initial learning in a given domain.

THE IMPORTANCE OF SCHOOLWIDE INVOLVEMENT

It strikes me, however, that response to intervention approaches such as that proposed by Fuchs and Fuchs (1997) would ultimately have to become schoolwide approaches that are fashioned through the active involvement of all school personnel working in concert with parents in developing effective educational and intervention programs. Thus, it is of some importance that researchers studying early reading programs in high-performing, high-poverty schools (Adler & Fisher, 2000) have identified the following key elements of school operations and programming common to these schools: (a) administrative and instructional leadership provided by knowledgeable professionals who help to develop and implement the literacy program; (b) a dynamic core of experienced and knowledgeable teachers who actively support and learn from one another; (c) shared responsibility for student success and schoolwide concern for early reading achievement within and across grades; (d) ongoing professional development supported by the leadership; (e) collaborative planning; (f) flexible and dynamic student grouping; (g) ongoing student assessment for instruction; (h) "safety nets" for struggling readers that include a variety of remedial formats (one-to-one, small group, etc.); and (i) balanced approaches to reading instruction that include both code- and meaning-oriented pedagogies. Because current approaches to identification and classification tend to exempt all but the child's ineptitude as the source of that child's learning difficulties, the probability of such schoolwide involvement and attendant success of students in a given school is greatly lessened.

CONCERNS ABOUT THE DIAGNOSTIC TEAM

Gresham's discussion of intervention-based classification models as well as his discussion of the role of the diagnostic team in classifying children for purposes of intervention and educational planning prompted thoughts about another concern that I have, which has to do with the expertise of the participating members of the diagnostic team charged with making judgements about who should and should not be classified as learning disabled. If Gresham's concern that only 29 states require elementary school teachers to take academic coursework in reading raises red flags (and I'll bet the same is true of math, writing, and other basic learning skills), so also should the fact that this problem, no doubt, occurs regarding other members of the diagnostic team, including administrators, special educators, school psychologists, and other professionals involved in classification and remedial planning. I don't have statistics of the type cited by Gresham, but I do have direct and rather extensive contact with special educators, school psychologists, and other professionals working in local school districts (e.g., speech pathologists, occupational and physical therapists), as well as experience as an academic. It is abundantly clear to me that these professionals are typically ill-equipped, in terms of the coursework to which they have been exposed, their background knowledge, and their practical experience with basic academic skills such as reading and math, to participate as members of a diagnostic team responsible for identifying the source(s) of a child's learning difficulties in these and other academic areas and for helping to develop intervention strategies for correcting them (but see Fish & Margolis, 1988). Educational administrators typically know even less. And, if intervention approaches to classification and educational planning are to become any more effective than current psychometrically based approaches, then significant change in the way these professionals are trained needs to take place, both before and after their academic training.

LENGTH AND INTENSITY OF REMEDIATION

Another point that might be usefully made has to do with a question raised by Gresham in his concluding remarks concerning the length and intensity of intervention that might be required for successful remediation. In discussing results obtained in recent intervention studies documenting that most poor readers can be successfully remediated through one-to-one intervention (Torgesen, Wagner, & Rashotte, 1999; Torgesen et al., 2001; Vellutino et al. 1996), Gresham asks "how much one might change or otherwise deviate from this effective treatment protocol and produce similar results" (Gresham, this volume). I would first like to point out, in response to this question, that in a study cited by Gresham (Vellutino et al., 1996), my colleagues and I found that although almost 70% of the poor readers who received daily one-to-one tutoring scored within the average range on measures of basic word-level skills after one semester of remediation, a little over 50% of the children who received 2 or 3 days a week of small-group, school-based remediation also scored within the average range over the same period. This finding is important because it suggests that many impaired readers can be successfully remediated with formats that are less intensive than one-to-one tutoring. Additional support for this suggestion comes from a recent article reporting results of a meta-analysis evaluating the effectiveness of one-to-one tutoring programs for struggling readers (Elbaum, Vaughn, Hughes, and Moody, 2000). In this article, several studies were reviewed in which the progress of children who received small-group intervention was found to be comparable to that of children who received one-to-one intervention. Similar results were reported in a recent review by Hiebert & Taylor (2000) and in an article by Santa & Hoien (1999). Such findings speak for the importance of distinguishing between children who can be readily remediated in a relatively short period, using more or less intensive formats, and children who will require long-term remediation using more intensive formats. Acquiring the means for making such distinctions is, of course, a research issue, but our data suggest that a child's initial response to intervention is a reasonably good barometer of whether he/she will prove to be readily remediated or difficult to remediate. Much of the research reviewed in Gresham's paper provides supporting evidence for promising approaches to distinguishing between impaired readers who are difficult to remediate and impaired readers who are readily remediated. (e.g., Fuchs and Fuchs, 1997).

EARLY IDENTIFICATION OF AT-RISK CHILDREN

Along these same lines, it is important to point out that the number of children classified as learning disabled might be appreciably reduced if children "at risk" for early reading difficulties were identified even before being exposed to formal reading instruction in first grade. Without laboring the point, my colleagues and I are currently conducting a study evaluating a "preventative approach" to early literacy development and the results are, thus far, promising (Scanlon et al., 2000). In this study, beginning kindergartners who were deficient in emergent literacy skills such as knowledge of the alphabet and phoneme awareness were given small-group remediation (three in a group) focusing on foundational phonological skills for 2 to 3 days a week over the kindergarten year. Preliminary results suggest that the number of children who experience reading difficulties in first grade can be significantly reduced through kindergarten intervention that provides them with foundational reading skills. Conversely, our data also suggest that children who experience reading difficulties in first grade, despite having been exposed to such kindergarten intervention, may well be accurately classified as learning disabled.

SOURCES OF OPPOSITION TO GRESHAM'S PROPOSAL

Finally, it is important to briefly discuss another issue that will inevitably need to be addressed in future discussions concerning intervention-based approaches as an alternative to currently used psychometric/exclusionary approaches to identification of learning disabilities—specifically, the large incentive for inflating the number of children placed in the learning disabled category. The primary incentive for classifying children as learning disabled comes, of course, from parents and teachers, who often view this classification as a necessary vehicle for procuring more intensive and more individualized instruction than can be provided in typical classroom settings. In addition, many parents want their children to be classified as learning disabled because they have come to believe that the advantages of this classification, in terms of such benefits as special accommodations on school exams, college entrance exams, and elimination of college course requirements, outweigh the disadvantages associated with the stigma of being so classified. This problem is becoming widespread and worthy of extensive empirical research. I know of no studies that have targeted this problem, but our contact with local school districts makes it clear that the problem is real. A related problem is the increasingly large number of college students who are requesting special accommodations such as additional time to take exams or complete assignments, on the strength of the claim that they are suffering from a learning disability. Again, I have no national statistics, but at our own university, there has been well over a 50% increase in the number of students receiving special accommodations such as those just mentioned.

There is also strong fiscal incentive for classifying children as learning disabled, given that school districts receive state and federal support for special education programs in direct proportion to the number of children given this classification. Still more incentive for classifying children as learning disabled inheres in state policies that allow school districts to remove children identified as handicapped from the statewide achievement testing programs, which often positively affects district assessment profiles (Allington & McGill-Franzen, 1989; Gartner & Lipsky, 1987).

Finally, I expect strong opposition from professionals and academics who are in the test construction business and who see an intervention-based approach to identification of learning disabilities and other impediments to learning as a threat to their professional interests and perhaps even their livelihoods (Naglieri, 2001; Vellutino, 2001). Similarly, I expect strong opposition from professionals who are wedded to both the medical model of diagnosis and biological conceptions of learning disability, and, who, because of their own limitations in diagnosing the source(s) of a child's learning difficulties and generating educational solutions to such difficulties, cannot conceive of an intervention-based approach to identification of learning disabilities in lieu of a psychometrically based approach. I would advise the professionals who will ultimately be concerned with this issue to be prepared to address such opposition along with the other important issues they will need to address, so aptly and eloquently articulated by Gresham.

Summary

In sum, Gresham's paper was extraordinarily well done and will, no doubt, provide an excellent platform on which to launch what promises to be an intense and prolonged discussion as to the relative merits of using intervention-based approaches to identification of learning disabilities as an alternative to contemporary psychometric/exclusionary approaches having the IQ-achievement discrepancy as their central defining criterion. The paper outlines the major problems associated with traditional approaches to identification as well as the important issues that need to be addressed for successful dialogue of the type that is needed to effect positive change in current classification practices. Aside from untoward imprecision in identifying basic causes of learning difficulties, such approaches provide no direction for educational and remedial planning. Thus, in my opinion, they have few redeeming graces and need to be replaced by more practical and cost-effective approaches such as those discussed by Gresham. His paper should provide both practitioners in the field and those officials who will ultimately be responsible for making relevant policy decisions with enough evidence and incentive to seriously consider the course of action he proposes.

References

Adler, M. A., & Fisher, C. W. (2000). *An initial cross-case analysis of early reading programs in high-performing, high-poverty schools: How school-wide structures make a difference.* Paper presented at the Annual Meeting of the American Educational Research Association, New Orleans, April.

Allington, R. (1993). *Reducing the risk: Integrated language arts in restructured elementary schools. Report Series 1.8.* Albany, NY: National Research Center on Literature Teaching and Learning.

Allington, R. L., & McGill-Franzen, A. (1989). Different programs, indifferent instruction. In D. Lipsky & A. Gartner (Eds.), *Beyond separate education: Quality education for all* (pp. 75–98). New York: Brookes

Coleman, J., Campbell, E., Hobson, C., McPartland, J., Mood, A., Weinfeld, F., & York, R. (1966). *Equality of educational opportunity.* Washington, DC: U.S. Government Printing Office.

Elbaum, B., Vaughn, S., Hughes, M. J., & Moody, S. W. (2000). How effective are one-to-one tutoring programs in reading for elementary students at risk for reading failure? A meta-analysis of the intervention research. *Journal of Educational Psychology, 92*(4), 605–619.

Fish, M. C., & Margolis, H. (1988). Training and practice of school psychologists reading assessment and intervention. *Journal of School Psychology, 26,* 399–404.

Fletcher, J. M., Shaywitz, S. E., Shankweiler, D. P., Katz, L., Liberman, I. Y., Stuebing, K. K., Francis, D. J., Fowler, A. E., & Shaywitz, B. A. (1994). Cognitive profiles of reading disability: Comparisons of discrepancy and low achievement definitions. *Journal of Educational Psychology, 86,* 6–23.

Fuchs, L., & Fuchs, D. (1997). Use of curriculum-based measurement in identifying students with learning disabilities. *Focus on Exceptional Children, 30,* 1–16.

Gartner, A., & Lipsky, D. K. (1987). Beyond special education: Towards a quality system for all students. *Harvard Educational Review, 57,* 367–395

Hiebert, E. H., & Taylor, B. M. (2000). Beginning reading instruction: Research on early interventions. In M. L. Kamil, P. B. Mosenthal, P. David Pearson, & R. Barr (Eds.), *Handbook of Reading Research: Volume III* (pp. 455–482). Mahwah, NJ: Erlbaum.

McGill-Franzen, A. (1994). Compensatory and special education: Is there accountability for learning and belief in children's potential? In E. H. Hiebert and B. M. Taylor (Eds.). *Getting reading right from the start: Effective early interventions* (pp. 13–35). Boston: Allyn and Bacon.

Naglieri, J. A. (2001). Do ability and reading achievement correlate? *Journal of Learning Disabilities, 34*(4), 304–305.

Santa, C. M., & Hoien, T. (1999). An assessment of Early Steps: A program for early intervention of reading problems. *Reading Research Quarterly, 34,* 54–79.

Scanlon, D. M., Vellutino, F. R., Small, S. G., & Fanuele, D. P. (2000, April). *Severe reading difficulties: Can they be prevented? A comparison of prevention and intervention approaches.* Paper presented at the Annual Meeting of the American Educational Research Association, New Orleans.

Siegel, L. S. (1988). Evidence that IQ scores are irrelevant to the definition and analysis of reading disability. *Canadian Journal of Psychology, 42,* 201–215.

Siegel, L. S. (1989). IQ is irrelevant to the definition of learning disabilities. *Journal of Learning Disabilities, 22,* 469–479.

Stanovich, K. E., & Siegel, L. S. (1994). Phenotypic performance profile of children with reading disabilities: A regression-based test of the phonological-core variable-difference model. *Journal of Educational Psychology, 86*(1), 24–53.

Torgesen, J. K., Alexander, A., Wagner, R., Rashotte, C., Voeller, K., & Conway, T. (2001). Intensive remedial instruction for children with severe reading disabilities: Immediate and long term outcomes from two instructional approaches. *Journal of Learning Disabilities, 34*, 33–58.

Torgesen, J. K., Wagner, R. K., & Rashotte, C. A. (1999). Preventing reading failure in young children with phonological processing disabilities: Group and individual responses to instruction. *Journal of Educational Psychology, 91*, 579–594.

Vellutino, F. R. (2001). Further analysis of the relationship between reading disability and intelligence. *Journal of Learning Disabilities, 34*(4), 306–310.

Vellutino, F. R, Scanlon, D. M., & Lyon, G. R. (2000). Differentiating between difficult to remediate and readily remediated poor readers: More evidence against the IQ Achievement discrepancy definition of reading disability. *Journal of Learning Disabilities, 33*(3), 223–238.

Vellutino, F. R., Scanlon, D. M., Sipay, E. R., Small, S. G., Pratt, A., Chen, R., & Denckla, M. B. (1996). Cognitive profiles of difficult to remediate and readily remediated poor readers: Early intervention as a vehicle for distinguishing between cognitive and experiential deficits as basic causes of specific reading disability. *Journal of Educational Psychology, 88*(4), 601–638.

ACKNOWLEDGMENTS

The data for my own research reported in this paper were collected as part of two research projects funded by the National Institute of Child Health and Human Development (NICHD). The first project was implemented under the auspices of a special center grant awarded to the Kennedy Krieger Institute of Johns Hopkins University (NICHD grant #P50HD25806). Martha B. Denckla was the principal investigator overseeing the various projects initiated under the grant. The research reported in this paper was part of Project IV (The Reading and Language Project) implemented under a subcontract directed by Dr. Frank R. Vellutino and Dr. Donna M. Scanlon of the Child Research and Study Center of the University at Albany. The second project was implemented under the auspices of NICHD grant #5RO1HD34598. Frank R. Vellutino and Donna M. Scanlon are the co-principal investigators on this project.

CHAPTER VII: EMPIRICAL AND THEORETICAL SUPPORT FOR DIRECT DIAGNOSIS OF LEARNING DISABILITIES BY ASSESSMENT OF INTRINSIC PROCESSING WEAKNESSES

Joseph K. Torgesen, Florida State University

Traditionally, the term *learning disabilities* has been used to refer to problems acquiring academic knowledge and skills that are caused by disorders in basic psychological processes. These processing weaknesses, in turn, are caused by dysfunction of the central nervous system (U.S. Department of Education, 1977). Further, these processing weaknesses are thought to have a strictly limited impact on cognitive development; they impede the acquisition of certain academic skills while leaving many other cognitive abilities to develop normally. This conceptualization is meant to differentiate children with specific learning disabilities from those who have learning problems in school for other reasons. The idea that the processing disabilities have a relatively narrow impact on cognitive development differentiates children with *specific* learning disabilities from those who have the kind of *general* learning weaknesses associated with mental retardation. The idea that the processing limitations are intrinsic, or constitutionally based, differentiates children with learning disabilities from children whose problems learning in school are the result of lack of opportunity or motivation to learn.

The issue of concern in this paper is whether we currently have sufficient scientific knowledge to recommend that schools adopt a method of identifying children with learning disabilities that involves direct measurement of the intrinsic processing disabilities that are the presumed heart of the disorder. At present, these children are identified for special education services primarily through methods that attempt to exclude other possible explanations for the academic problem in question. By requiring children to show a discrepancy between "general learning potential" as assessed by IQ tests and performance on measures of specific academic skills, current approaches attempt to rule out explanations for learning problems associated with low general learning aptitude. Current approaches are also supposed to rule out other potential causes of the learning problem such as lack of instructional opportunities (both home- and school-based), emotional disturbance, or sensory impairment. Our current consideration of alternative approaches to classification of children with learning disabilities is motivated by widespread dissatisfaction with the IQ discrepancy approach that derives from both theoretical and empirical issues (Fletcher et al., 1998; Siegel, 1989; Stanovich, 1991).

The alternative approach to be evaluated in this paper involves direct diagnosis of learning disabilities by measurement of the *intrinsic* processing or capacity weaknesses that are presumed to underlie the academic performance problems shown by these children. Although the concept of intrinsic processing weaknesses is central to current definitions of learning disabilities, federal regulations specifying operational criteria for classification of children with learning disabilities do not require a demonstration of specific processing weaknesses for the diagnosis to be made (U.S. Department of Education, 1992). Assessment of intrinsic processing weaknesses was not included as part of the operational criteria for diagnosis of learning disabilities in current regulations because there has been little consensus about what these deficient processes are or how to measure them (Hammill, 1990). In the absence of agreement about the nature of the intrinsic processing weaknesses responsible for specific learning disabilities, it has become a category defined by exclusion.

During the two decades since the original regulations that outlined the operational criteria to "objectively and accurately" identify children with learning disabilities were formulated (U.S. Department of Education, 1977, p. 250), there have been enormous advances in our scientific understanding of learning disabilities. Thus, it is important to consider whether we currently have sufficient knowledge to shift away from discrepancy-based approaches that emphasize diagnosis by exclusion to direct diagnosis of learning disabilities based upon assessment of intrinsic processing weaknesses. Information relevant to this question will be organized into six sections:

1. a definition of intrinsic processes with distinctions between them and other kinds of mental processes;
2. evidence for intrinsic processing weaknesses as the cause of specific learning disabilities;
3. advantages of a processing approach to diagnosis over current discrepancy-based approaches;
4. difficulties in the implementation of diagnosis based on direct assessment of intrinsic processes;
5. alternatives to classification based on assessment of intrinsic processes; and

6. threats to the concept of specific learning disabilities at the levels of science and educational practice of a decision to eschew assessment of intrinsic processes as part of classification procedures.

WHAT IS MEANT BY THE TERM "INTRINSIC PROCESSING" WEAKNESSES?

When I first began my study of children with learning disabilities in the spring of 1974, the field was in a state of considerable intellectual disarray. I remember coming home from the library one evening so confused about the meaning of the word *process* from my reading about children with learning disabilities, that I sat down and looked it up in the dictionary. The dictionary gave two definitions and an example that helped to fix the meaning of the word in my mind. The first definition was "a natural phenomenon marked by gradual changes that lead toward a particular result," and the second was "a series of actions or operations conducing to an end" (*Webster's Seventh New Collegiate Dictionary*, 1965). The example provided was of the Bessemer Steel Process—a set of well specified manufacturing operations that led to the production of steel. This definition makes it clear that a process is a set of steps, operations, or developing conditions that follow one another in a certain way and that lead to, or produce, a given outcome. Of course, it is not clear that the writers of the federal definition of learning disabilities had this definition in mind when they described learning disabilities as resulting from a disorder in one or more of the basic psychological processes. However, what was very clear in 1974, and what continues to be a problem in the current literature on learning disabilities, is that the term *process* is used in many different ways to describe a broad variety of problems shown by children with learning disabilities. It was this confusion about the term *process* that led those who formulated the popular definition proposed by the National Joint Committee on Learning Disabilities (NJCLD, 1988) to delete the phrase "basic psychological processes" from their definition. This omission did not change the essential meaning of the definition, however, as the NJCLD definition still contained language about learning disorders that were intrinsic to the individual and presumed to be caused by dysfunction of the central nervous system.

THE USE OF PROCESSING LANGUAGE IN DIFFERENT LEVELS OF EXPLANATION

One of the difficulties with the word *process* is that it is not tied to any particular level of explanation of human behavior. For example, a neurophysiologist might describe a problem arising from weaknesses in the processes involved in transmission of electrical impulses within neurons or across synapses, or with the transmission of information between the hemispheres of the brain. A neuropsychologist might describe primary deficits in visual-spatial-organizational processes or complex psychomotor processes. A cognitive psychologist trained within the information processing paradigm might explain a learning difficulty in terms of deficient processes operating within working memory or problems with rate of acquisition for certain types of information in long-term memory. Finally, an educator might describe a reading difficulty in terms of deficient alphabetic decoding processes or weak reading comprehension processes.

At what level of explanation are processing difficulties best described and studied in children with learning disabilities? There are three issues to be considered here. First, as one moves from descriptions at the neurophysiological level through the neuropsychological level and the cognitive level to descriptions at the educational level, the processing operations involved in the description become progressively easier to link to the actual academic performance problem that is being explained. Since, as we will see later, one of the most difficult challenges in describing academic performance problems in terms of intrinsic processing weaknesses is to be sure of the causal connection between processes and outcomes, processing descriptions that are as close as possible to the academic problem being explained have some inherent advantages. On the other hand, the higher one goes in the explanatory hierarchy (from neurophysiological to educational), the more difficult it is to be sure the processing differences used in the explanation are intrinsic, or constitutionally based, rather than learned through varying experiences. Finally, the measurement technology and expertise required to identify processing weaknesses also varies with the level of explanation. Assessment of processes occurring at the neuronal level requires highly specialized equipment and considerable technical training, while assessment of processing differences at the educational level require less technology.

Since one purpose of this paper is to consider whether it is practical, at this point in time, to recommend that the public school system in the United States classify children as learning disabled by identifying those with intrinsic processing weaknesses, measurement considerations are of obvious importance. It is also clear that the level of explanation we choose should be below the educational level, as that is simply a description of the learning outcome. For example, when genetic influences on variability in reading skill are discussed, no one seriously entertains the idea that there is a specific gene, or combination of genes, for reading *per se*. Similarly, few would agree that it is adequate to explain the problem by indicating the child has a disability in "the reading process." Rather, the most common current explanations of genetic influences on reading growth are that they directly affect the phonological component of natural language ability (Olson, 1999). That is, specific weaknesses in the ability to process phonological information are offered as an explanation for the reading difficulty, and phonological processing disabilities are conceptualized as intrinsic or constitutionally based limitations that are significantly heritable.

To provide additional context for considering which level of explanation is most viable for diagnostic and classification purposes, consider the levels of explanation required for complete understanding of any particular of learning disability (Torgesen, 1999). This discussion starts with the recognition that children can have learning problems in school for many reasons, and that the definition of learning disabilities is meant to focus our attention on one particular type of learning problem. Thus, a theory of learning disability must be consistent with the major elements of current definitions. The first step in the development of a coherent theory of learning disabilities is to specify the learning or performance problem that is to be explained by the theory. There cannot be a single coherent theory of learning disabilities because the term *learning disabilities* refers to a heterogeneous set of learning problems. It is not reasonable, for example, to expect the same theory to explain both difficulties acquiring word reading skills and difficulties with listening comprehension. Thus, the starting point for any coherent theory of learning disabilities must be a precise and focused description of the specific academic problem to be explained.

The first level of *explanation* in a coherent theory of any type of learning disability should be a description of the basic psychological processes that are the proximal cause of the academic learning problem. This is the first level at which we might reasonably begin to attach the word *intrinsic*. It is meant to identify the fundamental information processing limitations that cause the child to have difficulty acquiring specific academic skills. It is at this level of explanation that we have made enormous advances in the last 20 years. These advances have occurred not only in understanding the basic processes that underlie development, but also in identifying those processing limitations that produce individual differences in learning outcomes for children exposed to the same learning opportunities. The reason for these advances is that the information processing paradigm, as a way of studying and explaining human behavior, has matured during this time, and it has contributed important methodologies and theoretical constructs to the understanding of human learning and behavior.

The information processing approach is of fairly recent origin (Massaro, 1975), and was developed in the aftermath of successful simulation of human cognitive achievements (i.e., chess playing, numerical calculations) by computers. The availability of clear descriptions of the different processes by which computers solve human-like intellectual problems led researchers to the hope that similar descriptions of internal psychological events intervening between receipt of a stimulus and emission of a response might also be developed for humans. Thus, information processing accounts treat mental processes in terms of different operations that are performed on information. John Flavell, an eminent cognitive developmental psychologist, explained the paradigm this way:

> Like a computer, the (human) system manipulates or processes information coming in from the environment or already stored within the system. It processes the information in a variety of ways: encoding, recoding, or decoding it; comparing or combining it with other information; storing it in memory or retrieving it from memory; bringing it into or out of focal attention or conscious awareness, and so on…the ideal goal of the information-processing approach is to achieve a model of cognitive processing in real time that is so precisely specified, explicit, and detailed that it can actually be run successfully as a working program on a computer. (Flavell, Miller, & Miller, 1993, pp. 8–9).

From the point of view of information processing theory, processes are defined as sequences of mental actions or operations that transform and manipulate information between the time it enters as a stimulus and the time a response to it is selected and executed. Although, as we shall see, some information processing skills or capacities are clearly acquired through learning and experience, others may represent basic features of the biological "hardware" that would qualify as intrinsic or constitutionally-based features of an individual child's cognitive capabilities.

Once a theory of learning disabilities has identified the deficient psychological processing operations that are the proximal cause of the poor learning outcome, the next level of explanation must involve identification of the locus of neurological impairment that is a likely cause of the limitation in processing capacity. Again, this is a requirement of any theory that is consistent with current definitions. The locus of neurological impairment might be either structural (e.g., a difference in distribution, organization, or density of neurons, or presence of anomalous formations) or functional. If a functional limitation is identified, it might use concepts from neurophysiology, and when fully understood, would probably be described as a deficient neurophysiological process. One advantage of having a precise description of processing deficiencies at the psychological level is that it can provide guidance about where to look for impairments in the central nervous system. For example, the strong evidence that one common form of reading disabilities is caused by weaknesses in phonological processing ability has directed attention to the left temporal region of the brain, which is identified with speech processing, as a possible locus of central nervous system dysfunction in children with reading disabilities. Conversely, if no structural or functional anomalies are found in these areas, this should lead to additional theory development at the psychological level.

The last level of explanation required by a complete theory of learning disabilities involves specification of the etiology of the structural or functional impairment in the central nervous system causing the disability. Like the word *process*, the meaning of the word *constitutional* is not well specified in current definitions of learning disabilities. Use of the term in the context of other elements of the definition (e.g., they are not the result of extrinsic conditions such as cultural differences or lack of opportunities to learn) would suggest that it means something similar to *inherent*; it is a biologically based disability that is present when the child is born. The prototypical cause for this kind of disability would be genetic. That is, a child's genes would either lead to the development of information processing weaknesses present at birth or would influence the emergence of processing weaknesses arising during development. However, there are clearly other causal possibilities for intrinsic, constitutionally based processing weaknesses arising from dysfunction or damage to the central nervous system (Rourke, 1989). It is also possible for children to bring "intrinsic" processing disabilities with them to school that arise as a result of environmental conditions following birth (Hallahan, Kauffman, & Lloyd, 1996).

This extended excursion into learning disabilities theory is offered in support of the idea that processing disabilities conceptualized at the psychological level are potentially most useful for widespread identification and classification purposes. As we will see shortly, there is clear evidence for intrinsic psychological processing capabilities that are given as part of our genetic or biological make-up and that are also accessible to assessment outside the medical or biological laboratory. Thus, for the remainder of this paper, the focus will be to determine whether we currently have enough scientific knowledge to begin classifying children as learning disabled by direct assessment of the psychological processing weaknesses responsible for their observed learning difficulties. I will begin by making some important distinctions among different types of psychological processes.

DISTINCTIONS AMONG TYPES OF PSYCHOLOGICAL PROCESSES

One important distinction among psychological processing operations is that between processing sequences or capabilities that appear to function automatically as part of the biological "hardware" of the brain and those that are assembled as an adaptive response to the requirements of specific tasks. When humans enter the world, they are immediately capable of complex information processing activities in a number of domains. For example, newborn infants can perform the complex mental calculations required to localize sounds without seeing the sound source (Morrongiello, Fenwick, Hillier, & Chance, 1994; Wertheimer, 1961). The brain also seems "wired" to perceive phonemic contrasts categorically, which is of enormous assistance in acquiring receptive speech capabilities (Aslin, Jusczyk, & Pisoni, 1998; Eimas, Siqueland, Jusczyk, & Vigorito, 1971). Human beings also appear to process information about the frequency of events automatically, without really thinking about it or even intending to do it, and children as young as 5 years old are as effective as college students in retaining this kind of information (Hasher & Zacks, 1984).

One of the central themes of developmental psychology over the past 20 years is the increasing recognition that human beings are capable of much more behavioral complexity and complex information processing at very young ages than was previously thought. As Fischer and Bidell (1991) suggest:

> The behavioral abilities with which human beings are genetically endowed are far richer and more complex than traditional accounts of cognitive development imply. New research seems to have revealed rich sets of perceptual and cognitive abilities in infants and young children. ... these early abilities show the starting points from which cognitive development must emerge. As starting points, they set limits or constraints on what is possible and thereby help to channel the direction of development. (p. 200)

Flavell and his colleagues (Flavell et al., 1993) go on to point out that:

> We seem to be biologically prepared to do very specific kinds of information processing and very specific kinds of learning, with no apparent links between one set of processing mechanisms (e.g., those for discriminating speech sounds) and another (e.g., those for extracting numerical information). Different theorists talk about these highly specialized capacities in different ways... Common to the various conceptions, however, is an emphasis on domain specificity—these are processes that perform very specific tasks, not all-purpose learning mechanisms. (p. 336–353)

As suggested in the comments by Flavell and his colleagues, processes can be domain-specific or they can be domain-general. A good example of a domain-general learning process that is present from birth is the ability to form representations of objects or events so they can be recognized as familiar (Werner & Siqueland, 1978). The rate at which children can learn to recognize objects as familiar predicts their later general intelligence quite accurately (Rose, Feldman, & Wallace, 1992). This recognition capability is a domain-general process and thus exerts a relatively broad influence on cognitive development: Infants who are slow to habituate to an item on repeated presentation show slower rates of general cognitive development, resulting in lower measured intelligence at later points in development. Domain-general processes or capacities are not a good place to look for explanations of specific learning disabilities, because their effect on learning and performance is so pervasive. If a child is deficient in an important domain-general information processing skill, the likely result will be mild to serious mental retardation rather than development of a specific learning disability.

A third important distinction among different kinds of information processing activities is between automatic and controlled processes. Processes that require significant amounts of attention and conscious direction are labeled controlled, while those that require little, if any attention, are labeled automatic. Activities that are initially accomplished through controlled processing activities can eventually be accomplished via automatic processes as the brain establishes highly practiced information processing routines. A clear example of this change from controlled to automatic information processing occurs during the acquisition of reading skills. Whereas the first time a word is encountered in print it must be identified using a combination of controlled processes involving phonemic analysis and contextual constraints (Share & Stanovich, 1995), after the word has been read accurately several times, the brain forms a representation of its spelling that allows it to be recognized instantly and automatically, with almost no attention or effort involved (Ehri, 1998). This transition from controlled to automatic processes is important in development, because when automatic processes are employed, mental resources are freed to accomplish other tasks. In the case of reading, when word recognition occurs automatically, processing resources are freed to construct the meaning of the passage.

The distinction between automatic and controlled processes is important for the present discussion because it has important implications for assessment of processes and capacities in children with learning disabilities. For example, one of the strongest themes in developmental psychology over the past 20 years is that older children are more adaptive and efficient in the use of controlled information processing strategies to accomplish both novel and routine tasks (Siegler, 1998). Frequently, when older children perform better than younger children on a learning or memory task, it is not because the older child has greater learning or memory capacity *per se*, but because older children more successfully use the processing resources they have to adapt to the requirements of the task.

Another factor that affects measurement of basic psychological processes is that automatic processes can become more efficient with experience. For example, as children acquire more familiarity, or exposure, to different types of information, their processing of it becomes more and more efficient. Thus, one important explanation for the significant difference between younger and older children in their ability to remember sequences of numbers involves older children's greater familiarity with numbers: They process the numbers more automatically, and thus their apparent capacity for remembering them increases (Case, Kurland, and Goldberg,

1982). In this case, what might initially be interpreted as a difference in memory capacity between older and young children can be directly explained in terms of the older child's more automatic processing of the stimuli to be remembered. Siegler's (1998) discussion of differences between older and young children's processing experience, and its relationship to their apparent processing capacities, provides a cautionary note about the potential difficulties involved in directly assessing intrinsic processing or capacity limitations in children with learning disabilities:

> Developmental improvements in performance can be produced either by an increase in the child's resources or by a decrease in the resources the child expends in doing the task. How might the resources required to do a task decrease with development? The older children know more about numbers. This greater familiarity could help them remember the numbers more efficiently. They also know more strategies, such as rehearsal, for enhancing their recall. They also are more skillful in choosing when to use the strategies they know. Thus it is clear that older children can store more material in working memory, but it remains unknown (and perhaps unknowable) whether this is because of a change in the actual capacity of working memory or because of changes in knowledge and strategies that allow more material to be stored within the same capacity. (p. 189).

Ways in Which Psychological Processes Can Cause Individual Differences in Performance

Processing differences among children can affect learning and performance in a number of ways. For example, children can be different from one another in accuracy of processing for specific types of information. A good example of this type of processing difficulty is provided in the work of Paula Tallal and her colleagues (Tallal, 1980; Tallal, Stark, & Mellits, 1985). They have developed a theory to explain language disabilities by suggesting that some children have special difficulties processing rapidly changing or rapidly sequential auditory stimuli. This difficulty arises because these children's brains do not sample acoustic signals sufficiently rapidly to note changes of short temporal duration. Thus, the children perceive some speech contrasts, or other rapid temporal events, inaccurately.

Children's performance on a variety of tasks can also be affected by differences in processing speed. Wolf and Bowers (1999) have developed a hypothesis to explain certain kinds of reading difficulties in terms of limitations in visual processing speed for letters. They hypothesize that "slow letter (or digit) naming speed may signal disruption of the automatic processes which support induction of orthographic patterns, which, in turn, result in quick word recognition" (Bowers & Wolf, 1993),

p. 70). According to this explanation, if children are sufficiently slow at visual recognition of letters, it interferes with their ability to construct a mental representation of a word's spelling that will allow the word to be recognized automatically.

Children can also be different from one another in processing capacity, and this would certainly produce individual differences in performance on tasks that place demands on this capacity. Lee Swanson and his colleagues have conducted an extensive series of studies from which they propose that children with both reading and math disabilities suffer from a domain-general capacity limitation in working memory (Swanson & Ashbaker, 2000). This hypothesis will be discussed more completely in the next section.

Finally, differences in learning or performance can also result from children's use of inefficient processing sequences, or weaknesses in the coordination of processing components.

It is by now widely acknowledged that a reliable characteristic of many learning disabled children is that they frequently appear disorganized on tasks and often do not use efficient strategies to solve problems or acquire new information (Denckla, 1994; Meltzer, 1993). However, whether these problems in organization and strategy execution qualify as intrinsic processing limitations and primary causes of learning disabilities or whether they are a secondary characteristic arising as a reaction to early and chronic academic failure is a question that is not completely resolved (Kistner & Torgesen, 1987; Meltzer, 1993). One problem with strategy-based explanations of processing weaknesses in children with learning disabilities is that strategic, or controlled, processes are highly susceptible to modification through experience, motivation, and opportunities to learn (Siegler, 1998). In studying these kinds of processes, the researcher has an especially heavy burden to show that weaknesses in their execution and organization have a biological rather than an experiential basis.

SUMMARY

A major conclusion of this section is that the most productive level to search for intrinsic processing weaknesses in children with learning disabilities is the psychological or neuropsychological level. At this level of explanation, it is possible to identify processing capacities and skills that can be conceptually linked to the biological substrate (and would thus qualify as intrinsic to the child), but which are also potentially measurable outside a medical or biological laboratory. At this level, processes are defined as sequences of specific mental actions that transform and manipulate information between the time it enters as a stimulus and the time a response to it is selected and executed. It is important to note that these processes, or processing descriptions of behavior, are theoretical constructs. There is no claim that they are a veridical representation of specific neurological events. Rather, these processing descriptions are offered to help understand reliable patterns of human cognitive functioning, and they are an intermediate level of explanation between overt behavioral outcomes (e.g., extreme difficulties acquiring automatic recall of math facts or difficulties acquiring use of phonemic decoding skills in reading) and their biological underpinnings.

There is good evidence that humans are born with biological hardware capable of supporting complex information processing routines. Since they are present from birth, these biologically based processing capabilities are part of the child's constitutionally based information processing capability and are thus subject to the same kind of variability in speed, accuracy, or capacity as other biological endowments. It is processing capabilities that arise relatively early in development, that are domain-specific, and that are relatively automatic in execution and operation that are the most likely candidates for the kind of intrinsic processing weaknesses that are referred to in definitions of learning disabilities.

EVIDENCE FOR INTRINSIC PROCESSING WEAKNESSES AS THE CAUSE OF SPECIFIC LEARNING DISABILITIES

In order to justify a recommendation that children be identified as learning disabled by showing they have the kind of intrinsic processing weaknesses that are a central part of the definition, we must have reasonable evidence that the type of learning disability specified in the definition does, in fact, exist. In order to validate the theoretical elements in the definition of learning disabilities from a scientific perspective, all that is required is to show that children with neurologically based, intrinsic learning disabilities are a reality. Even one case of a child with this type of disorder can serve as an "existence proof" for the definition and concept.

However, validation of the definition from the perspective of learning disabilities as a field in special education (which can be considered a social-political-educational movement) is much more difficult. This type of validation requires nothing less than evidence that a *significant portion* of children currently being served in learning disabilities programs fit the essential elements of the definition. It is on this point that the theoretical assumptions of the definition are most frequently attacked. For example, Jim Ysseldyke and his colleagues have reported on a program of research showing that school-identified learning disabled children cannot be differentiated from other kinds of poor learners on the basis of their patterns of intellectual abilities (Ysseldyke, 2001). In his book *The Learning Mystique*, Gerald Coles (1987) also mounted an extensive attack on the idea that most school-identified learning disabled children have neurological problems as the basis of their learning difficulties. In fact, he is right in showing that the evidence for this idea is exceedingly weak.

In contrast, the evidence in support of the idea that constitutionally based, intrinsic processing weaknesses can produce important patterns of learning disability in specific children is very strong. I will now briefly review two coherent lines of research that provide support for the concept of learning disabilities as it is presently defined.

THE THEORY OF PHONOLOGICALLY BASED READING DISABILITIES

This theory, which is perhaps the most completely developed and widely supported current conceptualization of a specific learning disability type (Torgesen, 1999), starts with the observation that children identified as severely reading disabled most frequently experience extreme difficulties in acquiring word level reading skills. Even more specifically, the outcome to be explained by this theory is these children's inordinate difficulties mastering the alphabetic principle in learning to read (Rack, Snowling, & Olson, 1992; Stanovich & Siegel, 1994). These children have extreme difficulties learning to use grapheme-phoneme correspondences to decipher words they have not seen before in print.

The psychological explanation for this overt learning difficulty is that these children have difficulties processing the phonological features of words (Liberman, Shankweiler, & Liberman, 1989). These phonological processing difficulties manifest themselves on a variety of non-reading measures including tests of phonological awareness, rapid automatic naming, verbal short-term memory, and speech perception (Manis, McBride, Seidenberg, Doi, & Custodio, 1993; Stanovich & Siegel, 1994; Torgesen, 1999). Investigation of the relationships between these variables and reading growth has been the focus of intense study over the past two decades, and there is now a substantial body of both longitudinal-correlational (Wagner, Torgesen, & Rashotte, 1994; Wagner et. al, 1997) and experimental (Bradley & Bryant, 1985; Hatcher, Hulme, & Ellis, 1994; Lundberg, Frost, & Peterson, 1988) evidence indicating that differences among children on these language skills are *causally* related to variability in the rate at which children acquire early word reading abilities.

At the next level of explanation, the neurobiological locus of the specific processing weakness, there is consistent evidence indicating that poor readers exhibit disruption primarily but not exclusively in the left hemisphere serving language. Thus, neurobiologic investigations using postmortem brain specimens (Galaburda, Menard, & Rosen, 1994), brain morphometry (Filipek, 1996), and diffusion tensor magnetic resonance imaging (Klingberg et al., 2000) suggest that there are subtle structural differences in several regions of the brain between children who are learning to read normally and children with reading disabilities. There is also emerging evidence from a number of laboratories using functional brain imaging that indicates an atypical pattern of brain organization in children with reading disabilities. These studies show reductions in brain activity while performing reading tasks usually, but not always, in the left hemisphere (Shaywitz et al., 2000). In a recent summary of the evidence concerning the neurobiological substrate for specific reading disabilities, Zeffiro and Eden (2000) conclude that, "the combined evidence demonstrating macroscopic, morphologic, microscopic neuronal, and microstructural white matter abnormalities in dyslexia is consistent with a localization of the principal pathophysiological process to perisylvian structures predominantly in the left hemisphere" (p. 23). However these authors also hint at the possible need to enlarge our conceptualization of the biological differences between dyslexic and typical children by pointing out that there is emerging evidence for brain abnormalities in these children extending beyond the classically defined language areas.

At the level of etiology of the neurobiological and processing differences that cause difficulties acquiring accurate and fluent word reading skills, there is strong and consistent evidence that these kinds of information processing weaknesses are significantly heritable (Olson, 1999). That is, reading disabilities run in families, and a child with a parent who has a reading disability is approximately 8 times more likely to have a reading difficulty than a child of unaffected parents.

Although the theory of phonologically based reading disabilities is widely accepted at present, there are several interesting problems remaining that are relevant to the issues considered in this paper. The most fundamental question involves the nature of the specific processing limitation that interferes with performance on both reading and non-reading measures of phonological skill. For example, oral language measures of phonological awareness are strongly predictive of difficulties acquiring alphabetic reading skills, but phonological awareness is defined as a kind of knowledge and understanding about words and phonemes, not as a basic psychological processing capability (Wagner & Torgesen, 1987). In other words, deficits in phonological awareness are an outcome of processing weakness and are not a direct measure of an intrinsic processing disability. It is true that children must engage in phonological processing (the processing of phonological information) in order to succeed on measures of phonological awareness, but the processing required on phonological awareness tasks is also supported by knowledge about words and phonemes that is acquired through experience and instruction. The causal relationship between phonological awareness and reading is actually reciprocal (Ehri, 1989; Morais, Alegria, & Content, 1987; Perfetti, Beck, Bell, & Hughes,

1987); differences in initial levels of phonological awareness cause different success in learning to read, and different responses to early reading instruction cause further differences in growth of phonological awareness.

Currently the two leading hypotheses concerning the information processing weaknesses that causes performance difficulties on both measures of phonological awareness and alphabetic reading skill are a speech-specific perceptual processing problem (Studdert-Kennedy & Mody, 1995) and a more general problem processing rapidly changing or rapidly successive acoustic stimuli (Tallal, 1980). It is interesting that measures of neither of these information processing skills are used as widely as measures of phonological awareness to predict the emergence of reading difficulties in young children or to verify the diagnosis of specific reading disability in older children.

Another point of controversy within the theory of phonologically based reading disabilities at present concerns the question of whether rapid automatic naming tasks are primarily measures of phonological processing skill or whether they measure a different kind of processing capability that influences aspects of reading growth other than the initial attainment of accuracy in using alphabetic reading strategies. For example, Wolf and Bowers (Bowers, Golden, Kennedy, & Young, 1994; Wolf & Bowers, 1999; Wolf, 1991) and their colleagues have argued against viewing rapid automatic naming tasks as primarily phonological in nature, and instead they emphasize the visual and speed components of these tasks. They propose that rapid naming tasks assess the operation of a "precise timing mechanism" that is important in the formation of the visually based representations of words that allow them to be recognized as whole units in text. If Wolf and Bowers are correct, this would mean that that an additional (other than phonological), as yet unspecified processing weakness causes reading failure in some children.

A final issue that is important in the present context is that individual differences in phonological awareness, which is the primary measure of phonological processing capability used in research and diagnosis of reading disabilities, are only roughly 50% heritable. The other half of the variability in phonological awareness is produced by environmental factors, such as the language environment in the home and factors related to socioeconomic status (Hecht, Burgess, Torgesen, Wagner, & Rashotte, 2000). Further, we know that phonological awareness and reading have a reciprocal causal relationship (Wagner et al., 1997). Thus, in current practice, we have strong evidence that one of the most commonly used measures of children's intrinsic processing weaknesses in the phonological area is influenced both by constitutionally based differences in processing capability and by environmental/instructional factors at home and school.

THE NONVERBAL LEARNING DISABILITIES SYNDROME

Children with nonverbal learning disabilities (NLD) were originally identified by their particularly poor performance on mechanical arithmetic tasks (Rourke & Finlayson, 1978; Rourke, Young, & Flewelling, 1971). Over the past 30 years, Rourke and his colleagues have expanded their description of these children's academic difficulties to include problems with graphomotor skills (early problems with printing and cursive writing), difficulties in reading comprehension, mathematical reasoning, and tasks in science that involve complex concept formation. In Rourke's work, it is the *pattern* of strengths and weaknesses in academic skills, rather than their absolute levels, that is the most defining feature of the syndrome. Thus, children with NLD show striking weaknesses in math computation skills *relative* to their word recognition and spelling skills. Their deficits in reading comprehension are also relative to their much stronger word-level reading skills. These children show persistent difficulties in academic subjects that require problem solving and complex concept formation relative to their strengths on tasks that require simple rote learning. Children with NLD have also been shown to have quite severe social/behavioral problems.

Rourke's theory does not identify intrinsic cognitive deficits within an information processing model of mechanical arithmetic or other academic outcomes. Rather, he describes these children's intrinsic processing weaknesses in terms of a pattern of neuropsychological assets and deficits. The theory indicates how a core of primary neuropsychological difficulties involving tactile perception, visual-spatial-organizational skills, and complex psychomotor functions lead to a variety of difficulties with academic and social/behavioral outcomes.

Rourke's theoretical description of children with NLD also includes explicit discussion of areas of normal cognitive development. Early in development, these areas of strength include auditory perception, simple motor behaviors, and rote memory ability. Later, these intact areas of functioning produce normal levels of skill in phonological processing, receptive language, verbal knowledge and associations, and verbal output. As with outcomes at the academic and social skill level, it is the pattern of performance (strength versus weaknesses) that is most important in identifying children for the diagnosis of NLD. Thus, it is performance deficits on visual-spatial-organizational skills relative to performance on measures of vocabulary, or relative deficits on measures of complex motor versus simple motor skills, that are considered the most reliable indicators of the diagnosis.

The major locus of neurological impairment in children with NLD, according to Rourke's theory, is in the right cerebral hemisphere. Specifically, he states that "the necessary condition for the production of the NLD syndrome is the destruction or dysfunction of white matter that is required for intermodal integration. (For example, a significant reduction of callosal fibers or any other neuropathological state that interferes substantially with 'access' to right hemispheral systems [and thus, to those systems that are necessary for intermodal integration] would be expected to eventuate in the NLD syndrome)"(Rourke, 1988, p. 312).

According to the theory, each individual will manifest specific aspects of the NLD syndrome depending upon both the total amount of white matter that is affected and upon the location and stage of development at which the white matter was damaged.

In terms of etiology, Rourke views the NLD syndrome to be the "final common pathway" for a number of different conditions that produce white matter disease or dysfunction (Rourke, 1995). Examples of such conditions include head injury involving shearing of white matter, hydrocephaly, treatment of acute lymphocytic leukemia with large doses of X-irradiation for a long period of time, congenital absence of the corpus callosum, or significant tissue removal from the right cerebral hemisphere. Other etiologies that might produce the kind of white matter destruction or dysfunction associated with the NLD syndrome include teratogenic effects between conception and birth and extremely low birth weight itself. At present, there is no evidence that NLD is transmitted genetically, except as specific diseases that produce white matter damage may be transmitted genetically (Rourke, 1995).

If it is true that Rourke's neuropsychological assessments are valid measures of intrinsic cognitive processing weaknesses in children with NLD, then his approach to assessment could serve as a prototype for the type of process-oriented direct diagnosis of learning disabilities that is being discussed in this paper. The diagnosis does not depend on the presence of a discrepancy between general IQ and academic achievement, but rather on the identification of a pattern of strengths and weaknesses in neuropsychological functioning that are the core of the learning disability being identified. For Rourke, the diagnosis is made at the neuropsychological level, and the academic and social outcomes are simply the common expression or phenotype of the disorder (Rourke, 1995).

One continuing weakness of the theory of nonverbal learning disabilities, from the present point of view, is that it does not clearly specify how the cognitive, or neuropsychological, limitations of NLD children actually produce the primary academic symptoms such as difficulties with mechanical arithmetic. A useful addition to the theory would be the development of a more complete information processing model of their problems acquiring arithmetic skills. This model would add to the theory in two ways. First, it would help to refine our understanding of NLD children's specific difficulties in acquiring arithmetic skills in a way that might suggest remedial interventions. Second, it might also help to clarify or validate theoretical statements about the underlying cognitive limitations of NLD children. Such a model is important if tight theoretical links are to be established between the academic performance problem and the intrinsic cognitive disabilities of NLD children. A problem that is associated with this latter issue is that the theory has been developed primarily from clinical observation and interpretation of empirical data that is exclusively correlational. Although statements about causality in the theory are embedded within a comprehensive model of neuropsychological development, they have not been subject to rigorous analysis of causal relationships in longitudinal-correlational studies or treatment-intervention studies.

SUMMARY

There is very strong evidence that current definitions of learning disabilities are, in fact, a valid description of the learning difficulties of many children. For the theory of phonologically based reading disabilities, the strongest evidence for intrinsic cognitive weaknesses as the cause of the reading disability comes from the consistent evidence that the phonological component of reading skills is strongly heritable (Olson, 1999). For the NLD theory, this evidence comes from neuropsychological studies of brain-behavior relationships in which specific anomalies within the central nervous system have been reliably associated with patterns of performance on neuropsychological measures (Rourke, 1995).

In spite of this evidence for the validity of the intrinsic processing component of the definition, however, serious problems remain in terms of reliable assessment of the critical processing weaknesses that are causally related to the academic outcomes. In the case of phonologically based reading disabilities, the tasks that are most commonly used to predict reading disabilities or to establish the diagnosis in older children are not direct measures of the processing weaknesses that are fundamental to the disorder. In the case of NLD, evidence for causal relationships between the specific neuropsychological problems identified in the syndrome and the academic outcomes associated with the syndrome is still relatively weak.

ADVANTAGES OF A PROCESSING APPROACH TO DIAGNOSIS OVER CURRENT DISCREPANCY-BASED APPROACHES

If it were possible to reliably identify children with learning disabilities by directly assessing their intrinsic processing weaknesses, advantages over current aptitude-achievement discrepancy approaches would be apparent in three areas. First, it would allow identification of the learning disability very early in the instructional process so that preventive, rather than remedial, instruction could become the norm. We now know a great deal about the negative consequences to children of serious academic failure during the early years of schooling (Cunningham & Stanovich, 1998; Kistner & Torgesen, 1987; Stanovich, 1986), and discrepancy approaches to diagnosis require the child to show significant failure in basic academic subjects before the diagnosis can be made. Recent evidence (Torgesen, Rashotte, & Alexander, 2001) suggests that the costs of waiting to intervene for children who have serious reading disabilities may be enduring difficulties in reading fluency that are extremely difficult to overcome.

A second advantage of process assessment, or primary diagnostic, approaches over discrepancy-based approaches is that they will not arbitrarily exclude children from receiving instruction that is appropriate to their educational needs. For example, discovery of the core phonological problems associated with specific reading disability has had at least one unanticipated consequence. The ability to assess these core language problems directly has led to the discovery that the early word reading difficulties of children with relatively low general intelligence are associated with the same weaknesses in phonological processing that interfere with early reading growth in children who have large discrepancies between general intelligence and reading ability (Fletcher et al., 1994; Share & Stanovich, 1995; Stanovich & Siegel, 1994). This discovery is consistent with recent reports from intervention studies that general verbal ability does not predict growth in early word reading ability when differences in phonological ability are controlled (Torgesen et al., 1999; Vellutino et al., 1996). It is also consistent with findings that discrepant (IQ higher than reading ability) and non-discrepant (IQ similar to reading ability) groups show a similar rate of growth in word-level reading skill, both during early elementary school (Foorman, Francis, Shaywitz, Shaywitz, & Fletcher, 1997) and into early adolescence (Francis, Shaywitz, Stuebing, Shaywitz, & Fletcher, 1996).

Thus, to exclude children from special instruction designed to help them acquire good word-level reading skills because their reading ability is not significantly discrepant from their general intelligence level fails to recognize that they have the *same learning handicap* as children who score higher on tests of general intelligence. The learning handicap in both cases involves weaknesses in phonological processing ability. Children with this particular handicap respond equally well to explicit and intensive instruction in phonological awareness and phonemic decoding skills, regardless of their level of general intelligence (within the broadly "normal" range) (Torgesen et al., 1999).

The final potential advantage of an approach to diagnosis involving identification of basic processing weaknesses involves benefits for instruction. If we had full understanding of the component processes and knowledge required to perform specific academic tasks, and we could measure these component processes and knowledge accurately in children, this would be of enormous potential benefit for instruction. An example from the research on reading disabilities can serve to illustrate this potential in two ways.

Although we have already acknowledged that measures of phonological awareness do not directly assess an intrinsic processing disability, they do assess a kind of knowledge about phonemes and an ability to process them in specific ways that is causally related to ability to acquire alphabetic reading skills. Children who cannot successfully perform simple measures of phonological awareness in kindergarten are highly likely to experience difficulties learning to read (Wagner et al., 1997). There is also a powerful convergence of evidence (National Reading Panel, 2000) that special attention to stimulating phonemic awareness in young children (particularly those who have weaknesses in this area) helps them to learn to read more easily. Although instruction to build phonemic awareness does not necessarily remediate children's intrinsic weaknesses in phonological processing, it does help them to acquire a specific kind of knowledge and skill required in learning to read. So, even if a fundamental processing weakness is not directly remediable, knowing about its presence in specific children may direct our attention to the need for special and/or sustained instruction to build the specific reading or pre-reading skills that the processing weakness makes it difficult for the child to acquire.

An even more dramatic, albeit still speculative, approach to direct intervention for children's processing weaknesses is illustrated in the work of Tallal and her colleagues (Tallal et al., 1996; Merzenich et al., 1996). These investigators have reported success in directly modifying children's ability to process the rapidly changing or rapidly successive features of auditory signals. In effect, they claim to have a technique that can change the way the brain processes speech, and other auditory signals, so that perception and understanding of speech and language is improved. These effects have been documented primarily for language comprehension in children with severe language disabilities, but some evidence has also been reported that the method can lead directly to improvements in phonemic awareness (DeMartino, Espresser, Rey, & Habib, in press; Habib et al., 1999). This latter finding is consistent with the idea that the method may have some use in treating the core information processing deficits of children with developmental dyslexia. Because negative results for this method and its theory are also being reported (cf. McAnally, Hansen, Cornelissen, & Stein, 1997; Mody, Studdert-Kennedy, & Brady, 1997; Nittrouer, 1999), its applicability as a widely useful intervention technique for children with reading disabilities is still uncertain. Although the field of learning disabilities is rightfully wary of instructional methods that claim to affect basic processing capabilities and thus to improve academic learning outcomes (Hallahan

& Cruickshank, 1973; Hammill & Larson, 1974; Torgesen, 1979), we must remain open to genuine scientific achievements that may be powerfully beneficial to many children.

SUMMARY

Direct diagnosis of the processing weaknesses of children with learning disabilities has three important advantages over IQ-discrepancy approaches. First, a processing approach to diagnosis would not require that the child endure a period of failure in school before the diagnosis was made. This would encourage early intervention and prevention of learning difficulties so that many of the effects on learning attitudes and lost opportunities for academic growth that are the result of failure could be avoided. Second, direct assessment of processing weaknesses would allow instruction to be targeted to all children who have common learning handicaps, and not just to those who satisfy an arbitrary discrepancy criterion. Finally, identification of children's intrinsic processing weaknesses has the potential, at least, to help focus instruction in areas of greatest need.

DIFFICULTIES IN IMPLEMENTATION OF DIAGNOSIS BASED ON DIRECT ASSESSMENT OF INTRINSIC PROCESSING WEAKNESSES

From the material discussed thus far, it is clear that direct diagnosis of learning disabilities by assessment of the intrinsic processing limitations that cause them has a number of important advantages over current discrepancy-based approaches. Conceptually, the process assessment approach is more consistent with definitions that specify deficits in psychological processing capabilities as the proximal cause of poor academic outcomes in children with learning disabilities. As we have just seen, the process approach to diagnosis would also support early identification and intervention as well as targeting of instruction to both the children and in the specific cognitive/neuropsychological areas of greatest need. However, the utility of approaches that emphasize assessment of psychological processing strengths and weaknesses is also critically dependent upon a knowledge base about human learning and cognitive functioning that is not available now, nor is it likely to be available in the immediately foreseeable future. In this section I will briefly describe a range of difficulties that preclude the widespread use of process-oriented approaches to the diagnosis of learning disabilities in present practice.

THE KNOWLEDGE BASE REQUIRED TO SUPPORT PROCESS ASSESSMENT AS A DIAGNOSTIC APPROACH

Current federal regulations specify that children may be identified with learning disabilities that affect learning outcomes in any one of seven areas: 1) oral expression, 2) listening comprehension, 3) written expression, 4) basic reading skill, 5) reading comprehension, 6) mathematics calculation, or 7) mathematics reasoning. A well validated theory of each of these types of learning disorder is required to support the kind of diagnostic approach being evaluated in this paper. To justify diagnosing learning disabilities by assessing the intrinsic psychological processing weaknesses that supposedly underlie them, we must have a well-established understanding of the nature of those processes. Our theoretical understanding of each of these areas of learning disability must start with agreement about how the learning problem, at the outcome level, is to be specified. For example, what exactly is meant by a problem in "written expression"? Can children have more than one kind of problem in this area? If so, what are the several types (and how should each be measured)?

Next, we must be able to identify the specific psychological processing weaknesses that cause the problem with learning outcome. This is extremely difficult to do: It requires several lines of converging evidence to be at least reasonably confident about causality in psychological theory. For example, in the well developed theory of phonologically based reading disabilities, we have evidence from three lines of research that phonological weaknesses are causally related to problems acquiring basic reading skill. In the most convincing research, phonological processing weaknesses have been indexed by performance on measures of phonological awareness. Evidence that individual differences in phonological awareness are causally related to the early growth of alphabetic reading skills comes from: 1) both standard and causal modeling studies of longitudinal-correlational data (Mann, 1993; Stanovich, Cunningham, & Cramer, 1984; Wagner et al., 1994; Wagner et al., 1997); 2) studies showing that older reading disabled children are more impaired in phonological awareness than younger, normal readers matched to them on reading level (Bowey, Cain, & Ryan, 1992); and 3) true experiments that show improved growth in word-level reading skills as a result of prior training in phonological awareness (Cunningham, 1990; Hatcher, Hulme, & Ellis, 1994; Lundberg et al., 1988; Torgesen, Morgan, & Davis, 1992).

When performance on rapid automatic naming tasks is used as a marker for phonological processing difficulties (or some other processing disability), there are two sources of evidence for their causal role in the development of early word reading ability: 1) standard and causal modeling analyses of longitudinal-correlational data

(Felton & Brown, 1990; Wagner et al., 1994, Wagner et al., 1997; Wolf & Goodglass, 1986); and 2) differences between younger normal and older reading disabled children matched for reading level (Bowers et al., 1994).

There are beginning attempts to specify the psychological processing problems associated with other forms of academic failure (Berninger, 1994; Berninger & Graham, 1998; Geary, 1993; Geary, Hamson, & Hoard, 2000; Rourke, 1995), but none of these theories is as well developed as the theory of basic reading difficulties caused by phonological processing weaknesses. As an illustration of the difficulties involved in establishing causal relationships between intrinsic processing limitations and learning outcomes, consider the work of Lee Swanson and his colleagues in studying the role of domain-general capacity limitations in working memory as a cause of problems in word reading ability, reading comprehension, and math calculation skills. In a careful and extensive series of studies (Swanson, 1994; Swanson, 1999; Swanson & Alexander, 1997; Swanson & Sachse-Lee, in press), Swanson and his colleagues have shown that children with learning disabilities in either reading or math perform more poorly than typical learners on measures of working memory that require children to both store and process information at the same time. Because of specific correlational patterns in the data, Swanson argues that at least part of the math and reading difficulties of these children is caused by a domain-general limitation in working memory capacity. Apart from the difficulties inherent in arguing the presence of a constitutionally based *domain-general* processing weakness as the cause of *specific* learning disabilities, Swanson also must establish that this domain-general capacity limitation is the cause of the learning problems and has not, in fact, been caused by them. Thus far, none of the three categories of causal evidence described earlier consistently supports the hypothesis that constitutionally based, or inherent, domain-general limitations in working memory capacity actually cause specific learning disabilities in reading or math.

It is, in fact, very likely that almost all children with learning disabilities will show performance problems on complex measures of working memory, because these tasks draw so heavily on a variety of knowledge and skills that are acquired during successful learning experiences. Siegler (1998) makes explicit the difficulties involved in interpreting performance problems on these tasks when he describes the various factors that can contribute to differences between older and younger children on many memory tasks:

> One explanation is that older children have superior basic processes and capacities. In terms of the computer metaphor, this means that development occurs in the hardware of the system—its absolute information processing capacity or its speed of operation. A second explanation emphasizes strategies. Older children know a greater variety of strategies than young

children and use them more often, more efficiently, and more flexibly. A third explanation highlights metacognition—knowledge about one's own cognitive activities. Older children better understand how memory works; they use this knowledge to choose strategies and allocate memory resources more effectively. Finally, older children have greater prior knowledge of the types of content they need to remember or process; this greater content knowledge may be a major source of their superior memory. (p. 178)

It is easy to imagine how the functional capacity of working memory will be affected by the chronic learning failures experienced by children with learning disabilities. Since early failure affects motivation to learn or succeed in school, children become less engaged in putting consistent effort into school learning tasks (Kistner & Torgesen, 1987). Not only does this affect acquisition of new knowledge across many domains, but it also undermines growth in the control processes and strategies that help children adapt successfully when asked to perform complex tasks such as those used to measure working memory. In this way, it is plausible that domain-general limits in the *functional capacity* of working memory would be characteristic of many children with learning disabilities. While it is important to know about these domain-general limitations (because they will affect these children's adaptation to new learning challenges and limit their success on complex tasks), if they arise as a result of chronic failure caused by other domain-specific processing limitations, then they are secondary characteristics (Torgesen, 1993) and not the kind of intrinsic processing limitations specified in the definition.

In sum, to support the widespread application of a diagnostic process that involves the identification of intrinsic processing disabilities, we will need substantial concurrence about what the critical intrinsic processes are that affect every type of learning disability specified by the definition. For almost all of the learning and skill outcomes specified in the definition, it is possible to find an isolated study (or a single investigator) that purports to have discovered a unique processing disability to explain the learning difficulty. However, emerging speculative scientific understanding is not sufficient justification for advocating widespread, everyday measurement of these processes by school psychologists or diagnosticians. For this level of application, we require converging evidence from many different investigators, as well as compelling theoretical descriptions of the mechanisms by which the processing disability acts as a proximal cause of the learning difficulty.

DIFFICULTIES IN THE ASSESSMENT OF PSYCHOLOGICAL PROCESSES THEMSELVES

In his discussion of the difficulties involved in diagnosing the presence or absence of specific processing capabilities in children, Flavell (Flavell et al., 1993) described them as "many, varied, and very, very troublesome"(p. 320). In their most general form, these problems arise because of the complex organization and interactions among processes and knowledge in all academic learning and performance outcomes. As Flavell and his colleagues point out,

> the mind is a very highly organized device, one whose numerous 'parts' are richly interconnected to one another. It is not a collection or aggregate of unrelated cognitive components, but rather a complexly organized system of interacting components...each process plays a vital role in the operation and development of each other process, affecting it and being affected by it. This idea of mutual, two-way interactions among cognitive processes is an exceedingly important one. (p.3)

Any deficit in academic outcome or performance that fits the definition of a learning disability always involves a complex admixture of a processing weakness (or weaknesses) present at some point in development (perhaps not even concurrently present), an instructional context in which that processing weakness operates, the child's motivational and emotional reaction to the learning difficulties caused by the processing weakness, and the domain-specific knowledge acquired to support performance on the task. As children become older and acquire longer learning histories, measurement ambiguity increases until, when measuring a "psychological processing disability" in a 9-year-old child with suspected learning disabilities, it is extremely difficult to be certain that what we have identified is a constitutionally based, or intrinsic, processing disability.

With this general description of the complexities of cognitive diagnosis as a background, let us now consider three specific problems that make diagnosis of learning disabilities by identifying intrinsic processing weaknesses a daunting prospect. First, psychological processing weaknesses in school-aged children can be identified accurately only by multiple measurements that vary from one another in theoretically meaningful ways. For example, in order to establish that a child has specific difficulties processing rapidly changing or rapidly sequential aspects of the auditory signal (Tallal's temporal processing hypothesis), one would have to present a series of stimuli that required processing across varying temporal durations. Only if the child showed an aberrant effect of rapid, as opposed to slower changes, could one infer that the child was particularly affected at rapid rates of change. Since measurement of many of the basic processing skills underlying poor performance on academic tasks is likely to require very precise delivery of stimuli and/or precise measurement of response times under conditions that eliminate potentially distracting or confounding stimuli, there are likely to be enormous practical difficulties involved in assessing the basic processes and capacities that are alluded to in definitions of learning disabilities.

Another problem with assessing basic processes and capacities is that, as we attempt to assess them outside the context of the task for which they are purportedly required, we run a serious risk of distorting them. As Ericsson (in press) has pointed out, "when investigators design tasks that minimize the relevance of prior knowledge and eliminate redundant stimuli, all these factors combined are likely to induce processes mediating performance that have limited relevance to behavior in everyday life" (p. 12). In other words, humans adapt to the requirements of single, or simple tasks by trying to use the most efficient strategy possible. Strategies that enhance performance on a simple task might actually interfere when the processing skill supposedly measured by that task is embedded in a more complex task environment.

A final difficulty in diagnosing the basic psychological processing weaknesses responsible for difficulties in a particular academic domain is that performance on academic tasks, for which skill is acquired over time, is likely to depend on control processes or knowledge structures that are not required on simpler tasks. These more complex integrative or management processes and knowledge structures will not be assessed when single or elemental processes are measured. The example of long-term working memory is relevant here. When people are first exposed to tasks that are unfamiliar, their performance is tightly constrained by the limited capacity of their working memory. However, these rigid constraints of working memory tend to disappear once individuals have had sufficient skill-building experience with the tasks (Ericsson & Kintsch, 1995). Acquiring almost any academic skill involves acquisition of problem solving routines and knowledge structures that help one to appear more efficient in processing information on that task or in related domains. If relatively small differences in processing capacity or skill give rise to very different learning histories, or if different motivational patterns or learning opportunities produce similar differences in skill acquisition, children will manifest very different information processing skill profiles after several years. The essential point here is that acquisition of academic skills themselves has such an important effect on a child's processing capabilities that it becomes very difficult, indeed, to determine which processing weaknesses are intrinsic and which are acquired.

SUMMARY

There are two very difficult problems that severely limit the viability of approaches to the diagnosis of learning disabilities that depend upon identification of intrinsic or constitutionally based psychological processing weaknesses. The first problem is that we do not have a complete understanding of the psychological processing capabilities that are required to attain good learning outcomes in all the areas specified in the definition and regulations. Although individual psychologists, in school or private practice, often speculate about the specific processing weaknesses that underlie a child's academic performance problems, these speculations are most often not supported by reliable scientific evidence. They are a kind of "psychometric phrenology" that has limited diagnostic reliability or instructional usefulness.

The second problem involves technical issues that interfere with the valid assessment of basic psychological processing weaknesses within the complexly organized cognitive systems of children who have substantial learning histories. It is most difficult to know for certain whether performance problems on psychological tests reflect intrinsic processing limitations or whether performance is limited by deficits in acquired knowledge structures and acquired automatic processing routines.

Overall, the foundation for reliable and valid assessment of the intrinsic psychological processing weaknesses of children with learning disabilities is not strong enough to recommend it for widespread application in schools. The premature use of process-oriented approaches to diagnosis and treatment has lead the learning disabilities field down many blind alleys (Hallahan & Cruickshank, 1973; Torgesen, 1979) in the course of its history. Although there is now good evidence that current definitions of learning disabilities are valid for many children, we are still not ready to directly apply the concept of intrinsic processing weaknesses in the routine diagnosis of learning disabilities in school. We will now consider an alternative that, although it does not involve assessment of intrinsic processing weaknesses, is still consistent with the definition and may enable critical early interventions to be more widely applied for children with learning disabilities.

ALTERNATIVES TO CLASSIFICATION BASED ON ASSESSMENT OF INTRINSIC PROCESSES

To be considered as an improvement over current diagnostic procedures for children with learning disabilities, any alternative must meet several important criteria. First, it must support identification of children with learning disabilities before their academic failure has progressed to the point that it begins to have motivational/emotional consequences and produce secondary knowledge and skill deficits (Cunningham & Stanovich, 1998). We know enough about the advantages of early intervention to assert that whatever diagnostic criteria are selected, they should facilitate intervention to prevent children with learning disabilities from falling seriously behind their age peers in critical academic skills.

Second, new diagnostic criteria should support the delivery of appropriate instruction to all children, not just those who show an arbitrary level of discrepancy between one set of learning abilities and another. For example, current evidence suggests that *all* children who have weaknesses in phonological abilities require more explicit instruction in this area in order to learn to read (Foorman & Torgesen, in press). Further, level of discrepancy between general intelligence and phonological ability is not a powerful or unique predictor of how well children will profit from this type of instruction (Torgesen et al., 1999; Vellutino et al., 1996). In other words, one cannot argue that children who do not show a discrepancy between their phonological processing abilities and other cognitive abilities (i.e., general intelligence) do not have a very important learning disability that affects their ability to acquire accurate and fluent word-level reading skills. They clearly have such a disability, but they are excluded from services under procedures that require an aptitude-achievement discrepancy for identification.

Finally, new diagnostic procedures must meet broadly acceptable standards for psychometric reliability and validity. That is, the criteria established should be those that can be measured with reasonable reliability, and they should also be conceptually and empirically consistent with current definitions. If indicators of potential failure are used to identify children at risk for the development of learning disabilities once formal school instruction has begun, these indicators must have sufficient predictive validity to warrant their widespread use in early identification.

THE USE OF PROCESS-MARKER VARIABLES FOR EARLY IDENTIFICATION AND OF OUTCOME/ RESPONSE TO TREATMENT VARIABLES FOR LATER DIAGNOSIS

I made the point earlier that measures of phonological awareness are not direct measures of intrinsic or constitutionally based psychological processing weaknesses. Rather, individual differences in phonological awareness reflect both the operation of biologically based processing abilities and the learning opportunities to which a child has been exposed. On the one hand, if a child has a weakness in intrinsic phonological processing capability, phonological awareness will be weak in spite of ample preliteracy learning opportunities. On the other hand, if a child's preschool environment does not provide the kind of experiences that stimulate growth of beginning levels of phonological sensitivity and awareness, the emergence of phonological awareness will be delayed even if phonological processing abilities are relatively intact.

Even though measures of phonological awareness do not directly assess an intrinsic processing weakness, they are *markers* for the presence of a pre-literacy skill that is critical in learning to read. The same could be said for rapid automatic naming tasks; they are markers for a functional capability (arising from an interaction between intrinsic processing capabilities and experience) that is causally related to early reading growth. There is also substantial evidence that simple knowledge of letter-sound relationships in kindergarten, or the ability to "invent" phonetic spellings for words, has the same or even greater predictive power (Mann & Ditunno, 1990; Scarborough, 1998) for later reading growth. Thus, outcomes on these pre-reading skills are markers for early failure to acquire skills that are critical to the process of deciphering print. In essence, variability on these markers reflects the operation of both basic (intrinsic) processing capabilities and learning opportunities in the child's environment. Both the ability to acquire these skills and the actual presence of the skill itself in sufficient strength are predictive of response to future instruction in reading.

The alternative diagnostic scheme proposed here would facilitate early intervention through assessment of reliable and valid predictors of future difficulties acquiring essential academic skills. Measurement of these marker variables would allow us to identify children in need of more powerful instruction in a particular domain. Children would be initially identified for this special preventive instruction because they met some criteria of low performance on these marker (predictor) variables and were not classifiable as mentally retarded. The label *learning disabled* would not be assigned until some later point in development (perhaps 2nd or 3rd grade, or even later), but in the meantime, *every* child who was determined to require special instruction in reading, math, or writing on the basis of low performance on these marker variables, and who was not mentally retarded, would be eligible for special instructional services designed to maintain the child's academic growth (e.g., reading or pre-reading skills) within normal limits. During the period of early intervention (and before labels were assigned), response to instruction would be periodically assessed to examine the continuing need for the assignment of at-risk status and the associated special interventions to which the child had been assigned. Thus, every child who was failing to acquire critical pre-academic or academic skills at acceptable levels, and who was not classified as mentally retarded or some other primary classification, would be eligible for special education services under learning disabilities regulations. These children would not be officially labeled as learning disabled until later in development, but would have at-risk status and be eligible for services until their achievement fell within normal limits or they were officially labeled as learning disabled.

At whatever point in development it is judged proper to assign the official label of learning disabled, this designation would be applied to any child who fell below designated levels on measures of the learning outcomes specified in the definition and regulations and who also had general intelligence above some agreed-upon level. This level should probably be the same as the criteria for the diagnosis of mental retardation (i.e., IQ above 70), so that there would be continuity with earlier procedures for determining at-risk status and so that we would not automatically create a category of children critically behind in academic skills but who "fall through the cracks" between diagnostic categories. Additional processing or non-academic cognitive assessments would be part of the diagnostic criteria for learning disabilities only if it is clearly established that they provide information critical to further instruction, or if they predict future academic growth beyond the predictive power of the child's current academic levels.

The diagnostic and classification model I am proposing here is a combination of early assessment of marker variables for academic failure combined with ongoing assessment to determine response to treatment. At this point, I want to be very clear about one thing. This model will not guarantee that *only* children with intrinsic psychological processing disabilities will be identified as learning disabled. In fact, *there is no practical way to do that on a large-scale basis at present.* Stanovich and Siegel (1994) make this point in a powerful way when they sum up evidence against using IQ-discrepancy procedures to classify children as learning disabled:

> ...neither the phenotypic nor the genotypic indicators of poor reading are correlated in a reliable way with IQ discrepancy. If there is a special group of children with reading disabilities who are behaviorally, cognitively, genetically, or neurologically different, it is becoming increasingly unlikely that they can be easily identified by using IQ discrepancy as a proxy for the genetic and neurological differences themselves. Thus, the basic assumption that underlies decades of classification in research and educational practice regarding reading disabilities is becoming increasingly untenable. (p. 48)

Some would argue (Vellutino et al., 1996) that only children who do not respond adequately to well designed instruction can be considered classically learning disabled (in the sense that they have fundamental processing limitations). This is simply not true. For example, failure to respond to interventions could be the result of factors other than intrinsic processing deficits that are either not understood or not measured for each child. The only way to rule this out is to be completely sure one has accurately measured the entire knowledge and skill domains, as well as the motivational and emotional domains, as well as the environmental domains (support for learning outside the immediate instructional situation) that are relevant to achievement in the area being instructed. In a recent study of intensive preventive instruction in early reading skills, we (Torgesen et al., 1999) found that the three best independent predictors of response to the intervention were beginning levels of phonological processing ability, socioeconomic status of the child's parents, and classroom teacher ratings of attention and behavior. Further, the intrinsic processing disabilities that cause academic failure are almost certainly normally distributed in terms of their severity (Shaywitz, Escobar, Shaywitz, Fletcher, & Makuch, 1992). Children with mild intrinsic processing disabilities will respond to more intensive and explicit instruction, and those with more severe problems will respond less well. A good response to excellent instruction does not mean that the child does not have a constitutionally based processing disorder; it just means the particular instruction the child received was powerful enough to compensate for it.

In principle, any methodology that uses response to treatment as a way of classifying children as learning disabled has no greater chance of correctly identifying children with intrinsic learning disorders than do traditional assessment procedures. The children identified by the response-to-treatment method will be those who are most difficult to teach, no matter what the reason. For example, some estimates suggest that the variability in pre-school exposure to literacy learning opportunities can vary by as much as 1,000 hours in children from different home environments (Adams, 1990). If these estimates are close to being correct, and unless we can measure all the effects of the environmental difference before instruction begins, we cannot tell whether problems in responding to an intervention in kindergarten are the result of constitutionally based processing weaknesses or to unspecified weaknesses in the knowledge domains most relevant to the task being learned.

No method of educational or psychological assessment currently available can identify with certainty children who have intrinsically based psychological processing disorders. However, children who continue with severe learning difficulties after several years of appropriate early intervention are the ones most likely to have this kind of enduring learning disability. Thus, within present assessment capabilities, the method most likely to reliably identify the kind of children who are described in widely accepted definitions of learning disabilities involves early identification with process/outcome markers followed by careful monitoring of growth on critical skills in response to appropriate and consistent early interventions. This model clearly implies that our *methods of early identification and monitoring will develop and change as we learn more about the developmental course of each of the kinds of learning disability outcomes described in current definitions.* If the federal government were to specify which early markers of pre-academic development can be used to identify children for at-risk status to be served under learning disabilities regulations, this set of process/outcome markers would need to be periodically updated as new knowledge about emergent indicators of learning disabilities is developed.

Points of Vulnerability in the Proposed Classification Model

Two immediate points of vulnerability and difficulty with the classification model just presented are current levels of accuracy in identifying children at risk for learning disabilities and problems ensuring that children who are identified as at risk receive appropriate, research-based instruction delivered with sufficient intensity and skill. The model can easily break down, and create many difficulties for schools, children, and families, if identification for preventive instruction is not reasonably accurate and if preventive interventions are not optimal. There are a few facts relevant to these two issues to guide formation of policy in this area. First, if we want to ensure that a very high proportion of children at risk for the most serious reading difficulties (e.g., the bottom 10%) are identified in kindergarten for preventive instruction, we must be prepared to provide preventive instruction to more than 10% of children.

Two kinds of errors can be made when identifying children at risk for future reading failure. False positive errors are made when children who will eventually become good readers score below the cut-off score on the predictive instrument and are falsely identified as at risk. In general, the proportion of this type of error has ranged between 20% and 60%, with an average of around 45% (Catts, 1996; Scarborough, 1998). That is, almost half of the children identified during kindergarten as at risk turn out not to have serious reading problems by the end of first grade. False negative errors occur when children who later exhibit reading problems are identified as not being at risk. Typical percentages of false negative errors range from 10% to 50%, with an average of around 22%. That is, on average, current procedures fail to identify about 22% of children who eventually end up with serious reading difficulties (Catts, 1996; Scarborough, 1998).

In any given study, the relative proportion of false positive and false negative errors is somewhat arbitrary, since it depends on the level of the cut-off score. For example, we (Torgesen & Burgess, 1998) reported a significant reduction in the percentage of false negative errors within the same sample of children by doubling the number of children we identified as at risk. Our goal was to identify, during the first semester of kindergarten, the children most at risk to be in the bottom 10% in word reading ability by the beginning of second grade. When we selected the 10% of children who scored lowest on our predictive tests, our false negative rate was 42% (we missed almost half the children who became extremely poor readers). However, when we identified the 20% of children who scored lowest on our measures, the false negative rate was reduced to 8%. As a practical matter, if schools desire to maximize their chances for early intervention with the most impaired children, they should provide this intervention to as many children as possible. This is less of a waste of resources than it might seem at first glance, because, although many of the falsely identified children receiving intervention may not be among the most seriously disabled readers, almost all of them are likely to be below-average readers (Torgesen & Burgess, 1998).

It is also important to note that prediction accuracy increases significantly the longer a child has been in school. Prediction of reading disabilities from tests given at the beginning of first grade is significantly more accurate than from tests administered during the first semester of kindergarten (Scarborough, 1998; Torgesen, Burgess, & Rashotte, 1996). Given the widely varying range of children's pre-school learning opportunities, many children may score low on early identification instruments in the first semester of kindergarten simply because they have not had the opportunity to learn the skills. However, if pre-reading skills are actively taught in kindergarten, some of these differences may be reduced by the beginning of the second semester of school. Accuracy of identification of at-risk students can potentially be increased to 100% by frequent assessments of critical pre-reading and reading skills during the early elementary years. A model such as that established in Texas using the *Texas Primary Reading Inventory* (Texas Education Agency, 2000), in which a combination screening/assessment instrument is administered three times a year during kindergarten through 2nd grade will guarantee that any child who falls critically behind in important early literacy skills will be identified for extra supportive instruction.

The examples of assessment issues provided here have focused on reading, because that is the area we know the most about. However, Berninger and her colleagues (Berninger, in press; Berninger, Stage, Smith, & Hildebrand, 2001) have demonstrated the effectiveness of a "3-Tier Model for Prevention and Remediation" that involves early assessment to identify children at risk for difficulties in writing and math. The 3-Tier model is actually quite similar to the model being proposed here, except that it has an additional layer of intervention at the classroom level. In the simpler model I am proposing, I am assuming that classroom teachers are doing all they can to deliver high-quality, research-based instruction to all children, and that they are actively trying to accommodate individual differences in response to their instruction. If this is not the case, there will be far too many children requiring services under the learning disabilities regulations for the system to work effectively (Foorman & Torgesen, in press).

What do we know about the effectiveness of early interventions in preventing serious reading disabilities? We know, for example, that the best preventive interventions tested in research thus far typically reduce the percentage of children who are continuing be at risk for reading failure (defined as falling below the 30th percentile on critical word reading skills) at the end of first or second grade to about 2% to 6% of the population (Torgesen, 1999). We also know a great deal about the characteristics of effective instruction for children with learning disabilities (Foorman & Torgesen, in press; Swanson, Hoskyn, & Lee, 1999; Vaughn, Gersten, & Chard, 2000), and we know that they will frequently require instruction that is much more intensive and systematic than typical children if they are to attain reading levels within the normal range (Torgesen et al., 2001). One of the major challenges for politicians, school administrators, teachers, and parents in the model I have presented would be to ensure that all children who are at risk for learning disabilities receive appropriate and skillful instruction delivered with the right intensity for sufficient periods of time. A further challenge would be to ensure even greater levels of intensity and skill in instruction for children who do not respond successfully to the first layers of intervention.

As an example of what can be accomplished if excellent classroom instruction in reading is supplemented with more intensive instruction for children identified as at risk for reading failure, consider what happened at Hartsfield Elementary School over a period of 5 years (King & Torgesen, 2000). Hartsfield Elementary School serves a mixed population of school children of whom about 65% qualify for free and reduced lunch services and of whom about 65% are minority (primarily African-American). In the first year of the multiyear change project when only partially improved classroom instruction in reading was accomplished, 32% of the children obtained scores below the 25th percentile on a nationally standardized measure of word-level reading skills at the end of first grade. Once classroom instruction was more consistently high-quality and early identification procedures were in place, only 3.7% of the children fell below the 25th percentile at the end of first grade, and only 2.4% fell below this mark in second grade. In the present model, it would be those 2.4% of children who were still struggling to acquire basic reading skills who might be eligible for further assessment and diagnosis as learning disabled.

SUMMARY

The classification model being recommended in this paper is a two-stage or two-tier model that combines assessment of marker (predictor) variables with careful and continuous monitoring of children's response to early and subsequent interventions. Initially, children in first grade, kindergarten, or even preschool (depending on accuracy of predictive measures) would be identified for special preventive instruction under learning disabilities regulations if they performed below criterion on predictors of specific academic achievement and were not mentally retarded. These children would be assigned some kind of at-risk status to justify or certify their eligibility for these special services. The pre-academic or academic skills of these children would be assessed periodically (at least three times a year, perhaps more) to determine their continuing need for special services, and any child not being served could be identified for special services by referral and administration of similar tests. Any child not classified with some other primary disability (e.g., mental retardation, visual handicap) who was achieving below criterion on markers for at-risk status would be eligible for services.

Children would not be assigned the formal label of learning disabled until later in elementary school (perhaps 3rd grade or later). After receiving several years of special preventive instruction, a child could be certified as learning disabled if they continued to experience severe difficulties with any of the academic skills specified in the definition and regulations and if they attained a score on a measure of general learning ability above a given level. Any child with continuing severe academic difficulties who was not classified with some other primary disability (e.g., mental retardation, visual disabilities) would be considered learning disabled for purposes of instruction and accommodation. Additional processing or non-academic cognitive assessments would be part of the diagnostic criteria only if it is clearly established that they provide information critical to further instruction, or if they predict future academic growth beyond the predictive power of the child's current academic levels.

POTENTIAL THREATS TO CONCEPTS AND PRACTICES FROM THE PROPOSED DIAGNOSTIC APPROACH

The term learning disabilities is associated both with a social-political-educational movement and with a field of scientific research and study. Changes to common diagnostic practices as guided by federal regulations will have foreseeable and unforeseeable effects in both areas. As a social-political-educational movement, the field is associated with teacher training programs, parent and professional organizations, legal requirements for educational and workplace accommodations, status as a "handicapping condition," public and private school programs, etc. As a field of scientific inquiry, it is associated with research funding programs, professional identities of scientists, scientific journals and publications, research conventions and questions, etc. Changing the diagnostic criteria for learning disabilities in the manner suggested in this paper will have major impact in some of these areas and little impact in others. It is beyond the scope of this paper (to say nothing of the ability and knowledge of its writer) to give full consideration to all potential effects of a change such as the one proposed here. Nevertheless, a few of the more obvious consequences will be briefly discussed.

CONSEQUENCES FOR THE FIELD AS A SOCIAL-POLITICAL-EDUCATIONAL MOVEMENT

One of the most obvious consequences of a change in classification procedures such as the one being recommended here is a change in the characteristics of children being identified for special educational services under learning disabilities regulations. The group identified by these new procedures will be much more heterogeneous with regard to general intelligence. Further, many children currently served as learning disabled might not be served because the absolute level of their academic performance problem may not be sufficiently severe. In current practice, it is the size of the discrepancy between general intelligence and academic skill, rather than the absolute level of academic skill, that leads to a diagnosis of learning disability. Many children with average to above-average general intelligence are served as learning disabled because of the discrepancy between their level of reading skill and their level of general ability, even though the absolute level of their reading abilities is substantially higher than other children who show less of a discrepancy between IQ and reading level. If a criterion involving actual reading level were substituted for the currently used discrepancy criteria, it is obvious that many children with mild reading problems (but large discrepancies) would no longer be served as reading disabled (unless service delivery capacity was considerably expanded over present limits). It is also likely that the ethnic composition and socioeconomic status of children identified as having learning disabilities would shift more strongly toward minorities and lower socioeconomic status groups, because these groups tend to have fewer of the specific types of pre-school language experiences that support the growth of phonological awareness and other pre-academic skills (Whitehurst & Lonigan, 1998).

One of the most widely accepted conventions about learning disabilities is that they involve "unexpected" academic underachievement. The poor academic performance of these children is not expected given their general level of learning ability (as measured by IQ tests), adequate learning opportunities, and reasonable motivation for learning. The trouble with this concept in practice, at least for the development of reading skills, is that standard IQ measures are not equally predictive of all aspects of reading growth. Standard IQ measures are not good independent predictors of early word reading growth (Stanovich, Cunningham & Feeman, 1984; Torgesen et al., 1999), but they are good predictors of individual differences in reading comprehension (Stanovich et al., 1984) once word reading ability has been acquired. IQ measures are good predictors of reading comprehension scores in older children because IQ scores are heavily influenced by level of vocabulary and verbal skills, and this kind of knowledge is also required in reading comprehension. If IQ measures contained a more thorough assessment of phonological abilities and knowledge, they would also be very predictive of growth in early word reading skill. Thus, while general IQ (and particularly verbal IQ) does not lead to clear expectations for growth in early word reading ability, it does justify clear expectations for the ultimate level of reading comprehension that we may expect from individual children. Children with broad verbal and language comprehension abilities far below average cannot be expected to comprehend written material at average levels even if they can decipher all the words in print accurately.

Ultimately, our educational response to children, as well as our system of accommodation to their learning disability, will need to recognize a far greater range of individual differences than it currently does. For example, it is clear that a child with high levels of domain-related knowledge and verbal ability who cannot decipher words fluently should have this reading disability accommodated on tests in which the object is to demonstrate mastery and understanding of a given subject area. However, is there an appropriate accommodation for a child who can decipher the words accurately, but who does not have the domain-related knowledge and broad verbal ability that is required for good performance on the test? The problem, in terms of thinking through the implications of the presently proposed classification scheme, is that both of these students would probably be classified as learning disabled. The example suggests that the concept of accommodations for learning disabilities would need to be more finely developed and clearly articulated than it often is at present.

Another potential consequence of changing the classification criteria for learning disabilities to a system that does not explicitly contain discrepancy criteria is that it might lose its identity as a focus for political action and educational funding. As scientifically flawed and unfair as current discrepancy criteria are, they at least *attempt* to make a distinction between learning difficulties resulting from specific, constitutionally based processing weaknesses and learning difficulties that are the result of many other causes such as lack of motivation, lack of home support, or low general learning ability. Any classification procedure that does away with the discrepancy idea runs the risk of destroying the concept of learning disabilities in the minds of politicians and educators. The point being made in this paper is that it is not currently feasible to accurately identify children whose learning difficulty is the sole result of an intrinsically based processing disability, and we should not try to do so using invalid discrepancy-based procedures. By publicly acknowledging the problem in moving to a classification criteria that involves neither direct assessment of intrinsic processing weaknesses nor use of discrepancy criteria, we do run the risk of weakening the base for political and social action on behalf of children with developmental learning disabilities.

CONSEQUENCES FOR THE FIELD AS AN AREA OF SCIENTIFIC INQUIRY

In contrast to the potential consequences for learning disabilities as a political-social-educational movement, which do involve some serious risks, the change to more encompassing and inclusive criteria for classification of learning disabilities should have mostly positive consequences for the field as an area of scientific inquiry. Perhaps the most positive consequence is that it will underline the heterogeneity of children with learning disabilities in a way that will promote more careful specification of sample characteristics in research as they relate to the questions being asked.

It has long been recognized that researchers should not use school-defined samples of children with learning disabilities as the focus of research, for such samples are simply too heterogeneous to be the basis for coherent theory development (Senf, 1986; Stanovich, 1993; Torgesen, 1993). Since the study of learning disabilities is essentially the study of individual differences in learning and performance, samples should always be carefully selected in relationship to the particular question being addressed in the research. For example, if one wants to determine if weaknesses in a given ability or processing skill can cause a learning difficulty independently from levels of other important abilities (such as verbal or nonverbal intelligence, vocabulary, syntactic skill, general knowledge, etc.) then samples of learning disabled and nondisabled children should be carefully equated on the abilities being controlled. Without such methods, it is arguable that we may never have discovered the unique contributions of word-level reading problems or phonological processes to developmental dyslexia (reading disability), because lower IQ children so frequently also have problems in broad verbal ability and language comprehension (Torgesen, 1989). If the goal is to develop a theory of math disabilities, then only children with a specified type of math disability should be used in the research—and it would also be important to ask how levels of other abilities (such as general intelligence) affect the expression of the disability.

The major threat to the field of learning disabilities as an area of scientific inquiry would involve a potential loss of focused identity if research articles never contained the term learning disabilities but only mentioned topics like "problems with math fact retrieval in children of average intelligence," "difficulties in expressive language in young children with adequate receptive skills," or "factors involved in handwriting difficulties in young children." If a more inclusive definition of learning disabilities applied in the public schools created a loss of cohesion among researchers studying these children, this might make it more difficult to focus public attention on learning disabilities as an area for research funding. It might also create such diversity of focus in professional societies that the synergistic effects found in groups that gather to discuss common interests would be diluted.

SUMMARY

Changing procedures for the classification of children with learning disabilities in the manner suggested in this paper would have several clear consequences for the field of learning disabilities as an educational-social-political movement. First, the children identified for learning disabilities services in the school would become more heterogeneous with regard to level of general intelligence. This would require a more differentiated approach to the provision of accommodations than is presently the case, in which children often can receive accommodations simply because of their status as learning disabled. Second, children identified as at risk for learning disabilities on the basis of their performance on process/outcome measures would also be more likely to come from minority ethnic groups and homes of lower socioeconomic status. This would occur simply because children from these kinds of pre-school environments often enter school less well prepared on the critical markers, or predictors for various learning outcomes. Finally, unless service delivery capacity were substantially increased, many children now receiving learning disabilities services would no longer receive them. For example, a child with mild reading difficulties that are significantly discrepant from IQ can qualify for learning disabilities services under current IQ-discrepancy procedures. However, if absolute level of process/outcome scores or reading scores were used to identify children as reading disabled, the same child might not qualify because his or her scores would not be low enough. In order to serve all children who do not have another primary disability but whose learning difficulties in specific academic areas were severe enough to interfere with their ability to accomplish grade level work, there is no question that special instructional capacity for children with learning disabilities would need to be expanded.

The changes to classification procedures recommended in this paper might also impact the scientific study of learning disabilities, but these effects would probably be less severe or threatening than those to the education and politics of learning disabilities. Potentially, the changes could positively affect the scientific study of learning disabilities by forcing investigators to more carefully define their samples, and to select them in more principled ways. The major negative impact might arise from a loss of identity for the field as it divided into separate groups, each focusing on different kinds of learning difficulties.

References

Adams, M. (1990). *Beginning to read: Thinking and learning about print.* Cambridge, MA: MIT

Aslin, R. N., Jusczyk, P. W., & Pisoni, D. P. (1998). Speech and auditory processing during infancy: Constraints on and precursors to language. In W. Damon, K. Kuhn, & R. S. Siegler (Eds.), *Handbook of child psychology: Vol. 2: Cognition, perception & language* (5th ed., pp. 223–259). New York: Wiley.

Berninger, V., & Graham, S. (1998). Language by hand: A synthesis of a decade of research in handwriting. *Handwriting Review, 12,* 11–25.

Berninger, V. W. (1994). *Reading and writing acquisition: A developmental neuropsychological perspective.* Madison, WI: Brown & Benchmark.

Berninger, V. W., Stage, S. A., Smith, D. R., & Hildebrand, D. (2001). Assessment for reading and writing intervention: A 3-tier model for prevention and remediation. In J. W. Andrews, D. H. Saklofske, & H. L. Janzen (Eds.), *Handbook of psychoeducational assessment* (pp. 195–223). San Diego, CA: Academic Press.

Berninger, V. W. (in press). Best practices in reading, writing, and math assessment-intervention links: A systems approach for schools, classrooms, and individuals. In T. A. Grimes (Ed.), *Best practices in school psychology*. Bethesda, MD: National Association of School Psychologists.

Bowers, P. G., Golden, J., Kennedy, A., & Young, A. (1994) Limits upon orthographic knowledge due to processes indexed by naming speed. In V. W. Berninger (Ed.), *The varieties of orthographic knowledge, I: Theoretical and developmental issues* (pp. 173–218). Dordrecht, The Netherlands: Kluwer Academic Publishers.

Bowers, P. G., & Wolf, M. (1993). Theoretical links between naming speed, precise timing mechanisms and orthographic skill in dyslexia. *Reading and Writing: An Interdisciplinary Journal, 5,* 69–85.

Bowey, J. A., Cain, M. T., & Ryan, S. M. (1992). A reading-level design study of phonological skills underlying fourth-grade children's word reading difficulties. *Child Development, 63,* 999–1011.

Bradley, L., & Bryant, P. (1985). *Rhyme and reason in reading and spelling.* Ann Arbor: University of Michigan Press.

Case, R., Kurland, D. M., & Goldberg, J. (1982). Operational efficiency and the growth of short-term memory span. *Journal of Experimental Child Psychology, 33,* 386–404.

Catts, H. (1996, March). Phonological awareness: A key to detection. Paper presented at the conference titled The Spectrum of Developmental Disabilities XVIII: Dyslexia, Johns Hopkins Medical Institutions, Baltimore.

Coles, G. S. (1987). *The learning mystique: A critical look at "learning disabilities."* New York: Pantheon.

Cunningham, A. E. (1990). Explicit versus implicit instruction in phonemic awareness. *Journal of Experimental Child Psychology, 50,* 429–444.

Cunningham, A. E., & Stanovich, K. E. (1998). What reading does for the mind. *American Educator, 22*(Spring/Summer), 8–15.

DeMartino, S., Espresser, R., Rey, V., & Habib, M. (in press). The "temporal processing deficit" hypothesis of dyslexia: New experimental evidence. *Brain and Cognition.*

Denckla, M. (1994). Measurement of executive function. In G. Reid Lyon (Ed.), *Frames of reference for the assessment of learning disabilities: New views on measurement issues* (pp. 143–162). Baltimore, MD: Brookes Publishing.

Ehri, L. C. (1989). The development of spelling knowledge and its role in reading acquisition and reading disability. *Journal of Learning Disabilities, 22,* 356–365.

Ehri, L. C. (1998). Grapheme-phoneme knowledge is essential for learning to read words in English. In J. Metsala & L. Ehri (Eds.), *Word recognition in beginning reading* (pp. 3–40). Hillsdale, NJ: Lawrence Erlbaum Assoc.

Eimas, P. D., Siqueland, E. R., Jusczyk, P., & Vigorito, J. (1971). Speech perception in infants. *Science, 171,* 303–306.

Ericsson, K. A. (in press). The acquisition of expert performance as problem solving: Construction and modification of mediating mechanisms through deliberate practice. In J. E. Davidson & R. J. Sternberg (Eds.), *The psychology of problem solving.* Cambridge: Cambridge University Press.

Ericcson, K. A., & Kintsch, W. (1995). Long-term working memory. *Psychological Review, 102,* 211–245.

Felton, R., & Brown, I. S. (1990). Phonological processes as predictors of specific reading skills in children at risk for reading failure. *Reading and Writing: An Interdisciplinary Journal, 2,* 39–59.

Filipek, P. (1996). Structural variations in measures in the developmental disorders. In R. Thatcher, G. Lyon, J. Rumsey, & N. Krasnegor (Eds.), *Developmental neuroimaging: Mapping the development of brain and behavior* (pp. 169–186). San Diego, CA: Academic Press.

Fischer, K. W., & Bidell, T. (1991). Constraining nativist inferences about cognitive capacity. In S. Carey & R. Gelman (Eds.), *The epigenesis of mind: Essays on biology and cognition* (pp. 168–187). Hillsdale, NJ: Lawrence Erlbaum Assoc.

Flavell, J. H., Miller, P. H., & Miller, S. A. (1993). *Cognitive development* (3rd ed.). Englewood Cliffs, NJ: Prentice-Hall, Inc.

Fletcher, J. M., Francis, D. J., Shaywitz., S. E., Lyon, G. R., Foorman, B. R., Steubing, K. K., et al. (1998). Intelligent testing and the discrepancy model for children with learning disabilities. *Learning Disabilities Research & Practice, 13,* 186–203.

Fletcher, J. M., Shaywitz, S. E., Shankweiler, D. P., Katz, L., Liberman, I. Y., Fowler, A., et al. (1994). Cognitive profiles of reading disability: Comparisons of discrepancy and low achievement definitions. *Journal of Educational Psychology, 86,* 1–18.

Foorman, B. R., Francis, D. J., Shaywitz, S. E., Shaywitz, B. A., & Fletcher, J. M. (1997). The case for early reading intervention. In B. Blachman (Ed.), *Foundations of reading acquisition and dyslexia* (pp. 243–264). Mahwah, NJ: Lawrence Erlbaum Assoc.

Foorman, B. R., & Torgesen, J. K. (in press). Critical elements of classroom and small-group instruction promote reading success in all children. *Learning Disabilities Research and Practice*.

Francis, D. J., Shaywitz, S. E., Stuebing, K. K., Shaywitz, B. A., & Fletcher, J. M. (1996). Developmental lag versus deficit models of reading disability: A longitudinal individual growth curves analysis. *Journal of Educational Psychology, 88*, 3–17.

Galaburda, A. M., Menard, M., & Rosen, G. (1994). Evidence for aberrant auditory anatomy in developmental dyslexia. *Proceedings of the National Academy of Science, 91*, 8010–8013.

Geary, D. C. (1993). Mathematical disabilities: Cognitive, neuropsychological, and genetic components. *Psychological Bulletin, 114*, 345–362.

Geary, D. C., Hamson, C. O., & Hoard, M. K. (2000). Numerical and arithmetical cognition: A longitudinal study of process and concept deficits in children with learning disability. *Journal of Experimental Child Psychology, 77*, 236–263.

Hallahan, D. P., & Cruickshank, W. M. (1973). *Psycho-educational foundations of learning disabilities*. Englewood Cliffs, NJ: Prentice-Hall.

Hallahan, D. P., Kauffman, J. M., & Lloyd, J. W. (1996). *Introduction to learning disabilities*. Boston: Allyn and Bacon, 1996

Hammill, D. D. (1990). On defining learning disabilities: An emerging consensus. *Journal of Learning Disabilities, 23*, 74–84.

Hammill, D. D., & Larson, S. C. (1974). The efficacy of psycholinguistic training. *Exceptional Children, 41*, 5–14.

Hasher, L., & Zacks, R. T. (1984). Automatic processing of fundamental information: The case of frequency of occurrence. *American Psychologist, 39*, 1372–1388.

Hatcher, P., Hulme, C., & Ellis, A. W. (1994). Ameliorating early reading failure by integrating the teaching of reading and phonological skills: The phonological linkage hypothesis. *Child Development, 65*, 41–57.

Hecht, S. A., Burgess, S. R., Torgesen, J. K., Wagner, R. K., & Rashotte, C. A. (2000). Explaining social class differences in growth of reading skills from beginning kindergarten through fourth-grade: The role of phonological awareness, rate of access, and print knowledge. *Reading and Writing: An Interdisciplinary Journal, 12*, 99–127.

King, R., & Torgesen, J. K. (2000). *Improving the effectiveness of reading instruction in one elementary school: A description of the process.* Unpublished manuscript, Florida State University, Tallahassee, FL.

Kistner, J., & Torgesen, J. K. (1987). Motivational and cognitive aspects of learning disabilities. In A. E. Kasdin, & B. B. Lahey (Eds.), *Advances in clinical child psychology.* New York: Plenum Press.

Klingberg, T., Hedehus, M., Temple, E., Salz, T., Gabrieli, J., Moseley, M., & Poldrack, R. (2000). Microstructure of temporo-parietal white matter as a basis for reading ability: evidence from diffusion tensor magnetic resonance imaging. *Neuron, 25,* 493–500.

Liberman, I. Y., Shankweiler, D., & Liberman, A. M. (1989). The alphabetic principle and learning to read. In D. Shankweiler & I. Y. Liberman (Eds.), *Phonology and reading disability: Solving the reading puzzle* (pp. 1-33). Ann Arbor, MI: University of Michigan Press.

Lundberg, I., Frost, J., & Peterson, O. (1988). Effects of an extensive program for stimulating phonological awareness in pre-school children. *Reading Research Quarterly, 23,* 263–284.

Manis, F. R., McBride, C., Seidenberg, M. S., Doi, L., & Custodio, R. (1993, March). *Speech perception and phonological awareness in normal and disabled readers.* Paper presented at the meeting of the Society for Research in Child Development, New Orleans.

Mann, V. A. (1993). Phoneme awareness and future reading ability. *Journal of Learning Disabilities, 26,* 259–269.

Mann, V. A., & Ditunno, P. (1990). Phonological deficiencies: Effective predictors of future reading problems. In G. Pavlides (Ed.), *Dyslexia: A neuropsychological and learning perspective* (pp. 105–131). Sussex, UK: Wiley.

Massaro, D. W. (1975). *Experimental psychology and information processing.* Chicago, IL: Rand McNally.

McAnally, D. I., Hansen, P. C., Cornelissen, P. L., & Stein, J. F. (1997). Effect of time and frequency manipulation on syllable perception in developmental dyslexics. *Journal of Speech, Language, and Hearing Research, 40,* 912–924.

Meltzer, L. J. (1993). *Strategy assessment and instruction for students with learning disabilities.* Austin, TX: PRO-ED.

Merzenich, M. M., Jenkins, W. M., Johnston, P., Schreiner, C., Miller, S. L., & Tallal, P. (1996). Temporal processing deficits of language-learning impaired children ameliorated by training. *Science, 271,* 77–81.

Mody, M., Studdert-Kennedy, M., & Brady, S. (1997). Speech perception deficits in poor readers: Auditory processing or phonological coding? *Journal of Experimental Child Psychology, 64,* 199–231.

Morais, J., Alegria, J., & Content, A. (1987). The relationships between segmental analysis and alphabetic literacy: An interactive view. *Cahiers de Psychologie Cognitive, 7,* 414–438.

Morrongiell, B. A., Fenwick, K. D., Hillier, L., & Chance, G. (1994). Sound localization in newborn human infants. *Developmental Psychobiology, 27,* 519–538.

National Joint Committee on Learning Disabilities (1988). Letter to NJCLD member organizations.

National Reading Panel (2000). *Teaching children to read: An evidence-based assessment of the scientific research literature on reading and its implications for reading instruction.* National Institute of Child Health and Human Development, Washington, DC.

Nittrouer, S. (1999). Do temporal processing deficits cause phonological processing problems? *Journal of Speech, Language, and Hearing Research, 42,* 925–942.

Olson, R. K. (1999). Genes, environment, and reading disabilities. In R. J. Sternberg and L. Spear-Swerling (Eds.), *Perspectives on learning disabilities* (p. 3–22). New Haven: Westview Press.

Perfetti, C. A., Beck, I., Bell, L., & Hughes, C. (1987). Phonemic knowledge and learning to read are reciprocal: A longitudinal study of first grade children. *Merrill-Palmer Quarterly, 33,* 283–319.

Rack, J. P., Snowling, M. J., & Olson, R. K. (1992). The nonword reading deficit in developmental dyslexia: A review. *Reading Research Quarterly, 27,* 29–53.

Rose, S. A., Feldman, J. F., & Wallace, I. F. (1992). Infant information processing in relation to six-year cognitive outcome. *Child Development, 63,* 1126–1141.

Rourke, B. P. (1988). The syndrome of nonverbal learning disabilities: Developmental manifestations in neurological disease, disorder, and dysfunction. *The Clinical Neuropsychologist, 2,* 293–330.

Rourke, B. P. (1989). *Nonverbal learning disabilities: The syndrome and the model.* Guilford Publications, Inc.: New York.

Rourke, B. P. (1995). *Syndrome of nonverbal learning disabilities: Neurodevelopmental manifestations.* New York: Guilford Press.

Rourke, B. P., & Finlayson, M. A. J. (1978). Neuropsychological significance of variations in patterns of academic performance: Verbal and visual-spatial abilities. *Journal of Abnormal Child Psychology, 6,* 121–133.

Rourke, B. P., Young, G. C., & Flewelling, R. W. (1971). The relationships between WISC Verbal-Performance discrepancies and selected verbal, auditory-perceptual, and problem-solving abilities in children with learning disabilities. *Journal of Clinical Psychology, 27,* 475–479.

Scarborough, H. S. (1998). Early identification of children at risk for reading disabilities: Phonological awareness and some other promising predictors. In B. K. Shapiro, P. J. Accardo, & A. J. Capute (Eds.), *Specific reading disability: A view of the spectrum* (pp. 75–120). Timonium, MD: York Press.

Senf, G. M. (1986). LD research in sociological and scientific perspective. In J. K. Torgesen & B. Y. L. Wong (Eds.), *Psychological and educational perspectives on learning disabilities* (pp. 27–55). New York: Academic Press.

Share, D. L., & Stanovich, K. E. (1995). Cognitive processes in early reading development: A model of acquisition and individual differences. *Issues in Education: Contributions from Educational Psychology, 1,* 1–35.

Shaywitz, S. E., Escobar, M. D., Shaywitz, B. A., Fletcher, J. M., & Makuch, R. (1992). Evidence that dyslexia may represent the lower tail of a normal distribution of reading ability. *The New England Journal of Medicine, 326,* 145–150.

Shaywitz, S. E., Pugh, K. R., Jenner, A. R., Fulbright, R. K., Fletcher, J. M., Gore, J. C., et al. (2000). The neurobiology of reading and reading disability (dyslexia). In M. L. Kamil, P. B. Mosenthal, P. D. Pearson, & R. Barr (Eds.), *Handbook of reading research: Vol. III* (pp. 229–249). Mahwah, NJ: Lawrence Erlbaum Assoc.

Siegel, L. S. (1989). IQ is irrelevant to the definition of learning disabilities. *Journal of Learning Disabilities, 22,* 469–479

Siegler, R. S. (1998). *Children's thinking* (3rd ed.). Upper Saddle River, NJ: Prentice-Hall, Inc.

Stanovich, K. E. (1986). Matthew effects in reading: Some consequences of individual differences in the acquisition of literacy. *Reading Research Quarterly, 21,* 360–406.

Stanovich, K. E. (1991). Discrepancy definitions of reading disability: Has intelligence led us astray? *Reading Research Quarterly, 26,* 1–29.

Stanovich, K. E. (1993). The construct validity of discrepancy definitions of reading disability. In G. R. Lyon, D. B. Gray, J. F. Kavanagh, & N. A. Krasnegor (Eds.), *Better understanding learning disabilities* (pp. 273–308). Baltimore: Paul H. Brooks.

Stanovich, K. E., Cunningham, A. E., & Cramer, B. B. (1984). Assessing phonological awareness in kindergarten children: Issues of task comparability. *Journal of Experimental Child Psychology, 38,* 175–190.

Stanovich, K. E., Cunningham, A. E., & Feeman, D. J. (1984). Intelligence, cognitive skills, and early reading progress. *Reading Research Quarterly, 24,* 278–303.

Stanovich, K. E., & Siegel, L. S. (1994). Phenotypic performance profiles of children with reading disabilities: A regression-based test of the phonological-core variable difference model. *Journal of Educational Psychology, 86,* 24–53.

Studdert-Kennedy, M., & Mody, M. (1995). Auditory temporal perception deficits in the reading-impaired: A critical review of the evidence. *Psychonomic Bulletin Review, 2,* 508–514.

Swanson, H. L. (1994). Short-term memory and working memory: Do both contribute to our understanding of academic achievement in children and adults with learning disabilities? *Journal of Learning Disabilities, 27,* 34–50.

Swanson, H. L. (1999). What develops in working memory? A live span perspective. *Developmental Psychology, 35,* 986–1000.

Swanson, H. L., & Alexander, J. (1997). Cognitive processes as predictors of word recognition and reading comprehension in learning disabled and skilled readers: Revisiting the specificity hypothesis. *Journal of Educational Psychology, 89,* 128–158.

Swanson, H. L., & Ashbaker, M. (2000). Working memory, STM, articulation speed, word recognition, and reading comprehension in learning disabled readers: Executive and/or articulatory system? *Intelligence, 28,* 1–30.

Swanson, H. L., Hoskyn, M., & Lee, C. (1999). *Interventions for students with learning disabilities: A meta-analysis of treatment outcomes.* NY: The Guilford Press.

Swanson, H. L., & Sachse-Lee, C. (in press). Mathematical problem solving and working memory in children with learning disabilities: Both executive and phonological processes are important. *Journal of Experimental Child Psychology.*

Tallal, P. (1980). Auditory temporal perception, phonics, and reading disabilities in children. *Brain and Language, 9,* 182–198.

Tallal, P., Miller, S. L., Bedi, G., Byma, G., Wang, X., Nagarajan, S. S., Schreiner, C., et al. (1996). Language comprehension in language-learning impaired children improved with acoustically modified speech. *Science, 271,* 81–84.

Tallal, P., Stark, R. E., & Mellits, E. D. (1985). Identification of language-impaired children on the basis of rapid perception and production skills. *Brain and Language, 25,* 314–322.

Texas Education Agency. (2000). *Texas Primary Reading Inventory.* Austin, TX: Texas Education Agency.

Torgesen, J. K. (1979). What shall we do with psychological processes? *Journal of Learning Disabilities, 12,* 514–521.

Torgesen, J. K. (1989). Why IQ is relevant to the definition of learning disabilities. *Journal of Learning Disabilities, 22,* 484–487.

Torgesen, J. K. (1993). Variations on theory in learning disabilities. In R. Lyon, D. Gray, N. Krasnegor, and J. Kavenagh (Eds.), *Better understanding learning disabilities: Perspectives on classification, identification, and assessment and their implications for education and policy* (pp. 153–170). Baltimore: Brookes Publishing.

Torgesen, J. K. (1999). Phonologically based reading disabilities: Toward a coherent theory of one kind of learning disability. In R. J. Sternberg & L. Spear-Swerling (Eds.), *Perspectives on learning disabilities* (pp. 231–262). New Haven: Westview Press.

Torgesen, J. K., Alexander, A. W., Wagner, R. K., Rashotte, C. A., Voeller, K., Conway, T., & Rose, E. (2001). Intensive remedial instruction for children with severe reading disabilities: Immediate and long-term outcomes from two instructional approaches. *Journal of Learning Disabilities, 34,* 33–58.

Torgesen, J. K., & Burgess, S. R. (1998). Consistency of reading-related phonological processes throughout early childhood: Evidence from longitudinal-correlational and instructional studies. In J. Metsala & L. Ehri (Eds.), *Word recognition in beginning reading* (pp. 161–188). Hillsdale, NJ: Lawrence Erlbaum Assoc.

Torgesen, J. K., Burgess, S., & Rashotte, C. A. (1996, April). *Predicting phonologically based reading disabilities: What is gained by waiting a year?* Paper presented at the annual meeting of the Society for the Scientific Study of Reading, New York.

Torgesen, J. K., Morgan, S. T., & Davis, C. (1992). Effects of two types of phonological awareness training on word learning in kindergarten children. *Journal of Educational Psychology, 84,* 364–370.

Torgesen, J. K., Rashotte, C. A., & Alexander, A. (2001). Principles of fluency instruction in reading: Relationships with established empirical outcomes. In M. Wolf (Ed.), *Dyslexia, fluency, and the brain* (pp. 334–355). Parkton, MD: York Press.

Torgesen, J. K., Wagner, R. K., Rashotte, C. A., Rose, E., Lindamood, P., Conway, T., et al. (1999). Preventing reading failure in young children with phonological processing disabilities: Group and individual responses to instruction. *Journal of Educational Psychology, 91,* 579–593.

U.S. Department of Education. (1977). Definition and criteria for defining students as learning disabled. *Federal Register, 42,* 250.

U.S. Department of Education (1992). Assistance to states for the education of children with disabilities program and preschool grants for children with disabilities; Final rule. *Federal Register, 34*, CRF Parts 300 and 301.

Vaughn, S., Gersten, R., & Chard, D. J. (2000). The underlying message in LD intervention research: Findings from research syntheses. *Exceptional Children, 67*, 99–114.

Vellutino, F. R., Scanlon, D. M., Sipay, E. R., Small S. G., Pratt, A., Chen, R., et al. (1996). Cognitive profiles of difficult-to-remediate and readily remediated poor readers: Early intervention as a vehicle for distinguishing between cognitive and experiential deficits as basic causes of specific reading disability. *Journal of Educational Psychology, 88*, 601–638.

Wagner, R. K., & Torgesen, J. K. (1987). The nature of phonological processing and its causal role in the acquisition of reading skills. *Psychological Bulletin, 101*, 192–212.

Wagner, R. K., Torgesen, J. K., & Rashotte, C. A. (1994). The development of reading-related phonological processing abilities: New evidence of bi-directional causality from a latent variable longitudinal study. *Developmental Psychology, 30*, 73–87.

Wagner, R. K., Torgesen, J. K., Rashotte, C. A., Hecht, S. A., Barker, T. A., Burgess, S. R., et al. (1997). Changing causal relations between phonological processing abilities and word-level reading as children develop from beginning to fluent readers: A five-year longitudinal study. *Developmental Psychology, 33*, 468–479.

Webster's seventh new collegiate dictionary. (1965). Springfield, MA: G. & C. Merriam Company.

Werner, J. S., & Siqueland, E. R. (1978). Visual recognition memory in the preterm infant. *Infant Behavior and Development, 1*, 79–94.

Wertheimer, M. (1961). Psychomotor coordination of auditory-visual space at birth. *Science, 134*, 1692.

Whitehurst, G. J., & Lonigan, C. J. (1998). Child development and emergent literacy. *Child Development, 69*, 335–357.

Wolf, M. (1991). Naming speed and reading: The contribution of the cognitive neurosciences. *Reading Research Quarterly, 26*, 123–141.

Wolf, M. A., & Bowers, P. G. (1999). The double-deficit hypothesis for the developmental dyslexias. *Journal of Educational Psychology, 91*, 415–438.

Wolf, M., & Goodglass, A. (1986). Dyslexia, dysnomia, and lexical retrieval: A longitudinal investigation. *Brain and Language, 28*, 154–168.

Ysseldyke, J. (2001). Reflections on a research career: Generalizations from 25 years of research on assessment and instructional decision making. *Exceptional Children, 67*, 295–309.

Zeffiro, T. J., & Eden, G. (2000). The neural basis of developmental dyslexia. *Annals of Dyslexia, 50*, 1–30.

RESPONSE TO "EMPIRICAL AND THEORETICAL SUPPORT FOR DIRECT DIAGNOSIS OF LEARNING DISABILITIES BY ASSESSMENT OF INTRINSIC PROCESSING WEAKNESSES"

Virginia W. Berninger, University of Washington

This white paper addresses whether sufficient scientific knowledge exists to recommend that schools use direct assessment of intrinsic processing abilities to identify students with learning disabilities. The commentary on this paper is divided into three parts: (a) the issue at stake, (b) Torgesen's position, and (c) other points. This commentary reflects the multiple perspectives of the author as researcher (director of the Multidisciplinary Learning Disability Center and Writing Project, funded by the National Institute of Child Health and Human Development), trainer of school psychologists (professor of educational psychology), clinician who assesses children with developmental and learning differences (licensed clinical psychologist) and consults with schools, and former general and special educator.

ISSUE AT STAKE

Over the past three decades considerable research progress has been made in understanding the processes contributing to normal acquisition of reading, writing, and math, especially at the early stages of academic learning (Berninger & Richards, 2002). These same processes, if impaired, can interfere with normal acquisition of academic skills and result in a specific reading, writing, and/or math disability. Cognitive and developmental psychologists and medical doctors, such as developmental pediatricians and child neurologists, conducted this research. Although researchers in one domain may not be aware of the research in the other academic domains, research does exist across academic domains. Some research has focused on component skills within academic domains (e.g., word recognition accuracy and fluency, phonological decoding accuracy and fluency, and comprehension in reading; handwriting legibility and automaticity, spelling, and composition in writing; math fact retrieval, arithmetic algorithms, problem solving, and concepts in math). Other research has focused on the cognitive or neurodevelopmental processes that are related to a component skill in an academic domain (e.g., orthographic, phonological, and rapid automatic naming for word recognition; verbal reasoning, morphological and syntactic knowledge, and working memory for reading comprehension; orthographic and fine motor skills for handwriting; phonological and orthographic skills for spelling; planning, translating, and reviewing/ revising for composing; visual spatial, fine motor, language, short-term, long-term, and working memory skills, and math concepts for arithmetic algorithms and applications).

Because nationally normed, standardized measures are available for all these academic component skills and most of the related processes, it is reasonable to expect schools to describe a student's profile of academic and process skills as part of in-depth assessment. In addition, considerable research on early reading in the United States and other countries has documented the processes that best predict beginning reading. Researchers have developed measures of these processes for identifying students for the purpose of early intervention that are also now available to schools. Our review of the literature 5 years ago indicated that sufficient research had been conducted and replicated across laboratories to document that three language processes (phonological, orthographic, and rapid naming) predict beginning reading and are marker variables in the phenotype for specific reading disability (dyslexia) in which word reading and spelling skills are significantly underdeveloped compared to verbal comprehension. Subsequent research confirmed that these three language measures predict response to early intervention (e.g., Stage, Abbott, Jenkins, & Berninger, in press) and the phenotype for component reading and writing skills in child and adult dyslexics (Berninger, Abbott, Thomson, & Raskind, 2001).

However, a general principle should be kept in mind: Process measures are necessary but not sufficient and should not be used alone without the related component academic skills. The goal of service delivery is always to increase student-learning outcome in academic skills. Moreover, the work of Lynn and Doug Fuchs at Vanderbilt shows that the more frequently the academic progress is assessed, the greater the learning (reviewed in Berninger, 1998), demonstrating the need for more frequent monitoring of academic progress than the current mandate for a 3-year reassessment.

Torgesen is correct that contrasting intrinsic versus extrinsic processing is problematic because these processing skills are not just intrinsic to the individual and are responsive to instruction. That is, processing skills are the result of nature-nurture interactions in which genes and brain structures constrain learning but do not cause it independent of academic instruction (see special issue, summer 2001, in *Learning Disability Quarterly* on nature-nurture interactions in school learning). For example, brain-imaging research at the University of Washington showed that the brain could change in efficiency of phonological processing in response to phonologically driven intervention (Richards et al., 2000).

TORGESEN'S POSITION

Torgesen's position, as stated in this volume, is that as scientifically flawed and unfair as the current discrepancy criteria are, eliminating the discrepancy definition runs the risk of losing recognition of learning disability as a concept that can help educators and politicians understand the specificity of the learning problem: Despite normal intelligence, the student has a specific learning difficulty and other areas of development and functioning are in the normal range. Torgesen's caution about possible side effects in eliminating the discrepancy definition should be taken very seriously. Before eliminating the discrepancy definition altogether, it is important that the implications of a replacement scheme be well thought out. One such criterion might be: Will it serve the needs of *all* students with developmental and learning differences? One of the unfortunate consequences of the current classification scheme is that slow learners and those with neurologically based learning disabilities are short-shrifted because their learning problems are not appropriately described on the basis of IQ-achievement discrepancy (Berninger, 2001). At the same time, it is also important to serve the gifted students with learning disabilities (e.g., Yates, Berninger, & Abbott, 1994). The slower learners are more likely to be identified on the basis of absolute low achievement, whereas the gifted learning disabled are most likely to be identified on the basis of IQ-achievement discrepancy—thus the need for flexible criteria in serving the needs of all students (Berninger, Hart, Abbott, & Karovsky, 1992).

Torgesen recommends replacing the discrepancy definition with a two-stage or two-tier model that combines assessment of marker variables with careful and continuous monitoring of children's response to early and subsequent interventions. In the first tier, students would be labeled "at risk" to be eligible for special services. In the second tier, those students who continued to have difficulty despite intervention would be qualified for special services under the category of learning disabled. Research supporting this position is reviewed in Berninger (1998); Berninger, Stage, Smith, and Hildebrand (2001); Busse, Berninger, Smith, and Hildebrand (2001); and Berninger (in press). The first reference discussed a two-tier model, but the last three entertained a three-tier model in which the second tier becomes the third tier and a new second tier of collaborative problem solving is introduced. This new second tier is based on a growing practice in the schools in which the school psychologist works with the multidisciplinary team that includes classroom teachers in general education and uses curriculum-based assessment measures to identify at-risk students and to monitor their progress following modification of the general education program. For the remainder of this commentary, only the first tier (early intervention) and second tier (ongoing intervention for the most severely impaired) in Torgesen's model will be discussed.

In our view, IQ-achievement discrepancy is not relevant to the first tier, which should be made available to all struggling beginning readers in order to optimize the learning of all students. Discrepancy is relevant to some diagnoses at the second tier, for example, dyslexia, but it is not the only consideration in assessment of the more severe learning disorders. For those with specific learning disability, some degree of IQ-achievement discrepancy is usually present but specific language process marker deficits are also present. Thus, IQ should be part of the second tier assessment, but is only one variable to consider. Language process measures should also be administered along with measures of reading, writing, and math skills. Learning disabilities should never be diagnosed solely on the basis of profiles of subtests on intelligence tests (cf. Ysseldyke, 2001).

OTHER POINTS

Research on the processes that contribute to learning to read, write, and do math will continue. It is important that federal legislation allow for application of scientific advancements to assessment and intervention (e.g., in understanding processes in academic learning). For example, schools might be authorized to assess the language and neuropsychological processes that have already been validated but also acknowledge that others may be added in the future as the scientific evidence for them becomes available. For example, several research groups worldwide are now investigating morphological and syntactic processes; others are investigating low-level processes in the visual, auditory, and motor systems that may explain the learning problems of some children (Berninger & Richards, 2002). Progress has been made and continues to be made in understanding the role of attention, executive function, and memory processes in academic learning (Lyon & Krasnegor, 1996).

However, no matter what processes are found to be deficient it is still important that instruction be aimed at all the necessary components of curriculum at the appropriate developmental level (Berninger, 1998). The mistake of the diagnostic-prescriptive model was that isolated processes became the target of instruction. A systems approach that comprehensively addresses multiple components is needed if students are to acquire functional reading, writing, and math systems. For example, phonological awareness may be the deficit that interferes with learning to read, but still instruction should be aimed at phonological decoding, word automaticity, oral reading fluency, and comprehension as well as phonological

awareness. An analogy to illustrate the problem in designing instructional programs based on research on etiology (processing deficits) is the car engine that
breaks down because the spark plug misfires. Building a car engine requires more
components than a spark plug, but also awareness that the car will not move unless
the spark to ignite all the other parts is functional. (See Berninger, 1998, for further
discussion of the systems approach as an alternative to the diagnostic-prescriptive
model that was not supported by research.)

One of the unfortunate side effects of Public Law 94-142 and the Individuals with
Disabilities Education Act (IDEA) has been that schools are more focused on deciding whether students qualify for special education services than on conducting
careful differential diagnosis for those in the second tier with persistent, severe
learning problems (Berninger, 1998). When our Multidisciplinary Learning Disabilities Center first opened in 1995, we sent flyers to local special education teachers and school psychologists to send to parents of students with whom they worked.
The resulting referrals included students with mental retardation, pervasive developmental disorder, autism, specific language impairment, and slower learners as
well as some who meet the inclusion criteria for specific reading and/or writing
disability. Diagnostic confusion prevailed in the schools, and parents told us over
and over that what they really wanted was to understand the nature of their child's
problem (i.e., obtain a diagnosis) and to receive acknowledgement that there really
was a problem. The true dyslexics who met the inclusion criteria for research (but
found us through a network of parents) were often not being given services at
school because the schools said they were bright and not in as much need as the
low IQ children. Many parents were told that dyslexia does not exist; this refusal to
acknowledge a condition that crossed multiple generations of their families caused
these families a great deal of distress. Part of the reason for the diagnostic confusion may be that although the law requires multidisciplinary assessment, no provision was made for creating a conceptual framework for integrating assessment
information across disciplines for the purpose of differential diagnosis.

At the invitation of the International Dyslexia Association, I described such an
approach based on examination of student profiles *across developmental domains,
academic domains, and processing domains* (Berninger, 2001). In this approach, differential diagnosis of the most common learning differences (e.g., mental retardation, pervasive developmental disorder, autism, specific language impairment, slower
learning, specific learning disability—dyslexia, dysgraphia, dyscalculia, and other)
emerges from analysis of the individual profile. Just because all these learning disorders have phonological processing problems (and most do relative to the mean
for age or grade), it does not follow that all of these learning disorders have the
same etiology, instructional needs, or prognosis. Likewise, Pennington, Bennetto,
McAleer, and Roberts (1996) cautioned that executive function deficiencies are

found across many neuropsychiatric and developmental disorders such as early treated phenylketonuria, autism, attention deficit hyperactivity disorder, and fragile X syndrome in women. A single marker process variable in the reading, writing, or math phenotype does not define the disorder apart from its context in the profile of all the relevant neurological, neuropsychological, developmental, and academic domains. The marker process variables should be part of the second tier assessment process but not the only consideration. All in all, children would be served better if more attention were devoted to diagnosis in the second tier in addition to making a decision about whether a student qualifies for special education. Placement decisions and diagnosis are separate issues, but currently eligibility categories, which are not based on scientific research, and differential diagnosis, which should be based on scientific research, are confused; the confusion often leads to unfortunate lawsuits. In the author's experience as an expert witness, the *Diagnostic and Statistical Manual of Mental Disorders* (DSM–IV), which is grounded in scientific research, overrides the special educational eligibility categories, which are not diagnostic categories and are not grounded in scientific research and disciplinary knowledge.

The school psychologists we train report two major impediments to effective delivery of services to students with learning disabilities: overwhelming amounts of paperwork and artificial boundaries between general and special education. The system is driven by documenting in writing that legal procedures were followed to prevent lawsuits rather than by documenting the ongoing instructional interventions and individual progress in response to instruction. Prior to 1975, general educators were expected to serve the whole continuum of students in their classes (except for the severely impaired). More and more, special education is viewed as a dumping ground for students with any kind of learning difference. Policy is needed that rewards general and special educators for working together to document measurable academic progress. (See Berninger, in press, for an example of how such collaboration resulted in the lowest readers at the beginning of first grade achieving above the mean by the end of first grade).

To make the two-tier model recommended by Torgesen financially affordable requires a team effort and a two-tier funding mechanism. A systems level collaboration of the whole school is needed in which school psychologists, speech and language specialists, and special educators help administer and score the screening measures across all K-2 general education classrooms and work with teachers to either implement the specialized instruction in general education classrooms or supervise paraprofessionals to deliver the instruction in pull-out or before- or after-school models. The first tier is cost effective because schools that implement the first tier substantially reduce the number of students requiring second-tier intervention (see Stage's work reported in Berninger et al., 2001). Federal legislation should change funding policies so that schools receive a certain allocation of the special education money for implementing first-tier screening and early intervention that is not tied to qualifying any student for special education. The remaining allocation for implementing second-tier assessment and intervention should, however, be tied to specific students with severe learning problems despite early intervention; these students should receive thorough diagnostic assessments and frequent, ongoing monitoring of their educational progress, with modification of their instructional program if necessary.

REFERENCES

Berninger, V. (1998). *Process assessment of the learner: Guides for reading and writing intervention.* San Antonio, TX: The Psychological Corporation.

Berninger, V. (2001). Understanding the lexia in dyslexia. *Annals of Dyslexia, 51,* 23–48.

Berninger, V. (in press). Best practices in reading, writing, and math assessment-intervention links: A systems approach for schools, classrooms, and individuals. In A. Thomas & J. Grimes (Eds.), *Best practices in school psychology IV.* Bethesda, MD: National Association of School Psychologists.

Berninger, V., Abbott, R., Thomson, J., & Raskind, W. (2001). Language phenotype for reading and writing disability: A family approach. *Scientific Studies in Reading, 5,* 59–105.

Berninger, V., Hart, T., Abbott, R., & Karovsky, P. (1992). Defining reading and writing disabilities with and without IQ: A flexible, developmental perspective. *Learning Disability Quarterly, 15,* 103–118.

Berninger, V., & Richards, T. (2002). *Brain literacy for educators and psychologists.* New York: Academic Press.

Berninger, V., Stage, S., Smith, D., & Hildebrand, D. (2001). Assessment for reading and writing intervention: A 3-tier model for prevention and intervention. In J. Andrews, H. D. Saklofske, & H. Janzen (Eds.), *Ability, achievement, and behavior assessment: A practical handbook* (pp. 195–223). New York: Academic Press.

Busse, J., Berninger, V., Smith, D., & Hildebrand, D. (2001). Assessment for math talent and disability: A developmental model. In J. Andrews, H. Saklofske, & H. Janzen (Eds.), *Ability, achievement, and behavior assessment: A practical handbook* (pp. 225–253). New York: Academic Press.

Lyon, G. R., & Krasnegor, N. (1996). *Attention, memory, and executive function.* Baltimore, MD: Paul H. Brookes Publishing Co.

Pennington, B., Bennetto, L., McAleer, O., & Roberts, R. (1996). Executive functions and working memory: Theoretical and measurement issues. In G. R. Lyon & N. Krasnegor (Eds.), *Attention, memory, and executive function* (pp. 327–348). Baltimore, MD: Paul H. Brookes Publishing Co.

Richards, T., Corina, D., Serafini, S., Steury, K., Dager, S., Marro, K., et al. (2000). Effects of phonologically driven treatment for dyslexia on lactate levels as measured by proton MRSI. *American Journal of Radiology, 21*: 916–922.

Stage, S., Abbott, R., Jenkins, J., & Berninger, V. (in press). *Predicting response to early reading intervention using Verbal IQ, reading-related language abilities, attention ratings, and Verbal IQ-word reading discrepancy.* To appear in a special issue of *Journal of Learning Disabilities.*

Yates, C., Berninger, V., & Abbott, R. (1994). Writing problems in intellectually gifted children. *Journal for the Education of the Gifted, 18,* 131–155.

Ysseldyke, J. (2001). Reflections on a research career: Generalizations from 25 years of research on assessment and instructional decision-making. *Exceptional Children, 67,* 295–309.

A COMMENTARY ON "EMPIRICAL AND THEORETICAL SUPPORT FOR DIRECT DIAGNOSIS OF LEARNING DISABILITIES BY ASSESSMENT OF INTRINSIC PROCESSING WEAKNESSES"

Harold J. McGrady, Division for Learning Disabilities, Council for Exceptional Children

Torgesen's proposal to diagnose learning disabilities through the direct assessment of intrinsic processing weaknesses is a latter-day attempt to operationalize a long-held premise about learning disabilities. The assumption is that learning disabilities are the result of underlying brain dysfunctions that create deficiencies in certain processing skills that are prerequisite to specific types of learning. The proposed approach has promise, but not necessarily because it operationalizes the stated premise.

A validated taxonomy of intrinsic psychological processes is not yet available. Consequently, it cannot be determined that certain hypothesized processes qualify as intrinsic independent causal factors of specific learning disabilities. Torgesen concedes that scientists will need to reach "substantial concurrence about what the critical intrinsic processes are that affect every type of learning disability" (this volume) if measurement of intrinsic psychological processes is to be useful in diagnosis of learning disabilities. Because the necessary proof is not yet available, Torgesen concludes that "the foundation for reliable and valid measurement of the intrinsic psychological processing weakness of children with learning disabilities is not strong enough to recommend it for widespread application in schools" (this volume). This reviewer agrees.

However, Torgesen suggests an approach to assessment in the schools that may have benefit independent from any theory of intrinsic processing weaknesses. The screening and delayed diagnosis system that he proposes would be beneficial because: (1) it would identify potential problem learners early; (2) it would bring immediate intervention without the need for intensive diagnostic testing, thus capitalizing on critical periods of learning; (3) it would allow for extensive periods of diagnostic teaching; (4) it would not invoke the negative stigma associated with some disability labels; and (5) it would help the learning of all students. Torgesen has provided empirical evidence that such a system works. There would be pitfalls in the implementation of such a model, but it would be an improvement over present methodology. Following is a more detailed response to Torgesen's proposal.

DISCUSSION

Torgesen has addressed what may be one of the most critical and controversial core issues involving the concept of learning disabilities: the assumption that specific learning disabilities may be the result of weaknesses in underlying psychological processes. He calls them intrinsic processing *weaknesses* in the title of his paper, yet uses the term intrinsic processing *disabilities*. This semantic dissonance is significant, because it begs the question: Is the processing weakness *the* disability, i.e., the cause of a particular learning problem, such as a reading difficulty, or is the manifested learning problem the disability?

Torgesen supports the premise that certain academic problems may be the result of underlying disability in critical psychological process(es), with biological (genetic, neurological, or biochemical) factors as the root cause. Thus, the syllogism is as follows: A central nervous system defect causes a disability in certain information processing mechanisms, which in turn leads to a problem in performing certain learning tasks. Because children may fail to learn for a variety of different non-biological extrinsic reasons, such as inadequate exposure to information or inappropriate teaching, it is hypothesized that direct measurement of critical intrinsic processing mechanisms might be the best way to determine whether or not a child has a *true* learning disability.

Not only has Torgesen taken on this very demanding conceptual task, but he has also added an even more difficult dimension to his inquiry. He asks whether it is possible, given current levels of scientific knowledge, to use direct measures of intrinsic processing disabilities for the diagnosis of specific learning disabilities in the schools. In response to Torgesen's assertions, this reviewer has posed three questions: (1) Is there sufficient research evidence to convince the most skeptical scientist that intrinsic psychological processes[1] are the source of underlying disabilities for some youngsters who do not do well in various academic or social tasks? (2) Has he provided educational diagnosticians with sufficient data to persuade them that measures of such processes would be useful in their testing of students suspected of having learning disabilities? And (3) would the use of Torgesen's approach improve diagnosis and remedial instruction for students with specific learning disabilities?[2]

ARE WEAKNESSES IN INTRINSIC PSYCHOLOGICAL PROCESSES THE TRUE DISABILITIES?

Defining intrinsic psychological processes and their significance is a complicated task at best. Comparable to the "blind man and the elephant" parable, Torgesen clearly showed that definitions of intrinsic processing depend on one's particular professional perspective and the level(s) of processing being considered. There is need for a model that explains the entire hierarchical system that would be required for learning a particular set of behaviors, such as learning to read, as well as the components of that system. But Torgesen properly cautions the reader that any such theory of learning disabilities must account for the heterogeneous nature of this entity, as recognized by the National Joint Committee on Learning Disabilities (NJCLD) in their position paper on definition (NJCLD, 2001).

Torgesen's paper demonstrated a clear need for the development of an accurate taxonomy of intrinsic psychological processes. Without such a validated taxonomy, the task of establishing the site of a disability can only be determined through empirical evidence, i.e., relying on experience or observation alone without due regard for system and theory. Such being the case, the exercise of sound clinical judgment, although variable and subjective, might still be the most valid current way to determine presence or absence of a learning disability.[3]

We agree with Torgesen that the most likely model for defining learning disabilities is an information processing model. This approach is not new. An exemplary early attempt in the area of learning disabilities was the work of Chalfant and Scheffelin (1969). Their monograph was a review of research on central processing dysfunctions in children. They organized the review of research around topics such as "dysfunctions in the analysis of sensory information" (auditory, visual and tactile); dysfunctions in synthesis of sensory information (multiple stimulus integration and short-term memory); and dysfunctions in symbolic operations (auditory language, decoding written language, encoding written language, and quantitative language). Other iterations and modifications could be cited from ensuing literature. Furthermore, clinical reports are often based on such models. Modern advances in technology now make it more feasible to research this theory. With the advent of computers, theorists are now able to conceptualize learning and brain functions as analogous to a very sophisticated computer, an advancement over earlier telephone transmission notions or even more naïve mechanistic concepts.

Torgesen's discussion about the distinctions among types of psychological processes demonstrates the naïveté of advancing any simple information processing model. Noting that the factors of automaticity, domain specificity, and adaptation must be considered, it is clear that no simplistic model will suffice. This discussion should remind the reader of the importance of developmental factors, particularly critical periods for learning. Perhaps the best model for advancing this concept was the work of Maria Montessori (as reported by Standing, 1962). A physician who truly understood the biological bases for learning, Montessori stressed what she called "sensitive periods" for learning, presumably biologically based limitations. Her many examples from nature remind us that there may be critical periods in a child's life at which it is most advantageous to process certain types of information. In human learning for example, the younger a person is when exposed to a second language, the easier it is to learn to speak that language without a discernible accent. This developmental factor must be considered when examining the results of research about information processing mechanisms.

Perhaps the most salient point is Torgesen's admission that he does not know the answer to the question posed above: Are weaknesses in intrinsic psychological processes the true disabilities? He reports scientific evidence of individual differences in processing speed, sequencing, and capacity as several promising examples from research, but concludes that "whether these problems . . . qualify as 'intrinsic' processing limitations and primary causes of learning disabilities, or . . . a secondary characteristic arising as a reaction to early and chronic academic failure is a question that is not completely resolved" (this volume).

Torgesen recognizes the social and political factors that surround today's concept and use of the term *learning disabilities*. This reviewer has long recognized that "learning disabilities must be considered a sociopolitical entity" (McGrady, 1980, p. 513). But the political victories that have allowed educators to provide appropriate educational services to previously neglected students with learning disabilities have been tarnished. The term has been distorted through inappropriate application. Furthermore, the trend towards inclusive educational programs has resulted in an abandonment of the hallmark of special education: intensive individualized instruction. This reviewer has soundly criticized the misapplication of the term. "The term *learning disabilities* has been misused: sometimes overused, sometimes underused. Nationwide we are guilty of category abuse" (McGrady, 1987, p. 109). It is the objective scientific work like Torgesen's that may some day distinguish the real learning disabilities from those impostors that have been labeled as such for social or political expedience.

Torgesen's presentation of research in the area of phonological awareness indicates the potential pitfalls of designating the lack of a particular skill or behavior as the intrinsic processing weakness or the contributing factor to an academic problem. Although he states that "there is now a substantial body of . . . evidence indicating that differences among children on these language skills are causally related to variability in the rate at which children acquire early word reading abilities" (this volume), the reader is left to ponder whether the long list of studies cited truly can justify that conclusion. In fact, his own summary negates that conclusion. He states that: "we have strong evidence that one of the most commonly used measures of intrinsic processing weaknesses in the phonological area is influenced both by constitutionally based differences in processing capability and environmental/instructional factors at home and school" (this volume).

He does, however, provide the argument that there is increasing evidence to establish the neurobiological loci for certain behaviors. In this endeavor we often fail to recognize the works of earlier theorists, researchers, and clinicians. Much of the current evidence being gathered in laboratories is confirmation of brain-behavior relationships hypothesized at a time when technological sophistication might have been an oxymoron. The concept that Torgesen continues to follow is that learning disabilities are psychoneurological phenomena. There is a brain-behavior relationship that is the basis for all learning. The study of abnormal learners has the potential to contribute to our understanding of those relationships.

It was encouraging to see Torgesen include a discussion of nonverbal learning disabilities (NLD). Too often learning disabilities are associated only with failures in academic learning such as reading or writing. Recognition of NLD is not a new notion. My mentor and colleague, Helmer Myklebust, together with another colleague, Doris Johnson at Northwestern University, devoted an entire chapter to this topic in their seminal text on educational principles and practices for learning disabilities (Johnson and Myklebust, 1967). They dealt with topics such as motor learning, body image, spatial orientation, right-left orientation, and social imperception, as well as the symptoms that are so often associated with the "brain-injured child": distractibility, perseveration, and disinhibition. Many of these symptoms have more recently become associated with the designation of attention deficit hyperactivity disorder. Whether NLD are to be considered as distinct disabilities, comorbid conditions, or the causes of certain learning disabilities, it is important that they be studied thoroughly.

Torgesen expressed considerable favor with Rourke's work on NLD, especially since it is couched in neuropsychological terms, i.e., the research has included evidence to support certain brain-behavior connections. Rourke's studies represent a very salient principle in our attempt to understand the concept of learning disabilities. Rourke considers the pattern of neuropsychological assets and deficits (strengths vs. weaknesses) in a given child: comparison of a child's visual-spatial-organizational skills with performance on measures of vocabulary, or deficits on measures of complex motor versus simple motor skills. It is these types of comparisons that are often used in traditional clinical diagnosis. This approach highlights one of the prime criteria for the classical diagnosis of learning disabilities: determination of significant *intra*-individual differences.

But there is an important distinction in the types of comparisons made in the Rourke paradigm. The discrepancy comparisons are made *among* apparently discrete skills and abilities, not as a comparison of such skills with performance on a general estimate of intellectual potential—the traditional discrepancy formula approach. The research and clinical literature abound with comparisons that use various measures to determine a discrepancy, and most have been found wanting. If comparisons among measures are used as valid indicators that a significant intra-individual discrepancy is present, the comparisons must be among distinct skills in a hierarchy that measures different processes, skills, or abilities. That is the catch-22 of diagnosis for learning disabilities. Without the clearly validated hierarchy defined, any such comparisons will be suspect.

Torgesen has raised some very interesting questions. He has faithfully followed his attempt to confirm or deny the hypotheses about intrinsic processing. However, he has not yet discovered the base functions that would allow them to be used in diagnosis. This reviewer has posed the question: Are weaknesses in intrinsic psychological processes the true disabilities? The answer: We still don't know. The conclusion: This is a promising avenue for research, but "we have miles to go before we sleep."

CAN INTRINSIC PSYCHOLOGICAL PROCESSES BE MEASURED ADEQUATELY?

Some might say that there is no need to answer this question, because the first question has not yet been answered affirmatively. There is value, however, in considering the potential advantages and difficulties of implementing the processing approach to diagnosis, as Torgesen has done.

Professional diagnosticians in the field of learning disabilities have struggled for decades to find ways of measuring psychological processes in their regimen of tests. Even prior to the advent of Public Law (P.L.) 94-142, the Education for All Handicapped Children Act of 1975, we conducted a national study that addressed this issue (McGrady & Anderson, 1974). Our study sample consisted of schools in each of 38 states that had model learning disabilities projects sponsored by the Bureau of Education for the Handicapped.

In that study we found that 33 of the 38 sites (87%) professed to measure psychological processes in determining whether a child might have a learning disability. We were investigating decision-making processes used to establish eligibility for services at these learning disabilities model programs. We were curious to know whether they required evidence of deficiency in measured skills and/or a discrepancy relative to a measure of cognitive potential. We reviewed their use of both academic skills measures and psychological processes testing. The most prevalent practice in these centers was a requirement that a student display discrepant scores in *both* academics and psychological processes to qualify as learning disabled. Although the measures of psychological processes, such as memory, sound discrimination, and the like, might be considered crude by modern standards, it is clear that early practitioners in the schools were convinced that underlying psychological processes were important components in the diagnosis of learning disabilities. They were attempting to operationalize learning disabilities identification using pre-P.L. 94-142 thinking (McGrady, 1987). Torgesen's search for the Holy Grail of measurement regarding intrinsic psychological processes is simply a more sophisticated manifestation of early attempts to operationalize prevalent theories of learning disabilities.

In this search for answers, Torgesen lists a series of advantages to the processing approach: (1) early identification, to stimulate preventive intervention; (2) a reduction in arbitrary exclusions from remedial help; and (3) a better understanding of the component processes for instruction. These are each desirable implications. However, Torgesen may have been reaching beyond the data in certain conclusions. For example, he states that "measures of phonological awareness . . . assess a kind of knowledge about phonemes and an ability to process them in specific ways that is *causally* [my emphasis] related to ability to acquire alphabetic reading skills" (this volume). Considering the previous discussion, this statement may be a bit strong. In deference to Torgesen, however, he does clearly caution the reader that some of the approaches being researched and reported are "speculative."

Torgesen also enumerates the difficulties that would be encountered in order to implement direct assessment of intrinsic processing weaknesses. Significantly, that section is notably longer than the section on advantages. Torgesen recognizes that the more central, basic, or lower in the system the process to be evaluated, the greater the difficulty in obtaining useful measures. Furthermore, it is recognized that the central nervous system consists of many interconnections, creating a rich array of potential interactions among the processes.

What, then is the answer to our second question posed above: Can intrinsic psychological processes be measured adequately? Although citing some promising leads, the jury is still out on that answer. As Torgesen concludes: "the foundation for reliable and valid measurement of the intrinsic psychological processing weakness of children with learning disabilities is not strong enough to recommend it for widespread application in schools" (this volume).

CAN TORGESEN'S APPROACH IMPROVE DIAGNOSIS AND REMEDIAL INSTRUCTION FOR STUDENTS WITH LEARNING DISABILITIES?[4]

Not wanting to disband the major premise of this paper, Torgesen has suggested alternatives to classification based on assessment of intrinsic processes. Under his scheme, low performance on certain marker (predictor) variables, such as phonological awareness and rapid automatic naming, would qualify a student for "special preventive instruction." Those students who were judged to be mentally retarded or who belong to some other primary classification would be excepted. According to the system used in our previously cited study (McGrady & Anderson, 1974), this diagnostic approach would have been categorized as *diagnosis by exclusion*. In addition, however, to qualify for preventive instruction, the child would have to display evidence of processing deficits (not discrepancies). Thus, the procedures proposed by Torgesen comprise a deficit model. In order to be included in the special instruction (once the exclusive factors were discounted), the child would only need to show a weakness in one of the marker variables, disregarding comparisons to any other measure(s).[5]

An actual diagnosis would be delayed and dependent on the child's responsiveness to educational intervention. Torgesen's approach to the actual designation of a child as learning disabled is *diagnosis by trial teaching*, an approach that this reviewer feels is promising and demands further research and exploration. Torgesen refers to Vellutino's contention that "children who do not respond adequately to well designed instruction can be considered classically learning disabled" (this volume). Torgesen strongly disagrees with that position, indicating that many other variables would need to be considered before determining with finality that any youngster is truly learning disabled. His conclusion: "Any methodology that uses response to treatment as a way of classifying children as learning disabled has no greater chance of correctly identifying children with intrinsic learning disorders than do traditional assessment procedures" (this volume). That may be an overstatement. Torgesen contradicts his own conclusion when he recommends measurement of marker variables, followed by preventive instruction for those who show weaknesses in those predictors, with eventual identification as learning disabled only for those who do not respond. That sounds like diagnosis by trial teaching to this reviewer.

This reviewer agrees with Torgesen that important keys to whether such a system would work are the establishment of appropriate at-risk cut-off points and the appropriateness of early instructional intervention. He recommends a tiered instructional intervention system, using research-based instructional methods. Such an approach might prove to be the most efficient and valid diagnostic process.

Torgesen has stated an important presumption that would have significant effects on this approach:

> I am assuming that classroom teachers are doing all they can to deliver high-quality, research-based instruction to all children, and that they are actively trying to accommodate individual differences in response to their instruction. If this is not the case, there will be far too many children requiring services under the learning disabilities regulations for the system to work effectively." (this volume)

This reviewer does not believe that such a circumstance is the norm for schools today. Teachers will need to be trained to accomplish the kind of instruction that he suggests. We agree that, if all teachers were performing appropriately, fewer potential learning disabilities would be identified. Implementation of Torgesen's tiered instructional system could be a promising way of achieving that goal, i.e., reducing the numbers of students who need to be classified as learning disabled.

What, then, is the answer to this reviewer's third question: Will the alternative approaches to classification based on assessment of intrinsic psychological processes be of value in planning remedial education for students with learning disabilities? This reviewer's answer is "Yes, but not necessarily for the reasons stated." This approach would be beneficial because it would bring early intervention, research-based instruction, and focused individualized attention to problem learners. There is not sufficient proof to infer that intrinsic psychological processes would be measured or treated.

In the end, many practical factors may determine whether any system, no matter how valid, will work in implementation. To his credit, Torgesen has provided a useful discussion of possible consequences of using his suggested methodology to common practice.

As for the science, this reviewer strongly contends that basic research should continue independent of practices being used in the schools. Support for psychoneurological research should continue and be supplemented. But research into differential educational intervention must be increased significantly. Much progress has been made, but it will take a careful, long-term, coordinated, programmatic effort to research the many questions still unanswered.

REFERENCES

Chalfant, J. C., & Scheffelin, M. A. (1969). *Central processing dysfunctions in children: A review of research*. Washington, DC: NINDS Monograph No. 9.

Johnson, D. J., & Myklebust, H. R. (1967). *Learning disabilities: Educational principles and practices*. New York: Grune and Stratton.

McGrady, H. J. (1980). Communication disorders and specific learning disabilities. In R. J. Van Hattum (Ed.), *Communication disorders: An introduction* (pp. 509–561). New York: Macmillan.

McGrady, H. J. (1987). Eligibility: Back to basics. In S. Vaughn & C. S. Bos (Eds.), *Research in learning disabilities: Issues and future directions* (pp. 105–115). Boston: College Hill.

McGrady, H. J., & Anderson, C. S. (1974). *Screening and identification procedures in the child service demonstration programs*. Tucson, AZ: University of Arizona.

National Joint Committee on Learning Disabilities. (2001). *Collective perspectives on issues affecting learning disabilities* (2nd ed.). Austin, TX: Pro-Ed.

Standing, E. M. (1962). *Maria Montessori: Her life and work*. New York: New American Library of World Literature.

ENDNOTES

[1] The term *psychological processes* will be used when referring to these presumed intrinsic mechanisms. This respects the fact that the successful or unsuccessful implementation of those processes will lead to variant cognitive, social, behavioral, or educational outcomes.

[2] This reviewer wishes to commend Torgesen for using the term *specific* learning disabilities, stressing the important distinction from *general* learning disabilities. National polls consistently show that the public often confuses learning disabilities with mental retardation. Furthermore, school diagnosticians often dismiss this important criterion, i.e., that children with learning disabilities by definition must demonstrate average or above-average intellectual capacity or potential.

[3] This review does not consider the implications for regulatory changes related to the federal Individuals with Disabilities Education Act (IDEA) statute. However, if Torgesen's approach were to prove valid and practicable, regulatory changes would be in order. The fear of this reviewer would be that such changes would be driven more by political concerns than scientific knowledge and diagnostic accuracy.

[4] In answering these questions, this reviewer has purposefully avoided extensive discussion of the controversial discrepancy formula or diagnosis by exclusion methods that are commonly used for identifying youngsters with learning disabilities in the schools. The purpose of comments made in this review was simply to evaluate the methodology suggested by Torgesen. Attempts to assail the current approaches

merely confound the discussion. The processing approach needs to stand or fall on its own merits, not in comparison with other methodologies. If the suggested approach proves worthwhile, then comparisons to present procedures would be moot.

[5] Such an approach would not likely lessen the burden of the psychologist or educational diagnostician, who would still have to establish that the student did not qualify as mentally retarded, visually, or hearing impaired. Also, the direct measures of the so-called intrinsic processes might require more complex methodology than would be available or practicable in the schools.

BLURRING THE BOUNDARY: A COMMENTARY ON TORGESEN'S ARGUMENT FOR THE USE OF PROCESS MARKERS IN THE IDENTIFICATION OF LEARNING DISABILITIES

C. Addison Stone, University of Michigan

At either an implicit or explicit level, the notion of an intrinsic deficit in the processing of information has been central to the construct of specific learning disabilities throughout its early and more recent history. Long before Samuel Kirk (Kirk, 1962) proposed the term *learning disabilities* as a label for this elusive category of developmental inefficiencies, clinical reports of specific cases alluded to intrinsic or congenital causes. Hinshelwood's (1917) now famous accounts of congenital word blindness are good examples, as are Orton's (1937) accounts of spelling and oral language disorders. In fact, with few exceptions (e.g., Mann, REF), explicit categorical arguments *against* the concept of a processing deficit as a cause of learning disabilities have been made only by certain clinical and behavioral psychologists arguing for origins in atypical patterns of family dynamics (e.g., Green, 1989) or reinforcement of unwanted behaviors (e.g., Koorland, 1986) rather than in intrinsic deficits. Even those scholars who have argued strongly against the inclusion of a "process clause" in the learning disabilities definition have done so more out of a sense that the construct has little heuristic value for intervention than out of a conviction that it is an inherently misguided notion. Similarly, even the harshest critics of the field of learning disabilities (e.g., Coles, 1987; Poplin, 1988) have tended to acknowledge the existence of intrinsic process deficits in specific cases while focusing their discussion on the widespread over-extension of this core notion.

Given this history, it is neither surprising nor inappropriate that Torgesen argues in his paper on identification and assessment of learning disabilities for the central role of process deficits in assessment and identification. I tend to agree with Torgesen and other scholars (e.g., Wong, 1986) that the notion of process deficits has always been central to the construct of learning disabilities and that the field should strive to provide the notion with both the theoretical coherence and empirical validity that it deserves. Thus, I was a sympathetic reader of Torgesen's paper. However, as a clinician interested in diagnostic patterns and as a researcher interested in the social context of language and learning disabilities, I do have some concerns about the particular form of Torgesen's arguments. My concerns are sparked primarily by a sense that Torgesen is carving out too narrow a territory and that we need to broaden our vision of the origins and variety of process deficits. My argument, then, is for an expansion of Torgesen's position, not for its revision in any fundamental sense.

Torgesen's central argument, as I see it, is threefold. First, he argues that the notion of process deficits is central to the construct of learning disabilities and that recent research has provided solid evidence for the causal role of at least one process deficit (phonological processing) in at least one common type of learning disability (inefficient word recognition). Second, he argues that, although they are not pure or direct measures of processing, phonological awareness tasks are excellent markers for phonological processing deficits and that they should therefore play a central role in the assessment of reading disabilities. Finally, he argues that such markers (as well as, presumably, other markers) can and should be used to identify and guide intervention for children who are at risk for later learning disabilities long before they meet any criterion of academic failure.

I find myself in basic agreement with Torgesen's central arguments. However, I think that the discussion can and should be framed more broadly, for purposes of both science and policy. In particular, I would like to address two aspects of the argument: (a) the distinction between primary processing deficits and markers of those deficits, and (b) the relatively exclusive focus on phonological awareness as a means of early identification.

INTERACTIVE ORIGINS OF PROCESSING DEFICITS

In his discussion of the factors underlying the achievement problems of children with learning disabilities, Torgesen draws a distinction between processing deficits and markers of those deficits. At issue here is the need to distinguish between intrinsic characteristics of the child that are the underlying cause of the learning disability and a set of "pre-academic skills or capacities" that are indirect results of the manner in which the child and the child's environment have reacted to the core deficit but that are also causally related to academic learning problems. The major marker discussed by Torgesen is phonological awareness, which is based on an underlying deficit in phonological processing and which, in turn, is a key weakness related to early word recognition difficulties. Other markers he mentions are letter naming and rapid automatized naming.

Torgesen refers to process deficits as "fundamental information processing limitations." He notes that "some information processing skills or capacities are clearly acquired through learning and experience, others may represent basic features of the biological 'hardware' that would qualify as intrinsic or constitutionally based features of an individual child's cognitive capabilities" (this volume). His criteria for a process deficit are that it arises early in development, is domain-specific, and is relatively automatic in execution. In contrast, a marker is a derivative skill or "functional capability arising from an interaction between intrinsic processing capabilities and experience" (this volume).

Such a distinction has the virtue of conceptual clarity but, contrary to Torgesen's apparent intention, it may be more a distinction of degree than of kind. There is growing evidence that seemingly basic processing characteristics are the result of a complex interaction between genetic endowment and patterns of experiential stimulation. Torgesen cites Tallal's work (1980) on auditory temporal processing as an example of an intrinsic process. It is interesting to note, however, that the recent intervention efforts of Tallal and colleagues are predicated specifically on the increasingly accepted assumption of neural plasticity and the potential for change in the neural substrate as a result of targeted intervention (Merzenich et al., 1996).

Given this perspective, it becomes much more difficult to maintain a clear distinction between intrinsic process deficits and derivative cognitive markers. This difficulty is made all the clearer in the context of recent work on early patterns of parent-child interaction in various high-risk populations (Landry, Smith, Swank, & Miller-Loncar, 2000; Meadows, 1996; van Ijzendoorn, Goldberg, Kroonenberg, & Frenkel, 1992; van Ijzendoorn, Schuengel, & Bakermans-Kranenburg, 1999). Parents interact differently with their high-risk children both as an apparent response to signals from the infant (Crnic et al., 1983; Landry et al., 2000) and as an apparent response to the social stimulus value of a high-risk label (Donahue & Pearl, 1995). These interaction patterns can be identified quite early in the infant's life (Crnic, Ragozin, Greenberg, Robinson, & Basham, 1983; Landry et al., 2000) and persist (Donahue & Pearl, 1995; Landry et al. 2000). The implications of such interaction patterns are still unclear, but they certainly highlight the possibility that patterns of information processing, even in young infants, may be an interactive result of altered experience (Stone, Bradley, & Kleiner, in press).

In his discussion of possible experiential influences on children's cognitive and academic performance, Torgesen appears to assume that experiential influences are more relevant to the creation of controlled, strategic performance. This view is consistent with his emphasis in earlier writings on the role of experience in the creation of secondary characteristics of children with learning disabilities, such as maladaptive strategy use and poor motivation for learning (Kistner & Torgesen,

1987). However, both the evidence of early experiential influences on the behavioral patterns of very young infants and the fact that processes that are initially controlled may become automatized with repeated use (Siegler, 1998) suggest that early experience can indeed lead to altered patterns of automatic as well as controlled processing.

In arguing for the current need to focus on processing markers in the identification of children at risk for learning disabilities, Torgesen appears to hold out hope that we will eventually be able to abandon this approach in favor of the direct measurement of psychological processing. If by this we mean the measurement of relatively automatic processing, free of strategic overlay, I would agree. If we mean that we will eventually have a direct window into congenital, intrinsic processing, I am doubtful.

The immediate practical implications of this point are limited, but it may have important implications for future policy directions. Perhaps the most important implication is that the division between intrinsic processes, markers of those processes, and traditionally conceived secondary manifestations of a learning disability is a continuum, not a categorical distinction. Thus, identifying candidates for one of these aspects of learning disabilities will be a matter of pragmatic more than conceptual issues. Perhaps the clearest criteria will be the point of developmentally earliest measurement stability, ease of measurement, and predictive power. Such criteria might just as easily point to a traditional secondary characteristic (e.g., passivity) as to a cognitive process as Torgesen defines them. The implications of this fact warrant careful discussion in the context of research priorities and approaches to assessment.

MORE THAN PHONOLOGICAL AWARENESS

As mentioned above, in developing his argument for the role of psychological processes in typical and atypical learning, Torgesen is careful to delineate his criteria for what should count as a process. In addition, he is careful to establish criteria for what would count as necessary and sufficient evidence of the causal role of a specific process in normal and atypical learning. Finally, he is careful to point out that phonological processing is undoubtedly not the only type of process deficit that will be needed in a full account of specific learning disabilities. As other possible candidates, he mentions orthographic processing, working memory, and nonverbal processing, for example. He points out, however, that the evidence for the role of these other candidate processes in children's learning falls short of his criteria for theoretical clarity and/or causal adequacy. Thus, when he turns his attention to the issue of process markers as an implication of his discussion for policy and practice in the area of assessment and identification, his discussion narrows considerably and centers exclusively on phonological awareness, where he feels that the current evidence is adequate.

Torgesen's strategy follows a time-honored tradition of scientific parsimony, i.e., do not invoke constructs for which there is insufficient need or evidence. However sensible this approach might be in the laboratory, it presents a clear danger in the policy arena, a danger of premature closure. As we struggle to build a comprehensive theory of learning disabilities and as we turn our knowledge into practice, we encounter implications for both policy and human services. Torgesen's recommendation for assessment and early intervention, if followed literally, would identify only one type of learning disability, indeed only one type of reading disability. Although there is reason to believe that phonological processing is involved in some types of math problems as well as in word recognition and spelling (e.g., Geary, Hamson, & Hoard, 2000), Torgesen's recommendations result in a considerable narrowing of focus in terms of the range of problems identified. Torgesen is quite right that his suggested approach will lead to the identification of a larger number of children as at risk for reading disability than does the current discrepancy approach, especially when coupled with a lower IQ cutoff. However, many other children with difficulties in language and reading comprehension, mathematics, and content learning would not have the benefit of early identification afforded to children at risk for word recognition problems by Torgesen's approach. Thus, the frame would be correspondingly narrowed.

As I indicated above, Torgesen's suggestion is motivated by his interpretation of the status of current research. However, in reading Torgesen's rationale, I see a potential double standard: Why is working memory excluded as a process marker, for example, on the grounds that there is an experiential component to poor working memory, when Torgesen acknowledges a similar situation for phonological awareness? Working memory is probably also a marker, if not a process, at least by Torgesen's criteria. Moreover, it appears to represent prerequisite skills closely linked to language and reading comprehension as well as math, and thus might serve to identify a group of children who are at risk for learning disabilities and who overlap only partially with those identified by phonological awareness measures.

Similarly, although the evidence for orthographic processing is weaker than the evidence for phonological processing or working memory difficulties, the evidence for the double-deficit hypothesis is growing and difficult to ignore as a possible process marker. Other candidates for process markers also need greater attention, e.g., morphological awareness (Carlisle & Stone, in press; Mann, 1998), morphosyntactic awareness (Bowey, 1994; Leonard, 1998), quantitative reasoning ("number sense"; Geary et al., 2000), semantic associations (Bishop, 1997), and visual-spatial orientation (Harnadek & Rourke, 1994). I doubt that Torgesen would disagree with this point as a call for further research. However, my own feeling is that as we move to recommendations for policy implementation we cannot afford to ignore a broader list of process markers.

Thus, I am arguing for setting our criteria of scientific rigor at a different point on the continuum of evidential certainty. To do otherwise would prematurely disenfranchise a significant proportion of children with clinically significant learning disabilities.

CONCLUSIONS

In sum, I argue that there is danger in premature "boundary setting" for hypothesis generation and research funding, and for the types of children to be served. If we move to let science inform practice by reforming policy in a general way, we should err in the direction of principled inclusiveness and set reasonably generous standards of scientific rigor. Such inclusiveness is especially important in circumstances when there is room for legitimate differences of opinion regarding the ontological status of central constructs.

REFERENCES

Bishop, D. V. M. (1997). *Uncommon understanding: Development and disorders of language comprehension in children.* East Sussex, UK: Psychology Press.

Bowey, J. A. (1994). Grammatical awareness and learning to read: A critique. In J. J. F. ter Laak (Ed.), *Literacy acquisition and social context: The developing body and mind* (pp. 122–149). London: Harvester Wheatsheaf.

Carlisle, J. F., & Stone, C. A. (in press). The effects of morphological structure on children's reading of derived words in English. In E. Assink & D. Sandra (Eds.), *Reading complex words: Cross-language studies.* Kluwer.

Coles, G. (1987). *The learning mystique: A critical look at learning disabilities.* New York: Pantheon.

Crnic, K. A., Ragozin, A. S., Greenberg, M. T., Robinson, N. M., & Basham, R. B. (1983). Social interaction and developmental competence of preterm and full-term infants during the first year of life. *Child Development, 54,* 1199–1210.

Donahue, M. L., & Pearl, R. (1995). Conversational interactions of mothers and their preschool children who had been born pre-term. *Journal of Speech & Hearing Research, 38,* 1–9.

Geary, D. C., Hamson, C. O., & Hoard, M. K. (2000). Numerical and arithmetical cognition: A longitudinal study of process and concept deficits in children with learning disability. *Journal of Experimental Child Psychology, 77,* 236–263.

Green, R. (1989). "Learning to learn" and the family system: New perspectives on underachievement and learning disorders. *Journal of Marital and Family Therapy, 15,* 187–203.

Harnadek, M. C. S., & Rourke, B. P. (1994). Principal identifying features of the syndrome of nonverbal learning disabilities in children. *Journal of Learning Disabilities, 27,* 144–154.

Hinshelwood, J. (1917). *Congenital word blindness.* London: H. K. Lewis.

Ijzendoorn, M. H. van, Goldberg, S., Kroonenberg, P. M., & Frenkel, O. J. (1992). The relative effects of maternal and child problems on the quality of attachment: A meta-analysis of attachment in clinical samples. *Child Development, 63,* 840–858.

Ijzendoorn, M. H. van, Schuengel, C., Bakermans-Kranenburg, M. J. (1999). Disorganized attachment in early childhood: Meta-analysis of precursors, concomitants, and sequelae. *Development and Psychopathology, 11,* 225–249.

Kirk, S. A. (1962). *Educating exceptional children.* Boston: Houghton-Mifflin.

Kistner, J., & Torgesen, J. K. (1987). Motivational and cognitive aspects of learning disabilities. In A. E. Kasdin & B. B. Lahey (Eds.), *Advances in clinical child psychology* (pp. 289–334). New York: Plenum.

Koorland, M. A. (1986). Applied behavior analysis and the correction of learning disabilities. In J. K. Torgesen & B. Y. L. Wong (Eds.), *Psychological and educational perspectives on learning disabilities* (pp. 297–328). Orlando: Academic Press.

Landry, S. H., Smith, K. E., Swank, P. R., & Miller-Loncar, C. L. (2000). Early maternal and child influences on children's later independent cognitive and social functioning. *Child Development, 71,* 358–375.

Leonard, L. B. (1998). *Children with specific language impairment.* Cambridge, MA: MIT Press.

Mann, L. (1979). *On the trail of process.* New York: Grune & Stratton.

Mann, V. (1998). Language problems: A key to early reading problems. In B. Y. L. Wong (Ed.), *Learning about learning disabilities* (2nd ed., pp. 163–201). San Diego: Academic Press.

Meadows, S. (1996). *Parenting behaviour and children's cognitive development.* Hove, England: Psychology/Erlbaum.

Merzenich, M. M., Jenkins, W. M., Johnston, P., Schreiner, C., Miller, S. L., & Tallal, P. (1996). Temporal processing deficits of language-learning impaired children ameliorated by training. *Science, 271,* 77–81.

Orton, S. T. (1937). *Reading, writing, and speech problems in children.* New York: W. W. Norton.

Poplin M. S. (1988). The reductionistic fallacy in learning disabilities: Replicating the past by reducing the present. *Journal of Learning Disabilities, 21,* 389–400.

Siegler, R. (1998). *Children's cognitive development* (3rd ed.). Prentice-Hall.

Stone, C. A., Bradley, K., & Kleiner, J. (in press). The role of parental perceptions in the creation of learning opportunities for children with language/learning disabilities. In B. Y. L. Wong & M. Donahue (Eds.), *The social dimensions of learning disabilities.* Mahwah, NJ: Lawrence Erlbaum Assoc.

Tallal, P. (1980). Auditory temporal perception, phonics, and reading disabilities in children. *Brain and Language, 9,* 182–198.

Wong, B. Y. L. (1986). Problems and issues in the definition of learning disabilities. In J. K. Torgesen & B. Y. L. Wong (Eds.), *Psychological and educational perspectives on learning disabilities* (pp. 1–25). San Diego: Academic Press.

LEARNING DISABILITIES IS A SPECIFIC PROCESSING DEFICIT, BUT IT IS MUCH MORE THAN PHONOLOGICAL PROCESSING

H. Lee Swanson, University of California–Riverside

In my opinion, the case for learning disabilities (LD) rests on three assumptions: (a) Learning difficulties are not due to inadequate opportunity to learn, to general intelligence, or to physical or emotional/behavioral disorders, but are due to basic disorders in specific cognitive information processes; (b) these specific information processing deficits are a reflection of neurological, constitutional, and/or biological factors; and (c) these specific information processing deficits underlie a limited aspect of academic behavior. Thus, to assess LD at the cognitive level, systematic efforts are made to detect: (a) normal psychometric intelligence, (b) below-normal achievement in some academic skills, (c) below-normal performance in specific cognitive processes (i.e., phonological awareness, working memory), (d) that optimal instruction has been presented but deficits in isolated processes remain, and (e) that processing deficits are not directly caused by environmental factors or contingencies (e.g., socioeconomic status). Unfortunately, the identification of LD has been clouded by current practices that focus on uncovering a significant discrepancy between achievement in a particular academic domain and general psychometric intellectual ability (see Hoskyn & Swanson, 2000, for a review of this literature). This approach has questionable validity and other approaches must be formalized. The alternative approach suggested by Torgesen as well as others (see Swanson, 1987, special issue on information processing) is to focus on process assessment. The model for theory testing suggested by Torgesen consonant with my own (see Swanson, 1988b; also see Torgesen, 1988, for rebuttal).

There are several aspects of Torgesen's paper in which we are kindred spirits. There are other points in which we differ. The parts I agree with are as follows: (1) The processing difficulties of students with LD have a constitutional base that in turn influences functional processing (i.e., the primary problems are in the hardware

Response to "Empirical and Theoretical Support for Direct Diagnosis of Learning Disabilities by Assessment of Intrinsic Processing Weaknesses"

and not the software); (2) absolute levels of intelligence and reading must be used in defining LD (e.g., average IQ but reading is below normal—I prefer that full scale IQ is above 85, but reading and/or math standard scores are below 85); (3) intensive remedial training is critical to the assessment process (see Swanson, 1988b, for a discussion of this issue); and (4) several experimental researchers have long ago abandoned school-based discrepancy models in their selection of participants for study.

My specific concerns in this extremely short analysis relate to Torgesen's (a) representation of the causal role of domain-general processing, and (b) overemphasis on phonological skills as theoretical bases for instruction. The purpose of outlining my concerns are to complement his work.

I. What Is Meant by Domain-Specific vs. Domain-General "Intrinsic" Processes?

The paper by Torgesen is unclear about how domain-general processes play a causal role in LD. Torgesen suggests that a causal model cannot be invoked and that domain-general processes are a result of poor achievement. I will briefly outline the causal model and then quickly review the results of several empirical studies. Before I do, it is necessary in lay terms to compare the tasks emphasized by Torgesen and those emphasized by myself. Simply stated, some children with LD perform poorly on tasks that require accurate and/or speedy recognition or recall of strings of letters, numbers, real words, and pseudowords. These tasks have a "read in and read out" quality to them, i.e., few demands are placed on long-term memory to infer or transform the information. One common link among these tasks is the ability to store and/or access the sound "structure" of language (hereto referred to as phonological processing). Torgesen sees these skills as important, as I do. However, some children with LD also do poorly on tasks that place demands on attentional capacity (for example, holding a person's address in mind while listening to instructions about how to get there, listening to a sequence of events in a story while trying to understand what the story means, locating a sequence of landmarks on a map while determining the correct route, listening to specific word features among several in one ear and suppressing the same features in the other ear, and so on; cf. Swanson & Alexander, 1997). All these tasks have the quality of interference (a competing memory trace that draws away from the targeted memory trace) and monitoring (decisions related to the allocation of attention to the stimulus that is under consideration together with the active consideration of several other stimuli whose current status is essential for successfully completing the task). Tasks that require the retrieval of information in the face of interference and active monitoring tap what has been referred to in the literature as working memory (WM).

Our causal model as cited in Swanson and Siegel (2001b) is as follows:

Limitations in WM capacity have a neurological/biological base. These limitations are multifaceted as to the psychological operations they influence. Limitations in WM capacity cause LD. However, these limitations disrupt only certain cognitive operations (a cognitive operation involves manipulating, representing, storing, and/ or allocating of attentional resources) when high demands are placed on processing. When performance demands on various tasks directly tax the WM capacity of individuals with LD, deficiencies related to accessing of speech-based information and/or the monitoring of attentional processes emerge. These two areas of deficiencies are related to components of WM referred to in Baddeley's model (Baddeley & Logie, 1999) as the phonological loop and the executive system. Individuals with LD do *not* suffer all aspects of the phonological loop (e.g., they have relatively normal abilities in producing spontaneous speech and have few difficulties in oral language comprehension) or the executive system (e.g., they have normal abilities in planning and sustaining attention across time). Those aspects of the phonological system that appear particularly faulty for individuals with LD relate to accurate and speedy access of speech codes and those aspects of the executive system that appear faulty are related to the concurrent monitoring of processing and storage demands and the suppression of conflicting (e.g., irrelevant) information. Deficiencies in these operations influence performances in academic domains (reading comprehension, mathematics) that draw heavily upon those operations. Deficiencies in these operations are not due to academic achievement or psychometric IQ because problems in WM capacity remain when achievement and IQ are partialed out or controlled in a statistical analysis. In addition, regression modeling shows these limitations in WM are *independent* of limitations in phonological processing. Children with LD do well in some academic domains because (a) those domains do not place heavy demands on WM operations, and/or (b) they compensate for WM limitations by increasing domain-specific knowledge and/or their reliance on environmental support. (pp. 1–2)

In Torgesen's behalf, part of the confusion in adequately capturing the involvement of a domain-general system in LD is related to the confusion in the literature as to what such a system entails. Cognitive operations that operate independent of (or are not directly moderated by) verbal or visual-spatial skills have been referred to as domain-general processes. Domain-general processing is a misnomer, however, because operations that cut across verbal and visual spatial skills are multifaceted. In cognitive terms, these operations are referred to as central executive processing and reflect a diversity of activities (12 are listed in Swanson & Siegel, 2001b, such as planning, allocating attention, and quickly accessing information from long-term memory). These processes draw from several regions of the brain but are associated primarily with the prefrontal cortex (e.g., Smith & Jonides, 1999). There are emerging studies showing that children with LD have problems related to activities in this part of the brain (e.g., Lazar & Frank, 1998). No doubt, the part of the brain involved is biased by the type of task used to assess the neurological bases of LD (if studies of reading primarily use phonological measures to test theory, then obviously prefrontal areas of the cortex are less involved).

A review of the experimental literature (Swanson & Siegel, 2001a, b) shows that children with LD yield (a) poor performance on complex divided attention tasks; (b) poor monitoring, such as an inability to suppress (inhibit) irrelevant information; and (c) depressed performance across verbal and visual-spatial tasks that require concurrent storage and processing. These executive processes significantly predict reading and math performance even when phonological processes, age, and psychometric IQ are partialed out in the analysis (see Swanson & Siegel, 2001b, for a review). More importantly, deficiencies in WM remain when achievement is partialed from the analysis. Thus, these processes are not secondary or merely functional aspects of processes at the phonological level as Torgesen suggests.

We have provided a rebuttal to some of the typical arguments against such a WM model, e.g., deficits are due to attention deficit hyperactivity disorder (ADHD), low intelligence, domain-specific knowledge, or low order processes such as phonological coding (see Swanson & Siegel, 2001a, for a review). We find (as do independent laboratories) that (a) children with normal IQ can have executive processing deficits; (b) some LD readers suffer executive processing deficits that do not overlap with the deficits attributed to children with ADHD (e.g., WM deficits emerge in LD readers but not ADHD children of normal intelligence); (c) significant differences in WM remain between LD and non-LD participants when achievement, domain-specific knowledge, and psychometric intelligence are partialed from the analysis; (d) the causal basis of attention between LD and ADHD children (as well as manifestations) differs; and (e) some subtypes of LD readers (such as those with problems in reading comprehension) have executive processing deficits but not phonological deficits. We also suggest that in the flush of enthusiasm of causal modeling in studies of LD, very few of these studies have (a) tested alternative models, (b) used valid measures of WM, and (c) discussed how the distribution effects influenced the magnitude of correlations.

Linda Siegal and I (Swanson & Siegel, 2001b) have recently reviewed approximately two decades of research showing that WM deficits are fundamental problems of children and adults with LD across a large age-span. These WM problems predict difficulties in reading and mathematics and to some degree writing (text generation). There are three important conclusions related to this review. First, depending on the academic task, age, and type of learning disability, operations related to both general and specific WM systems are involved in LD. At the domain-specific level, the research clearly shows that students with LD in reading and/or math suffer WM deficits related to the phonological loop, a component of WM that specializes in the retention of speech-based information. We also found that this system is of service in complex cognition, such as reading comprehension, problem solving, and writing. However, the research also clearly showed that this simple subsystem is *not* the only primary structural aspect of WM that is deeply rooted in more complex activities experienced by children and adults with LD. In situations that place high demands on processing, which in turn place demands on controlled attentional processing capacity (such as monitoring limited resources, suppressing conflicting information, and updating information), children and adults with LD are at a clear disadvantage when compared with their chronologically aged-matched normal achieving counterparts. (Controlled attention is defined as the capacity to maintain and hold relevant information in the face of interference or distraction.) More important, these deficits are sustained when measures of articulation speed, verbal short-term memory, reading scores, and (most importantly) phonological processing are partialed from the analysis. Thus, LD students' executive system (monitoring activities linked to their capacity for controlled sustained attention) is clearly impaired. This impaired capability for controlled processing manifested itself across demanding visual-spatial and verbal WM tasks, and therefore reflects a domain-general deficit.

However, we qualify our findings. First, students with LD are proficient in some aspects of executive processing. For example, students with LD can set up a series of subgoals for successful task solution (see Swanson, 1993, for review). Second, the importance of the executive and phonological system in predicting reading performance is related to age. As children age, the executive system plays more of a primary role in separating good and poor readers than at the younger ages. Finally, students with LD experience problems in WM processes unrelated to achievement. Fundamental processing deficits exist even when reading and/or math ability is partialed from our analysis (Swanson, 1999c).

II. Teaching Deficiency or Processing Deficiency?

I have stated elsewhere that the importance of phonological processing training (at least in isolation) has been greatly overstated (Swanson, 1999a). My observation is that when treatment conditions systematically include a highly structured core of instructional components (e.g., systematic repeated and explicit practice, advanced organizers, sequencing, teacher modeling, consistent probing; see Swanson, 1999b, for review), the contribution related to the degree or intensity of phonological instruction is difficult to evaluate when predicting performance on real word recognition tasks. In reviewing this literature, I outlined three additional concerns with the reading intervention literature that includes students with LD that cloud definitive conclusions: (a) Several outcome measures in reading instruction studies are confounded with treatment activities; (b) effect sizes on transfer measures (e.g., word recognition) are not necessarily related to intense one-to-one phonics instruction (see Swanson, 1999b); and (c) funding practices have not been directed toward an inclusive understanding of LD (e.g., less work has been done on the cognitive basis of reading comprehension than on word attack deficits). Before I provide my comments on a related issue, I would like to make two statements. First, research in the last few years has done much to change our focus on the importance of directly instructing children in phonological skills. Torgesen's research (as well as those of others) makes a significant contribution to our knowledge about effective reading instruction. Second, traditional assessment procedures seldom provide information that assesses the stability or durability of intrinsic cognitive processing deficits under instructional conditions. Torgesen's model does much to put instruction in the context of the assessment process. If an individual at risk for LD has an inability to remember (i.e., access) specific aspects of language (phonological information), then clear documentation must be provided that they have been systematically provided with direct instruction in those aspects of language. This is in line with my previous recommendations that dynamic assessment as well as intensive instruction be used to identify children with normal IQs who are unresponsive to instruction (Swanson, 1988a, 1988b).

This latter point is the focus of my concern. Torgesen is critical of Vellutino et al.'s (1996) assertion that only children who do not respond adequately to well-designed instruction are considered "classically learning disabled (in the sense that they have fundamental processing limitations)" (this volume). I agree with Vellutino et al.'s assertion and find Torgesen's argument unconvincing. Torgesen argues that socioeconomic status, parent support, and other variables influence outcomes. No doubt they do. However, if children suffer from an intrinsic processing deficit (phonological processing that is constitutionally based), then one would expect marginal outcomes even when socioeconomic status, parent support, and other variables are controlled. For example, a child who is blind from birth, asked to produce the correct sound from a visual stimulus in otherwise well designed treatments, is going to have difficulty encoding visual information even when motivation and other environmental factors are controlled. Likewise, well-designed instruction in phonological processing may produce some positive results, but if LD is related to a constitution-based disorder as suggested by Torgesen throughout this paper, clearly there should be some serious constraints in performance when compared with other academic domains or even to other children with poor reading skills. One criterion for measuring resistance to change is effect size between the control and experimental condition. Effect sizes above 0.80 are considered substantial, those above 0.60 are considered moderate, and those below 0.20 are considered small. Based on these criteria, one would not expect substantial changes in a core deficit (i.e., effect sizes would not be expected to be greater than 0.20).

Unfortunately, there is weak support for the assumption that performance on phonological measures are less likely to change (yield lower effect sizes) than performance in other domains or processes. We (Swanson & Hoskyn, 1998) found in a meta-analysis of 180 group design studies that when controls were made on methodological variables (e.g., variation in components of instruction, teacher effects), the magnitude of change (as measured by effect size) in word recognition and phonological skills was in the same range as a number of other domains (e.g., memory, writing, intelligence scores, global achievement, mathematics). We found with LD samples that outcomes on standardized phonological measures and word recognition measures are in the magnitude of 0.62 and 0.57, respectively (see p. 289). Finding such high outcomes for phonological measures I think argues (at least partially) in favor of an environmentally based (teaching-based) deficit. We have also recently reviewed all the published studies on reading (Necoechea & Swanson, in progress) funded by the National Institute of Child Health and Human Development and found that the typical effect size on standardized phonological processing measures (e.g., pseudowords) is approximately 0.65. These are extremely high effect sizes (at least when compared to other domains) for an area considered to reflect a processing deficit that has a constitutional base. I must qualify this observation. I believe that intensive direct phonics instruction is necessary for those students who need it—a large group of children with LD and children with other reading problems need it. However, if response to treatment outcomes is a good test of theory (see Swanson & Hoskyn, 1998), then I don't think his model is convincing, at least as related to the phonological processing measures.

Another problematic aspect of emphasizing a phonological model is that the magnitude of outcomes on transfer measures as a function of phonological processing instruction (reading of real words as opposed to direct skill measures, e.g., word attack or pseudoword reading) is not clear. In a review of several studies that include real word recognition, we found that when treatment components that include a basic instructional core are entered first into a regression model in predicting word recognition, segmentation training and individual instruction did not enter significantly in predicting outcomes (Swanson, 1999b). An excellent study by Foorman et al. (1997) also found that when socioeconomic status and IQ were controlled, variations in reading instruction (analytic phonics, synthetic phonics vs. whole word) did *not* significantly predict real word reading. Such findings raise questions about the primary importance of phonological training (at least as it relates to the unit of word analysis) as it applies to improving word recognition.

My point is not to dispute the fact that phonological processing is a fundamental processing deficit or that intensive phonological instruction is important. Rather, I would argue that a stubborn resistance to change in a specific psychological process after intense systematic instruction is a critical base for validating the cognitive basis of LD.

SUMMARY

Overall, Torgesen has provided a compelling paper on the importance of phonological processing. However, I think we should not discount findings related to other processes that contribute significant variance to reading, mathematics, and writing. I argue that for some ages and tasks, phonological processes are no more important than isolated operations related to an executive system. I also think that some qualifications are necessary when arguing for intensive phonological instruction.

REFERENCES

Baddeley, A. D., & Logie, R. H. (1999). Working memory: The multiple component model. In A. Miyake & P. Shah (Eds.), *Models of working memory: Mechanisms of active maintenance and executive control* (pp. 28–61). New York: Cambridge University Press.

Foorman, B. R., Francis, D. J., Winikates, D., Mehta, P., Schatshneider, C., & Fletcher, J. M. (1997). Early interventions for children with reading disabilities. *Scientific Studies of Reading, 3,* 255–276.

Hoskyn, M., & Swanson, H. L. (2000). Cognitive processing of low achievers and children with reading disabilities. A selective meta-analytic review of the published literature. *School Psychology Review, 29,* 102–119.

Lazar, J. W., & Frank, Y. (1998). Frontal systems dysfunction in children with attention-deficit/hyperactivity disorder and learning disabilities. *Journal of Neuropsychiatry & Clinical Neurosciences, 10,* 160–167.

Smith, E. E., & Jonides, J. (1999). Storage and executive processes in the frontal lobes. *Science, 283* (5408), 1657–1661.

Swanson, H. L. (1987). Information processing theory: A commentary and future perspective. *Journal of Learning Disabilities, 20,* 100–140.

Swanson, H. L. (1988a). Comments, countercomments and new thoughts. *Journal of Learning Disabilities, 21,* 289–297.

Swanson, H. L. (1988b). Towards a metatheory of learning disabilities. *Journal of Learning Disabilities, 21,* 196–209.

Swanson, H. L. (1993). An infornlation processing analysis of learning disabled children's problem solving. *American Education Research Journal, 30,* 861–893.

Swanson, H. L. (1999a). Has the importance of phonological awareness training been greatly overstated. *Issues in Education: Contributions from Educational Psychology, 5,* 125–138.

Swanson, H. L. (1999b). Reading research for students with LD: A meta-analysis of intervention outcomes. *Journal of Learning Disabilities, 32,* 504–532.

Swanson, H. L. (1999c). Reading comprehension and working memory in skilled readers: Is the phonological loop more important than the executive system? *Journal of Experimental Child Psychology, 72,* 1–31.

Swanson, H. L., & Alexander, J. (1997). Cognitive processes as predictors of word recognition and reading comprehension in learning disabled and skilled readers: Revisiting the specificity hypothesis. *Journal of Educational Psychology, 89,* 128–158.

Swanson, H. L., & Hoskyn, M. (1998). Experimental intervention research for students with learning disabilities: A meta-analysis of treatment outcomes. *Review of Educational Research, 68,* 277–321.

Swanson, H. L. & Siegel, L. (2001a). Elaborating on working memory and learning disabilities: A reply to commentators. *Issues in Education: Contributions from Educational Psychology.*

Swanson, H. L., & Siegel, L. (2001b). Learning disabilities as a working memory deficit. *Issues in Education: Contributions from Educational Psychology.*

Torgesen, J. (1988). Applied research and metatheory in the context of cognitive theory. *Journal of Learning Disabilities, 21,* 271–274.

Vellutino, F. R., Scanlon, D. M., Sipay, E. R., Small, S. G., Pratt, A., Chen, R. S., & Denkla, M. B. (1996). Cognitive profiles of difficult-to-remediate and readily remediated poor readers: Early intervention as a vehicle for distinguishing between cognitive and experiential deficits as basic causes of specific reading disability. *Journal of Educational Psychology, 88,* 1–38.

CHAPTER VIII: CLINICAL JUDGMENTS IN IDENTIFYING AND TEACHING CHILDREN WITH LANGUAGE-BASED READING DIFFICULTIES

Barbara W. Wise & Lynn Snyder, University of Colorado

I. INTRODUCTION

Expert educators continuously evaluate their students' performance, adapting instructional programs to be as effective as possible for each child. This paper considers the information educators need to make these adaptations. The term *educator* refers here to professionals along the whole cascade of teaching services, from general classroom teachers, to learning specialists in smaller reading or special education settings, to therapists and specialists working one on one with the student experiencing difficulty. Because of reading's critical role in learning and because of the prevalence of reading problems in children referred for special education, the paper focuses on decisions educators make about children with specific reading disabilities (SRDs), with specifically poor comprehension, or both. We consider these separately, because different kinds of language deficits underlie the two kinds of reading problems.

Research from the last twenty years clearly suggests how to screen, identify, teach, and evaluate children with language-based reading difficulties. We refer to some of this research in this paper. However, the chapter mainly considers the clinical judgments that expert educators add to this knowledge to recognize children with learning disabilities and to construct and evaluate their educational programs. We explore some training and classroom management ideas to help teachers work towards this goal without exhaustion. The chapter closes by recommending that educators and researchers collaborate to evaluate and improve treatments and scale up the best treatments, so that more and more children will receive effective methods and practices for their needs.

II. ISSUES IN IDENTIFICATION

Given the potential social stigma (Sapon-Shevin, 1987; Smith & Nagle, 1995) and sometimes reduced teacher expectations (Tauber, 1998) that can be caused by labeling a child as having a learning disability, why do we still advocate using the label? Clearly, labels can be justified only if they are reliable, valid, and useful (Pennington, 1991). A label is reliable if it identifies a learning difference that remains stable across many tests and settings. A label of a learning disability is valid if it identifies a learning difference related to processes intrinsic to the learner. It is valid and instructionally useful if children with that label benefit from treatments theoretically compatible with the identified underlying processes more than from other treatments. Demonstrated advantages for such treatments are indeed what justify and require the continued identification of children with valid, instructionally useful labels. Many labels (e.g., visual or auditory closure difficulties) that were applied in the early 1970s and the treatments that accompanied those labels did not prove either valid or helpful, and they have thankfully fallen out of use (Hammill, 1972; Vaughn, Gersten, & Chard, 2000).

In this paper we focus on variability within two major learning disability labels, both involving reading difficulties, because reading is so crucial for success in schools and because reading disabilities are so prevalent in special education settings (Langenberg, 2000). Much well-controlled research covered in this report identifies core deficits underlying many cases of reading disabilities and indicates reliable tests that can discriminate children with and without the deficits. Research has also identified aspects of theoretically valid programs that help such children more than other programs do. All this research yields practical recommendations about screening, teaching, and evaluating the progress of these children.

We focus first on SRD, often called dyslexia (Lyon, 1995), the most prevalent learning disability. It is usually based on underlying core deficits in phonological (or speech-sound based) processing. Problems in phoneme awareness (the ability to identify and manipulate sounds inside syllables) and phonological decoding (the sounding out of words) are abilities that suffer when phonological processing is weak, and these weaknesses lead directly to problems in word reading. Children with weak phonological processes also struggle secondarily with reading comprehension, for two reasons. First, comprehension suffers when they misread words. Second, comprehension can still fail if remedied word reading remains so slow and effortful that it uses too much attention (Perfetti, 1985). Children whose reading comprehension is hindered solely by phoneme awareness and decoding comprehend well when listening to stories, but have problems when reading the stories themselves.

On the other hand, a less common group of children with specifically poor comprehension struggle with formulating main ideas, summaries, and inferences both when they listen to stories and when they read them themselves. The difficulties appear despite these children's normal phoneme awareness and decoding skills. These comprehension problems seem usually to relate to underlying core deficits in higher-level language skills, such as difficulties with non-literal meaning, vocabulary, and syntax.

Of course, real children with language-based reading problems present with unique profiles with different combinations of deficits and strengths that should affect the design of their optimal instructional program. Their abilities vary in phonological processes (phonemic awareness, memory, and naming speed, discussed later), with or without problems in higher language skills. Their profiles and their programs should also vary depending on strengths and weaknesses in other reading-related abilities such as orthographic memory, attention, and motivation. Verbal IQ, vocabulary, educational background, emotional and behavioral factors, and the home literacy environment also affect each child's profile.

Are there other ways to have difficulty with reading that are not based on language-based learning disabilities? Certainly there are! Other causes of reading difficulties include attention problems, inconsistent education, and problems due to learning to read in a second language. Other children struggle with reading due to mental retardation, sensory deficits, or emotional problems. These children's classroom behaviors, screening, diagnosis, and treatment differ from those of the children with learning disabilities who are the focus of this paper. Their reading should be instructed concurrently with or following the treatment of their primary deficit.

III. RESEARCH IN IDENTIFICATION AND INSTRUCTION FOR SPECIFIC READING DISABILITIES

Identification

The last three decades of research have yielded a positive history and an optimistic future for the identification and treatment of SRDs. Research in the 1970s moved away from definitions and treatments based on underlying perceptual deficits, such as "visual or auditory closure or figure-ground difficulties" (Hammill, 1972; Vaughn et al., 2000; Vellutino, 1979). Later research moved the field beyond the "exclusionary" definition of Public Law 94-142, which said all that reading disabilities were not but not what they were (Lyon, 1995). The current working definition of SRD results from the work of seven professional organizations, including the National Institute of Child Health and Human Development (NICHD). It identifies a core deficit in phonological or analytic language processes, involving awareness and efficiency in using speech-based codes, underlying most cases of SRD (Lyon, 1995). According to this research-based, working definition:

> Dyslexia is one of several distinct learning disabilities. It is a specific language-based disorder of constitutional origin characterized by difficulty in single word decoding, usually reflecting insufficient phonological processing. The difficulties in single word decoding are often unexpected in relation to age and other cognitive abilities; they are not the result of generalized developmental disability or sensory impairment. Dyslexia is manifested by variable difficulty with different forms of language, often including, in addition to problems in reading, a conspicuous problem with acquiring proficiency in writing and spelling.

Twin and family studies in behavioral genetics (e.g., Gayan et al., 1995; Olson, Forsberg, Gayan, & DeFries, 1999; Scarborough, 1990) and research in the function and structure of the brain (Frith, 1997; Hynd & Hiemenz, 1997; Shaywitz, 1996; Zeffiro & Eden, 2000) both suggest a constitutional origin for SRDs. Reading-level match studies support a causal role for phonological deficits, since older children with SRD perform worse in phoneme awareness and phonological decoding than do younger normal readers who read real words at equivalent levels (Olson, Wise, Conners, Rack, & Fulker, 1989; Rack, Snowling, & Olson, 1992). Furthermore, phoneme awareness in kindergarten is one of the strongest predictors (along with letter knowledge) of reading through elementary school (Adams, 1990). Finally, intervention studies validate training in phoneme awareness and decoding. This training, when integrated and applied to reading accurately in context, leads to gains beyond phonological skills into reading itself (Hatcher, Hulme, & Ellis, 1994; Lovett et al., 1994; Torgesen, Wagner, & Rashotte, 1997; Wise, Ring, & Olson, 2000).

It is important to note that the phonological deficits underlying SRDs, and indeed the category itself, are a matter of degree, as with all cognitive processes. No absolute level of phoneme awareness clearly defines how many children have SRDs. The percentage of children that will be identified depends entirely on the criteria set. Research estimates in the 1980s tended to include the lowest 10% of readers with average or above-average IQ. More recently, Lyon cited findings by the Shaywitz's and other researchers to suggest that as many as 20% of children have phonological skills weak enough that reading is one of the most difficult tasks they will have to master in school (Lyon, 1999). The criteria chosen for identification will depend on how many children society decides it can afford to provide with the intensive, individualized instruction required by the appropriate special education that has been so eloquently described by Zigmond (1997).

We propose that the more educators know, the stronger their programs become, and that the better supported they are by technology and personnel, the more children can be identified early and helped efficiently. Lyon (1999) describes strong advantages for early intervention: 90–95% success for students who begin remediation before third grade versus 25% success for children who do not begin until nine years of age. Thus, the earlier children are recognized for risk, the more children can be helped, whether with appropriate instruction in the classroom, with supplemental intensive small group instruction, or with remedial special education services.

What Instruction for Children With SRD Should Include

Research suggests that interventions for children at risk for SRD should at least improve their deficient phoneme awareness, decoding, and fluency (Kame'enui, Simmons, & Coyne, 2000). We now report research on the remediation of these deficits as well as problems in comprehension that result for children with reading disabilities.

Improving deficient phoneme awareness and decoding. Research has not identified a "best" method to improve phoneme awareness (Wise, Ring, & Olson, 1999; Wise, Ring, Sessions, & Olson, 1997) or decoding or fluency (Hall & Moats, 1999). However, these studies do suggest components that should be included in programs for children with phonological deficits. These children need first to recognize and manipulate sounds easily within words (phoneme awareness), in order then to learn and use the "alphabetic principle" at the base of the English sound-to-print system (Liberman & Shankweiler, 1985). If a child cannot easily analyze the difference in the order of sounds in, for example "fist" vs. "fits," the child must memorize each word as a whole unit. After children have improved in phoneme awareness, they can learn to decode the English print-to-sound system and master decoding and word reading.

Aiming for transfer of phonological training. The studies cited above and the experiences of educators suggest that well-structured phonological training should help children make substantial gains in phonological decoding and accurate word reading. The fact is that many researchers and educators are indeed succeeding in helping more and more poor and non-readers become accurate readers. Justified satisfaction from this progress should not, however, lead us to be smug. Yes, many studies have found impressive differential effects in phonological and word level skills from interventions with explicit vs. less explicit phonological training (Hatcher et al., 1994; Lovett et al., 1994; Torgesen et al., 1997; Wise, Ring, & Olsen, 2000). However, these studies had difficulty showing similar differential gains in reading rate and in comprehension. These researchers also reported a discouraging lack of transfer of differential gains one and two years after treatment ended, relative to the less explicit treatments. Other researchers suggest that children need to apply the skills in well-structured programs, balancing foundation-level skills with work in automaticity and application in accurate reading for meaning in context (Brady & Moats, 1997; Snow, Burns, & Griffin, 1998).

Educators who work one on one, who are able to individualize their instruction, and who can keep students as long as they need to ensure independent use of self-correction and comprehension strategies have some students who maintain gains after treatment (Uhry, 1997; Wise, 2001). However, designing studies of long-term transfer can raise ethical concerns, if researchers must withhold the most effective treatment for a comparison control condition long enough to show follow-up differences two or five years later. If progress from treatments differs significantly after one year at post-test, is it ethical to withhold the better treatment from a control group? On the other hand, the research community needs long-term follow-up to be sure that treatments differ. The research and clinical communities need to grapple with this dilemma to find creative solutions and to consider how to interpret current studies that have not attempted long-term follow-up (Viall, 2001).

Improving fluency and automaticity. The research reported in the last section converges with other research findings to suggest that mastering phoneme awareness and decoding are necessary, but not sufficient, components of early reading instruction (Wise, 1999). If a child labors at decoding words accurately, s/he will not do so when reading for pleasure. Indeed, until foundation-level skills become automatic, most children with reading disabilities will experience more work than pleasure in reading.

In pilot studies, Wise, Olson, and Ring (2000) were surprised how suddenly and completely engaged children with reading disabilities became with very simple programs that speeded practice with words the children had previously mastered for accuracy. Many researchers are using computer programs to practice repeated speeded readings of high frequency words and sub-word units to improve automaticity (Blok, Oostdam, Otter, & Overmaat, in press; Lewin, 1997; Van Daal & Van der Leij, 1994; Wolf, Miller, & Donnely, 2000). Computer programs seem to be ideal to help reading become automatic. Future research may suggest which children will profit most from this kind of instruction.

Improving comprehension for students with specific reading disabilities. Vaughn and colleagues have studied comprehension instruction in small groups of students with learning disabilities, with large effect sizes (Vaughn et al., 2000). Vaughn and her colleagues (2000) and Williams (1993) emphasize extensive practice *at appropriate instructional reading levels* for children with decoding difficulties.

Except for adjusting reading levels for decoding difficulties, their research is relevant for children with comprehension problems without word recognition problems. Therefore, we report the studies later, in the section on specific comprehension difficulties.

Effects of naming speed deficits. While the above research suggests ways to improve word recognition, automaticity, and comprehension for most children with learning disabilities, some children retain a slow reading rate. Certainly it is good that such children read better than they did before remediation, but their continued slow reading reduces their enjoyment of reading and probably hampers comprehension. These children may be those that are most resistant to treatment, with "double deficits" in phoneme awareness and in "naming speed" (Felton, 2001; Wolf, 1999). They currently challenge researchers and teachers.

Naming speed tasks typically require children to name as many pictured objects, colors, or letters as quickly as they can. Poor naming speed can exist alone or coexistent with poor phoneme awareness or with the higher-level language problems of specifically poor comprehenders reported in the next section. Wolf believes that children with good phoneme awareness but slow naming speeds are not only slow readers, but also poor comprehenders (Wolf, Bowers, & Biddle, 2000). Research has not yet clarified exactly what underlies slow naming speed, but it is surely language related. It appears to depend at least on slow speech rates and probably on slow lexical access (Scarborough, 1998b; Wolf, Bowers, & Biddle, 2000).

It is interesting to puzzle through how these underlying language skills predict progress in reading. Phoneme awareness is the strongest predictor of reading progress through elementary school (Wagner, Torgesen, & Rashotte, 1994). Scarborough (1998a) also found that phoneme awareness ability in kindergarten predicted success at the end of second grade in reading. Scarborough also concurs with many other researchers (e.g., Felton & Brown, 1990) who have shown that those who are poor readers in first and second grades tend to remain poor readers into junior high. Predicting forward from second grade testing, Scarborough found that simple literacy scores predicted eighth grade reading better than any other variable. Interestingly, adding phoneme awareness or phonological decoding to the equation at second grade did not improve these predictions. Only when rapid serial naming in second grade was added to second grade literacy did the prediction become more precise about who would struggle with reading and comprehension in eighth grade. This fits Wolf's picture that phonological deficits are more amenable to remediation, while children with "double deficits" in phoneme awareness and naming speed seem more resistant to treatment. On the other hand, phoneme awareness ability in second grade was the best predictor of eighth grade *spelling* ability.

These kinds of recent findings have turned researchers' attention to naming speed, with a resulting increase in the number of studies on rapid serial naming. Two important questions arise: Can rapid naming be improved, and if so, will its improvement affect reading performance? Suppose naming speed is impossible to change. If that proves to be the case, researchers and educators will look to revising instructional programs to accommodate slow reading and naming speed. In current practice, such revised programs encourage using assistive technology for reading and writing, reducing amounts of printed work, and providing alternative methods of demonstrating learning for children who read and write slowly and with great effort.

On the other hand, it is not yet time to give up on improving the reading rates of children who are slow at serial naming. Most of the research field has been aware of the significant effects of naming speed for less time than it has been aware of the importance of phonological deficits. It is certainly worth seeing what the field can come up with to help these children. Wolf, Denckla, Bowers, and Felton have suspected the importance of naming speed for far longer than most researchers (Wolf, Bowers, & Biddle, 2000). Repeated readings and guided reading have been shown to improve fluency, but rapid naming was usually not measured in these studies (Felton, 2001). Wolf, Miller, et al. (2000) are devising computer programs that they hope will help improve reading rates by working on fluency and on elaborating vocabulary. They believe that the more routes a child has to retrieve a word, the faster his retrieval may be, though this reasonable conjecture has not yet been proven.

The previous discussion suggests that the expert educator will assess, teach, and monitor progress in fundamental skills, build automaticity with speeded practice, and provide extensive opportunities to apply skills in context at instructional levels. S/he does this while teaching and supporting comprehension and while encouraging independent reading and writing away from the classroom to ensure transfer. Accomplishing this in individualized programs is the goal of the expert educator, who begins to sound like a superhero! In a later discussion on modifying instruction to meet individual needs, we examine research and suggest how s/he may accomplish this with neither supernatural powers nor exhaustion. Before considering these ideas in practice, we want to contrast the profiles of children with specifically poor comprehension to those of the children we have been discussing thus far.

IV. THE IDENTIFICATION OF CHILDREN WITH SPECIFIC COMPREHENSION PROBLEMS

Gough and Tunmer's (1986; Gough, Hoover, & Peterson, 1996) simple model of reading describes reading as interactions among decoding and language comprehension skills. The majority of research on children with reading disabilities, summarized in the previous section, has focused on their poor decoding skills, the weak phonological representations that underlie them, and their resulting secondary problems in reading comprehension. On the other hand, a growing body of research has identified a group of children who have normal decoding skills but whose comprehension is nonetheless weak, demonstrating a specific weakness in the other half of Gough's equation. However, researchers debate the identity of this group and the deficits that underlie their reading comprehension problems.

Building an Understanding of a Text

Children with good comprehension build the "gist" or overall meaning of a text as they read, while children with specific problems in reading comprehension do this less readily. Many researchers studying reading comprehension here in the United States have focused on children with more generalized reading deficits, a group whose performance lagged both in decoding and comprehension (e.g., Snyder & Downey, 1991). Consequently, as Stothard and Hulme (1996) point out, studying reading comprehension combined with generalized deficits may have obscured the understanding of the nature of many children's specific reading comprehension problems. In contrast, a group of colleagues from "across the pond," in the United Kingdom, have focused their research on children with deficient reading comprehension despite normal decoding skills. They refer to this group of children as poor comprehenders or what we will term children with specific comprehension problems or difficulties.

In one of the early studies conducted by this group, Yuill and Oakhill (1991) found that when children with specific comprehension problems listened to short stories, they recalled verbatim details as accurately as their peers with good comprehension did. However, the same children lagged behind their peers in describing the gist of the stories. Over time, this body of research has characterized the language and processing strengths and weaknesses of these children with increasing clarity and precision (Nation, Adams, Bowyer-Crane & Snowling, 1999; Nation & Snowling, 1998a, 1998b; Oakhill, 1983, 1993; Stothard & Hulme, 1992, 1995, 1996; Yuill & Oakhill, 1988a, 1988b, 1991).

Problems Constructing Inferences

Oakhill's early work (1984) compared aspects of the reading comprehension of children with good and poor reading comprehension, all of whom demonstrated normal decoding skills on standardized measures. She found that the children with poor comprehension were less accurate than the skilled readers at answering questions about text they had read, both for information stated explicitly in the text and for information that was implicit and required the construction of inferences. When the text was made available to the children during questioning, children with poor comprehension improved in their ability to answer questions about explicit information, but remained deficient in answering questions that required the construction of inferences. It is worth noting that inspection of the types of inferences used in this study revealed that many of them were lexical inferences that relied on context for interpretation.

Constructing inferences requires drawing from a fund of general knowledge, so it is conceivable that children with poor comprehension simply lack basic information. Cain (1994), however, found that these children failed to construct the inferences needed to understand a text even when the relevant knowledge was made available to them. Similarly, Cain and Oakhill (1998) found that even when children with poor comprehension could demonstrate the general knowledge necessary for inferences, they could not draw relations between sentences. Further, their performance was significantly worse than the performance of children matched to them on either comprehension or on chronological age, who did not differ from one another.

In other studies, poor comprehenders also showed difficulty resolving pronominal reference to antecedents in text (Oakhill & Yuill, 1986; Yuill & Oakhill, 1991). This occurred with and without memory loads and with and without gender cues. The children struggled to provide pronouns in a gap-filling response, though they did this better for simple than for complex inferences. These findings suggest that the difficulty these children experience may reside at least partly in a failure to attend to or use available pronominal cues, such as gender.

In sum, the research suggests that children with specific comprehension problems have difficulty constructing inferences and handling pronominal reference. The latter difficulty may be related to the construction of inferences, because pronouns provide cohesion in connected text (Halliday & Hasan, 1976) as do inferences. These findings, then, may be symptomatic of the same underlying deficit in constructive processing.

Problems of Specifically Poor Comprehenders Are Not Related to Short-Term Memory

Countless studies in psychology suggest that verbal short-term memory is supported by phonological processes (Conrad, 1964; Gathercole & Baddeley, 1993). The weak phonological processes of children with SRD, described earlier in the chapter, result in poor decoding and limit their available resources while reading text and also make their phonologically based short-term memory less efficient. Perfetti's (1985) "bottleneck theory" suggests that these children need to deploy so many resources to decoding that insufficient resources remain in a limited capacity system to construct a well-formed understanding of text. On the other hand, children with specifically poor comprehension are defined as having phonological decoding skills that are within normal limits, and one would suspect should also have efficient short-term memory. Indeed, Oakhill (1982) found no significant differences between children with poor and good comprehension on forward or backward digit span tests.

Perfetti, Marron, and Foltz (1996) noted that many of the studies conducted by our British colleagues characterized "normal" decoding skills on the basis of the *Neale Analysis*, a measure that assesses word decoding within connected text. They observed that in one study using the *Neale,* Yuill and Oakhill (1991) found that their poor comprehenders did not lag behind normal readers in speed or accuracy for reading real words, but did differ in reading non-words, usually defined as phonological decoding. This decoding difference confounds the findings for this sample. On the other hand, research from Stothard and Hulme (1992, 1996) and others (e.g., Nation et al., 1999) provides ample evidence that children do exist with poor comprehension without underlying phonological deficits. These samples of children with poor comprehension demonstrated similar performance on reading rates and on many phonologically related tasks (including non-word reading, spoonerisms, and spelling) as chronological age matches who were skilled at comprehension. Yet, their comprehension skills were significantly lower, as were their higher-level verbal skills, than those of their age matches. Perfetti's objections to Yuill and Oakhill's use of word reading in context as a phonological measure were well reasoned. Nevertheless, the above studies by Hulme and Snowling and colleagues constitute considerable evidence supporting the existence of children with specifically poor comprehension without the phonological and short-term memory deficits characteristic of children with SRD.

Lexical and Semantic Language Processing Deficits

The recent work of Nation and colleagues (Nation et al., 1999) sheds considerable light on the underlying language and processing weaknesses of children with specifically poor comprehension. Looking at the phonological and semantic contributions to short-term memory in children with poor and good comprehension, these researchers found that children with poor comprehension resembled children with good comprehension in their ability to recall real and non-word strings. They also demonstrated similar word and non-word reading accuracy. Their recall of abstract words, however, was considerably worse than the recall of children with good comprehension. Further, their spatial but not their listening spans were similar to those of children with good comprehension. Nation et al. suggest that their poor recall of abstract words and poor listening spans for sentences suggests an underlying, non-phonological language impairment.

In recent years, a common theme has emerged regarding the underlying language weaknesses of children with unique deficits in reading comprehension. Increasing evidence points to deficits in lexical and semantic processing skills. Stothard and Hulme (1996) found that children with poor comprehension had significantly lower verbal IQs on the Wechsler Intelligence Scale for Children–Revised (WISC-R) than either their age peers with good comprehension or their younger comprehension-level matches. On the other hand, they did not differ from their peers in performance IQ. Closer inspection of the data showed marked differences in their scores on the Vocabulary and Similarities subtests of the WISC-R, both of which are highly related to lexical-semantic knowledge. This profile was quite different from that of children with SRD. Nation and Snowling's (1998b) study of lexical priming in children with specific comprehension deficits also demonstrated an effect of poorly developed semantic knowledge. They found that children with specifically poor reading comprehension demonstrated priming effects for highly associated word pairs (e.g., *cat-dog*), but not for pairs with lower association strength. Further, the findings of Nation et al. (1999) discussed earlier demonstrated significant differences in these children's ability to recall abstract words. These findings all underscore what seem to be impoverished lexical and other semantic representations.

Lastly, Nation and Snowling (1998a) also examined the degree to which three groups of children were able to use context to facilitate their comprehension. They found that children with specific comprehension problems were poor at using context to facilitate reading comprehension, in contrast to children with decoding problems or to children with normal reading. In sum, accruing evidence points to impoverished lexical and other semantic representations in children with specific comprehension problems. These problems affect their ability to build a coherent and cohesive understanding of stories and other text, the very bedrock of reading comprehension.

Is This Just a Matthew Effect?

Cain and Oakhill (1998) suggested that the poor inferential skills of children with specific comprehension deficits could reflect another instance of Stanovich's Matthew effect (1986), that the "rich get richer and the poor get poorer." Cain and Oakhill reasoned that poor comprehenders probably read less and certainly with worse comprehension than normal readers do, because of their difficulties integrating information within a coherent text structure. Reduced exposure to reading would further delay the development of inferential text processing skills and elaboration of new vocabulary, since both lexical and inferential skills increase with increased reading exposure. Yet these children have been shown to perform worse in constructing inferences than younger children who comprehend at the same level (Cain & Oakhill, 1998). Since the older poor comprehenders would likely have more exposure to print than their younger matches, as well as more time for words to elaborate within their lexicons, this finding contradicts the Matthew effect and any effect exerted by chronological age. These poor comprehenders struggle with constructing well-formed, coherent representations from what they read, more likely due to reduced or sparse lexical and other semantic representations.

A Clinical Profile

The studies discussed here provide increasing support for underlying semantic-lexical language deficits in children with specific comprehension problems. Accruing evidence supports a clinical profile of impoverished semantic representations, especially at the lexical level, that underlie poor comprehension, in the face of normal decoding skills and normal short-term phonological memory. Educators and clinicians expert in this area will thus be sensitive to those children who show difficulties with story recall, summarization, and discussion whether listening to or reading stories. The informed educator will evaluate their ability to construct the gist of what has been read, handle pronoun reference, and draw inferences. The educator will check for weaknesses in their lexical abilities, particularly with abstract words. Also, if an IQ test has been administered revealing a low verbal IQ in contrast to performance IQ, the educator will watch for the above difficulties.

V. Research on Instruction for Children With Poor Comprehension

Researchers and educators have studied the reading problems of children with SRDs for many years. They have used this time to refine a working definition of SRD to include the converging evidence supporting underlying core deficits in phonological processes. While most intervention research with children with SRDs has focused on improving their deficient phonological and word reading processes, some studies have focused on improving comprehension among these students or on students with general learning disabilities. Vaughn and her colleagues have taught metacognitive, self-questioning strategies in small groups to improve comprehension for students with learning disabilities, with large effect sizes (0.98 to 1.33; Vaughn et al., 2000). These researchers also reviewed others' comprehension training programs. They synthesized the important components of the most successful programs, including:

1. teaching students how to summarize key points in a paragraph in their own words (Jenkins, Heliotus, Stein, & Haynes, 1987),
2. asking questions to activate relevant background information (Billingsly & Wildman, 1988),
3. teaching self-monitoring (Graves, 1986),

4. teaching students to ask questions about the structures of stories (story grammars) and to tell the main theme of a story (Williams, Brown, Silverstein, and deCani, 1994), and

5. small group instruction (Vaughn, Hughes, Moody, & Elbaum, in press), with extensive practice at reading levels that ensured successful word recognition were also important in improving comprehension. Follow-up results were not reported in this synthesis.

Williams and colleagues (Williams, 1993; Williams et al., 1994; Wilder & Williams, in press) studied the effects of teaching diverse samples of students with severe learning disabilities to identify themes. Set within a paradigm of explanation and modeling by the teacher, with guided and with independent activities, this training taught students to identify plot components and then to identify themes of stories being read. Not only did the students with learning disabilities experience significant gains, but in this study they also maintained these gains over the long term.

Promising work in reading comprehension instruction "anchored" with multimedia presentations and computer and Internet explorations is being conducted by a large team of researchers at Vanderbilt University. For example, Kinzer and Cammack (2001) extended this work to study its viability to support comprehension for children with learning disabilities. In their study, groups of children analyzed multimedia "anchors" to help segment, organize, discuss, write about, and publish documents about elements in a unit of study. In this study, children with learning disabilities in inclusion classrooms increased their understanding of the material and their ability to participate in class with this kind of support.

Given their more recent identification, intervention studies that have focused specifically on children with comprehension problems without significant word-reading problems have also been more recent. The field has not yet fully converged on how to identify such children, nor on the deficits that underlie the problem. Consequently, relatively few studies have explored the effects of treatment for children with specific comprehension deficits. Most of these studies conducted thus far have been by Yuill, Oakhill, and their colleagues.

In an initial treatment study, Yuill and Oakhill (1988b) compared the effects of three different types of training for children with specific comprehension deficits. They studied the effects of three approaches: one that encouraged the development of inferential skills, one that had children answer comprehension questions about stories they had read, and one that emphasized the decoding of words in text. The inference-focused approach provided activities that emphasized developing lexical inferences, generating questions about the text, and formulating predictions about missing information. After two months of training, children given inference training improved significantly in reading comprehension compared with the other two groups who showed no significant improvement in comprehension. These techniques seem quite compatible with those suggested by Vaughn and colleagues (2000) for children with reading disabilities. Similarly, they are consistent with Swanson's (2001) meta-analysis of training studies using strategy instruction vs. direct instruction with diverse samples of students with learning disabilities. He found that strategy instruction, using techniques such as questioning and elaboration, was effective in improving comprehension among children with problems in comprehension. On the other hand, direct instruction of the skills that support decoding was most effective in improving word recognition for children with deficits in word reading.

Another early study by Yuill and Josceleyne (1988) studied the effects of providing organizational cues and cueing strategies (using pictures, captions, and book titles to enhance comprehension) on the reading comprehension of children with good and poor comprehension. Children with specific comprehension deficits improved their reading comprehension markedly following this treatment. In a different type of treatment study, Yuill (1996) compared the effect of training using riddles to resolve ambiguities for children with specific comprehension deficits and for skilled readers. She found a significant effect of ambiguity training on reading comprehension for both groups of readers.

In short, focused intervention that uses strategies to address skills related to semantic memory seems to improve reading comprehension performance for children with specific comprehension deficits. Research in this area, though promising, has been limited and does not consider the question of enduring post-treatment gains. Recall also that Perfetti et al. pointed out that the test for reading words in context used by Yuill & Oakhill (1991) did not rule out phonological deficits in one of their samples. Since this test is widely used by these researchers from the United Kingdom, their samples may have included some children with mild phonological deficits. Training studies with more precisely defined samples such as those of Stothard and Hulme (1992, 1996), and Nation et al. (1999) will help identify the most effective techniques for these children. The lexical and semantic deficits indicated in the best of the research reviewed above suggest that work on vocabulary—particularly non-literal meaning, pronominal reference, and inference construction—should be valuable aspects of remediation for these children.

VI. CLINICALLY RECOGNIZING CHILDREN WITH LANGUAGE-BASED READING DISABILITIES

This section of the paper deals with how the expert educator uses classroom behaviors and miscue analysis to recognize children who have language-based reading disabilities, either in decoding or in poor comprehension. It also identifies the screening measures the educator might want to use next. We expect that teachers easily notice those students who act out, act extremely discouraged, fail to pay attention, or fail to turn in assignments, and that they would therefore look at these students further. In the following section, we discuss what to look for in the reading and writing of these students and of other more compliant students whose frustrations from learning difficulties may be less apparent. It is our belief that modifications to instructional programs can begin immediately from these observations and screening. Continued observation of problems despite program modifications should lead to a referral for further testing by trained diagnosticians, to refine and modify treatment design. For instance, some children may have attention deficits not just secondary to their reading problems, but as primary ones, which may benefit from behavior management or medication. How much overlap exists between reading disabilities and attention deficits depends on the criteria used for assessment of each problem (DeFries, Filipek, Fulker, Olson, Pennington, et al., 1997; Pennington, 1991) and we will discuss this later in the paper. Yet we also concur with Fuchs and colleagues, that the best instruction will use continuing inductive assessment based on classroom performance, rather than limiting expectations and prescriptions to what is found by the best of diagnostic pretesting (Fuchs, Fuchs, & Hamlett, 1994).

Recognizing Language-Based Learning Disabilities from Classroom Behaviors

Do teachers recognize children at risk for language-based reading disabilities? How effective are classroom teachers at recognizing children at risk for learning problems? Gresham, MacMillan, and Bocian (1997) found that teachers were quite successful at differentiating "at-risk" students from control students from referred samples, with 95% accuracy, which would result in 5% of children being falsely identified as at risk. Within the at-risk group, however, the teachers could not differentiate children with IQ-discrepant learning disabilities from "slow learners" whose low achievement was consistent with their 76 or higher IQ. On the other hand, most researchers (e.g., Shaywitz, Fletcher, Holohan, & Shaywitz, 1992; Siegel, 1992; Stanovich, 1991) suggest that IQ discrepancy is not a crucial distinction, because both groups of children respond similarly to appropriate, intensive reading instruction. A later study by Gresham and colleagues (Bocian, Beebe, MacMillan, & Gresham, 1999) confirmed that teachers identified most children at risk for poor behavior and performance, even if they did not always fit IQ-discrepant definitions. Another study with 612 students found that using a WISC profile did not separate children with learning disabilities from children without them, nor did it robustly predict academic achievement among children with learning disabilities (Watkins, Kush, & Glutting, 1997). All these studies suggest that teachers are actually better at predicting children with learning problems than are diagnoses that rely on performance discrepancies from IQ.

The fact that many teachers reliably recognize children at risk is hopeful. Screening test data and miscue analyses of reading and spelling can only help them refine their instructional programming for children at risk for different kinds of reading problems, until or unless further testing becomes available. For a long time, Siegel (1992) and Stanovich (1991) have suggested that poor phonological performance should dictate who gets phonological training, rather than IQ discrepancy formulae. Siegel found that children with phonological problems benefited from phonological training, regardless of IQ within an educable range. Siegel suggests looking for children who read nonsense words worse than they read real words, rather than those who read lower than their IQ expectation. Similarly, finding children with good decoding who do not "get" the gist of stories or passages should be the clue for recognizing children at risk for specific comprehension problems.

Recognizing children with phonological deficits from miscue analysis. Sensitive teachers will inspect children's behaviors in oral reading and in classroom dictation to see which children need intensive phonological work. Errors in weekly spelling tests will reveal many children with phonological problems. However, teachers must realize that some children may be able to memorize words for the weekly test, but show bizarre spellings in their daily work. These children may have high motivation and a strong orthographic memory. Strengthening their underlying phonological foundation and phonics skills will provide a more balanced system as well as help them remember spellings beyond their weekly tests.

What kinds of errors might reflect only inexperience or use of contextual strategies, and not necessarily relate to phonological deficits? Many children without processing deficits sometimes guess a word in reading from its first sound and context, either from their own lack of experience, from inattention to earlier instruction, or from applying a strategy they have been taught to use. Many children with average phonological skills may make vowel errors in reading and spelling, either because they have had little or no background in phonics, or they have not paid attention during phonics lessons. Moats (1995b) suggested that older children's vowel spelling errors and problems knowing when to double letters in spelling do not necessarily indicate phonological problems. Percentages of vowel and doubling errors were not higher among children with phonological deficits than children with milder problems. Learning to master vowel spellings and consonant doubling is a part of spelling development typical of all children. On the other hand, Post, Foorman, and Hiscock (1997) did find that younger (second and third grade) children with phonological difficulties did show more problems in the accurate production of vowels and the perception of vowel distinctions than normally reading children. Thus, vowel errors probably deserve a second look. Children with spelling errors only in doubling or suffix rules should benefit from learning about phonics and word structure, but probably do not require intensive work in phoneme awareness.

What characterizes the errors of children with phonological deficits? Recall that such children have trouble analyzing, segmenting, and blending sounds within syllables. Their phonological system appears indistinct or poorly specified (Elbro, Borstrom, & Petersen, 1998; Snowling, 2000). If this is so, their word reading and spelling errors should reflect less distinct phonological representations in the kinds of errors they make and the kinds of sound combinations that give them trouble. Children who cannot easily hear the order of sounds in words are likely to leave sounds out or get them out of order in reading and especially in spelling. Moats (1995b) found that the spelling errors of most children with dyslexia seemed to follow similar developmental patterns as very early spellers (Treiman, 1993). Moats also examined the quality of the spelling errors of adolescents with severe phonological deficits compared to children with less severe deficits. She found that children with severe deficits had much higher percentages of errors of consonant omissions and substitutions, sound order changes, and difficulties with morphological endings of –ed and –s. The less deficient spellers had higher percentages of errors in doubling consonants, using familiar orthographic patterns, or using silent e. Sawyer, Kim, and Wade (2000) found that for most students, spelling and reading abilities tend to be at similar levels. Students with phonological deficits had spelling profiles that tended to lag further and further behind their reading levels. However, Sawyer et al. did find errors similar to Moats (1995a, b) among their most severely deficient spellers, reflecting systematic consonant coding errors seemingly linked to poor phoneme differentiation and/or production. They recommended that these most severely deficient spellers might benefit from instruction targeting how sounds are articulated in association with phonics.

Let us sum up some things a teacher may notice in reading and writing behaviors that suggest phonologically-based learning difficulties, in students who have and who have not shown behavioral frustrations or lack of attention. In reading, teachers can look for children who comprehend much better when listening to stories than when reading stories at the same level of difficulty. In reading, they are likely to guess words from context, to have poor decoding, to be slow, and to avoid reading. Examining daily written work or giving a classroom dictation with unknown words that contain consonant clusters and more than one syllable may also help teachers identify these children. In free, unstudied spelling, teachers can look for sound substitutions, additions, omissions, and sounds out of order, especially from phonologically difficult consonant blends containing nasals *(m, n, ng)*, liquids *(l, r)*, or fricatives *(f, v, th, s, z, sh)* (Moats, 1995). These errors are not diagnostic for first graders, but they become more so as children grow older.

Recognizing the Varied Profiles of Children With Phonological Deficits

Again, real children have a whole variety of strengths and challenges that all affect their performance and their optimal program. What differences in abilities affect how a child with a phonological deficit will appear? Of course, the severity of the deficit and the presence of other language strengths matter. Children with mild deficits may be close to grade level in reading and with some reversals and omissions in their spelling. They may respond very well in small group instruction in class and indeed may serve as good peer tutors for other children.

Children with high vocabulary and syntax but very low phonological processing. Children may have severe phonological deficits but very high vocabulary and other higher-level language skills. These children may be grade level readers with atrocious spelling. They are often missed by special education, because their deficits are not devastating in terms of keeping up with class work. But their spelling and reading both benefit remarkably from improving their phoneme awareness, phonics, and knowledge of word structures with much practice in application into writing. Children who can spell and write fluently generally enjoy writing more (Berninger, Vaughn, Abbot, Abbott, Rogan, et al., 1997). Such children can also help with using small group instruction well in a classroom setting, by helping with individualization in phonics small group work, because they often learn the material rapidly and enjoy acting as tutors or coaches in small group activities.

Children with attention deficit as well as phonological deficits. While all children with reading disabilities will have profiles that vary depending on other deficits and strengths, a commonly sighted overlap is the "comorbidity" of attention deficits with SRDs (DeFries et al., 1997; Pennington, 1991; Pennington et al., 1993). Classroom observation of differences can be very difficult here. Many children with SRDs may quit paying attention and start acting out due to frustration with not being able to read. Indeed, recent research suggests that many children with attention deficit without hyperactivity may have this problem secondarily to reading disabilities (Pennington et al., 1993). On the other hand, many children with attention deficits with hyperactivity may read poorly because they have been unable to focus on and remember what has been taught. Both sets of children will profit from a well-structured approach to reading, but children with adequate phoneme awareness will not need the intensive phonological work. Screening for phonological deficits and examining errors for consonant omissions and reversals will suggest who does and who does not require intensive phonological training. If phonological training is done well and intensively, and the child does not respond well to this treatment and does not retain what s/he is taught, this may suggest attention problems. Such a child should be referred for further diagnosis, with an eye towards possible use of medications or other modifications.

Children with deficits in phonological memory. Most, though not all, children with deficits in phoneme awareness have poor phonological recoding in working memory. These children have problems with following more than two directions at a time and with math facts, and many have problems with ordered concepts such as the alphabet, months, seasons, and days of the year. A recent training study by Van Kleek, Gillam, and McFadden (1998) demonstrated that training in phonemic awareness results in improved phonological memory, unlike an alternative training program in rhyming. Many teachers find that work with concrete manipulatives and mnemonic devices aids memory, though we cannot cite specific research supporting this practice. Providing children with appropriate "assistive technology" can scaffold for poor memory, whether that technology is as simple as number lines and math facts tables or as advanced as using calculators and electronic reminder systems.

Children with poor orthographic memory. Although all children with severe reading disabilities require extensive practice for success, those with poor orthographic memories require phenomenal amounts of practice (Van Daal & Reitsma, 1993). Computer technology, repeated readings, and using visualization tricks for spelling may all be helpful additions to programs for such children. Children with stronger orthographic memories and high vocabularies can look like miracles with the speed of their progress, once the phonological deficits are remedied and they are given lots of opportunity for practice to get their new skills applied and automatic.

"Treatment resisters." Children with weak rapid naming, phoneme awareness, memory, and decoding in screening and testing appear to be those who turn out to be most "resistant to treatment" (Felton, 2001; Scanlon & Vellutino, 1997; Torgesen et al., 1997; Wolf & Katzir-Cohen, 2001). Most programs have helped these children improve their decoding, but they have not helped them achieve grade-level reading rates or comprehension. These children are our biggest continuing challenge. In class, they may have an especially hard time coming up with words in oral language. Current research suggests that speeded practice, vocabulary elaboration, repeated reading, and computer-assisted speeded practice may improve reading speed and comprehension (Wolf, 1999; Wolf, Bowers, & Biddle, 2000). Further research is certainly needed to clarify how best to help these children. For now, these children are prime candidates for programs modified to include reduced printed work and assistive technology for reading and writing and note-taking, such as Kurzweil Readers, TextHelp, or Dragon Dictate. They should also be allowed alternative ways to demonstrate competence besides written tests.

Recognizing Children With Specifically Poor Comprehension

How will the teacher recognize the student with specific comprehension deficits from their classroom behaviors? These children will often have problems following directions. Their oral reading performance will be appropriate for their age and grade level, but they will struggle retelling the stories they have read. They can often remember details in stories, but have a hard time constructing gist, so they do very poorly at summarizing or drawing inferences (Oakhill & Yuill, 1991). Children with this difficulty are often identified at later grade levels than children with phonological deficits. This happens because many of the stories read at first and early second grade have very simple plots and characters and do not provide much opportunity for drawing inferences from implicit information. These children may also demonstrate other problems handling nonliteral meaning. Often, they may not understand jokes or riddles (Yuill, 1996), laughing later than the other children in the class, not at all, or at surprising times. Similarly, they may not understand multiple meanings of words. In fact, they may seem quite concrete in their thinking relative to other children, especially by the third or fourth grade. They will also have trouble with arithmetic word problems, both in tracking the succession of facts and in constructing the problem space.

Screening for Reading Disabilities

Many school-based literacy programs screen kindergartners and first graders for possible risk of failure in reading. The reasoning behind this practice is that there is mounting evidence that by the end of third grade most students who have been identified as poor readers fail to catch up with their peers with normal reading skills (Lyon, 1999). In fact, some educators contend that we must identify children at risk for failure in reading and begin intervention no later than kindergarten (Kame'enui et al., 2000). Because this sensitive window of time in which educators may best be able to make a difference in these students' lives seems rather short, the concern is how to best identify at-risk students this early in their school experience.

Screening programs are designed to be the first step in the process of identifying children at risk for reading failure. This first step is a coarse-grained sifting of all students to pull out those with some degree of risk, who are likely to fall in the lower two standard deviations of the normal distribution. Not all of these children will demonstrate SRD or be at risk for specific comprehension problems. Rather, the screening process will also identify students who are at risk because of inadequate exposure to print and other aspects of literacy for a wide variety of reasons such as cultural differences, the effects of language impairment, and histories of hospitalization.

The purpose of screening is to pull out students thought to be at risk, to provide them with extra intensive instruction, and to conduct additional assessment for more specific identification if they lag behind peers in this instruction (Badian, 2000). Screening is neither a comprehensive nor complete process and does not, in itself, constitute the diagnostic process. Furthermore, screening measures will also misidentify some children as being "at risk" for reading failure who performed poorly for other reasons, e.g., coming down with a cold, having insufficient sleep the night before, and so on. Such identifications are considered "false positives." On the other hand, the screening may fail to identify some children who are at risk, but who scored better than expected because the child may have overheard another student's answers or because the screening measure was not sufficiently discriminating or was administered incorrectly. These "passes" are called "false negatives." A good screening measure minimizes the occurrence of both. In fact, screening measures should provide information on their "hit rates," that is, the percentage of false negatives and false positives obtained during their standardization testing. The expert teacher looks for a screener that reports this type of information and that minimizes both types of risk. Logic helps in this process: choose the screener that minimizes the false negatives, which miss children who need treatment. The expert teacher knows that false positives can always be weeded out with diagnostic assessment or formative evaluation at a later date.

Screening for potential problems of any kind typically involves testing students for proficiency in skills prerequisite to success in that area. For example, when speech and language therapists screen kindergartners for speech and language disorders, they sample each child's ability to understand and produce age-appropriate vocabulary and grammar and to discriminate and produce age-appropriate speech sounds. Similarly, screening for risk of reading failure involves sampling each child's ability to perform at some level on the skills thought to be fundamental in learning to read.

In the last decade, journals have reported large-scale prospective longitudinal studies of children (Scarborough, 1991) and well-developed screening and diagnostic studies with longitudinal follow-up (Badian, 2000; Wagner et al., 1994). Converging findings have identified clearly the foundation-level skills that are key to success in reading and that are compromised in children who struggle with learning to read. The consensus seems to be that phoneme awareness, alphabet knowledge, and automaticity with the code are crucial to learning to read. For this reason, most screening programs sample at least the first two of these skills. Many researchers also advocate the inclusion of a test of rapid naming (e.g., Wagner, Torgesen, & Rashotte, 1999), based on the findings of Scarborough (1991) and Wolf (1999).

A recent kindergarten screening study (Catts, Fey, Zhang, & Tomblin, 2001) has taken the steps necessary to assemble the type of screening for risk of reading failure that meets the standards we have just discussed. Catts and colleagues used a large prospective sample (more than 1,600 children) and sampled many foundation-level skills. Next, they identified the variables that best predicted success in reading at the end of the second grade and used them to form a composite score. They reported levels of hit rates with different weightings of the key variables in this composite. Most helpfully, they provided a weighting by hit rate report, which allows expert teachers to determine how to screen with some sense of security in the outcome. The key variables identified in this screening include measures of serial rapid naming, phonemic awareness, letter identification, verbal memory (sentence imitation), and maternal education level. This cluster of testing and the formula provided to construct a composite prediction score appears to be the most comprehensive, simple, and reliable screening available to date.

The majority of the screening studies from the last 20 years indicate that at the kindergarten level, letter identification from screenings is consistently one of the most potent predictors of later success in learning to read. Consistent with this observation, Catts et al. found in their (2000) screening study that much, but not all, of the variance in reading scores at the end of the second grade was accounted for by children's early letter identification scores.

In addition, considerable research supports that phonemic awareness is crucial to the child's ability to crack the code and read text. As we indicated earlier, most of the prospective studies using comprehensive assessments found that phonemic awareness is the other strongest predictor of later reading. There are several measures of phonemic awareness that are easy, quick, and reliable to administer. These include Rosner's (1975, 1993) phonemic elision task, Catts' (1993) version of the same task, and Wagner et al.'s (1999) tests of phonemic awareness.

An important caveat in this discussion is that screenings are unlikely to find all students at risk for failure. The expert teacher should thus be alert to identifying additional children during the ongoing formative evaluation that is part of good teaching. Looking for specific comprehension problems has not been considered in most screenings, perhaps because these problems are usually recognized in more advanced reading, in third grade or above. An astute teacher might keep an eye open for younger children with relatively weak vocabulary or other semantic difficulties. Research can soon consider how and when best to screen children for lexical and semantic difficulties.

In summary, screening is only a first step in the identification process, and it comes with risks related to hit rates. Recent studies like the one by Catts and his colleagues provide a new level of confidence in screening for reading disabilities with an empirically based decision-making matrix that includes hit rates and sensitivity indices. Despite this new information, screening is still not a perfect science. To be useful, it should be followed by teachers' ongoing formative evaluation with supplemental intensive instruction and by diagnostic assessment if the evaluation shows a child's progress still lagging behind peers. We will briefly discuss how expert educators use the information from diagnostic assessments, before we give fuller coverage to ongoing formative evaluation in the classroom and resource room.

Diagnostic Assessment of Reading Disabilities

Like screening, diagnostic assessment is not a perfect science. Unlike screening, assessment allows more time with students and larger samples of all their reading-related skills and behavior. This additional detailed information offers further precision and security in identifying children with reading disabilities, characterizing their problems, and designing appropriate programs. These issues are covered at length in other white papers presented at the Learning Disabilities Summit. Because diagnostic assessment requires time and resources, we concur with many of the authors in this book that referral for special education diagnosis follow failure to respond to supplemental treatment variation based on observation and screening. This kind of decision can be made only with ongoing formative evaluation.

We would like to discuss here factors that influence how expert teachers interpret and use findings from a student's diagnostic assessment, in light of the profiles identified for children with SRD vs. specific comprehension problems. The crux of this concern centers on distinctions made among different profiles of children with specific reading disabilities and the remarkably different clinical profile of children with comprehension problems. These profiles also vary against a background of general intelligence and basic communicative language skills.

In many states, children with reading disabilities are currently identified with a discrepancy formula, where the student's performance on one or more measures of academic achievement is significantly discrepant from performance on a test of general cognition. Earlier in the paper, we discussed how the validity of the basic assumption that underlies using IQ to establish a significant discrepancy has been called into question and debated over the last decade (Gresham et al., 1997; Shaywitz et al., 1992; Siegel, 1992; Stanovich, 1991; Watkins et al., 1997). A consensus is growing recommending the abandonment of an IQ discrepancy from definitions of learning disabilities.

The cognitive criteria look somewhat different for children with specific comprehension problems. Earlier, we noted that these children, in fact, often have verbal IQs that are significantly lower than their performance IQs. Thus, children with poor comprehension may have even more problems meeting a discrepancy criterion than do children with phonological deficits. Nation et al. (1999) contend that these children may, in fact, have specific language impairment (SLI) and not a reading disability per se. If so, these children certainly have a specific subtype of SLI not typically seen in school-age children. On the other hand, the lexical and other semantic memory and integration deficits reported for these children are certainly deficits in language processing, and the deficits clearly compromise their reading comprehension. Thus, while both types of disabilities are language-based, a diagnostic distinction between SRD and a subtype of SLI is justifiable in terms of our earliest discussion, in that it identifies children who have different instructional needs. It is also clear that evaluating poor listening comprehension and related verbal abilities can yield perfectly adequate markers for specifically poor comprehension without requiring IQ testing.

VII. Implementing Clinical Judgments in Evaluation and Modification of Instruction

Improving Teachers' Expertise

The expert teacher attends to each child's needs, based on the strengths and weaknesses observed from screening, ongoing classroom observation, and diagnostic testing. For teachers to make the kinds of judgments and modifications we have been advocating, they clearly need a strong knowledge base in language and in all aspects of reading. Brady and Moats (1997) and many others support continuing education to help teachers learn as much as they can about reading and language. Indeed, McCutchen (1997) found that the more teachers knew about the structure of language, the better progress their students made in reading. By definition, special education should be specially individualized for each child's profile and instructional level (Zigmond, 1997). Teachers who can individualize and use guided directed questioning can help children become actively engaged in all aspects of reading, so they in effect learn to become their own teachers (Swanson, 1999). Vaughn and colleagues (2000) caution that "teachers need to plan and reflect on their instruction to ensure that it is explicit and intensive, so that students with LD are not robbed of valuable learning time."

However, many special education teachers have not been observed to implement "best practice" systematic phonological instruction for children with reading disabilities, even though the same teachers spoke of its importance more than they had three years previously (Moody, Vaughn, Hughes, & Fisher, 2000). More shockingly, these researchers found that though the resource teachers they observed taught in small groups, they did not individualize instruction even by selecting appropriately leveled reading material for the children in these groups. Clearly, many teachers also need to learn more about how to individualize instruction.

Schools of education can begin to offer and require more courses in language, reading, and individualizing instruction for all elementary teachers and all special education teachers. School districts can provide inservice training for teachers to help support and enrich their knowledge in this area. CASELINK is an exciting attempt by the Office of Special Education Projects to provide further training via the Internet to help teachers discuss particular case management, using problem-based learning (Gerber, English, & Singer, 1999). We believe similar web-based instruction can improve teacher education and support in areas of improving expert knowledge about phonology, comprehension, reading, and composition to help more teachers become experts.

Individualizing Instruction With Ongoing Assessment

Meta-analyses have highlighted the most important components of remedial programs for children with learning difficulties. Effective programs sequence materials at appropriate individualized levels to ensure success, use directed questioning that promotes thinking aloud about strategies, include extensive practice, and instruct children in groups of six or less at a time (Swanson, 1999; Vaughn et al., 2000). Vaughn reports interesting studies that suggest that a one-to-three teacher-student ratio with highly qualified teachers can be as effective as one-on-one (Vaughn et al., in press), and that paired reading and peer-tutoring small groups are quite effective ways of managing small groups (Elbaum, Vaughn, Hughes, Moody & Schumm, 2000). Interestingly, students with learning difficulties especially benefited by taking the role of tutor in peer-tutoring situations, either with younger or with same-age tutees. These ideas, along with the possibilities of using easily individualizable computer programs and learning kits, suggest ways that may help teachers provide the kind of sequenced instruction at levels guaranteed for success that these articles recommend.

The clear educational goal for children with learning disabilities, as outlined by Swanson (1999) and Vaughn et al. (2000), is to design instruction for small groups of children, working at instructional levels, with lots of appropriate practice, and with directed questioning that helps them discover and use appropriate learning strategies. This is no easy feat in resource rooms of three to nine children, nor certainly in classrooms of up to 30 diverse learners. Different researchers are studying how to help teachers use classroom-based assessment to modify and to adapt instruction continuously to the needs of their students.

In 1984, Fuchs and Fuchs found that teachers are not particularly adept at assessing student performance from informal assessments of children's classroom work, usually tending to overrate their abilities. Also, the continual adjustment of assessment to accomplish the goal of providing appropriately leveled instruction can be overwhelming in time demands: up to 148 minutes a day! These kinds of problems led the Fuchs and their colleagues to devise computer assessment programs that not only helped teachers assess progress, but offered "expert" advice about modifying programs for students not making progress (Fuchs, Fuchs, & Hamlett, 1994). Expert systems considered information about students' work habits and teachers' curricular priorities, availability of additional teacher time, use of aides and peers with stronger skills, and other implementation concerns of the teacher. The systems also analyzed students' performance. In reading, students were assessed on the quality of decoding, fluency, and comprehension performance. The system identified up to two instructional strategies for each area. About 33 teachers each participated in fields of math, spelling, and reading. One third of the teachers used no software, one third used the curriculum-based measurement without the expert advice, and one third used computer-based measurement plus computerized expert advice. Students in the computer conditions interacted twice a week with the computer for learning assessment.

Results of the studies suggested that computerized assessment was helpful to teachers and students. At least in math, children whose teachers used the software made more progress than children in control groups did, and students whose teachers used the expert as well as the measurement software achieved the most. In reading, the computerized measures led to teachers adjusting their teaching more and led to greater gains than the control condition. However, the expert advice led to an advantage only on one reading recall outcome measure. It seems possible to us that the "expert" assessment and programming advice can be improved to achieve a similar result in reading with deeper knowledge about the structures of English phonology, orthography, morphology, semantics and grammar; it is certainly a worthy goal for further research.

While this use of technology seems extremely promising, it is also enlightening to read of Kame'enui and colleagues' (2000) work in helping teachers apply continuous assessment and adaptive education at the level of a school system without the benefit of technology. The schools in a system in western Oregon decided how to teach phoneme awareness, decoding, and automaticity to children at risk for failure, within the limits of each "host school's" needs. Kame'enui agrees that we need to consider the needs of the individual child, which is certainly the goal of the ideal teacher. Yet he reminds us that if the aim is long-lasting improvements, we must set programming changes within a schoolwide improvement model.

Kame'enui et al.'s (2000) program had schools agree on how to analyze individual performance and plan instruction groups, design interventions, and meet biweekly to monitor progress and adjust instruction. Teachers monitored beginning readers (kindergarten to third grade) in fall, winter, and spring and assessed at-risk children monthly. They measured kindergartners on onset recognition, phonemic segmentation fluency, and nonsense word fluency. All children received direct instruction in reading for at least 30 to 45 minutes, with at-risk children receiving a double dose. Intensive intervention groups had no more than five students in each. While this study had no control group, we include it to see how Kame'enui has taken on the idea of scaling up the ideas from single-setting research to affect an entire school system. We have also been quite excited to learn in this Initiative of other scaled-up systems that include (1) early screening for children at risk, (2) "best practices" of intensive direct instruction in phonology and reading in kindergarten and first grade, with (3) extra time in intensive small group work for those children at risk (Grimes, 2001; Marston, 2001). Special education referrals in these systems occur only after failure to respond to this extra intensive instruction, and the systems are reporting great success in reading and reductions in referrals to special education.

We have mentioned how computer technology can help teachers with formative assessments, but technology can also play an important role in individualizing instruction. In the last decade, different studies have demonstrated that well-designed computer programs can help improve different skills including phoneme awareness, decoding, spelling, supported text reading, comprehension, and automaticity, by assessing ongoing performance and reviewing or advancing students based on pre-programmed criteria for success (Kinzer & Cammack, 2001; Segers & Verhoeven, 2001; Verhoeven & Irausquin, 2001; Wise, Ring, et al., 2000; Wolf, Miller, et al., 2000). This literature has most recently been reviewed and meta-analyzed by Blok and colleagues (in press) in the Netherlands, where almost half the studies that passed the criteria for his meta-analysis were conducted. Computers are ideal for the repeated and speeded practice that many children with learning difficulties need. Some programs already marketed in this country successfully individualize instruction in phonological skills, speed skills to automatic levels, and some offer speech-support for reading in context. The most powerful products available at this time, however, are those in assistive technology that can read text aloud to help children with slow reading skills, that can help with writing or spelling with ever-improving ability to turn speech to text, and that can help with study skills.

It seems clear that educational technology of the future will build on the researched and the marketed successes of this last decade. Advances in computer animation, speech recognition, and speech recognition within specific domains will empower future software. This kind of technology is now being developed and evaluated at the Center for Spoken Language Research (CSLR) at the University of Colorado, directed by Cole. The authors of this paper are members of the development team, along with other researchers from five sites and with teachers and administrators from Colorado, who help design and evaluate the programs.

The CSLR project is designing engaging tutorial activities that improve foundation-level skills and automaticity in ways that integrate fully with interesting, interactive books. The books practice, assess, and prescribe skills for instruction or review with the tutorials. The tutorials assess and practice foundation-level skills to mastery and then to automaticity and assign choices of books where students apply the patterns they have mastered. Tutorials and books have animated coaches who give intelligent hints and ask directed questions to encourage strategic thinking about word reading, vocabulary, and comprehension. The programs report children's errors and progress to teachers and provide copies of some books and of successfully read or spelled word lists to take home to read to a parent (see the CSLR web site at the University of Colorado). Programs like these and others (e.g., Kinzer & Cammack, 2001; Wolf, Miller, et al., 2000) should help teachers individualize and work in small groups and help researchers study which methods work best, for which children, and for how long.

Cole estimates that reliable speech recognition for children's reading of single words may materialize within five years, with recognition of specific errors in reading in context a bit further off. Whenever scientists accomplish this, computerized instruction will be able to reach new heights of helping children detect errors and actively engage in focused problem solving. All this will help extend the resources of the overstretched expert teachers we discuss in this paper. It will expand their knowledge of students' performance, allowing them to modify and tailor their students' programs with confidence, based on information about daily performance and with newly freed time for individualized and small-group work.

VIII. Summary and Future Challenges

Current knowledge about the needs of children with language-based learning disabilities is strong enough to support teachers in recognizing children with different needs in reading and in selecting and adapting programs for them that have been shown to be helpful. Clearly, teachers of reading, whether in the general classroom, in Title I programs, or in special education, can all improve their effectiveness by continuing to expand and deepen their knowledge of reading, language, and how to individualize instruction. It also seems obvious that well-trained aides and technical support can already extend the resources of teachers.

Future research should improve our understanding of specific comprehension deficits and should refine our understanding of the best practices for particular children with varied reading profiles. That research will be more effective and applicable if teachers and researchers collaborate to design and evaluate the effectiveness of programs for different children in different settings. Studies cited earlier by the Fuchs' (1994) and by Kame'enui and colleagues (2000) seem to point the way for effective collaboration that will expand and refine our ability to deliver the optimal program for each student.

In the meantime, however, enough knowledge and resources exist to move more of us to expert levels. The studies summarized in this paper suggest or are consistent with the following guidelines for those who teach reading to children:

1. Screen and identify children early, to modify children's programs as early as possible for the best chances of success.
2. Give extra intensive small group instruction with "best practices" to all at-risk children as early as possible, so only those who do not succeed with this instruction need to receive special education in later years.
3. From treatments that are consistent with research, choose those that you can teach with understanding and excitement.
4. Evaluate and modify programs as you go, based on children's performance.
5. Ground reading instruction in your deep and expanding knowledge of language.
6. Teach, read, and write with children in a rich environment that encourages the exploration of language, expansion of vocabulary, and active problem solving and construction of meaning, in small groups where children themselves have learned to provide positive focused hinting and questioning support for each other.
7. Practice and practice newly instructed skills and strategies accurately in and out of context, aiming first for mastery and then for application, fluency, and automaticity.
8. Encourage children to transfer their knowledge and skills in activities, puzzles, and reading for enjoyment beyond the school environment.
9. Encourage a culture of reading, thinking, and learning in and beyond your classroom.

Each incipient expert teacher has the power to impact not only the children s/he teaches, but also colleagues, who will recognize the impact of instruction that is individualized to meet student needs and modified with repeated assessment as students progress. Impassioned and informed teaching, coupled with imaginative and well-designed research, will help us meet the challenge of helping every child to become an independent and eager reader.

References

Adams, M. (1990). *Beginning to read* (pp. 31–56). Cambridge, MA: MIT Press.

Badian, N. (2000). Do preschool orthographic skills contribute to the prediction of reading? In N. Badian (Ed.), *Prediction and prevention of reading failure* (pp. 31–56). Baltimore, MD: York Press.

Berninger, V., Vaughn, K., Abbot, R., Abbott, S., Rogan, L., Brooks, A., & Reed, E. (1997). Treatment of handwriting problems in beginning writers: Transfer from handwriting to composition. *Journal of Educational Psychology, 89,* 652–666.

Billingsley, B., & Wildman, T. (1988). The effects of prereading activities on the comprehension monitoring of learning disabled adolescents. *Learning Disabilities Research, 4,* 36–44.

Blok, H., Oostdam, M., Otter, M., & Overmaat, M. (in press). Computer-assisted instruction in support of beginning reading instruction: A review. *Review of Educational Research.*

Bocian, K., Beebe, M. E., MacMillan, D. L., & Gresham, F. M. (1999). Competing paradigms in learning disabilities and the variations in the meaning of discrepant achievement. *Learning Disabilities Research, 14,* 1–14.

Brady, S., Fowler, A., Stone, B., & Winbury, N. (1994). Training phonological awareness: A study with inner-city kindergarten children. *Annals of Dyslexia, 24,* 26–59.

Cain, K. (1994). An investigation into comprehension difficulties in young children. Unpublished doctoral thesis, University of Sussex, England.

Cain, K., & Oakhill, J. (1998). Comprehension skill and inference-making ability: Issues of causality. In C. Hulme & R. Joshi (Eds.), *Reading and spelling: Development and disorders* (pp. 329–342). Mahwah, NJ: Lawrence Erlbaum Associates.

Catts, H. (1993). The relationship between speech-language impairments and reading disabilities. *Journal of Speech and Hearing Research, 36,* 948–958.

Catts, H., Fey, M., Zhang, X., & Tomblin, J.B. (2001). Estimating the risk of future reading difficulties in kindergarten children: A research-based model and its clinical implication. *Language, Speech, & Hearing Services in Schools, 32,* 38–50.

Conrad, R. (1964). Acoustic confusions in immediate memory. *British Journal of Psychology, 55,* 75–84.

DeFries, J., Filipek, P., Fulker, D., Olson, R., Pennington, B., Smith, S., & Wise, B. (1997). Colorado Learning Disabilities Center. *Learning Disabilities: A Multidisciplinary Journal, 8,* 7–20.

Elbaum, B., Vaughn, S., Hughes, M., Moody, S., & Schumm, J. (2000). How reading outcomes of students with disabilities are related to instructional grouping formats: A meta-analytic review. In R. Gersten, E. Schiller, & S. Vaughn (Eds.), *Contemporary Special Education Research* (pp. 105–135). Mahwah, NJ: Lawrence Erlbaum Associates.

Elbro, C., Borstrom, I., & Petersen, D.K. (1998). Predicting dyslexia from kindergarten: The importance of distinctness of phonological representations of lexical items. *Reading Research Quarterly, 33,* 36–60.

Felton, R. (2001). Students with three types of severe reading disabilities: Introduction to the case studies. *Journal of Special Education, 35,* 122–124.

Felton, R., & Brown, I. (1990). Phonological processes as predictors of specific reading skills in children at risk for reading failure. *Reading & Writing, 2,* 39–59.

Frith, U. (1997). Brain, mind, and behaviour in dyslexia, in C. Hulme & M. Snowling (Eds.), *Dyslexia: Biology, cognition, & intervention.* London: Whurr Publishing.

Fuchs, D., & Fuchs, L. (1998). Researchers and teachers working together to adapt instruction for diverse learners. *Learning Disabilities Research & Practice, 13,* 126–137.

Fuchs, L., & Fuchs, D. (1984). Criterion-referenced assessment without measurement: How accurate for special education? *Reading and Special Education, 5,* 29–32.

Fuchs, L., Fuchs, D., & Hamlett, C. L. (1994). Strengthening the connection between assessment and instructional planning with expert systems. *Exceptional Children, 6,* 138–146.

Fuchs, L., Fuchs, D., Hamlett, C., & Hasselbring, T. (1987). Using computers with curriculum-based monitoring: Effects on teacher efficiency and satisfaction. *Journal of Special Education Technology, 8,* 14–27.

Gathercole, S., & Baddeley, A. (1993). *Working memory and language.* Hillsdale, NJ: Lawrence Erlbaum Associates.

Gayan, J., Olson, R., Cardon, L., Smith, S., Fulker, D., Kimberling, W., Pennington, B., & DeFries, J. C. (1995). Quantitative trait locus for different measures of reading disability. *Behavioral Genetics, 25,* 266.

Gerber, M., English, J., & Singer, G. (1999). Bridging between craft and academic knowledge: A computer supported problem based learning model for professional preparation in special education. *Teacher Education and Special Education, 22,* 100–113.

Gough, P. B., Hoover, W. A., & Peterson, C. (1996). A simple view of reading. In C. Cornoldi & J. Oakhill (Eds.), *Reading comprehension difficulties: Processes and intervention* (pp 1–14). Mahwah, NJ: Lawrence Erlbaum Associates.

Gough, P., & Tunmer, W. (1986). Decoding, reading and reading disability. *Remedial and Special Education, 7,* 6–10.

Graves, A. W. (1986). Effects of direct instruction and metacomprehension training on finding main ideas. *Learning Disabilities Research, 1,* 90–100.

Gresham, F., MacMillan, D., & Bocian, K. (1997). Teachers as "tests": Differential validity of teacher judgements in identifying students at-risk for learning difficulties. *School Psychology Review, 26,* 47–60.

Grimes, J. (2001, August). *Responsiveness to interventions: The next step in special education identification, service, and exiting.* Paper presented at the LD Summit, Washington, DC.

Hall, S., & Moats, L. (1999). *Straight talk about reading.* Chicago: Contemporary Books.

Halliday, M. A. K., & Hasan, R. (1976). *Cohesion in English.* New York: Longman.

Hammill, D. (1972). Training visual perceptual processes. *Journal of Learning Disabilities, 5,* 552–559.

Hatcher, P., Hulme, C., & Ellis, A. (1994). Ameliorating early reading failure by integrating reading and phonological teaching: The phonological linkage hypothesis. *Child Development, 65,* 41–57.

Hynd, G., & Hiemenz, J. (1997). Dyslexia and gyral morphology variation. In C. Hulme & M. Snowling (Eds.), *Dyslexia: Biology, cognition, & intervention.* London: Whurr Publishing.

Jenkins, J., Heliotis, J., Stein, M., & Haynes, M. (1987). Improving reading comprehension by using paragraph restatements. *Exceptional Children, 54,* 54–59.

Kame'enui, E., Simmons, D., & Coyne, M. (2000). Schools as host environments: Toward a school-wide reading improvement model. *Annals of Dyslexia, 50,* 31–52.

Kinzer, C., & Cammack, D. (2001). *Scaffolding for story comprehension: Increasing student understanding and participation in an inclusion classroom.* Paper presented at Interactive Literacy Education International Workshop, Nijmegen, the Netherlands.

Langenberg, D. (2000). *Report of the National Reading Panel: Teaching children to read. (Reports of the subgroups).* Washington, DC: National Institute of Child Health and Human Development.

Lewin, C. (1997). Test-driving CARS: Addressing issues in the evaluation of computer-assisted reading software. *Journal of Computing in Education, 8,* 111–132

Liberman, I., & Shankweiler, D. (1985). Phonology and problems of learning to read and write. *Remedial & Special Education, 6,* 8–17.

Lovett, M., Borden, S., DeLuca, T., Lacerenza, L., Benson, N., & Brackstone, D. (1994). Treating the core deficits of developmental dyslexia: Evidence of transfer-of-learning. *Developmental Psychology, 30,* 805–822.

Lyon, G. R. (1995). Toward a definition of dyslexia. *Annals of Dyslexia, 45,* 3–30.

Lyon, G. R. (1999). Reading development, reading disorders, and reading instruction: Research-based findings. *Language, Learning, and Education, 6,* 8–16.

Marston, D. (2001, August). *A functional and intervention-based assessment approach to establishing discrepancy for students with learning disabilities.* Paper presented at the LD Summit, Washington, DC.

McCutchen, D. (1997). The links between teacher training and student learning. Paper presented at the annual meeting of the International Dyslexia Association, San Francisco, CA.

Moats, L. C. (1995a). *Spelling: Development, disability, and instruction.* Baltimore: York Press.

Moats, L. C. (1995b). Spelling error interpretation: Beyond the phonetic/dysphonetic dichotomy. *Annals of Dyslexia, 43,* 174–185.

Moody, S. W., Vaughn, S., Hughes, M. T., & Fischer, M. (2000). Reading instruction in the resource room: Set up for failure. *Exceptional Children, 66,* 305–316.

Nation, K., Adams, J. W., Bowyer-Crane, N., & Snowling, M. (1999). Working memory deficits in poor comprehenders reflect underlying language impairments. *Journal of Experimental Child Psychology, 73,* 139–158.

Nation, K., & Snowling, M. (1998a). Individual differences in contextual facilitation: Evidence from dyslexia and poor reading comprehension. *Child Development, 69,* 996–1011.

Nation, K., & Snowling, M. (1998b). Semantic processing and the development of word recognition skills: Evidence from children with reading comprehension difficulties. *Journal of Memory and Language, 39,* 85–101.

Oakhill, J. (1982). Constructive processes in skilled and less-skilled comprehenders. *British Journal of Psychology, 73,* 13–20.

Oakhill, J. (1983). Instantiation in skilled and less-skilled comprehenders. *Quarterly Journal of Experimental Psychology, 35A,* 31–39.

Oakhill, J. (1984). Inferential and memory skills in children's comprehension of stories. *British Journal of Educational Psychology, 54,* 31–39.

Oakhill, J., & Yuill, N. (1986). Pronoun resolution in skilled and less skilled comprehenders: Effects of memory load and inferential complexity. *Language and Speech, 29,* 25–36.

Oakhill, J., & Yuill, N. (1991). Remediation of reading comprehension difficulties. In M. Snowling & M. Thomson (Eds.), *Dyslexia: Integrating theory and practice.* London: Whurr.

Olson, R., Forsberg, H., Gayan, J., & DeFries, J. (1999). A behavioral-genetic analysis of reading disabilities and component processes. In R. M. Klein & P. A. McMullen (Eds.), *Converging methods for understanding reading and dyslexia* (pp. 133–153). Cambridge, MA: MIT Press.

Olson, R. K., Wise, B. W., Conners, F., Rack, J., & Fulker, D. (1989). Specific deficits in component reading and language skills: Genetic and environmental influences. *Journal of Learning Disabilities, 22,* 339–348.

Pennington, B. (1991). *Diagnosing learning disorders: A neuropsychological framework.* New York: Guilford Press.

Pennington, B., Groisser, D., & Welsh, M. (1993). Contrasting cognitive deficits in attention deficit hyperactivity disorder vs. reading disability. *Developmental Psychology, 29,* 522–523.

Perfetti, C. (1985). *Reading ability.* Oxford, England: Oxford University Press.

Perfetti, C., Marron, M., & Foltz, P. (1996). Sources of comprehension failure: Theoretical perspectives and case studies. In C. Carnoldi & J. Oakhill (Eds.), *Reading comprehension difficulties: Processes and intervention.* Mahwah, NJ: Lawrence Erlbaum Associates.

Post, Y., Foorman, B., & Hiscock, M. (1997). Speech perception and speech production as indicators of reading difficulty. *Annals of Dyslexia, 47,* 1–25.

Rack, J., Snowling, M., & Olson, R. (1992). The nonword reading deficit in developmental dyslexia: A review. *Reading Research Quarterly, 27,* 28–53.

Rosner, J. (1975 1st ed, 1993 3rd ed). *Helping children overcome learning difficulties.* New York: Walker & Co.

Sapon-Shevin, M. (1987). Learning disabled/gifted: The politics of contradiction. In B. M. Franklin (Ed.), *Learning disabilities: Dissenting essays.* New York: Falmer Press.

Sawyer, D., Kim, J., & Wade, S. (2000). Applications of Frith's developmental phase model to the process of identifying at-risk beginning readers. In N. Badian (Ed.), *Prediction and prevention of reading failure*. Baltimore, MD: York Press.

Scanlon, D., & Vellutino, F. (1997). A comparison of the instructional backgrounds and cognitive profiles of good, average, and poor readers who were initially identified as at risk for reading failure. *Scientific Studies of Reading, 1*, 191–216.

Scarborough, H. (1990). Very early language deficits in dyslexic children. *Child Development, 61*, 1728–1743.

Scarborough, H. (1991). Antecedents to reading disability: Preschool language development and literacy experiences in children from dyslexic families. *Reading and Writing, 3*, 219–233.

Scarborough, H. (1998a). Predicting the future achievement of second graders with reading disabilities: Contributions of phonemic awareness, verbal memory, rapid naming, and IQ. *Annals of Dyslexia, 48*, 115–136.

Scarborough, H. (1998b, April). *What underlies rapid serial naming?* Presentation at the Society for the Scientific Study of Reading, San Diego, CA.

Segers, E., & Verhoeven, L. (2001). *Emergent literacy enhancement*. Paper presented at Interactive Literacy Education International Workshop, Nijmegen, the Netherlands.

Shaywitz, S. (1996, November). Dyslexia. *Scientific American*, 98–104.

Shaywitz, S., Fletcher, J., Holahan, J., & Shaywitz, B. (1992). Discrepancy compared to low achievement definitions of reading disability: Results from the Connecticut longitudinal study. *Journal of Learning Disabilities, 25*, 639–648.

Siegel, L. (1992). An evaluation of the discrepancy definition of dyslexia. *Journal of Learning Disabilities, 25*, 618–629.

Smith, D. S., & Nagle, R. J. (1995). Self-perceptions and social comparisons among children with LD. *Journal of Learning Disabilities, 6*, 364–371.

Snow, C., Burns, M., & Griffin, P. (1998). *Preventing reading difficulties in young children: Report of the National Research Council*. Washington, DC: National Academy Press.

Snowling, M. (2000). *Dyslexia* (2nd ed.). Oxford, UK: Blackwell Publishers

Snyder, L., & Downey, D. (1991). The language-reading relationship in normal and reading-disabled children. *Journal of Speech and Hearing Research, 34*, 129–140.

Stanovich, K. (1986). Matthew effects in reading: Some consequences of individual differences in acquisition of literacy. *Reading Research Quarterly, 21,* 360–497.

Stanovich, K. (1991). Discrepancy definitions of reading disability: Has intelligence led us astray? *Reading Research Quarterly, 26,* 1–29.

Stothard, S., & Hulme, C. (1992). Reading comprehension difficulties: The role of language comprehension and working memory. *Reading and Writing, 4,* 245–256

Stothard, S., & Hulme, C. (1995). A comparison of phonological skills in children with reading comprehension difficulties and children with decoding difficulties. *Journal of Child Psychology and Psychiatry, 36,* 399–408.

Stothard, S., & Hulme, C. (1996). A comparison of reading comprehension and decoding difficulties in children. In C. Cornoldi & J. Oakhill (Eds.), *Reading comprehension and difficulties: Processes and intervention.* Mahwah, NJ: Lawrence Erlbaum Associates.

Swanson, H. L. (1999). *Interventions for students with learning disabilities: A meta-analysis of treatment outcomes.* New York: Guilford.

Swanson, H. L. (2001). Reading intervention research outcomes and students with learning disabilities: What are the major instructional ingredients for successful outcomes? *Perspectives, 27,* 18–20.

Tauber, R. T. (1998). Good or bad: What teachers expect from students they generally get! Washington, DC: ERIC Clearinghouse on Teaching and Teacher Education.

Torgesen, J., Wagner, R., & Rashotte, C. (1997). Prevention and remediation of severe reading disabilities: Keeping the end in mind. *Scientific Studies of Reading, 1,* 217–234.

Treiman, R. (1993). *Beginning to spell.* New York: Oxford.

Uhry, J. (1997). Case studies of dyslexia: Young readers with rapid serial naming deficits. In C. K. Leong & R. M. Joshi (Eds.), *Cross-language studies of learning to read and spell* (pp. 71–88). Dordrecht, Netherlands: Kluwer Academic Publishers.

Van Daal, V., & Reitsma, P. (1993). Effects of practice with segmented and whole-word feedback in disabled readers. *Journal of Research in Reading, 13,* 133–148.

Van Daal, V., & Van der Leij, A. (1994). Computer-based reading and spelling practice for children with LD. *Journal of Learning Disabilities, 25,* 186–195.

Van Kleeck, A., Gillam, R., & McFadden, T. U. (1998). A study of classroom-based phonological awareness training for preschoolers with speech and/or language disorders. *American Journal of Speech-Language Pathology, 7,* 65–76.

Vaughn, S., Gersten, R., & Chard, D. (2000). The underlying message in LD intervention studies: Findings from research syntheses. *Exceptional Children, 67,* 99–114.

Vaughn, S., Hughes, M., Moody, S., & Elbaum, B. (in press). Instructional grouping for reading for children with learning disabilities. *Intervention in School and Clinic.*

Vellutino, F. (1979). *Dyslexia: Theory and research.* Cambridge, MA: MIT Press.

Verhoeven, L., & Irausquin, R. (2001). *Multi-agent based support for poor readers.* Paper presented at Interactive Literacy Education International Workshop, Nijmegen, the Netherlands.

Viall, J. T. (2001). The "M" in multisensory structured language instruction. *Perspectives, 27,* 3.

Wagner, R. K., Torgesen, J., & Rashotte, C. (1994). The development of reading-related phonological processing abilities. *Developmental Psychology, 30,* 73–87.

Wagner, R., Torgesen, J., & Rashotte, C. (1999). *Comprehensive Test of Phonological Processing (CTOPP).* Austin, TX: Pro-Ed.

Watkins, M., Kush, J., & Glutting, J. (1997). Discriminant and predictive validity of the WISC-III acid profile in children with learning disabilities. *Psychology in the Schools, 34,* 309–19.

Wilder, A. A., & Williams, J. P. (in press). Students with severe learning disabilities can learn higher-order comprehension skills. *Journal of Educational Psychology.*

Williams, J. P. (1993). Comprehension of students with and without learning disabilities: Identification of themes and idiosyncratic text representations. *Journal of Educational Psychology, 85,* 631–641.

Williams, J., Brown, L., Silverstein, A., & deCani, J. (1994). An instructional program in comprehension of narrative themes for adolescents with learning disabilities. *Learning Disability Quarterly, 17,* 205–331.

Wise, B. (1999). The promise and limits of phonological training for children with specific reading disabilities. *ASHA Division 1: Language, Learning, & Education Newsletter, 6,* 22–24.

Wise, B. (2001). The indomitable dinosaur builder (how she overcame her phonological deficit and learned to read instructions, and other things). *Journal of Special Education, 35,* 134–144.

Wise, B., Olson, R., & Ring, J. (2000, February). *Transfer from phonological training in children with reading disabilities.* Paper presented at Pacific Coast Research Conference, San Diego, CA.

Wise, B. W., Ring, J., & Olson, R. K. (1999). Training phonological awareness with and without explicit attention to articulation. *Journal of Experimental Child Psychology, 72,* 271–304.

Wise, B. W., Ring, J., & Olson, R. K. (2000). Individual differences in gains from computer-assisted remedial reading. *Journal of Experimental Child Psychology, 77,* 197–235.

Wise, B. W., Ring, J., Sessions, L., & Olson, R. K. (1997). Phonological awareness with and without articulation: A preliminary study. *Learning Disability Quarterly, 20,* 211–225.

Wolf, M. (1999). What time may tell: Towards a new conceptualization of developmental dyslexia. *Annals of Dyslexia, 49,* 3–28.

Wolf, M., Bowers, P., & Biddle, K. (2000). Naming speed processes, timing, and reading: A conceptual review. *Journal of Learning Disabilities, 33,* 322–324.

Wolf, M., & Katzir-Cohen, T. (2001). Reading fluency and its intervention. *Scientific Studies in Reading, 5,* 211–219.

Wolf, M., Miller, L., & Donnelley, K. (2000). The Retrieval, Automaticity, Vocabulary Elaboration, Orthography (RAVE-O): A comprehensive fluency-based reading intervention program. *Journal of Learning Disabilities, 33,* 375–386.

Yuill, N. (1996). A funny thing happened on the way to the classroom: Jokes, riddles and metalinguistic awareness in understanding and improving poor comprehension in children. In C. Cornoldi & J. Oakhill (Eds.), *Reading comprehension difficulties: Processes and intervention* (pp. 193–220). Mahwah, NJ: Lawrence Erlbaum Associates.

Yuill, N., & Josceleyne, T. (1988). Effects of organizational cues and strategies on good and poor comprehenders' story understanding. *Journal of Educational Psychology, 80,* 152–158.

Yuill, N., & Oakhill, J. (1988a). Understanding of anaphoric relations in skilled and less skilled comprehenders. *British Journal of Psychology, 79,* 173–186.

Yuill, N., & Oakhill, J. (1988b). Effects of inference training on poor reading comprehension. *Journal of Applied Cognitive Psychology, 2,* 33–45.

Yuill, N., & Oakhill, J. (1991). *Children's problems in text comprehension: An experimental investigation.* Cambridge, England: Cambridge University Press.

Zeffiro, T. J., & Eden, G. (2000). The neural basis of developmental dyslexia. *Annals of Dyslexia, 50,* 1–30.

Zigmond, N. (1997). Educating students with disabilities: The future of special education. In J. W. Lloyd, E. J. Kame'enui, & D. Chard (Eds.), *Issues in educating students with disabilities* (pp. 377–390). Mahwah, NJ: Lawrence Erlbaum Associates.

ACKNOWLEDGMENTS

1. The Office of Special Education Projects for inviting us to write the paper and providing support for it,

2. The National Science Foundation for an ITR-HCI grant IIS-0086107: Creating the Next Generation of Animated Conversational Agents, to Ron Cole at the Center for Spoken Language Research (CSLR) at the University of Colorado, which also partially supported its writing,

3. The National Institute of Child Health and Human Development for support from grants HD 11683 and HD 22223 to Richard Olson and Barbara Wise;

4. Boulder Valley Schools staff and students for participation and support of some of the research reported in this chapter,

5. Our research assistant, Nikki Davis, for finding so many good articles, and

6. Our colleague Dr. Ron Cole of CSLR for encouraging us to write it.

CULTURE IN LEARNING:
THE NEXT FRONTIER IN READING DIFFICULTIES RESEARCH[1]

Alfredo J. Artiles, Vanderbilt University

A clear message in Wise and Snyder's review of the literature is that we possess solid and promising evidence about the nature and treatment of language-based reading disabilities. They also argue this knowledge base can be translated into useful information to identify and treat students' reading difficulties. Wise and Snyder present a cogent summary of research on two groups of language-based reading difficulties, namely specific reading disabilities (SRDs) and difficulties associated with poor language comprehension. The authors summarize the knowledge base on identification and teaching for each group and discuss its clinical applications; for example, they identify miscues and behaviors that might reflect language-based disabilities. The charge for my response is to offer "additional perspectives and/or research." Thus, I discuss three interrelated aspects that place culture at the center of learning processes and that can enrich the next generation of language-based reading difficulties research.

WHAT IS THE PHENOMENON UNDER STUDY? FROM READING TO THE PRACTICE OF LITERACY

The current emphasis on discrete psycholinguistic processes (e.g., phonemic awareness, efficiency in using speech-based codes) might inadvertently imply that reading is a unitary process when in reality multiple perceptual, cognitive, linguistic, emotional, and social processes are involved. People use reading competencies in complex social and institutional milieu to achieve goals. Future research must address questions that frame reading beyond psycholinguistic aspects because reading is both competence and performance. Scribner (1997) explained that "a performance framework of analysis requires attention not only to a *reader* and a *text* but to the *task* the reader is trying to fulfill through engagement with a text" (p. 191) (emphasis in original). A core principle in this view is that reading is situated in readers' sociocultural contexts, which in turn implies reading research be located in the realm of literacy and its practice, "where mind and society meet" (Scribner, 1997, p. 190). Literacy is embedded in sociocultural, institutional, and political practices; hence, the practice of literacy integrates oral and written language with "nonlanguage 'stuff,' that is, with ways of acting, interacting, feeling, valuing, thinking, and believing, as well as with various sorts of nonverbal symbols, sites, tools, objects, and technologies" (Gee, 1999, p. 356). In this view, the unit of analysis is the person-using-reading-competencies-in-a-sociocultural-context-for-specific-purposes. Unfortunately, research on language-based reading difficulties has emphasized discrete psycholinguistic processes and thus, it focuses on the individual reader engaged with isolated school-like tasks. It is not surprising, therefore, that the reviewed research shows little "differential gains in reading rate and in comprehension... [and] a discouraging lack of transfer of differential gains in one and two years after treatment ends, relative to the less explicit treatments" (Wise & Snyder, this volume).

I am not suggesting the study of reading competencies is unimportant; rather, I argue future research ought to examine goal-directed reading performance in a wider range of productive literacy practices so that we can begin to map out similarities and differences in the underlying processes involved in people's everyday literacy practices (Scribner, 1997). This will help us understand, for example, how a student's lack of ability in school literacy tasks, as documented by traditional approaches, does not necessarily preclude the student's ability to perform other literacy practices in and out of school contexts.

In addition to naturalistic inquiry, this vision calls for a new generation of experimental research with strong external validity. As a consequence, two issues arise, namely the challenges of achieving ecological validity and operationalizing the notion of context. Ecological validity is defined as "the extent to which behavior sampled in one setting can be taken as characteristic of an individual's cognitive processes in a range of other settings" (Cole, 1996, p. 222). Ecologically valid inquiry must meet three conditions: (a) target situations that are authentic to the person's routine experiences, (b) work in settings that accurately resemble the individual's sociocultural everyday milieu, and (c) align the person's definition of the situation (i.e., experiment conditions and outcomes) with the study's definition (Cole, 1996). One way to enhance ecological validity is to use Scribner's notion of "locating the experiment" as a way to achieve symmetry between experimental tasks and everyday practices. She recommended a three-step process: (a) conduct ethnographic analyses of people's everyday activities in a target context, (b) gather detailed descriptions of literacy-related tasks as performed during the routine activities, and (c) use such descriptions to generate models of the underlying processes involved in the target tasks and to test the models in experimental conditions and interviews.

In turn, the notion of "context" is key in a practice-based view of literacy and reading. But how do we define "context," what is included in context, and where do we locate the boundary between "context" and the "behavior(s)" under scrutiny? Goodwin and Duranti (1992) identified three central issues in the analysis of context. First, it is fundamental that such analysis takes the perspective of participants whose behavior is being studied. Second, what counts as context for participants is shaped by the culturally specific activities performed during the event being examined. Third, "participants are situated within multiple contexts which are capable of rapid and dynamic change as the events they are engaged in unfold" (p. 5).

Because participants' perspectives and their contexts are important in the study of reading competencies and performance, it is germane to ask who is included in reading research, what do we know about these individuals' cultural histories, and what role does culture play in their learning processes? I address these questions next.

WHO IS INCLUDED IN READING DIFFICULTIES RESEARCH? OR HOW TO ACCOUNT FOR CULTURE IN LEARNING

Contemporary special education placement patterns suggest three trends: (a) a sizable number of students are referred to special education due to reading difficulties; (b) although special education legislation includes nondiscriminatory safeguards so that learning difficulties caused by environmental, cultural, or economic disadvantages are not interpreted as disabilities, minorities are over-represented in high incidence disabilities, including learning disabilities (LD); and (c) most students with reading difficulties are placed in the LD category. Based on these trends, it is understandable to find a large proportion of poor minority students in programs for language-based reading difficulties. Yet, the research on reading difficulties is troublingly silent about the presence of minorities.

At the heart of this silence is the fact that special education's treatment of culture has been problematic. First, researchers have ignored culture. My colleagues and I found that most of the contemporary LD research does not attend to culture and sociocultural factors; the same pattern has been documented in psychology and language development research. In fairness to Wise and Snyder, aside from the fact they cautioned their review did not cover reading "problems due to [among other things] learning to read in a second language, or problems due to inconsistent education" (this volume), reading research silence about minorities seems to be symptomatic of a larger problem in special education, namely the invisibility of ethnic minorities and culture in research practices.

Second, when culture is taken into account, it is regarded as an independent variable and/or defined from a deficit perspective, or both. For instance, it is assumed membership in an ethnic group has a causal effect on people's worldviews, values, and learning styles; hence, we hear for example that Latinos are field-dependent thinkers. Culture is also cast in a negative light. Thus, we learn that the culture of poverty or being a culturally diverse individual (meaning ethnic minority) exacerbates the risks for school failure—note this view equates culture with ethnicity, class status, or both. These views of culture are problematic because they are overly deterministic, ignore culture's dynamic and instrumental nature, and stress a unidimensional view, disregard within-group diversity, and imply only minority groups possess culture. As we know, this assumption has negative overtones since to be an ethnic minority means to be poor, a low achiever, and a second-class citizen.

I argue for a more complex view of culture that integrates multiple locations and honors its dynamic nature. Culture is located in the minds of individuals (e.g., values, knowledge structures, beliefs) *as well as* in the practices, artifacts, rituals, rules for social interactions, and roles that groups develop over time to accomplish common purposes (Cole, 1996). The former view of culture assumes people appropriate a cultural tool kit in their (ethnic, linguistic, gender, or class) communities. This tool kit embodies the unique cultural history and the developmental goals valued by community members.[2] Rogoff (1990) concluded cultural values play a major role in the desired cognitive skills and goals of development. In fact, she reminded us that even Piaget conceded that the endpoint of development—its goals and valued skills—is not universal; it depends on local circumstances and aspirations. In turn, the latter view of culture explains how people use this tool kit to navigate social situations, to negotiate and function in institutional settings.

From this perspective, we find multiple cultures in any given classroom as embodied in the cultural tool kit that each person brings to school and the cultures that are created as students, teachers, and school staff interact over time; these are the cultures that define what counts as competent performance, the rules and rituals teachers and students abide by to orchestrate participation structures during classroom discourse, and the ideal (values, beliefs, norms) and material (tests, rating scales, observation protocols) artifacts that are sanctioned to define identities such as deprived, gifted, or language-delayed.

This more complex understanding of culture implies human development and learning are imbued in cultural media. For this reason, future research must be grounded in a systematic understanding of the role of culture in learning and its sociohistorical origins. Research suggests that lack of attention to these crucial premises can have negative consequences. For instance, Heath (1983) showed how cultural discontinuities in literacy and discourse practices between the home and community and the school mediated poor and minority students' reading difficulties and had consequences for the quality of their participation in school activities. Similarly, reading research's overemphasis on psycholinguistic skills precludes us from seeing the mediating contributions of cultural practices. Gee (1999) illustrates this point by noting the emphasis of the 1998 National Research Council's (NRC's) report about reading difficulties on the correlation between phonological awareness and success in learning to read and its neglect of the equally significant correlation between early language abilities (receptive and expressive vocabulary, ability to recall and comprehend sentences and stories, ability to engage in verbal interactions) and future success in reading. Iin fact, language abilities and phonological awareness are also correlated. This research further suggests family, community, and school cultural practices can enhance these language abilities (Gee, 1999).

The good news about the association between early language abilities and future reading success is that all children (including poor and minority kids) come to school with a wealth of literacy practices that include vocabulary, grammar, and understandings of stories (Hymes, 1996). The bad news is that the traditional cultures of classrooms and schools place a differential value on the language abilities of distinct groups. Many educational authorities, for example, assume ethnic minorities enter school without the linguistic abilities needed for success in school. Interestingly, there is research that speaks to this assumption.

For instance, Labov documented variability in African-American linguistic competence as a function of situational factors such as the race of the examiner and the organization of social relations in the assessment situation. There is also evidence about the complexity of African-American Vernacular English as reflected in its history of independent development, systematic phonology, syntax, tense and aspect system, lexical semantics, and distinctiveness from other English dialects (Labov, 1982; Stockman, 1995). Likewise, Michaels and Cazden (1986) documented how differences in narrative styles of African American and White students had distinct consequences (in terms of teacher approval) for each group during "sharing time." Unlike African Americans, Replace students' styles aligned with the teacher's sanctioned style.

This evidence challenges the long-standing deficit view about African Americans' Vernacular English and the twin assumption that African Americans' language differences constitute learning difficulties (including reading problems), as reflected in high-profile legal cases (Labov, 1982). This evidence also reminds us a community's language is more than phonemes and grammar. Every language has varieties and styles, ways of using it, sociohistorical antecedents, and political status (Hymes, 1996).

An implication of this scholarship is that future reading difficulties research be situated in everyday literacy practices, include the various groups represented in the educational system (including minorities) who bring multiple language varieties, and acknowledge that language uses, including reading performance, often constitute acts of identity carried out in cultural-historical settings by members of disenfranchised groups. This evidence further implies that just as educators need to apply research findings in their practice, they also need to possess a complex understanding of the interplay between learning and culture.

How Do Teachers Make Informed Clinical Judgments? Toward a Hybrid Metaphor

Practitioners' clinical judgments about student learning difficulties have important consequences. For instance, we know the vast majority of referred students are found eligible for special education services. We also know minority students represent a large proportion of these cases. To complicate matters, evidence suggests clinical judgments are made in complex socioeconomic and historical landscapes. This is evidenced in the NRC reading panel's finding that school poverty level is a better predictor of reading difficulties than early phonemic awareness; as we know, poor schools serve predominately minority populations and school poverty is associated with poor schooling such as unqualified teachers, scarcity of resources, and low quality of instruction. Miscommunication between teachers and students is also a potential problem, especially if they come from distinct speech communities and particularly if there are differences in key areas such as articulation, grammar, and knowledge of their respective cultures.

Social psychological research provides insights on the complex dynamics and consequences of decisions, actions, and interactions. Stereotypes about racial minorities are pervasive in our society to the point that stigmatized individuals can be stereotyped automatically; a stereotype can "unconsciously, affect one's actions, thoughts, and emotions... When we are in a hurry... distracted or cognitively overloaded... when the situation is ambiguous... stereotypes can shape our response to the stereotyped, even when we are otherwise low in prejudice ... and even when we are members of the stereotyped group (Crocker, Major, & Steele, 1998, p. 535). This research also shows stigmatized groups are usually aware of negative stereotypes, an awareness that may have nefarious consequences depending on the context and task at hand—a case in point is the negative effect of stereotype threats on the test performance of African Americans, independent of their ability or past performance level (Crocker et al., 1998).

How does this complex web of influences mediate practitioners' clinical judgments to identify reading difficulties? It should be clear we cannot afford to conceptualize practitioners' judgments as the mere application of a knowledge base produced under controlled conditions. Although practitioners have at their disposal a wealth of information about reading skill profiles, we have little evidence on how practitioners take into account cultural influences as they screen and make judgments about students' classroom behaviors, inference construction processes, narrative crafting, and text comprehension processes.

My point is not that research should document White educators' responsibility in minority students' plight; instead, we need to study why well-intentioned people such as most educators are still creating conditions that maintain school inequality. One important task becomes, therefore, to develop a model of teacher judgments based on a hybrid metaphor that integrates a cognitive dimension as well as the sociocultural and historical contexts of practitioners' work. This hybrid metaphor will enable us to trace how educators use research findings for varying purposes, with particular populations of students, and in distinct cultural contexts. In addition, it should incorporate a moral and ethical dimension that is mindful of the historical and political trajectories of minority students in the educational system and society.

This research program should also focus on *teacher learning about diversity* in various subject matters, in this case reading and literacy. Recent scholarship on conceptions of learning as a situated, distributed, and social phenomenon can inform this research program. As we broaden the conception of teacher learning, this research would document how teachers' use of ideal tools (beliefs, values, theory, knowledge base), contexts, and social practices mediate students' reading difficulties.

CONCLUSION

I comment briefly on two implications for brevity's sake. First, our scholarly community will have to reformulate the goals of literacy. Scribner identified three metaphors, namely literacy as adaptation (it stresses the survival and pragmatic value of literacy), literacy as power (it focuses on the link between literacy learning and group advancement), and literacy as a state of grace (it bestows the literate individual with special virtues). We must ask, which metaphor should guide reading difficulties research? The search for a literacy metaphor to guide reading difficulties research must capitalize on the possibilities afforded by a diverse society and ultimately aim to, as Scribner suggested, broaden our vocabulary of metaphors.

Second, my proposal compels us to revisit the definition of "good research" and it forces us to face the longstanding tension between the goals of basic versus applied research. Our challenge is to develop a research program that synthesizes basic understanding and use. Such a paradigm will force researchers to acknowledge that power issues and the societal status of minorities as "different" often mediate access to literacy and reading performance (Gee, 1999). A research program that integrates these goals and concerns can generate a knowledge base that will allow us to fulfill the promise of education in a democratic nation, namely full and meaningful citizenship for all members of society.

REFERENCES

Cole, M. (1996). *Cultural psychology.* Cambridge, MA: Harvard University Press.

Crocker, J., Major, B., Steele, C. (1998). Social stigma. In D. T. Gilbert, S. T. Fiske, & G. Lindzey (Eds.), *The handbook of social psychology* (4th ed., Vol. II) (pp. 504–553). Boston, MA: McGraw-Hill.

Gee, J. P. (1999). Reading and the new literacy studies: Reframing the National Academy of Sciences report on reading. *Journal of Literacy Research, 31,* 355–374.

Goodwin, C., & Duranti, A. (1992). Rethinking context: An introduction. In A. Duranti & C. Goodwin (Eds.), *Rethinking context: Language as an interactive phenomenon* (pp. 1–42). New York: Cambridge University Press.

Heath, S. B. (1983). *Ways with words: Language, life and work in communities and classrooms.* Cambridge, England: Cambridge University Press.

Hymes, D. (1996). Report from an underdeveloped country: Toward linguistic competence in the United States. In R. Singh (Ed.), *Towards a critical sociolinguistics* (pp. 151–194). Philadelphia, PA: John Benjamins Publishing Co.

Labov, W. (1982). Objectivity and commitment in linguistic science: The case of the Black English trial in Ann Arbor. *Language in Society, 11,* 165–201.

Michaels, S., & Cazden, C. B. (1986). Teacher/child collaboration as oral preparation for literacy. In B. B. Schieffelin & P. Gilmore (Eds.), *The acquisition of literacy: Ethnographic perspectives.* Norwood, NJ: Ablex.

Rogoff, B. (1990). *Apprenticeship in thinking: Cognitive development in social context.* New York: Oxford University Press.

Scribner, S. (1997). The practice of literacy: Where mind and society meet. In E. Tobach, R. J. Falmagne, M. B. Parlee, L. M. W. Martin, & A. S. Kapelman (Eds.), *Mind and social practice: Selected writings of Sylvia Scribner* (pp. 190–205). New York: Cambridge University Press.

Stockman, I. J. (1995, March). *The social-political construction of science: Evidence from language research on African American children.* W. E. B. Du Bois Distinguished Visiting Lecturer Series. The City University of New York.

ENDNOTES

[1] I acknowledge the support of the COMRISE Project at the University of Virginia under grant #H029J60006 awarded by the U.S. Department of Education, Office of Special Education Programs. I am grateful to Mike Rose and Stan Trent for their feedback on earlier versions of this response.

[2] Within-group diversity is equally important in this discussion but I focus only on the cultural histories of groups (cultural homogeneity) due to space constraints.

CLINICAL JUDGMENTS IN IDENTIFYING AND TEACHING CHILDREN WITH READING DISABILITIES: ANOTHER PERSPECTIVE

Barbara Bateman

The knowledgeable, competent expert clinicians envisioned by Wise and Snyder are the dream of professionals and the answer to the prayers of millions of parents of children with reading disabilities. However, the realities of the identification and teaching of children with reading disabilities under the Individuals with Disabilities Education Act (IDEA) in the public schools of this nation are too often another matter altogether. This public school reality is the perspective explored here.

Five and a half million school aged children were identified as disabled under IDEA in 1998-99 (U.S. Department of Education, 2001). Slightly more than half of these have a specific learning disability (SLD). Well over 75% of the SLD students have reading disabilities, and all but a small percentage of the 2.8 million SLD children attend public schools. Wise and Snyder's ideal clinicians likely practice in private school and clinics. They are infrequently found employed in public schools.

IDEA includes students with reading disabilities under the category of "specific learning disabilities" that may occur in reading, math, written expression, oral expression, or listening comprehension. In IDEA, 'reading disabilities and all other SLDs are treated alike. Both terms—reading disabled and SLD—are used here to denote the children of concern.

IDENTIFICATION

Since IDEA was passed in 1975 (then known as P.L. 94-142 and later as the Education for All Handicapped Children Act), it has been no secret that public school personnel, in general, have been extraordinarily hesitant to exercise clinical judgment, instead relying on standardized test scores to identify children who have

SLD. The misapprehensions about legal processes that underlie this reluctance are beyond this discussion. The result, however, is that the only students with reading disabilities served (beyond Chapter One) are those found IDEA-eligible. For decades now, professionals and parents alike have encountered these public school systems willing to provide special services only to those students who have been formally and legally identified as IDEA-eligible. How has it happened that schools have lost or failed to acquire the responsibility for trying to meet the unique needs of all students, even if they don't "qualify" under a federal law? Untold thousands of times, parents have been told by school personnel that "The only way we can serve your child is if she is found eligible as a special education student."

According to IDEA, every eligibility decision is to be based on a full and individual evaluation that assesses *all* areas related to a child's suspected disability and is sufficiently comprehensive to identify *all* of the child's special education and related service needs, whether or not they are commonly linked to the disability category (34 C.F.R. §300.532). Reading disabilities are usually based on core deficits in phonological processing, a fact that has been well known and widely accepted for about 20 years and with which Wise and Snyder deal in depth. Nevertheless, it is rare that a public school evaluation includes any examination of phonological processing or any other aspect of reading beyond word reading and comprehension as measured by standardized tests. An intelligence test usually completes the evaluation. An incomplete and superficial evaluation leads to similar program recommendations. The purpose of the required evaluation is twofold: (a) to determine if the student meets the definitional criteria, and if so, (b) to determine all of the student's educational needs.

The IDEA legal definition of SLD is the beginning point for examining the "everyday reality" perspective on identification of reading disabilities. That definition is found in three parts in the IDEA regulations. First, an SLD is one of the 13 named disability categories:

> ...the term child with a disability means a child evaluated ... as having mental retardation, a hearing impairment, a visual impairment including blindness, serious emotional disturbance (hereafter referred to as emotional disturbance), an orthopedic impairment, autism, traumatic brain injury, an other health impairment, a specific learning disability, deaf-blindness, or multiple disabilities, and who, by reason thereof, needs special education and related services. (34 C.F.R. §300.7(a)(1))

In this regulation, SLD is a recognized category of disability while neither dyslexia or reading disability *per se* appears. In addition to having a specified disability, every eligible student must also need special education. Not all children with reading disabilities meet this latter requirement.

In a second definition, SLD, including dyslexia, is *described*, but not operationalized. SLD is

> a disorder in one or more of the basic psychological processes involved in understanding or in using language, spoken or written, that may manifest itself in an imperfect ability to listen, think, speak, read, write, spell, or to do mathematical calculations, including conditions such as perceptual disabilities, brain injury, minimal brain dysfunction, dyslexia, and developmental aphasia.

The term does not include learning problems that are primarily the result of visual, hearing, or motor disabilities, of mental retardation, of emotional disturbance, or of environmental, cultural, or economic disadvantage (34 C.F.R.§300.7(c)(10)).

Third, the *operational* SLD definition states that

(a) A team may determine that the child has a specific learning disability if

  (1) The child does not achieve commensurate with his or her age and ability levels in one or more of the areas listed in paragraph (a)(2) of this section, if provided with learning experiences appropriate for the child's age and ability levels; and

  (2) The team finds that a child has a severe discrepancy between achievement and intellectual ability in one or more of the following areas: (i) oral expression, (ii) listening comprehension, (iii) written expression, (iv) basic reading skill, (v) reading comprehension, (vi) mathematics calculation, (vii) mathematics reasoning.

(b) The team may not identify a child as having a specific learning disability if the severe discrepancy between ability and achievement is primarily the result of

  (1) a visual, hearing, or motor impairment;

  (2) mental retardation;

  (3) emotional disturbance; or

  (4) environmental, cultural or economic disadvantage (34 C.F.R. §300.541).

These IDEA regulations, taken together, require three separate determinations in the identification of a student with SLD: (1) whether there is a severe discrepancy between ability and achievement in one of the seven named areas; if so, (2) whether the discrepancy is believed by the team to be due to a learning disability rather than to other factors, and if so, (3) whether the student needs special education. Each of these three determinations—discrepancy, causality, and special education—requires brief but important rethinking.

Discrepancy

The present legal requirement that IDEA eligibility requires a severe discrepancy between ability and achievement is controversial and undergoing scrutiny. Nevertheless, it is presently the law and has been so for more than 25 years. In the publicly funded sector, a reading disabled child's legal entitlement to essential reading services depends upon a team's decision that a severe discrepancy exists, and so this population may be slightly different from that seen in clinics and private schools. In a denial of the role, importance, and validity of the clinical judgment that Wise and Snyder present so cogently, most states and school districts have created and/ or employed a mathematical formula to examine discrepancy. These formulas determine whether a given difference between two (and *only* two) test scores meets a certain statistical likelihood of occurring, absent a "true" difference of a predetermined magnitude.

The fervent desire of many evaluation team members is for a magical, easy to use, and legally permissible formula to decide whether a given discrepancy between ability and achievement in reading is "severe." There is no such formula. None is magical, and if one is relied upon, it is not legal. No child can be reduced to two test scores. Yet that is exactly what every discrepancy formula does. Even if that procedure were allowed for some children, a child with SLD would be one of the last for whom it would make sense.

For just a moment, consider Joe who is starting the 7th grade when the evaluation team begins its eligibility determination. During the past few weeks, Joe was given a variety of reading tests, and he earned standard scores ranging from 63 to 85, percentile rankings from 1 to 34, and grade equivalents from 2.7 to 4.5. Suppose Joe has also taken the Wechsler Intelligence Scale for Children–III (WISC–III) twice and earned verbal IQs of 94 and 102, performance IQs of 90 and 97, and full scale IQs of 93 and 99.

If Joe's lowest reading score were compared to his highest IQ, the discrepancy would be larger than if the highest reading score were compared to the lowest IQ. Even if only one reading and one cognitive ability score is available, the problem is the same. Either score could be at either end of Joe's true range of scores. Again, no child should be reduced to two scores.

What should happen? Each team member should form a professional, clinical opinion as to the child's ability and achievement status. One member might conclude that Joe's reading is very slow and labored at a middle third to low fourth grade level and that Joe's ability is average, and, therefore, conclude that Joe ought to be reading near grade level. Since Joe reads four years below that, this team member says Joe has a severe discrepancy. Someone else might argue that Joe's performance IQ of 90 is not significantly discrepant from his reading test standard score of 85. The first team member has avoided the "two-score pitfall"; the second has not. The first exercised clinical judgment; the second could have had a machine pick and compare Joe's highest achievement and lowest ability scores.

Only if the machine possessed the research-based knowledge and clinical expertise outlined by Wise and Snyder should this determination be entrusted to it. Proponents of reliance upon a mathematical formula (especially of the regression type) for the identification of a reading disability have responded to a perceived need to control, in the short term, the costs of providing special services to children with reading disabilities. The long-term cost of not providing services is arguably far higher. An additional reason that public school personnel prefer to rely on a formula in eligibility decisions is that there is no ambiguity inherent in cutoff score established by a formula, and therefore, less room for discussion, argument, and disagreement about eligibility. However, reliance upon formulas is contrary to law and common sense and is an undeserved slap in the face of clinical expertise. On the other hand, if the fact is the team lacks clinical knowledge and expertise with SLD, reliance on a formula may not be the worst option.

CAUSALITY

If an evaluation team does not find a severe discrepancy, the LD eligibility inquiry is over. If they do find one, the next question is what caused it. Most teams are comfortable excluding mental retardation, sensory and motor impairments, and serious emotional disturbance. What is more difficult is distinguishing a learning disability from environmental, economic, or cultural disadvantage. The team too often lacks the experience to reliably and comfortably distinguish a reading disability from a reading delay.

The intent of the IDEA exclusion requirement is to ensure that the discrepancy is due not to something else but to a reading disability, as so well characterized by Wise and Snyder. All of the characteristics of a reading disability, especially phonological and rapid naming deficits, should be thoroughly examined. However, the wealth of information now available regarding disabilities in decoding and comprehension is seldom considered even briefly by teams. Eligibility and program decisions are almost always made solely on standardized test scores with little attention to far more important data.

SPECIAL EDUCATION

To be IDEA eligible, a student who has a learning disability must also need special education (34 C.F.R. §300.7(a)(1)), which is defined as "specially designed instruction" to meet the unique needs of the child (34 C.F.R. §300.26(a)(1)). Specially designed instruction, in turn, is defined as "adapting, as appropriate to the needs of an eligible child under this part, the content, methodology, or delivery of instruction" (34 C.F.R. §300.26(b)(3)).

If a student needs only modifications to regular education that require no specially designed instruction, the student is not IDEA eligible. So it is properly possible that a student is SLD in one district and not in another, as a function of the nature and quality of the regular education programs.

TEACHING

Wise and Snyder do not distinguish sharply between special education and general education settings, personnel, or instruction for children who have reading disabilities. If and when all general education instruction in beginning reading (K-3) is consistent with today's best practices, many fewer students will need remediation, and the distinction between general and special education may become less important than it is today.

Unless a student has been identified as a special education student or is served by another special, federally funded program, she is unlikely to receive either intensive or individualized reading instruction. The need for labeling a child, in most districts, is therefore very real when special education services are needed.

INSTRUCTIONAL SETTING

Even if a student with a reading disability is eligible to receive special education reading, there is no guarantee that the instruction will be recognizable as special education. In a chapter that should be read by every educator, Zigmond (1997) asks:

> Is having two teachers in the classroom the same as providing special education? Is being helped through a writing assignment by a competent second-grade peer (study buddy) the same as getting a special education? Is any instruction delivered by a person certified in special education what is meant by receiving a special education? Is learning what everyone else learns, and doing what everyone else does the same as receiving a special education? Is planning instruction and modifying instruction based on stereotypic generalizations rather than individual assessment data what we mean by special education? (p. 384)

She continues:

> special education is, first and foremost, instruction focused on individual need. It is carefully planned. It is intensive, urgent, relentless, and goal directed. It is empirically supported practice, drawn from research. To provide special education means to set priorities and select carefully what needs to be taught. It means teaching something special and teaching it in a special way. To provide special education means...defining the special education curriculum appropriate for each student that will be designated on the annual IEP. To provide special education means monitoring each student's progress... and taking responsibility for changing instruction when the monitoring data indicate that sufficient progress is not being made. (p. 385)

INSTRUCTION

Wise and Snyder report that "research has indicated that interventions for children at risk for SRD should aim at least at improving their deficient phonological awareness, decoding, and fluency."(this volume). Again, sadly, few public school students with reading disabilities (except those included in research or special projects) receive interventions focused on either phonological awareness, decoding, or fluency.

Similarly, it is unusual to find a public school that offers intensive, individual, or small group instruction in any synthetic, systematic, sequential, multisensory phonics program. When parents of children with learning disabilities who have been identified as needing such a program request that the public school provide it, the answer is typically, "No." Some parents feel so strongly that their child needs such reading instruction that they go to a due process hearing over the issue. Invariably, whether or not it prevails, a district spends substantially more on the hearing than it would have cost to provide the program requested by the parent.

Wise and Snyder report that successful programs for students who have comprehension problems teach students to summarize key points in their own words, ask questions, self-monitor, and tell the main theme of a story. These techniques, unlike those needed to teach accurate and fluent decoding, are widely implemented. However, arguably only a fraction of the students receiving these comprehension techniques need them. Many of the public school children receiving instruction in comprehension actually have difficulty only with decoding. Whenever it is said of a child that, "She can't understand what she reads, but if it is read to her, she has no problem," the odds are high that the problem is in decoding, not comprehension. Too often, low "comprehension" scores on standardized tests are accepted at face value with no recognition that inadequate decoding leads directly to these scores.

CONCLUSION

The plight of public school students who have reading disabilities will be relieved by better training, recruitment, and retention of more clinicians like those described by Wise and Snyder. Many of us believe that this must include a restoration of special education. Zigmond (1997) has expressed this aptly and forcefully:

> Special education was once worth receiving; it could be again. In many schools, it is not now. Here is where practitioners, policymakers, advocates, and researchers in special education need to focus—on defining the nature of special education and the competencies of the teachers who will deliver it. Here is where the research-to-practice gulf must be bridged. Here is the issue we must resolve, or the hard-fought promise of IDEA will be empty, indeed. (p. 389)

REFERENCES

U.S. Department of Education. (2001). *Twenty-second annual report to Congress on the implementation of the Individuals with Disabilities Education Act.* Washington, DC: Author.

Zigmond, N. (1997). Educating students with disabilities: The future of special education. In J. W. Lloyd, E. J. Kame'enui, & D. Chard (Eds.), *Issues in education students with disabilities* (pp. 377–390). Mahwah, NJ: Lawrence Erlbaum Associates.

CLINICAL JUDGMENT IN THE
ASSESSMENT OF LEARNING DISABILITIES

Karen J. Rooney, Educational Enterprises, Inc.

Working with children, their teachers, and their families has influenced my view of assessment and has taught me the importance of the process. The process must be appropriate, respectful and informative so that the data obtained is relevant to the questions being asked and sufficient to result in recommendations for change. As a practitioner, the faces of hundreds of children I have assessed float through my mind. I see the eager 7-year-old boy who became so concerned when he could not understand the directions to the task that his lip began to tremble, the 14-year-old girl who simply said "I don't know" to large numbers of items on many subtests, the 10-year-old boy who finished every item just inside the outer limits of time so two additional hours had to be scheduled, the 16-year-old girl who was being recruited for a college basketball scholarship but whose reading was at the third grade level, and the 13-year-old boy who was suspended from school because he spent the day in the library so he "could learn something." These children are very different from each other though their standard score profile might be similar. Clinical judgment can be defined as the human element in testing and is the critical component needed to make sense of scores in the context of the individual being evaluated.

Though reading disabilities do comprise the largest percentage of identified learning disabilities (National Reading Panel, 2000), the definition of learning disabilities covers a much broader spectrum. In addition to reading, the areas of listening, speaking, writing, reasoning, and mathematical abilities fall under the rubric of learning disabilities (Hammill, 1990). An initiative investigating clinical judgment in the assessment of learning disabilities needs to include a discussion of current practices as well as these other areas in the definition.

DISCUSSION OF CURRENT PRACTICES

Though standardized testing is the hallmark of assessment for identification (Haney, 1985), the use of professional judgment (Keogh & Speece, 1996), informal approaches to identification and ongoing diagnostic-prescriptive teaching has gained popularity (Tindal & Marston, 1990). The use of standardized assessment as currently practiced has come under close scrutiny because of several concerns about its use with children with learning disabilities.

First, the psychometric problems with standardized tests have been well-documented in the literature (Morris, 1993; Salvia & Ysseldyke, 1991). The use of tests that do not measure what we think they are measuring, that may not produce the same results again, or that cannot be generalized will be detrimental to the process and may even cause harm to the child.

Second, the impact of a learning disability is not removed from the assessment process. The specific learning disability may not only hinder performance but also put the child at risk, because standardized procedures do not allow for the extra explanation that may help the child better understand the question, directions, or task to be more successful. The deficit scores, then, are combined into composite or cluster scores to be used to predict potential.

Third, though research has not supported the use of discrepancy formulas and IQ testing in the identification process (Fletcher, Francis, Shaywitz, Lyon, Foorman, et al., 1998; Vellutino, Scanlon, & Lyon, 2000), the practice is widespread in the field (Frankenberger & Harper, 1987; Mercer, King-Sears, & Mercer, 1990) and can be a rigid gatekeeper if the emphasis is placed on the severity of the discrepancy. In addition, the lack of a consistent standard (Lyon, 1996) required for identification causes some children to be learning disabled in one school system but not in another.

Fourth, numerical profiles provide limited information about the types of errors, the quality of the performance, or the level of language development in the actual response. Often, the real information remains in the protocols while the report summarizes the performance numerically.

Issues in the Use of Clinical Judgment

For clinical judgment to be effective, the clinician needs to have adequate training in tests and measurement (Davis & Shephard, 1983; Ross, 1990) but also needs to have the appropriate background in the areas being measured to be able to plan an appropriate assessment, use qualitative analysis to interpret data, and make relevant recommendations (Moats, 1994b).

A second issue is related to diversity. The influence of culture and English as a second language on the assessment process must be understood and incorporated into the analysis. Cultural influence can affect interpretation of questions, social judgment, and decision-making (Patton, 1992), which can be a negative factor when responses are scored according to strict, standardized answer keys. English as a second language can result in problems with language processing that are extrinsic to the child though the scores may reflect deficit areas that could be misinterpreted in the identification process (Kaufman, 1990). The limited availability of tests in a variety of languages, inaccuracies in translation, inappropriate norm samples, test bias (McLoughlin & Lewis, 1990) and shortages of well-trained clinicians who are fluent in the language and immersed in the culture of the child being evaluated are serious concerns (Ochoa, Gonzalez, Galarza, & Guillemard, 1996).

Topics in Addition to Reading Disability

Attention, Learning Disabilities, and Reading Disabilities

Recent studies have found an overlap between learning disabilities and attention disorders as being as high as 70% (Mayes, Calhoun, & Crowell, 2000). Rates of comorbidity of attention disorders with reading disability were found to range from 25% to 40% (Dykman & Ackerman, 1991). The work of Felton and Wood (1989); Shaywitz, Shaywitz, and Fletcher (1992); and Bonofina, Newcorn, McKay, Koda, and Halperin (2000) also substantiates the connection between attention disorders and reading disability. The inclusion of data on attentional variables in the diagnosis and treatment of reading disability across the continuum of skills, not just phonological processing, needs to be part of the assessment process.

Listening

Clinicians must be very sensitive to observations that suggest the presence of a receptive language disorder as a contaminating factor that must be considered in the analysis of scores. For example, a child who is asked to define the word "grave" and who responds with the answer "courageous" is not demonstrating a vocabulary error but is providing feedback that the child is clearly at risk for inaccurate interpretation of questions, directions, and communication presented orally. A continuum of listening skills at the level of the phoneme, word, sentence, question, and discourse (Johnson, 1994) and inclusive of memory, social interchange, syntactic processing, and semantic processing needs to be measured (Johnson, 1994).

Speaking (Oral Expressive Language)

Expressive language disorders can make it difficult for a child to demonstrate his or her knowledge under standardized conditions, so observation, samples, and clinical judgment take on greater importance. Some of the tests that are more technically sound do not provide adequate information about expressive language and some of the measures that provide more information are not psychometrically sound (Moats, 1994b). In addition, the complexity of the language task, which ranges from word level analysis such as retrieval, pronunciation, word knowledge, word selection (variety of words used), and use of multiple meanings to organizational issues such as syntax, semantics, pragmatics, and sequencing, makes more formal assessment less compatible with the goal of the evaluation. In order to obtain relevant information, the use of language samples of sufficient size (Wren, 1985) in conjunction with research-based scoring criteria (Johnson, 1994; Moats, 1994b) is strongly recommended to augment standardized data.

Writing

The assessment of writing involves a multitude of systems (Berninger, Mizokawa, & Bragg, 1991); however, for the purpose of this paper, the scope will be narrowed to include handwriting, spelling, and written expression.

Handwriting. The obvious goal of handwriting is legibility but rate of production is also an important component for fluent writing. Berninger (1994) recommends that the two components be assessed separately but both are important to detect the more classic motor production problem associated with writing disability (dysgraphia). Children with dysgraphia diagnose themselves fairly accurately by saying, "I have the ideas but I just can't get them down on paper." The case for developmental output failure has been clearly made by Levine, Oberkaid, and Meltzer (1981); however, formal tests to assess handwriting are few in number so informal assessment based on visual inspection is typically used.

Spelling. The study of spelling has taken on a precision that has improved assessment practices but has also uncovered the multifaceted nature of the task (Graham, 1999) as well as the tenacity of spelling disorders (Bruck, 1987).

Moats (1994a) recommends that spelling be measured using dictation lists as well as a sample of spontaneous writing. The dual approach is important because of the discriminatory value to differentiate spelling errors from other factors such as divided attention. Moats (1994a) also described the components of a well-designed assessment. The assessment should include a sample of the orthographic, sound-symbol, and morphophonemic patterns of English, have a range that allows for analysis in small increments, use qualitative analysis of the performance, have a measure of internal consistency and reliability, be representative of what children are expected to learn in school, have concurrent validity, and meet psychometric scaling criteria.

Written Expression. The measurement of written expression may be the most challenging for objective measurement since the matrix of variables defies adequate quantification as a process. Variables such as word selection, word usage, word sequencing, sentence organization, paragraph cohesion, transitioning, and fluency combine with the influence of factors related to attention, working memory, sequential memory, and long term memory as well as such constructs as task demands, motivation, task-persistence, and self-esteem to make appropriate assessment an elusive goal. The overwhelming complexity of the goal makes the use of standard procedures such as the aptitude-achievement model inappropriate (Lyon, 1987). Qualitative analysis, observation, and clinical judgment are necessary simply because of the "nature of the beast" being tamed.

In addition to the linguistic view of writing, the presence or absence of strategies to support written expression needs to be assessed. Observing the strategies employed by the child may be helpful to assess organizational needs as well as provide information about cognitive processing weaknesses that must be supported. Research on the use of strategies has shown such techniques to be successful to improve written expression (Graham, 1999; Harris & Graham, 1996).

With the advancements in technology (Greenwood & Reith,1994), a discussion of writing can not exclude assessment with and without the use of technology. Currently, assessment has not kept pace with the production of performance measures with and without the use of technology, but the need to do so is imminent. With the increase in technology available at home and in school (Hauser & Malouf, 1996), information about a child's writing when technology is used is important for planning for appropriate accommodation (MacArthur, 1988; Outhred, 1989) and may have significant implications for identification as well as remediation.

Reasoning (Metacognition or Executive Function)

Denckla (1994) has demonstrated the connection between executive function and learning disabilities. Denckla states that executive processing is linked to learning disabilities in ways similar to language or spatial abilities and is included under the definition as one of the psychological processes, particularly related to thinking and reasoning (Denckla, 1994). The extensive investigation of metacognition and the use of self-monitoring, self-regulation, and self-instruction has provided research that documents effective educational interventions for students with metacognitive weaknesses (Deshler, Schumaker, & Lenz, 1984; Hallahan, 1980; Hallahan, Kauffman, & Lloyd, 1999; Rooney, 1998; Swanson, 1999). Behaviors related to these important areas need to be observed and documented since measurement of academic skills and IQ does not provide sufficient data for analysis of executive functioning (Denckla, 1994).

Mathematical Abilities and Nonverbal Learning Disabilities

As with other subjects, poor schooling (Russell and Ginsberg, 1984) and familial factors (Shalev, Manor, Kerem, Ayali, Badichi, et al., 2001) play a role in math disorders but patterns indicating math weaknesses have also been identified (Bryant, Bryant, & Hammill, 2000). Though patterns have been identified, the behaviors can be confounded by many factors such as quality of instruction (Russell & Ginsberg, 1984), supervision of homework (Fleischner, 1994), and the pace of instruction (Carnine, 1991), so clinical judgment is needed to rule out causative factors extrinsic to the child.

Problems with right hemisphere functioning have also been associated with social skill deficits (Badian, 1992; Harnadek & Rourke, 1994) that have historically been assessed through the use of peer ratings, self-report measures, and behavior checklists. These measures require the use of caution and must depend on clinical judgment because of psychometric issues related to validity, reliability, and intentionality of the reporter (Bryan, 1997).

A Concern about Re-evaluation and Transition

When students are re-evaluated during high school, transition planning becomes an integral part of the process; however, some students transitioning to college have not had re-evaluations that are comprehensive enough to meet the criteria for identification at the collegiate level (The Association of Higher Education and Disability, 1997). Unless the students have resources to obtain additional testing, eligibility for services or access to accommodations that enabled them to be successful at the secondary level may be denied. Research needs to look at the prevalence of this problem and the implications for policy change.

SUMMARY

Historically, the pendulum in education has often taken a "one or the other" swing but this tendency has been detrimental. The discussion in this paper as well as the White Paper by Wise and Snyder clearly argue for the use of clinical judgment by well-trained professionals; however, the logical solution is an assessment that provides enough formal and informal information to truly describe the child being evaluated. The clinician, then, can connect those pieces of data into patterns and arrange those patterns into an accurate description of the child. Once this authentic picture emerges, effective planning and implementation of interventions that are both appropriate and sufficient to create real change in the life of that child can begin.

REFERENCES

Association on Higher Education and Disability, The. (1997). *Guidelines for documentation of a learning disability in adolescents and adults.* Columbus, OH: AHEAD.

Badian, N. A. (1992). Nonverbal learning disability, school behavior and dyslexia. *Annals of Dyslexia, 42,* 159–178.

Berninger, V. (1994). Future directions for research on writing disabilities: Integrating endogenous and exogenous variables. In G. Reid Lyon (Ed.), *Frames of reference for the assessment of learning disabilities* (pp. 419–439). Baltimore, MD: Paul H. Brookes Publishing Co.

Berninger, V., Mizokawa, D., & Bragg, R. (1991). Theory-based diagnosis and remediation of writing disabilities. *Journal of School Psychology, 29,* 57–79.

Bonafina, M. A., Newcorn, J. H., McKay, K. E., Koda, V. H., & Halperin, J. M. (2000). ADHD and reading disabilities: A cluster analytic approach for distinguishing subgroups. *Journal of Learning Disabilities, 33,* 297–307.

Bruck, M. (1987). The adult outcomes of children with learning disabilities. *Annals of Dyslexia, 37,* 252–263.

Bryan, T. (1997). Assessing the personal and social status of students with learning disabilities. *Learning Disabilities Research & Practice, 12,* 63–76.

Bryant, D. P., Bryant, B. R., & Hammill, D. D. (2000). Characteristic behaviors of students with LD who have teacher-identified math weaknesses. *Journal of Learning Disabilities, 33,* 168–177, 199.

Carnine, D. (1991). Reforming mathematics instruction: The role of curriculum materials. *Journal of Behavioral Education, 1,* 37–57.

Davis, W. A., & Shepard, L. A. (1983). Specialists' use of tests and clinical judgement in the diagnosis of learning disabilities. *Learning Disability Quarterly, 6,* 128–138.

Denckla, M. B. (1994). Measurement of executive function. In G. Reid Lyon (Ed.), *Frames of reference for the assessment of learning disabilities* (pp. 117–142). Baltimore, MD: Paul H. Brookes Publishing Co.

Deshler, D. D., Schumaker, J. B., & Lenz, B. K. (1984). Academic and cognitive interventions for LD adolescents, Part I. *Journal of Learning Disabilities, 17,* 108–117

Dykman, R. A., & Ackerman, P. T. (1991). ADD and specific reading disability: Separate but often overlapping disorders. *Journal of Learning Disabilities, 24,* 96–103.

Felton, R. H., & Wood, F. B. (1989). Cognitive deficits in reading disability and attention deficit disorder. *Journal of Learning Disabilities, 22,* 3–22.

Fleischner, J. E. (1994). Diagnosis and assessment of mathematics learning disabilities. In G. Reid Lyon (Ed.), *Frames of reference for the assessment of learning disabilities* (pp. 441–458). Baltimore, MD: Paul H. Brookes Publishing Co.

Fletcher, J. M., Francis, D. J., Shaywitz, S. E., Lyon, G. R., Foorman, B., Stuebing, K. K., & Shaywitz, B. A. (1998). Intelligent testing and the discrepancy model for children with learning disabilities. *Learning Disabilities Research & Practice, 13,* 186–203.

Frankenberger, W., & Harper, J. (1987). States' criteria and procedures for identifying learning disabled children: A comparison of 1981-82 and 1985-86 guidelines. *Journal of Learning Disabilities, 20,* 118–121.

Graham, S. (1999). Handwriting and spelling instruction for students with learning disabilities: A review. *Learning Disability Quarterly, 22,* 78–98.

Greenwood, C. R., & Reith, H. J. (1994). Current dimensions of technology-based assessment in special education. *Exceptional Children, 61,* 105–113.

Hallahan, D. P. (1980). Teaching exceptional children to use cognitive strategies. *Exceptional Children Quarterly, 1,* 1–102.

Hallahan, D. P., Kauffman, J. M., & Lloyd, J. W. (1999). *Introduction to learning disabilities.* Boston: Allyn & Bacon.

Hammill, D. D. (1990). On defining learning disabilities: An emerging consensus. *Journal of Learning Disabilities, 4,* 336–342.

Haney, W. (1985). Making testing more educational. *Educational Leadership, 43,* 4–13.

Harnadek, M. C. S., & Rourke, B. P. (1994). Principal identifying features of the syndrome of nonverbal learning disabilities in children. *Journal of Learning Disabilities, 27,* 144–154.

Harris, K. R., & Graham, S. (1996). Making the writing process word: Strategies for composition and self-regulation. Cambridge, MA: Brookline.

Hauser, J., & Malouf, D. B. (1996). A federal perspective on special education technology. *Journal of Learning Disabilities, 29,* 504–511.

Johnson, D. (1994). Measurement of listening and speaking. In G. Reid Lyon (Ed.), *Frames of reference for the assessment of learning disabilities* (pp. 203–227). Baltimore, MD: Paul H. Brookes Publishing Co.

Kaufman, A. S. (1990). *Assessing adolescent and adult intelligence.* Boston, MA: Allyn and Bacon.

Keogh, B. K., & Speece, D. L. (1996). Learning disabilities within the context of schooling. In D. L. Speece & B. K. Keogh (Eds.), *Research on classroom ecologies: Implications for inclusion of children with learning disabilities* (pp. 1–14). Mahwah, NJ: Lawrence Erlbaum Associates, Inc.

Levine, M., Oberklaid, F., & Meltzer, L. (1981). Developmental output failure: A study of low productivity in school-aged children. *Pediatrics, 67,* 18–25.

Lyon, G. R. (1987). Learning disabilities research: False starts and broken promises. In S. Vaughan & C. Bos (Eds.), *Research in learning disabilities: Issues and future directions* (pp. 69–85). San Diego, CA: College Hill Press.

MacArthur, C. A. (1988). The impact of computers on the writing process. *Exceptional Children, 54,* 536–542.

Mayes, S. D., Calhoun, S. L., & Crowell, E. W. (2000). Learning disabilities and ADHD: Overlapping spectrum disorders. *Journal of Learning Disabilities, 33,* 417–424.

McLoughlin, J. A., & Lewis, R. B. (1990). *Assessing special students* (3rd ed.). Columbus, OH: Merrill.

Mercer, C. M., King-Sears, P., & Mercer, A. R. (1990). Learning disabilities definitions and criteria used by state education departments. *Learning Disability Quarterly, 13,* 141–152.

Moats, L. C. (1994a). Assessment of spelling in learning disabilities research. In G. Reid Lyon (Ed.), *Frames of reference for the assessment of learning disabilities* (pp. 333–349). Baltimore, MD: Paul H. Brookes Publishing Co.

Moats, L. C. (1994b) Honing the concepts of listening and speaking. In G. Reid Lyon (Ed.), *Frames of reference for the assessment of learning disabilities* (pp. 229–241). Baltimore, MD: Paul H. Brookes Publishing Co.

Morris, R. (1993). Issues in empirical versus clinical identification of learning disabilities. In G. R. Lyon, D. B. Gray, J. F. Kavanaugh, & N.A. Krasnegor (Eds.), *Better understanding learning disabilities: New views from research and their implications for education and public policies* (pp. 273–307). Baltimore, MD: Paul Brookes Publishing Co.

National Reading Panel. (April, 2000). *Report of the National Reading Panel: Teaching children to read* (NIH Publication No. 00-4654). Bethesda, MD: National Institute of Child Health and Human Development, National Institutes of Health.

Ochoa, S. H., Gonzalez, D., Galarza, A., & Guillemard, L. (1996). The training and use of interpreters in bilingual psycho-educational assessment: An alternative in need of study. *Diagnostique, 21,* 19–22.

Outhred, L. (1989). Word processing: Its impact on children's writing. *Journal of Learning Disabilities, 22,* 262–264.

Patton, J. M. (1992). Assessment and identification of African American learners with gifts and talents. *Exceptional Children, 59,* 150–159.

Rooney, K. J. (1998). *Independent strategies for efficient study.* Richmond, VA: Educational Enterprises, Inc.

Ross, R. P. (1990). Consistency among school psychologists in evaluating discrepancy scores: A preliminary study. *Learning Disability Quarterly, 13,* 209–219.

Russell, R., & Ginsburg, H. P. (1984). Cognitive analysis of children's mathematics difficulties. *Cognition and Instruction, 1,* 217– 244.

Salvia, J., & Ysseldyke, J. E. (1991). Assessment in special and remedial education (5th ed.). Boston: Houghton Mifflin.

Shalev, R. S., Manor, O., Kerem, B., Ayali, M., Badichi, N., Friedlander, Y., & Gross-Tsur, V. (2001). Developmental dyscalculia is a familial learning disability. *Journal of Learning Disabilities, 34,* 59–65.

Shaywitz, B. A., Shaywitz, S. E., & Fletcher, J. M. (1992). The Yale Center for the Study of Learning and Attention Disorders. *Learning Disabilities: A Multidisciplinary Journal, 3,* 1–12.

Swanson, H. L. (1999). Instructional components that predict treatment outcomes for students with learning disabilities: Support for a combined strategy and direct instruction model. *Learning Disabilities Research & Practice, 14,* 129–140.

Tindal, G. A. & Marston, D. B. (1990). *Classroom-based assessment: Evaluating instructional outcomes.* Columbus, OH: Merrill Publishing Company.

Vellutino, F. R., Scanlon, D. M., & Lyon, G. R. (2000). Differentiating between difficult-to-remediate and readily remediated poor readers: More evidence against IQ-achievement discrepancy definition of reading disability. *Journal of Learning Disabilities, 33,* 223–238.

Wren, C. T. (1985). Collecting language samples from children with syntax problems. *Language, Speech, and Hearing Services in Schools, 16,* 83–102.

RESPONSE TO "CLINICAL JUDGMENTS IN IDENTIFYING AND TEACHING CHILDREN WITH LANGUAGE-BASED READING DIFFICULTIES"

Maryanne Wolf, Tufts University

INTRODUCTION

In an ideal world all children with learning disabilities would be assessed and taught by "expert clinicians" and teachers, and all of these clinicians and teachers would have read the final draft of Barbara Wise and Lynn Snyder's white paper. It is a paper worth writing, reading, and expanding, which is the task of the present response. It has become an unexpected pleasure to have been assigned the responsibility of reflecting upon this paper's contents and presenting perspectives "left out or not well represented." After a brief summary of the white paper, I will address two related areas in identification and intervention, both because of my personal knowledge of these areas, and because they include research too new to be known by the authors, albeit alluded to in their review.

SUMMARY

There is a highly useful surface structure to this paper in which Wise and Snyder provide an overview of two decades of well-known research on the screening, identification, evaluation, and teaching of learning disabled children. The basis of selection of the research is purposeful and explicit: these are studies every clinician should know and apply to their students. Studies vary widely in perspective with no one prevailing view or bias: an important and impressive achievement.

The deep structure of the paper is still more significant, whether or not by conscious design. The authors model in their paper the goals they have for "expert clinicians": that is, the careful selection and application of research principles that are appropriate for the identification, ongoing assessment, and teaching of particular groups of children who have language-based reading disabilities and/or reading comprehension deficits. The paper closes with a set of guidelines that should be mandatory reading to clinicians and teachers alike. It is my opinion that the authors do a deft, masterful job in a paper that I will assign to each of my graduate-level students.

NEW AREAS OF RESEARCH

There are no good papers without lacunae. I will emphasize two areas that are only partially represented in this paper: first, the use of naming-speed or serial naming tasks in the early identification of reading disabilities, and second, the importance of new approaches to fluency and comprehensive intervention. In both instances I will be supplementing Wise and Snyder's paper with new research that is only now becoming available.

Identification

There is complete consensus that phonological awareness tasks like the ones discussed in Wise and Synder (e.g., phoneme deletion, segmentation, phoneme manipulation) are one of the two best predictors of later reading disabilities in the English language. Naming speed tasks are, however, either the second or the first best predictor, depending on the language system, the age, and the subtype of reading disabilities. Undiscussed in this white paper is the rather extraordinary finding that in languages with transparent orthographies (e.g., German, Dutch, Finnish, and Spanish) and with varied scripts (e.g., Hebrew) naming speed is the single best predictor of later reading performance. Most recently, an equally surprising finding in the cross-linguistic research was presented at the 2001 meeting of the Society for Scientific Study of Reading: It now appears that naming speed is the best single predictor of reading disabilities in Chinese, with that language's morphophonemic elements.

This cross-linguistic prediction research is only one part of a larger body of work pointing to (a) the theoretical importance of conceptualizing naming-speed deficits as independent of phonological processing deficits, and (b) the practical importance of including tests of naming speed in early screening. For many years naming-speed deficits were subsumed under the phonological rubric and not considered an *index* of a second core deficit. We now know from extensive studies that deficits in naming speed represent an additional, largely independent predictor of reading disability (Ackerman & Dykman, 1993; Badian, 1995, 1996a, b; Berninger, Abbott, Billingsley, & Nagy, 1998; Bowers, Steffy, & Tate, 1998; Breznitz, 2001; Denckla & Rudel, 1974, 1976a, b; Grigorenko, Wood, Meyer, Hart, Speed, et al., 1997; Lovett, Steinbach, & Frijters, 2000; McBride-Chang & Manis, 1996; Meyer, Wood, Hart, & Felton, 1998; Snyder & Downey, 1995; Spring & Capps, 1974; Torgesen, Wagner, Rashotte, Burgess, & Hecht, 1997; Wimmer, 1993; Wolf, Bally, &

Morris, 1986; Wolf & O'Brien, 2001). The consequences of a second core deficit are not trivial. If phonological and naming-speed processes represent two independent sources of breakdown, there are critical implications for diagnosis, subtyping efforts, and, most importantly in the design of intervention that is tailored to the individual, as suggested by Wise and Snyder.

In recent years Bowers and I (Bowers & Wolf, 1993; Wolf, 1991; Wolf & Bowers, 1999, 2000; Wolf, Bowers, & Biddle, 2000) have developed an alternative conceptualization of developmental reading disabilities to the well-known phonological core deficit view. This conceptualization incorporates both phonology and naming-speed processes as two major sources of reading breakdown. Bowers and I found that within the well-known heterogeneity of dyslexic readers there are three major subtypes who can be characterized by the presence, absence, or combination of the two core deficits in phonology and naming speed. In other words, there are poor readers who have only phonological deficits without differences in naming speed. Conversely, there are readers who have adequate phonological and word attack skills, but who have early naming-speed deficits and later comprehension deficits. Important for identification efforts, these are the children who would be missed by the vast majority of our diagnostic batteries, because their decoding is slow but accurate. The most intractable subtype is characterized by both deficits; children with both or "double deficits" represent the most severely impaired subtype in all aspects of reading, particularly in reading fluency.

This part of the story is what we call the **Double-Deficit Hypothesis** (see Special Issue on the Double-Deficit Hypothesis in Wolf & Bowers, 2000). Extensive data by many colleagues now replicate the existence of these three subtypes of impaired readers, and in several language systems (e.g., German, Dutch, Finnish, and Hebrew). But there are interesting surprises that are emerging. For example, in English, Lovett, Steinbach, and Frijters (2000) studied a large sample of clinically referred severely impaired readers and found that more than half are double-deficit with the remainder fairly equally split across the single deficit subtypes. By contrast, Breznitz (personal correspondence, December 13, 2000) reports that out of 375 dyslexic children studied in Hebrew, the overwhelming majority would be double-deficit readers, with 56 naming-speed readers, and with only 15 readers classified with solely phonological deficits. Deeney, Gidney, Wolf, and Morris (1999) also report differences in subtype distribution for African-American impaired readers who speak Vernacular English. There appear far more double-deficit and phonological subtypes in this population than the distribution of subtypes for Caucasian and African-American children who do not speak Vernacular English.

The accumulating data on independent subtypes has led to the most important theoretical and applied implications of the Double-Deficit Hypothesis—that is, the necessity to understand the role of rate of processing and fluency in reading development and the need to create reading intervention that addresses these issues. Until this time, reading disabled children with single phonological deficits were adequately treated with current programs emphasizing phonological awareness and decoding. However, the other two subtypes of disabled readers with their explicit problems in naming speed, reading fluency, and comprehension, were *not* adequately remediated. It is important to realize that reading-impaired children with fluency issues do not have sufficient time to allocate to inferential and comprehension processes. It is highly likely that these children make up at least one significant portion of the children called "treatment resisters" by Torgesen, Wagner, & Rashotte (1994). This is because our phonological-based interventions are necessary but insufficient treatments for fluency-based issues.

Lyon and Moats (1997) succinctly summarize the problem that has begun to surface with fluency problems: "Improvements in decoding and word reading accuracy have been far easier to obtain than improvements in reading fluency and automaticity. This persistent finding indicates there is much we have to learn about the development of componential reading skills and how such skills mediate reading rate and reading comprehension."

Wise and Snyder accurately describe children with "double-deficits" as "our biggest continuing challenge" (this volume) and offer several suggestions for treatment. They are, however, less aware of rate-deficit children who are almost invisible until third grade comprehension demands in reading overwhelm their slower processing speed. In the next section on intervention, I will outline some ongoing, cutting-edge research that is specifically designed to meet the particular fluency and comprehension needs of the double-deficit disabled reader and the rate-deficit reader. Very importantly, this work may also prove especially useful—with its inclusion of semantic and orthographic treatment components—for two other groups of children discussed by Wise and Snyder: 1) children with comprehension problems and impoverished semantic representations, and 2) children with weak orthographic memory.

The Importance of Fluency in Reading Intervention

In a superb recent review of fluency literature, Meyers and Felton (1999) described the consensual view of fluency as "the ability to read connected text rapidly, smoothly, effortlessly, and automatically with little conscious attention to the mechanics of reading such as decoding." This approach to fluency accurately captures the last two decades of researchers' views on the end-goal of fluency—effortless reading with good comprehension (see Carver, 1990; LaBerge & Samuels, 1974; Perfetti, 1985).

There are increasingly apparent problems with this view. With the exception of Berninger et al. (2001), Lyon and Moats (1997), and Kame'enui, Simmons, Good, and Harn (2001), few current researchers have perceived the need to define fluency either in terms of its component parts or its various levels of reading subskills— letter, letter pattern, word, sentence, and passage. Together with Kame'enui et al. (2001), we suggest a figure-ground shift for the conceptualization of fluency: that is, as a **developmental process**, as well as an outcome. In an essay on fluency for a special issue on this topic just appearing in *Scientific Studies of Reading*, Katzir-Cohen and I (Wolf & Katzir-Cohen, 2001) review the modern history of reading fluency research and use the following developmental definition:

> In its beginnings, reading fluency is the product of the initial develop-ment of accuracy and the subsequent development of automaticity in underlying sublexical processes, lexical processes, and their integration in single-word reading and connected text. These include perceptual, pho-nological, orthographic, and morphological processes at the letter-, let-ter-pattern, and word-level; as well as semantic and syntactic processes at the word-level and connected-text level. After it is fully developed, read-ing fluency refers to a level of accuracy and rate, where decoding is rela-tively effortless, where oral reading is smooth and accurate with correct prosody, and where attention can be allocated to comprehension. (p. 219)

Such a developmental, more encompassing view of reading fluency has profound implications for prevention, intervention, and assessment, as discussed by Wise and Snyder. For within a developmental perspective, efforts to address fluency should start at the beginning of the reading acquisition process, not after reading is al-ready acquired (as with most current fluency instruction). The importance of work-ing preventatively before difficult fluency problems ever begin is a major theme in the recent studies by Torgesen, Rashotte, and Alexander (2001) and by Kame'enui et al. (2001).

As Stahl recently has described (Stahl, Heubach, & Crammond, 1997), most cur-rent efforts in fluency do not work within a prevention framework, but rather are based largely on the Repeated Reading technique (Dahl, 1974; Dowhower, 1994; Samuels, 1985; Young, Bowers, & MacKinnon, 1996). From the developmental con-text we are working from, such a treatment is an important and efficacious tool when used at a particular phase of fluency development, but would be insufficient by itself to address the development of rapid processing in the multiple, sublexical systems, as well as the development of higher-level, semantic (vocabulary) systems.

Over the last five years we have been developing an experimental, developmental approach to fluency instruction. The RAVE-O program (Retrieval, Automaticity, Vocabulary Enrichment, and Orthography) simultaneously addresses both the need for automaticity in phonological, orthographic, morphosyntactic, and semantic systems and also the importance of teaching *explicit connections* among these systems. The program emerged as the result of an NICHD-funded collaboration by Morris, Lovett, and Wolf to investigate the efficacy of several theory-based treatments for different dyslexia subtypes. Described in detail in Wolf, Miller, and Donnelly (2000), the RAVE-O program was designed with three goals for each child: first, accuracy and automaticity in sublexical and lexical levels; second, increased accuracy and fluency in word attack, word identification, and comprehension; and third, a transformed attitude towards language.

The program is taught only in combination with a program that teaches systematic, phonological analysis and blending (see Lovett et al., 2000). Children are taught a group of *core words* each week that exemplify critical phonological, orthographic, and semantic principles. First, the multiple meanings of core words are introduced in varied semantic contexts. Second, children are taught to connect the phonemes in the core words with the trained orthographic patterns in RAVE-O. For example, children are taught individual phonemes in the phonological program (like *a*, *t*, and *m*) and *orthographic chunks* with the same phonemes in RAVE-O (e.g., *at* and *am* along with their word families).

There is daily emphasis on practice and rapid recognition of the most frequent orthographic letter patterns in English that we believe would be particularly efficacious for children with poor orthographic memory, as discussed in the white paper. Computerized games (such as Speed Wizards, Wolf & Goodman, 1996) were designed to allow for maximal practice and to increase the speed of orthographic pattern recognition (i.e., onset and rime) in a fun fashion.

There is a simultaneous emphasis on vocabulary and retrieval, based on earlier work in vocabulary development that suggests that one retrieves fastest what one knows best (see Beck, Perfetti, & McKeown, 1982; German, 1992; Kame'enui, Dixon, & Carnine, 1987; Wolf & Segal, 1999). Vocabulary growth is conceptualized as essential to both rapid retrieval (in oral *and* written language) and also to improved comprehension, an ultimate goal in the program. Retrieval skills are taught through a variety of ways including a set of metacognitive strategies called the "Sam Spade

Strategies." I believe that the principles underlying this component of RAVE-O have important implications to offer clinicians working with children with lower verbal IQs and weak semantic representations as described by Wise and Snyder.

With regard to comprehension, a series of very short stories, called *Minute Mysteries*, accompany each week of RAVE-O and directly address the fluency aspects involved in comprehension in several ways. The controlled vocabulary in the timed and untimed stories both incorporates the week's particular orthographic patterns and also emphasizes the multiple meanings of the week's core words. In addition, the stories provide a superb vehicle for repeated reading practice, which, in turn, helps fluency in connected text. Thus, the Minute Mysteries are multipurpose vehicles for facilitating fluency in phonological, orthographic, and semantic systems, at the same time that they build comprehension skills. In this way all knowledge systems that were taught explicitly earlier in the week in separate domains are being called upon to work together in order to comprehend a story.

There is an additional system too little discussed by many of us, including Wise and Snyder (who are nevertheless known experts in it!)—that is, the affective-motivational one. The secret weapon of the RAVE-O program is the deceptive cover of *whimsy* over the program's systematicity. There is a daily emphasis for the teacher and the student on having fun with words, which I believe is one of the most important elements in the clinician-student relationship.

Other Comprehension Principles

There are several major researchers conducting important work in comprehension who were not discussed by Wise and Snyder but who deserve a clinician's attention. For example, Canadian psychologist Maureen Lovett and her colleagues (Lovett et al., 1996) compared two comprehension programs with different goals to ascertain what program works best for which learning disabled child. They first designed a text comprehension program that could address the needs of children with insufficient knowledge bases (which would include the children with low IQs) and inadequate familiarity with different story structures, expository text conventions, etc. A second experimental program was based on the reciprocal teaching methods of Palincsar and Brown (1984) and used four explicit strategies to enhance comprehension: summarizing, clarifying, questioning, predicting. Lovett and her colleagues found that *both* approaches were effective with disabled readers. They concluded that the use of metacognitive strategies for comprehension work with reading disabled children was an important addition to the teacher's repertoire, and to my mind, the clinician's repertoire.

CONCLUSION

Wise and Snyder ended their white paper with seven guidelines that I said at the outset of my response should be learned, if not memorized, by every clinician and teacher. I would like to add another. The history of dyslexia research, the documented heterogeneity of reading disabled children, and the complex, developmentally changing structure of the reading process compel researcher and clinician alike to reject any notion that there will ever be one explanation for dyslexia or one best treatment for all children. The implication of this statement for the expert clinician and for all of us who work with children with learning disabilities is that we must become active, vigilant consumers of that research that will best guide the selection of assessment and intervention tailored to meet *each* child's partially unique profile of strengths and weaknesses, at each developmental stage of reading acquisition. That would be indeed a powerful contribution to an ideal world for children with learning disabilities.

REFERENCES

Ackerman, P. T., & Dykman, R. A. (1993). Phonological processes, confrontation naming, and immediate memory in dyslexia. *Journal of Learning Disabilities, 26*, 597–609.

Badian, N. (1995). Predicting reading ability over the long-term: The changing roles of letter naming, phonological awareness and orthographic processing. *Annals of Dyslexia: An Interdisciplinary Journal, XLV*, 79–86.

Badian, N. (1996a). Dyslexia: A validation of the concept at two age levels. *Journal of Learning Disabilities, 29*(1), 102–112.

Badian, N. (1996b). Dyslexia: a validation of the concept at two age levels. *Journal of Learning Disabilities, 29*, 102–112.

Beck, I. L., Perfetti, C. A., & McKeown, M. G. (1982). Effects of long-term vocabulary instruction on lexical access and reading comprehension. *Journal of Educational Psychology, 74*, 506–521.

Berninger, V. W., Abbott, R. D., Billingsley, F., & Nagy, W. (2001). Processes underlying timing and fluency of reading: Efficiency, automaticity, coordination, and morphological awareness. In M. Wolf (Ed.), *Dyslexia, Fluency, and the Brain* (pp. 383–414). Timonium, MD: York Press.

Bowers, P. G., Steffy, R., & Tate, E. (1988). Comparison of the effects of IQ control methods on memory and naming speed predictors of reading disability. *Reading Research Quarterly, 23*, 304–309.

Bowers, P., & Wolf, M. (1993). Theoretical links among naming speed, precise timing mechanisms, and orthographic skills in dyslexia. *Reading and Writing: An International Journal, 5,* 69–85.

Breznitz, Z. Personal correspondence (December 13, 2000).

Breznitz, Z. (2001). The role of inter-modality temporal features of speed of information processing in asynchrony between visual-orthographic and auditory-phonological processing. In M. Wolf (Ed.), *Dyslexia, Time, and the Brain* (pp. 245–276). Timonium, MD: York Press.

Carver, R. P. (1990). *Reading rate: A review of research and theory.* Boston: Academic Press, Inc.

Dahl, P. (1974). *An experimental program for teaching high speed word recognition and comprehension skills* (Final Report Project #3-1154). Washington, DC: National Institute of Education.

Deeney, T., Gidney, C., Wolf, M., & Morris, R. (1999). *Phonological skills of African-American reading-disabled children.* Paper presented at 6th Annual Meeting of the Society for the Scientific Study of Reading, Montreal, Canada.

Denckla, M. B., & Rudel, R. G. (1974). Rapid automatized naming of pictured objects, colors, letters, and numbers by normal children. *Cortex, 10,* 186–202.

Denckla, M. B., & Rudel, R.G. (1976a). Naming of objects by dyslexic and other learning-disabled children. *Brain and Language, 3,* 1–15.

Denckla, M. B., & Rudel, R. G. (1976b). Rapid automatized naming (R.A.N.): Dyslexia differentiated from other learning disabilities. *Neuropsychologia, 14,* 471–479.

Dowhower, S. L. (1994). Repeated reading revisited: Research into practice. *Reading and Writing Quarterly: Overcoming Learning Difficulties, 10,* 343–358.

German, D. J. (1992). Word-finding intervention in children and adolescents. *Topics in Language Disorders, 13*(1), 33–50.

Grigorenko, E., Wood, F., Meyer, M., Hart, L., Speed, W., Shuster, A., & Pauls, D. (1997). Susceptibility loci for distinct components of developmental dyslexia on chromosomes 6 and 15. *American Journal of Human Genetics, 60,* 27–39.

Kame'enui, E. J., Dixon, R. C., & Carnine, D. W. (1987). Issues in the design of vocabulary instruction. In M. G. McKeown and M. E. Curtis (Eds.), *The nature of vocabulary acquisition* (pp. 129–145). Hillsdale, NJ: Lawrence Erlbaum Associates.

Kame'enui, E. J., Simmons, D. C., Good, R. H., & Harn, B. A. (2001). The use of fluency-based measures in early identification and evaluation of intervention efficacy in schools. In M. Wolf (Ed.), *Dyslexia, fluency, and the brain* (pp. 307–332). Timonium, MD: York Press.

LaBerge, D., & Samuels, S. J. (1974). Toward a theory of automatic information processing in reading. *Cognitive Psychology, 6,* 293–323.

Lovett, M. W., Border, S. L., Warren-Chaplin, P. M., Lacerenza, L., DeLuca, T., & Giovinazzo, R. (1996). Text comprehension training for disabled readers: An evaluation of reciprocal teaching and text analysis training programs. *Brain and Language, 54(3),* 447–480.

Lovett, M. W., Steinbach, K. A., & Frijters, J. C. (2000). Remediating the core deficits of developmental reading disability: A double-deficit perspective. *Journal of Learning Disabilities, 33(4),* 334–358.

Lyon, G. R., & Moats, L. C. (1997). Critical conceptual and methodological considerations in reading intervention research. *Journal of Learning Disabilities, 30,* 578–588.

McBride-Chang, C., & Manis, F. (1996). Structural invariance in the associations of naming speed, phonological awareness, and verbal reasoning in good and poor readers: A test of the double deficit hypothesis. *Reading and Writing, 8,* 323–339.

Meyer, M. S., Wood, F. B., Hart, L. A., & Felton, R. H. (1998). Selective predictive value of rapid automatized naming in poor readers. *Journal of Learning Disabilities, 31,* 106–17.

Palincsar, A. S., & Brown, A. L. (1984). Reciprocal teaching of comprehension-fostering and comprehension-monitoring activities. *Cognition and Instruction, 1(2),* 117–175.

Perfetti, C. A. (1985). *Reading ability.* New York: Oxford University Press.

Samuels, S. J. (1985). Automaticity and repeated reading. In J. Osborn, P.T . Wilson, & R.C. Anderson (Eds.), *Reading education: Foundations for a literate America* (pp. 215–230). Lexington, MA: Lexington Books.

Snyder, L., & Downey, D. (1995). Serial rapid naming skills in children with reading disabilities. *Annals of Dyslexia, 45,* 31–50.

Spring, C., & Capps, C. (1974). Encoding speed, rehearsal, and probed recall of dyslexic boys. *Journal of Educational Psychology, 66,* 780–786.

Stahl, S., Heubach, K., & Crammond, B. (1997). Fluency-oriented reading instruction. *Reading Research Report, 79,* 1–38.

Torgesen, J., Rashotte, C., & Alexander, A. (2001). The prevention and remediation of reading fluency problems. In M. Wolf (Ed.), *Dyslexia, fluency, and the brain* (pp. 333–356). Timonium, MD: York Press.

Torgesen, J. K., Wagner, R. K., & Rashotte, C. A. (1994). Longitudinal studies of phonological processing and reading. *Journal of Learning Disabilities, 27,* 276–286.

Torgesen, J. K., Wagner, R. K., Rashotte, C. A., Burgess, S., & Hecht, S. (1997). Contributions of phonological awareness and rapid automatic naming ability to the growth of word-reading skills in second to fifth grade children. *Scientific Studies of Reading, 1,* 161–185.

Wimmer, H. (1993). Characteristics of developmental dyslexia in a regular writing system. *Applied Psycholinguistics, 14,* 1–34.

Wolf, M. (1991). Naming speed and reading: The contribution of the cognitive neurosciences. *Reading Research Quarterly, 26,* 123–141.

Wolf, M., Bally, H., & Morris, R. (1986). Automaticity, retrieval processes, and reading: A longitudinal study in average and impaired readers. *Child Development, 57,* 988–1000.

Wolf, M., & Bowers, P. (1999). The "double-deficit hypothesis" for the developmental dyslexias. *Journal of Educational Psychology, 91,* 1–24.

Wolf, M., & Bowers, P. (2000). Naming-speed processes and developmental reading disabilities: An introduction to the Special Issue on the Double-Deficit Hypothesis. *Journal of Learning Disabilities, 33*(4), 322–324.

Wolf, M., Bowers, P., & Biddle, K. R. (2000). Naming-speed processes, timing, and reading: A conceptual review. *Journal of Learning Disabilities, 33,* 387–407.

Wolf, M., & Goodman, G. (1996). *Speed Wizards.* Computerized reading program. Tufts University and Rochester Institute of Technology.

Wolf, M., & Katzir-Cohen, T. (2001). Reading fluency and its intervention. *Scientific Studies in Reading, 5(3),* 211-239.

Wolf, M., Miller, L., & Donnelly, K. (2000). RAVE-O. *Journal of Learning Disabilities, 33*(4), 375–386.

Wolf, M., & O'Brien, B. (2001). On issues of time, fluency and intervention. In A. Fawcett (Ed.), *Dyslexia: Theory of practice* (pp. 124–140). London: Whurr Publishing.

Wolf, M., & Segal, D. (1999). Retrieval-rate, accuracy, and vocabulary elaboration (RAVE) in reading-impaired children: A pilot intervention program. *Dyslexia: An International Journal of Theory and Practice, 5,* 1–27.

Young, A., Bowers, P., & MacKinnon, G. (1996). Effects of prosodic modeling and repeated reading on poor readers' fluency and comprehension. *Applied Psycholinguistics, 17,* 59–84.

ACKNOWLEDGMENTS

I wish to acknowledge the essential support of NICHD grant OD30970-01A1 to me and my collaborators, Robin Morris and Maureen Lovett, during ongoing intervention research. I always wish to thank present and past members of the Center for Reading and Language Research: Heidi Bally, Kathleen Biddle, Theresa Deeney, Katharine Donnelly-Adams, Wendy Galante, Calvin Gidney, Julie Jeffery, Terry Joffe, Tami Katzir-Cohen, Cynthia Krug, Lynne Miller, Mateo Obregon, and Alyssa Goldberg-O'Rourke. The work cited in this paper could never have been done without their efforts.

CHAPTER IX: IS "LEARNING DISABILITIES" JUST A FANCY TERM FOR LOW ACHIEVEMENT? A META-ANALYSIS OF READING DIFFERENCES BETWEEN LOW ACHIEVERS WITH AND WITHOUT THE LABEL

Douglas Fuchs and Lynn S. Fuchs, Peabody College of Vanderbilt University; Patricia G. Mathes, University of Texas—Houston Health Science Center; Mark W. Lipsey and P. Holley Roberts, Peabody College of Vanderbilt University

This paper has two parts. The first part has three purposes: (a) to provide a brief history of how a formal definition of learning disabilities (LDs) was determined; (b) to explore how politics and research during the past two decades has influenced how people think about the validity of the LD construct; and (c) to explain why a quantitative synthesis, or meta-analysis, was necessary to determine whether low achievers with and without the LD label were more alike or different. The second part of this chapter describes method, results, and implications of the meta-analysis.

HISTORY, POLITICS, AND THE LD CONSTRUCT

In 1978, the first author of this paper went to Milwaukee to the annual conference of the Association of Children with Learning Disabilities (now Learning Disabilities Association) to present his just-completed dissertation research. Because it was his first professional meeting, he remembers it well. But it is memorable for an additional reason: Less than 3 years before, advocates had convinced Congress to include LD as a category of exceptionality in the Education for All Handicapped Children Act, and the celebratory greetings and congratulatory backslapping among advocates and practitioners, as well as their excitement and optimism, pulsed through the meeting rooms, hallways, and bars of the crowded conference hotel.

Contributing to the conference-goers' upbeat mood was their confidence in the validity of the LD construct. Throughout the 1970s, most practitioners, parents, and academics firmly believed that LD represented a discrete classification of exceptionality marked by two unique features: "unexpected" learning failure and "specific" learning failure (e.g., Kavale, 1987; Kavale & Forness, 1998). The child with "unexpected" learning failure was perceived by parents and teachers as generally competent. The learning difficulty was both surprising and puzzling. "Specific" learning failure suggested neurological dysfunction and processing deficits, which were presumed to cause severe problems in reading, writing, or math (e.g., Kavale & Forness).

There were at least two reasons to view "unexpected" and "specific" learning failure as a conceptual anchor and rallying cry for the field. First, as far back as the 1890s, physicians W. Pringle Morgan and John Hinshelwood separately described "the seemingly paradoxical inability of some children of average and superior intelligence to master academic concepts" (Lyon, 2001), a phenomenon documented more extensively by another physician, Samuel Orton, in the 1920s and 1930s (Hallahan & Mercer, 2001).

Second, in 1975, Rutter and Yule reported findings from an epidemiological study that seemed to buttress the clinical observations of Morgan, Hinshelwood, and Orton. Rutter and Yule measured the IQ and reading performance of all 9- and 14-year-olds on the Isle of Wight. The researchers regressed the children's IQ scores on their reading scores to produce a distribution of IQ-predicted reading performance. Scores above the mean represented overachievement (i.e., exceeding prediction); scores below the mean indicated underachievement (i.e., beneath prediction). Whereas such a distribution should resemble a Gaussian curve, with overachievement occurring as frequently as underachievement, Rutter and Yule reported a "hump" at the lower end of the distribution, which, they said, indicated that "extreme degrees" of reading underachievement occur at a greater rate than should be expected (Rutter & Yule, 1975, p. 185). When Rutter and Yule compared the "underachievers" to the children whose low reading performance was commensurate with their equally low IQ scores (i.e., "low achievers"), they found that the underachievers were different "in terms of sex distribution, neurological disorder, and pattern of neuro-developmental deficit" (p. 194). Further, the underachieving readers had a worse prognosis for reading and spelling and a better prognosis for mathematics. These findings led Rutter and Yule to suggest that the group of underachievers, or children with "specific reading retardation," was distinctly different from the group of low achievers, or "generally backward readers." Findings appeared to confirm "unexpected" and "specific" learning failure as a valid marker of students with LD (Fletcher, 1995).

And yet, clinicians' and researchers' affirmation of the LD construct, and the general buoyancy of the advocates, belied longstanding concerns. For example, as described by Hallahan and Mercer (2001), the question of prevalence had been a point of contention since the early 20th century when Hinshelwood argued that fewer than 1 in 1,000 students might have "word blindness," or reading disabilities, and Orton countered that a more accurate ratio was 1 in 10. (As indicated below, some policymakers today suggest a 1-in-4 prevalence rate for reading disabilities.)

An obvious reason for such disparate estimates is that there has never been agreement on an LD definition. For a century, the field has tried unsuccessfully to invoke the central nervous system to explain the disorder. Hinshelwood, for example, required that a diagnosis of word blindness be associated with obvious pathology. Orton dismissed this criterion, noting the impossibility of distinguishing pathological from nonpathological cases (see Hallahan & Mercer, 2001). In the early 1960s, the federal government and Easter Seals cosponsored several task forces on LD, the first two of which focused on definitional issues. Task Force I, composed mostly of medical professionals, defined LD in terms of minimal brain dysfunction. The education professionals who constituted Task Force II rejected this definition "because special educators in the field of learning disabilities must base educational management and teaching strategies on functional diagnostic information" (Haring & Bateman, cited in Hallahan & Mercer, p. 34). This task force's substitute definition proposed in part that "Children with learning disabilities are those (1) who have educationally significant discrepancies among their sensory-motor, perceptual, cognitive, academic, or related developmental levels which interfere with the performance of educational tasks; (2) who may or may not show demonstrable deviation in central nervous system functioning; and (3) whose disabilities are not secondary to general mental retardation, sensory deprivation, or serious emotional disturbance" (Haring & Bateman, cited in Hallahan & Mercer). With minor modification, this language became part of the U.S. Office of Education definition in 1977.

Because the definition did not include criteria by which practitioners could identify children with LD, the federal government proposed regulations to operationalize it. The government's strategy was to suggest a "severe discrepancy" between intelligence and achievement as the primary criterion, or marker, for identification. In 1977, the government wrote that educators may determine that children have a specific learning disability if they receive appropriate learning experiences for their age and ability and still do not achieve commensurate with their age or ability levels in oral expression, listening comprehension, written expression, basic reading skill, reading comprehension, mathematics education, or mathematics reasoning.

This guideline, however, was viewed as insufficient by many state education agencies. Most adopted the federal government's severe discrepancy idea (Frankenberger & Fronzaglio, 1991; Mercer, King-Sears, & Mercer, 1990), but defined it in their own way. In 1983, the federal government tried again by convening the Work Group on Measurement Issues in the Assessment of LD. Its primary mission was to determine "[w]hat constitutes a severe discrepancy, from a statistical perspective between aptitude and achievement" (Mastropieri, 1987, p. 29). The Work Group found that (a) states had indeed adopted many varieties of measurement formulas for identifying a severe discrepancy, and (b) some of these formulas were not only excessively complex but mathematically incorrect. The Work Group recommended that practitioners regress an aptitude measure on an achievement measure to produce a predicted achievement score, and that "discrepancy" should be defined as the difference between actual and predicted achievement.

However, even this effort was criticized sharply. "The...discrepancy model," wrote Willson (1987), "is basically an atheoretical, psychologically uninformed solution to the problem of LD classification. For LD to move forward...statistical models...need to be replaced by constructs firmly grounded in psychological theories of learning" (p. 28; also see Lyon, 1987).

1980s: The Politicization of LD

These concerns percolated more or less quietly in the U.S. Office of Education, state education agencies, and academe until the 1980s. Then two things happened to cause a much greater number of educators and politicians to question the validity of the LD construct.

Special Education's Soaring Enrollments and Cost

Between 1977 and 1994, the number of students with disabilities increased from 3.7 million to 5.3 million "despite... [the fact] that overall public school enrollment [remained] roughly constant over this period" (Hanushek, Kain, & Rivkin, 2001, p. 7). These numbers represented an increase from 8.3 to 12.2% of the general student population. Virtually all of the growth came from increases in students classified as LD, a group that grew from 22 to 46% of all special-needs children over this period (Hanushek et al., p. 7). Hanushek and Rivkin (1997, cited in Hanushek et al.) suggested that "special education accounted for roughly 20% of the increase in per student spending during the 1980s, slightly less than double the share of special education students" (p. 7). These developments did not escape the attention of school boards, school superintendents, politicians, and other stakeholders in public education, some of whom began calling for an immediate downsizing of special education (e.g., Viadero, 1991).

The Regular Education Initiative

Another event dramatizing and deepening LD concerns was the Regular Education Initiative (REI), a reform movement bold and comprehensive in design. One of its founders was Madeleine Will who, in the 1980s, was assistant secretary of Education in the Office of Special Education and Rehabilitation Services. She was also the mother of a son with Down's syndrome and, more than anything else, she wanted to dramatically increase the number of children with disabilities in regular schools and classrooms. In 1986, she circulated a paper entitled "Educating children with learning problems: A shared responsibility," which became a manifesto of sorts of the movement. Will and other REI supporters (notably her friend, Margaret Wang, and Wang's colleagues, Maynard Reynolds and Herbert Walberg) were critical of what they perceived as special education's empire-building and profligate spending (e.g., Wang & Walberg, 1988); its use of putatively stigmatizing labels such as "mental retardation" and "behavior disorders" (e.g., Reynolds, Wang, & Walberg, 1987); and its separation of special-needs children from nondisabled peers, which they characterized as undemocratic (e.g., Wang & Walberg) and racist because of the overrepresentation of children of color in many resource rooms and self-contained classes (e.g., Lipsky & Gartner, 1989; Stainback & Stainback, 1988). Moreover, REI supporters claimed little was "special" (e.g., Sleeter, 1998; Spear-Swerling & Sternberg, 1998) or effective (e.g., Biklen & Zollers, 1986; Gartner & Lipsky, 1989; Wang & Walberg) about special education instruction.

The REI's distinctiveness, however, was not its litany of complaints against special education, or its goal of accelerating the mainstreaming of special-needs children. Instead, its noteworthiness was its broader aim of transforming general education into a more instructionally responsive system capable of accommodating a large majority of children with disabilities and thereby reducing the size and cost of special education. The Adaptive Learning Environments Model (ALEM; e.g., Wang & Birch, 1984), cooperative learning (e.g., Stevens, Madden, Slavin, & Farnish, 1987), reciprocal teaching (Palincsar & Brown, 1984), and other instructional programs designed for mainstream classrooms were advanced as proven means to such an ambitious end. REI advocates believed that the remaking of general education would require (a) massive professional development, which, they assumed, would be financed by the dollars saved from downsizing special education, and (b) a redefinition of the role of special educators, away from direct service and toward "collaborative consultation" and "coteaching" alongside classroom teachers. Both the professional development and the new roles for special educators would require a major reconfiguration of separate administrative systems (i.e., general education, special education, Title I, and English as a second language) into a "unified" system (see McLaughlin & Warren, 1992).

Will and many other REI backers viewed children with LD as most appropriate among all students with disabilities for placement in transformed mainstream classrooms. There were at least two reasons for this. First, students with LD were understood by many to represent the mildest form of disability and, hence, they were seen as having the best chance of making it in the mainstream. Second, students with LD occupied the resource and self-contained classrooms coveted by advocates of children with mental retardation. In other words, some REI supporters reasoned that, if students with LD were mainstreamed, then many children with mental retardation could move from special schools to the more normal settings vacated by the children with LD. When LD advocates expressed skepticism about regular education's willingness and ability to accommodate the unique learning needs of many students with disabilities—a central assumption of REI supporters—a vigorous debate ensued (e.g., Bryan & Bryan, 1988; Fuchs & Fuchs, 1988a, 1988b; Hallahan, Keller, McKinney, Lloyd, & Bryan, 1988; Kauffman, 1989; Lloyd, Repp, & Singh, 1991; Reynolds, 1988; Wang & Walberg, 1988). This debate, in turn, further politicized the LD construct, as well as a good portion of LD research, which, deliberately or otherwise, contributed to the growing perception that LD was an invalid category of exceptionality.

LD Research

At least three lines of research in the 1980s addressed the LD construct. The first documented considerable variation of LD definitions and operationalizations across states (e.g., Gerber & Semmel, 1984; Mercer et al., 1990). Definitions differed in many ways: (a) the operationalization of discrepancy (e.g., standard scores for IQ minus standard scores for achievement vs. the regression of IQ on achievement); (b) the size of the discrepancy (e.g., 1.0 SD vs. 2.0 SDs); and (c) the choice of IQ and achievement tests. A popular and provocative way of expressing the findings from this work was to say something like "a child qualifying as LD in one state very well may have been excluded from the category in a neighboring state because of varying state regulations" (see Gerber & Semmel, 1984). In certain cases, some argued, the LD designation hinged more on the school district than the state in which one resided because of differences in regulations between districts within the same state (e.g., Peterson & Shinn, 1997).

Second, related work showed that many teachers purposely disregarded definitional rules and regulations to ensure special education for their students (e.g., Gottlieb, Alter, Gottlieb, & Wishner, 1994; MacMillan, Gresham, & Bocian, 1998; MacMillan, Gresham, Siperstein, & Bocian, 1996; Shepard & Smith, 1983). Gottlieb et al., for example, randomly selected 175 children with LD from six school districts and 165 elementary and middle schools in a large metropolitan area. Ninety percent of this group received some form of public assistance. The mean IQ of the sample was

81.4 (*SD* = 13.9). Students with LD in resource classes had higher IQ scores (*M* = 86.6) than those in self-contained classes (*M* = 75.0). Such scores, as well as teacher interviews, indicated that "children...classified as learning disabled...exhibit[ed] a generalized failure in their academic work rather than specific inefficiencies of cognitive processes or deficiencies in circumscribed academic subject matter" (p. 458). Only 15% met conventional identification criteria. Gottlieb et al. wrote, "Were the significant discrepancy feature of the learning disability definition observed, it would be extremely difficult to obtain with IQ scores so low" (p. 458).

"Why," asked Gottlieb et al. (1994), "is the severe discrepancy component of the definition so frequently ignored by school professionals?" They responded, "Our...discussions...with urban practitioners suggest that discrepancies are knowingly ignored...to marshall...resources for low-achieving (LA) students. Assessment staff and decision makers acknowledge that much of the school failure exhibited by children is more likely attributed to the effects of poverty...than to a 'learning disability' as defined in state regulations. Nevertheless...an educational fiction is agreed [on] to provide eligibility for special education services and programs. The current state of urban education, so woefully underfunded relative to its needs, provides students little access to intensive resources outside special education" (p. 459).

A third area of research in the 1980s reported considerable overlap in performance on various aptitude and educational tests between low achievers with and without the LD label (e.g., Ysseldyke, Algozzine, Shinn, & McGue, 1982) and between students with LD and Title I (high-poverty) students (e.g., Jenkins, Pious, & Peterson, 1988). Ysseldyke and colleagues (1982), and others, concluded from this work that virtually no important educational difference existed between students with LD and garden-variety poor achievers, that LD was an "oversophistication" of the concept of low achievement (e.g., Algozzine, 1985; Algozzine & Ysseldyke, 1983). Such a claim motivated others to conduct similar research, a point to which we will return.

In aggregate, the research on the variability of state definitions of LD, teachers' disregard for these definitions, and the overlap in performance between low achievers with and without the LD label promoted a widely held view that an LD designation was essentially arbitrary (see Coles, 1987; Doris, 1993; Finlan, 1994; Klatt, 1991; Pugach, 1988; Reynolds, 1991; Reynolds, Wang, & Walberg, 1987; Skrtic, 1991; Sleeter, 1986; Wang, Reynolds, & Walberg, 1994/1995; Ysseldyke, Algozzine, & Epps, 1983; Ysseldyke, Algozzine, Richey, & Graden, 1982; Ysseldyke, Algozzine, Shinn, & McGue, 1982). Writing in 1983, following completion of a program of research associated with their federally funded, 5-year Institute for Research on Learning Disabilities, Ysseldyke and colleagues spoke for many when they wrote, "After five years of trying, we cannot describe, except with considerable lack of precision, students called LD. We think that LD can best be defined as 'whatever society wants it to be, needs it to be, or will let it be' at any point in time. We think [LD] researchers have compiled an interesting set of findings on a group of students who are experiencing academic difficulties, who bother their regular classroom teachers and who have been classified by societally sanctioned labelers in order to remove them, to the extent possible, from the regular education mainstream" (Ysseldyke et al., 1983, cited in Hallahan & Mercer, 2001, p. 50).

Summary

REI advocates, therefore, promoted the idea that all children with an LD label were simply low achievers. They further claimed that because so-called children with LD did not have unique learning needs, they, together with their nondisabled peers, could profit from the ALEM, cooperative learning, and other presumably proven instructional programs for the mainstream. To ensure all low-performing children's academic well-being, REI supporters argued that special educators should be re-tooled as consultants and coteachers. In these new roles, they would spend much of their time in the mainstream. The ALEM, cooperative learning, and similar programs, combined with in-class support, would in turn permit the responsible decertification of children with LD and a dramatic downsizing of special education. Despite such innovative ideas to strengthen mainstream classrooms and shrink special education, REI supporters could neither convince a critical mass of general educators to support their strategies (see Pugach & Sapon-Shevin, 1987) nor persuade important stakeholders in the disability community that general education would be willing and able to respond appropriately to the unique learning needs of students with disabilities.

1990s: The NICHD Group

In the 1990s, an "NICHD group" became the most important voice expressing dissatisfaction with current LD definitions and encouraging fundamental change in our thinking about LD. The "NICHD group" refers in part to the principal investigators of learning disabilities centers funded by the National Institute of Child Health and Development (NICHD) and to Reid Lyon, the branch chief who supervises and coordinates their work. Our descriptor for this group is admittedly imprecise because we include researchers without NICHD funding who have conducted similar research, and we have little reason to believe everyone in the group thinks alike on all issues. Nevertheless, the group's work is sufficiently cohesive and important for us to regard it as an entity, and sufficiently tied to NICHD for us to use the acronym as an adjective. This group is different from the REI advocates in many ways. The NICHD group consists mostly of developmental, experimental, clinical, and neuropsychologists; REI advocates were largely special educators. The NICHD group focuses mostly on reading disabilities; REI supporters focused on the broad range of learning disabilities. Perhaps the most important difference between the groups is that the NICHD group claims to recognize the legitimacy of the LD construct. Lyon et al. (2001) have written, "Few would disagree that 5% or more of our school-age population experience difficulties with language and other skills that would be disruptive to academic achievement. The concept of LD is valid" (p. 7). What is invalid, says the NICHD group, are the definitions and operationalizations of the construct, which, they insist, must be reconceptualized.

The Argument Against IQ Discrepancy As a Valid LD Marker

Many concerns exist about IQ discrepancy as a definition or operationalization of LD, several of which already have been described. In addition, there are statistical problems (e.g., Willson, 1987) and the rejection by many of IQ as a meaningful estimate of overall intellectual potential (e.g., Spear-Swerling & Sternberg, 1998). The NICHD group's principal interest in the IQ discrepancy has been to explore the criterion validity of the "two-group hypothesis"; that is, the belief that qualitative differences exist between (a) children whose poor reading is discrepant from their IQ and (b) children whose poor reading is not discrepant from their IQ. This work has included a review of earlier studies conducted by others, secondary analyses of extant work, and the implementation of primary research.

"Earlier studies," wrote Fletcher (1995), "provided at best equivocal evidence for the validity of the two-group hypothesis. Many studies yielded null results, while other studies observed small but statistically significant differences between the two groups" (p. 16). Fletcher dismissed this earlier research with the claim that it suffers from methodological weaknesses that compromise its findings. In recent years, the NICHD group has conducted at least four studies on IQ discrepancy and the validity of the two-group hypothesis (Fletcher et al., 1994; Foorman, Francis, & Fletcher, 1995; Francis, Shaywitz, Stuebing, Shaywitz, & Fletcher, 1996; Stanovich & Siegel, 1994). Two of these studies (Fletcher et al. and Francis et al.) used extant data from Shaywitz and colleagues' Connecticut Longitudinal Study (Shaywitz, Escobar, Shaywitz, Fletcher, & Makuch, 1992). The four studies are noteworthy for (a) their researcher-defined samples, (b) their broad selection of concurrent child measures, and (c) the systematic way in which the studies build on each other. Each of these studies fails to support the two-group hypothesis. Moreover, authors of these studies have argued that many related investigations have demonstrated that "IQ scores do not predict who is able to benefit from remediation" (Siegel, 1999, p. 312). Or, as Fletcher put it, "There is no evidence that low-IQ and high IQ poor readers respond differently to treatment" (p. 41). Hence, the NICHD group contends that predictive and concurrent validity studies indicate that poor readers characterized by an IQ-achievement discrepancy are no different from poor readers without this discrepancy in terms of most reading-related skills.

The Argument for Phonological Deficits As a Valid LD Marker

Share, McGee, and Silva (1991, cited in Fletcher, 1995) have written, "Professional preoccupation with IQ...is liable to obscure those significant advances achieved over the last 15 years in the field of reading research...to identify domain-specific factors...that are more potent than all-purpose measures, such as IQ. More importantly, these domain specific factors go much further than IQ in helping us understand and deal with reading failure" (p. 43). One important domain-specific factor, according to the NICHD group, is phonological processing. According to Fletcher (1995), Morris et al. (1998), Share et al. (1991), Siegel (1989, 1999), Stanovich (1999), Stanovich, Siegel, and Gottardo (1997), Torgesen, Morgan and Davis (1992), Vellutino et al. (1996), Wagner et al. (1997), and others, phonological processing figures prominently among the information-processing operations that are believed to underlie severe problems in word recognition. The NICHD group claims that phonological deficit should be recognized as a valid LD marker.

Further, they estimate about 25% of the student population demonstrates phonological deficits and argue that all of these children should be understood as reading disabled: "We have chosen to combine the [reading disabled] designation with children who (a) meet criteria for LD and typically receive services through special education; and (b) read below the 25th percentile but who do not qualify for the diagnosis of LD and often receive services through compensatory education [because] data [indicate] little difference between the two groups in the proximal causes of their reading difficulties" (Lyon et al., 2001, pp. 3–4).

Twenty-five percent of 50 million school-going children equals 12.5 million students. Together with approximately 3 million special-needs children who are not LD, this recommendation produces a population of students with disabilities of about 15.5 million, more than 2.5 times the number currently served under the Individuals with Disabilities Education Act (IDEA). With 12.5 million children identified as LD, one might expect strong political pressure to reconceptualize this large group in terms of "nondisabled students in need of more effective general instruction."

The key to more effective instruction, says the NICHD group, is early identification and prevention. In his March 8, 2001, testimony before the U.S. House Subcommittee on Education and the Workforce, Lyon asked, "Can children with reading problems overcome their difficulties?" He answered, "Yes, the majority...can learn to read at average or above levels, but only if they are identified early and provided with systematic, explicit, and intensive instruction in phonemic awareness, phonics, reading fluency, vocabulary, and reading comprehension strategies" (p. 3). Moreover, he informed Congress, "Sufficient data exist to guide the development and implementation of early identification and prevention programs for children at-risk for LD" (p. 2). Early identification and prevention, says the NICHD group, should occur in general education: "Given that the underlying causes of most reading difficulties are similar for children regardless of whether they are currently served in special or compensatory education programs, we argue that the most valid and efficient way to deliver this early intervention in reading is as part of regular education" (Lyon et al., 2001, p. 20). However, a "major problem with such efforts is that special educators who typically provide instruction to children with LD have not been integrated into the early identification and prevention initiatives. It is important that both regular and special education embrace these efforts..." (Lyon et al., 2001, p. 36).

Similarities Between the NICHD and REI Groups

Many of the NICHD group's views about and policy recommendations for children with LD (and, more generally, for special education) are strikingly similar to those advanced by REI adherents in the 1980s. Both groups (a) are critical of special education effectiveness; (b) recommend that special education dollars should be combined with Title I dollars and possibly other funding streams to support the professional development necessary to strengthen general education's capacity to accommodate all low achievers; (c) argue that, with this accomplished, many special-needs children will be in mainstream classrooms, thereby permitting a reduction in the size and cost of special education nationwide; and (d) promote the notion that special educators' roles must change. REI adherents argued that special educators should become consultants and coteachers; the NICHD group recommends that they become heavily involved in early identification and prevention.

Most important, both groups view LA children with and without the LD label as the same children. For the NICHD group, "all low achievers are LD"; for the REI group, "all children with LD are low achievers." Although the NICHD group claims to believe in the validity of the LD construct, its critique of LD definitions and operationalizations seems to raise fundamental questions about the category. For example, Lyon et al. (2001) ask rhetorically, "Is the definition of LD that guides assessment and diagnostic practices too general and ambiguous to ensure accurate identification of younger students? Are the constructs and principles inherent in the definition of LD [invalid]? Are the diagnostic practices biased against the identification of younger, poor, or ethnically different children with LD?" (p. 7). To each question, they answer "yes." Similarly, Fletcher (1995) has written: "We have shown that the two-factor [poor readers with and without the LD label] classification implicit in the Federal Register definition lacks validity" (pp. 45–46). The NICHD group's dismissal of the distinction between low achievers with and without the LD label would seem to encourage a reconceptualization of children with LD—a subsumption of these children into a much larger, nondisabled group (i.e., the 12.5 million poor readers who, according to the NICHD group, require early identification and intensive prevention in general education). Hence, statements of support for the LD construct notwithstanding, the NICHD group, like the REI group before it, appears to be questioning whether the LD category deserves continued support.

META-ANALYSIS

Need for a Meta-Analysis

Since Morgan's and Hinshelwood's pioneering work at the turn of the last century, there has been disagreement about the nature of LD. In the past two decades, as its prevalence and the associated costs of special education to local and state governments have escalated, these discussions have taken on a high-stakes tone. Many interested parties are now openly questioning the meaningfulness (and usefulness) of the LD construct. Researchers have played an important role in this discourse. Using *researcher-identified* samples, the NICHD group has repeatedly demonstrated that poor readers with and without an IQ-achievement discrepancy have more in common (e.g., phonological deficits) than not. On this basis, the NICHD group and others argue that the IQ-achievement discrepancy should *not* be a criterion in LD identification.

According to Gottlieb, MacMillan, Shepard, and Ysseldyke and their respective colleagues, however, many school districts deliberately disregard discrepancy information. In contrast to the NICHD group's research, Ysseldyke and his associates used *practitioner-identified* samples to explore whether low achievers with and without the label are different from each other. Across a series of studies, they reported no educationally important differences between the two groups. This provocative claim inspired many others to try to replicate their work. Findings have been inconsistent, and for good reason: Investigators have explored different performance domains (e.g., reading achievement vs. classroom behavior); chosen dissimilar measures within a given domain (e.g., reading comprehension vs. phonemic awareness); used contrasting definitions of LD (e.g., IQ greater than or equal to 90 vs. IQ greater than or equal to 70) and low achievement (e.g., teacher judgment vs. cutoff scores); involved demographically different student groups (e.g., low vs. middle vs. high socioeconomic status; urban vs. suburban vs. rural); and based their statistical comparisons on different metrics (e.g., degree of overlap vs. mean performance).

Bottom line: There is no consensus as to whether the two groups of low achievers—those whom the schools have labeled and those who remain unlabeled—are distinguishable.

If a comprehensive review of the empirical evidence shows that students with the LD label cannot be distinguished from their LA, nonlabeled classmates, then it would seem only reasonable to support the abolition of this disability category. After all, the logical alternative would be to declare all LA students learning disabled, an assertion that we believe would make little economic, political, or legal sense. On the other hand, if a systematic review of research shows that the school-identified LD group performs more poorly, in both a statistically significant and educationally meaningful sense, then we can assume that the two groups represent different populations of students. Such a result may lend weight to the view that students with the LD label have different educational needs, in degree or kind, which might be addressed only within special education (e.g., Mather & Roberts, 1994; National Joint Committee on Learning Disabilities, 1994).

With these and other questions in mind, we have identified and quantitatively synthesized the extant literature in the domain of reading. We have chosen this domain for several reasons. First, a majority of studies comparing LA students with and without the LD label focus on reading. Second, most children with LD are identified as such because of chronic reading problems. Third, reading difficulty strongly affects overall school achievement (e.g., Stanovich, 1986).

In searching the scientific literature on reading, we coded each study that met our inclusion criteria and we analyzed the resulting data base. In the following sections, we summarize these methods and our results. We provide detailed information on the development of our coding system. For a thorough description of the literature search and data analysis, see Fuchs, Fuchs, Mathes, Lipsey, and Roberts (2001).

METHOD

Inclusion Criteria and Search Strategies

Our goal was to identify all published and unpublished studies in which the reading achievement of LD and LA nondisabled students could be compared. A study was defined by its participants: If two or more studies were conducted on the same students, the studies were counted as one. In a similar way, a single article could report more than one study if it included different samples of students with LD.

For inclusion, a study had to meet five criteria:

1. It had to present reading data.
2. Those data had to be reported separately for LD and LA groups.
3. Whenever the LD group included a mixture of students with high-incidence disabilities, students with LD had to constitute at least 85% of the group.
4. Participants had to be school age (i.e., kindergarten through grade 12).
5. The study had to report data necessary for calculating effect sizes (ESs).

To identify studies that met these criteria, we undertook a comprehensive search of journal articles, Educational Resources Information Center (ERIC) documents, and dissertations in Dissertations Abstracts International (DAI) produced between January 1975 and December 1996. This search comprised three phases: a manual search of journals, two computerized database searches (ERIC and DAI), and an ancestral search of titles in the references of identified investigations. Eighty-six studies met our inclusion criteria.

Coding the Studies

To systematically derive information from the studies, we developed a coding form in two phases. As we initially read the studies, it was unclear which study characteristics would eventually prove worthy of coding. Therefore, in Phase 1, we described many study features, knowing some would later be discarded. We began by reading a considerable portion of the research and becoming familiar with the typical range of study features described. We then developed a first-draft coding form with which we independently coded a sample study—Shinn, Ysseldyke, Deno, and Tindal (1986). After debriefing, we developed a second draft and accompanying code book. Then, we independently coded four studies, including Shinn et al. (1986) for a second time. After coding each study, we again discussed each item on the coding form. Throughout this process, definitions of codes were refined and decision rules about handling ambiguous situations were determined.

At this point, we began coding studies. However, within a couple of weeks, unacceptably low levels of interrater agreement indicated a need for more precise definitions, so the coding form was revised again. As a result, 30 articles that had already been coded with the second draft had to be recoded. A 16-page coding form emerged from Phase 1 (contact the first author for the final coding form). Using this iteration of the form, five studies were coded with interrater agreement of 90% or better on each study.

Then, the remaining journal articles and ERIC documents were coded independently. During this coding process, to check whether the raters were continuing to code in the same way, they completed independently the same set of 13 studies. Agreement on each exceeded 85%.

Recognizing the temptation to make reasonable inferences about information not clearly presented in studies, we instituted a no-guessing rule: If uncertainty arose about how to code an item, it was left blank. Later, an author determined the code. If questions still remained, the codes were discussed until consensus was achieved.

Approaching data entry, it became apparent that the 16-page coding form was too detailed; it contained codes inappropriate or irrelevant for many studies. Therefore, in Phase 2, the form was reduced to 45 codes that would be entered into the computer. During this scaling-down process, we added one code, "reading," which was redefined by various subdomains (e.g., phonological awareness, lexical retrieval, reading readiness).

The final coding form differed in appearance from the 16-page version because it was briefer and designed to match the computer spreadsheet. So, for example, both coding form and spreadsheet now displayed one line of data for every reading measure in a study.

Selected study codes were then transferred from the 16-page coding form to the briefer, final form. Before beginning this process, two coders independently transferred the codes of five studies from one form to the other, immediately checking accuracy. One coder then transferred the codes of all previously coded studies to the final coding form. An independent coder then checked this transfer of codes for every study.

Codes for 86 studies were entered into an electronic spreadsheet. To ensure accuracy, two checkers examined the spreadsheet item by item. As one person read the data base entry, the second person checked the information on the coding form.

Computation of Individual ESs

Typically, ES was computed as the standardized mean difference (d index): the difference between the means of the comparison groups divided by the pooled standard deviation (Hedges & Olkin, 1985). This formula represents LD-LA differences scaled in the uniform metric of standard deviation units. A positive ES reflects higher performance by the LA group. As recommended by Hedges (1981), this ES formula was adapted to yield an unbiased estimate of the underlying

population effect. Whereas a majority of studies presented the information necessary to compute ES using the basic formula, some studies presented other comparison statistics. In such cases, ES was estimated from those other statistics.

Aggregation of ES Within Studies

We aggregated two or more ESs in the same study, if those ESs were identical on
eight variables: reading subdomain, research design, sample size for LD, sample
size for LA, grade level, and IQ (Full Scale, Verbal, and Performance). Thus, any
two ESs in the same study that did not match exactly on these eight dimensions
were judged to be independent, with one important exception. In a few instances,
subgroups of a sample differed in size, but were identical with respect to the remaining seven variables. In these cases, ESs associated with these subsamples were
eliminated. Also eliminated at this point were seven studies in which LD and LA
students were matched on reading achievement or reading achievement and IQ.
ESs from the remaining 79 studies were included in the meta-analysis.

Preliminary Analyses

We undertook four preliminary analyses to formulate decisions about which data,
in what form, should be incorporated into the major analyses. First, we examined
the effect of four types of study designs: (a) descriptive/one point in time, (b) de-
scriptive/change over time, (c) intervention/posttest only, and (d) intervention/
change over time. We decided to conduct analyses on only one type, which had the
vast majority of ESs: the descriptive/one-point-in-time studies ($n = 202$).

Second, we examined whether and if so how to consolidate data across the reading
subdomains. We found that five reading domains (decoding isolated words, reading connected text, reading comprehension, overall reading, and vocabulary) yielded
ES values sufficiently similar, as indexed by their central tendencies, to be considered comparable. However, the remaining domains (phonological awareness, rapid
automatized naming, and reading readiness) were comparable neither with the
other five domains listed previously nor with each other. The mean covariate-
adjusted ESs for these three domains, respectively, were 0.05, 0.26, and −0.40. Thus,
we did not combine these three domains with the remaining five domains or with
each other. This left 172 ESs.

Third, with this smaller data base, we identified independent samples that contributed more than one ES. These records were aggregated by averaging all variables
(except the reading subdomain). Because all other variable values in the averaged
records were identical, a single record was produced for each independent sample.

This resulted in a data file of 112 records, each representing an independent sample with an ES in one of the five reading subdomains or a mean ES averaged over two or more of the five subdomains.

Finally, the distribution of the 112 ESs revealed outliers at both ends. To reduce the possibly distorting effect of these outliers, we windsorized them. Two ESs less than −1.00 were increased to −1.00; five ESs greater than 1.75 were reduced to 1.75. Doing so had a minimal effect on the overall mean ES.

RESULTS

Are the ESs Homogeneous?

Our first major analysis indicated considerable disagreement among the studies with respect to the magnitude of the differences between LD and LA groups in reading performance: The Q statistic indicated substantially greater variability among ESs than would be expected from sampling error alone, $Q(111) = 535.75$, $p < 0.001$. This finding led us to explore which study characteristics might be associated with variation in ES.

How Might We Consolidate the Large Number of Study Features?

Before examining the relation between study features and ESs, we consolidated some study features. First, based on analyses we conducted, we consolidated our definitions of LD and LA samples to five levels of LD/LA definitional pairings; this resulted in 109 ESs.

Second, we conducted several focused factor analyses on sets of variables that seemed to be related conceptually and were better represented as multivariate composites. A varimax-rotated solution seemed to fit these variables nicely. We thereby reduced the LD-LA student comparability data to three factors: achievement, which incorporated variables related to reading comparability; demographic characteristics, including age, race, and socioeconomic status (SES); and gender comparability, IQ, and SES comparability. We refer to these three factors as (a) achievement comparability, (b) demographic comparability, and (c) gender comparability, respectively.

Finally, we conducted another factor analysis to examine relations among variables describing the research method used for constructing the LD-LA samples. This analysis produced a sensible two-factor solution. The first factor showed a co-occurrence of the following: (a) lower IQ scores, (b) higher grade levels for the LD sample, and (c) referral of LA samples for special education testing. We called this factor "other sample features." The second factor cleanly combined the two variables describing whether the samples were district or researcher identified. We called this factor "identification source."

How Do the Clustered Study Features Relate to ESs? We used weighted least-squares regression, weighting each ES by the inverse of its variance. Our pool of predictor variables included the LD/LA definitional pairings, the five factor scores (reading comparability, demographic comparability, gender comparability, other sample features, and identification source), the three locale variables, technical adequacy, test format, study quality, and date of study. Predictors were entered simultaneously; then, the weakest was dropped and the model was refit. We repeated this process until all remaining variables were significant.

The regression model accounted for a statistically significant 41% of the variance among the ESs. The following variables made significant, independent contributions to the prediction of ES.

First, measurement format contributed to the prediction of ES, with a beta of 0.34. ESs were greater for the timed than the untimed measurement formats. For example, on tests requiring students to work in a fixed time (such as the Stanford Achievement Test or curriculum-based measurement), the difference between students with and without LD was larger than when tests permitted students as much time as they needed (e.g., Woodcock Reading Mastery Tests). This was true across reading domains.

Second, other sample features contributed to the prediction of ES, with a beta of 0.16. ESs were greater for LD samples with lower IQ and with higher LD grade; ESs were greater when LAs had been referred but had never qualified as appropriate for special education.

Third, LD/LA definitional pairings contributed to the prediction of ES. ESs were greater when LD samples were defined by discrepancies and when LA samples were defined by teacher judgment; the associated beta was 0.51. ESs were smaller when LD samples were identified by multidisciplinary team judgment and when LA samples were defined by data-driven methods; the associated beta was −0.27.

Fourth, the three comparability factors contributed to the prediction of ES. ESs were greater when achievement and demographics were not comparable for LD and LA samples; the associated beta was 0.13. ESs were greater when gender and, to a lesser extent, IQ and SES were comparable; the corresponding beta was 0.08.

Finally, methodological study quality contributed to the prediction of ES, with somewhat greater ESs for lower quality studies. The associated beta was 0.12.

WHAT DOES THIS META-ANALYSIS TELL US?

Across the many substantive and methodological variables associated with studies in this meta-analysis, ESs demonstrated considerable heterogeneity. Analyses were, however, successful in identifying a large proportion of the variance among ESs. Ten variables operated independently to explain the variation. In particular, three variables maximized the degree of reading impairment associated with the LD label and, therefore, provide insight into the theoretical nature of the disability. They also may help practitioners and researchers develop more effective assessment and intervention procedures for students with LD, as well as more precise measures of treatment success.

On the basis of these meta-analytic findings, we offer three conclusions, which may guide future research and practice. First, across the many different ways in which students become identified as LD, results leave no doubt that these students' reading achievement differs dramatically from other LA, nondisabled students. Averaged across all the methodological and substantive variations in the studies, the mean effect size was 0.61 standard deviations units. This effect is sizable; it means than 72% of the LA population performs better in reading than the mean of the LD population. Moreover, regarding ESs for timed measurements, whereby students were required to perform (i.e., read aloud, read silently, answer questions, match words to meanings) within a fixed time, the ESs increased to well beyond one full standard deviation unit. And, in a similar way, when LD and LA samples had been identified using data-based methods, the overall ES of 0.61 rose to beyond a full standard deviation unit. Findings, therefore, suggest that researchers and school personnel in fact do identify as LD those children who have appreciably more severe reading problems compared to other low-performing students who go unidentified. As with any comparison of two populations, some overlap between these populations occurs; that overlap, however, is not sufficient to call the LD label into question. Consequently, in light of the more severe magnitude of LD students' reading problems, it seems reasonable and desirable that more intensive forms of reading instruction be directed at this group of students.

Second, the ESs associated with timed tests were larger than those associated with untimed tests. The beta associated with this effect was an impressive 0.34. This strong effect associated with timed measurement format suggests theoretical and practical implications. Failure at achieving automaticity may represent an important characteristic of students with LD, which may be associated with the low performance on rapid-naming tasks (Wolf, 1991) of many of these children. The possibility that difficulties in achieving automaticity may represent a key feature of students with LD warrants additional study. Methods of identifying LD children might incorporate timed reading assessments to focus on students' failure to achieve automatic word-reading performance. In addition, with respect to treatment, researchers should develop methods for helping students with LD transition from accurate to automatic word reading. Finally, results suggest that the effectiveness of interventions for students with LD should be evaluated at least in part by how they influence students' performance on timed reading measurements.

Finally, results underscore the importance of objective measurement of reading performance in the identification process. Larger differences between LD and LA students emerged when definitional and selection criteria for inclusion to studies relied on objective forms of reading measurement—that is, the administration of tests. By contrast, when individual or team judgment was involved, differences between LD and LA samples on reading measures grew smaller. On one hand, this finding provides a basis for questioning human judgment in the identification process. On the other hand, it suggests that other considerations, such as a focus on social behavior, may play a viable role in the identification of children whose overall performance profiles warrant special treatment. Practitioners should be mindful of the advantages and disadvantages associated with reliance on nonobjective forms of input to the multidisciplinary team process. Future research should continue to identify which types of nonobjective data may be important in the identification process and should continue to examine the role of social behavior deficits and the possibility of comorbidity in children with LD.

REFERENCES

Algozzine, B. (1985). Low achiever differentiation: Where's the beef? *Exceptional Children, 52,* 72–75.

Algozzine, B., & Ysseldyke, J. E. (1983). Learning disabilities as a subset of school failure: The oversophistication of a concept. *Exceptional Children, 50,* 242–246.

Biklen, D., & Zollers, N. (1986). The focus of advocacy in the LD field. *Journal of Learning Disabilities, 19,* 579–586.

Bryan, J. H., & Bryan, T. H. (1988, April). *Where's the beef?* Paper presented at the annual meeting of The Council for Exceptional Children, Washington, DC.

Coles, G. (1987). *The learning mystique: A critical look at "learning disabilities."* New York: Pantheon.

Doris, J. L. (1993). Defining learning disabilities: A history of the search for consensus. In G. R. Lyon, D. B. Gray, J. F. Kavanagh, & N. A. Krasnegor (Ed.), *Better understanding learning disabilities: New views from research and their implications for education and public policies* (pp. 97–115). Baltimore: Brookes.

Finlan, T. G. (1994). *Learning disability: The imaginary disease*. Westport, CT: Bergin & Garvey.

Fletcher, J. M. (1995, May). *Diagnostic utility of intelligence testing and the discrepancy model for children with learning disabilities: Historical perspectives and current research*. Paper presented at the IQ Testing and Educational Decision Making Workshop, National Research Council, National Academy of Sciences.

Fletcher, J. M., Shaywitz, S. E., Shankweiler, D. P., Katz, L., Liberman, I. Y., Stuebing, K. K., Francis, D. J., Fowler, A. E., & Shaywitz, B. A. (1994). Cognitive profiles of reading disability: Comparisons of discrepancy and low achievement definitions. *Journal of Educational Psychology, 86*(1), 6–23.

Foorman, B. R., Francis, D. J., & Fletcher, J. M. (1995, March). *Growth of phonological processing skill in beginning reading: The lag versus deficit model revisited*. Paper presented at the Society for Research on Child Development, Indianapolis, IN.

Francis, D. J., Shaywitz, S. E., Stuebing, K. K., Shaywitz, B. A., & Fletcher, J. M. (1996). Developmental lag versus deficit models of reading disability: A longitudinal, individual growth curves analysis. *Journal of Educational Psychology, 88*(1), 3–17.

Frankenberger, W., & Fronzaglio, K. (1991). A review of states' criteria for identifying children with learning disabilities. *Journal of Learning Disabilities, 24,* 495–500.

Fuchs, D., & Fuchs, L.S. (1988a). Evaluation of the Adaptive Learning Environments Model. *Exceptional Children, 55*(2), 115–127.

Fuchs, D., & Fuchs, L.S. (1988b). Response to Wang and Walberg. *Exceptional Children, 55*(2), 138–146.

Fuchs, D., Fuchs, L. S., Mathes, P. G., Lipsey, M. W., & Roberts, P. H. (2001). Is "learning disabilities" just a fancy term for low achievement? A meta-analysis of reading differences between low achievers with and without the label. Paper presented at the Office of Special Education Program's LD Initiative Conference, August 27–29, Washington, DC.

Gartner, A., & Lipsky, D. K. (1989). *The yoke of special education: How to break it*. Rochester, NY: National Center on Education and the Economy. (ERIC Document Reproduction Service No. ED 307 792)

Gerber, M. M., & Semmel, M. I. (1984). Teacher as imperfect test: Reconceptualizing the referral process. *Educational Psychologist, 19*, 137–148.

Gottlieb, J., Alter, M., Gottlieb, B. W., & Wishner, J. (1994). Special education in urban American: It's not justifiable for many. *The Journal of Special Education, 27*, 453–465.

Hallahan, D. P., Keller, C. E., McKinney, J. D., Lloyd, J. W., & Bryan, T. (1988). Examining the research base of the regular education initiative: Efficacy studies and the ALEM. *Journal of Learning Disabilities, 21*, 29–35.

Hallahan, D. P., & Mercer, C. D. (2001). *Learning Disabilities: Historical Perspectives*. Washington, DC: Office of Special Education Programs, U.S. Department of Education.

Hanushek, E. A., Kain, J. F., & Rivkin, S. G. (2001, March). *Inferring program effects for specialized populations: Does special education raise achievement for students with disabilities?* Unpublished manuscript.

Hedges, L. V. (1981). Distribution theory for Glass's estimator of effect size and related estimators. *Journal of Educational Statistics, 6*, 490–499.

Hedges, L. V., & Olkin, I. (1985). *Methods of meta-analysis*. Newbury Park, CA: Sage.

Jenkins, J. R., Pious, C. G., & Peterson, D. L. (1988). Categorical programs for remedial and handicapped students: Issues of validity. *Exceptional Children, 55*, 147–158.

Kauffman, J. M. (1989). The Regular Education Initiative as Reagan-Bush education policy: A *trickle*-down theory of education of the hard to teach. *The Journal of Special Education, 23*, 256–278.

Kavale, K. A. (1987). Theoretical issues surrounding severe discrepancy. *Learning Disabilities Research, 3*(1), 12–20.

Kavale, K. A., & Forness, S. R. (1998). The politics of learning disabilities. *Learning Disability Quarterly, 21*(4), 245–273.

Klatt, H. J. (1991). Learning disabilities: A questionable construct. *Educational Theory, 41*, 47–60.

Lipsky, D. K., & Gartner, A. (1989). *Beyond separate education: Quality education for all*. Baltimore: Paul Brookes.

Lloyd, J. W., Repp, A. C., & Singh, N. N. (Eds.), (1991). *The regular education initiative: Alternative perspectives on concepts, issues, and models*. Sycamore, IL: Sycamore.

Lyon, G. R. (1987). Severe discrepancy: Theoretical, psychometric, developmental, and educational issues. *Learning Disabilities Research, 3*(1), 10–11.

Lyon, G. R., Fletcher, J. M., Shaywitz, S. E., Shaywitz, B. A., Torgesen, J. K., Wood, F. B., Schulte, A., & Olson, R. (2001). *Rethinking Learning Disabilities*. Hudson Institute.

MacMillan, D. L., Gresham, F. M., & Bocian, K. M. (1998). Discrepancy between definitions of learning disabilities and school practices: An empirical investigation. *Journal of Learning Disabilities, 31*(4), 314–326.

MacMillan, D. L., Gresham, F. M., Siperstein, G. N., & Bocian, K. M. (1996). The labyrinth of I.D.E.A.: School decisions on referred students with subaverage general intelligence. *American Journal on Mental Retardation, 101*, 161–174.

Mastropieri, M. A. (1987). Statistical and psychometric issues surrounding severe discrepancy: A discussion. *Learning Disabilities Research, 3*(1), 29–31.

Mather, N., & Roberts, R. (1994). Learning disabilities: A field in danger of extinction? *Learning Disabilities Research and Practice, 9*, 49–58.

McLaughlin, M., & Warren, S. (1992, September). *Issues and options in restructuring schools and special education programs*. College Park, MD: The Center for Policy Options in Special Education. (ERIC Document Reproduction Service No. ED 350 774)

Mercer, C. D., King-Sears, P., & Mercer, A. R. (1990). Learning disabilities definitions and criteria used by state education departments. *Learning Disability Quarterly, 13*, 141–152.

Morris, R. D., Shaywitz, S. E., Shankweiler, D. P., Katz, L., Stuebing, K. K., Fletcher, J. M., Lyon, R. G., Francis, D. J., & Shaywitz, B. A. (1998). Subtypes of reading disability: Variability around a phonological core. *Journal of Educational Psychology, 90*, 347–373.

National Joint Committee on Learning Disabilities. (1994). A reaction to "full inclusion": A reaffirmation of the right of students with learning disabilities to a continuum of services. In *Collective Perspectives on Issues Affecting Learning Disabilities: Position Papers and Statements*. Austin, TX: Pro-Ed.

Palincsar, A. M., & Brown, A. L. (1984). Reciprocal teaching of comprehension monitoring activities. *Cognition and Instruction, 2*, 117–175.

Peterson, K., & Shinn, M. R. (1997). *An examination of competing models of learning disabilities identification practice: The role of achievement context in school-based decision making*. Unpublished paper.

Pugach, M. (1988). Special education categories as constraints on the reform of teacher education. *Journal of Teacher Education, 39*(3), 52–59.

Pugach, M., & Sapon-Shevin, M. (1987). New agendas for special education policy: What the national reports haven't said. *Exceptional Children, 53*, 295–299.

Reynolds, M. C. (1988). Reaction to the JLD special series on the Regular Education Initiative. *Journal of Learning Disabilities, 21*, 352–356.

Reynolds, M. C. (1991). Classification and labeling. In J. W. Lloyd, A. C. Repp, & N. N. Singh (Eds.), *The regular education initiative: Alternative perspectives on concepts, issues, and models* (pp. 29–41). Sycamore, IL: Sycamore.

Reynolds, M. C., Wang, M. C., & Walberg, H. J. (1987). The necessary restructuring of special and regular education. *Exceptional Children, 53*, 391–398.

Rutter, M., & Yule, W. (1975). The concept of specific reading retardation. *Journal of Child Psychology and Psychiatry*, 16, 181–197.

Shaywitz, S. E., Escobar, M. D., Shaywitz, B. A., Fletcher, J. M., & Makuch, R. (1992). Evidence that dyslexia may represent the lower tail of a normal distribution of reading disability. *The New England Journal of Medicine, 326*, 145–150.

Shepard, L., & Smith, M. L. (1983). An evaluation of the identification of learning disabled students in Colorado. *Learning Disability Quarterly, 6*, 115–127.

Shinn, M. R., Ysseldyke, J. E., Deno, S. L., & Tindal, G. A. (1986). A comparison of differences between students labeled learning disabled and low achieving on measures of classroom performance. *Journal of Learning Disabilities, 19*, 545–552.

Siegel, L. S. (1989). I.Q. is irrelevant to the definition of learning disabilities. *Journal of Learning Disabilities, 22*, 469–478.

Siegel, L. S. (1999). Issues in the definition and diagnosis of learning disabilities: A perspective on Guckenberger v. Boston University. *Journal of Learning Disabilities, 32*, 304–319.

Skrtic, T. M. (1991). *Behind special education: A critical analysis of professional culture and school organization.* Denver: Love.

Sleeter, C. E. (1986). Learning disabilities: The social construction of a special education category. *Exceptional Children, 53*, 46–54.

Sleeter, C. E. (1998). Yes, learning disabilities is political; what isn't? *Learning Disability Quarterly, 21*, 289–296.

Spear-Swerling, L., & Sternberg, R. J. (1998, January). Curing our "epidemic" of learning disabilities. *Phi Delta Kappan*, 397–401.

Stainback, S., & Stainback, W. (1988). Letter to the editor. *Journal of Learning Disabilities, 21*, 452–453.

Stanovich, K. E. (1986). Matthew effects in reading: Some consequences of individual differences in the acquisition of literacy. *Reading Research Quarterly, 21*, 360–406.

Stanovich, K. E. (1999). The sociopsychometrics of learning disabilities. *Journal of Learning Disabilities, 32*, 350–361.

Stanovich, K. E., & Siegel, L. S. (1994). Phenotypic performance profile of children with reading disabilities: A regression-based test of the phonological-core variable-difference model. *Journal of Educational Psychology, 86,* 24–53.

Stanovich, K. E., Siegel, L. S., & Gottardo, A. (1997). Converging evidence for phonological and surface subtypes of reading disability. *Journal of Educational Psychology, 89,* 114–127.

Stevens, R. J., Madden, N. A., Slavin, R. E., & Farnish, A. M. (1987). Cooperative integrated reading and composition: Two field experiments. *Reading Research Quarterly, 22,* 433–454.

Torgesen, J. K., Morgan, S. T., & Davis, C. (1992). Effects of two types of phonological awareness training on word learning in kindergarten children. *Journal of Educational Psychology, 84,* 364–370.

Vellutino, F. R., Scanlon, D. M., Sipay, E. R., Small, S. G., Pratt, S., Chen, R., & Denckla, M. B. (1996). Cognitive profiles of difficult-to-remediate and readily remediated poor readers: Early intervention as a vehicle for distinguishing between cognitive and experiential deficits as basic causes of specific reading disability. *Journal of Educational Psychology, 88*(4), 601–638.

Viadero, D. (1991, June 12). States turn to special education programs for budget cuts. *Education Week,* p. 16.

Wagner, R. K., Torgesen, J. K., Rashotte, C. A., Hecht, S. A., Barker, T. A., Burgess, S. R., Donohue, J., & Garon, T. (1997). Changing relations between phonological processing abilities and word-level reading as children develop from beginning to skilled readers: A five-year longitudinal study. *Developmental Psychology, 33,* 468–479.

Wang, M. C., & Birch, J. W. (1984). Comparison of a full-time mainstreaming program and a resource room approach. *Exceptional Children, 51,* 33–40.

Wang, M. C., Reynolds, M. C., & Walberg, H. J. (1994/1995). Serving students at the margins. *Educational Leadership, 52,* 12–17.

Wang, M. C., & Walberg, H. J. (1988). Four fallacies of segregationism. *Exceptional Children, 55,* 128–137.

Willson, V. L. (1987). Statistical and psychometric issues surrounding severe discrepancy. *Learning Disabilities Research, 3*(1), 24–28.

Wolf, M. (1991). Naming speed and reading: The contribution of the cognitive neurosciences. *Reading Research Quarterly, 26,* 123–141.

Ysseldyke, J. E., Algozzine, B., Richey, L., & Graden, J. (1982). Declaring students eligible for disability services: Why bother with the data? *Learning Disability Quarterly, 5*(1), 37–43.

Ysseldyke, J. E., Algozzine, B., Shinn, M. R., & McGue, M. (1982). Similarities and differences between low achievers and students classified learning disabled. *The Journal of Special Education, 16,* 73–85.

RESPONSE TO "IS 'LEARNING DISABILITIES' JUST A FANCY TERM FOR LOW ACHIEVEMENT? A META-ANALYSIS OF READING DIFFERENCES BETWEEN LOW ACHIEVERS WITH AND WITHOUT THE LABEL"

Donald D. Deshler, University of Kansas

INTRODUCTION

There has been a dramatic rise in the percentage of children counted by educators as having a learning disability (LD) since 1976–1977, when schools were first required to track students enrolled in programs offering LD services. Specifically, the percentage of students labeled as LD has grown from 1.8% in 1976–1977 to 5.2% today. Moreover, more than half of all students receiving special education services are classified as having an LD compared to only 22% a quarter century ago. This marked increase in the number of students being identified as eligible for LD services underscores the importance of finding an answer to the question posed by Fuchs et al.: "Is learning disabilities just a fancy term for low achievement?" In essence, if the two groups cannot be differentiated scientifically or theoretically, there is no defensible way to justify why one segment of this low achieving (LA) group receives special services (under the Individuals with Disabilities Education Act [IDEA]) whereas the other does not have access to these services. Yet if special services were made available to all students who are designated as low achievers, it would be extremely problematic from an economic and policy standpoint.

The purpose of this paper is to respond to some of the key points raised directly by the authors or suggested by the conclusions they advance. Specifically, the following topics will be addressed: (a) the soundness of Fuchs et al.'s methodology; (b) the notion that students with LD are different from low achievers "in kind"; (c) the merits and limitations of focusing on the reading domain alone; and (d) the role of a developmental perspective in understanding the LD construct.

Prior to addressing these topics, it is important to acknowledge the effective job the authors have done in positioning their meta-analysis within a historical context. It is vital that any new proposal for change is viewed in light of our field's history—we cannot afford to overlook lessons we have learned in the past and sometimes quickly forget or ignore. The authors wisely devoted a significant portion of their paper to describing the factors and trends they considered to be the historical forerunners of the circumstances and dilemmas educators and policymakers are facing in today's educational climate. One minor point, however: The contributions of Siegel (1989) and Stanovich (1989) were very significant in framing cogent arguments about the limitations of IQ in LD identification frameworks. The historical picture presented in this paper would have been more complete if their contributions had been noted.

THE SOUNDNESS OF THE METHODOLOGY

The authors offered a solid rationale for applying meta-analysis to the literature they were reviewing, including extensive details about the conceptual framework they used as well as the procedures and decision rules they followed. Overall, the procedures were logical, and it is clear that great care was taken to make consistent and valid decisions in selecting and categorizing the literature and analyzing and interpreting the results. However, regardless of the care taken in conceptualizing and conducting a meta-analysis, the findings and conclusions that emerge from such an analysis must be viewed with caution. Like any methodology, meta-analysis presents certain limitations to researchers that should be fully understood by the consumers.

A couple of factors should be noted because of their potential influence on the data. First, in Appendix C, the authors reported that "the correlation between the LD and LA groups was rarely available, it was estimated to be .80 when not provided" (this volume). Much of the study's core findings are contingent on this correlation being accurate; yet as the authors point out, it was "rarely available." This estimated figure was used to determine the effect sizes. While the authors clearly report in the appendix the decision rule they followed in dealing with these missing data, this limitation should have been more prominently discussed in the text to ensure that readers were aware of this estimation and its potential effects on the data.

Second, Fuchs et al. used several different formulas to determine the effect size, each relying on different components from the source studies. This raises obvious questions as to the comparability of the results. That is, different outcomes drawn from the many studies reviewed required considerable modification to translate the data into a form used as comparable in the meta-analysis. For example, the source documents offered gain scores that were "occasionally ... presented for analysis," *t* tests were reported for gain scores "in a few studies," and effect size was determined from the F score "on occasion." While the meta-analysis was based on the "best data" available, it is important to view the conclusions drawn from the meta-analysis in light of these potential limitations.

The Notion That Students with LD Are Different from Low Achievers in Kind

The finding that students with the LD label, especially in the upper grades, demonstrate large differences in reading performance on timed tests, and the authors' contention that the differences noted may be one of kind and not merely degree, is noteworthy from both a theoretical and an instructional perspective. It will be important to cross-validate this finding in future studies with adequate controls. However, it is perhaps of even greater theoretical interest to determine the reasons *why* students with the LD label perform more poorly on these measures. For example, is it due to underlying psychological processing differences (e.g., difficulties with attention, association, short-term memory, retrieval, or encoding)? The design of powerful intervention programs that are appropriately tailored to the unique qualitative differences of students with the LD label will be greatly enhanced if researchers have a clear understanding of these underlying factors.

The authors' contention that this group of students should become the responsibility of special education is reasonable. However, in order for special educators to effectively address the unique and pressing needs of these students, they must be prepared to provide the specially designed instruction that, according to IDEA, should characterize all of special education (Public Law 105-17, 1997). Evidence suggests that many special education teacher training programs today are not preparing teachers to be the type of diagnostic-prescriptive specialists who are able to provide individually designed instructional programs (Kozleski, Mainzer, & Deshler, 2000; Peterson & Beloin, 1998). Rather, special educators are primarily being trained in the skills related to teaming with general education teachers to ensure that *all* students in the general education classroom succeed (Baker & Zigmond, 1995). Regrettably, the LD field has witnessed a major reconfiguration in how services are provided to students with LD. Namely, placement in the general education classroom is mistakenly equated with access to and success in the general education curriculum. The confusion between *place* (that is, the general education classroom) and *instructional conditions* (that is, the conditions necessary to enable students to be successful in responding to the requirements of the general education curriculum) has led to a dramatic narrowing of how services are conceptualized on behalf of students with LD. Specifically, the types of support services that are most frequently made available to students with LD come in the form of (a) consultation with the general education teacher by a special educator; (b) co-teaching by a general and a special educator in the general education classroom; and (c) various accommodations or adaptations of the general education curriculum and assessments. Each of these services is aimed at helping students with LD "make it through" the general education curriculum and pass the tests (Deshler et al., 2001). In a word, these services typically lack the intensive and uniquely focused emphasis on teaching students the skills and strategies they need to become learners who can independently negotiate and respond to the demands of the curriculum. As Kauffman (1999) so powerfully summarized this situation:

> ...if we are going to help students with disabilities, we are going to have to change course. We cannot continue to avoid focusing on instruction. We cannot continue to suppose that consultation and collaboration will somehow make up the deficit in instruction. We cannot rely on substitutes for specialized, individualized, intensive, relentless instruction that special education is supposed to be in all cases but actually is today in too few cases. This kind of education is very expensive and highly visible. As such, it is out of step with today's sociopolitical currents. (p. 251)

THE MERITS/LIMITATIONS OF FOCUSING ON THE READING DOMAIN ALONE

Fuchs et al. provide a reasonable rationale for focusing their meta-analysis on a very narrow subset of reading behaviors. Clearly, conducting a meta-analysis on all seven domains (oral expression, listening comprehension, written expression, basic reading skills, reading comprehension, mathematics calculations, and mathematics reasoning) included within the LD definition would be unreasonable, because of the magnitude of the task and the limited literature that exists in some of the domain areas. However, the authors follow a practice that has become increasingly common among researchers and commentators on LD during the past decade. That is, to make their research manageable and understandable, they study a relatively narrow subset of skill behaviors (e.g., in this case, a subset of reading behaviors), but then overgeneralize their conclusions to include the entirety of the LD construct. This practice has characterized much of the work conducted by the National Institute for Child Health and Human Development (NICHD) group, for example. Again, while it not only understandable but necessary for researchers to study only a limited subset of the seven factors at any one time, it is incumbent upon them not to overgeneralize their findings on a small subset of behaviors within a single domain (e.g., reading decoding) to the entire LD construct. The existence of very unique differences between LD and LA students in other domain areas is, at least theoretically, very likely.

Until careful work is done across each of the domain areas, it is important to exercise caution to ensure that research findings are not inappropriately overgeneralized. The likelihood of policymakers or practitioners making hasty or incorrect decisions based on limited data sets that have been overgeneralized is great when the limitations are not clearly and forcefully delineated.

Further, as individuals with LD mature into adolescence and adulthood, their competence will be judged in ways that extend far beyond a narrow set of reading skills. In other words, their disability may be manifested in ways not seen during their younger years because of the changing dynamics of the school and work settings in which they must function (Mellard, 2000). Based on a series of studies in the workplace, Murnane, Willett, and Levy (1995) and Murnane and Levy (1996) have identified a set of "new basic skills" that are required to earn a middle-class wage in the United States. These skills include the ability to: (a) read at the ninth-grade level or higher; (b) do math at the ninth-grade level or higher; (c) solve semi-structured problems where hypotheses must be formed and tested; (d) work in groups with persons of various backgrounds; (e) communicate effectively, both orally and in writing; and (f) use personal computers.

It is clear from this list of expectations that individuals whose disabilities are in areas other than or in addition to reading will encounter "unexpected" and "specific" learning failure as they try to respond to academic and employment demands (Fletcher, 1995; Kavale, 1987; Kavale & Forness, 1998). Hence, it is essential that our study of LD extend beyond limited subsets of behaviors if we are to adequately understand the varying ways in which LD may be manifested at different ages and across settings and contexts.

THE ROLE OF A DEVELOPMENTAL PERSPECTIVE IN UNDERSTANDING THE LD CONSTRUCT

The authors of this paper are to be commended for acknowledging some of the developmental effects of the LD condition. Their data have underscored the importance of differing performance patterns at different age levels (i.e., students with LD became more discrepant from LA peers as grade levels increased). Early in the history of the LD field, most funding initiatives were directed at younger students with the assumption (or hope) that if treatment was provided at a young age, many of the manifestations of LD would be minimized or avoided altogether in later years (Kirk & Elkins, 1975). However, research has shown that adolescents and adults with LD have enduring and unique characteristics that are manifested in differing ways as development and setting demands change (e.g., Alley, Schumaker, Deshler, Clark, & Warner, 1983; Brinckerhoff, Shaw, & McGuire, 1992; Mellard & Deshler, 1991; Schumaker & Deshler, 1984, 1987).

In light of the increased problems experienced by the older students in their study, Fuchs et al. add their voice to others, especially those of the NICHD team (e.g., Lyon & Fletcher, 2001), who have so effectively made the case for early identification and intervention. While these goals are important and laudable, there is a potential danger in overemphasizing early treatment at the expense of interventions at later ages. That is, the calls for these early intervention efforts "may be misinterpreted as implying that by doing the early intervention, most of the problems presented by students with LD will be ameliorated. While this is certainly a desired outcome, it is much more likely that the problems will persist and continue to be manifested in older ages as well. Thus, there are two reasons for not putting all of our field's eggs in the early identification and intervention basket.

First, even though an impressive array of reading interventions has been developed for younger students (e.g., Foorman, Francis, Novy, & Liberman, 1991; Torgesen, Morgan, & Davis, 1992), it is unlikely that these methods will be successfully implemented *to scale* nationally given our schools' poor track record of implementing educational innovations (e.g., Elmore, 1996; Fullan, 1993; Knight, 1998). In spite of the effectiveness of the existing set of interventions, the problems of bringing any innovation to broad-scale implementation with fidelity is remote (Cuban, 1984). Because of the enormous challenges of effecting large-scale implementations, there will be many students who will not receive the intervention and will move on to later grades with significant, un-addressed deficits. Second, even if children with LD do receive quality interventions during their early years, in all likelihood, their disability will endure into adolescence and adulthood. The need for equally effective intervention strategies for these older individuals is as great as if not greater than the need for interventions for younger children, because of all the emotional overlays that generally emerge as individuals mature and continue to encounter significant failure (Shaw, McGuire, & Brinckerhoff, 1994). Hence, it is critical that the LD field has a research and intervention agenda that is designed to address multiple aspects of the condition of LD across multiple age ranges. As compelling as the case for early intervention can be, if that case is made at the expense of addressing the equally problematic and unique set of problems presented by older-aged individuals, the long-term effects of such a policy will be devastating for thousands of individuals with LD.

CONCLUSION

Fuchs et al. have made a significant contribution to our understanding of an important reading dynamic among children labeled as LD. Their argument of differences in kind versus degree is compelling and will provide helpful direction for future research. Based on the information presented on the subset of reading behaviors, they have shed meaningful light on the question of whether "LD is just a fancy name for low achievement." However, in order to fully answer the question, similar research is needed in domain areas other than reading. In short, the important contributions of Fuchs et al. must be viewed in light of the totality of the LD construct, with the recognition that LD is a multidimensional construct.

The findings of this meta-analysis will be enhanced when additional studies are done that identify the relevant combination of variables in human learning that act together to influence outcomes. Multidisciplinary and multiagency-supported efforts will be needed to effectively study the broad array of variables that interact to influence typical student learning (Bransford, Brown, & Cocking, 2000). When a disability is present to compound matters, the need for multiple perspectives and innovative methodologies is especially great in order to achieve significant breakthroughs in our understanding of both learning and failure to learn.

REFERENCES

Alley, G. R., Schumaker, J. B., Deshler, D. D., Clark, F. L., & Warner, M. M. (1983). Learning disabilities in adolescents and young adult populations: Research implications (Part II). *Focus on Exceptional Children, 15*(9), 114.

Baker, J., & Zigmond, N. (1995). The meaning and practice of inclusion for students with learning disabilities: Themes and implications from the five cases. *Journal of Special Education, 29*(2), 163–180.

Bransford, J. D., Brown, A. L., & Cocking, R. R. (2000). *How people learn: Brain, mind, experience, and school*. Washington, DC: National Academy Press.

Brinckerhoff, L. C., Shaw, S. F., & McGuire, J. M. (1992). Promoting access, accommodations, and independence for college students with learning disabilities. *Journal of Learning Disabilities, 25*(7), 417–429.

Cuban, L. (1984). *How teachers taught: Constancy and change in American classrooms 1890–1980*. New York: Longman.

Deshler, D. D., Schumaker, J. B., Lenz, B. K., Bulgren, J. A., Hock, M. F., Knight, J., et al. (2001). Ensuring content-area learning by secondary students with learning disabilities. *Learning Disabilities Research and Practice, 16*(2), 96–108.

Elmore, R. F. (1996). Getting to scale with good educational practice. *Harvard Educational Review, 66*(1), 1–26.

Fletcher, J. M. (1995, May). *Diagnostic utility of intelligence testing and the discrepancy model for children with learning disabilities: Historical perspectives and current research*. Paper presented at the IQ Testing and Educational Decision Making Workshop, National Research Council, Washington, DC: National Academy of Sciences.

Foorman, B. R., Francis, D. J., Novy, D. M., & Liberman, D. (1991). How letter-sound instruction mediates progress in first-grade reading and spelling. *Journal of Educational Psychology, 83*, 456–469.

Fullan, M. (1993). *Changing forces: Probing the depths of educational reform.* New York: The Falmer Press.

Individuals with Disabilities Education Act (IDEA) Amendments of 1997. Public Law 105-17.

Kauffman, J. M. (1999). Commentary: Today's special education and its message for tomorrow. *Journal of Special Education, 32*(4), 244–254.

Kavale, K. A. (1987). Theoretical issues surrounding severe discrepancy. *Learning Disabilities Research, 3*(1), 12–20.

Kavale, K. A., & Forness, S. R. (1998). The politics of learning disabilities. *Learning Disability Quarterly, 21*(4), 245–273.

Kirk, S., & Elkins, J. (1975). Characteristics of children enrolled in child service demonstration centers. *Journal of Learning Disabilities, 8*, 630–637.

Knight, J. (1998). Do schools have learning disabilities? *Focus on Exceptional Children, 30*(9), 1–14.

Kozleski, E., Mainzer, R., & Deshler, D. (2000). *Bright futures for exceptional learners: An agenda to achieve quality conditions for teaching and learning.* Reston, VA: Council for Exceptional Children.

Lyon, G. R., & Fletcher, J. M. (2001, Summer). Early warning system. *Education Matters,* 23–29.

Mellard, D. F. (2000). Education and the new disability paradigm: Researching the educational environment. In *The new paradigm on disability: Research issues and approaches.* Washington, DC: National Institute on Disability and Rehabilitation Research.

Mellard, D. F., & Deshler, D. D. (1991). Education of exceptional persons: Learning disabilities. In M. C. Alkin (Ed.), *Encyclopedia of educational research* (6th ed., pp. 67–83). Washington, DC: American Educational Research Association.

Murnane, R. J., & Levy, F. (1996). *Teaching the new basic skills: Principles for educating children to thrive in a changing economy.* New York: The Free Press.

Murnane, R. J., Willett, J. B., & Levy, F. (1995). The growing importance of cognitive skills in wage determination. *Review of Economics and Statistics, 77*(2), 251–266.

Peterson, M., & Beloin, K. S. (1998). Teaching the inclusive teacher: Restructuring the mainstream course in teacher education. *Teacher Education and Special Education, 21*(4), 306–318.

Schumaker, J. B., & Deshler, D. D. (1984). Setting demand variables: A major factor in program planning for the LD adolescent. *Topics in Language Disorders Journal, 4*(2), 22–40.

Schumaker, J. B., & Deshler, D. D. (1987). Implementing the regular education initiative in secondary schools—A different ball game. *Journal of Learning Disabilities, 2*(1), 36–42.

Shaw, S. F., McGuire, J. M., & Brinckerhoff, L. C. (1994). College and university programming. In P. J. Gerber & H. B. Reiff (Eds.), *Learning disabilities in adulthood: Persisting problems and evolving issues* (pp. 141–151). Boston: Andover Medical Publishers.

Siegel, L. S. (1989). IQ is irrelevant to the definition of learning disabilities. *Journal of Learning Disabilities, 22*(8), 472–480.

Stanovich, K. E. (1989). Has the learning disabilities field lost its intelligence? *Journal of Learning Disabilities, 22*(8), 465–472.

Torgesen, J. K., Morgan, S. T., & Davis, C. (1992). Effects of two types of phonological awareness training on word learning in kindergarten children. *Journal of Educational Psychology, 84*, 364.

RESPONSE TO "IS 'LEARNING DISABILITIES' JUST A FANCY TERM FOR LOW ACHIEVEMENT? A META-ANALYSIS OF READING DIFFERENCES BETWEEN LOW ACHIEVERS WITH AND WITHOUT THE LABEL"

Ann Kornblet, St. Louis, MO

As a parent of children with learning disabilities (LD), I was hopeful when the Office of Special Education Programs (OSEP) started the process to open discussion on the identification and assessment of children with LD. As we gear up for another reauthorization of the law that protects our children (the Individuals with Disabilities Education Act [IDEA]), it is evident that once again it will be a task of supreme effort. So the discussion at OSEP, with their work group proceeding to gather the most current information on the key issues surrounding LD, seems especially on target.

We who have been through the reauthorization process before know that various forces and special interests begin to nip at real or perceived problems and to position their organizations and special interests long before the actual reauthorization process begins. With the numbers in the LD category continuing to grow for a variety of reasons, this time around we are facing questions about the validity of the condition itself. We cannot be distracted from the basic obligations of protecting the rights of students with LD, of working for earlier identification, of securing a complete continuum of appropriate services, of ensuring access to the general education curriculum, and of seeking the best professional preparation and in-service. It is hoped that basic understanding, coordinated efforts, and thoughtful change will emerge from the white papers and surrounding discussions.

Fuchs et al. have taken an extensive look at the research on basic reading performance in students with LD and students named low achievers. With the current interest in reading, the surrounding controversy on why some children are not learning to read, and the reading research being used as a tool to make or change policy, this analysis, because it uses reading studies, could provide a strong answer to low achievement = LD proponents.

The authors give a historical overview of the discussions surrounding the condition of LD and its definition. It is necessary to distinguish between the terms *definition* and *condition*, since we are concerned with defining the condition while understanding that the definition is not the condition. Webster's Dictionary (1998) states, "definition – the act of defining; a brief and precise description of a thing by its properties; an explanation of the signification of a word or term" (p. 116) and "condition – particular mode of being; situation; a state; that which is requisite to be done, happen, exist, or be present in order for something else being done; taking place, or happening" (p. 93).

The condition that is termed *learning disabilities* goes beyond a description of the presentation of academic symptoms that occur at a point in time. It is understood that those symptoms are the result of dysfunction over time and are broader than the manifestation of academic deficits.

The white paper reviews the changes that occurred in the field in the 1980s, with the appearance of the Regular Education Initiative and with it the damaging term "mild" disability used to describe LD. It was the beginning of loose interpretation of the IDEA regulations by states and school districts, with implementation in the states being quite different from the law and its intent. Regular education schools were unable to address the problems of diversity and overcrowded classrooms, were not adjusting to the needs of children growing up in a fast changing society, and were not supporting and training teachers for this new kind of student. As a result, communities allowed their schools to begin shifting more and more students into special education.

It was also a time when dramatic generalized statements about inclusive research were seen more in the journals and when critics of special education were able to increase their numbers and add to the growing dissension in the field. Certainly, the OSEP-funded research centers that developed and disseminated strategies on how to teach students with LD were a bright spot in that decade. Now, the need is great for the U.S. Department of Education to make research in LD a top priority, along with commitment to superior professional preparation programs and strong, mandated, ongoing in-service.

The next section of the white paper summarizes the role the National Institute for Child Health and Human Development (NICHD) and its research centers played in "encouraging fundamental change in our thinking of LD" (Fuchs et al., this volume). Most are aware of the importance of the work that has come out of the NICHD LD centers. How the research has been used, misused, quoted, and misquoted is another discussion. NICHD has brought to the attention of the public the problems in our classrooms in beginning and early reading. We cannot praise NICHD enough for this accomplishment.

In the discussions on low achievement and LD cited in the white paper, it becomes apparent that sound bites, volatile phrases, and generalizations do not answer the questions that need to be answered. We must not assume that low achievement and LD are the same only because test groups responded to the same basic reading skill training. Some of the differences Fuchs et al. cite are severity of deficit, increased differences over time, and different responses to timed and un-timed tests. LD is not domain limited, nor can LD be studied looking at low achievement alone. Surely by now the field and the public understand that LD does not mean a present and/ or future of low achievement and failure.

The history and discussion set the stage for the full description of the meta-analysis. The task was a large one, with different studies and research using different tests and definitions and with samples defined in assorted ways. From the outside looking in, this white paper showcases the need for defining and accepting what is valid research and what constitutes best practice in the field of educational research.

The conclusions of this study must be stated in clear language. From this summit and the following discussions must come plans for research wider in scope. The discussion of LD cannot center around early reading alone. The discussion of eligibility criteria must encompass all factors that are used, or should be used, in the diagnosis of LD. It is most important that all children who need help in school receive it. It is inappropriate to send all children who need help in school to special education. It is not right to suggest that students with LD no longer need the guidance a true diagnosis gives. It is inappropriate to suggest that students with LD will receive the support they need from general education in its present form.

We cannot lose the category of LD as described by the definition in federal law. Implementation of the regulations must be carried out to reflect the intent of the law. Change must not happen based on generalizations. As we cannot generalize the needs of a child, we cannot generalize the differences in our states and school systems as they implement the law. The focus on reading that has come to the forefront can be used to bring the two educational systems to a working partnership, but a partnership must strengthen, not weaken. The need for specialized training and a continuum of services based on the individualized education plan becomes more important, not less.

REFERENCES

Random House Webster's School and Office Dictionary. (1998). New York: Random House, Inc.

LEARNING DISABILITIES AND LOW ACHIEVEMENT ARE NOT MEANING-FULLY DIFFERENT CATEGORIES FOR CLASSIFICATION OR TREATMENT OF READING DISABILITIES

Louisa C. Moats, University of Texas–Houston

The meta-analysis of studies comparing low achievers and students with learning disabilities (LD) by Fuchs et al. (see also Fuchs, Fuchs, Mathes, & Lipsey, 2000a; Fuchs, Fuchs, Mathes, Lipsey, & Eaton, 2000b) examined and compared the reading performance of underachieving children with and without the LD label given by school evaluation teams. The researchers found several differences between these groups and they contend that special education has selected and served the poorest readers in the LD category. In their introductory statement of purpose, Fuchs et al. express concern that those who have argued against using an IQ-achievement discrepancy to classify children as LD may also aim to do away with the LD category in special education. They also fear that the demise of a discrepancy criterion for LD classification could result in the adoption of a simple achievement cut-off for special education eligibility. In fact, leading critics of IQ-discrepancy formulas such as Linda Siegel, Keith Stanovich, Reid Lyon, Jack Fletcher, Frank Vellutino, and others have not called for elimination of the LD category and, with the exception of Siegel, do not endorse a simple low achievement definition. Instead they are asking the field to confront and change ineffective, discriminatory, and scientifically indefensible policies and practices that have emanated from current conceptions of LD—reasons that are not contradicted by the results of the Fuchs analysis.

Fuchs et al. found that students who are placed into school-based LD programs perform more poorly in reading than low achieving students who do not qualify for special education services. Not surprisingly, students classified as LD in the schools also do more poorly than non-special education students on timed tests of oral reading known to be excellent measures of overall reading skill. Furthermore, Fuchs et al. found that students classified as LD showed worsening achievement deficits with age in comparison to non-labeled students. The majority of students who make their way into special education under the LD guidelines appear to have severe and chronic reading problems that typically do not improve over time.

The Fuchs analysis did not address the fundamental question of classification validity that plagues every aspect of special education for students with LD. Two other meta-analyses recently conducted by Hoskyn and Swanson (2000) and by Stuebing et al. (submitted manuscript) were designed to address related but dissimilar questions: Are discrepancy-based definitions of reading disabilities and low achievement valid for classification purposes? Are poor readers without IQ-achievement discrepancies and poor readers with IQ-achievement discrepancies different from one another with regard to the core cognitive deficits that predict and explain poor reading? Are they different with regard to related characteristics such as the presence of language deficits, spelling and writing problems, or emotional and behavioral problems? Do children who belong to each group respond differently to evidence-based instruction? Are their long-term growth patterns different?

Fuchs et al. and these other two analyses appear on the surface to have yielded contradictory results. These, however, can be easily explained because the hypotheses, inclusion criteria, and purposes of the analyses differed. Unlike the non-discrepant poor readers in the Fuchs study, the low achievement group in the other two meta-analyses were defined a priori with cut-off scores. In Stuebing et al. (2001), the dependent variables used to study effect sizes for group comparisons were not the same as the IQ and reading measures used to constitute the groups. This fact, in and of itself, explains the effect size difference observed by Fuchs et al. and prevents it from addressing the validity of the discrepancy- based classification. Stuebing et al. found negligible differences between LD and low achieving groups for behavior (effect size 0.05) and achievement (effect size 0.12), but a small difference in cognitive ability (effect size 0.30), the latter finding similar to Hoskyns and Swanson (2000). The differences in cognitive ability were in the expected direction (students with LD having higher ability). In all three meta-analyses, there was substantial similarity between the discrepant LD and non-discrepant low achieving groups, especially with regard to phonological awareness and rapid naming—those cognitive attributes that positively define the most common reading disorders. Those variables, the common denominators in reading disability, were eliminated by the Fuchs group and did not influence the aggregate effect size that reportedly differentiated their groups. Spelling skills, oral reading, real word decoding, and pseudoword decoding were slightly lower in poor readers who were IQ-discrepant in the Stuebing et al. study and the Hoskyns and Swanson study, and Stuebing et al. did not base their estimates on measures used to select the groups, where large differences are assured. On the dependent variables less central to the reading process (e.g., concept formation, nonverbal IQ), the two groups were more heterogeneous. As expected, the discrepant LD group tended to score higher on tests correlated with intellectual ability. The evidence-based studies by Hoskyns and Swanson (2000) and Stuebing et al. (2001) concluded that there was little evidence supporting the validity or relevance of the two-group classification of poor readers for either identification or treatment, echoing many consensus-based reviews of these issues (Aaron, 1997; Fletcher et al., 1994; Fletcher et al., 1998; Siegel, 1992; Stanovich, 1993; Stanovich & Siegel, 1994).

Reading proficiency, regardless of IQ, is predicted by performance on tasks measuring phonological awareness and phonological memory, rapid naming, and knowledge of word meanings. Moreover, printed word recognition accuracy and speed accounts for much of the variance in reading comprehension in poor readers of all ages (Share & Stanovich, 1995). Nonverbal, visual-spatial and executive function measures rarely account for much of the unique variance in reading achievement, even though they may be higher in discrepancy-defined poor readers. Most importantly, neither full-scale nor performance IQ measures predict differential response to treatment in IQ-discrepant and low achieving subgroups (Torgesen et al., 2001; Vellutino et al., 2000).

Children with reading disabilities show variable difficulties with different forms of language (Lyon, 1995; Morris et al., 1998). Some experience impairments of specific phonological skills and remain able to manage other language-based academic demands. These individuals are often referred to clinically as prototypical dyslexics. Many others, however, experience related language and cognitive challenges to varying degrees with varying combinations of symptoms. The more pervasive the child's language and cognitive difficulties, the less likely that the child will meet the IQ-achievement discrepancy criteria for LD classification, even though it is fair to assume that a child with generalized language and vocabulary deficiencies would be equally in need of evidence-based intervention. The problem we have created is that higher IQ children's needs are more often recognized, if not productively remediated, and lower IQ children's needs are passed over, even though IQ levels have little to do with response to instruction or prognosis, at least as far as reading is concerned (Fletcher et al., 1998).

Prominent critics of IQ discrepancy criteria are not attacking the legitimacy of the LD category. In contrast, Stuebing et al. state specifically that LD exists and that reading disability is definable on the basis of well-researched criteria that specify the cognitive-linguistic characteristics of the disorder. I and other researchers who seek changes in policy and practice support the existence of the category of LD. LD exists and students affected by it need better professional services so that their lives can be as productive as possible. We do, however, advocate changes in policy and practice commensurate with what the field has gleaned from rigorous research.

Certainly the overall record of special education in serving the needs of LD students, especially those with reading and language disabilities, is difficult to defend (Moody, Vaughn, Hughes, & Fischer, 2000; Vaughn, Moody, & Shuman, 1998). The following are the aspects of identification and treatment that are most in need of change.

USE OF VALID PRACTICES IN REGULAR CLASSROOMS

Instruction that emphasizes critical components at critical times, beginning in pre-kindergarten and kindergarten, reduces the incidence of reading failure that requires special services (National Reading Panel, 2000).

ASSESSMENT AND CLASSIFICATION OF READING DISORDERS

The relevant variables for classification of a reading disorder are phonological awareness, phonological memory, rapid naming, vocabulary knowledge, speed and accuracy of real and non-word reading, and oral passage reading fluency. Spelling, writing, and oral language comprehension might be added to this list. Children should be screened in kindergarten and re-screened several times each year if they are exhibiting weaknesses in critical skills. Cognitive testing should not be necessary to access effective reading and language instruction. Curriculum-based assessment of relevant skills and a focus on student progress should be routine in every primary classroom. Children with problems should be placed, without delay, in preventive and remedial programs taught by well-prepared teachers. Currently these practices are the exception, not the norm.

INCENTIVES FOR EARLY INTERVENTION

Education funding should be structured so that children can be served without the delays and hurdles of the special education eligibility process. Too many children have failed unnecessarily before services are ever provided. For example, the formality of an individualized education plan could be delayed until 4th grade if intensive instruction is being carried out with good results. If a student is not receiving appropriate instruction that results in satisfactory improvement, parents and guardians should be able to access a reasonable stipend for clinic-based, Internet-based, or university-based services of their choice. At present, parents who can afford such choices take them; parents of lower socioeconomic status cannot exercise choice so easily. This inequity should change.

PREPARATION OF READING TEACHERS WITH SKILLS IN STRUCTURED LANGUAGE TEACHING

Reading teachers who specialize in explicit, structured teaching of language must be recruited, prepared, and supported by public education. If they are not, parents will continue to press for the right to such services provided by private practitioners at public expense. At present, licensing standards and professional regulation for academic language therapists, to include coursework, supervision, documented effectiveness, and continuing education requirements, have been developed almost exclusively in the private sector by professional associations and institutes such as the International Multisensory Structured Language Education Council. These groups should be given more say in the licensing of public school reading and special education teachers, whose professional preparation has yet to reflect our growing knowledge of the causes, correlates, consequences and treatments of language-based reading disabilities.

REFERENCES

Aaron, P. G. (1997). The impending demise of the discrepancy formula. *Review of Educational Research, 67,* 461–502.

Fletcher, J. M., Francis, D. J., Shaywitz, S. E., Lyon, G. R., Foorman, B. R., Stuebing, K. K., & Shaywitz, B. A. (1998). Intelligent testing and the discrepancy model for children with learning disabilities. *Learning Disabilities Research & Practice, 13,* 186–203.

Fletcher, J. M., Shaywitz, S. E., Shankweiler, D. P., Katz, L., Liberman, I. Y., Fowler, A., Francis, D. J., Stuebing, K. K., & Shaywitz, B. A. (1994). Cognitive profiles of reading disability: Comparisons of discrepancy and low achievement definitions. *Journal of Educational Psychology, 86,* 1–18.

Fuchs, D., Fuchs, L. S., Mathes, P. G., & Lipsey, M. W. (2000a). Reading differences between low-achieving students with and without learning disabilities: A meta-analysis. In R. Gersten, E. P. Schiller, & S. Vaughn, *Contemporary special education research* (pp. 105–136). Mahwah, NJ: Lawrence Erlbaum Assoc.

Fuchs, D., Fuchs, L. S., Mathes, P. G., Lipsey, M. W. E., & Eaton, S. (2000b). A meta-analysis of reading differences between underachievers with and without the disability label: A brief report. *Learning Disabilities, 10,* 1–4.

Hoskyn, M., & Swanson, H. L. (2000). Cognitive processing of low achievers and children with reading disabilities: A selective meta-analytic review of the published literature. *The School Psychology Review, 29*(1), 102–119.

Lyon, G. R. (1995). Toward a definition of dyslexia. *Annals of Dyslexia, 45,* 3–30.

Moody, S. W., Vaughn, S. R., Hughes, M. T., & Fischer, M. (2000). Reading instruction in the resource room: Set up for failure. *Exceptional Children, 16,* 305–316.

Morris, R. D., Stuebing, K. K., Fletcher, J. M., Shaywitz, S. E., Lyon, G. R., Shankweiler, et al. (1998). Subtypes of reading disability: Variability around a phonological core. *Journal of Educational Psychology, 90,* 347–373.

National Reading Panel. (2000). *Teaching children to read: An evidence-based assessment of the scientific research literature on reading and its implications for reading instruction.* Washington, DC: National Institute of Child Health and Human Development.

Share, D. L., & Stanovich, K. E. (1995). Cognitive processes in early reading development: Accommodating individual differences into a model of acquisition. *Issues in Education: Contributions From Educational Psychology, 1,* 1–57.

Siegel, L. S. (1992). An evaluation of the discrepancy definition of dyslexia. *Journal of Learning Disabilities, 25*(10), 618–629.

Stanovich, K. E. (1993). Dysrationalia: A new specific learning disability. *Journal of Learning Disabilities, 26,* 501–515.

Stanovich, K. E., & Siegel, L. S. (1994). Phenotypic performance profiles of children with reading disabilities: A regression-based test of the phonological-core variable difference model. *Journal of Educational Psychology, 86,* 24–53.

Stuebing, K. K., Fletcher, J. M., LeDoux, J. M., Lyon, G. R., Shaywitz, S. E., & Shaywitz, B. A. (2001). *Validity of IQ-discrepancy classification of reading disability: A meta-analysis.* Paper submitted for publication.

Torgesen, J. K., Alexander, A. W., Wagner, R. K., Rashotte, C. A., Voeller, K. K. S., & Conway, T. (2001). Intensive remedial instruction for children with severe reading disabilities: Immediate and long-term outcomes from two instructional approaches. *Journal of Learning Disabilities, 34,* 33–58.

Vaughn, S. R., Moody, S. W., & Shuman, J. S. (1998). Broken promises: Reading instruction in the resource room. *Exceptional Children, 64,* 211–225.

Vellutino, F. R., Scanlon, D. M., Sipay, E., Small, S., Pratt, A., Chen, R., & Denckla, M. (1996). Cognitive profiles of difficult to remediate and readily remediated poor readers: Early intervention as a vehicle for distinguishing between cognitive and experiential as basic causes of specific reading disability. *Journal of Educational Psychology, 88,* 601–638.

RESPONSE TO "IS 'LEARNING DISABILITIES' JUST A FANCY TERM FOR LOW ACHIEVEMENT? A META-ANALYSIS OF READING DIFFERENCES BETWEEN LOW ACHIEVERS WITH AND WITHOUT THE LABEL"

Alba A. Ortiz and James R. Yates, The University of Texas at Austin

The Fuchs et al. meta-analysis of reading differences between low achieving (LA) students and students with learning disabilities (LD) represents quality scholarship of a nature rarely possible in the academy. The issues are well represented and the study has several features that make it an excellent vehicle for discussion of the distinction between low achievement and LD:

1. The authors objectively identified one of the largest databases to examine the differences between low achievement and LD. The study represents an enormous commitment of time and resources not ordinarily available for, or committed to, research studies in the field of special education.

2. The authors describe the data, its availability, and its format in ways that should facilitate replication or further inquiry, generation of additional research questions, and development of other recommendations.

3. The authors clearly describe how they controlled for, eliminated, or at least identified, potential sources of bias.

4. Their detailed description of procedures and analyses should minimize the type of criticisms that commonly plague research efforts such as these.

5. The design, procedures, and findings represent a conservative approach; the authors take great care to identify the limitations of their work and do not overstate their findings.

6. The study presents an unusual clarity of writing that facilitates the readers' understanding of the study, the findings, and the recommendations. The information contained in this report will be easily understood by researchers and practitioners alike.

We agree with the overall conclusion that LD is not just a fancy term for low achievement; the authors make an excellent case for this conclusion.

We would, however, like to raise an additional set of issues relative to the applicability of the recommendations to culturally and linguistically diverse learners, focusing specifically on English Language Learners, students who have such limited command of English that they cannot profit from general education instruction provided in English without support. We do so fully cognizant that this issue was not directly treated in the paper (except perhaps with regard to classification of students by race/ethnicity or economic status). This is understandable in that there is virtually no research on English Language Learners with LD. This is a plea, then, to support research on this population.

COMPARABILITY OF SAMPLES

That effect sizes were larger when the age and race of the LD and LA samples were dissimilar, and when gender and IQ were similar, underscores the importance of controlling the demographic comparability of LD and LA samples. This is an important point, not only because of the dramatically changing demography of the student population in the United States. More importantly, though, some of the author's recommendations will be difficult to implement and may have unintended, negative consequences if applied to English Language Learners. In 1998, almost 40% of the 46,792,000 public school students in grades 1 through 12 were students of color (National Center for Education Statistics, 2000). About 10 million of these students lived in households where languages other than English were spoken, 75% of whom were Spanish speakers (Waggoner, 1994). Language minority students will soon represent the majority school population in more than 50 major U. S. cities (Teachers of English to Speakers of Other Languages, 1997). This linguistic diversity is expected to continue given that 90% of recent immigrants come from non-English speaking countries (Hans, Baker, & Rodriguez, 1997) and that fertility rates are higher for minority women than for white women, with Hispanics having the highest rates (Villaruel, Imig, & Kostelnik, 1995).

Efforts to improve the reading achievement of culturally and linguistically diverse learners, and of English Language Learners specifically, is hampered by the limited information available about how these students learn to read in their native language or in English (August & Hakuta, 1997) or about strategies and approaches that lead to effective literacy skills for these students. While research on literacy instruction for English Language Learners is scarce, that related to limited English proficient students with reading-related LD is virtually non-existent. Few states have specific guidelines for assessing English Language Learners for special education eligibility and limited data are available on effective instruction for students who qualify. There is also a serious shortage of bilingual special education and related services personnel or special educators with English as a second language expertise. Until we develop the knowledge base, it will be virtually impossible to distinguish the effects of limited English proficiency from low achievement or LD.

PERFORMANCE OF LD STUDENTS IS LOWER AND BECOMES MORE DISCREPANT OVER TIME

The authors found that the reading scores of 73% of the LA population were above the average reading scores for LD students. Moreover, the performance of the LD group become more discrepant over time. The authors suggest that students with poor reading skills read less, and thus are more likely to suffer cumulative deficits in critical areas such as vocabulary, background information, and text-structure awareness. These skills are associated with skilled reading comprehension. As the authors state, these findings reinforce the importance of early identification and intervention.

We concur with this conclusion. Prevention and early intervention efforts can help poor readers; with appropriate intervention, LA students will likely show progress; those with LD will be "weeded out" because they do not respond to intervention. This will allow earlier identification of students with disabilities, eliminating the common practice of waiting for students to demonstrate a discrepancy significant enough to qualify them for special education services. It is critical that research focus on identifying effective prevention and pre-referral intervention activities and the resources required for the implementation of such efforts.

Historically, the purpose of pre-referral intervention has been to prevent unnecessary special education referrals and placements (Fuchs, Fuchs, Bahr, Fernstrom, & Stecker, 1990; Garcia & Ortiz, 1988). All too often, pre-referral activities occur too late to be effective in distinguishing disabled from non-disabled students. By the time teachers request pre-referral assistance, their interest in problem solving is half-hearted and with good reason. Research shows that if students are more than a year below grade level, even the best remedial or special education programs are unlikely to be successful (Slavin & Madden, 1989). Teachers view pre-referral intervention as a barrier to having students tested for special education. In reality, general education's failure to intervene in a timely fashion, not the presence of a disability, may be the real source of students' difficulties. Thus, committing resources to prevention and early intervention and involving general educators in these efforts is crucial. While no one disagrees with this, it is difficult to point to concrete examples of prevention and early intervention programs that have proved effective over time, and it is difficult to access resources that describe how such efforts are designed, launched, and sustained over time. The field needs such information.

TIMED TESTS MEASURE READING COMPETENCE MORE ACCURATELY

Timed tests may measure overall reading competence more accurately and thus be a better index of reading performance than untimed tests. The authors suggest that timed tests appear to be better measures of automaticity and thus are preferable to untimed tests, especially given that automaticity represents a more difficult challenge for LD students. This recommendation poses two issues for English Language Learners. The recommendation cannot be implemented unless appropriate reading assessments are available in the student's native language. The Texas legislature recently implemented a requirement that the reading progress of all students in kindergarten through 3rd grade be assessed, using instruments selected from a Texas Education Agency list of approved tests; these tests were deemed to have appropriate psychometric properties. In the case of Spanish speakers, the largest language minority group in the state, only one test initially made the list (although there was a lot of controversy as to whether it was a technically sound instrument). The Agency has funded a project to develop an appropriate reading measure for students in bilingual education programs who are initially taught to read in Spanish; no such instruments are available in other languages. So, timed tests in the students' native languages, appropriately normed for U.S. students, are not available, making it difficult to implement this recommendation. If the student is limited English proficient, then a timed test of English reading performance would be inappropriate. Publishing companies and state departments of education must make appropriate instruments available to assess the reading performance of English Language Learners. We concur that it is of prime importance to conduct research on interventions that help students transition from accurate to automatic word reading in the native language and in English as second language literacy.

OBJECTIVE MEASURES MORE ACCURATE THAN TEACHER JUDGMENT

Relying on teacher judgment was not as promising as using objective measures in identifying students with LD. This represents a double whammy for English Language Learners. There is a lack of appropriate instruments, making objective measurement difficult; teacher (and multidisciplinary team) judgments permit variables unrelated to academic performance to influence decision making. Studies of referral, assessment, and placement of culturally and linguistically diverse learners in special education reveal that teachers and other personnel are not able to distinguish linguistic differences and characteristics of second language acquisition from language or learning disorders (e.g., Ortiz et al., 1985; Ortiz, García, Wheeler, & Maldonado-Colón, 1986). Further, the data gathered to inform special education decisions are inadequate for the purposes of distinguishing disabilities from linguistic and cultural differences, resulting in culturally and linguistically diverse students being inaccurately labeled as having disabilities. Neither objective measurement nor educator judgment works well in identification of LD among this population.

We concur that there is a need to study what types of non-objective data can be useful in decision making. This research agenda should include developing systems that allow for systematic documentation of prevention and early intervention efforts and for monitoring reading acquisition in the native language, English, or both. Also needed are ways to help teachers and team members interpret data from multiple sources (objective and non-objective), not only in terms of academic performance but also from the standpoint of the influence of variables such as native language and English proficiency, cultural characteristics, economic status, and opportunities to learn.

NEED FOR SPECIAL EDUCATION

We concur that it is increasingly difficult for general education teachers to accommodate the range of student characteristics, needs, interests, motivations, and so forth that they routinely encounter in their classrooms. For low-performing students, who by definition require remedial instruction, there is an inherent contradiction between the principle of high academic standards for all students and the reality that some students require intensive, direct, skill instruction to get them back on track; while remediation is taking place, these students may not profit as much as expected from the instruction being provided their peers. We continue to be hampered by the standardization of programs and curricula, testing programs, the 9-month school calendar, grade levels, and the expectation that all students will learn the same material, in the same way, in the same timeframe—while, at the same time, we hammer away at teachers asking them to recognize and respect individual differences. Different general education structures are needed for struggling learners. Examples of structures that work in addressing the needs of struggling learners must be more widely disseminated; otherwise, we will continue to struggle with distinguishing low achievers from students with LD.

The same case can be made for students with disabilities. A study conducted by McLaughlin, Henderson, and Rhim (1998) found that teachers had difficulty figuring out how to provide students with disabilities access to a broad and balanced curriculum, how to focus instruction, and how to balance competing priorities. Teachers reported that they had difficulty finding the time to teach the content required by standards-based reforms while, at the same time, teaching other, more basic skills that might actually be more important in the long-term, given a student's disabilities (McLaughlin, Nolet, Rhim, & Henderson, 1999). These concerns highlight the need to provide teachers time to plan and collaborate as well as professional development opportunities to support their involvement in standards-based reform. These concerns may also support the need for special education. Such instruction might be more effective when, as the authors suggest, "the right resources are in place, such as a proficient teacher with a caseload small enough to permit differentiated instruction" (p. 63). For English Language Learners, however, special education teachers must be able to simultaneously address the students' disability-related needs and their language status. Otherwise, special education instruction will be as ineffective as general education instruction.

TEACHER TRAINING

Finally, there is much to be said about the need to revamp both general and special education personnel preparation programs so that graduates can effectively respond to the reality of today's schools—a changing demography, large numbers of under-achieving students, standards-based reform, high stakes accountability systems, elimination of social promotion, mainstreaming, inclusion, and so forth. It is beyond the scope of this response to elaborate on this particular issue, but we would like to make one observation. The reform of teacher education cannot happen without support to update the knowledge and skills of university faculty. General education teacher trainers cannot address disability issues without training; neither they nor special education teacher trainers can address linguistic and cultural diversity without appropriate preparation. Those of us in higher education are not required to pursue continuing professional development as are most public school teachers and administrators. If we choose to do so, we oftentimes do it at our own expense, which constitutes a disincentive given the low salaries of education professors. There is a critical need to support higher education faculty development in order to improve teacher training.

REFERENCES

August, D., & Hakuta, K. (1997). *Improving schooling for language minority children: A research agenda.* Washington, DC: National Research Council, National Academy Press.

Fuchs, D., Fuchs, L. S., Bahr, M. W., Fernstrom, P., & Stecker, P. M. (1990). Prereferral intervention: A prescriptive approach. *Exceptional Children, 56*(6), 493–513.

Garcia, S. B., & Ortiz, A. A. (1988). Preventing inappropriate referrals of language minority students in special education. *New Focus, 5.* Wheaton, MD: National Clearinghouse for Bilingual Education.

Han, M., Baker, D., & Rodriguez, C. (1997). *A profile of policies and practices for limited English proficient students: Screening methods, program support, and teacher training [SASS 1993-94, NCES 97-472].* Washington, DC: U. S. Department of Education, National Center for Education Statistics.

McLaughlin, M. J., Henderson, K., & Rhim, L. M. (1998). *Snapshots of reform: How five local districts are interpreting standards based reform for students with disabilities.* Alexandria, VA: Center for Policy Research on the Impact of General and Special Education Reform.

McLaughlin, M. J., Nolet, V., Rhim, L. M., & Henderson, K. (1999). Integrating standards: Including all students. *Teaching Exceptional Children, 31*(3), 66–71.

National Center for Education Statistics. (2000). *The condition of education.* Washington, DC: U. S. Department of Education.

Ortiz, A. A., García, S. B., Holtzman, W. H., Jr., Polyzoi, E., Snell, W. E., Jr., Wilkinson, C. Y., et al. (1985). *Characteristics of limited English proficient Hispanic students in programs for the learning disabled: Implications for policy, practice, and research.* Austin, TX: The University of Texas, Handicapped Minority Research Institute on Language Proficiency.

Ortiz, A. A., García, S. B., Wheeler, D., & Maldonado-Colón, E. (1986). *Characteristics of limited English proficient students served in programs for the speech and language handicapped: Implications for policy, practice, and research.* Austin, TX: The University of Texas, Handicapped Minority Research Institute on Language Proficiency.

Slavin, R. E., & Madden, N. A. (1989, February). What works for students at risk: A research synthesis. *Educational Leadership,* 4–13.

Villaruel, F. A., Imig, D. R., & Kostelnik, M. J. (1995). Diverse families. In E. Garcia & B. McLaughlin (Eds.) with B. Spokek & O. Saracho, *Meeting the challenge of linguistic and cultural diversity in early childhood education* (pp. 103–124). New York: Teachers College Press.

Waggoner, D. (1994). Language minority school-age population now totals 9.9 million. *NABE News, 18*(1), 1, 24–26.

SPECIFIC LEARNING DISABILITIES: BUILDING CONSENSUS FOR IDENTIFICATION AND CLASSIFICATION

BACKGROUND

The original goal for the Learning Disabilities Initiative was to synthesize current research and make that information available to educators, parents, and policy makers to serve as a foundation for future discussions and decision making regarding the identification of children with learning disabilities (LD). Because of the large amount of information and variable opinions throughout this volume, the Office of Special Education Programs (OSEP) recognized the need for consensus regarding the key issues in identifying children with LD. Selected researchers in the field of LD, including authors of the white papers and response papers and members of the LD Initiative Work Group (see sidebar), reviewed the empirical evidence contained in the nine papers and synthesized the implications of this knowledge base for policy, practice, and technical assistance.

The researchers formulated eight consensus statements regarding the identification and assessment of children with LD. In addition, they delineated topics requiring further clarification or additional research as well as recommendations for policy makers to consider. These consensus statements, additional topics of discussion, and issues for reauthorization and implementation of the Individuals with Disabilities Education Act (IDEA) are discussed below.

AREAS OF CONSENSUS

The process of building consensus can take many forms. For the purposes of this work, the researchers defined consensus as a statement or set of statements that each researcher was willing to stand by and support. Knowing that the discussion surrounding some issues would lead to full consensus, while the discussion of other issues would not, the researchers included an option for majority and minority

RESEARCHERS
Lou Danielson Renee Bradley

Don Deshler, University of Kansas	Margo Mastropieri, George Mason University
Jack Fletcher, University of Texas, Houston	Dan Reschly, Vanderbilt University
Doug Fuchs, Vanderbilt University	Rune Simeonsson, University of North Carolina
Frank Gresham, University of California, Riverside	Joseph Torgesen, Florida State University
Dan Hallahan, University of Virginia	Sharon Vaughn, University of Texas
Joseph Jenkins, University of Washington	Barbara Wise, University of Colorado
Kenneth Kavale, University of Iowa	

points of view regarding a particular statement. Although many important issues were addressed throughout the papers, they decided that consensus on every issue was not realistic.

Eight consensus statements, including one statement with a minority opinion, were developed and are contained in the following sections of this chapter. The consensus statement appears at the beginning of each section in italics and is followed by a summary of the researchers' discussion that preceded the development of the statement.

Concept of SLD

Strong converging evidence supports the validity of the concept of specific learning disabilities (SLD). This evidence is particularly impressive because it converges across different indicators and methodologies. The central concept of SLD involves disorders of learning and cognition that are intrinsic to the individual. SLD are specific in the sense that these disorders each significantly affect a relatively narrow range of academic and performance outcomes. SLD may occur in combination with other disabling conditions, but they are not due primarily to other conditions, such as mental retardation, behavioral disturbance, lack of opportunities to learn, or primary sensory deficits.

IDEA currently recognizes 13 categories under which a child can be identified as a child with a disability: autism; deaf-blindness; deafness; emotional disturbance; hearing impairment; mental retardation; multiple disabilities; orthopedic impairment; other health impairment; specific learning disability; speech or language impairment; traumatic brain injury; and visual impairment including blindness. There was immediate consensus that SLD should continue to exist as a separate category identifying a child as a child with a disability. There was also consensus on referring to this type of disability as a "specific learning disability" to emphasize the difference between children with SLD and those with general learning difficulties. The field of SLD is often viewed as fragmented because knowledge based on research—what we know works—is not always implemented in practice. One of the ongoing challenges in the identification of children with SLD is the variation in implementing the current definition and regulations regarding identification.

The group agreed that disorders of learning arise from intrinsic factors and result in neurobiological deficits in the brain. However, there was some discussion regarding the extent to which external factors, such as poverty and lack of learning opportunities, also influence brain development. Confounding the impact of these variables is the fact that some children in the classroom and in research settings do not respond to instruction, even with sufficient learning opportunities. Such confounding factors notwithstanding, all researchers agreed that children with SLD exhibit average to above-average intelligence across many domains, but have specific deficits within a narrow range of performance.

Exclusionary factors are also relevant to classification because, according to the researchers, a child should not be identified as having specific learning disability unless other factors such as lack of exposure to high-quality instruction have been ruled out. Exclusionary criteria can also prevent inappropriate identification of children. At present, IQ scores are the most common means for exclusion from classification as having SLD due to mental retardation. However, additional empirical evidence is needed regarding methods used to exclude children on the basis of behavioral disturbance, lack of opportunities to learn, and primary sensory deficits. The importance of paying attention to the needs and circumstances of children with limited English proficiency and from different cultural and ethnic groups was also discussed.

The Responsibility of Special Education to Children with SLD

Students with SLD require special education. As defined in IDEA, the term "special education" means specially designed instruction, at no cost to the parents, to meet the unique needs of a child with a disability (§300.26).

All of the researchers strongly believed in the need for, and importance of, providing special education and related services to all students identified with a specific learning disability who have been found eligible for special education and related services and for whom, on the basis of an individual evaluation, special education and related services have been determined necessary. However, the group expressed concern about the prevalence of faulty classification procedures currently being implemented in many school districts across the country. These faulty procedures have resulted in special education becoming a "catchall" for low-performing students, whether or not they have a disability. Special education should not be viewed as necessary for all low-performing students. Schools need to implement systemic models of prevention that address (1) primary prevention: the provision of high-quality education for all children; (2) secondary prevention: targeted scientifically based interventions for some children who are not responding to primary prevention; and (3) tertiary prevention: the provision of intensive individualized services and interventions for those children who have not responded to high-quality instruction or subsequent intervention efforts. It is this third group of children—those who have failed to respond to high-quality instruction and scientifically based interventions—that the researchers considered to be children with disabilities who require special education services.

Current classification criteria need to be improved to ensure that appropriate special education and related services are available to appropriately identified students who require them. Also needed is a common understanding among regular and special educators regarding the purposes of special education and related services and the relationships of those services to the provision of high-quality instruction and interventions. The field has gravitated away from the specifically designed instruction for students in need of that instruction, originally intended as the purpose of special education, and there is a need to reaffirm special education's original intent. Additional challenges in the current system include the misconceptions that special education is a place and that special education services are based on a specific categorical label. There is a need to reemphasize that special education should not be a set of services linked to a specific category or place, but instead should be linked to the individual needs of the child and delivered in an environment based on the needs of that child.

Lifelong Disorder

SLD are frequently experienced across the life span with manifestations varying as a function of developmental stage and environmental demands.

The terms "developmental stage" and "environmental demands," as opposed to "academic demands," need to be used to support the concept that SLD are lifelong and not evident in academic settings alone. Demands placed on an adult with SLD in the workforce can be quite different from demands placed on a child in the classroom. Successful remediation in one area of difficulty will not necessarily preclude an individual with SLD from experiencing difficulties and a need for additional intervention in that area or another area in the future.

Prevalence Rates

It is difficult to know the true prevalence rate of SLD. However, based on reading research, conducted largely in the elementary grades, we know that:

* *High-quality classroom instruction is a way to meet many of the educational needs of individuals with learning difficulties.*

* *Supplemental intensive small-group instruction can reduce the prevalence of learning difficulties.*

Even with the above interventions, approximately 6 percent of students may exhibit SLD and will need special education intervention.

Prevalence rates for students with SLD involving math and written expression are difficult to estimate given the current lack of research evidence.

The national prevalence of students currently classified under the criteria for SLD ranges between 5 to 6 percent of the total school-age population. However, identification rates vary significantly across different states and districts. For example, in Georgia less than 3 percent of students receive special education services as students with SLD. However, in Rhode Island, 7 percent of students are currently classified as having SLD.

Because of variability in identification procedures, it is difficult to know the true prevalence of SLD. Current research in early reading estimates that 2 to 6 percent of students will not make adequate progress in early reading even when provided with the highest quality regular education instruction. Nationally, the risk for reading problems ranges from 20 to 80 percent of all children. The most recent data from the National Assessment of Educational Progress shows that 37 percent of students in fourth grade do not have the adequate reading skills necessary to complete grade-level work. However, even with adequate resources and supplemental instruction, approximately 6 percent of students will require special education and related services for their SLD. Unfortunately, research on additional academic areas has not received the same amount of attention as has research on early reading.

IQ/Achievement Discrepancy

> *Majority: IQ/achievement discrepancy is neither necessary nor sufficient for identifying individuals with SLD. IQ tests do not need to be given in most evaluations of children with SLD.*
>
> *There should be some evidence that an individual with SLD is performing outside the ranges associated with mental retardation, either by performance on achievement tests or by performance on a screening measure of intellectual aptitude or adaptive behavior.*
>
> *Minority: Aptitude/achievement discrepancy is an appropriate marker of SLD, but is not sufficient to document the presence or absence of underachievement, which is a critical aspect of the concept of SLD.*

At present, there is often a significant disconnect between definition, classification, and the subsequent intervention provided to students who are found eligible to receive special education services under the present classification criteria for SLD. In most schools across the country, the regular education teacher is the individual primarily responsible for making referrals for special education services. This initial referral is the first and most critical step in a process involving a multidisciplinary team that considers the results of psychometric tests, reviews the student's school history, determines whether the child qualifies as a student with a disability, and plans services based on the student's needs. Typically, the multidisciplinary team uses classification criteria that require a discrepancy between measured ability (IQ) and achievement in the classroom as well as formal and informal assessments of educational need. It is important to recognize that the determination of eligibility is a to-pronged process that is based on both the presence of a disability and educational need. Some children who are potentially eligible for special education services may not need them because they are able to function adequately or may only require minimal support, which can be obtained through Section 504.

The current method for determining discrepancy often varies from state to state and district to district. This level of variation is problematic if services are based on particular labels versus the individual needs of the child. Under these conditions, a student who would qualify for services as a student with mental retardation in one locality may qualify in other localities for services under the SLD category, or may not qualify at all.

The validity of the IQ/achievement discrepancy and its link to intervention has been debated in the field for some time. The IQ/achievement discrepancy approach has become outdated and no longer reflects the current research. This approach was originally developed in the late 1970s when Congress required the U.S. Bureau of Education of the Handicapped to limit the number of students identified as requiring special education services for SLD. The primary goal of this approach was originally intended to limit the total population served under this category.

Today, there is considerable disagreement among practitioners and researchers alike on the usefulness of the discrepancy approach. Although many IDEA stakeholders in the field reject the use of a discrepancy approach because it does not identify the students they believe are in most need of services, many others continue to depend on psychometric tests as a way of corroborating their clinical judgment. The majority of researchers agreed that use of IQ tests is neither necessary nor sufficient as a means of classifying students with SLD. However, a minority viewpoint cautioned that the field of SLD could be compromised by eliminating the discrepancy approach because it may be an appropriate marker for unexpected underachievement, which is one measure of SLD. In addition, several researchers expressed concern regarding the lack of a viable alternative to the current process and the ability to implement that process with fidelity on a large scale within schools.

The results of a number of recent reading studies comparing children with discrepancies to those who are poor achievers but have no discrepancy found that the characteristics of these two groups of children were more similar than different. These results—if confirmed by further research—beg the question of whether or not students who show a discrepancy have a greater need for services than those whose disability is not manifested in a discrepancy. The more important question, however, is whether or not effective interventions differ between these two groups of children.

Processing Deficit

Although processing difficulties have been linked to some SLD (e.g., phonological processing and reading), direct links with other processes have not been established. Currently available methods for measuring many processing difficulties are inadequate. Therefore, systematically measuring processing difficulties and their link to treatment is not yet feasible.

Processing deficits should be eliminated from the criteria for classification because no clear measure or understanding of processing deficits currently exists. Although evidence exists that individuals with SLD have processing limitations, methods for measuring the presence of processing difficulties and devising appropriate interventions for those deficits have yet to be established.

Response to Intervention

> *There should be alternative ways to identify individuals with SLD in addition to achievement testing, history, and observations of the child. Response to quality intervention is the most promising method of alternative identification and can both promote effective practices in schools and help to close the gap between identification and treatment. Any effort to scale up response to intervention should be based on problem-solving models that use progress monitoring to gauge the intensity of intervention in relation to the student's response to intervention. Problem-solving models have been shown to be effective in public school settings and in research.*

The researchers agreed that response to intervention had considerable promise as a tool for improving current approaches to the identification and classification of SLD. There are multiple possibilities for how to plan and implement interventions for students with SLD. However, views vary on how to evaluate responsiveness to these interventions. One suggestion was to administer norm-referenced assessment batteries at the beginning and end of every school year. Another suggestion was to set a standard (e.g., the 25th percentile) that all students must perform at or above; any student who did not meet the standard would receive intensive intervention as early as possible and his or her responsiveness to this intervention could be monitored by administering fall, winter, and spring assessments. Continuous progress monitoring in which more frequent assessments of progress are made (e.g. weekly) was also viewed as promising. However, concern existed about both approaches because of the lack of personnel trained in progress monitoring and implementation of research-based interventions.

While the concept of responsiveness to intervention is a viable alternative to the current classification approach, further research is needed before the field can move toward adopting this approach on a large-scale basis. If discrepancy is eliminated as a requirement for a diagnosis of SLD, an alternative problem-solving approach may be a viable option. Such an approach may include the following:

- Student demonstrates low achievement.

- There is an insufficient response to effective research-based interventions. A systematic plan for assessing change in performance must be established prior to intervention.

- Exclusion factors such as mental retardation, sensory deficits, serious emotional disturbance, language minority children (where lack of proficiency in English accounts for measured achievement deficits), and lack of opportunity to learn should be considered.

Major considerations for any alternative to the current identification procedures must include a process that is research-based, efficient, and effective, and protects rights of children and parents to access needed services. Current thinking also emphasizes the need to embed such a problem-solving model in the context of a three-tiered model of prevention to provide effective interventions at the primary, secondary, and tertiary levels for all children.

Research on the response-to-intervention problem-solving process should include the selection of interventions, determination of the duration and intensity of the intervention, and defining what amount of change (progress) is viewed as adequate. Because responsiveness to interventions involves extensive time and expense, additional cost-benefit analyses of the alternative identification procedure will be needed to determine its utility.

Effective Interventions for Students with SLD

There is strong evidence that there are interventions that are effective for many individuals with SLD when implemented with consistency, appropriate intensity, and fidelity.

Despite this knowledge, there are interventions for individuals with SLD that are demonstrably ineffective but are still being used.

A solid research base on effective interventions has been developed for students with SLD, particularly in the area of early reading. However, there is a great need to more effectively communicate this knowledge to practitioners to ensure that all students receive instruction based on research-validated methods. Reasons for the poor implementation of these methods include inadequate teacher preparation, poor professional development, and the lack of overall school environments that support the use of research-based methods. Additional research about effective interventions is needed in the areas of mathematics, written expression, and listening comprehension.

ADDITIONAL TOPICS DISCUSSED

Additional issues related to identifying children with SLD were also discussed. Although the researchers were not directed to come to consensus about these topics, they articulated some important points for further discussion and clarification. The following section describes the researchers' discussions about the relationship between regular education and special education, the role of clinical judgment, and teacher preparation.

Relationship between Regular Education and Special Education

In an ideal system that ensures that no child is left behind, early screening, early intervention, continuous monitoring of progress, and specially designed instruction are needed. However, questions arise concerning who is responsible for the delivery of these services. Historically, regular education and special education have been viewed as two separate systems. Discussion on this topic focused on how to systematically increase the capacity of general educators to educate all students and how to move away from the traditional perception of a dual system. Among their varied roles, special educators should serve in a consultative role to regular educators in a systemic pre-referral intervention process before a child is referred for evaluation for special education. By serving in this capacity, special educators could share interventions, accommodations, and strategies with general educators and could ensure that some interventions are implemented prior to referral for special education. Given the critical need for, and advantages of, early screening and early intervention, such a process may facilitate early access to specialized services and possible special education identification. Concerns exist about whether special educators with classroom responsibilities would have the time to serve as both expert instructors and consultants and whether implementing interventions in regular education under current funding levels would diminish funding that supports special education. Some states have already decided to fund the delivery of early intervention services, but this practice is not in place in every state. The recently reauthorized Elementary and Secondary Education Act (No Child Left Behind) may assist with this problem. Research on the effectiveness of pre-referral interventions is mixed, though recent research indicates that high-quality pre-referral can lead to a reduction of inappropriate referrals to special education.

The Role of Clinical Judgment

Clinical judgment is an integral component of the decision-making process in special education, from pre-referral to identification to placement. Clinical judgment is required in interpreting and evaluating multiple sources of information related to disability classification and treatment. These judgments must be based on consideration of data and must be consistent with the multiple sources of information provided. For example, clinical judgment is involved in decisions about the following:

- Whether or not behavior or academic performance warrants initial referral;

- Selection and interpretation of achievement tests;

- Assessment of whether high-quality education interventions were applied;

- Assessment of other influences on performance, such as mental retardation, emotional disturbance, and language differences; and

- Determination of whether response to intervention is sufficient.

Because clinical judgment is a critical component in the appropriate identification of children who need special education services, it must be exercised in a responsible way. There is a continuing national need to address clinical judgment skills in teacher training and professional development programs, and to set standards for balancing the relative importance of clinical judgment and evaluating results when making educational placement decisions. To improve this aspect of the decision-making process, pre-service and in-service professional development programs must teach and enhance these critical skills.

Teacher Preparation

Both pre-service and in-service training are essential to developing the competency of educators. However, many teachers obtain more information about teaching and instruction from the mass media than from professional journals, textbooks, or research-based resources available on the Internet. In addition, many teacher training institutions are not teaching scientifically based practices. As an example, one participant stated that graduates of a particular curriculum and instruction program were taught to be skeptical about phonics instruction—a practice with strong research validation. Both pre-service and in-service teacher preparation programs for all teachers require dramatic improvements. Beyond an emphasis on the dissemination of research-based practices, teacher preparation programs should infuse information about screening and formative assessment procedures, specific content-area instruction methodologies, and methods of individual and small-group instruction into the curricular for all educators, not just for special educators. Toward that end, OSEP, other offices within the U.S. Department of Education, and professional organizations should increase their efforts and continue to support the dissemination of research-based practices especially given the goals of No Child Left Behind.

Areas Needing Additional Research

The researchers also discussed current research findings and identified areas where additional research is needed. New research findings have the potential to drive policy decisions, refine current classification and identification procedures, and improve service delivery in the field of special education and SLD. Thus, the researchers believed that their discussion was timely as Congress moves toward the upcoming reauthorization of IDEA.

The researchers determined that in order to answer some of the more difficult questions regarding improving the identification process for children with SLD, further research is needed in the following areas:

- Methods to assess responsiveness to intervention.

- Measures of intervention quality.

- How to scale up the use of research-based practices.

- Markers for early identification of students who are likely to be unresponsive to intervention including younger children.

- Research in content areas beyond reading. The knowledge base concerning effective practices in mathematics, written expression, and listening comprehension is not adequate, especially in relation to early reading.

- How would a change in the identification of SLD influence students across the age profile? How are SLD manifested throughout the life span?

- What steps should be taken if a student is not making progress in special education?

- What is the impact of early identification and intervention on cost, referral to special education, and intensity of services over time?

FUTURE ISSUES FOR REAUTHORIZATION AND IMPROVED IMPLEMENTATION

The researchers reflected on the issues under discussion and formulated a set of issues for the larger education community to consider during the reauthorization of IDEA and in the continued efforts to improve not only identification but also results for children with SLD. Effective and efficient implementation of future changes to IDEA will require a comprehensive evidence-based discussion of the following issues:

1) Consider making identification procedures less complex while placing more emphasis on assessing student achievement. Focus on treatment validity and accountability for student learning rather than process compliance.

2) School districts should evaluate special education programs using student outcomes. Schools should focus on monitoring a child's progress over time.

3) If discrepancy is eliminated as a requirement for SLD, the alternative process needs to be efficient and based on the best we know, while protecting the rights of children and parents to access needed services.

4) Build accountability into the regulations. It is imperative to have data to document what has been done to improve a child's performance.

5) Implementation of research-based practices regarding instruction, assessments, and interventions must be more rigorous.

6) Provide guidelines to districts on instructional practice. Provide information about what we know about effective and ineffective practices.

7) Redefine the types of SLD: Combine reading comprehension and basic reading skills into the category of *Reading* (e.g., fluency, accuracy, and comprehension). Combine math calculation and mathematical reasoning into *Mathematics* (e.g., calculation and problem solving). Maintain *Written Expression* (e.g., composition and spelling) and *Listening Comprehension*, but eliminate *Oral Expression*.

8) Exclusion factors should be stated as follows: "SLD is not due primarily to mental retardation, behavioral disturbance, lack of opportunities to learn, or primary sensory deficits."

CONCLUSION

The original goal for the Learning Disabilities Initiative was to synthesize the current research on identification and make that information available to educators, parents, and policy makers to serve as a foundation for future discussions and decision making regarding the identification of children with learning disabilities. The work of this group of researchers was intended to follow up on the work of the LD Summit by focusing on areas of consensus and disagreement related to the identification and classification of children with SLD and summarizing the work of the OSEP LD

Initiative. The researchers agreed that the current process for identification and classification requires substantial review by policy makers, parents, researchers, and practitioners. In addition, they concluded that the regular and special education communities, working in concert, must address issues related to providing a high-quality education for all children, including addressing the needs of those with SLD.

OSEP is committed to continue working on improving the identification of children with learning disabilities. As part of its commitment, OSEP recently funded the National Research Center on Learning Disabilities. This Center will conduct some of the research needed to continue to improve special education services for children with learning disabilities and will work to bring the best of what we know, including the research represented in this volume, to teachers, administrators, families, and policy makers. The successful transfer of research to practice is the critical link to ensure that children with learning disabilities are being appropriately identified and served.

CURRENT IDEA DEFINITION—
SPECIFIC LEARNING DISABILITY 300.7(C)(10)

Specific learning disability is defined as follows:

i) General. The term means a disorder in one or of the basic psychological processes involved in understanding or in using language, spoken or written, that may manifest itself in an imperfect ability to listen, think speak, read, write, spell, or to do mathematical calculation, including conditions such as perceptual disabilities, brain injury, minimal brain dysfunction, dyslexia and developmental aphasia.

ii) Disorders not included. The term does not include learning problems that are primarily the result of visual, hearing, or motor disabilities or mental retardation, of emotional disturbance, or of environmental cultural or economic disadvantage.

CURRENT IDEA REGULATIONS: CRITERIA FOR DETERMINING THE EXISTENCE OF A SPECIFIC LEARNING DISABILITY 300.541

a) a team may determine that a child has a specific learning disability if

1) The child does not achieve commensurate with his or her age and ability levels in one or more of the areas listed in paragraph (a)(2) of this section, if provided with learning experience appropriate for the child's age and ability levels; and

2) The team finds that a child has a severe discrepancy between achievement and intellectual ability in one or more of the following areas:

i) Oral expression

       ii) Listening comprehension
      iii) Written expression
      iv) Basic reading skill
      v) Reading comprehension
      vi) Mathematics calculation
      vii) Mathematics reasoning

b) the team may not identify a child as having a specific learning disability if the severe discrepancy between ability and achievement is primarily the result of—

1) A visual, hearing, or motor impairment

2) Mental retardation

3) Emotional disturbance

4) Environmental, cultural, or economic disadvantage

RESOURCES AND ORGANIZATIONS
ON SPECIFIC LEARNING DISABILITIES

Association for Higher Education and Disability (AHEAD)
Stephen Smith, Executive Director
University of Massachusetts at Boston
100 Morrissey Boulevard
Boston, MA 02125
www.ahead.org

Council for Learning Disabilities (CLD)
Ann Ryan, Executive Director
PO Box 40303
Overland Park, KS 66204
www.cldinternational.org

Division for Children's Communication Development (DCDD)
Council for Exceptional Children
Diane Paul-Brown, Executive Director
1920 Association Drive
Reston, VA 22091

International Reading Association (IRA)
Alan Farstrup, Executive Director
800 Barksdale Road
PO Box 8139
Newark, DE 19714-8139
www.reading.org

National Associat of School Psychologists (NASP)
Susan Gorin, Executive Director
4340 East West Highway
Suite 402
Bethesda, MD 20814
www.nasponline.org

National Research Center on Learning Disabilities
Vanderbilt University
Peabody College, Box 328
Nashville, TN 37203

American Speech-Language-Hearing Association (ASHA)
Frederick T. Spahr, Executive Director
10801 Rockville Pike
Rockville, MD 20852-3279
www.asha.org

Division for Learning Disabilities (DLD)
Council for Exceptional Children
Hal McGrady, Executive Director
1770 Scottsdale Avenue
Columbus, OH 43235
www.dldcec.org

International Dyslexia Association (IDA)
Thomas Viall, Executive Director
8600 LaSalle Road
Chester Building, Suite 382
Baltimore, MD 21286
www.interdys.orh

Learning Disabilities Association (LDA)
Jane Browning, Executive Director
4156 Library Road
Pittsburgh, PA 15324-1349
www.ldaamerica.org

National Center for Learning Disabilities (NCLD)
James H. Wendorf, Executive Director
381 Park Avenue South
Suite 1401
New York, NY 10016
www.ld.org

U.S. Office of Special Education Programs
www.ed.gov/offices/OSERS/OSEP

NAME INDEX

Numbers in parenthesis are endnote numbers. Complete reference appears in italic type.

A

Aaron, P. B., 252, *258*

Aaron, P. G., 191, 192, 194, 224, 238, *239*, 403, 404, *407*, 450, 452, *453*, 459, *464*, 779, *781*

Abbott, R., 127, *138*, 464, *464*, 476, 483, 485, 489, *508*, 616, 617, *621, 622*, 671, *683*, 726, 729, *732*

Abbott, S., 671, *683*

Aboitz, F., 45, *57*

Abt Associates, 37, *52*

Ackerman, P., 370, *407*

Ackerman, P. T., 216, *239*, 715, *720*, 726, *732*

Adams, G., 255, *258*

Adams, J. W., 212, 213, *245*, 661, 663, 664, 667, 677, *686*

Adams, M., 43, *52*, 103, 106, *138*, 169, *171*, 194, 224, *239*, 595, *603*, 656, *683*

Adler, M. A., 558, *562*

Ahonen, T., 217, *246*

Al Otaiba, S., 121, 122, 123, 136, *142*

Alegria, J., 578, *608*

Alexander, A., 103, 127, *146*, 156, *160, 161*, 313, 316, *332*, 482, 483, 485, 487, 500, 502, 505, 506, *518*, 522, *529*, 538, *545*, 556, 559, *564*, 582, 598, *611*, 729, *735*, 779, *782*

Alexander, D., 70, *73*, 256, *260*

Alexander, J., 587, *610*, 644, *651*

Alexson, J., 377, *422*

Algozzine, B., 35, *65*, 91, 92, *97*, 205, *239*, *250*, 251, 255, *258*, 291, *332*, 373, 379, 387, 389, 390, 391, 392, 393, 394, *407, 408*, 411, *425*, 430, *435*, 451, 452, *453*, 455, 474, 475, *519*, 532, *546*, 743, *756, 761, 762*

Allee, T., 376, *425*

Alley, G., 35, 62, 99, *140*, 767, 769

Allington, R., 128, *138*, 404, *417*, 561, 557, *562*

Allison, R., 538, *544*

Allor, J. H., 122, *143*

Allsopp, D., 189, *244*, 288, 294, 296, *331*, 361, *368*, 374, 398, *417*, 470, 473, *515*

Alspaugh, J., 375, *408*

Alter, M., 291(1), 295, 305, 306, 318, 324, *329*, 333(1), 388, *413*, 468, *511*, 532, *543*, 742, 743, *758*

American Psychiatric Association, 253, 254, *258*

Ames, L. B., 398, *408*

Anderson, C. S., 628, 630, *632*

Anderson, L. M., 354, *358*

Anderson, P. L., 4(3), *52*, 65

Anderson, R. C., 104, *138*

Andrews, J. E., 50, 51, *52*, 86, *86*

Anthony, H. M., 354, *358*

Apicella, A. M., 45, *57*

Appelbaum, M. I., 394, *421*

Applebee, A. N., 273, *277*

Armstrong, S., 523, *529*

Arter, J., 479, *507*

Ashbaker, M., 575, *610*

Ashcraft, M. H., 215, *239*

Asher, S. R., 323, *327*

Aslin, R. N., 571, *603*

Association for Children with Learning Disabilities, 39, 41, *52*

Association on Higher Education and Disability, The, 718, *719*

August, D., 784, *788*

M

SUBJECT INDEX

M